Henry James
A Bibliographical Catalogue
of a Collection of Editions
to 1921

Henry James
A Bibliographical Catalogue of a Collection of Editions to 1921

DAVID J. SUPINO

Second Edition, Revised

LIVERPOOL UNIVERSITY PRESS

First published 2006 by
Liverpool University Press
4 Cambridge Street
Liverpool L69 7ZU

Copyright © 2006, 2014 David J. Supino

The right of David J. Supino to be identified as the author of this work has been asserted by him in accordance with the Copyright, Designs and Patents Act, 1988

All rights reserved. No part of this book may be reproduced, stored in a retrieval system, or transmitted, in any form or by any means, electronic, mechanical, photocopying, recording, or otherwise, without the prior written permission of the publisher.

British Library Cataloguing-in-Publication data
A British Library CIP record is available

ISBN 978-1-84631-862-7

Typeset by Koinonia in Golden Cockerel
Printed and bound in the European Union by Henry Ling Ltd

For Linda
Who *still* believes that all this is a bit "dusty".

"This is a book ... [that] will be read only by the initiate. If we be hystericals, we have at least our weakness in common. Let us therefore shut the door and compare our symptoms, for we are all fools together."
Michael Sadleir, *Excursions in Victorian Bibliography* (Chaundy & Cox: London, 1922), 2.

"The form of a bibliographical description should ideally be so full that previous unsuspected variation in the structure of the book can be brought to light by checking a variant copy against the description."
Fredson Bowers, *Principles of Bibliographical Description* (St Paul's Bibliographies: Winchester, 1994), 370.

Contents

Acknowledgements	ix
Preface to the Second Edition	xiii
Preface	xvii
List of Titles	xxviii
References	xxi
Illustrations	xxxiii
Catalogue of the Collection	1
Appendix A: A Note on J. R. Osgood	610
Appendix B: A Note on Tauchnitz's James Editions	614
Appendix C: A Bundle of Letters: Points	618
Appendix D: Second Edition, American Issue of *The Portrait of a Lady*: Points	620
Appendix E: A Note on the Text of *The Portrait of a Lady*	624
Appendix F: The Publishers of James's Non Pirated Editions	626
Appendix G: Documents bearing on the Terms relative to the New York Edition	629
Appendix H: James Titles Listed for Sale in The Times Book Catalogue of 1905	633
Index to Stories and Tales; First Magazine and Subsequent Book Publication 1875–1923	635
General Index	642

Acknowledgements

This Catalogue would not have been possible without the help and support of a number of people, to whom I am most grateful. Foremost among them is Richard S. Loomis, Jr. of Sumner & Stillman from whom, over a period of more than twenty years, many of the books in this Catalogue were acquired. He was also most helpful in making editorial suggestions and assisted in the solution of a number of bibliographical problems, not the least identifying the first seven impressions of the American edition of *The Portrait of a Lady*, in an article which I co-authored with him.

I am also greatly indebted to Roger Stoddard of the Houghton Library, Philip Horne of University College, London, Steve Jobe, and G. Thomas Tanselle whose encouragement of this project spurred me on; and to Kenneth E. Carpenter, not only for editorial guidance but for his thoughtful and insightful discussion of bibliographical issues, including elucidating the murky waters of the definitions of impression, issue and state.

It should be underscored that none of these gentlemen is responsible for whatever are the defects of, or errors in, this Catalogue.

I would also like to thank numerous book dealers from whom I acquired some of the books catalogued here: among them, Steve Weissman, who first set me on the path of Henry James when I acquired from him a fine copy of the multi-volume *The Princess Casamassima* in 1988; Edward Maggs and the late John Manners of Maggs Brothers Ltd.; Sophie Schneiderman; James Cummins; Young's Antiquarian Books; Anthony Neville; Jarndyce; Tiger Books; John Updike Rare Books; Blackwell's; William Reese; Ursus Books and Prints, Ltd.; Thomas A Goldwasser Rare Books; The Brick Row Book Shop; Richard Gekoski; Simon Finch Rare Books; Marlborough Rare Books Ltd.; Bernard Quaritch, Ltd.; Johnnycake Books; and others too many to mention. Their role in the preservation of English literature is too often ignored.

ACKNOWLEDGEMENTS

I would like to thank Anthony Cond, Director of the Liverpool University Press, and his staff for their indispensable assistance in bringing this Catalogue to fruition; and the archivists Elizabeth James of The British Library, Peter Accardo at the Houghton Library, Jean Rose of the Random House Group Archive and Library, and Joel Silver of the Lilly Library, as well as and Anny Cheng, Jennifer Hamilton and Philip Parkinson who did invaluable research for me.

Finally I would like to thank Stacey and Vicky Moore of Moore & More Printing, for their skill and patience in printing multiple revisions of drafts of this Catalogue.

The following institutions and person have kindly granted permission to publish information and quotations contained in this Catalogue: the Lilly Library, Indiana University, Bloomington, Indiana, for permission to publish information in the Methuen & Co. Archive, and also to use a ledger page from the Methuen & Co. Ledger, Volume 1, page 424 as an illustration on the dustjacket; the British Library, London, for permission to publish information contained in the Macmillan & Co. Production Ledgers (also known as Editions Books), and to quote from the correspondence of J.B. Pinker in the Macmillan & Co. Archive; Macmillan-Palgrave to quote from letters in *The Correspondence of Henry James and the House of Macmillan*, and *The Selected Letters of Henry James to William Gosse*, and to publish information contained in the Macmillan Editions Book and "Cards" in their archive at Basingstokes; the Oxford University Press for permission to cite information, and quote from, *A Bibliography of Henry James*, by Leon Edel and Dan Laurence, and to quote, from *International Copyright Law and the Publisher in The Reign of Queen Victoria*, by Simon Nowell-Smith; the Houghton Library, Harvard University to use information, and quote from documents, in the Houghton, Mifflin Archive; The Yale University Press and The Bibliographical Society of America for permission to cite information contained in, and quote from, *The Bibliography of American Literature*, Volume 5, produced by Jacob Blanck; Bay James, of the Estate of Henry James, to quote from the letters of Henry James, and have access to the information on James in The Random House Group Archive; The Random House Group, Ltd. for permission to publish information contained in the William Heinemann Archive, the Chatto & Windus Archive, and the Martin Seeker Archive at the Random House Group Archive and Library at the University of Reading; the Princeton University Library for

ACKNOWLEDGEMENTS

permission to publish information in, and quote from, the Charles Scribner's Sons Archive, Manuscript Division, Department of Rare Books and Special Collections; and the National Library of Scotland, Edinburgh, for permission to publish information from the Blackwood Archive.

Preface to the Second Edition

This Catalogue of a collection of Henry James's editions and impressions published during the period 1875 to 1921 (and in a few cases later) is a significant expansion of the first edition of this Catalogue. Besides covering many more volumes, this edition is in some ways a quite different work. The major difference is the inclusion of information on the printing and publishing history of James titles, as revealed by searches in publishers' archives. The aim of this collection, and the revised edition of this Catalogue which describes it, is to obtain all possible printings of James's works and to record them together with the publishers' records of those printings. As a result of this research, I believe this revised edition of the Catalogue represents one of the few attempts to trace out in detail the publishing history of an author's texts in combination with a description of the books themselves.

This revised edition catalogues almost 1000 volumes (as compared to the 775 volumes catalogued in the first edition), including the addition of some rarities, such as the Ashendene Press edition of *Refugees in Chelsea*, and copies of the very rare first impression of *Daisy Miller: a Study*, published by Harpers in its Half-Hour series, in both wrappers and cloth, to name just two titles. But what the publishers' records also make clear, particularly in the case of James's American publishers, is that the numerous reprintings of many of his works makes it almost impossible that all of them will be recovered, since many of these reprintings were of a quite small number of copies, and are copies which are most difficult to find as most book dealers, nstitutional libraries, and collectors consider them to be of negligible or no importance.

The principal publishers' archives searched were those of Macmillan & Co. (both the London and New York houses), Houghton, Mifflin & Co. (including the records of firms it acquired: J. R. Osgood & Co., Houghton, Osgood & Co., and the second J. R. Osgood & Co.), Harper & Brothers, Scribner's Sons, Methuen, William Heinemann, and less important (in terms of the number of James titles published)

PREFACE TO THE SECOND EDITION

the archives of Martin Secker, Chatto & Windus, and William Blackwood.

The results of these searches have been uneven. The archives of Macmillan (London) at The British Library, London, those of Houghton, Mifflin and its predecessor firms at the Houghton Library, Harvard, and those of Scribners at the Firestone Library, Princeton, are treasure troves of information. It is amazing to learn, for example, that the plates of the first American edition of *The Portrait of a Lady* were in constant use by Houghton, Mifflin from 1881 through 1917, for a total of thirty-two impressions. On the other hand the records of Macmillan (New York) and William Heinemann at the University of Reading (England) revealed little or no information. In one unfortunate instance a publisher refused access to its publishing records citing the inconvenience and cost of allowing access, but in general archivists and librarians have been most helpful in ferreting out information.

The unfortunate fact is that since the 1950s when Jacob Blanck and Edel & Laurence compiled their bibliographies, institutional libraries, at least until more recently, sought the archives of publishers more for correspondence with authors rather than for publishing records. Because of this, and because of consolidations within the publishing industry in the 1970s and later, many publishing records, such as royalty legers, sheet stock books, cost books and other such documents, which Jacob Blanck and Edel and Laurence undoubtedly consulted in writing their bibliographies, have been lost or destroyed. They were probably seen as having little value, particularly in relation to the library space they took up. The records of the printing history of James titles published by Harpers (18 titles published in America) exists, unfortunately, only indirectly in the royalty records for the years 1879 through 1897. In the case of William Heinemann, the Ledger for the years 1898 through 1905 is missing, so there is no information on the four James titles it published during those years. In other cases such records were lost in wars or natural disasters. The records of Duckworth & Co. (which published the English edition of *In the Cage*), and Ward, Lock & Co. (which published the unauthorized first English edition of *The American*), for example, were lost in a war and in fires.

Nevertheless the records that have survived, together with the books themselves, as recorded in this revised Catalogue do present a

PREFACE TO THE SECOND EDITION

picture of publishing and printing in the late Victorian and Edwardian eras, and point up both the similarities and differences between the practices of English and American publishers during this period, albeit through the perspective of the texts of one author. In addition, these records have enabled a far more precise identification of editions and impressions subsequent to the first, which in the first edition of this Catalogue were in numerous instances merely identified as "impressions later than the first".

There is much more to be learned. Perhaps others may be able to unearth records that I have not been able to find or have overlooked. *The Complete Letters of Henry James*, will surely add important new information on the publication and revision of his works. Thus far, that project at The University of Nebraska, with seven volumes published, covers only the years 1855–1878.

In furtherance of future James scholarship, the collection on which this Catalogue is based is being donated to The Beinecke Rare Book and Manuscript Library at Yale University, where it will be kept together as a collection for scholars (both academic and others) to use as a basis for research. I am most grateful to G. Thomas Tanselle who suggested and facilitated this donation, and to the enthusiasm with which E. C. Schroeder, Nancy Kuhl and Sarah Fisher of the Beinecke received it.

David J. Supino

Preface

A bibliography, particularly one of works with a printing history as complex as those of Henry James, is never finished. New binding states are discovered, errors that have crept in are corrected, the importance of dust-jackets is recognized, and differing interpretations by bibliographers of the same data are narrowed or resolved.

There are two bibliographies of the works of Henry James in current use: that of Jacob Blanck in the *Bibliography Of American Literature*, (New Haven: Yale University Press, 1969) Volume 5, 117–181 (hereafter BAL) and that of Leon Edel and Dan H. Laurence, *A Bibliography of Henry James*, Third Edition, revised with the assistance of James Rambeau (Oxford: Clarendon Press, 1982) (hereafter E&L). In addition, Todd and Bowden's *Tauchnitz: International Editions in English, 1841–1955* (New York: Bibliographical Society of America, 1988) (hereafter T&B) describes James's Tauchnitz editions.

However, both E&L and BAL suffer from certain inadequacies, not the least of which is that they have not been revised for many years, and are in different ways of limited scope. T&B, on the other hand, because it is comprehensive and covers all Tauchnitz editions, not just those of James, is seldom referred to. Unfortunately, Tauchnitz editions are largely ignored by James collectors.

SCOPE OF THE CATALOGUE

It is believed that this Catalogue is a useful adjunct to the existing James bibliographies in several respects. It, of course, corrects a number of errors in the existing literature. In addition, it is of greater scope (there are over 700 entries) as it is the only bibliography of James's works that covers in detail, that is with full bibliographical descriptions, all the editions, impressions, issues, and states published in English to 1921, by which date most of James's writings

PREFACE

of significance (except his letters) had been published.[1] It covers not only English and American editions, but colonial and Continental editions as well. It is the first attempt to describe in detail dust-jackets on James's works. And finally, it incorporates information bearing on American and English printing history in the period 1875 to 1921.

This Catalogue is not, of course, a traditional "census" bibliography, that is one that is the product of comparing the copies in the major institutional libraries. But curiously enough the traditional "census" bibliography also has its limitations. One is that the process employed in gathering information – making notes on copies in one institution and comparing those notes with copies in other institutions – is prone to omission because detail can easily be overlooked. Secondly, it can easily lead to the inadvertent "conflation" of what are in fact separate impressions or states. Considerable evidence that that has indeed been the case can be found in this Catalogue. Further, with its emphasis on the "ideal" first impression of the first edition, that is, "the most perfect state of the book as the printer or publisher finally intended to issue it… ." Bowers, 113, leads to a narrowness of scope which, among other things, tends to ignore or mask the whole commercial process of Victorian book production. It also has a tendency to ignore valuable information that subsequent impressions and editions can shed on what is the first impression or edition. Finally, there is a further limitation imposed by a search of institutional libraries for information to create a bibliography that is also enumerative. That is the fact that the rare book departments of libraries (and many high end "rare" book dealers) are seldom interested in or have on their shelves impressions other than the first.

Three things, it is believed, have helped in overcoming some of the possible shortcomings of the "catalogue" approach. First and foremost is that the work of BAL and Edel and Laurence created the foundation on which to build.

Second is the fact that this Catalogue is based on a collection the entirety of which is in one location. This allows a far more detailed and comparative examination of the books it catalogues, and has resulted in the discovery of important information previously overlooked.

---

1 In a few instances this time limit has been exceeded; either because the inclusion of a post 1921 impression answered certain questions (e.g. 64.13.0), or because a multi-volume edition was published over time, some volumes of which were published post 1921 (e.g. 86.1.0 and 86.2.0).

PREFACE

The third is the resource provided by the internet. With hundreds of booksellers having their holding posted on web pages it is possible to discover different copies of a given title (but given the fact that internet-based book descriptions are notoriously faulty, only after telephone or e-mail inquiries as to specific points), and also to have access to booksellers who might have copies of later impressions and editions. It is estimated that three quarters of the books in this Catalogue were found through internet searches over a period of fifteen years. Thus it is arguable that an internet sourced single-site collection can be as comprehensive a basis for a bibliography as that afforded by library searches.

A further word is in order on the subject of publishers' dust-jackets. Dust-jackets (as well as slipcase boxes) on Nineteenth and early Twentieth Century English and American publications have been, until fairly recently, a neglected subject. BAL makes no mention of them. E&L notes only that "[No] attempt has been made to record dust-jackets except in two [actually three] instances." In part this may be due to their rarity, or the notion that dust-jackets, being removable, are not "part of" the book. In the case of BAL, besides the unavailability of dust-jackets in institutional libraries, perhaps they were ignored because it could not be demonstrated conclusively that the dust-jacket and the book went together. In the case of E&L, it would appear that dust-jackets are only an appropriate subject of an author bibliography when the dust-jacket has an authorial connection, in short a blurb on it written by the author.

The earliest James dust-jacket in this collection is on the first English edition of *French Poets and Novelists* (1878). Actually, it is amazing that any early dust-jackets survived, given both their fragile nature and their early purpose, which seems primarily to have been to protect the book until it reached the ultimate consumer. Pre 1890 dust-jackets are indeed rare, as this Catalogue shows. The whole subject of dust-jackets has been admirably treated by G. Thomas Tanselle in Book-Jackets, Blurbs, and Bibliographers, *The Library* (Fifth Series, Vol. XXVI, No. 2, June 1971) 91–134.[2]

2 This has been superseded by G. Thomas Tanselle's: *Book-Jackets: Their History, Form, and Use* (Charlottesville: The Bibliographical Society of the University of Virginia, 2011), which includes a list of some 1800 examples of dust-jackets and other book coverings spanning the period 1779–1901 on which his analysis is based. It is the definitive work on the subject, and is likely to remain so for many decades.

PREFACE

A further telling point is illustrated by my experience in attempting to research James dust-jackets at the British Library. Eagerly expecting to find a great collection, I was told that they did not exist: in the early 1960s all the books in the Library had been stripped of their dust-jackets. Those prior to 1925 were destroyed; those subsequent to that date were bundled by year and sent to the Victoria & Albert to gather dust in one of its outlying repositories; see Tanselle 18, note 42. Implicit here is the assessment of those times that dust-jackets belong more properly to the domain of the decorative arts rather than to serious bibliography.

This view is being revised. An early and more balanced, if cautious, view is stated by Fredson Bowers: "If one is willing to go into such fine points – and I see no reason why not, if one is interested – jackets have their states as have bindings." Bowers, 416. Bibliographies of authors whose works are principally written in the Twentieth Century generally include a record of dust-jackets. The difference in monetary value between a book with or without its dust-jacket is great, a fact appreciated by the book trade. But more importantly, the dust-jacket, I would submit, can provide a great deal of information about the book itself. It also provides a further window on the history and evolution of the book trade and its practices. In fact dust-jackets on James's works exemplify rather neatly their transition over time from a protective medium to an important marketing and advertising tool.

THE ORDER AND FORM OF THE ENTRIES

This Catalogue has been compiled to be not incompatible with entry numbers used in E&L's bibliography, which is by far the most accessible, complete and widely referred to bibliography of James's works. As a consequence, this Catalogue covers only those *titles* recorded by E&L in Section A (Original Works), and therefore omits certain works included in BAL but not in E&L, which are for the most part works for which James wrote the preface (e.g. BAL 10598), which James translated (e.g. BAL 10592) or to which he made a contribution (e.g. BAL 10624). These are, in totality, approximately thirty-five in number, but arguably are not of great significance, and many of them, no doubt, were printed elsewhere in the James canon.

Within each section (that is under each title) the order of the editions, impression and states is chronological in the order of

PREFACE

impression of the sheets of the book,[3] with, however, the following extension: if, for example, the first English edition was published before the American edition, then the English edition is recorded first in this Catalogue, followed, in chronological order of impressions of all the other English editions, impressions and states (including The Times Book Club binding states and colonial impressions); these are followed in turn by the first appearance of the American publication followed, in chronological order of publication, by all other American editions, impressions and states. The converse is true when the American edition was published first. Colonial impressions and issues of colonial sheets bound for the domestic market are recorded among the English issue in the chronological order of the impressions. Continental editions are uniformly recorded at the end of each entry, that is after the English and the American editions. In the case of sheets of any particular impression being issued at successive times (as is not infrequently the case with the prevalence of batch binding) the chronological order of publication (to the extent ascertainable) within such impression, but prior to the next impression or edition, is observed.

Within each title the entries are numbered sequentially with no numerical break between the English, American and continental entries. Each entry is numbered first with the section number, followed by the number for that entry followed by a zero. The zero is present to permit subsequent supplements to, or editions of, this Catalogue to include additional interpolated entries without changing the numbers of the existing ones. In a few instances interpolated entries have been used in this Catalogue (e.g. 8.11.5) in order to permit the inclusion of copies that were found too late to permit the extensive numbering changes they would entail were they to be included as non-interpolated entries.

DESCRIPTIVE FORMULA

No single descriptive formula could be followed in this Catalogue for each entry, as it would result in unnecessary repetition.

Broadly speaking there are two types of entries: the fully descriptive entry and the follow-on entry. The full descriptions include:

---

3 In some cases (e.g. 24.6.0 and 24.7.0) a later binding up of first impression sheets with a new (substituted) title-page will precede a later impression of sheets with an earlier dated title-page.

transcription of the title-page, size (by which is meant page size, not the size of the binding), collation, contents, binding and inserted ads, inscriptions, bookplates, binder's and bookseller's tickets, dust-jacket, if present, and finally any applicable commentary. The follow-on entry basically describes the differences between the book under consideration and the fully described book. Usually the full descriptive entry is for the first edition, first impression, and the follow-on entries are for later states, issues or impressions. However, if a book that is an edition or impression subsequent to the first is sufficiently different as to make comparative reference to the first impression cumbersome or confusing, then a full description is given of that subsequent edition or impression. Although this may result in a certain unwelcome diversity to the entries, it is felt that on balance it is better than undue repetition or confusion.

TITLE-PAGE

In the fully descriptive entries, or in follow-on entries where the title-page is described, the title-page is described in quasi facsimile. In such descriptions line endings are denoted by a vertical line rather than a forward slash to avoid confusion with the English convention of the forward slash used to divide pounds, shillings and pence. Type style other than roman (e.g. italic and Gothic) and words or ornaments printed in color are noted at the end of the pertinent line within square brackets. Title-page type dimensions have been noted where differences have been found, and have proved useful in differentiating between impressions and identifying resettings. See for example the first and second impressions of the first edition of *The American*, and the first and second American impressions of the second edition, of *The Portrait of a Lady*.

SIZE

Unless otherwise noted, sizes given are the of the leaves of the book not of the casing (unless otherwise specified). When uncut leaves are present the size recorded is that of the largest leaf.

PREFACE

COLLATIONAL FORMULA

Until after 1900 English printers of editions in this Catalogue uniformly signed their books with letters of the Latin alphabet (23 letters, omitting "J", "V" and "W"). In contrast, American printers of editions in this Catalogue for the most part signed their books with Arabic numerals. However, a not insubstantial number of American printers used all 26 letters in signing, or alternatively by, what seems to have been the recommended practice, 25, that is all letters except "J"; see Thomas MacKellar, *The American Printer*, 13th edition (Philadelphia: Mackellar, Smith & Jordan, 1882), 135 and 216. The first editions of *A Passionate Pilgrim* and *Transatlantic Sketches*, for example, used all 26 letters, while the second edition, revised, of *Roderick Hudson* is signed with 25 of the 26 letters (omitting "J").

Using in this context the standard bibliographical convention, recommended by Bowers, of ignoring the omitted letters and writing a collational formula of A–Z to mean 23 signatures seems to invite confusion. Jacob Blanck discusses this issue lucidly and at some length in the Preface to Volume I of BAL, and concludes that rather than following the Bowers convention, it creates greater certainty to use a formula "to set down precisely what we see." This conclusion seems eminently sensible and is followed here.

PAGINATION FORMULA

Pagination is given in this Catalogue for each entry where a collation is provided. Inferred page numbers are not intended to imply that the printer would have numbered them in this way had the printer chosen to number them. They are here used solely to symbolize the pages within the structure of the book.

Preliminary leaves which are not numbered are given inferred pagination (usually roman numerals, unless the first numbered page of the preliminary leaves or of the text suggests otherwise) within square brackets. These preliminary leaves are separated from the rest of the pagination by a comma. The initial fly-title is treated as part of the preliminary leaves. Blank preliminary and terminal leaves not preceded or followed, respectively, by printed pages, and which are part of the sheets of the book are recorded by an italicized page total within square brackets at the beginning or end of the pagination sequence, except in the case of preliminary leaves where following numbered pages require them to be given inferred pagination.

Text pages if unnumbered are given inferred page numbers in square brackets, but only in the case of the first and last page of the text, and (separately) the verso of the last page of the text if the text ends on a recto. Unnumbered pages within the text are not identified in the pagination formula. In the single case where the last page of the text pages has been misnumbered, the correct page number is given in the pagination formula, and the error noted in the entry.

Final, unnumbered pages after the text that are part of the sheets of the book are given inferred pagination when they have printing on them, or are the blank versos in a printed sequence. Thus, for example, three pages of ads on two leaves after the text which are part of the last signature would also include the inferred pagination for these three pages and the blank last page, and would be given inferred page numbers sequential with the text even if the printer had separately numbered the pages of the ads starting a new sequence.

If the sheets of the book are used as an endpaper, whether a free endpaper or a pastedown, that is the endpaper is not a binder's insertion, these pages are included in the pagination formula; see for example entry 25.5.0.

The pagination formula excludes endpapers (except as noted above), binder's fly-leaves, ads not part of the sheets of the book, such as inserted ads or publisher's catalogues, and all tipped in plates or other plates and insertions not a part of the printer's numbering sequence.[4] However, where there are leaves of the book that are not included by the printer in the numbering sequence, that fact is both noted and the number of such leaves quantified so that the collation given can be seen to cohere to the pagination given. A case in point would be illustrations not tipped in and printed on the sheets of the book that are disregarded in the printer's numbering sequence.[5]

---

[4] Bowers recommends that all inserts be included in the collation, and by extension in the pagination formula. Bowers, pp. 235–241. This recommendation has been followed in the case of all inserts with text on them, such as inserted "publisher's notes", singleton title-pages, and inserted frontispieces. However, in some cases where inserted illustrations are numerous, such as the first edition of *Italian Hours*, 67.1.0 (with 63 full-page illustrations tipped in and not reckoned in the pagination), to include all in the collation and pagination formulas would cumbersome and confusing. Instead it is thought that noting the actual number of such inserts is sufficient.

[5] In such cases the number of pages that are disregarded in the printer's

PREFACE

BINDINGS

A full description of bindings has been given in this Catalogue. This includes description of cloth type and color, the decoration and lettering on the covers and spine (with particular attention to the publisher's imprint), endpapers color and type of paper, text paper type and watermarks if present, edge treatment (trimming, gilding or other coloring), binder's fly-leaves[6] and inserted ads not part of the sheets of the book and inserted publisher's catalogues, and (where important) whether the book is sewn or stapled. If no mention is made in the binding description as to whether a book is sewn or stapled, it is sewn. Parenthetically, it is interesting to note during most of this period the English preference for untrimmed pages and the American preference for trimmed pages.

Probably the most subjective part of the binding description is the binding color, in part because so many bindings changed color over time due to the fugitive nature of the dyes used (especially the purples which tend to turn to a shade of brown), fading and harsh environmental conditions. This is exemplified in the case of the first binding states of *A Passionate Pilgrim, Transatlantic Sketches, Roderick Hudson* and *The American*. E&L records *A Passionate Pilgrim* and *Roderick Hudson* as appearing in both rust-brown and terra-cotta bindings, and *Transatlantic Sketches* and *The American* as appearing in a rust-brown binding. In point of fact, all four titles appeared in terra-cotta and none in rust-brown, a fact confirmed by BAL. E&L's confusion on this issue was the result of not taking into account the effects of the environment on the binding color. In this catalogue color is consequently described as seen, but with an eye to the possible changes in color over time (and never judging by the color of the spine). Where the original color was evidently different this has been noted.

---

numbering sequence are noted, and also are added at the end of the pagination formula indicating the total number of pages so disregarded, e.g. "plus 86"; see 23.15.0.

6 With regard to binder's fly leaves, when such fly-leaves are present in any volume, their presence is noted in the binding description. When such fly-leaves are not preset, their absence is not noted in the binding description; except, however, when in a sequence of impression of an edition some of the impressions have fly-leaves and others do not, then both the presence and absence of fly-leaves is noted in the binding descriptions. Whereas American publishers frequently used fly-leaves, English publishers of James's works in the period covered by this Catalogue seem, for the most part, to have eschewed their use.

PREFACE

Common, and hence more readily understandable, color nomenclature has been used rather than the more scientific but less accessible ISCC-NBS method of designating color with reference to the Centroid color charts.

Similarly, in describing book cloth, reference has been to common descriptive nomenclature advocated by Philip Gaskell, *A New Introduction to Bibliography* (Oxford: Oxford University Press, 1972), 240–247, rather than the more scientific but perhaps less accessible system of cloth grains and designations used by BAL.[7]

ENDPAPERS AND TEXT PAPER

In this Catalogue both the type as well as color of the endpapers and the type of paper on which the text is printed are described as parts of the binding description. Differences between text paper, and to a somewhat lesser extent endpapers, of copies of the same edition are helpful in establishing the differences between, and perhaps the sequence of, impressions or states.

In the case of colored or patterned endpapers, the color or pattern is described, and in the case of other endpapers, the shade and type of paper (e.g. white wove or laid) is specified. Where reference is made to coated endpapers, the implicit meaning is a color on a coated white paper. In the case of the text paper, the type of paper is specified (wove or laid), unless a special paper was used, in which case the special paper is described. Also, when present, watermarks in the paper are recorded, and when it is relevant the thickness of the paper is also described.

In most instances of endpapers that are not colored or patterned, the paper is described as white unless some other description is clearly warranted, even though it is sometimes very difficult to tell whether a given paper was originally white or whether the off-white shade may have resulted from discoloration or oxidation over the years.

In general, E&L describes endpapers by color only, not paper type, and ignores, with just a few exceptions, the type of paper on which the text is printed, even when, as is the case for the first American

---

[7] It should be noted that the study of bookcloth has been much advanced by Andrea Krupp's detailed study: *Bookcloth in England and America, 1823–1850* (The Bibliographical Society of America, 2008).

PREFACE

edition of *What Maisie Knew*, a watermark on the text paper may be an important element in distinguishing between the first and the second and later impressions. BAL describes both the color and paper type of endpapers, as well as the text paper but not in all instances (compare, for example, BAL 10671 with BAL 10674).

DUST-JACKETS

All dust-jackets in this catalogue have been described with the books with which they are associated. The description of the dust-jacket comes after the description of the binding, and is the last part of the book which is described. The description of dust-jackets is ordered as follows: paper type and color, design, and the text of the front cover, the spine, the back cover, the front inner flap and, last, the rear inner flap.

ERRORS AND OMISSIONS

On the subject of the inevitable errors that have been committed in this Catalogue, I can do no better than quote Jacob Blanck: "There remains one element ... saved for the last: Error. It is a time honored custom of bibliographers to disclaim perfection and the tradition is respected. In doing so I am not moved by modesty. I simply recognize man's limitations, my own in particular, and trust that others will have the charity to do the same. By all means inform me of errors as they are discovered... ." Preface, xli.

It is said that no bibliography will ever be complete, a view with which I can obviously and heartily concur, and of which this Catalogue is proof. There are obvious omissions in this Catalogue, for the simple reason that copies could not be found even though the omission is known or suspected. In addition, there is always what is out there that one does not know about or even suspect. Bibliography is full of quiet surprises. But that is part of the thrill of the hunt.

David J. Supino

List of Titles

Ambassadors, The	58
American: A Comedy, The	35
American, The	4
American Scene, The	63
Art of Fiction, The	25
Aspern Papers, The	32
Author of Beltraffio, The	26
Awkward Age, The	53
Better Sort, The	57
Bostonians, The	28
Bundle of Letters, A	13
Collective Edition of 1883, The	20
Confidence	11
Daisy Miller: A Comedy	18
Daisy Miller: A Study	8
Dairy of a Man of Fifty, The	14
Embarrassments	46
English Hours	62
Essays in London and Elsewhere	40
Eugene Pickering	10
Europeans, The	7
Finer Grain, The	68
Foreign Parts	2
French Poets and Novelists	5
Gabrielle de Bergerac	80
Golden Bowl, The	60
Guy Domville	43
Hawthorne	12
Henry James Yearbook, The	69
International Episode, An	9
In the Cage	51

LIST OF TITLES

Italian Hours	67
Ivory Tower, The	77
John Delavoy	50
Julia Bride	66
Landscape Painter, A	83
Lesson of the Master, The	36
Little Tour in France, A	23
London Life, A	33
Madonna of the Future, The	10
Master Eustace	85
Middle Years, The	79
Notes and Reviews	87
Notes of a Son and Brother	72
Notes on Drawings by George Du Maurier	22
Notes on Novelists	73
Novels and Stories of Henry James, The	86
Novels and Tales of Henry James, The	64
Other House, The	47
Outcry, The	70
Partial Portraits	30
Passionate Pilgrim, A	1
Pictures and Text	38
Pictures and Other Passages from Henry James	76
Point of View, The	17
Portrait of a Lady, The	16
Portraits of Places	21
Princess Casamassima, The	29
Private Life, The	39
Question of Our Speech, The	61
Question of the Mind, The	75
Real Thing, The	37
Refugees in Chelsea	84
Reverberator, The	31
Roderick Hudson	3
Sacred Fount, The	55
Sense of the Past, The	78
Siege of London, The	19
Small Boy and Others, A	71
Soft Side, The	54

LIST OF TITLES

Spoils of Poynton, The	48
Stories Revived	27
Tales of Three Cities	24
Terminations	45
Theatricals	42
Theatricals: Second Series	44
Transatlantic Sketches	2
Tragic Muse, The	34
Travelling Companions	82
Two Magics, The	52
Uniform Tales of Henry James, The	74
Views and Reviews	65
Washington Square	15
Watch and Ward	6
What Maisie Knew	49
Wheel of Time, The	41
William Wetmore Story and His Friends	59
Wings of the Dove, The	56
Within the Rim	81

References

American Printer	Thomas MacKellar, *The American Printer: A Manual of Typography* (Philadelphia: MacKellar, Smith & Jordan, thirteenth edition, 1882).
Anesko	Michael Anesko, *"Friction Within the Market" Henry James and the Profession of Authorship* (New York and Oxford: Oxford University Press, 1986).
BAL	*Bibliography of American Literature*, Volume 5 (New Haven: Yale University Press, 1969).
Ball	Douglas Ball, *Victorian Publishers' Bindings* (London: The Library Association, 1985).
Bowers	Fredson Bowers, *Principles of Bibliographical Description* (Winchester: St. Paul's Bibliographies, 1994).
CLHJ	*The Complete Letters of Henry James, 1855–1872*, 2 volumes; *1872–1876*, 3 volumes; *1876–1878*, 2 volumes (Lincoln and London: University of Nebraska Press, 2006, 2009, 2011, 2012, and 2013).
CWJ	*Correspondence of William James: William and Henry*, 3 volumes (Charlottesville and London: University Press of Virginia, 1992–1994).
EC	*The English Catalogue of Books*, 1875–1925.
E&L	Leon Edel and Dan H. Laurence, *A Bibliography of Henry James*, Third Edition, revised with the assistance of James Rambeau (Oxford: Clarendon Press, 1982).
Gaskell	Philip Gaskell, *A New Introduction to Bibliography* (New York and Oxford: Oxford University Press, 1972).
HJL	Leon Edel, *The Letters of Henry James*, 4 volumes (Cambridge: The Belknap Press 1974–1984).
Horne	Philip Horne, *Henry James: A Life in Letters* (London: Allen Lane The Penguin Press, 1999).
Kramer	Sidney Kramer, *A History of Stone & Kimball and Herbert S. Stone & Co., with a Bibliography of Their Publications 1893–1905* (Chicago: The University of Chicago Press [1940]).

REFERENCES

MBC	*A Bibliographical Catalogue of Macmillan and Co.'s Publications from 1843 to 1889* (London and New York: Macmillan and Co., 1891).
MEB	*Macmillan Editions Book*, 946 page ledger with index, the Macmillan Archive, Department of Manuscripts, British Library (not catalogued).
MPL	Macmillan Production Ledgers, 1892–1939, the Macmillan Archive, Department of Manuscripts, British Library (Add Mss 55909–55925, 1892–1924).
Moore	Rayburn S. Moore, *The Correspondence of Henry James and the House of Macmillan 1877–1914* (Baton Rouge: Louisiana State University Press, 1993).
Nowell-Smith	Simon Nowell-Smith, *International Copyright Law and the Publisher in the Reign of Queen Victoria* (Oxford: The Clarendon Press, 1968).
PC	*Publishers' Circular*
Sadleir	Michael Sadleir, *XIX Century Fiction*, 2 volumes (Cambridge: The University Press, 1951).
Tanselle	G. Thomas Tanselle, *Book-Jackets: Their History, Forms, and Use* (Charlottesville: The Bibliographical Society of the University of Virginia, 2011).
T&B	William Todd and Anne Bowden, *Tauchnitz International Editions in English, 1841–1955* (New York: Bibliographical Society of America, 1988).
Tomlinson & Masters	William Tomlinson and Richard Masters, *Bookcloth 1823–1980* (Mellor Stockport, Dorothy Tomlinson, 1996).
Wolff	Robert Lee Wolff, *Nineteenth Century Fiction*, 5 volumes (New York and London: Garland Publishing, Inc., 1981).

Illustrations

	Plate Number
A Passionate Pilgrim	1
Transatlantic Sketches	2
The American	3
The American	4
French Poets and Novelists	5
An International Episode	6
Washington Square	7
The Portrait of a Lady	8
The Portrait of a Lady	9
The Collective Edition of 1883	10
Portraits of Places	11
Tales of Three Cities	12
The Bostonians	13
The Princess Casamassima	14
The Princess Casamassima	15
The Reverberator	16
A London Life	17
The Real Thing	18
The Spoils of Poynton	19
What Maisie Knew	20
In the Cage	21
The Two Magics	22
The Awkward Age	23
The Awkward Age	24
The Ambassadors	25
The Question of Our Speech	26
Julia Bride	27
Italian Hours	28
The Outcry	29
Gabrielle De Bergerac	30
Traveling Companions	31
Times Book Club bindings	32

Catalogue of the Collection

1. *A PASSIONATE PILGRIM*

1.1.0. *A Passionate Pilgrim*, first edition, first impression, first binding state, one volume, Boston 1875.

A | PASSIONATE PILGRIM, | AND OTHER TALES. | BY | HENRY JAMES, Jr. | [publisher's device] | BOSTON: | JAMES R. OSGOOD AND COMPANY, | Late Ticknor & Fields, and Fields, Osgood, & Co. | 1875.

Size: 7 $7/16''$ x 4 $13/16''$.

Collation: [1^2, 2–21^{12}, 22^6], signed as [A]^8, B–Z, AA–EE^8 and [1]^{12}, 2–20^{12}, 21^8; pp. [1–6], [7]–496.

Contents: [1–2] title-page, verso copyright notice and printer's imprint: "Copyright, 1875, | By JAMES R. OSGOOD & CO. | University Press: Welch, Bigelow, & Co., | Cambridge."; [3–4] "CONTENTS.", verso blank; [5–6] divisional fly-title, verso blank; [7]–496 text.

Binding: green sand-grain cloth over bevelled boards, with the front and back covers decorated in blind with a single-rule frame within a wider single-rule border. The spine, which is lettered and decorated in gilt, reads "[thick followed by a thin rule] | A | Passionate | Pilgrim | ETC. | [decorative rule] | H. James Jr. | J. R. Osgood & Co [with no period after the last "o"] | [thin followed by a thick rule]". The endpapers are of brown coated paper, and the text is printed on wove paper. All edges are trimmed, and the top edge is stained brown. It is sewn, not stapled. There are binder's fly-leaves of wove paper at both the front and the back.

Illustrated Plate 1.

E&L records four colors for the bindings on the first binding state of this title: green, deep purple, terra-cotta, and dark rust-brown. It is highly likely that what E&L records as rust-brown is in fact not a separate color but merely a darkened copy of the terra-cotta binding. Anecdotal evidence suggests that during the period 1871–1877, the life of the first J. R. Osgood firm, Osgood used only green, purple, and terra-cotta bindings not only on James's works, but also on the works of other authors. In this connection, it should be noted that BAL does not record a rust-brown copy of the first binding state of this title or, for that matter, of *Transatlantic Sketches*, *Roderick Hudson*, or *The American*, the other three James titles published by J. R. Osgood & Co. in this period, all of which E&L records as having, among other colors, rust-brown bindings. However, during the period 1880 to 1885, the life of the second Osgood firm, Osgood issued James titles in a number of other colors, including blue, ochre, and various shades of brown and green.

See Appendix A: A Note on J. R. Osgood.

Printing history. Houghton Mifflin Archive. First edition: Ms Am 2030.2 (23), 15 and Ms Am 2030(17), 116: *first* [Osgood] *impression* January 27, 1875, 1510 copies, 1435 bound between January 28, 1875, and before June 1, 1882, and a further 37 on June 3, 1882; published January 31, 1875; notation: "Author's Plates"; *second impression* [and first Houghton, Mifflin impression] July 25, 1882, 160 copies, 154 bound between September 13, 1892, and July 3, 1883; *third impression* August 21, 1883, 158 copies all bound between September 4, 1883, and October 28, 1884; *fourth impression* February 20, 1885, 154 copies, 153 bound between March 5, 1885, and November 12, 1886. Ms Am 2030(18), 136: *fifth impression* April 7, 1888, 152 copies, 151 bound between April 30, 1888, and February 28, 1891. Ms Am 2030(19), 153: *sixth impression* April 18, 1892, 158 copies, 154 bound between April 25, 1892, and March 21, 1895. Ms Am 2030(21), 220: *seventh impression* June 21, 1897, 156 copies, 150 bound between July 12, 1897, and June 13, 1900. Ms Am 2030(22), 218: *eighth impression* July 26, 1901, 150 copies, 149 bound between October 28, 1901, and July 2, 1904; *ninth impression* April 12, 1905, 155 copies, 153 bound between April 22, 1905, and February 9, 1906; *tenth impression* July 10, 1907, 157 copies, 155 bound between July 25, 1907, and May 29, 1908. Ms Am 2030(23), 213: *eleventh impression* May 22, 1908, 153 copies, 151 bound between December 15, 1908, and January 24, 1911; *twelfth impression* June 21, 1912, 271 copies, 265 bound between August 26, 1912, and August 4, 1916; *thirteenth impression* May 8, 1917, 154 copies, 152 bound between May 31, 1917, and April 23, 1918; *fourteenth impression* August 5, 1919, 283 copies, 266 bound between January 29, 1920, and March 3, 1921; notation: "9/5/19 ptd. 290 jackets"; *fifteenth impression* February 15, 1922, 511 copies, 496 bound between May 25, 1922, and April 23, 1926; notations "2/16/22 ptd. 547 jackets", "10/29/23 ptd. 554 jackets n[ew] s[tyle]", "[copies printed] 4282".

Priced at $2.00, which price was unchanged through 1905.

It is generally believed that his title was not published in England. However, *The Times Book Club Catalogue of 1905*, at 414 records: "*A*

A PASSIONATE PILGRIM

Passionate Pilgrim ... Pub. 3s. 6d.; our price, 2s. 8d." Some of the tales it contains were published in *The Collective Edition of 1883*, 20.1.0–20.5 0, in *The Novels and Tales of Henry James* (New York Edition), 64.1.0–64.3.0, and all were included in *The Novels and Stories of Henry James*, 86.1.0–86.2.0; see Index to James's Stories and Tales.

Total production costs of the first impression were $1938.67. The cost of the stereotype plates was $641.17. This includes $596.42 for the plates, $26.00 for 52 hours work correcting the plates, $13.75 for 11 wood boxes to store the plates and $5.00 for "Berry dies". The other (variable) cost were in total $1297.50, which includes $319.50 for 35 10/20 reams of 23 ½" x 40" paper, $63.00 for printing 1500 copies, $300 for "Copyright" [probably an estimate of royalties], $300 for advertising and $315.00 for binding; see Ms Am 2030.2(25) and Ms Am 2030.2(20), 308. Total costs were $1.30 per bound copy, or $.86 per bound copy without the plates, and $.66 for each unbound copy, again without the plates. The retail selling price was $2.00, which after discounts to booksellers and jobbers (40%) left no profit (based on full costs) for the first impression. But these figures give a good indication of the substantial economies of reprinting and batch binding, as with a cost of only $.86 per bound copy for subsequent impressions the margin of profit would be about 40%.

1.2.0. *A Passionate Pilgrim*, first edition, first impression, first binding state, one volume, Boston 1875.

This copy is identical in all respects to the first edition, first impression, first binding state, 1.1.0, except that it is bound in purple dotted-line-grain cloth.

E&L describes this cloth as fine-cross-ribbed, but in this Catalogue it is described as dotted-line-grain, the nomenclature used by Phillip Gaskell. Gaskell, 241 Fig. 87. BAL's equivalent is FL cloth.

1.3.0. *A Passionate Pilgrim*, first edition, first impression, first binding state, one volume, Boston 1875.

This copy is identical in all respects to the first edition, first impression, first binding state, 1.1.0, except that it is bound in terra-cotta dotted-line-grain cloth. The top edge is stained ochre.

1.4.0. *A Passionate Pilgrim*, first edition, first impression, second binding state, one volume, Boston 1875.

The title-page, size, collation and contents are identical to those of the first edition, first impression, first binding state, 1.1.0.

Binding: green sand-grain cloth over bevelled boards, lettered and decorated as described in 1.1.0 for the first binding state, except that the publisher's imprint present at the foot of the spine is "Houghton, Osgood & Co." The endpapers are of brown coated paper, and the text is printed on wove paper. All edges are trimmed, and the top edge is stained ochre. It is sewn, not stapled. A binder's fly-leaf of wove paper is at both the front and the back.

The bookplate of the James collector Paul Lemperly is on the front pastedown.

1.5.0. *A Passionate Pilgrim*, first edition, first impression, second binding state, one volume, Boston 1875.

This copy is identical to the first edition, first impression, second binding state, 1.4.0, except that it is bound in terra-cotta sand-grain cloth.

On the front binder's leaf is the pencil inscription "M. N. Tuckerman – | June – / 80 | Brookline–", and on the front pastedown is the bookplate of Oliver Brett (later Lord Esher).

Illustrated Plate 1.

1.6.0. *A Passionate Pilgrim*, first edition, first impression, third binding state, one volume, Boston 1875.

Size: $7\,3/8''$ x $4\,13/16''$.

Title-page, collation, and contents are identical to those of the first edition, first impression, first binding state, 1.1.0.

Binding: green sand-grain cloth over bevelled boards, lettered and decorated identically to 1.1.0, except that the publisher's imprint present at the foot of the spine is "Houghton, Mifflin & Co." The ampersand in the publisher's imprint on the spine has a flat rather than a rounded top. The endpapers are of brown coated paper, and the text is printed on wove paper. A binder's fly-leaf of wove paper is at both

A PASSIONATE PILGRIM

the front and the back. All edges are trimmed, and the top edge is stained ochre. It is sewn, not stapled.

Illustrated Plate 1.

1.7.0. *A Passionate Pilgrim*, first edition, first impression, fourth binding state, one volume, Boston 1875.

Size: 7 3/8" x 4 3/4".

The title-page, collation, and contents are identical to those of the first edition, first impression, first binding state, 1.1.0.

Binding: sage-green linen-grain cloth, lettered in red-brown with decoration in red-brown, sage-green, and gilt on the front cover and spine. The title on the front cover and spine is in red-brown within a gilt panel with a pronounced maze-like background pattern. The publisher's imprint at the foot of the spine reads: "Houghton Mifflin & Co." The ampersand in the publisher's imprint has a flat rather than a rounded top. The endpapers are of a tan floral design on white-coated paper, and the text is printed on wove paper. A binder's fly-leaf of wove paper is at both the front and the back. All edges are trimmed, and the top edge is stained ochre. It is sewn, not stapled.

On the recto of the front binder's fly-leaf is the inscription: "Mrs C. C. Holt [or Hall] | from | Ed [illegible] | Jan[uar]y 23/83".

Illustrated Plate 1.

This binding is uniform with that on the first American impression of the second edition of *The Portrait of a Lady* (1881), 16.5.0.

With respect to the binding on this copy, note that: "During the 1880s Houghton, Mifflin's dominant purpose was to reduce its indebtedness. ... [Mifflin] achieved his purpose by following three major policies – acquisition of fresh partnership capital, *reworking the lists inherited from Hurd & Houghton and Houghton, Osgood*, and cautious investment in new writers" (emphasis added). Ellen B. Ballou, *The Building of the House: Houghton Mifflin's Formative Years* (Boston: Houghton Mifflin Company, 1970), 303. One of the authors "reworked" was Henry James. In order to capitalize on the success of *The Portrait of a Lady*, of which 6093 copies were printed in 1881–1882, and a further 500 in 1883, Houghton, Mifflin in the period 1882 to 1886 issued remaining first impression sheets or reprints (from Osgood plates) of the seven James titles acquired from

Osgood. Six of these (*A Passionate Pilgrim, Transatlantic Sketches, Roderick Hudson, The American, The Europeans* and *Confidence*) were issued in bindings uniform with the first American impression of the second edition of *The Portrait of a Lady* (1881). These uniform bindings were issued in chocolate-brown, tan, and pea-green diagonal-fine ribbed cloth. It is probable that all these titles were issued in all three cloth colors. In two instances, *A Passionate Pilgrim* (1.7.0) and *The Portrait of a Lady* (16.13.0), sage-green and olive-green linen-grain cloth were also used. *Watch and Ward*, because its small physical size made it unsuitable for a similar binding, was issued in a binding uniform with the original Osgood binding, except in the case of the first edition, fifth impression, 6.8.0.

1.8.0. *A Passionate Pilgrim*, first edition, later impression, one volume, Boston 1882.

A | PASSIONATE PILGRIM, | AND OTHER TALES. | BY | HENRY JAMES, Jr. | [shield-shaped publisher's device] | BOSTON: | HOUGHTON, MIFFLIN AND COMPANY. | The Riverside Press, Cambridge. [in Gothic type] | 1882.

Size: 7 3/8" x 4 3/4"

Collation: $[1]^{12}$ $2-20^{12}$ 21^8, also signed as $[A]^8$ B–Z AA–EE^8; pp. [1–6], [7]–496.

Contents: [1–2] title-page, verso copyright notice: "Copyright, 1875, | By JAMES R. OSGOOD & CO."; [3–4] "CONTENTS", verso blank; [5–6] divisional fly-title, verso blank; [7]–496 text.

Binding: pea-green diagonal-fine-ribbed cloth, lettered in red-brown with decoration in red-brown, pea-green, and gilt on the front cover and spine. The title on the front cover and spine is in red-brown within a gilt panel with a pronounced maze-like background pattern. The publisher's imprint at the foot of the spine reads: "Houghton Mifflin & Co." The ampersand in the publisher's imprint has a flat rather than a rounded top. The endpapers are of a tan floral design on white-coated paper, and the text is printed on wove paper. A binder's fly-leaf of wove paper is at both the front and the back. All edges are trimmed, and the top edge is stained light brown. It is stapled, not sewn.

On the title-page is the signature "Saul S. Gray". On the front free endpaper is a small pink bookseller's ticket reading: "W. B. CLARKE & CARRUTH, | Booksellers, | BOSTON, MASS."

A PASSIONATE PILGRIM

The text block is 1 5/32″ thick (without boards).

This binding is uniform with that on the first American impression of the second edition of *The Portrait of a Lady* (1881), 16.5.0.

1.8.1. *A Passionate Pilgrim*, first edition, second impression, one volume, Boston and New York 1882.

The title page, size, collation, and contents are identical to those of the first edition, second impression, 1.8.0.

Binding: tan diagonal-fine-ribbed cloth, lettered and decorated on the front cover and spine identically to 1.8.0. The title on the front cover is in red-brown within a gilt panel with a pronounced maze-like background pattern. The ampersand in the publisher's imprint at the foot of the spine has a flat rather than a rounded top. The endpapers are of chocolate-brown coated paper, and the text is printed on wove paper. A binder's fly-leaf of wove paper is at both the front and the back. All edges are trimmed, and the top edge is stained brown. It is sewn not stapled.

1.8.3. *A Passionate Pilgrim*, first edition, unrecorded impression between the third and fourth impressions, one volume, Boston 1884.

The title-page, size, collation, and contents are identical to those of the first edition, second impression, 1.8.0, except that the title-page is dated 1884 at the foot.

Binding: identical to that on 1.8.0. The endpapers are of a tan floral design on white-coated paper, and the text is printed on wove paper. A binder's fly-leaf of wove paper is at both the front and the back. All edges are trimmed, and the top-edge is stained light brown. It is sewn, not stapled.

On the front binder's fly-leaf is an inscription dated: "March 31 '86."

1.8.5. *A Passionate Pilgrim*, first edition, sixth impression, one volume, Boston and New York, 1892.

A | PASSIONATE PILGRIM, | AND OTHER TALES. | BY | HENRY JAMES, Jr. | SIXTH EDITION. | [oblong publisher's device of a piper under a tree within a frame] | BOSTON: | HOUGHTON, MIFFLIN AND COMPANY. | New York: 11 East Seventeenth Street. [in sans-serif] | The Riverside Press, Cambridge. [in Gothic type] | 1892.

Size: 7 3/8" x 4 7/8".

Collation:[12]^{12} 2–20^{12} 21^8, also signed as [A]^8 B–Z AA–EE^8; pp. [1–4] [5–6], [7]–496.

Contents: [1–2] title-page, verso copyright notice and printer's imprint: "Copyright, 1875, | By JAMES R. OSGOOD & CO. | The Riverside Press, Cambridge, Mass., U. S. A. [in italic] | Printed by H. O. Houghton & Company."; [3–4] "CONTENTS.", verso blank; [5–6] divisional fly-title, verso blank; [7]–496 text.

Binding: chocolate-brown diagonal-fine-ribbed cloth, lettered in red-brown and decorated in chocolate-brown, red-brown, and gilt on the front cover and spine. The title on the front cover and spine is in red-brown within a gilt panel with a pronounced maze-like background pattern. The publisher's imprint on the spine reads: "HOUGHTON | MIFFLIN [dot] & [dot] CO." The ampersand in the imprint is like a figure "8", and has a rounded rather than a flat top. The endpapers are of white laid paper, and the text is printed on wove paper. A binder's fly-leaf of wove paper is at both the front and the back. All edges are trimmed, and the top edge is stained brown. It is sewn not stapled.

This binding is uniform with that on the first American impression of the second edition of *The Portrait of a Lady* (1881), 16.5.0.

On the front binder's fly-leaf is the inscription "C. K. Barry | 1895."

1.9.0. *A Passionate Pilgrim*, first edition, tenth impression, one volume, Boston and New York [n.d., 1907].

A PASSIONATE PILGRIM | AND OTHER TALES | BY | HENRY JAMES, Jr. | [publisher's device of a piper under a tree not within a frame] | BOSTON AND NEW YORK | HOUGHTON, MIFFLIN AND COMPANY | The Riverside Press, Cambridge [in Gothic type]

Size: 7 3/8" x 4 7/8".

Collation: [1–31^8 32^2], signed as [A]^9 B–Z AA–DD^8 EE^9, and [1]^{13} 2–20^{12} 21^9; pp. [i-ii] [1–6], [7]–496 [497–498].

Contents: [i-ii] blank, verso ad within a single-rule frame headed: "By Henry James [in Gothic type]", listing 18 titles with dollar prices, the last dated being *The Question of Our Speech* and *English Hours* (both

1905); [1–2] title-page, verso "Copyright, 1875, | By JAMES R. OSGOOD & CO. | Copyright, 1903, | By HOUGHTON, MIFFLIN & CO. | All rights reserved. [in italic]"; [3–4] "CONTENTS.", verso blank; [5–6] divisional fly-title, verso blank; [7]–496 text; [497–498] blank leaf.

Binding: green vertical-rib-grain cloth, lettered and decorated in gilt on the front cover and spine. The front cover has within a single-rule border an elaborate centered cartouche within which is the title and author's name separated by a decorative rule. The spine reads: "[rule] | A PASSIONATE | PILGRIM ETC. | [decorative rule] | HENRY JAMES | HOUGHTON | MIFFLIN CO. | [rule]". The back cover has a single-rule border in blind. The endpapers are of white wove paper, and the text is printed on wove paper. There are no binder's fly-leaves. All edges are trimmed and the top edge appears to be stained light yellow-ochre.

This binding is uniform with that on the first American edition of *The Spoils of Poynton* (1897), 48.6.0, on which it first appeared.

This impression was printed from the first edition plates, with a reset title-page and, on the verso, the addition of the 1903 copyright information and the reservation of rights. This impression was probably printed in 1907, the first printing of this title after *The Question of Our Speech* and *English Hours* were first published (October 1905).

1.10.0. *A Passionate Pilgrim*, first edition, eleventh or twelfth impression, one volume, Boston and New York [n.d., 1908 or 1912].

The title-page, size, collation, and contents are identical to those of the first edition, tenth impression, 1.9.0, except that the publisher's imprint at the foot of the title-page reads: "HOUGHTON, MIFFLIN COMPANY | The Riverside Press Cambridge [in Gothic type]".

Binding: brown vertical-rib-grain cloth lettered and decorated identically to 1.9.0. The endpapers are of white laid paper, and the text is printed on wove paper. There are no binder's fly-leaves. All edges are trimmed, and the top edge appears to be stained ochre.

On the front pastedown is the bookplate of Edward Stewart Gifford Jr.

The change in the publisher's name (dropping the "and") on the title-page indicates that this copy is a later printing than 1.9.0.

A PASSIONATE PILGRIM

1.11.0. *A Passionate Pilgrim*, first edition, thirteenth or later impression, one volume, Boston and New York [n.d., 1917 or later].

A PASSIONATE PILGRIM | AND OTHER TALES | BY | HENRY JAMES, Jr. | [oblong publisher's device of a piper under a tree not within a frame] | BOSTON AND NEW YORK | HOUGHTON MIFFLIN COMPANY | The Riverside Press Cambridge [in Gothic type]

Size: $7\,7/16''$ x $5''$.

Collation: $[1-15^{16}\,16^{10}]$, signed as $[A]^9$ B–K^8 $[L]^8$ M-Z AA–DD^8 EE^9 and $[1]^{13}$ $2-20^{12}$ 21^9; pp. [i-ii] [1–6], [7]–496 [497–498].

Contents: [i-ii] blank, verso ad within a single-rule frame headed: "By Henry James [in Gothic type]", listing 17 titles without dollar prices, the last dated being *Italian Hours*; [1–2] title-page, verso copyright notice and reservation of rights: "COPYRIGHT, 1875, BY JAMES R. OSGOOD & CO. | COPYRIGHT, 1903, BY HOUGHTON, MIFFLIN & CO. | COPYRIGHT, 1917, BY HENRY JAMES | ALL RIGHTS RESERVED"; [3–4] "CONTENTS.", verso blank; [5–6] divisional fly-title, verso blank; [7]–496 text; [497–498] blank leaf.

Binding: glazed smooth blue cloth, lettered in gilt and decorated in black and gilt. The front cover, within a black double-rule border within which is a black single-rule frame, reads: "[horizontal decorative device of rules, dots and flowers] | A PASSIONATE | PILGRIM ETC. | [small four cornered device] | HENRY [dot] JAMES | [horizontal decorative device of rules, dots and flowers]". The spine, which is lettered in gilt, and decorated in gilt with an oblong frame within which are five decorative ovals in each of which is a stem of flowers, reads: "A | PASSIONATE | PILGRIM | ETC. | [small decorative device] | HENRY | JAMES". The back cover is neither lettered nor decorated. The endpapers are of white wove paper, and the text is printed on wove paper. There are no binder's fly-leaves. The top and fore-edges are trimmed, and the bottom edge is rough trimmed.

This impression was printed from the first edition plates (forty-two years or more after the first impression was printed), with changes to the ad on [ii] (including eliminating the dollar prices), the title-page and the title-leaf verso, and the elimination of the signature mark "L" on 177.

This binding is uniform with that on the third edition of *Roderick Hudson*, (1916), 3.16.0; the first edition, later impression, of *The American* (undated), 4.14.0; the first American edition, later impression of *The Europeans* (undated), 7.15.0; the first published edition, later impression, of *Daisy Miller: A Comedy* (undated), 18.11.0; the third American edition, first separate impression, of *The Portrait of a Lady* (1916), 16.20.5; the first edition, fourth impression, of *The Siege of London* (undated), 19.12.0; the first edition, later impression and the first edition, sixteenth impression of *A Little Tour in France* (both undated), 23.9.5 and 23.9.7; and the first edition, later impression, of *The Spoils of Poynton* (undated), 48.9.0.

✠

2. *TRANSATLANTIC SKETCHES*

2.1.0. *Transatlantic Sketches*, first edition, first impression, first binding state, one volume, Boston 1875.

TRANSATLANTIC SKETCHES. | BY | HENRY JAMES, Jr. | [monogram publisher's device] | BOSTON: | JAMES R. OSGOOD AND COMPANY, | Late Ticknor & Fields, and Fields, Osgood, & Co. | 1875.

Size: $7\,^{7}/_{16}$" x $4\,^{3}/_{4}$.

Collation: $[1]^{12}$ 2–16^{12} 17^{10}, also signed $[A]^{8}$ B–Y^{8} $[Z]^{2}$; pp. [i]–vi, [7]–401 [402], [403–404]. Note that the printer used the entire alphabet (except Z) in this collation. The first page of the text is [7], the preceding page (the last of the prelims) is paginated vi.

Contents: [i-ii] blank, verso ad for *A Passionate Pilgrim* headed: "BY THE SAME AUTHOR. [in sans-serif]"; [iii–iv] title-page, verso copyright notice and printer's imprint: "Copyright, 1875. | By JAMES R. OSGOOD & CO. | University Press: Welch, Bigelow, & Co., | Cambridge."; [v]–vi "CONTENTS", continued on verso; [7]–401 text; 401 at foot printer's imprint: "[long rule] | Cambridge: Electrotyped and Printed by Welch, Bigelow, & Co."; [402] blank; [403–404] blank leaf.

Binding: purple fine dotted-line-grain cloth over bevelled boards, with the front and back covers decorated in blind with a single-rule frame within a wider single-rule border. The spine, which is lettered and decorated in gilt, reads: "[thick followed by a thin rule] | Transatlantic | Sketches | [decorative rule] | H. James Jr. | J. R. Osgood & Co [with no period after last "o"] | [thin followed by a thick rule]". The endpapers are of brown coated paper, and the text is printed on wove paper. A binder's fly-leaf of wove paper is at both the front and the back. All edges are trimmed, and the top edge is stained gray.

The verso of [1]₃ with the pagination "vi", immediately followed by the first page of the text paginated [7] is also present in all copies catalogued in entries 2.2.0 through 2.10.8.

Printing history. Houghton Mifflin Archive. First edition: Ms Am 2030.2(23), 155: *first* [Osgood] *impression* April 21, 1875, 1578 copies, 1565 bound between April 23, 1875, and June 3, 1882; published April 29, 1875; notation "Author's Plates". Ms Am 2030(17), 116: *second impression* [and first Houghton, Mifflin impression] July 31, 1882, 158 copies, 154 bound between December 7, 1882, and July 3, 1883; *third impression* March 21, 1884, 162 copies, 165 [*sic*] bound between June 4, 1884, and May 31, 1886. Ms Am 2030(18), 136: *fourth impression* April 9, 1888, 160 copies, 155 bound between April 30, 1888, and January 29, 1892. Ms Am 2030(19), 153: notation September 25, 1892, "balance Sept 27/92 [of fourth impression] 31". Ms Am 2030(20), 173: *fifth impression* July 27, 1893, 156 copies, 154 bound between August 11, 1893, and June 2, 1898. Ms Am 2030(21), 220: *sixth impression* March 30, 1900, 158 copies, 154 bound between August 24, 1900, and May 8, 1905. Ms Am 2030(22), 218: *seventh impression* February 14, 1906, 151 copies, 150 bound between February 21, 1906, and September 23, 1907; *eighth impression* June 30, 1910, 161 copies, 157 bound between August 10, 1910, and June 14, 1920.

Priced at $2.00, which price was unchanged through 1905. This title was not published in England.

As indicated above, James paid for the plates. The cost of the plates was $532.71,[8] which includes $482.02 for the initial production of the plates, $31.00 for 62 hours of corrections, $11.25 for 9 boxes to house the plates, $2.94 for "Berry dies" and $5.50 for a further 11 hours of corrections.

James, in returning the corrected proofs of this title to the printers, insisted that each chapter must start on a fresh page. CHJL 1872–1876, Volume 2, 210.

---

8 However, in a letter from James to Osgood, dated 18 August 1875, James states that Osgood has billed him $555.07 for "the stereotyped plates of Transatlantic Sketches &c." CLHJ, 1872–1876, Volume 2, 231.

2.2.0. *Transatlantic Sketches*, first edition, first impression, first binding state, one volume, Boston 1875.

This copy is identical in all respects to the first edition, first impression, first binding state, 2.1.0, except that it is bound in green sand-grain cloth.

Illustrated Plate 2.

2.3.0. *Transatlantic Sketches*, first edition, first impression, first binding state, one volume, Boston 1875.

This copy is identical in all respects to the first edition, first impression, first binding state, 2.1.0, except that it is bound in green sand-grain cloth.

On the title-page in blue ink is a stamp, $1\,1/8''$ in diameter, of two concentric circles that reads: "H. O. Houghton & CO. | CAMBRIDGE, MASS. | SEP | 28 | 1878 [the date being centered in the inner circle]."

2.4.0. *Transatlantic Sketches*, first edition, first impression, first binding state, one volume, Boston 1875.

This copy is identical in all respects to the first edition, first impression, first binding state, 2.1.0, except that it is bound in terra-cotta fine dotted-line-grain cloth. The top edge is stained yellowish-gray.

2.5.0. *Transatlantic Sketches*, first edition, first impression, second binding state, one volume, Boston 1875.

The title-page, size, collation, and contents are identical in all respects to those of the first edition, first impression, first binding state, 2.1.0.

Binding: green sand-grain cloth over bevelled boards, lettered and decorated as described in 2.1.0, except that the rule between the title and the author's name on the spine is plain, not decorative, and that the publisher's imprint at the foot of the spine reads: "Houghton, Osgood & Co." The endpapers are of brown coated paper, of a darker brown than those on the above copies of the first binding state, and the text is printed on wove paper. There are no binder's fly-leaves. All edges are trimmed.

On the front free endpaper is the inscription: "Elizabeth D. Keing [or

Kling?] | March 1879 | New York". On the front pastedown is the book-plate of Frederic Bronson.

This second binding state is not noted in E&L, and while BAL 10530 speculates that such a binding might exist ("Query: Also bound with the Houghton, Osgood & Company spine imprint?"), he did not find such a copy. The firm was named Houghton, Osgood & Co. during the period 1878–1880, and the inscription on the endpaper coincides with these dates.

2.6.0. *Transatlantic Sketches*, first edition, first impression, second binding state, one volume, Boston 1875.

This copy is identical in all respects to the first edition, first impression, second binding state, 2.5.0, except that it is bound in purple fine sand-grain cloth, and on the spine the rule between the title and the author's name is plain not decorative. There are no binder's fly-leaves. All edges are trimmed, and the top edge is stained ochre.

On the first page of the text at the top is the pencil inscription: "A. Pardee Jr. | Aug. 1879."

2.7.0. *Transatlantic Sketches*, first edition, first impression, second binding state, one volume, Boston 1875.

This copy is identical in all respects to the first edition, first impression, second binding state, 2.5.0, except that it is bound in terra-cotta fine-sand-grain cloth and the rule on the spine between the title and the author's name is plain not decorative. A binder's fly-leaf of wove paper is at both the front and the back.

Illustrated Plate 2.

2.8.0. *Transatlantic Sketches*, first edition, first impression, third binding state, one volume, Boston 1875.

The title-page, size, collation, and contents are identical to those of the first edition, first impression, first binding state, 2.1.0.

Binding: terra-cotta sand-grain cloth over bevelled boards, lettered and decorated as described in 2.1.0, except that the rule on the spine between the title and author's name is a plain rather than a decorative rule, and the publisher's imprint at the foot of the spine reads: "Houghton, Mifflin & Co." The endpapers are of brown coated paper, and the text is printed on wove paper. A binder's fly-leaf of wove paper is at both the front and the back. All edges are trimmed.

Illustrated Plate 2.

2.9.0. *Transatlantic Sketches*, first edition, first impression, fourth binding state, one volume, Boston 1875.

Size: 7 3/8" x 4 3/4".

The title-page, collation, and contents are identical to those of the first edition, first impression, first binding state, 2.1.0.

Binding: chocolate-brown diagonal-fine-ribbed cloth, lettered in red-brown and decorated in red-brown, chocolate-brown, and gilt. The title on the front cover and spine is in red-brown within a gilt panel with a pronounced maze-like background pattern. The publisher's imprint at the foot of the spine reads: "Houghton Mifflin & Co." The ampersand in the imprint has a flat rather than a rounded top. The endpapers are of white-coated wove paper with an overall floral pattern printed in beige (this patterned endpaper is also seen on the copies of the second edition, revised, first and second American issues, of *Roderick Hudson*, below, and the second edition, first American impression, of *The Portrait of a Lady*, all of which are also bound uniformly with this title). The text is printed on wove paper. A binder's fly-leaf of wove paper is at both the front and the back. All edges are trimmed, and the top edge is stained ochre.

On the front pastedown is the bookplate of Oliver Brett (later Lord Esher).

Illustrated Plate 2.

This binding is uniform with that on the first American impression of the second edition of *The Portrait of a Lady* (1881), 16.5.0. The floral endpapers, the uniform binding, and the 1882 date on the title-pages of the uniformly bound *A Passionate Pilgrim*, *The Portrait of a Lady* and the copy of *Transatlantic Sketches* catalogued below, would suggest that this copy was bound in 1882.

TRANSATLANTIC SKETCHES

2.10.0. *Transatlantic Sketches*, first edition, second impression, one volume, Boston 1882.

TRANSATLANTIC SKETCHES. | BY | HENRY JAMES, Jr. | [shield shaped publisher's device] | BOSTON: | HOUGHTON, MIFFLIN AND COMPANY. | The Riverside Press, Cambridge. [in Gothic type] | 1882.

Size: 7 3/8" x 4 3/4".

Collation: $[1]^{12}$ $2–16^{12}$ 17^{10}, also signed as $[A]^8$ $B–X^8$ Y^{10}; pp. [i]–vi, [7]–401 [402] [403–404].

Contents: [i–ii] blank, verso and ad within a single-rule frame headed: "MR JAMES'S WRITINGS.", listing 8 titles with dollar prices, the last dated being *The Portrait of a Lady*; [iii–iv] title-page, verso copyright notice: "Copyright, 1875. | By JAMES R. OSGOOD & CO. | CAMBRIDGE: PRINTED AT THE RIVERSIDE PRESS."; [v]–vi "CONTENTS", verso continuation of contents; [7]–401 text; [402] blank; [403–404] blank leaf.

Binding: pea-green diagonal-fine-ribbed cloth, lettered in red-brown and decorated in red-brown, pea-green, and gilt on the front cover and spine. The title on the front cover and spine is in red-brown within a gilt panel with a pronounced maze-like background pattern. The publisher's imprint at the foot of the spine reads: "Houghton Mifflin & Co." The ampersand in the publisher's imprint has a flat rather than a rounded top. The endpapers are of a floral tan design on white-coated paper, and the text is printed on wove paper. A binder's fly-leaf of wove paper is at both the front and the back. All edges are trimmed, and the top edge is stained brown. It is sewn not stapled.

On the front pastedown is a label which reads: "Private Library | of | James Walter Young."

2.10.5. *Transatlantic Sketches*, first edition, fourth impression, one volume, Boston 1888.

TRANSATLANTIC SKETCHES. | BY | HENRY JAMES, Jr. | FOURTH EDITION. | [shield shaped publisher's device] | BOSTON: | HOUGHTON, MIFFLIN AND COMPANY. | The Riverside Press, Cambridge [in Gothic type] | 1888.

The size, collation, and contents are identical to those of the first edition, second impression, 20.10.0, except for "FOURTH EDITION" and the date 1888 on the title-page.

Binding: tan diagonal-fine-ribbed cloth, lettered and decorated identically to 2.10.0, except that the publisher's imprint at the foot of the spine reads: "HOUGHTON | MIFFLIN [dot] & [dot] CO." The ampersand in the imprint is like a figure "8" and has a rounded rather than a flat top. The title on the front cover and spine is within a gilt panel with a pronounced maze-like background pattern. The endpapers are of white laid paper, and the text is printed on wove paper. A binder's fly-leaf of wove paper is at the front, but none at the back. All edges are trimmed, and the top edge is stained light brown.

On the front binder's fly-leaf is the inscription "C. K. Barry. | 1895."

This binding is uniform with that on the first American impression of the second edition of *The Portrait of a Lady* (1881), 16.5.0.

2.10.6. *Transatlantic Sketches*, first edition, fourth impression, one volume, Boston 1888

The title-page, size, collation, and contents are identical to those of the first edition, fourth impression, 2.10.5.

Binding: dark-brown diagonal-fine-ribbed cloth, lettered and decorated identically to 2.10.5, including the publisher's imprint at the foot of the spine and the gilt panel on the front cover. The endpapers are of white coated woven paper with an overall floral pattern printed in beige, and the text is printed on wove paper. A binder's fly-leaf of wove paper is at the front, but none at the back. All edges are trimmed, and the top edge is stained dark brown.

2.10.8. *Transatlantic Sketches*, first edition, seventh impression, one volume, Boston and New York [n.d., 1906].

TRANSATLANTIC SKETCHES. | BY | HENRY JAMES, Jr. | [oblong publisher device of a piper under a tree within a single-rule frame] | BOSTON AND NEW YORK | HOUGHTON, MIFFLIN AND COMPANY | The Riverside Press, Cambridge [in Gothic type].

Size: $7\,3/8''$ x $5''$.

Collation: [A]^8 B–V^8 [W]^8 X–Y^8 [Z]^2, also signed as [1]^{12} 2–16^{12} 17^{10}; pp. [i]–vi, 7–401 [402] [403–404].

Contents: [i–ii] blank, verso ad within a frame headed: "By Henry James [in Gothic type]", listing 18 James titles with dollar prices, the last dated being *The Question of Our Speech* and *English Hours* (both 1905); [iii–iv] title-page, verso copyright notice, reservation of rights, and impression: "Copyright, 1875, | By JAMES R. OSGOOD & CO. | Copyright, 1903, | By HOUGHTON, MIFFLIN & CO. | All rights Reserved. [in italic] | SEVENTH IMPRESSION"; [v]–vi "CONTENTS", verso contents continued; [7]–401 text; [402] blank; [403–404] blank leaf.

Binding: brown vertical rib-grain cloth, lettered and decorated in gilt on the front cover and spine. The front cover has within a single-rule border an elaborate centered cartouche within which the title an author's name separated by a decorative rule. The spine reads: "[rule] | TRANSATLANTIC | SKETCHES | [decorative rule] | HENRY JAMES | HOUGHTON | MIFFLIN & CO." The ampersand in the publisher's imprint is stylized, and is like a Greek π. The back cover has a single-rule border in blind. The endpapers are of white laid paper, and the text is printed on wove paper. A binder's fly-leaf is at the front, but none at the back. The top edge is trimmed, and stained light-brown, and the other edges are rough-trimmed.

This binding is uniform with that on the first American edition of *The Spoils of Poynton* (1897), 48.6.0, on which it was first issued.

2.11.0. *Foreign Parts*, first continental edition, revised, first impression, one volume, Leipzig 1883.

FOREIGN PARTS. | BY | HENRY JAMES, | AUTHOR OF | "DAISY MILLER," "THE PORTRAIT OF A LADY," ETC. | AUTHORIZED EDITION. [in italic] | LEIPZIG BERNHARD TAUCHNITZ | 1883.

Size: 6" x 4 1/4".

Collation: [1]^8 2–20^8; pp. [1]–8, [9]–318 [319–320].

Contents: [1–2] series half-title, verso ad listing 9 James titles, the last dated being *The Portrait of a Lady*; [3–4] title-page, verso blank; [5–6] authorization "NOTE", verso blank; [7]–8 "CONTENTS", verso continuation of contents; [9]–318 text; [319–320] blank leaf.

Binding: rebound in half vellum, marbled paper boards with vellum fore-corners, and with gilt lettering and a floral design on the spine. The spine reads: "JAMES | [rule] | FOREIGN | PARTS | [rule]". The endpapers are of marbled paper, and the text is printed on wove paper. All edges are trimmed and stained red, and a red ribbon marker is bound in. A binder's fly-leaf of wove paper is at the front, but none at the back. It lacks the original dated wrappers and the publisher's catalogue of ads at the end.

This copy is signed by Henry James on the title-page and inscribed "Julia G Robins | Florence | Feby 1887", in what appears to be James's hand, on the front binder's fly-leaf. James was in Florence between some time in early January 1887 and February 20, 1887; see Leon Edel, *The Middle Years* (Philadelphia and New York: J.B. Lippincott Company, 1962), 208–212.

This is a revised edition of *Transatlantic Sketches*, with omissions.

See T&B 2164a. T&B records one edition with two impressions of this title, the first with 9 titles and the second with 13 titles on the half-title-leaf verso. This copy, with nine titles conforms to the description given in T&B for the first impression, but without its dated wrappers and catalogue the issue date cannot be precisely determined. Inexplicably, leaf 20_4, pages [319–320], which is an integral part of the last signature, lacks the printer's imprint called for by T&B on the recto and is a blank; see 2.12.0.

See also Appendix B: A Note on Tauchnitz's James Editions.

2.12.0. *Foreign Parts*, first continental edition, revised, first impression, later binding state, one volume, Leipzig 1883.

The title-page and collation are identical to those of the first continental edition, revised, first impression, 2.11.0.

Size: 6 $7/16''$ x 4 $5/8''$.

Contents: [1–2] series half-title, verso ad listing 9 James titles, the last dated being *The Portrait of a Lady*; [3–4] title-page, verso blank; [5–6] authorization "NOTE.", verso blank; [7]–8 "CONTENTS.", verso continuation of contents; [9]–318 text; [319] printer's imprint: "PRINTING OFFICE OF THE PUBLISHER. [between two rules]"; [320] blank.

Binding: buff wove paper wrappers, cut flush, with lettering on the front cover in black within a black single-rule frame which is decorated with a flower-like device at each of the four corners with lettering above and below the frame. The spine is lettered in black between a series of eight pairs of thick and thin black rules. The back cover, which is also lettered in black, reads: "December 1889. | TAUCHNITZ

EDITION. | [rule] | Latest Volumes: | [followed by a list of 29 titles, but without their corresponding Tauchnitz issue numbers, the last title listed being *For One and the World* by M. Betham-Edwards] | A complete Catalogue of the Tauchnitz | Edition is attached to this work. | [long rule] | Bernhard Tauchnitz, Leipzig; | And sold by all booksellers." The inner front and back wrappers are blank. A 16-page publisher's catalogue, dated January 1895, is bound in at the end.

On the series half-title is the ink inscription: "Pamela O. Clapp | Geneva, August 1898".

T&B 2164a records one edition with two impressions of this title. The earliest issue having a wrapper dated July 1883. T&B does not record an issue with a December 1889 wrapper. This copy is of the first impression but of a binding state later than the first.

2.13.0. *Foreign Parts*, first continental edition, revised, second impression, later binding state, one volume, Leipzig 1883.

The title-page, size, and collation are the same as those of the first continental edition, revised, first impression, later binding state, 2.12.0.

Contents: identical to those of 2.12.0, except that the half-title-leaf verso ad lists 13 rather than 9 titles, the last dated being *A Little Tour in France*, and on [319] the printer's imprint is present.

Binding: buff wove paper wrappers, cut flush. The lettering and decoration on the front cover and spine is the same as that of 2.12.0, except that the title and author's name on the front cover are in bold sans-serif type. The back cover reads: "December 1912. | Tauchnitz Edition. | [rule] | Latest Volumes | [followed by a list of 24 titles with each title preceded by its Tauchnitz issue number] | [long rule] | The Tauchnitz Edition is sold by all Booksellers and Rail- | way Libraries on the Continent, price of each volume M1, 60 or | francs 2,00 sewed, M2, 20 or francs 2, 75 cloth (Original-Leinen- | band), M3,00 or francs 3, 75 in elegant soft binding (Original- | Geschenkband). A complete Catalogue of the Tauchnitz Edition is | attached to this work. [all the foregoing in italic]". The inner front and back wrappers are blank. No publisher's catalogue is bound in at the end.

T&B 2164b records the second impression of this title as having 13 James titles listed on the verso of the half-title-leaf. That entry records the earliest wrapper being dated January 1906, but does not record a wrapper dated December 1912. It is difficult to date this impression; one can only state that it was printed after the first impression of *A Little Tour in France* (1885) and before January 1906, the earliest wrapper date on this impression recorded in T&B 2164b, as no other James titles were published by Tauchnitz between 1885 and 1912.

2.13.5 *Foreign Parts*, first continental edition, revised, second impression, later binding state, one volume, Leipzig 1883.

The title-page, size, and collation are the same as those of the first continental edition, first impression, later binding state, 2.12.0.

Contents: identical to those of 2.12.0, except the title-leaf verso lists 9 rather than 13 titles, the latest dated being *A Little Tour in France*, and on [319] the printer's imprint is present.

Binding: buff wove wrappers, cut flush, with lettering on the front cover in black within a double-rule frame, the outer rule being wider than the inner, which frames are divided into three panels by thin double rules. The lettering in the upper panel reads: "TAUCHNITZ EDITION | COLLECTION OF BRITISH AND AMERICAN AUTHORS | VOL. 2164". The middle panel reads: "FOREIGN PARTS | BY | HENRY JAMES [all the foregoing in sans-serif] | IN ONE VOLUME | LEIPZIG: BERNHARD TAUCHNITZ | PARIS: LIBRAIRIE HENRY GAULON, 39, RUE MADAME". The lower panel reads: "The Copyright of this Collection is purchased for Continental Circulation | only and the volumes therefore may not be introduced into Great Britain | or her Colonies." Below the frame reads: "A complete cataloguer of the Tauchnitz Edition, with a list of the latest additions | on page 1 is attached to this volume [all in italic]". The spine, also lettered in black between a series of eight pairs of thick and thin black rules, and between rules six and seven reads: "PRICE | M1. 80". The back cover, also lettered in black, reads at the top: "TAUCHNITZ EDITION | Latest Volumes | 4–6 new volumes are published regularly every month [in italic] | November 1926", followed by a list of volumes 4756 to 4726, in descending numerical order. Bound in at the end is a 32 page catalogue dated on [1] "October 1928".

3. RODERICK HUDSON

3.1.0. *Roderick Hudson*, first edition, first impression, first binding state, one volume, Boston 1876 [1875].

RODERICK HUDSON. | BY | HENRY JAMES, Jr. | [monogram publisher's device] | BOSTON: | JAMES R. OSGOOD AND COMPANY, | Late Ticknor & Fields, and Fields, Osgood, & Co. | 1876.

Size: 7 $^{5}/_{16}$" x 4 $^{13}/_{16}$".

Collation: [1^2 2–21^{12} 22^2], signed as π^2 1–30^8 31^2; pp. [i–iv], [1]–482 [483–484].

Contents: [i–ii] title-page, verso copyright notice and printer's imprint: "Copyright, 1875, | By H. O. Houghton & Co. and James R. Osgood & Co. | RIVERSIDE, CAMBRIDGE: | STEREOTYPED AND PRINTED BY | H. O. HOUGHTON AND COMPANY."; [iii–iv] "CONTENTS.", verso blank; [1]–482 text; [483–484] blank leaf.

Binding: green sand-grain cloth over bevelled boards, with the front and back covers decorated in blind with a single-rule frame within a wider single-rule border. The spine, which is lettered and decorated in gilt, reads: "[thick followed by thin rule] | Roderick | Hudson | [rule] | H. James Jr. | J. R. Osgood & Co." | [thin followed by a thick rule]". The endpapers are of brown coated paper, and the text is printed on wove paper. A binder's fly-leaf of wove paper is at both the front and the back. All edges are trimmed.

BAL 10531 has identified three typographical errors in the text of this impression: on page 12, line 6 ("illustratd"), page 16, line 3 ("to her") and page 447 line, line 11 ("Casamassina").

Printing history as recorded in the Houghton Mifflin Archive. First edition: Ms Am 2030.2(23), 155: *first impression* November 10, 1875, 1572 copies, 1553 bound between November 17, 1875, and January 28, 1882; published November 20, 1875; notations: "printed by H. O. H & Co." and "Plates melted May 23, 1894". Ms Am 2030(17), 116: *second impression*[9] March 27, 1882, 250 copies, 242 bound May 2 and 3, 1882; *third impression* September 10, 1882, 248 copies "+ 5 imperfect", 252 [sic] bound between September

---

9 This record is as reflected in the Houghton, Mifflin Ledgers. In actuality, as is discussed in detail later, what is recorded as the second through the nineteenth impressions are not separate impressions but batches of sheets printed by Macmillan in England and shipped to Houghton, Mifflin in America.

RODERICK HUDSON

20, 1882, to February 5, 1884; *fourth impression* September 9, 1884, 245 copies, 248 [sic] bound between October 18, 1884, and November 12, 1886; notation to second through fourth impressions: "Printed by Macmillan". Ms Am 2030(18), 135: *fifth impression* July 11, 1888, 150 copies, 143 bound between July 13, 1888, and March 1, 1890; notation: "Printed by Macmillan & Co." Ms Am 2030(19), 157: *sixth impression* February 25, 1891, 76 copies, 76 bound April 4, 1891, and 1 "lev[ant]". June 3, 1892; *seventh impression* June 20, 1892, received from Macmillan & Co. 150 copies, 138 bound between November 1, 1892, and July 6, 1893. Ms Am 2030(20), 174: *eighth impression* February 23, 1895, received from Macmillan & Co., 150 copies of 841, 158 [sic] bound between March 25, 1895, and June 15, 1899. Ms Am 2030(21), 220: *ninth impression* March 27, 1899, received from Macmillan & Co. 100 copies and June 6, 1899, received from Macmillan & Co. 50 copies, 148 bound between July 6, 1899, and August 24, 1900; notation: "[total to date] 2991". Ms Am 2030(22), 218: *tenth impression* March 9, 1901, received from Macmillan & Co. 61 copies, all bound April 16 and 30, 1901; *eleventh impression* July 29, 1901 [sic, 1902?], received from Macmillan & Co. 250 copies, all bound between August 22, 1902, and May 4, 1904; notation: "new size"; *twelfth impression* January 6, 1905, received from Macmillan & Co. 250 copies, 251 [sic] bound between February 3, 1905, and June 9, 1905; *thirteenth impression* August 31, 1906, received from Macmillan & Co. 250 copies, 252 [sic] bound between October 16, 1906, and June 27, 1907; *fourteenth impression* anuary 20, 1908, received from Macmillan & Co. 250 copies, 249 bound between February 28, 1908, and September 24, 1908; notation: "printed in England on last page"; *fifteenth impression* January 4, 1909, received from Macmillan & Co. 250 copies, all bound between January 21, 1909, and March 3, 1910; notation: "printed in England on last page". Ms Am 2030(23), 213: *sixteenth impression* April 14, 1910, received from Macmillan & Co. 250 copies, 251 [sic] bound between June 9, 1910, and May 31, 1911; *seventeenth impression* February 2, 1912, received from Macmillan & Co. 250 copies, all bound April 4, 5 and 6, 1912; notation: "3/28/12 ptd. 302 cancel title and note"; *eighteenth impression* October 4, 1913, received from Macmillan & Co. 252 copies, 250 bound between December 18, 1913, and January 17, 1914; *nineteenth impression* July 6, 1915, received from Macmillan & Co. 252 copies, 251 bound between September 13, 1915, and January 4, 1916; notation: "5/24/15 ptd. 372 titles"; *twentieth impression* August 9, 1917, "New [second American] Edition", 1038 copies, 1028 bound between August 27, 1917, and February 1, 1921; notation: "8/27/17 ptd. 1040 jackets"; *twenty-first impression* February 7, 1922, 524 copies, 519 bound on March 1, 1922, and August 16, 1926; notations: "2/7/22 ptd. 526 jackets", "New Edition" and "[total copies printed] 6868".

Priced at $2.00, which price was unchanged through 1905.

Printing history as recorded in the Macmillan Archive. The Houghton, Mifflin record cited above is clarified by the printing history of *Roderick Hudson* in the Editions Book of Macmillan & Co. MEB, 267 records the following: June 1879 a first (and sole) impression of 500 copies of the three volume first English edition, revised (note that the 1875 text of the first American edition was not published in England); March 1880 the first impression of 1500 copies of the one volume second English edition, revised; with a second impression of 2,000 copies in June 1888. There were no further printings for the English market. However, starting in July 1902 (with what was recorded by Houghton, Mifflin as the eleventh impression) there are recorded nine further printings by Macmillan's English printer from the plates of the second English edition, revised for "Amer. Edn ptd. for Houghton, Mifflin & Co." Seven of these printings are of 250 copies, and two are of 252 on the following dates: July 1902; January 1905; August 1906; January and December 1908; April 1910; January 1912; September 1913; and July 1913. There is the notation : [plates] "dest. Feb. /21".

From the above it is clear that the "second" through the "nineteenth" impressions in the Houghton, Mifflin records do not represent American impressions, but are rather batches of sheets imported from England. The "twentieth" and "twenty first" impressions are Houghton, Mifflin printings (a new edition).

James's dislike of the first edition text was clearly known to Houghton, Mifflin prior to 1882. On November 23, 1881, James wrote to Houghton, Mifflin: "I had some talk with one of your gentlemen (in Park St.,) which appeared to be all that is necessary to be said just now in relation to *Roderick Hudson*. I desire that the American [first] edition of the book should remain for the present out of print. The English edition [second edition, revised of 1879] is virtually a new book, & a very superior one; & it is only in that form that I wish to present it again to the American public". Horne, Letter 61.

To accommodate James and no doubt to avoid the expense of creating a new set of plates based on the revised text, Houghton, Mifflin imported English sheets. Sheets of the one volume 1880 second English edition, revised, first impression were used, with new prelims, for the 1882 and 1885 American issues (three issues in all, 3.8.0–3.10.0). These are thought to correspond to the "second" (1882), "third" (1882) and "fourth" (1884) impressions in the Houghton, Mifflin records. They comprise in total 740 sets of sheets, or almost half those printed in 1880 by Macmillan. They are described as the second edition, revised, *first impression*, first through the third American issues.

What is referred to in the Houghton, Mifflin records as the "fifth impression" of 1888 (with the notation printed "[by] Macmillan & Co.") through the "tenth impression" are further importations aggregating 740 sets of Macmillan sheets. In all probability these were of the *second impression* of the second English edition which was printed in 1888, the imported sheets again accounting for almost half the Macmillan second impression. A copy of this first American issue of the second impression with an 1888 date on the title-page has not been found. But the "sixth impression" of 1891 is clearly a further importation of sheets of the second English edition, second impression of 1888, as the printing history on the title-page verso references the 1888 impression. It constitutes the second American issue of the second impression; see 3.11.0.

These six "impressions" (the fifth through the tenth) are the first (1888) through the sixth (1901) American issues of the *second impression* of the second English edition, revised.[10]

The "tenth impression", that is the sixth American issue, published by Houghton, Mifflin in 1901 must have exhausted Macmillan's surplus supply of its 1888 second impression sheets. To provide further sheets, Macmillan in the period July 1902, to July 1915, printed for Houghton, Mifflin nine further impressions aggregating 2254 sets of sheets; see 3.11.7 through 3.15.0. Each of these impressions was of 250 (two were of 252) sets of sheets. None of these impressions were published in England. These constitute the *third* through the *eleventh* impressions of the second edition, revised.

In 1916 Thomas Nelson and Sons published a new cheap edition, priced at 7d., which was reprinted in 1921, priced at 2s.; see note following 4.21.5.

On August 9, 1917, Houghton, Mifflin printed a "New Edition" with a first impression of 1038 copies of *Roderick Hudson* (with James's preface)

---

10 This is based on the assumption that the shipments of March and June 1899 were used for a single issue, which is implied by the numbering of the "impressions".

from the American plates used to print that title in the *Novels and Tales of Henry James* (the New York Edition, 1907–1909), and on August 27, 1917, printed 1040 dust-jackets.¹¹ This is the fourth edition of *Roderick Hudson*, as a stand-alone volume; see 3.16.0. This separate impression has been classified as the first separate impression of the third edition. A second impression of 524 copies of this edition was printed on February 7, 1922. This was part of the 1922 reprinting of the *The Novels and Tales of Henry James*; see the printing history in 64.

3.2.0. *Roderick Hudson*, first edition, first impression, first binding state, one volume Boston 1876 [1875].

This copy is identical in all respects to the first edition, first impression, first binding state, 3.1.0, except that it is bound in terra-cotta dotted-line-grain cloth.

On the front pastedown is the bookplate of Oliver Brett (later Lord Esher).

3.3.0. *Roderick Hudson*, first edition, first impression, first binding state, one volume, Boston 1876 [1875].

This copy is identical in all respects to the first edition, first impression, first binding state, 3.1.0, except that it is bound in dark plum dotted-line-grain cloth.

This cloth color is not recorded in E&L or BAL. E&L records copies in green patterned sand-grain, and deep rust-brown and terra-cotta fine bead-grain cloth. BAL records copies in green C (sand-grain) and terra-cotta FL (dotted-line-grain) cloth only.

3.4.0. *Roderick Hudson*, first edition, first impression, second binding state, one volume, Boston 1876 [1875].

The title-page, size, collation, and contents are identical to those of

---

11 The entry for "New Edition" in Ms Am 2030(23), 213 is slightly ambiguous. Although the entry is headed at the top "Rcvd from Macmillan & Co.", there are no dates of receipts of the sheets of the "New Edition" from Macmillan as there are for other "impressions" in this entry. In addition, there is no corresponding entry in the Macmillan Production Ledgers referring to such a printing. It seems clear that this "New Edition" was printed by Houghton, Mifflin. This is corroborated by the copy described in 3.16.0.

RODERICK HUDSON

the first edition, first impression, first binding state, 3.1.0.

Binding: terra-cotta sand-grain cloth over bevelled boards, lettered and decorated identically to 3.1.0, except that the publisher's imprint at the foot of the spine reads: "Houghton, Osgood & Co." The endpapers are of brown coated paper, and the text is printed on wove paper. A binder's fly-leaf of wove paper is at both the front and the back. All edges are trimmed.

The bookplate of Edwin W. Coggeshall is on the front pastedown.

3.5.0. *Roderick Hudson*, first edition, first impression, second binding state, one volume, Boston 1876 [1875].

This copy is identical in all respects to the first edition, first impression, second binding state, 3.4.0, except that it is bound in dark green sand-grain cloth. The endpapers are of brown coated paper, and the text is printed on wove paper. A binder's fly-leaf of wove paper is at the front, but none at the back. All edges are trimmed.

3.6.0. *Roderick Hudson*, first edition, first impression, second binding state, one volume, Boston 1876 [1875].

This copy is identical in all respects to the first edition, first impression, second binding state, 3.4.0, except that it is bound in plum dotted-line-grain cloth. The endpapers are of brown coated paper, and the text is printed on wove paper. A binder's fly-leaf of wove paper is at the back, but none at the front. All edges are trimmed.

3.7.0. *Roderick Hudson*, first edition, first impression, third binding state, one volume, Boston 1876 [1875].

The title-page, size, collation, and contents are identical to those of the first edition, first impression, first binding state, 3.1.0.

Binding: green sand-grain cloth over bevelled boards, lettered and decorated as described in 3.1.0, except that the publisher's imprint at the foot of the spine reads: "Houghton, Mifflin & Co." The endpapers are of brown coated paper, and the text is printed on wove paper. A binder's fly-leaf of wove paper is at the front, but none at the back. All edges are trimmed.

On the recto of the binder's fly-leaf at the front is the inscription: "Hugh Jevis | Cambridge; Harvard College | [double rule] | '84'".

Not recorded in E&L, but noted in BAL 10531.

3.8.0. *Roderick Hudson*, second edition, revised, first impression, first American issue, one volume, Boston and New York 1882.

RODERICK HUDSON. | BY | HENRY JAMES, JR. | REVISED EDITION. [in italic] | [shield shaped publisher's device] | BOSTON: | HOUGHTON, MIFFLIN AND COMPANY. | NEW YORK: 11 EAST SEVENTEENTH STREET. | THE RIVERSIDE PRESS, CAMBRIDGE. [in Gothic type] | 1882.

Size: 7 3/8" x 4 3/4".

Collation: $[A]^8$ ($\pm[A]_{1,2}$) B–I K–U X^8 Y^8(–$Y_{7,8}$); pp. [1–4], [5]–347 [348]. A_1 and A_2 are cancels. The two excised leaves, Y_7 and Y_8, are the four pages of English ads.

Contents: [1–2] title-page, verso copyright notice: "Copyright, 1875. | By H. O. HOUGHTON & CO., and JAMES R. OSGOOD & CO. | Copyright, 1882. | By HENRY JAMES, JR."; [3–4] "NOTE. | 'Roderick Hudson' was originally published in 1875. | It has now been minutely revised, and has received a large | number of verbal alterations. Several passages have been | rewritten.", verso blank; [5]–347 text; [348] centered, printer's imprint: "LONDON | R. CLAY, SONS, AND TAYLOR, | BREAD STREET HILL".

The text of the "Note" on [3] differs slightly from that in the second edition, revised, English issue, 3.17.0, in that the words "in Boston" have been deleted.

Binding: pea-green diagonal-fine-ribbed cloth lettered and decorated in red-brown, green, and gilt. The title on the front cover and spine is in red-brown within a gilt panel with a pronounced maze-like background pattern. The publisher's imprint at the foot of the spine reads: "Houghton Mifflin & Co." The ampersand has a flat rather than a rounded top. The endpapers are of white-coated paper on which is printed an overall floral pattern in beige. The text is printed on wove paper. A binder's fly-leaf of wove paper is at both the front and the back. All edges are trimmed, and the top edge is stained brown. It is stapled, not sewn. There is no catalogue of ads at the end.

This binding is uniform with that of the second edition, first American impression of *The Portrait of a Lady* (1881), 16.5.0.

3.9.0. *Roderick Hudson*, second edition, revised, first impression, second (?) American issue, one volume, Boston and New York 1882.

The title-page, size, collation and contents of this copy are identical to those of the second edition, revised, first impression, first American issue, 3.8.0, except that the title-leaf verso has commas rather than periods after each of the two copyright years.

Binding: tan diagonal-fine-ribbed cloth, with lettering and decoration in red-brown, tan, and gilt. The title on the front cover and spine is in red-brown within a gilt panel with a pronounced maze-like background pattern. The publisher's imprint at the foot of the spine reads: "Houghton Mifflin & Co." The ampersand in that imprint has a flat rather than a rounded top. The endpapers are of white-coated paper on which is printed an overall floral pattern in beige. The text is printed on wove paper. A binder's fly-leaf of wove paper is at both the front and the back. All edges are trimmed, and it is sewn, not stapled. Bound in at the end is an undated 16-page paginated publisher's catalogue of ads, [1] of which is headed: "STANDARD AND POPULAR | LIBRARY BOOKS [in Gothic type] | SELECTED FROM THE CATALOGUE OF [in italic capitals] | HOUGHTON, MIFFLIN AND CO.", listing 8 titles by James with dollar prices on page 9. This catalogue is printed on a slightly thicker paper than that used in the body of the book.

This binding is uniform with that of the second edition, first American impression, of *The Portrait of a Lady* (1881), 16.5.0. These identical ads also appear at the end of the uniformly bound second edition, fifth, sixth and (with slight variations) seventh American impressions of *The Portrait of a Lady*, 16.13.0–16.16.0, but are present there not as an inserted catalogue but as part of the signatures of the book.

3.10.0. *Roderick Hudson*, second edition, revised, first impression, third American issue, one volume, Boston 1885.

The title-page, size, collation (including the cancels and excisions), and contents are identical to those of the first edition, revised, first impression, first American issue, 3.8.0, except that the title-page is dated 1885 rather than 1882, and the copyright notice on the verso of the title-leaf has a comma rather than a period after each of the two copyright years.

Binding: chocolate-brown diagonal-fine-ribbed cloth lettered and decorated in red-brown, chocolate-brown, and gilt. The title on the front cover and spine is in red-brown within a gilt panel with a pronounced maze-like background pattern. The publisher's imprint at the foot of the spine reads: "Houghton Mifflin & Co." The ampersand in that imprint has a flat rather than a rounded top. The endpapers are of white-coated paper on which is printed an overall floral pattern in beige, and the text is printed on wove paper. A binder's fly-leaf of wove paper is at both the front and the back. All edges are trimmed, and it is sewn, not stapled. There is no catalogue of ads at the end.

On the front free endpaper is a small label, lettered in black, reading: "W.B. CLARKE & CARRUTH | BOOKSELLERS STATIONERS | BOSTON". On the front pastedown is the bookplate that reads: "From the Library of | Dave Hennen Morris | New York".

3.11.0. *Roderick Hudson*, second edition, revised, second impression, second American issue, one volume, Boston and New York 1891.

RODERICK HUDSON | BY | HENRY JAMES, Jr. | Boston and New York [in Gothic type] | HOUGHTON, MIFFLIN, [sic] & COMPANY | THE RIVERSIDE PRESS, CAMBRIDGE | 1891

The title-leaf is a cancel, and the new tipped-in title-leaf measures $7\,1/8''$ in height, $3/16''$ less than the height of the rest of the pages in this copy. There is no publisher's device on the title-page.

Size: $7\,5/16'' \times 4\,3/4''$.

Collation: $[A]^8\,(\pm[A]_2)$ B–I K–U $X^8\,Y^8(-Y_{7,\,8})$; [1–4], [5]–347 [348].

Contents: [1–2] half-title, verso publisher's device of Macmillan [sic]; [3–4] title-page, verso blank; [5]–347 text; [348] printer's imprint: "LONDON | R. CLAY, SONS, AND TAYLOR, | BREAD STREET HILL." There is no copyright notice, and the "NOTE" is not present.

Binding: chocolate-brown diagonal-fine-ribbed cloth, lettered and decorated in red-brown, chocolate-brown, and gilt. The title on the front cover and spine is red-brown within a gilt panel with a pronounced maze-like background pattern. The publisher's imprint at the foot of the spine reads: "HOUGHTON | MIFFLIN [dot] & [dot] CO". The ampersand is like a figure "8" and has a rounded rather than a flat top. The endpapers are of white laid paper, and the text is printed on wove paper. A binder's fly-leaf of wove paper is at both the front and the back. All edges are trimmed, and the top edge is stained light brown. It is sewn, not stapled.

On the front free endpaper is the inscription: "Edith Lowenstene | 46 West 73 | N.Y.C."

This copy is made up of sheets of the second edition, revised, second English impression (the yellowback, 3.19.0) imported between 1888 and 1901, with a new title-leaf [3–4].

3.11.1. *Roderick Hudson*, second edition, revised, second impression, second American issue, one volume, Boston and New York, 1891.

The title-page, size, collation, and contents of this copy are identical to the second edition revised, second impression, second American issue, 3.11.0, except that the length of the title-leaf is 6 $^{15}/_{16}$", seven-sixteenth of an inch less than the height of the rest of the pages in this copy.

Binding: pea-green diagonal-fine-ribbed cloth, lettered and decorated identically to 3.11.0. It has endpapers of white laid paper and the text is printed on wove paper. A binder's fly-leaf of wove paper is at both the front and the back. All edges are trimmed, and the top edge is stained ochre.

3.11.3. *Roderick Hudson*, second edition, revised, second impression, third American issue, one volume, Boston and New York, 1892.

RODERICK HUDSON. | BY | HENRY JAMES, JR. | [oblong publisher's device of a piper under a tree within a frame] | BOSTON AND NEW YORK: | HOUGHTON, MIFFLIN AND COMPANY. | The Riverside Press, Cambridge. [in Gothic type] | 1892.

Size: 7 $^{1}/_{8}$" x 4 $^{13}/_{16}$".

Collation: $[A]^8([-A]_1 \pm [A]_2)$ B–I K–U X^8 Y^8 $(-Y_{7,8})$; pp. [3–4], [5]–347 [348].

The excised leaf, $[A]_1$, was the Macmillan half-title; $[A]_2$ is the new title-leaf; $[Y_{7,8}]$ the excised Macmillan ads; see 3.19.0.

Contents: [1–2] excised; [3–4] title-page, verso copyright notice, "NOTE" and printing history: "Copyright, 1879, | By HENRY JAMES. | NOTE. | 'Roderick Hudson' was originally published in Boston in | 1875. It has now been minutely revised, and has received a | large number of verbal alterations. Several passages have been | rewritten. | First Edition, 3 vols. crown 8vo, 1879. | New Edition, 1 vol. crown 8vo, 1880. | New Edition, 1 vol. globe 8vo, 1888."; [5]–347 text; [348] printer's imprint: "Richard Clay and Sons, Limited, | LONDON AND BUNGAY."

Binding: tan diagonal-fine-ribbed cloth, lettered in red-brown with decoration in red-brown, tan, and gilt. The title on the front cover and spine is in red-brown within a gilt panel with a pronounced maze-like background pattern. The publisher's imprint at the foot of the spine reads: "HOUGHTON | MIFFLIN [dot] & [dot] CO." The ampersand is like a figure "8", and has a rounded rather than a flat top, and the period after "CO" is a small dash. The endpapers are of white laid paper, and the text is printed on thin wove paper. A binder's fly-leaf of wove paper is at both the front and the back. All edges are trimmed, and the top edge is stained brown. It is sewn not stapled.

On the front binder's fly-leaf is the inscription "C. K. Barry. | 1895."

This copy is made up of sheets of the second English impression (the yellowback) with a new title-page, [3]. The text of title-leaf verso, [4], is that of the English yellowback impression except that the printer's imprint has been eliminated, and it has been reset in smaller type (brevier rather than long primer used in the yellowback).

3.11.5. *Roderick Hudson*, second edition, revised, second impression, fourth American issue, one volume, Boston and New York 1895.

Size: $7\,^1/_{16}"$ x $4\,^{13}/_{16}"$.

Title-page, collation, and contents are identical to the second edition, revised, third American issue, 3.11.3, except that the title-page is dated 1895.

Binding: olive-green vertical-rib-grain cloth, lettered and decorated in gilt on the front cover and spine. The front cover has within a single-rule border an elaborate centered cartouche within which are the title and the author's name separated by a decorative rule. The spine reads: "[rule] | RODERICK | HUDSON | [decorative rule] | HENRY JAMES | HOUGHTON | MIFFLIN [dot] & [dot] CO". The publisher's imprint on the spine is in sans-serif. The back cover has a single-rule border in blind. The endpapers are of laid paper, and the text is printed on thin wove paper. A binder's fly-leaf of wove paper, slightly thicker than the text paper, is at both the front and the back. All edges are trimmed.

On the recto of the front free endpaper is an ink inscription dated "January, 1899."

This binding is uniform with that on the first American edition of *The Spoils of Poynton* (1897), 48.6.0, on which it was first used. This suggests that the sheets of this copy were bound-up in 1897 or later.

3.11.6. *Roderick Hudson*, second edition, revised, second impression, fifth or sixth American issue, one volume, Boston and New York [n.d., probably between 1899 and 1901].

The title-page is identical to that of the second edition, revised, second impression, third American issue, 3.11.3, except that it has no date at the foot.

Size: $7\,^{11}/_{16}''$ x $4\,^{3}/_{4}''$.

Collation: identical to that of the second American issue, 3.11.0, except that leaf A_1, [1–2], is present.

Contents: identical to those of the first American issue, 3.11.1, except [1–2], a blank leaf, is present, and, as is the case of the third American issue, 3.11.5, the title-leaf verso, [4], is identical to that of the English second edition, revised, second impression (yellowback).

Binding: pea-green vertical rib-grain cloth, lettered and decorated in gilt on the front cover and spine. The front cover has within a single-rule border an elaborate centered cartouche within which is the title and author's name separated by a decorative rule. The spine reads: "[rule] | RODERICK | HUDSON | [decorative rule] | HENRY JAMES | HOUGHTON | MIFFLIN & CO." The ampersand in the publisher's imprint is stylized, and is like a Greek π. The back cover has a single rule border in blind. The endpapers are of white laid paper, and the text is printed on thin wove paper. There are no binder's fly-leaves. All edges are trimmed, and the top edge is stained light brown.

Like the preceding three American issues of the second edition, second impression, this issue is of sheets of the yellowback, with a reset title-leaf. The text of title-leaf verso, [4], is that of the English yellowback impression except that the printer's imprint has been eliminated and it has been reset in smaller type (brevier rather than long primer used in the yellowback).

This binding is uniform with that on the first American edition of *The Spoils of Poynton* (1897), 48.6.0.

3.11.7. *Roderick Hudson*, second edition, revised, fourth impression, one volume, Boston and New York 1905.

Roderick Hudson | By | Henry James | [oblong publisher's device of a piper under a tree not within a frame] | BOSTON AND NEW YORK | HOUGHTON, MIFFLIN AND COMPANY | The Riverside Press, Cambridge [in Gothic type] | 1905

Size: $7\,7/16''$ x $4\,15/16''$.

Collation: $[A]^8$ B–I K–U X^8 Y^6; pp. [1–4], [5]–347 [348].

Contents: [1–2] half-title, verso blank; [3–4] title-page, verso copyright notice: "Copyright [in italic] | 1879 | By Henry James.", and "NOTE." as in 3.11.3, but with different line endings; [5]–347 text; [348] printer's imprint: "Richard Clay and Sons, Limited, | BREAD STREET HILL, E. C., AND | BUNGAY, SUFFOLK."

Binding: olive-green vertical rib grain cloth, lettered and decorated identically to the second impression, fourth American issue, 3.11.5, except that the ampersand in the publisher's imprint on the spine is stylized like the Greek π. The endpapers are of white laid paper, and the text is printed on coarse wove paper. A binder's fly-leaf of wove paper is at both the front and the back. All edges are trimmed, and the top edge is stained brown.

Unlike 3.11.5 this copy is not made up of sheets of the yellowback. It is made up of imported sheets of an English printing (250 sets of sheets) in January 1905, all of the sheets of which were imported to America; see printing history 3.1.0.

3.12.0. *Roderick Hudson*, second edition, revised, sixth impression, one volume, Boston and New York 1908.

The title-page, collation, and contents are identical to those of the second edition, revised, fourth impression, 3.11.7, except that the title-page is dated 1908 at the foot, the printer's imprint is at the foot of 347, not on [348], and on [348] there is the legend "Printed in Great Britain. [in italic]"

Binding: brown vertical-rib-grain cloth, lettered and decorated in gilt on the front cover and spine. The front cover has within a single-rule border an elaborate centered cartouche within which is the title and author's name separated by a decorative rule. The spine reads: "[rule] | RODERICK | HUDSON | [decorative rule] | HENRY JAMES | HOUGHTON | MIFFLIN CO. | [rule]". The back cover has a single-rule border in blind. The endpapers are of white laid paper, and the text is printed on coarse wove paper. There are no binder's fly-leaves. The top edge is trimmed, and the other edges are untrimmed.

This binding is uniform with that on the first American edition of *The Spoils of Poynton* (1897), 48.6.0. The paper used in this copy is quite thick and coarse, and is very different from the thinner smoother paper used in previous impressions of the second edition, American issues. It seems that in the fifth and subsequent impressions that Macmillan printed for Houghton, Mifflin (all of the sheets of which were exported to America) Houghton, Mifflin requested thicker paper to make the copies bulkier. The text block of this and the subsequent impressions are $1\,3/16''$ thick as against $3/4''$ for the previous American issues.

The sixth impression (250 sets of sheets) was printed in January 1908, and the seventh (also 250 sets of sheets) in December 1908.

3.13.0. *Roderick Hudson*, second edition, revised, eight impression, one volume, Boston and New York 1910.

The title-page, size, collation, and contents of this copy are identical to those of the second edition, revised, sixth impression, 3.12.0, except that the title-page is dated 1910.

Binding: identical to 3.12.0, except that there is a binder's fly-leaf of wove paper at both the front and the back.

The eighth impression (250 sets of sheets) was printed in England in April 1910.

3.14.0. *Roderick Hudson*, second edition, revised, tenth or eleventh impression, one volume, Boston and New York [n.d., 1913 or 1915].

RODERICK HUDSON | BY | HENRY JAMES | [oblong publisher's device of a piper under a tree not within a frame] | BOSTON AND NEW YORK | HOUGHTON MIFFLIN COMPANY | The Riverside Press Cambridge [in Gothic type]

The size, collation, and contents of this copy are identical to those of the second edition, revised, sixth impression, 3.12.0, except that there is no date on the title-page, the printer's imprint on 347 reads: "PRINTED IN GREAT BRITAIN BY R. CLAY AND SONS, LTD., | BRUNSWICK ST., STAMFORD ST., LONDON, S. E., AND BUNGAY SUFFOLK.", and [348] is blank.

Binding: brown vertical-rib-grain cloth, lettered and decorated identically to 3.12.0. The endpapers are of white laid paper, and the text is printed on wove paper. A binder's fly-leaf of wove paper is at both the front and the back. All edges are trimmed, and the top edge is stained ochre.

On the title-page is the ink inscription: "Sarah & Stanley Bright | Cedar Hill Farm | Spring 1916."

3.15.0. *Roderick Hudson*, second edition, revised, tenth or eleventh impression, one volume, Boston and New York [n.d., 1913 or 1915].

This copy is identical in all respects to the second edition, revised, tenth or eleventh impression, 3.14.0, except that it is bound in green vertical-rib-grain cloth.

On 347 there is the pencil notation: "April 21 . 22 . 1917".

3.16.0. *Roderick Hudson*, third edition, first separate impression, one volume, Boston and New York 1917.

RODERICK HUDSON | BY | HENRY JAMES | [oval publisher's device] | BOSTON AND NEW YORK | HOUGHTON MIFFLIN COMPANY | The Riverside Press Cambridge [in Gothic type] | 1917

Size: $7\,^7/_{16}''$ x $5''$.

Collation: [unsigned, $1^6\,2^8\,3–18^{16}\,19^8$]; pp. [2] [1π–4π] [i–xxii], 1–526 [527–528].

Contents: blank leaf; 1π–2π blank, verso ad within a single-rule frame for works "By Henry James [in Gothic type]", listing 17 titles, the last dated being *Italian Hours*; 3π–4π half-title, verso blank; [i–ii] title-page, verso copyright notice: "Copyright, 1875, by H. O. Houghton & Co., and | James R. Osgood & Co. | Copyright, 1882, by Henry James, Jr. | Copyright, 1903, by Houghton, Mifflin & Co. | Copyright, 1907, by Charles Scribner's Sons | Copyright, 1917, by Henry James"; [iii–iv] "NOTE", verso blank; v–[xx] PREFACE; [xxi–xxii] half-title, verso blank; 1–[527] text; [528] printer's imprint: "The Riverside Press [in Gothic type] | CAMBRIDGE [dot] MASSACHUSETTS | U.S.A [*sic*]".

Binding: glazed smooth blue cloth, lettered and decorated in black and gilt. The front cover, within a black double-rule border within which is a black single-rule frame, is lettered and decorated in gilt, and reads: "[horizontal decorative device of rules, dots and flowers] | RODERICK | HUDSON | [small four-cornered device] | HENRY [dot] JAMES | [horizontal decorative device of rules, dots and flowers]". The spine, which is lettered in gilt, and decorated in gilt with an oblong frame within which are five decorative ovals in each of which is a stem of flowers, reads: "RODERICK | HUDSON | [small decorative device] | HENRY | JAMES". The back cover is blank. The endpapers are of white wove paper, and the text is printed on wove paper of two different weights: signatures [11–19] are printed on a significantly heavier paper than signatures [1–10]. The top edge is gilt, and the other edges are trimmed.

The preface and text of this impression were printed from the plates of Volume I of *The Novels and Tales of Henry James* (The New York Edition). There was only one impression of this title printed from these plates prior to this 1917 printing. Although The New York Edition was published by Scribner's, the plates of that Edition were controlled by Houghton, Mifflin; see Anesko, 147. The use of paper of two different weights may have been due to the paper shortage in World War I.

For bindings uniform with this binding, see 1.11.0.

Noted in BAL 10792.

3.17.0. *Roderick Hudson*, first English edition, revised, three volumes, London 1879.

RODERICK HUDSON. | BY | HENRY JAMES, Jr. | IN THREE VOLUMES. [in italic] | VOL. I. [II.] [III.] | REVISED EDITION. [in sans-serif] | London: [in Gothic type] | MACMILLAN AND CO. | 1879.

Size: $7\,^5/_{16}''$ x $4\,^7/_8''$.

Collation: Volume I: $[A]^2$ B–I K–R^8 S^1; pp. [i–iv], [1]–258. Volume II: $[A]^1$ B–I K–S^8 T^2 U^1; pp. [i–ii], [1]–277 [278]. Volume III: $[A]^1$ B–I K–R^8 S^4; pp. [i–ii], [1]–263 [264].

Contents: Volume I: [i–ii] title-page, verso printer's imprint: "LONDON: | PRINTED BY WILLIAM CLOWES AND SONS, | STAMFORD STREET AND CHARING CROSS."; [iii–iv] "NOTE." | "'Roderick Hudson' was originally published in | Boston, in 1875. It has now been minutely revised, | and has received a large number of verbal alterations. | Several passages have been rewritten.", verso blank; [1]–258 text. Volume II: [i–ii] title-page, verso printer's imprint as on Volume I title-leaf verso; [1]–277 text; [278] printer's imprint as on Volume I title-leaf verso. Volume III: [i–ii] title-page, verso printer's imprint as on Volume I title-leaf verso; [1]–263 text; [264] printer's imprint as on Volume I title-leaf verso.

Binding: dark blue fine-bead-grain cloth, with a double-rule border and curved edge panel in black on the front covers, and in blind on the back covers. The curved-edge panels measure $6\,^1/_{16}''$ x $3\,^3/_{16}''$. The space between the inner border and the panel is $^9/_{16}''$. The spines, which are decorated in black and gilt and lettered in gilt, read: "[rule]|[row of dots] |[rule]|RODERICK|HUDSON|H. James Jr|VOL. I [II][III]|[publisher's device in gilt]|Macmillan & Co.|[rule]|[row of dots]|[rule]". The "o" in "Co" is raised above a line. The endpapers are of brown coated paper, and the text is printed on wove paper. The top edges are untrimmed, the bottom edges are trimmed, and the fore-edges are rough trimmed. It is stapled, not sewn. A 40-page publisher's catalogue, dated May 1879, is bound in at the end of Volume I, paginated [1] 2–35 [36–40], the last page being blank except for the printer's imprint.

Both E&L A3b and BAL 10542 record two binding variants of this impression, with slightly different page sizes and a slightly different dimension of the curved panel on the front covers. Priority of states is not determined. The omission of a copyright notice in this edition, as well

RODERICK HUDSON

as the first impression of the one volume second edition is curious.

Advertised by Macmillan in PC, June 17, 1879, 475: "NEW BOOKS BY HENRY JAMES, Jr. RODERICK HUDSON. 3 vols. crown 8vo. 31s. 6d. [Just ready.[sic]"; and announced in PC July 1, 1879 under the heading "NEW WORKS PUBLISHED FROM JUNE 17 TO 30. .... James (H.) – Roderick Hudson. Revised edit. 3 vols. post 8vo. 31s. 6d. (vide Adv. 267) Macmillan .... A Novel first published in Boston in 1875."

English printing history. Macmillan Archive. MEB, 267, records one impression of the first (three volume) edition, 500 copies printed in June 1879, and records two impressions of the second (one volume) English edition, the first in March 1880 of 1500 copies, and the second in June 1888 of 2,000 copies. A portion of the sheets of both impressions of the second edition were exported to America; see printing history following 3.1.0. The sheets of the second impression of the second edition that were not exported were used for the yellowback; see 3.19.0.

A third English edition of *Roderick Hudson* was published in 1883 (and reprinted in 1886) as part of *The Collective Edition of 1883*; see 20.1.0–20.4.0. A fourth English edition was published by Thomas Nelson & Sons, Ltd. in 1916; see note following 4.21.5. A fifth English edition was published as Volume I of *The Novels and Stories of Henry James* in 1921; see 86.1.0–86.2.0.

3.18.0. *Roderick Hudson*, second English edition, revised, first impression, one volume, London 1880.

RODERICK HUDSON. | BY | HENRY JAMES, JR. | NEW EDITION. [in sans-serif] | London: [in Gothic type] | MACMILLAN AND CO. | 1880.

Size: $7\,^{1}/_{2}''$ x $4\,^{15}/_{16}''$.

Collation: A–I K–U X–Y^8; pp. [1–4], [5]–347 [348] [349–352].

Contents: [1–2] half-title, verso publisher's device; [3–4] title-page, verso "NOTE." text as in 3.17.0, but with different line endings; [5]–347 text; [348] centered, the printer's imprint: "LONDON | R. CLAY, SONS, AND TAYLOR, | BREAD STREET HILL."; [349–352] ads, headed: [349] "WORKS BY HENRY JAMES, JUN. [in sans-serif], [350–352] on each page headed: "MACMILLAN'S POPULAR NOVELS. [in sans-serif]".

Binding: dark green-blue fine-bead-grain cloth lettered and decorated in gilt, black, and in blind uniform with the second English edition of *The American* (1879), 4.17.0. There is no lettering on the front or back covers. The spine reads: "RODERICK | HUDSON | H. JAMES Jr. [all the foregoing in italic] | Macmillan & Co." The "o" in "Co" is raised above a dot. The endpapers are of dark brown coated paper, and the text is printed on wove paper. The top and fore-edges are untrimmed, and the bottom edge is rough trimmed. A 40-page publisher's catalogue, dated October 1879, is bound in at the end, paginated '[1] 2–35 [36–40], the last page being blank except for the printer's imprint.

Noted but not described in BAL 10754.

3.19.0. *Roderick Hudson*, second English edition, revised, second impression (yellowback), London 1888.

RODERICK HUDSON | BY | HENRY JAMES, | London [in Gothic type] | MACMILLAN AND CO. | AND NEW YORK | 1888

Size: 6 7/8″ x 4 5/8″.

Collation: $[A]^8$ B–I K–U X–Y^8; pp. [1–4], [5]–347 [348] [349–352].

Contents: [1–2] half-title, verso publisher's device; [3–4] title-page, verso copyright notice, "NOTE", printing history and printer's imprint: "Copyright [in italic] | 1879 | By Henry James | "NOTE." text as in 3.17.0, but without a comma after "Boston" | First Edition, 3 Vols. Crown 8vo, 1879. | New Edition, 1 Vol. Crown 8vo, 1880. | New Edition, 1 Vol. Globe 8vo, 1888. [printing history, except numerals, all in italic] | Richard Clay and Sons, Limited, London and Bungay."; [5]–347 text; [348] printer's imprint: "Richard Clay and Sons, Limited, | London and Bungay."; [349–352] ads, headed: [349–350] "BY THE SAME AUTHOR.", [351] "MACMILLAN & CO.'S PUBLICATIONS | [rule] | The Golden Treasury Series. [in Gothic type]", and [352] "MACMILLAN'S GLOBE LIBRARY. [in sans-serif]"

Binding: ivory boards with an elaborate floral design in red and black on the front and back covers, signed on the right of both covers "L. F. Day". The front cover also has a central red panel on which is printed in black: "Roderick | Hudson". The back cover has a similar red panel on which is printed in black, on a black outlined triangular scroll device: "Macmillan | & Co. [the "o" being raised with a dot under it]". The spine, which is lettered in black within a red panel, reads: "RODERICK | HUDSON | HENRY | JAMES [author's name in sans-serif]", and at the foot in red within a small black panel: "MACMILLAN & Co". The endpapers are of white wove paper, and the text is printed on wove paper. All edges are trimmed. There are no ads on the endpapers.

On the front free endpaper is the inscription: "A. G. Carter | May 1900."

The cover design is the standard Macmillan design for two shilling issues. Regarding this design, Frederick Macmillan wrote to James on April 3, 1888: "We have just begun the publication of a new series of Two Shilling Editions of novels bound in paper boards in a style which we think is as showy as the ordinary 'yellowback' but not as vulgar. ... I send a copy of one of the new 2/-. editions by this post so that you can see the kind of appearance I am proposing for you." Moore, 137.

It is tempting to speculate that L. F. Day was a member of the firm Day & Son (or its successor), specializing in the printing of chromolithographs, and that the paper covering of this copy was separately printed by that firm by the chromolithographic process; see Ball, 101, 175. Also Gaskell, 268.

3.20.0. *Roderick Hudson*, first continental edition, first (sole) impression, later binding state, two volumes, Leipzig 1879.

RODERICK HUDSON. | BY | HENRY JAMES, Jr. | AUTHORIZED EDITION. [in italic] | IN TWO VOLUMES. | VOL. I. [II.] | LEIPZIG | BERNHARD TAUCHNITZ | 1879.

Size: 6 $^{7}/_{16}$" x 4 $^{5}/_{8}$".

Collation: Volume I: [1]^8 2–19^8 20^4; pp. [1–6], [7]–312. Volume II: [1]^8 2–18^8; pp. [1–4], [5]–288.

Contents: Volume I: [1–2] series half-title and half-title, verso ad for "TAUCHNITZ EDITION. | By the same Author", listing 3 titles; [3–4] title-page, verso blank; [5–6] "NOTE", verso blank; [7]–312 text; 312 at foot printer's imprint: "[rule] | PRINTING OFFICE OF THE PUBLISHER. [off center to the right]". Volume II: [1–2] series half-title and half-title, verso blank; [3–4] title-page, verso blank; [5]–288 text; 288 at foot printer's imprint as on 312 of Volume I.

Binding: buff wove paper wrappers, cut flush, with lettering on the front covers in black within a black single-rule frame which is decorated with floral devices at each of the four corners with lettering above and below the frame. The spines are also lettered in black between a series of eight pairs of thin and thick black rules. The back covers, which are also lettered in black, read: Volume I: "December 1899. | Tauchnitz Edition. | [rule] | Latest Volumes:" followed by a list of 24 titles, the last dated being *Mr. Jack Hamlin's Meditations*, etc. by Bret Harte. Volume II: "January 1900. | Tauchnitz Edition | [rule] | Latest Volumes:" followed by a list of 24 titles, the last of which is *One Year* by Dorothea Gerard. Beneath the list of titles on the back covers of both volumes, below a long rule, there reads: "The Tauchnitz Edition is to be had of all Book- | sellers and Railway Libraries on the Continent, price | M 1, 60. or 2 francs per volume. A complete Cata- | logue of the Tauchnitz Edition is attached to this work." A 32-page paginated publisher's catalogue, dated October 1, 1903, is bound in at the end of Volume II.

See BAL 10545 and T&B 1842 and 1843. Wrappers and catalogue with these dates not recorded in T&B. *Mr. Jack Hamlin's Meditations* was first published by Tauchnitz in 1899, and *One Year* in 1900. T&B records one edition with one impression of this title.

3.21.0. *Roderick Hudson*, first continental edition, first (sole) impression, later binding state, two volumes, Leipzig 1879.

The title-pages, collations, and contents are identical to those of the first continental edition, first impression, 3.20.0.

Size: 6 3/8″ x 4 3/8″.

Binding: buff wove paper wrappers, cut flush, with lettering on the front covers in black within a double-rule frame, the outer rule being wider than the inner, which frame is divided into three panels by thin double rules. The lettering in the upper panel reads: "TAUCHNITZ EDITION | COLLECTION OF BRITISH AND AMERICAN AUTHORS | VOL. 1842 [1843]". The middle panel reads: "RODERICK HUDSON | BY | HENRY JAMES [all the foregoing in sans-serif] | IN TWO VOLUMES | VOL. 1 [2] | LEIPZIG: BERNHARD TAUCHNITZ | PARIS: LIBRAIRIE HENRY GAULON, 39, RUE MADAME". The lower panel reads: "The Copyright of this Collection is purchased for Continental Circulation | only and the volumes may therefore not be introduced into Great Britain | or her Colonies. (See also pp. 3–6 of the

Large Catalogue.)" Below the frames reads: "EACH VOLUME SOLD SEPERATELY". The spines are also lettered in black between a series of eight pairs of thick and thin black rules, and between rules six and seven reads: "PRICE | M 6.00". The back covers, also lettered in black reads at the top "TAUCHNITZ EDITION", below which is a single-rule frame composed of dots within which reads: "The following volumes issued since September 29th | 1919 are the first modern works published in the | Tauchnitz Edition after a long interruption. Other | books by famous contemporary writers will follow | in regular short intervals. | [followed by a single column listing of volumes 4527 through 4538]". Below the frame of dots reads: "LATEST VOLUMES: | [followed by a listing of volumes 4522 through 4526] | [rule] | In consequence of the steady increase in the cost of all materials | the publishers are compelled to raise the price of the Tauchnitz | Editions to M 6.00 sewed, and M 10.00 bound. This increase of | price is only intended as a temporary measure [all following the rule in italic]." The insides of the front and back covers are blank. No catalogue is bound in at the end of either volume.

This is a 1920 binding-up of 1879 first impression sheets. The highest numbered volume noted on the back covers, 4538 (Arnold Bennett's *Paris Nights*), was first published by Tauchnitz in 1920. Wrappers of this date are not recorded in T&B.

In April 1914, Tauchnitz changed the appearance of the front covers of its collection, these volumes being examples of that changed appearance. The references on the back covers to a "long interruption" refer to the war years during which period German censors prohibited the publication of modern English and American works. Note that the price per volume has risen to M 6.00 from M 1.60 in October 1903. It had risen to M 2.00 in August 1918, and then rose in M 1.00 increments to M 6.00 in 1919. By January 1922, the price per volume was M 16.00; see T&B pp. 609–616 and 950.

4. *THE AMERICAN*

4.1.0. *The American*, first edition, first impression, first binding state, one volume, Boston 1877.

THE AMERICAN. | BY | HENRY JAMES, Jr. | [monogram publisher's device] | BOSTON: | JAMES R. OSGOOD AND COMPANY, | Late Ticknor & Fields, and Fields, Osgood, & Co. | 1877.

On the title-page the publisher's imprint has a barely perceptible partial period after "Co", that is more like a speck or imperfection in the paper than a properly formed period, and the distance between the bottom of "HENRY JAMES" to the bottom of "1877" is 3.40".

Size: 7 3/8" x 4 7/8".

Collation: $[1–19^{12}\ 20^{12}\ (–20_{12})]$, signed as $[1]^8\ 2–29^8\ 30^7$; pp. [1–4], [5]–473 [474] [475–478].

Contents: [1–2] blank, verso ad within a single-rule frame headed: "MR. JAMES'S WRITINGS.", listing 4 titles: *A Passionate Pilgrim*, *Transatlantic Sketches*, *Roderick Hudson* and *The American*, with dollar prices, in "bevelled boards"; [3–4] title-page, verso copyright notice and printer's imprint: "Copyright, 1877, | By H. O. Houghton & Co. and James R. Osgood & Co. | RIVERSIDE, CAMBRIDGE: | STEREOTYPED AND PRINTED BY | H. O. HOUGHTON AND COMPANY."; [5]–473 text; [474] blank; [475–478] two blank leaves.

Binding: terra-cotta dotted-line-grain cloth over bevelled boards, with the front and back covers decorated in blind with a single-rule frame within a wider single-rule border. The spine, lettered and decorated in gilt, reads: "[thick followed by a thin rule] | The | American | [rule] | H. James Jr. | J. R. Osgood & Co. | [thin followed by a thick rule]". The endpapers are of brown coated paper, and the text is printed on wove paper. A binder's fly-leaf of wove paper is at the front, but none at the back. All edges are trimmed, and the top edge is stained ochre.

On the front free endpaper is the inscription: "Leonard F. Beckwith | from Helene | New York 1877 | May".

BAL notes: "There is a possibility that the copies first printed do not have a period following the co in the title-page imprint but positive proof of this is lacking and further study is indicated." The barely perceptible period on the title-page of this copy and 4.2.0, the absence

THE AMERICAN

of a full period on the title-page of 4.3.0, and the presence of a period on the title-page of 4.4.0 suggest that it may be correct. But as BAL states "further study is indicated".

American printing history. Houghton Mifflin Archive. First edition: Ms Am 2030.2(23), 155: *first* [Osgood] *impression* April 30, 1877, 1008 copies, 1004 bound on May 2 and May 10, 1877; *second impression* May 18, 1877, 514 copies, 495 bound between May 22 and July 12, 1877; *third impression* August 29, 1877, 504 copies, 514 [*sic*] bound between September 14, 1877, and September 11, 1878. Ms Am 2030(16), 127: *fourth* [first Houghton, Osgood] *impression* November 22, 1878, 270 copies, 284 [*sic*] bound between November 26, 1878, and April 16, 1879; *fifth impression* May 31, 1879, 278 copies, 284 [*sic*] bound between June 6, 1879, and December 1, 1879; *sixth impression* January 30, 1880, 274 copies, 285 [*sic*] bound between January 24, 1880, and January 21, 1881; *seventh* [first Houghton, Mifflin] *impression* October 29, 1881, 274 copies, 273 bound between November 23, 1881, and December 11, 1882. Ms Am 2030(17), 117: *eighth impression* December 22, 1882, 280 copies, 263 bound between January 3 and August 29, 1883; *ninth impression* January 8, 1884, 275 copies, 269 bound between March 22, 1884, and January 10, 1885. Ms Am 2030(18), 136: *tenth impression* May 3, 1886, 154 copies, 157 [*sic*] bound between May 14, 1886, and September 22, 1888; *eleventh impression* January 5, 1889, 280 copies, 279 bound between January 22, 1889, and February 12, 1892 (plus one "lev[ant] on June 3, 1892); notation: "[total copies] 4111". Ms Am 2030(20), 173: *twelfth impression* January 23, 1893, 156 copies, 152 bound between January 23, 1893, and April 10, 1894. Ms Am 2030(21), 221: *thirteenth impression* August 24, 1895, 154 copies, 155 [*sic*] bound between September 4, 1895, and February 24, 1897; *fourteenth impression* December 15, 1898, 152 copies, 150 bound between December 23, 1898, and December 14, 1899; *fifteenth impression* February 20, 1900, 144 copies, 147 [*sic*] bound on June 28, 1900, and January 21, 1901. Ms Am 2030(22), 218: *sixteenth impression* February 17, 1902, 148 copies, 146 bound between July 16, 1902, November 28, 1903; *seventeenth impression* September 22, 1904, 159 copies, 154 bound on October 10, 1904, and March 11, 1905; *eighteenth impression* June 26, 1905, 268 copies, 265 bound between July 14, 1905, and July 3, 1906; *nineteenth impression* April 24, 1907, 277 copies, 282 [*sic*] bound between May 8, 1907, and March 18, 1908; *twentieth impression* October 22, 1908, 268 copies, 256 bound between January 19, 1909, and September 1, 1909; *twenty-first impression* May 17, 1910, 284

THE AMERICAN

copies, 275 bound between June 2, 1910, and March 16, 1911. Ms Am 2030(23), 213: *twenty-second impression* June 20, 1912, 281 copies, 290 [*sic*] bound between August 22, 1912, and April 26, 1913; *twenty-third impression* May 4, 1914, 279 copies, 274 bound between May 12, 1914, and [illegible] 1915; *twenty-fourth impression* December 20, 1914, 282 copies, 277 bound on December 31, 1915, and April 13, 1916; *twenty-fifth impression* July 27, 1916, 529 copies, 516 bound between September 25, 1916, and March 13, 1917; *twenty-sixth impression* May 7, 1918, 533 copies, 507 bound between June 14, 1918, and March 24, 1920; *twenty-seventh impression* December 22, 1919, 524 copies, 514 bound between February 24, 1920, and February 26, 1920; notation: "[total copies] 8265".

Priced at $2.00, which price was unchanged through 1905.

PC records that copies of the first edition of *The American* were imported into England and sold at 10s. 6d.; see PC, June 16, 1877, 418 and 426.

For the second American edition, see *The Novels and Tales of Henry James*, 64.1.0.

In 1922, Houghton, Mifflin, with Scribner's and the James estate's permission, made a duplicate set of plates of The New York Edition of *The American*, and used these plates to print several separate impressions of that title as a "trade" edition and as part of its Riverside Literature Series; see 4.14.5.

4.2.0. *The American*, first edition, first impression, first binding state, one volume, Boston 1877.

The title-page, size, collation, and contents are identical to those of the first edition, first impression, first binding state, 4.1.0 (including the distance between the bottom of "HENRY JAMES" and the bottom of "1877 and the barely perceptible period after "Co" on the title-page),

Binding: plum dotted-line-grain cloth over bevelled boards, lettered and decorated identically to 4.1.0. The endpapers are of brown coated paper, and the text is printed on wove paper. A binder's fly-leaf of wove paper is at the front, but none at the back. All edges are trimmed, and the top edge is stained ochre.

On the title-page is the pencil inscription "M. E. Hister | 1877".

THE AMERICAN

4.3.0. *The American*, first edition, first impression, first binding state, one volume, Boston 1877.

The title-page, size, collation, and contents are identical to those of the first edition, first impression, first binding state, 4.1.0 (including the distance between the bottom of "HENRY JAMES" and the bottom of "1877 on the title-page), except that the publisher's imprint on the title-page has no period after "Co".

Binding: Kelly green dotted-line-grain cloth over bevelled boards, lettered and decorated identically to 4.1.0. The endpapers are of brown coated paper, and the text is printed on wove paper. There are no binder's fly-leaves. All edges are trimmed, and the top edge is stained light brown.

4.4.0. *The American*, first edition, first impression, first binding state, one volume, Boston 1877.

This copy is identical to the first edition, first impression, first binding state, 4.1.0, (including the distance between the bottom of "HENRY JAMES" and the bottom of "1877" on the title-page), except that the publisher's imprint on the title-page has a full period after "Co".

Binding: terra-cotta dotted-line-grain cloth over bevelled boards, lettered and decorated identically to 4.1.0. The endpapers are of brown coated paper, and the text is printed on wove paper. A binder's fly-leaf of wove paper is at the front, but none at the back. All edges are trimmed, and the top edge is stained ochre.

BAL 10532 records a second binding state with the spine imprint "HOUGHTON, OSGOOD & CO." However, it is doubtful that the spine imprint is all in capitals.

A Note on Some of the Binding States of the American First Edition of *The American*

There is a conflict between the evidence provided by the Houghton, Mifflin Archive as to the binding record for the first two impressions of *The American* and the physical evidence of the books themselves.

The Houghton Mifflin Archive records that the first impression of *The American* was printed for J.R. Osgood & Co. on April 30, 1877, a printing of 1008 copies, of which 1004 were bound on May 2 and May 10, 1877. J.R. Osgood & Co. was recapitalized on January 1, 1878 and its name changed to Houghton, Osgood & Co. on that date. In May 1880 the assets of Houghton, Osgood & Co. were acquired by Houghton, Mifflin & Co. Yet despite the fact that by May 10, 1877, all but four copies of this impression had been bound in J.R. Osgood bindings, third and fourth binding states of the first impression have been found in Houghton, Mifflin bindings (4.5.0 and 4.6.0), which seemingly could have been so bound only after May 1880.

BAL 10532 also records a second binding state of the first impression with a Houghton, Osgood binding (not found), which would present a similar problem of conflict, as 495 of its printing of 514 copies were bound between May 22 and July 12, 1877, and none are recorded as being bound thereafter.[12]

The only possible way of reconciling this conflict is to assume that some of the J.R. Osgood copies of the first impression were rebound by Houghton, Osgood in or after January 1878 and by Houghton, Mifflin in or after May 1880. However, the record is silent on this assumption; see 11.5.0 as a recorded instance of rebinding by Houghton, Mifflin.

The third impression of *The American* (4.7.0 and 4.8.0) does not present the same conflict. Although 504 copies were printed on August 29, 1877 prior to the recapitalization of J.R.Osgood & Co., it was bound in the period September 14, 1877, to September 11, 1878, and the recapitalization (and name change to Houghton, Osgood & Co.) took place between those dates.

4.5.0. *The American*, first edition, first impression, third binding state, one volume, Boston 1877.

The title-page, size, collation, and contents are identical to those of the first edition, first impression, first binding state, 4.1.0 (including the distance between the bottom of "HENRY JAMES" and the bottom of "1877" on the title-page), except that the publisher's imprint on the title-page has a full period after "Co".

Binding: dark green sand-grain cloth over bevelled boards, with the

---

12 It is possible that ten copies of the second impression were bound as part of the third impression, as only 504 copies of the third impression were printed whereas the record indicates that 514 were bound.

THE AMERICAN

front and back covers decorated in blind with a single-rule frame within a wider single-rule border. The spine, lettered and decorated in gilt, reads: "[thick followed by a thin rule] | The | American | [rule] | H. James Jr. | Houghton, Mifflin & Co. | [thin followed by a thick rule]". The ampersand in the printer's imprint has a flat rather than a rounded top. The endpapers are of brown coated paper, and the text is printed on wove paper. A binder's fly-leaf of wove paper is at the front, but none at the back. All edges are trimmed, and the top edge is stained ochre.

4.6.0. *The American*, first edition, first impression, fourth binding state, one volume, Boston 1877.

The title-page is identical to that on the first edition, first impression, first binding state, 4.1.0, (including the distance between the bottom of "HENRY JAMES and the bottom of "1877"), except that the publisher's imprint has a full period after "Co."

Size: 7 3/8" x 4 3/4".

The collation and contents are identical to those of 4.1.0 (including the presence of the ad on [2] listing the same four titles, with dollar prices).

Binding: tan diagonal-fine-ribbed cloth, with lettering in red-brown and decoration in red-brown, tan, and gilt on the front cover and spine. The title on the front cover and spine is in red-brown within a gilt panel with a not very pronounced maze-like background pattern. The publisher's imprint at the foot of the spine reads: "Houghton Mifflin & Co." The ampersand has a flat rather than a rounded top. The endpapers are of chocolate-coated paper, and the text is printed on wove paper. A binder's fly-leaf of wove paper is at the front, but none at the back. All edges are trimmed, and the top edge is stained brown. It is stapled, not sewn. There are no ads bound in at the end.

On the front pastedown is the armorial bookplate of Charles Henry Coster.

This binding is uniform with that of the second edition, first American impression of *The Portrait of a Lady* (1881), 16.5.0, and this together with the fact that it is stapled would indicate it was issued in the period 1881–1882.

THE AMERICAN

Based on the fact that the ad on [2] is the same as that appearing on [2] of the first impression, that the title-page dimensions are the same as those of the copies of the first impressions, above, and that the edition is not specified on the title-page (see below), it is likely that the sheets of this copy are of the first impression.

4.7.0. *The American*, first edition, second impression, first binding state, one volume, Boston 1877.

The title-page is identical to that of the first edition, first impression, first binding state, 4.1.0, except that "SECOND EDITION." appears between the author's name and the publisher's device, there is a full period after "Co" in the publisher's imprint, and the distance between the bottom of "HENRY JAMES" and the bottom of "1877" is 3.701" (approximately $3\,^{22}/_{32}$").

Size: $7\,^{5}/_{16}$" x $4\,^{7}/_{8}$".

The collation and contents are identical to those of 4.1.0, including the presence of the ad on [2] listing the same four titles with dollar prices and the absence of the last leaf, [20$_{12}$], which is excised; see BAL 10532.

Binding: Kelly green dotted-line-grain cloth over bevelled boards, lettered and decorated identically to 4.1.0, including the publisher's imprint at the foot of the spine which reads: "J. R. Osgood & Co." The endpapers are of brown coated paper, and the text is printed on wove paper. A binder's fly-leaf of wove paper is at the front, but none at the back. All edges are trimmed, and the top edge is stained ochre.

It is clear from the title-page type dimension of this and the third impression that this title-page has been reset and is not just overprinted.

Neither E&L nor BAL notes a copy with "SECOND EDITION", or "THIRD EDITION" on the title-page and dated 1877. However, BAL 10532 records that the publisher's records show three impressions in 1877 (April 30, May 18, and August 29), but was unable to distinguish between the three impressions.

4.8.0. *The American*, first edition, second impression, first binding state, one volume, Boston 1877.

The title-page and size are identical to those of the first edition, second impression, first binding state, 4.7.0.

[52]

The collation and contents are identical to those of first edition, first impression, first binding state, 4.1.0, including the presence of the ad on [2] listing the same four titles with dollar prices and the absence of the last leaf, [20$_{12}$], which is excised.

Binding: terra-cotta dotted-line-grain cloth over bevelled boards, lettered and decorated identically to 4.1.0, including the publisher's imprint at the foot of the spine which reads: "J. R. Osgood & Co." The endpapers are of brown coated paper, and the text is printed on wove paper. A binder's fly-leaf of wove paper is at the front, but none at the back. All edges are trimmed.

4.9.0. *The American*, first edition, third impression, first binding state, one volume, Boston 1877.

The title-page is identical to that of the first edition, second impression, first binding state, 4.7.0, including the distance between the bottom of "HENRY JAMES" and the bottom of "1877", except that "THIRD EDITION" is present between the author's name and the publisher's device.

Size: 7 $^{5}/_{16}$" x 4 $^{3}/_{4}$".

The collation and contents are identical to those of the first edition, first impression, first binding state, 4.1.0.

Binding: terra-cotta dotted-line-grain cloth over bevelled boards, lettered and decorated identically to 4.1.0, including the publisher's imprint at the foot of the spine which reads: "J. R. Osgood & Co." The endpapers are of brown coated paper, and the text is printed on wove paper. A binder's fly-leaf of wove paper is at the front, but none at the back. All edges are trimmed.

On the title-page is the inscription: "R. Neilson | 1/8/78".

4.10.0. *The American*, first edition, third impression, second binding state, one volume, Boston 1877.

The title-page and size are identical to those of the first edition, third impression, first binding state, 4.9.0.

The collation and contents are identical to those of the first edition, first impression, first binding state, 4.1.0.

Binding: terra-cotta dotted-line-grain cloth over bevelled boards, lettered and decorated identically to 4.1.0, except that at the foot of the spine the publisher's imprint reads: "Houghton, Osgood & Co." The endpapers are of brown coated paper, and the text is printed on wove paper. A binder's fly-leaf of wove paper is at the front, but none at the back. All edges are trimmed.

4.11.0. *The American*, first edition, fourth impression, binding state A, one volume, Boston 1879.

THE AMERICAN. | BY | HENRY JAMES, Jr. | FOURTH EDITION. | [shield shaped publisher's device] | BOSTON: | HOUGHTON, OSGOOD AND COMPANY. | The Riverside Press, Cambridge. [in Gothic type] | 1879.

Size: 7 5/16" x 4 3/4".

The collation is identical to that of the first edition, first impression, first binding state, 4.1.0.

Contents: [1–2] blank, verso ad within a single-rule frame headed: "MR. JAMES'S WRITINGS.", listing 6 titles with dollar prices, the same 4 titles as are present on the similar ad on [2] in the first edition, first impression, plus *Watch and Ward* and *The Europeans*; [3–4] title-page, verso copyright notice and printer's imprint: "Copyright, 1877, | by H. O. Houghton & Co. and James R. Osgood & Co. | RIVERSIDE, CAMBRIDGE: | STEREO- TYPED AND PRINTED BY | H. O. HOUGHTON AND COMPANY."; [5]–473 text; [474] blank; [475–478] two blank leaves.

Binding: green dotted-line-grain cloth over bevelled boards, lettered and decorated identically to 4.1.0, except that the publisher's imprint at the foot of the spine reads: "Houghton, Osgood & Co." with an initial "H" which extends below the other letters in the imprint, and an ampersand that is in lower not upper case. The text is printed on wove paper. Two binder's fly-leaves of different weight wove paper are at the front, and one at the back. All edges are trimmed, and speckled red-brown.

This copy has been re-cased, and white wove paper endpapers substituted for the original brown-coated endpapers, and remnants of the brown-coated endpapers are visible at the edges of the present endpapers.

THE AMERICAN

See printing history, 4.1.0, which records the fourth impression as having been printed on November 22, 1878, and bound between November 26, 1878, and April 16, 1879. For a binding with the same publisher's imprint, see 7.9.0.

4.11.1. *The American*, first edition, fourth impression, binding state B, one volume, Boston 1879.

The title-page, size, collation, and contents are identical to those of the first edition, fourth impression, 4.11.0.

Binding: terra-cotta dotted-line-grain cloth over bevelled boards, lettered and decorated identically to the first edition, first impression, 4.1.0, except that the publisher's imprint at the foot of the spine reads: "Houghton, Osgood & Co." with an initial "H" which does not extend below the other letters in the imprint, and an ampersand that is upper not lower case. The endpapers are of brown coated paper, and the text is printed on wove paper. A binder's fly leaf of wove paper is at the front, but none at the back. All edges are trimmed, and the top edge is stained light brown.

4.11.2. *The American*, first edition, fifth impression, one volume, Boston 1880.

THE AMERICAN. | BY | HENRY JAMES, Jr. | FIFTH EDITION. | [shield shaped publisher's device] | BOSTON: | HOUGHTON, OSGOOD AND COMPANY. | The Riverside Press, CAMBRIDGE. [in Gothic type] | 1880.

Size: $7\,^{7}/_{16}''$ x $4\,^{9}/_{16}''$.

The collation is identical to that of the first edition, first impression, first binding state, 4.1.0.

The contents (including the ad [2]) are identical to those of the first edition, fourth impression, 4.11.0, except that "FIFTH EDITION" and the date 1880 appear on the title-page.

Binding: dark green sand-grain cloth over bevelled boards, lettered and decorated identically to 4.1.0, except that the publisher's imprint at the foot of the spine reads: "Houghton, Osgood & Co." The endpapers are of chocolate-brown coated paper, and the text is printed on wove paper. A binder's fly-leaf of wove paper is at the front, but none at the back. All edges are trimmed, and the top edge is stained light brown.

See printing history 4.1.0 which records the fifth impression as being printed on May 31, 1879 and the sixth impression on January 30, 1880.

4.11.7. *The American*, first edition, eleventh impression, one volume, Boston 1889.

THE AMERICAN. | BY | HENRY JAMES, Jr. | ELEVENTH EDITION. | [shield shaped publisher's device] | BOSTON: | HOUGHTON, MIFFLIN AND COMPANY. | The Riverside Press, Cambridge. [in Gothic type] | 1889.

Size: $7\,3/8''$ x $4\,3/4''$.

Collation: $[1-19^{12}\,20^{10}\,(-20_{10})]$, signed as $[1]^8\,2-29^8\,30^5$; pp. [1–4], [5]–473 [474].

Contents: [1–2] blank, verso ad within a single rule frame headed: "MR. JAMES'S WRITINGS.", under which are 5 lines of a quoted review followed by a list of 8 James titles with dollar prices, the last dated being *The Portrait of a Lady*; [3–4] title-page, verso copyright notice and printer's imprint: "Copyright, 1877, | By H. O. Houghton & Co. and James R. Osgood & Co. | RIVERSIDE, CAMBRIDGE: | STEREOTYPED AND PRINTED BY | H. O. HOUGHTON AND COMPANY."; [5]–473 text; [474] blank.

Binding: brown diagonal-fine-ribbed cloth, lettered and decorated on the front cover and spine in red-brown, brown, and gilt. The title on the front cover and spine is in red-brown within a gilt panel with a pronounced maze-like background pattern. The publisher's imprint at the foot of the spine is in red-brown (not gilt) and reads: "HOUGHTON | MIFFLIN & CO." The ampersand in the imprint is stylised, and is like a Greek π. The endpapers are of white wove paper, and the text is printed on wove paper. Two binder's fly-leaves of wove paper are at the back, but none at the front. All edges are trimmed, and the top edge is stained brown. It is sewn, not stapled.

On [1] is the ink inscription "Maribel Hartman | May 10, 1892."

This binding is uniform with that of the first American impression of the second edition of *The Portrait of a Lady* (1881), 16.5.0.

THE AMERICAN

4.11.8. *The American*, first edition, fifteenth impression, one volume, Boston 1900.

THE AMERICAN. | BY | HENRY JAMES, Jr. | [oblong publisher's device of a piper under a tree within a frame] | BOSTON: | HOUGHTON, MIFFLIN AND COMPANY. | The Riverside Press, Cambridge. [in Gothic type] | 1900.

Size: 7 3/8" x 4 15/16".

Collation: $[1]^8$ $2-29^8$ 30^6; pp. [1–4], [5]–473 [474] [475–476].

Contents: [1–2] blank, verso ad within a single-rule frame headed: "Henry James's Books. [in Gothic type]", listing 16 titles with dollar prices, the last dated being *The Spoils of Poynton*; [3–4] title-page, verso copyright notice and printer's imprint: "Copyright, 1877, | By H. O. Houghton & Co. and James R. Osgood & Co. | The Riverside Press, Cambridge, Mass., U. S. A. [in italic] | Printed by H. O. Houghton & Company."; [5]–473 text; [474] blank; [475–476] blank leaf.

Binding: green vertical-rib-grain cloth, lettered and decorated in gilt on the front cover and spine. The front cover has within a single-rule border an elaborate centered cartouche within which are the title and the author's name separated by an ornamental rule. The spine reads: "[rule] | THE | AMERICAN | [ornamental rule] | HENRY JAMES | HOUGHTON | MIFFLIN & CO. | [rule]" The ampersand in the publisher's imprint is stylised, and is like the Greek π. The back cover has a single-rule border in blind. The endpapers are of cream laid paper, and the text is printed on wove paper. A binder's fly-leaf of wove paper is at the front, but none at the back. All edges are trimmed, and the top edge is stained brown.

This binding is uniform with that of the first American edition, first impression of *The Spoils of Poynton* (1897), 48.6.0, on which it was first issued.

4.12.0. *The American*, first edition, twenty-first impression, one volume, Boston [n.d., 1910].

THE AMERICAN. | BY | HENRY JAMES, JR. | [oblong publisher's device of a piper under a tree not within a frame] | BOSTON: HOUGHTON MIFFLIN COMPANY. | The Riverside Press, Cambridge. [in Gothic type]

On the title-page the publisher's device and the publisher's imprint (but not the rest of the printing) slope slightly downward to the right.

THE AMERICAN

Size: 7 3/8″ x 4 15/16″.

Collation: [1]⁸ 2–29⁸ 30⁶; pp. [1–4], [5]–473 [474] [475–476].

Contents: [1–2] blank, verso an ad within a single-rule frame headed "By Henry James [in Gothic type]", listing 17 titles without dollar prices, the last dated being *Italian Hours*; [3–4] title-page, verso copyright notice: "Copyright, 1877, | By H. O. Houghton & Co. and James R. Osgood & Co."; [5]–473 text; [474] blank; [475–476] blank leaf.

Binding: brown vertical-rib-grain cloth, lettered and decorated in gilt on the front cover and spine. The front cover has within a single-rule border an elaborate centered cartouche within which is the title and author's name separated by a decorative rule. The spine reads: "[rule] | THE | AMERICAN | [decorative rule] | HENRY JAMES | HOUGHTON | MIFFLIN CO. | [rule]". The back cover has a single-rule border in blind. The endpapers are of white wove paper, and the text is printed on wove paper. There are no binder's fly-leaves. The top edge is trimmed and stained ochre, the bottom edge is trimmed, and the fore-edge is rough trimmed.

This binding is uniform with the first American edition of *The Spoils of Poynton* (1897), 48.6.0, on which it was first issued.

This impression, which has *Italian Hours* listed among James's works in the ad on page [2], was probably printed in 1910, the year after the publication of that title; see printing history, 4.1.0, which records the twentieth impression as being printed on October 22, 1908 and the twenty-first on May 17, 1910. Throughout the volume there is a great deal of evidence of the poor state of the plates. Houghton, Mifflin and Company changed its imprint to Houghton Mifflin Company when it incorporated in 1908. Ellen B. Ballou, *The Building of the House: Houghton Mifflin's Formative Years* (Boston: Houghton Mifflin Company, 1970) 493–494.

4.13.0. *The American*, first edition, twenty-first impression, one volume, Boston [n.d., 1910].

The title-page, size, collation, and contents are identical to those of the first edition, twenty-first impression, 4.12.0, including on the title-page the slight slope downward to the right of the publisher's device and the publisher's imprint.

Binding: olive-green vertical-rib-grain cloth lettered and decorated identically to 4.12.0. The endpapers are of white wove paper, and the text is printed on wove paper. There are no binder's fly-leaves. The top edge is trimmed and stained gray, the bottom edge is trimmed, and the fore-edge is rough trimmed.

Dust-jacket: very thin tan wove paper, printed in black. The front and rear covers and the front and back inner flaps are blank. The spine, part of which is missing, seems to replicate the lettering on the spine of the book.

This copy is probably of the same impression as 4.12.0.

4.14.0. *The American*, first edition, twenty second or later impression, one volume, Boston [n.d., 1912 or later].

Size: 7 $^7/_{16}$″ x 5″.

The title-page, collation, and contents are identical to those of the first edition, twenty-first impression, 4.12.0, including the ad on [2] without dollar prices.

Binding: glazed smooth blue cloth, lettered in gilt and decorated in black and gilt. The front cover, within a black double-rule border within which is a black single-rule frame, reads: "[horizontal decorative device of rules, dots and flowers] | THE AMERICAN | [small four-cornered device] | HENRY [dot] JAMES | [horizontal decorative device of rules, dots and flowers]". The spine, which is lettered in gilt, and decorated in gilt with an oblong frame within which are five decorative ovals in each of which is a stem of flowers, reads: "THE | AMERICAN | [small decorative device] | HENRY | JAMES". The back cover is blank. The endpapers are of white wove paper, and the text is printed on wove paper. There are no binder's fly-leaves. The top edge is gilt, and the other edges are untrimmed.

For bindings uniform with this binding see 1.11.0.

4.14.5. *The American*, second American edition, first (?) separate impression, one volume, Boston [n.d., 1922?].

Riverside College Classics [in Gothic type] | THE AMERICAN | BY | HENRY JAMES | [oval publisher's device of a piper under a tree] | HOUGHTON MIFFLIN COMPANY | BOSTON NEW YORK

CHICAGO SAN FRANCISCO | The Riverside Press Cambridge [in Gothic type]

Size: 7 $^{13}/_{16}$″ x 4 $^{9}/_{16}$″.

Collation: [unsigned, 1–17^{16}]; pp. [i–ii], 1–540 [541–542].

Contents: [i–ii] title-page, verso copyright notice and printer's imprint: "COPYRIGHT, 1877, BY H. O. HOUGHTON & CO. AND JAMES R. OSGOOD & CO. | COPYRIGHT, 1907, BY CHARLES SCRIBNER'S SONS | The Riverside Press [in Gothic type] | CAMBRIDGE [dot] MASSACHUSETTS | PRINTED IN THE U.S.A."; 1–[540] text; [541–542] blank leaf.

Binding: red fine vertical rib-grain cloth, decorated in blind on the front cover with a single-rule border centered within which is an oval publisher's device. The back cover is neither lettered nor decorated. The spine, which is lettered and decorated in gilt, reads: "[single rule] | THE | AMERICAN | [decorative device of a tree] | HOUGHTON | MIFFLIN CO." The endpapers are of cream wove paper, and the text is printed on wove paper. There are no binder's fly-leaves. All edges are trimmed.

The text of this impression is printed from the same plates as were used to print Volume II of *The Novels and Tales of Henry James* (The New York Edition), 64.1.0, but James's preface is not included in this impression. James had extensively revised the text of *The American* for the New York Edition; see printing history following 4.1.0

4.15.0. *The American*, first English edition, unauthorized, one volume, London [n.d., 1877].

THE AMERICAN. | BY | HENRY JAMES, Jr. | [publisher's device] | London: [in Gothic type] | WARD, LOCK & CO., | WARWICK HOUSE, | DORSET BUILDINGS, SALISBURY SQUARE.

Size: 6 $^{15}/_{16}$″ x 4 $^{1}/_{2}$″.

Collation: [A]^8 B–I K–U X–Z AA–EE^8; pp. [1–4], [5]–435 [436] [437–448].

Contents: [1–2] half-title, verso ad headed: "FAVOURITE AUTHORS, | BRITISH AND FOREIGN.", listing the first 29 titles issued in that series in "Crown 8vo., Fancy Boards, 2s. each"; [3–4] title-page, verso ad headed: "HOUSEHOLD AND RAILWAY NOVELS.", listing the first 30 titles issued in that series; [5]–435 text; 435 at foot printer's imprint: "[rule]

THE AMERICAN

| Butler & Tanner, The Selwood Printing Works, Frome and London."; [436] blank; [437–448] 12 pages, paginated [1] 2–12, of undated ads.

Binding: red diagonal-fine-ribbed cloth, with "The American|by Henry James, Junr. [the "r" in "Junr."is raised above two dots]" in the cloth color within a gilt rectangle imposed on an elaborate design of a bunch of flowers in black within a double-ruled border in black on the front cover. The spine is decorated with a similar design in black of flowers, with the title and author in the cloth color within gilt rectangle, and with the printer's imprint "WARD LOCK & CO (the "O" being inside the "C") at the foot of the spine. The back cover has a double-rule border in blind with a centered blind-stamped decorative device. The endpapers are of pale yellow-coated paper, and the text is printed on wove paper. All edges are trimmed, and the top edge is stained ochre.

Illustrated Plate 3.

The collation and contents of this copy are exactly the same as the yellowback of this title in the British Library (except for the anomalous extra leaf of ads only seen in the British Library copy), and as described in E&L A4b for the unauthorized yellowback edition of 1877, including the printer's imprint after a rule at the bottom of 435 and the ads on the verso of the half-title ("FAVOURITE AUTHORS | BRITISH AND FOREIGN", 29 titles listed), on the verso of the title-page ("HOUSEHOLD AND RAILWAY NOVELS", 30 titles listed), and on the last 6 leaves of signature EE, being paginated [1] 2–12 (principally devoted to various Beaton publications). There is no indication in this or the following two copies of damage to the type which would probably occur if the plates were stored for a number of years. As a working hypothesis, it is possible that this copy (and the two copies recorded below) were published prior to the publication of the yellowback recorded by E&L as being the first impression. This would be consistent with the well established practice of English publisher's during this period of avoiding cannibalization of sales of the more expensive editions by only issuing cheaper ones after the more expensive had been absorbed by the market; see Alexis Weedon, *Victorian Publishing: The Economics of Book Production for a Mass Market 1836–1916* (Aldershot: Ashgate Publishing Limited, 2003), 141–156.

E&L A4b notes that impressions from the same plates as the first unauthorized yellowback edition were published as part of the Select Library of Fiction series in 1888 or 1889, including an issue in red cloth gilt. Examined copies of other titles in the Select Library of Fiction series all bear the series title on the top of the front cover and the top of the spine, and have ads at the end listing the titles issued in that series, including *The American* as number 519.

One of the examined copies of the Select Library of Fiction (not this title) had on the front free endpaper an inscription dated September 1886, and ads at the back for that series listing *The American* as number 519. This would indicate that the "Select Library of Fiction" publication of *The American* was in 1885 or 1886, not in 1888 or 1889 recorded in E&L A4b. Ward, Locke purchased The Select Library of Fiction from W. H. Smith and Son in 1885.

Nothing in this copy suggests that it was issued as part of the "Copyright Novel Series" which E&L records as announcing the publication of this title in 1894. As BAL 10532 records, the 1894 impression was published by Ward, Lock & Bowden, not Ward, Lock & Co.

The text of this pirated edition is very corrupt.

English printing history: There is no information on the printing history of the Ward, Lock "pirated" edition of *The American*, as Ward, Lock's records were partially destroyed in a fire, and those that escaped the fire were destroyed during the bombing of London during World War II.

MEB, 265, records that the Macmillan second English edition (authorized) was printed in a single impression of 1250 copies by Dickens & Evans in February 1879. It was published by Macmillan on March 11, 1879, priced at 6s. Although it is recorded that the impression was printed from "P [standing type] & M [moulds were made]", the moulds were never used to produce plates. These moulds were destroyed in May 1924.

A third English edition of *The American* was published in 1883 (reprinted in 1886) as part of *The Collective Edition of 1883*; see 21.1.0 and 21.4.0. A fourth English edition was published in 1909 by Thomas Nelson and Sons, reprinted in 1918 or 1919; see 4.21.5. A fifth English edition was published as Volume II of *The Novels and Stories of Henry James* in 1921; see 86.1.0–86.2.0.

PC, issue of March 17, 1879, 215, under the heading "NEW WORKS PUBLISHED FROM 1 TO 15." lists: "James (H.) – The American Post

THE AMERICAN

8vo. pp. 350, 6s. [vide Adv. 147] Macmillan." PC, same issue, 220, has a Macmillan ad for "NEW BOOKS" including *The American* "This day."

4.16.0. *The American*, first English edition, unauthorized, one volume, London [n.d., 1877].

The title-page, size, collation, and contents (including the ads) are identical to those of the first English edition, unauthorized, 4.15.0.

Binding: terra-cotta diagonal-fine-ribbed cloth, lettered ad decorated identically to 4.15.0. The endpapers are of pale yellow-coated paper, and the text is printed on wove paper. All edges are trimmed, and the top edge is stained brown.

On the front free endpaper is the inscription: "Sam Atkinson | Savile Town". On the front pastedown is a small circular green ticket that reads: "J. Malmshaw | Bookseller, Stationer, &c. Dewsbury."

Illustrated Plate 3.

4.16.5. *The American*, first English edition, unauthorized, one volume, London [n.d., 1877].

The title-page, size, collation, and contents are identical to those of the first English edition, unauthorized, 4.15.0 and 4.16.0, except that the first signature is $[A]^8$ $(-[A]_1)$, that is the half-title leaf is not present. In addition, leaf $2E_7$, pages 9 and 10 of the terminal ads, has been torn out of this copy but leaving the remnants of a stub.

Binding: royal-blue diagonal fine-ribbed cloth, with lettering and decoration identical to those on 4.15.0 and 4.16.0. The endpapers are of pale yellow-coated paper, and the text is printed on wove paper. All edges are trimmed, and the top edge is stained ochre.

On the front free endpaper and on the rear pastedown is the signatures: "Mrs Leverton Tattershalle".

4.17.0. *The American*, second English edition (authorized, 1879), binding state A, one volume, London 1879.

THE AMERICAN. | BY | HENRY JAMES, Jr. | London: [in Gothic type] | MACMILLAN AND CO. | 1879.

Size: $7\,3/8''$ x $5''$.

THE AMERICAN

Collation: [A]⁸ B–I K–U X–Y⁸; pp. [1–4], [5]–350 [351–352]. The last leaf Y$_8$, [351–352], is ads.

Contents: [1–2] half-title, verso publisher's device; [3–4] title-page, verso printer's imprint: "CHARLES DICKENS AND EVANS, | CRYSTAL PALACE PRESS."; [5]–350 text; 350 at foot printer's imprint: "[rule] | CHARLES DICKENS AND EVANS CRYSTAL PALACE PRESS."; [351–352] ad headed: "BY THE SAME AUTHOR." for *The Europeans* and *Daisy Miller*, verso ad headed: "The Works of Charles Kingsley."

Binding: dark blue-green fine-bead-grain cloth, with two decorative stamped bands in black, gilt, and the cloth color on the front cover and spine continuing across the back cover in blind. There is no lettering on the front or back covers. The spine, which is lettered in gilt, reads: "[decorative band] | THE | AMERICAN | H. JAMES Jr. [all the foregoing in italic] | [decorative band] | Macmillan & Co." The "o" in "Co" is raised above a line. The endpapers are of brown coated paper, and the text is printed on wove paper. The top edge is untrimmed, the fore-edge is rough trimmed, and the bottom edge is trimmed. It is stapled, not sewn. Bound in at the end is a 40-page publisher's catalogue, the first 35 pages of which are paginated, dated December 1879.

Illustrated Plate 4.

A Note on Bindings Uniform with that of the Second English Edition of *The American*

This is the first appearance (on a James work) of this binding, which was used by Macmillan on eleven James titles published in England between 1879 and 1888.[13] These were for the most part one-volume second editions of titles (novels) previously published in multi-volume editions. The exceptions to this were the two-volume second English editions of *The Madonna of the Future* (1880) and *Stories Revived* (1885).

13 These titles are: *The American* (1879), *The Europeans* (1879), *Roderick Hudson* (1880), *The Madonna of the Future* (1880), *Daisy Miller* (1880), *Washington Square* (1881), *The Portrait of a Lady* (1882), *Stories Revived* (1885), *The Bostonians* (1886), *The Princess Casamassima* (1886) and *The Reverberator* (1888). The use of this binding by Macmillan was by no means exclusive to James's works. See, for example, *Lady Hester* by Charlotte M. Yonge, one volume, Macmillan & Co. 1873. Five other James titles first published by Macmillan in this period are in bindings not uniform with that of the second English edition of *The American*. These are: *Hawthorne* (1879), *The Collective Edition of 1883*, *Portraits of Places* (1883), *Tales of Three Cities* (1884), and *Partial Portraits* (1888).

THE AMERICAN

It was also used on later impressions of the two or three-volume-in-one first editions of *The Europeans*, *The Bostonians* and *The Princess Casamassima*.

There are in fact two variants of this binding used on the seven of these titles published between 1879 and 1882. The first variant, variant A, has the author's name on the spine styled as "H. JAMES Jr." Variant A copies generally have brown coated endpapers and early dated catalogues bound in at the end. The second variant, variant B, has the author's name styled "HENRY JAMES", which, depending on the thickness of the volume, may be on one or two lines. Variant B copies generally have dark green or black coated endpapers and late dated or no catalogues bound in at the end. The change in style is due to the fact that James dropped the "Jr." from his name after the death of his father in December 1882.

It appears that early bindings-up (through 1882) of first impression sheets used variant A bindings, while later (post-1882) bindings up of these same first impression sheets used Variant B bindings. An example of this is *The Europeans*. The two-volumes-in-one first edition, second impression (7.3.0) and the one-volume second English edition with a publisher's catalogue dated November 1878 (7.4.0) are both in variant A bindings and have brown coated endpapers. The variant B binding (7.5.0) is of first impression sheets with dark green coated endpapers and with no catalogue bound in at the end. Similarly the one-volume second edition, second impression, of *Daisy Miller: A Study* with ads bound in dated "15.9.99" is in a variant B binding with dark green coated endpapers (8.21.0). The second English edition, first impression, of both *The American* and *The Portrait of a Lady* appear in both variant A and B bindings, the variant A bindings having brown coated endpapers and early dated catalogues (when catalogues are present), and the variant B bindings having dark green endpapers and catalogues dated 1896 and 1901, respectively.

It therefore seems that when a variant B binding appears on first impression sheets of the seven titles first printed before 1883, it is a post-1882 binding-up of those sheets.

The four James titles published by Macmillan after 1882 that were issued in bindings uniform with the second English edition of *The American* all appear in variant B bindings only, with the author's name on the spine as "HENRY JAMES" on either one or two lines.

4.18.0. *The American*, second English edition (authorized, 1879), binding state A, one volume, London 1879.

The title-page, size, collation, and contents are identical to those of the second English edition (authorized), binding state A, 4.17.0.

Binding: identical to that on 4.17.0. The endpapers are of brown coated paper, and the text is printed on wove paper. The top edge is untrimmed, the fore-edge is rough trimmed, and the bottom edge is trimmed. It is stapled not sewn. Bound in at the end is a 24-page paginated publisher's catalogue dated December 1881.

On the front pastedown is the armorial bookplate of David Garnett.

4.19.0. *The American*, second English edition (authorized, 1879), binding state A, one volume, London 1879.

The title-page, size, collation, and contents are identical to those of the second English edition (authorized), binding state A, 4.17.0.

Binding: identical to that on 4.17.0, except that the "o" in "Co" in the publisher's imprint is raised above a dot. The endpapers are of brown coated paper, and the text is printed on wove paper. The top edge is untrimmed, the fore-edge is rough trimmed, and the bottom edge is trimmed. No ads are bound in at the end.

4.20.0. *The American*, second English edition (authorized, 1879), binding state B, one volume, London 1879.

The title-page, size, collation, and contents are identical to those of the second English edition (authorized), binding state A, 4.17.0.

Binding: dark blue-green fine-bead-grain cloth, decorated in gilt on the front cover and spine identically to 4.17.0. The spine, which is lettered in gilt, reads: "[decorative band] | THE | AMERICAN | HENRY JAMES [all the foregoing in italic] | [decorative band] | MACMILLAN & Co." The "o" in "Co" is raised above a dot. The endpapers are of green-black coated paper, and the text is printed on wove paper. The top edge is untrimmed, the fore-edge is rough trimmed, and the bottom edge is trimmed. It is sewn, not stapled. The title on the spine tilts slightly upwards to the right. No ads are bound in at the end.

Illustrated Plate 4.

THE AMERICAN

4.21.0. *The American*, second English edition (authorized, 1879), binding state B, one volume, London 1879.

The title-page, size, collation, and contents are identical to those of the second English edition (authorized), binding state A, 4.17.0, except that this copy lacks the last leaf, Y_8, [351–352] (ads).

Binding: identical (including the lettering on the spine) to the binding on the second English edition (authorized), binding state B, 4.20.0. The endpapers are of dark green-black coated paper, and the text is printed on wove paper. The top edge is untrimmed, and the other edges are trimmed. It is sewn, not stapled. Bound in at the end is a 56-page paginated publisher's catalogue, dated January 1896.

The armorial bookplate of J. J. Storrow is on the front pastedown.

4.21.5. *The American*, fifth English edition, second (?) impression, one volume, London [n.d., 1918 or 1919].

The American | HENRY JAMES | THOMAS NELSON AND | SONS [all the foregoing within a decorative mirror panel]

Size: 6 1/8" x 4 1/8".

Collation: π^2 [1]^{16} 2–15^{16}; pp. [i–iv], [1]–456 [457–480].

Contents: [i–ii] ad under the heading: "UNIFORM WITH THIS VOLUME [in italic]", listing 26 titles including Conrad's *Romance*, but none by James; verso frontispiece signed at lower left "STEPHEN | REID 1909", [iii–iv] title-page, verso publisher's device; [1]–456 text; [457–480] unpaginated and undated ads [457–466] headed on [457]: "Uniform with this Volume and same Price.|[rule]|NELSON LIBRARY | OF COPYRIGHT NOVELS.|[rule]|A Few Recent Volumes. [in italic]", listing on [457] Conrad's *Romance*, but no works by James; [467] ad headed: "THE NELSON LIBRARY | CONDENSED LIST", listing *Romance*, but no works by James; [468–475] ads headed: "NELSON | SHILLING LIBRARY"; [476] ad headed: "CONDENSED LIST OF|THE VOLUMES."; [477–480] ads headed "NELSON|SIXPENNY CLASSICS."

Binding: bright red vertical rib-grain cloth. The front cover is decorated in blind with a double-rule border centered within which is a wreath with bow and pendant containing the intertwined letters "LN". The back cover is neither lettered nor decorated. The spine, which is lettered and decorated in gilt, reads: "The | American [in swash italic] | [small heart shaped device] | HENRY | JAMES [all the foregoing within a gilt-rule panel] | [wreath with pendant as on the front cover] | NELSON'S | LIBRARY [in italic] | decorative rule". The endpapers are of cream wove paper, the leaves $\pi_{1,2}$ are of coated paper, and the text is printed on poor quality wove paper. All edges are trimmed.

The text of this edition is that of The New York Edition (see discussion below), but it has been reset.

A Note on the Fourth English Edition of *The American*, and Other James Works that Nelson's Obtained Permission to Publish

In 1909, Thomas Nelson and Sons, Ltd., acquired from Macmillan the rights to publish *The American* as a cheap reprint. The impetus to sell the reprint rights came from James (who had been approached by Nelson) which paid him £135 for his consent. His agreement, however, was "on the basis of the text used being that of our [Macmillan's] Definitive Edition" and that "the book would be used without the preface now indefeasibly attached to the Edition presentation of it." Moore, Letter 283; see also Moore, Letters 284, 285 and 286. Nelson first published *The American* in 1909. EC, 1909 records that it was published in that year priced at 7d.

However, it appears that this copy is not of the first impression of the cheap 1909 edition. The rights to Conrad's *Romance*, which is listed as a cheap edition in the ads on [i] and [457] of *The American*, were acquired by Nelson from Smith, Elder & Co. in 1909, but it was published by Nelson in that year in a volume that sold for 7s., clearly not a cheap format. *Romance* was not published in a cheap format until it was reprinted in April 1918, priced at 1s. 6d.; see William Cagle, Draft Bibliography of Joseph Conrad (not published). The fact that the ad on [457] characterized *Romance* as a "recent" addition to Nelson Library of Copyright Novels (i.e. cheap novels), suggests that this copy of *The American* is a 1918 or 1919 reprint of the 1909 edition, a suggestion reinforced by the very poor quality of the text paper probably resulting from the paper shortage during WWI.

The American was not the only James novel that Thomas Nelson and Sons had acquired the right to publish. In May 1920, probably in connection with the forthcoming 35 volume *Novels and Stories of Henry James*, Frederick Macmillan inquired of J. B. Pinker, the agent for James's literary executors, what agreements with others had been made with respect to other James works. On May 14, 1920, Pinker replied that arrangements had been made with Nelson's with respect to "five [actually six]" titles in addition to *The American*. In a letter to Macmillan of May 26, 1920, Pinker elaborated on this:

> The Henry James agreements are dated March 29th 1909 ("*The American*"), December 16, 1915 ("*Roderick Hudson*") and May 3, 1917 ("*Daisy Miller*" "*The Bostonians*" "*Princess Casamassima*" "*The Tragic Muse*" "*The Madonna of the Future*"). The first of these agreements became terminable in 1914, the second will become terminable on July 25, 1921 while the agreement [of May 3, 1917] for the five books provides for a five year lease of each book from the date of its publication. "*Daisy Miller*" was published in May 1918 but the remaining four books have not yet been published.[14]

EC records that Thomas Nelson published *Roderick Hudson*, priced at 7d., in 1916, *Daisy Miller*, priced at 6d., in 1918, and *The Tragic Muse* and a further impression of *Roderick Hudson*, both priced at 2s., in 1920.

4.22.0. *The American*, first continental edition, first impression, two volumes, Leipzig 1878.

THE AMERICAN. | BY | HENRY JAMES Jr. | AUTHORIZED EDITION. [in italic] | IN TWO VOLUMES. | VOL. I. [II.] | LEIPZIG | BERNHARDT TAUCHNITZ | 1878.

Size: 6 $^{1}/_{16}$" x 4 $^{5}/_{16}$".

Collation: Volume I: $[1]^8$ $2–18^8$; pp. [1–6], [7]–288. Volume II: $[1]^8$ $2–18^8$; pp. [1–4], [5]–288.

Contents: Volume I: [1–2] series half-title, verso blank (there being no ad); [3–4] title-page, verso blank; [5–6] assent to publication, verso blank; [7]–288 text; 288 at foot and offset to the right printer's imprint: "[rule] | PRINTING OFFICE OF THE PUBLISHER." Volume II: [1–2] series half-title, verso blank (there being no ad); [3–4] title-page, verso blank; [5]–288 text; 288 at foot and offset to the right printer's imprint as in Volume I.

Binding: rebound as one volume in half-leather with marbled paper over boards (together with the first continental edition, first impression, of

---

14 Macmillan Archive, Mss 54905, Vol. ccx, ff. 83, 84 and 85.

FRENCH POETS AND NOVELISTS

The Madonna of the Future). The endpapers are of light-blue coated paper, and all edges are trimmed and red speckled.

T&B 1713 and 1714 records three impressions of one edition of this title. The first has no ad on the verso of the series half-title of Volume I (as in this copy), the second has 13 titles listed on the verso of the series half-title of Volume I, and the third has 14 titles listed on the verso of the series half-title of Volume I. There is no ad on the verso of the series half-title of Volume II in any of the three impression.

❧✢❧

5. FRENCH POETS AND NOVELISTS

5.1.0. *French Poets and Novelists*, first edition, binding state A, one volume, London 1878.

FRENCH|POETS AND NOVELISTS.|BY|HENRY JAMES Jr.|London [in Gothic type]|MACMILLAN AND CO.|1878.|[The Right of Translation and Reproduction is Reserved.] [in italic within brackets].

Size: $7\,7/16''$ x $4\,15/16''$.

Collation: [A]^4 B–I K–U X–Z AA–EE^8 FF^4; pp. [i–viii], [1]–439 [440].

Contents: [i–ii] half-title, verso publisher's device; [iii–iv] title-page, verso copyright notice: "COPYRIGHT.|HENRY JAMES JR.|1878. [all but date in italic]"; [v–vi] "NOTE.", verso blank; [vii–viii] "CONTENTS.", verso blank; [1]–439 text; [440] printer's imprint: "LONDON:|R. CLAY, SONS, AND TAYLOR,|BREAD STREET HILL, E. C."

The number 2 missing from the pagination 280, as noted in BAL 10534.

Binding: dark blue smooth-bead-grain cloth. The front and back covers are neither lettered nor decorated. The spine, which is lettered in gilt, reads: "FRENCH | POETS | AND | NOVELISTS | H. JAMES Jr. | Macmillan & Co." The "o" in "Co" is raised with a dot under it, and the imprint is $1\,1/8''$ wide. The endpapers are of white wove paper, and the text is printed on wove paper. The top edge is untrimmed, and the other edges are rough trimmed.

Dust-jacket: gray-blue wove paper, printed in black. The front cover reads: "FRENCH POETS [offset to the left]| AND NOVELISTS [offset to the right] | H. JAMES Jr. [in smaller capitals offset to the right]".

FRENCH POETS AND NOVELISTS

The spine reads: "FRENCH | POETS | and | NOVELISTS | H. JAMES Jr. | MACMILLAN & CO. [all centered]". The back cover is blank as are the front and rear inner flaps. The dust-jacket is ⅛" shorter than the cover of the book, the front inner flap extends to within ⁷⁄₁₆" of the book's front inner gutter, and the rear inner flap extends to ⅛" of the book's rear inner gutter.

Inscribed in ink on the front free endpaper: "Mrs Hattie J. Vauhoni | with Regards of | Iws. | July 18. 1879." This inscription has partially transferred itself onto the front innerflap, which indicates that the dust-jacket was on the book when the inscription was written.

Illustrated Plate 5. Tanselle 78.6 and plate 12.

This title was the first James work published by Macmillan; see note on James' relationship with Macmillan following 34.8.0. This copy was owned by James Gilvarry, and was sold at Christie's on February 7, 1986, lot 90.

Printing history: Macmillan Archive. MEB, 266, records that the first edition of *French Poets and Novelists* was printed in February 1878 from standing type in a single impression of 1250 copies. It was priced at 8s. 6d. The type was then dispersed. Five years later, in October 1883, Macmillan purchased from Tauchnitz the plates of the continental edition and, using these plates for its second edition of this title, printed with them five impressions: 1,000 copies in January 1884; 1,000 in January 1893; 500 in March 1904; 500 in August 1908; and a final impression of 500 in August 1919. Macmillan destroyed the Tauchnitz plates in 1923 (month not recorded). The first impression from the Tauchnitz plates was priced at 4s. 6d, and the second at 5s. MEB does not record the pricing of the last three impressions. James gave away 65 copies of the first impression; see CLHJ 1876–1878, Vol. 2, 57.

MPL 55909, at 37, records a print and paper order for 1,000 copies on November 14, 1892; MPL 55915, at 102, records a similar order for 500 copies and 525 envelopes on March 9, 1904; MPL 55918, at 4, records a similar order of 500 copies and 525 envelopes on July 24, 1908; and MPL 55923, at 110, records a similar order for 500 copies and 550 envelopes on July 10, 1919.

It is generally accepted that no American edition of *French Poets and Novelists* was published during the period covered by this Catalogue; see E&L A5a and A5d. BAL 10534 records that two copies [presumably of the English edition] were deposited for copyright in Washington in 1878. In the April 16, 1878, issue of PC, 270, under the heading "AMERICAN NEW BOOKS" there appears the entry: "James (H.) – French Poets and Novelists. 12mo. (New York) London 12s. 6d." BAL believes this listing is erroneous.

5.2.0. *French Poets and Novelists*, first edition, binding state B, one volume, London 1878.

The title-page, size, collation, and contents are identical to those of the first edition, binding state A, 5.1.0, including the "2" being dropped from the pagination of 280.

Binding: dark blue smooth linen-grain cloth. The front and back covers are neither lettered nor decorated. The spine, which is lettered in gilt but undecorated, reads: "FRENCH | POETS | AND | NOVELISTS | H. JAMES Jr. | Macmillan & Co." The printer's imprint is 1 $^{3}/_{8}$" wide, and the "o" in "Co" is set above a dot. It has endpapers of white wove paper, and the text is printed on wove paper. The top edge is untrimmed, and the other edges are rough trimmed.

These two binding variants are not recorded in BAL or E&L. The reference in Sadleir 1291 to variants, with "J" in "James" a drop-cap, is not applicable to the copies recorded in 5.1.0 and 5.2.0.

5.3.0. *French Poets and Novelists*, second English edition, first impression, one volume, London 1884.

FRENCH | POETS AND NOVELISTS | BY | HENRY JAMES | London [in Gothic type] | MACMILLAN AND CO. | 1884

Size: 7 $^{7}/_{16}$" x 4 $^{7}/_{8}$".

Collation: π^4 1–21^8 22^4; pp. [2] [i–vi], [1]–344.

Contents: blank leaf; [i–ii] half-title, verso publisher's device; [iii–iv] title-page, verso blank; [v–vi] "CONTENTS.", verso blank; [1]–344 text; 344 at foot printer's imprint: "Printed by R. & R. Clark, Edinburgh. [all except that printer's name in italic]".

Binding: greenish-black smooth cloth, with a single-rule border in blind on the front and back covers. The spine, which is lettered and decorated in gilt, reads: "[rule] | French | Poets | and | Novelists | Henry

James | Macmillan & Co. | [rule]". The publisher's imprint at the foot of spine has an initial capital "M", an initial capital "C" and a lower case "o" raised above a line. The endpapers are of white wove paper, and the text is printed on wove paper. The top and fore-edges are untrimmed, and the bottom edge is trimmed.

As indicated by correspondence between James and Macmillan, James made some further revisions to the Tauchnitz text for this edition; see Moore, letters 105 and 106, and HJL, III, 11.

Noted in BAL 10758.

5.4.0. *French Poets and Novelists*, second English edition, second impression, one volume, London 1893.

The title-page is identical to that of the second English edition, first impression, 5.3.0, except that the publisher's imprint and date at the foot reads: "London [in Gothic type] | MACMILLAN AND CO. | AND NEW YORK | 1893".

Size: 7" x 4 ¾".

The collation and contents are identical to those of the second English edition, first impression, 5.3.0, except as noted above for the title-page, and the title-leaf verso which reads: "First Edition (Crown 8vo) 1878; Second, 1884 | Reprinted (Globe 8vo) 1893. [all but dates in italic]". On 344 at the foot the printer's imprint reads: "Printed by R. & R. Clark, Edinburgh. [all but printer's name in italic]".

Binding: smooth maroon cloth, with a single-rule border in blind on the front and back covers. The spine, which is lettered and decorated in gilt, reads: "[rule] | French | Poets | and | Novelists | Henry | James | MACMILLAN & Co. | [rule]". The publisher's imprint at the foot of the spine is in capitals of uniform size except, except that the "o" in "Co" is raised above a line. The endpapers are of white wove paper, and the text is printed on wove paper. All edges are untrimmed.

Another copy has been examined which is identical to this copy of the second impression, except that stamped in pink ink on the title-page beneath the publisher's imprint is: "PRINTED IN GT. BRITAIN". This would suggest that this copy was exported, possibly to America.

5.5.0. *French Poets and Novelists*, second English edition, third impression, one volume, London 1904.

The title-page is identical to that of the second English edition, first impression, 5.3.0, except that the publisher's imprint and date at the foot reads: "London [in Gothic type] | MACMILLAN AND CO., Limited | NEW YORK: THE MACMILLAN COMPANY | 1904 | All rights reserved [in italic]".

The size, collation, and contents are identical to those of 5.3.0, except as noted above for the title-page, and the title-leaf verso which reads: "First Edition (Crown 8vo) 1878; Second, 1884 | Reprinted (Globe 8vo) 1893, 1904 [all but dates in italic]".

Binding: identical to that on the second English edition, second impression, 5.4.0.

5.6.0. *French Poets and Novelists*, second English edition, fourth impression, one volume, London 1908.

The title-page is identical to that of the second English edition, first impression, 5.3.0, except that the publisher's imprint and date at the foot reads: "MACMILLAN AND CO., LIMITED | ST. MARTIN'S STREET, LONDON | 1908".

Size: $7\,^1\!/_{16}''$ x $4\,^3\!/_4''$.

The collation and contents are identical to those of 5.3.0, except as noted above for the title-page, and the title-leaf verso which reads: "First Edition (Crown 8vo) 1878; Second, 1884 | Reprinted (Globe 8vo) 1893, 1904, 1908 [all but dates in italic]". On 344 at the foot the printer's imprint reads: "Printed by R. & R. Clark, Limited, Edinburgh. [all but printer's name in italic]"

Binding: smooth maroon cloth, with a single-rule border in blind on the front and back covers. The spine, which is lettered and decorated in gilt, reads: "[rule] | FRENCH | POETS | AND | NOVELISTS | HENRY | JAMES | MACMILLAN & Co. | [rule]". The publisher's imprint at the foot of the spine is in capitals of uniform size, except for the final "o" which is raised above a dot. The endpapers are of white wove paper, and the text is printed on wove paper. All edges are untrimmed. Bound in at the end is a 4-page unpaginated catalogue of "The Eversley Series." This is the only James title listed in the catalogue.

On the front free endpaper is the signature of M. E. Pitblads.

FRENCH POETS AND NOVELISTS

5.6.5. *French Poets and Novelists*, second English edition, fifth impression, one volume, London 1919.

The title-page is identical to that of the second English edition, first impression, 5.3.0, except that the publisher's imprint and date at the foot read "MACMILLAN AND CO., LIMITED | ST. MARTIN'S STREET, LONDON | 1919.

Size: 7 $^1/_{16}$" x 4 $^{11}/_{16}$".

The collation and contents are identical to those of 5.3.0, except as noted above for the title-page, and the title leaf verso which reads: "First Edition (Crown 8vo) 1878; second, 1884 | Reprinted (Glove 8vo) 1893, 1904, 1908, 1919 [all but dates in italic]". On 344 at the foot the printer's imprint reads: "Printed by R. & R. Clark, Limited, Edinburgh. [all but printer's name in italic]".

Binding: smooth maroon cloth, lettered and decorated identically to the second English edition, fourth impression, 5.6.0. The endpapers are of white wove paper, and the text is printed on wove paper. The top and bottom edges are untrimmed, and the fore-edge is rough trimmed. There are no ads bound in at the end.

5.7.0. *French Poets and Novelists*, first continental edition, one volume, Leipzig 1883.

FRENCH | POETS AND NOVELISTS. | BY | HENRY JAMES, | AUTHOR OF | "DAISY MILLER," "THE PORTRAIT OF A LADY," | ETC. ETC. | AUTHORIZED EDITION. [in italic] | LEIPZIG | BERNHARD TAUCHNITZ | 1883.

Size: 6 $^1/_2$" x 4 $^5/_8$".

Collation: π^4 1–21^8 22^4; pp. [i–viii], [1]–344.

Contents: [i–ii] series half-title, verso ad headed: "TAUCHNITZ EDITION. | By the same Author," listing 10 titles; [iii–iv] title-page, verso blank; [v–vi] "NOTE.", verso blank; [vii–viii] "CONTENTS.", verso blank; [1]–344 text; 344 at the foot offset to the right printer's imprint: "[rule] | PRINTING OFFICE OF THE PUBLISHER."

Binding: buff wove paper wrappers, cut flush, with lettering and decoration on the front and back covers and spine in black. The front cover is decorated with a black single-rule frame with floral devices at each of the four corners, with lettering within, as well as above and below the frame. The back cover is headed "February 1905.|Tauchnitz Edition.|[rule]|Latest Volumes:" listing 26 titles in a single column, the last of which is 3789/90, *The Prodigal Son* by Hall Caine. The insides of the front and back covers are blank. The spine reads: "[two thick and thin rules]|BRITISH|AUTHORS|TAUCHNITZ|EDITION [in italic]| [thick and thin rule] VOL. 2181.|[thick and thin rule]|JAMES|16.|[thick and thin rule]|FRENCH|POETS AND|NOVELIST|[thick and thin rule]|PRICE|M 1, 60.|[two thick and thin rules]". A 32-page paginated publisher's catalogue, dated October 1, 1906, is bound in at the end.

On the back cover stamped in red is: "T. H. ROUSSY, LIBRAIRIE ANGLAISE, LAUSANNE".

See T&B 2181, which records only one Tauchnitz edition with a single impression. It is likely that Tauchnitz did not reprint this title because the plates were sold to Macmillan in October 1883, and used by Macmillan to produce the impressions of the second English edition recorded above, all of which were printed by R. & R. Clark of Edinburgh. However, Tauchnitz continued to issue first impression sheets periodically for at least 24 years.

This wrapper date not recorded in T&B.

5.8.0. *French Poets and Novelists*, first continental edition, one volume, Leipzig 1883.

The title-page is identical to that of the first continental edition, 5.7.0.

Size: 6" x 4 $^{5}/_{16}$".

Collation: π^4 ($\pm\pi_4$) 1–21^8 22^4 ($\pm 22_1$); pp. [2] [i–vi], [1]–344. The recto of the cancellans π_4 is the contents page, the verso being blank. The recto and verso of the cancellans 22_1 are pages 337–38 of the text.

Contents: blank leaf; [i–ii] title-page, verso blank; [iii–iv] "NOTE", verso blank; [v–vi] "CONTENTS", verso blank; 1–344 text; 344 at foot offset to the right "[rule]|PRINTING OFFICE OF THE PUBLISHER."

Binding: white paper over bevelled boards. Elaborately decorated on the front and back covers with a wide gilt filigree band at top and foot, all within a single-rule red border with two red rules and two gilt rules immediately below the top band and above the lower band, leaving an undecorated white center panel. The spine, which is also elaborately decorated and lettered in gilt, has two rules at the top of the spine, followed by a filigree band, two further rules, the author's surname, a short rule, the title, two further rules, a wide filigree band, with four further rules at the foot. There is no publisher's imprint on the spine. The endpapers are of vertical-ribbed black silk over white wove paper with an overall fleur-de-lis and dot design in gilt, and the text is printed on wove paper. All edges are trimmed and stained red. A binder's fly-leaf is at the back, but none is at the front. A red ribbon marker is bound in.

The cancellation of π_4 appears to have taken place to be able to substitute a blank page in place of the half-title. It is not clear why 22_1 was cancelled.

It appears that this binding is a bookseller's binding, the elaborateness of which permitted the bookseller to sell the volume to tourists at a price greatly in excess of the then normal price for Tauchnitz volumes of 1.60 marks or 2 francs.

✤

6. WATCH AND WARD

6.1.0. *Watch and Ward*, first edition, first impression, one volume, Boston 1878.

WATCH AND WARD. | BY | HENRY JAMES Jr. | [ornamental rule] | BOSTON: | HOUGHTON, OSGOOD AND COMPANY. | The Riverside Press, Cambridge. [in Gothic type] | 1878.

Size: $5\,^3/_4$" x $4\,^3/_{16}$".

Collation: [unsigned, 1–13^8 14^8 (–14$_8$)]; pp. [1–4], [5]–219 [220] [221–222]. The last leaf, [14$_7$], is blank, as noted in BAL 10535 for the first of two impressions.

Contents: [1–2] title-page, verso copyright notice, reservation of rights and printer's imprint: "Copyright, 1878. | By HENRY JAMES Jr. | All rights reserved. [in italic] | University Press: Welch, Bigelow, & Co., | Cambridge."; [3–4] "NOTE. | 'Watch and Ward' first appeared in the | *Atlantic Monthly* in the year 1871. It has | now been minutely revised, and has received | many verbal alterations. | April, 1878.", verso blank; [5]–219 text; 219 at foot printer's imprint: "[rule] | Cambridge: Electrotyped and Printed by Welch, Bigelow, & Co."; [220] blank; [221–222] blank leaf.

WATCH AND WARD

Binding: terra-cotta diagonal-fine-ribbed cloth, with two elongated decorative gilt rules and lettering in gilt on the front cover, with blocking on the front and back covers in blind, and lettering in gilt and decoration in gilt with blocking in blind on the spine. The spine reads: "Watch | and | Ward | [rule] | H. James Jr. | Houghton, Osgood & Co." The endpapers are of tan-coated paper, and the text is printed on wove paper. A binder's fly-leaf of wove paper is at the front, but none at the back. All edges are trimmed and stained red.

Printing history. Houghton Mifflin Archive. First edition: Ms Am 2030(16), 127: *first* [Houghton, Osgood] *impression* May 18, 1878, 1,000 copies, all bound between May 21 and June 11, 1878; *second impression* July 25, 1878, 280 copies, 276 bound between August 1, 1878, and October 31, 1878; *third impression* April 23, 1879, 280 copies, 286 [*sic*, 287] bound between May 5, 1879, and February 15, 1883. Ms Am 2030(17), 117: *fourth* [first Houghton, Mifflin] *impression* May 5, 1883, 160 copies, 155 bound between June 1, 1883, and July 23, 1885; notation: "[total copies] 1720". Ms Am 2030(18), 136: *fifth impression* May 4, 1887, 162 copies, 159 bound between May 31, 1887, and April 26, 1892. Ms Am 2030(20), 174: *sixth impression* March 15, 1893, 160 copies, 152 bound between June 29, 1893, and May 19, 1897; notation: "Transf 50". Ms Am 2030(21), 221: March 31, 1899, notation: "Bal[ance] 50" sets of sheets, bound September 15, 1899; notations: "[total copies] 2042", and "Plates melted June 30, 1909".

Priced at $1.50 in cloth, which price was unchanged through 1905. This title published in 1886 in the Riverside Pocket Series (see 6.8.0) was priced at $.50.

Watch and Ward was not published in England until it appeared in 1923 as part of Volume XXIV of *The Novels and Stories of Henry James* (1921–1923), 86.1.0– 86.2.0. However, copies of the American edition were imported into England. The issue of PC for June 17, 1878 under the heading "AMERICAN NEW BOOKS" records: "James (H.) – Watch and Ward 18mo. (Boston) London, 6s. 8d."

6.2.0. *Watch and Ward*, first edition, first impression, one volume, Boston 1878.

The title-page, size, collation, and contents of this copy are identical to those of the first edition, first impression, 6.1.0.

Binding: bright green diagonal-fine-ribbed cloth, with lettering and

WATCH AND WARD

decoration on the front and back covers and spine identical to that on 6.1.0 (including the publisher's imprint "Houghton, Osgood & Co." at the foot of the spine). The endpapers are of dark blue-black coated paper, and the text is printed on wove paper. A binder's fly-leaf of wove paper is at the front, but none at the back. All edges are trimmed and stained red.

6.3.0. *Watch and Ward*, first edition, first impression, one volume, Boston 1878

This copy is identical to the first edition, first impression, 6.2.0, except that the endpapers are of light tan-coated paper.

6.4.0. *Watch and Ward*, first edition, second impression, one volume, Boston 1878.

The title-page and size are identical to the first edition, first impression, 6.1.0.

Collation: [unsigned, 1–13^8 14^6]; pp. [1–4], [5]–219 [220].

Contents: identical to 6.1.0, except that the final blank leaf, [221–222] is not present in this impression.

Binding: dark terra-cotta diagonal-fine-ribbed cloth, with lettering and decoration on the front and back covers and spine identical to that on 6.1.0. The endpapers are of tan-coated paper, and the text is printed on wove paper. A binder's fly-leaf of wove paper is at both the front and the back. All edges are trimmed and stained red.

BAL 10535 records the second impression with this collation.

6.5.0. *Watch and Ward*, first edition, third impression, first binding state, one volume, Boston 1879.

The title-page is identical to that of the first edition, first impression, 6.1.0, except that it is dated 1879 at the foot. The title-leaf verso is identical to that of 6.1.0.

Collation: [unsigned, 1–13^8 14^4, 15^2]; pp. [1–4], [5]–219 [220]. This collation is not noted in E&L or BAL.

The size and contents are as described for 6.1.0 (including the printer's imprint at the foot of 219), except that the final blank leaf, [221–222], in the first impression is not present in this impression.

WATCH AND WARD

Binding: bright green diagonal-fine-ribbed cloth, lettered and decorated on the front and back covers and spine identically to 6.1.0 (including the publisher's imprint "Houghton, Osgood & Co." at the foot of the spine). The endpapers are of tan-coated paper, and the text is printed on wove paper. A binder's fly-leaf of wove paper is at both the front and the back. All edges are trimmed and stained red.

Not recorded in BAL. The fact that the last signature in this copy is [15^2], the publisher's imprint at the foot of the spine reads: "Houghton, Osgood & Co." and the title-page is dated 1879, indicates that this copy is of the third or a later impression. This copy, and the copies of this title recorded below, disprove E&L's assertion that later impressions than the first all have a last signature [14^6].

6.6.0. *Watch and Ward*, first edition, third impression, second binding state, one volume, Boston 1879.

The title-page, size, collation, and contents are identical to those of the first edition, third impression, first binding state, 6.5.0.

Binding: bright green diagonal-fine-ribbed cloth, lettered and decorated in gilt on the front cover and spine, and decorated in blind on the front and back cover and spine are identically to the first edition, first impression, 6.1.0, except that the elongated decorative rules in gilt at the top and foot of the front cover are lacking, and the publisher's imprint at the foot of the spine reads: "Houghton, Mifflin & Co." The endpapers are of tan-coated paper, and the text is printed on wove paper. A binder's fly-leaf of wove paper is at both the front and the back. All edges are trimmed and stained red.

6.7.0. *Watch and Ward*, first edition, fourth impression, one volume, Boston 1883.

WATCH AND WARD. | BY | HENRY JAMES Jr. | [short decorative rule] | BOSTON: | HOUGHTON, MIFFLIN AND COMPANY. | The Riverside Press, Cambridge. [in Gothic type] | 1883.

Size: $5^{7}/8''$ x $4^{1}/8''$.

Collation: [unsigned, 1–13^8 14^4 15^2]; pp. [1–4], [5]–219 [220].

Contents: [1–2] title-page, verso copyright notice and reservation of rights: "Copyright, 1878. | By HENRY JAMES Jr. | All rights reserved. [in italic]"; [3–4] "NOTE." as in 6.1.0, verso blank; [5]–219 text; 219 at foot no printer's imprint; [220] blank.

Binding: bright green diagonal-fine-ribbed cloth, lettered and decorated in gilt on the front cover and spine, and decorated in blind on the front and back covers and spine identically to the first edition, first impression, 6.1.0, except that it lacks the elongated decorative rules in gilt at the top and foot of the front cover, and the publisher's imprint on the spine reads: "Houghton Mifflin & Co." The endpapers are of tan-coated paper, and the text is printed on wove paper. A binder's fly-leaf of wove paper is at the front, and a double binder's fly-leaf of wove paper at the back. All edges are trimmed and stained red.

6.8.0. *Watch and Ward*, first edition, unrecorded impression between the fourth and fifth recorded impressions, one volume, Boston and New York 1886.

Riverside Pocket Series [in Gothic type] | [rule] | WATCH AND WARD | BY | HENRY JAMES, JR. | [publisher's device of a piper under a tree within a frame] | BOSTON AND NEW YORK | HOUGHTON, MIFFLIN AND COMPANY | The Riverside Press, Cambridge [in Gothic type] | 1886.

Size: 6 ½″ x 4 ⅛″.

Collation: [unsigned, 1–7^{16}]; pp. [i–ii] [1–4], [5]–219 [220] [221–222].

Contents: [i–ii] blank, verso ad within a single-rule frame headed: "Henry James's Books. [in Gothic type]" listing 8 titles; [1–2] title-page, verso copyright notice and reservation of rights: "Copyright, 1878. | By HENRY JAMES Jr. | All rights reserved. [in italic]"; [3–4] "NOTE." as in the first edition, first impression, 6.1.0, verso blank; [5]–219 text; 219 at foot no printer's imprint; [220] blank; [221–222] ad headed: "Riverside Classics. [in Gothic type]" listing 9 titles, verso ad headed: "The Riverside Paper Series. [in Gothic type]" listing 13 titles.

Binding: olive-green smooth cloth over boards, cut flush (thus exposing the gray bare edge of the boards), with no lettering or decoration on the front or back covers. On the spine is a paper label, printed in brown, which reads: "JAMES | [rule] | WATCH | AND WARD | [rule] | Riverside | Pocket | Series [series title all in Gothic type] | [leaf device]". The endpapers are of buff wove paper with ads printed in red headed on the front pastedown: "The Riverside Aldine Series.", on the recto of the front free endpaper: "The Riverside Pocket Series.", on the verso of the rear free endpaper: "New Publications.", and on the rear pastedown: "The Riverside Paper Series.". The text is printed on wove paper. A binder's fly-leaf of wove paper is at both the front and the back. The top edge is stained ochre.

This impression was printed from the first edition plates, with a new title-page, the printer's imprint removed from the title-page verso and from 219, and the addition of the ads on [221–222]; see printing history 6.1.0 which records the fourth impression as having been printed on May 5, 1883 and the fifth on May 4, 1887, which, given the date on the title-page and the collation of this copy, would indicate that it is of a separate impression, unrecorded in the printing record, which was printed between the fourth and fifth recorded impressions.

6.9.0. *Watch and Ward*, first edition, fifth impression, one volume, Boston 1887.

WATCH AND WARD. | BY | HENRY JAMES Jr. | SIXTH EDITION [*sic*] | [short decorative rule] | BOSTON: | HOUGHTON, MIFFLIN AND COMPANY. | The Riverside Press, Cambridge. [in Gothic type] | 1887.

Size: $5\,3/4''$ x $4\,1/8''$.

Collation: [unsigned, 1–13^8 14^6]; pp. [1–4], [5]–219 [220].

Contents: [1–2] title-page, verso copyright notice and reservation of rights: "Copyright, 1878. | By HENRY JAMES Jr. | All rights reserved. [in italic]"; [3–4] "NOTE." as in the first edition, first impression, 6.1.0, verso blank; [5]–219 text; 219 at foot no printer's imprint; [220] blank.

Binding: terra-cotta diagonal-fine-ribbed cloth, lettered and decorated in gilt on the front cover and spine, and blocked in blind on the front and back covers and spine identically to 6.1.0, except that it lacks the elongated decorative rules in gilt at the top and foot of the front cover. The spine, which is lettered and decorated in gilt and in blind, reads: "Watch | and | Ward | [rule] | H. James Jr. [all the foregoing in gilt] | HOUGHTON | MIFFLIN [dot] & [dot] CO [publisher's imprint in blind]". The ampersand is not stylized. The endpapers are of black coated paper, and the text is printed on wove paper. A binder's fly-leaf of wove paper is at both the front and the back. All edges are trimmed and stained red.

THE EUROPEANS

See printing history 6.1.0, which records that the fifth impression was printed on May 4, 1887 and the sixth (and last) on March 15, 1893. However when one includes the unrecorded impression, 6.8.0, this would be the sixth, as is stated on the title-page.

6.10.0. *Watch and Ward*, first edition, sixth impression, Boston 1893.

The title-page is identical to that of the first edition, fifth impression, 6.9.0, except that "SEVENTH EDITION. [*sic*]" is present between the author's name and the decorative rule, and it is dated 1893 at the foot.

The size, collation, and contents are identical to those of 6.9.0.

Binding: bright green diagonal-fine ribbed cloth. The front cover is decorated, lettered and blocked identically to 6.1.0, but entirely in blind and without the elongated decorative rules at the top and foot of the front cover. The back cover is blocked in blind. The spine, which is lettered in gilt and in blind, and blocked in blind, reads: "Watch | and | Ward | [rule] | H. James Jr. [all the foregoing in gilt] | HOUGHTON | MIFFLIN [dot] & [dot] CO [publisher's imprint in blind]". The endpapers are of white laid paper, and the text is printed on wove paper. A binder's fly-leaf of wove paper is at both the front and the back. All edges are trimmed and stained red.

There were only six recorded impressions of the first edition printed, the sixth being printed on March 15, 1893, however, when one includes the unrecorded impression, 6.8.0, this would be the seventh impression, as is stated on the title-page.

7. THE EUROPEANS

7.1.0. *The Europeans*, first edition, first (?) impression, two volumes, London 1878.

No copy in the collection; see 7.2.0 for textual differences possibly sufficient to distinguish the first and second impressions, although the evidence for priority seems weak.

English printing history. Macmillan Archive. MEB, 266, records that there were three impressions of the two-volume first English edition of *The Europeans*, of 250 copies each. The first was in September 1878, the second in October 1878, and the third in November 1878. All three were printed from standing type, and the first two impressions were priced at 21s. for the two volumes. The third impression is thought to be seen only as two volumes bound as one; see 7.3.0. Stereotype plates were made for printing the one-volume second edition, of which there was only one impression of 1,000 copies in April 1879. It was priced at 6s. Macmillan destroyed the plates in March 1918.

A third English edition of *The Europeans* was published in 1883 (reprinted in 1886) as part of *The Collective Edition of 1883*; see 20.1.0–20.5.0. A fourth English edition was published as Volume III of *The Novels and Stories of Henry James* in 1921; see 86.1.0–86.2.0.

7.2.0. *The Europeans*, first edition, second (?) impression, two volumes, London 1878.

THE EUROPEANS. | A Sketch. [in Gothic type] | BY | HENRY JAMES, Jr. | IN TWO VOLUMES. [in italic] | VOL. I. [II.] | London: [in Gothic type] | MACMILLAN AND CO. | 1878.

Size: $7 \frac{1}{4}''$ x $4 \frac{7}{8}''$.

Collation: Volume I: [A]^2 B–I K–R^8; pp. [i–iv], [1]–255 [256]. Volume II: [A]^2 B–I K–S^8; pp. [i–iv], [1]–272.

Contents: Volume I: [i–ii] half-title, verso publisher's device; [iii–iv] title-page, verso printer's imprint and copyright notice: "Bungay: [in Gothic type] | CLAY AND TAYLOR, PRINTERS. | [Copyright.] [in italic, within brackets]"; [1]–255 text; [256] blank. Volume II: [i–ii] half-title, verso publisher's device; [iii–iv] title-page, verso printer's imprint and copyright notice as on Volume I title-leaf verso; [1]–272 text; 272 at foot printer's imprint: "CLAY AND TAYLOR, PRINTERS, BUNGAY."

Binding: bright blue sand-grain cloth. The front covers are decorated in black with a panel with curved corners within a double-rule border, and the back covers are decorated similarly in blind. The spines, which are decorated in black and gilt and lettered in gilt, read: "[two black rules separated by a row of black dots] | THE | EUROPEANS | H. JAMES Jr. | Vol. I [II] | [publisher's device] | Macmillan & Co. | [two black rules separated by a row of black dots]". The "o" in "Co" is raised above a dot. The endpapers are of brown coated paper, and the text is printed on wove paper. The top edges are untrimmed,

THE EUROPEANS

and the other edges are trimmed. It is stapled, not sewn. A 40-page (38 pages of which are paginated) publisher's catalogue, dated June, 1878, is bound in at the end of Volume I.

The chapter number in the running head on the rectos of pages 171–191 of Volume I is incorrectly printed IV rather than V. Also in Volume I the last line of 77 reads "say.", the last line of 83 reads "doorway." and the last line of 156 reads "indiscriminately,". In Volume II the last line of 101 reads "moment," and on 272 five lines of text are present.

See BAL 10536. BAL is uncertain as to the identification of the three printings, offering his solution "not as a final but as a contribution to a final solution." Presumably positive identification of the first impression could be made if a copy with a September 1878 inscription could be found. The distinguishing features suggested by BAL (sufficient for possible identification) of the first and second impressions are as follows.

Possible First Impression
Volume I
p. 77 last line ends "say"
p. 83 last line ends "door way."
p. 156 last line ends
   "indiscriminately"
Volume II
p. 272 four lines of text present.

Possible Second Impression

p. 77 last line ends "say."
p. 83 last line ends "doorway."
p. 156 last line ends
   "indiscriminately,"

p. 272 five lines of text present.

7.3.0. *The Europeans*, first edition, third impression, sheets of the two volumes of the first edition bound in one volume, London 1878.

THE EUROPEANS. | A Sketch. [in Gothic type] | BY | HENRY JAMES, Jr. | IN TWO VOLUMES. [in italic] | VOL I. [II.] | London [in Gothic type] | MACMILLAN AND CO. | 1878.

Size: 7 3/8" x 4 7/8".

Collation: Volume I sheets: [A]² B–I K–R⁸; pp. [i–iv], [1]–255 [256]. Volume II sheets: [A]² B–I K–S⁸; [i–iv], [1]–272.

Contents: Volume I pages: [i–ii] half-title, verso publisher's device; [iii–iv] title-page, verso printer's imprint: "Bungay [in Gothic type] | CLAY AND TAYLOR, PRINTERS. | [Copyright.] [in italic, within brackets]"; [1]–255 text; [256] blank. Volume II pages: [i–ii] half-title, verso publisher's device; [iii–iv] title-page, verso printer's imprint as on Volume I title-leaf verso; [1]–272 text; 272 at foot printer's imprint: "[rule] | BUNGAY: CLAY AND TAYLOR, PRINTERS."

In the Volume I sheets the chapter number in the running head on pages 177–191 (rectos only) is incorrectly printed "IV" rather than "V", and on pages 195 and 213 is incorrectly printed "Y" rather than "V". In the Volume II sheets there are five lines of text on 272, and at the foot of 272 the printer's imprint is beneath a rule.

Binding: dark blue-green bead-grain cloth, lettered and decorated in gilt, black and in blind uniform with the second English edition of *The American* (1879), 4.17.0. There is no lettering on the front and back covers. The spine, lettered in gilt, reads: "THE | EUROPEANS | H. JAMES Jr. [all the foregoing in italic] | Macmillan & Co." The "o" in "Co" is raised above a dot. The endpapers are of brown coated paper, and the text is printed on wove paper. The top edge is untrimmed, and the other edges are trimmed. The signatures, as in the two volume first and second impressions, are stapled, not sewn. No catalogue of ads is bound in at the end.

This copy conforms in all respects to what is described in BAL 10536 as the third printing of the first edition, which printing is noted only as "a two-volumes-in-one production; not as part of a two-volume set."

7.4.0. *The Europeans*, second English edition, binding state A, one volume, London 1879.

THE EUROPEANS. | A Sketch. [in Gothic type] | By HENRY JAMES, Jr. | NEW EDITION. [in italic] | London: [in Gothic type] | MACMILLAN AND CO. | 1879.

Size: 7 3/8" x 4 7/8".

Collation: [A]² B–I K–U X–Z AA⁸ BB⁶; pp. [i–iv], [1]–373 [374] [375–380].

Contents: [i–ii] half-title, verso publisher's device; [iii–iv] title-page, verso printer's imprint and copyright notice: "Bungay [in Gothic type] | CLAY AND TAYLOR, PRINTERS | [copyright.] [in italic, within brackets]"; [1]–373 text; [374] printer's imprint as on title-leaf verso; [375–380] undated ads, being the last three leaves of signature BB.

Binding: dark blue-green bead-grain cloth, lettered and decorated in gilt, black, and in blind uniform with the second English edition of

THE EUROPEANS

The American (1879), 4.17.0. There is no lettering on the front or back covers. The spine, which is lettered in gilt, reads: "THE | EUROPEANS | H. JAMES Jr. [all the foregoing in italic] | Macmillan & Co." The "o" in "Co" is raised above a line. The endpapers are of chocolate-brown coated paper, and the text is printed on wove paper. The top edge is untrimmed, and the other edges are rough trimmed. A 40-page (38 pages of which are paginated) publisher's catalogue, dated November 1878, is bound in at the end.

Noted but not described in BAL 10536.

7.5.0. *The Europeans*, second English edition, binding state B, one volume, London 1879.

This copy is identical to the second English edition, binding state A, 7.4.0, including the ads on [375–380], except that the spine, which is lettered in gilt, reads: "THE | EUROPEANS | HENRY JAMES [all the foregoing in italic] | MACMILLAN & Co." The publisher's imprint on the spine is in uniform capitals, except that the "o" in "Co" is raised above a dot. The endpapers are of dark green coated paper, and the text is printed on wove paper. The top edge is untrimmed, and the other edges are rough trimmed. No publisher's catalogue is bound in at the end.

This is a later binding-up of first impression sheets. On the style of this binding, see the note following 4.17.0.

7.5.5. *The Europeans*, second English edition, The Times Book Club binding state, London 1879.

Size: 7 1/4" x 4 7/8".

The title-page, collation, and contents, including the ads on [375–380], are identical to those of the second English edition, binding state A, 7.4.0.

Binding: bright orange smooth-linen-grain cloth. The front cover has a single-rule black border. The back cover is neither lettered nor decorated. The spine, which is lettered and decorated in black, reads: "[rule] | The | Europeans | HENRY JAMES [all the foregoing in italic] | [circular The Times Book Club device] | [rule]". The endpapers are of cream laid paper, and the text is printed on wove paper. All edges are trimmed. There is no catalogue of ads bound in at the end.

THE EUROPEANS

7.6.0. *The Europeans*, first American edition, first impression, binding state A, one volume, Boston 1879 [1878].

THE EUROPEANS. | A Sketch. [in Gothic type] | BY | HENRY JAMES, Jr. | [shield shaped publisher's device] | BOSTON: | HOUGHTON, OSGOOD AND COMPANY. | The Riverside Press, Cambridge. [in Gothic type] | 1879.

Size: $7\,3/8''$ x $4\,13/16''$.

Collation: $[1^2\ 2\text{--}12^{12}\ 13^{10}]$, signed as $\pi^2\ 1\text{--}17^8\ 18^6$; pp. [2] [i–ii], [1]–281 [282] [283–284]. This collation is recorded in BAL 10537 as the "1st (and 2nd?) Printing" of three; see discussion under the third impression, 7.10.0.

Contents: blank leaf, [i–ii] title-page, verso copyright notice, reservation of rights and printer's imprint : "Copyright, 1878, | By HOUGHTON, OSGOOD AND COMPANY | All rights reserved. [in italic] | RIVERSIDE, CAMBRIDGE: | STEREOTYPED AND PRINTED BY | H.O.HOUGHTON AND COMPANY."; [1]–281 text; [282] blank; [283–284] blank leaf.

Binding: terra-cotta dotted-line-grain cloth over bevelled boards, with front and back covers decorated in blind with a single-rule frame within a wider single-rule border. The spine, which is lettered and decorated in gilt, reads: "[thick followed by a thin rule] | The | Europeans | [rule] | H. James Jr. | Houghton, Osgood & Co. | [thin followed by a thick rule]". The initial "H" in the publisher's imprint at the foot of the spine does not extend below the other letters in the imprint and the ampersand is in upper not lower case. The endpapers are of chocolate-brown coated paper, and the text is printed on wove paper. A binder's fly-leaf of wove paper is at both the front and the back. All edges are trimmed, and the top edge is stained ochre.

On the front binder's fly-leaf is the inscription: "F. L. Higginson | 1878 [year underscored]". Higginson was a member of a prominent Boston family, active in business and owner of the famous F.L. Higginson House built from 1881 to 1883, which is still standing. The 1878 date of this inscription corroborates the fact that this copy is of the first impression; see American printing history, below. Both BAL and E&L record first impression copies in terra-cotta, dark green and light (Kelly) green cloth. BAL records the cloth as FL (dotted-line-grain), and E&L records it as fine-cross-ribbed.

THE EUROPEANS

American printing history. Houghton Mifflin Archive. First edition: Ms Am 2030(16), 127: *first* [Houghton, Osgood] *impression* October 7, 1878, 1558 copies, 1553 bound between October 9 and October 21, 1878; *second impression* December 24, 1878, 286 copies, 286 bound between January 2, 1879, and March 19, 1879; *third impression* April 21, 1879, 282 copies, 280 bound between April 30, 1879, and December 1, 1879; *fourth impression* January 20, 1880, 278 copies, 275 bound between January 20, 1880, and November 16, 1880. Ms Am 2030(17), 116: *fifth* [first Houghton, Mifflin] *impression* February 14, 1882, 280 copies, 279 bound between March 8, 1882, and June 3, 1883; *sixth impression* August 30, 1883, 272 copies, 293 [*sic*] bound between September 27, 1883, and June 28, 1886. Ms Am 2030(18), 136: *seventh impression* June 12, 1886, 158 copies, 121 bound between June 28, 1886, and January 11, 1890. Ms Am 2030(19), 153: *eighth impression* September 16, 1890, 158 copies, 189 [*sic*] bound between November 12, 1890, and July 6, 1893. Ms Am 2030(20), 173: *ninth impression* July 23, 1894, 154 copies, 151 bound between July 30, 1894, and October 21, 1898. Ms Am 2030(21), 220: *tenth impression* April 21, 1900, 154 copies, 158 [*sic*] bound between June 13, 1900, and March 15, 1904. Ms Am 2030(22), 218: *eleventh impression* April 25, 1905, 150 copies, 149 bound on May 8, 1905, and February 7, 1906; *twelfth impression* February 27, 1908, 148 copies, 144 bound on March 7, 1908, and March 31, 1909; *thirteenth impression* January 24, 1911, 159 copies, 155 bound on February 1, 1911, and April 29, 1913; notation: "[total copies] 4037". Ms Am 2030(23) 213: *fourteenth impression* December 31, 1915, 161 copies, 163 [*sic*] bound between March 31, 1916, and August 11, 1916; *fifteenth impression* August 12, 1919, 281 copies, 275 bound between January 30, 1920, and November 30, 1921; *sixteenth impression* October 2, 1923, 278 copies, 271 bound between October 30, 1923, and September 28, 1925; notation: "New Style [of binding?]"; *seventeenth impression* April 27, 1927, 532 copies, 511 bound between June 11, 1927, and May 1, 1934; notation: "[total copies printed] 5289".

Priced at $1.50, which price was unchanged through 1905.

7.6.5. *The Europeans*, first American edition, first impression, binding state B, one volume, Boston 1879.

The title-page, size, collation, and contents are identical to those of the first American edition, first impression, binding state A, 7.6.0.

Binding: terra-cotta dotted line-grain-cloth with lettering and decoration identical to those on 7.6.0 (although the cloth is somewhat darker), except that the publisher's imprint at the foot of the spine has an initial "H" which extends below the other letters in the imprint, and the ampersand is in lower not upper case.

7.7.0. *The Europeans*, first American edition, first impression, one volume, Boston 1879 [1878].

The title-page, size, collation, and contents are identical to those of the first American edition, first impression, binding state A, 7.6.0.

Binding: dark green dotted-line-grain cloth over bevelled boards, with lettering and decoration identical to 7.6.0. The endpapers are of chocolate-brown coated paper, and the text is printed on wove paper. A binder's fly-leaf of wove paper is at the back, but none at the front. All edges are trimmed, and the top edge is stained ochre.

7.8.0. *The Europeans*, first American edition, second impression, binding state A, one volume, Boston 1879.

The title-page and size are identical to those of the first American edition, first impression, binding state A, 7.6.0.

Collation: [1^1 2–12^{12} 13^8 14^1], signed as π^1 1–17^8 18^5; pp. [i–ii], [1]–281 [282]. The title-leaf is a singleton, as is the last leaf, 281–[282]. This collation is not recorded in either E&L or BAL.

Contents: [i–ii] title-page, verso copyright notice, reservation of rights and printer's imprint as in 7.6.0; [1]–281 text; [282] blank.

Binding: terra-cotta dotted-line-grain cloth over bevelled boards, with lettering and decoration identical to that on 7.6.0 (including the publisher's imprint at the foot of the spine). The endpapers are of chocolate-brown coated paper, and the text is printed on wove paper. Two binder's fly-leaves of wove paper are at both the front and the back. All edges are trimmed.

7.9.0. *The Europeans*, first American edition, second impression, binding state B, one volume, Boston 1879.

The title-page and size are identical to those of the first American edition, first impression, binding state A, 7.6.0.

The collation and contents are identical to those of the first American edition, second impression, binding state A, 7.8.0.

THE EUROPEANS

Binding: dark green sand-grain cloth over bevelled boards, with lettering and decoration identical to that on 7.6.0, except that the publsher's imprint at the foot of the spine has an initial "H" which extends below the other letters in the imprint, and the ampersand is in lower not upper case. The endpapers are of chocolate-brown coated paper, and the text is printed on wove paper. Two binder's fly-leaves of wove paper are at both the front and the back. All edges are trimmed, and the top edge is stained brown.

7.10.0. *The Europeans*, first American edition, third impression, first binding state, one volume, Boston 1879.

The title-page and size are identical to those of the first American edition, first impression, binding state A, 7.6.0.

Collation: $[1^{12}(\pm 1_1)\ 2\text{–}11^{12}\ 12^{12}(-12_{12})]$, signed as $\pi^1\ 1\text{–}17^8\ 18^6$; pp. [i–ii], [1]–281 [282][283–284]. The title-leaf, $[1_1]$, is a cancel.

Contents: [i–ii] title-leaf, verso copyright notice, reservation of rights and printer's imprint as in 7.6.0; [1]–281 text; [282] blank; [283–4] blank leaf.

Binding: Kelly green dotted-line-grain cloth over bevelled boards, with lettering and decoration identical to 7.6.0. The endpapers are of chocolate-brown coated paper, and the text is printed on wove paper. A binder's fly-leaf of wove paper is at the front, but none at the back. All edges are trimmed.

On the recto of the front binder's fly-leaf is the inscription: "Laura [letter illegible] S. Garnett | from her mother | Christmas | 1883."

BAL 10537, which records the collation as "$[1\text{–}12]^{12}$. Leaf $[12]_{12}$ excised or pasted under the end paper", identifies copies such as this copy as of the "2nd (3rd?) Printing", noting that: "in the only examined copy of this printing the title leaf $[1]_1$ appears to be a singleton and is not conjugate with $[1]_{12}$." This is not the case in this copy, which suggests that the title-leaf is a cancel. However, there is no discernible difference between this title-leaf and that of the first impression.

BAL 10537 also identifies three impressions dated 1879, but identifies only two collations, supposing that the first and possibly the second impressions have the same collation, or alternatively that the second and third impressions have the same collation. It is therefore possible that copies 7.8.0 and 7.9.0, with a collation not recorded in BAL, are of the second impression, and that each of the first three impressions has a different collation.

In summary, the three collations are:

> first impression: $[1^2\ 2\text{–}12^{12}\ 13^{10}]$, signed as $\pi^2\ 1\text{–}17^8\ 18^6$; pp. [2] [i–ii], [1]–281 [282] [283–284].
> second impression: $[1^1\ 2\text{–}12^{12}\ 13^8\ 14^1]$, signed as $\pi^1\ 1\text{–}17^8\ 18^5$; pp. [i–ii], [1]–281 [282].
> third impression: $[1^{12}(\underline{+1}_1)\ 2\text{–}11^{12}\ 12^{12}(-12_{12})]$, signed as $\pi^1\ 1\text{–}17^8\ 18^6$; pp. [i–ii], [1]–281 [282] [283–284].

7.10.5. *The Europeans*, first American edition, third impression, second binding state, one volume, Boston and New York 1879.

Size: $7\,7/16''$ x $4\,3/4''$.

The title-page, collation, and contents are identical to those of the first American edition, third impression, first binding state, 7.10.0.

Binding: blue-green diagonal-fine-ribbed cloth, with lettering and decoration in red-brown, blue-green, and gilt. The title on the front cover and spine is in red-brown within a gilt panel with a pronounced maze-like background pattern. The publisher's imprint at the foot of the spine reads: "Houghton Mifflin & Co." The ampersand in the imprint is not stylized. The endpapers are of a very light-tan floral design on white coated paper, and the text is printed on wove paper. There are no binder's fly-leaves. All edges are trimmed, and the top edge is stained light brown. It is sewn, not stapled.

This binding is uniform with that of the first American impression of the second edition of *The Portrait of a Lady* (1881), 16.5.0. It was first used by Houghton, Mifflin on a James work in 1881. Floral endpapers were not used on a James work published in America before late 1882. It is likely that this binding-up of third impression sheets was in 1882 or 1883, although the printing record states that all of the sheets (except two sets) were bound by December 1, 1879. It is possible that some copies of this impression were rebound by Houghton, Mifflin after it acquired Houghton, Osgood in May 1880.

THE EUROPEANS

7.11.0. *The Europeans*, first American edition, fourth impression, one volume, Boston 1880.

The title-page and size are identical to those of the first American edition, first impression, 7.6.0, binding state A, except that the title-page is dated 1880 at the foot.

Collation: $[1-11^{12}\ 12^{12}(-12_{12})]$, signed as $\pi^1\ 1-17^8\ 18^6$; pp. [i–ii], [1]–281 [282] [283–284].

Contents: [i–ii] title-page, verso copyright notice, reservation of rights and printer's imprint as in 7.6.0; [1]–281 text; [282] blank; [283–284] blank leaf.

Binding: terra-cotta sand-grain cloth over bevelled boards, lettered and decorated identically to 7.6.0. The endpapers are of chocolate-brown coated paper, and the text is printed on wove paper. A binder's fly-leaf of wove paper is at the front, but none at the back. All edges are trimmed, and the top edge is stained ochre.

On the title-page is the ink inscription: "L. E. Opdycke | from my mother Xmas 1881."

7.12.0. *The Europeans*, first American edition, seventh impression, one volume, Boston and New York 1886.

THE EUROPEANS. | A Sketch. [in Gothic type] | BY | HENRY JAMES, Jr. | SEVENTH EDITION. | [shield shaped publisher's device] | BOSTON AND NEW YORK: | HOUGHTON, MIFFLIN AND COMPANY. | The Riverside Press, Cambridge. [in Gothic type] | 1886.

Size: 7 3/8" x 4 3/4".

Collation: $[1^1\ 2-13^{12}\ 14^4]$, signed as $\pi^2\ 1-18^8\ [19]^3$; pp. [i–iv], [1]–281 [282] [283–294].

Contents: [i–ii] blank leaf, verso an ad within a single-rule frame, headed: "MR. JAMES'S WRITINGS.", with 5 lines of a quoted review followed by a list of 8 James titles with dollar prices, the last dated being *The Portrait of a Lady*; [iii–iv] title-page, verso copyright notice, reservation of rights and printer's imprint as in the first American edition, first impression, binding state A, 7.6.0; [1]–281 text; [282] blank; [283–294] 12 pages of ads, paginated [1]–12, headed on [1]: "Works of Fiction | Published by | Houghton, Mifflin and Company, | 4 Park Street., Boston; 11 E. 17th St., New York."

THE EUROPEANS

Binding: tan diagonal-fine-ribbed cloth, with lettering and decoration in red-brown, tan, and gilt. The title on the front cover and spine is in red-brown within a gilt panel with a pronounced maze-like background pattern. The publisher's imprint at the foot of the spine reads: "HOUGHTON | MIFFLIN [dot] & [dot] CO". The ampersand in the imprint is like a figure "8" and is larger than the other letters. The endpapers are of a light-tan floral design on white coated paper, and the text is printed on wove paper. A binder's fly-leaf of thin wove paper is at both the front and the back. All edges are trimmed, and the top edge is stained ochre.

This binding is uniform with that of the first American impression of the second edition of *The Portrait of a Lady* (1881), 16.5.0.

7.12.5. *The Europeans*, first American edition, eighth impression, one volume, Boston and New York [n.d., 1890].

THE EUROPEANS. | A Sketch. [in Gothic type] | BY | HENRY JAMES, Jr. | EIGHTH EDITION. | [shield shaped publisher's device] | BOSTON AND NEW YORK: | HOUGHTON, MIFFLIN AND COMPANY. | The Riverside Press, Cambridge. [in Gothic type]

Size: 7 3/8" x 4 13/16".

Collation: $[1–17^8\ 18^8\ (–18_8)]$, signed as $\pi^2\ 1–17^8\ 18^6\ (–18_6)$; pp. [i–iv], [1]–281 [282].

Contents: [i–ii] blank, verso an ad within a single rule frame, headed: "Henry James's Books.", listing 13 titles followed by "The above thirteen 12mo volumes, in box, $22.00.", followed by two further titles, *The Tragic Muse* and *Watch and Ward*, all with dollar prices; [iii–iv] title-page, verso copyright notice, reservation of rights and printer's imprint: "Copyright, 1878, | By HOUGHTON, OSGOOD AND COMPANY | All rights reserved. [in italic] | The Riverside Press, Cambridge, Mass., U S A. [*sic*, in italic] | Printed by H. O. Houghton & Company."; [1]–281 text; [282] blank.

Binding: chocolate-brown diagonal-fine-ribbed cloth, lettered and decorated identically to the first American edition, seventh impression, 7.12.0. The title on the front cover and spine is within a gilt panel with a pronounced maze-like background pattern. The endpapers are of white laid paper, and the text is printed on wove paper. A binder's fly-leaf of laid paper is at the front and of wove paper at the back (pasted on to the stub of [18$_8$]). All edges are trimmed, and the top edge is stained brown.

On the front binder's fly-leaf is the inscription "C. K. Barry | 1895."

This binding is uniform with that of the first American impression of the second edition of *The Portrait of a Lady* (1881), 16.5.0.

The 1890 date is suggested by inclusion in the ad of *The Tragic Muse* (published in June 1890) and the printing history which records that the eighth impression was printed on September 16, 1890.

7.12.9. *The Europeans*, first edition, ninth impression, first issue, one volume, Boston and New York [n.d., 1894]

THE EUROPEANS. | A Sketch. [in Gothic type] | BY | HENRY JAMES, Jr. | NINTH EDITION. | [oblong publisher's device of a piper under a tree within a frame] | BOSTON AND NEW YORK: | HOUGHTON, MIFFLIN AND COMPANY. | The Riverside Press, Cambridge. [in gothic type]

Size: 7 $^{5}/_{16}$" x 4 $^{7}/_{8}$".

Collation: [1–18^8], signed as π^2 1–17^8 18^6; pp. [i–iv], [1]–281 [282] [283–284].

Contents: [i–ii] blank, verso an ad within a single rule frame, headed: "Henry James's Books. [in Gothic type]", listing 13 titles followed by: "The above thirteen 12 mo volumes, in box, $22.00.", followed by two further titles, *The Tragic Muse* and *Watch and Ward*, all with dollar prices; [iii–iv] title-page, verso copyright notice, reservation of rights and printer's imprint: "Copyright, 1878, | By HOUGHTON, OSGOOD AND COMPANY | All rights reserved. [in italic] | The Riverside Press, Cambridge, Mass., U S.A. [*sic*, in italic] | Printed by H. O. Houghton & Company."; [1]–281 text; [282] blank; [283–284] blank leaf.

In the last line of 227 the word "being" has a broken "b".

Binding: blue-green diagonal-fine-ribbed cloth, lettered and decorated identically to the first American edition, seventh impression, 7.12.0. The title on the front cover and spine is within a gilt panel with a pronounced maze-like background pattern. The endpapers of white laid paper, and the text is printed on wove paper. A binder's fly-leaf of laid paper is at the front and of wove paper at the back. All edges are trimmed, and the top edge is stained light brown.

THE EUROPEANS

This binding is uniform with that of the first American impression of the second edition of *The Portrait of a Lady* (1881), 16.5.0, except for being blue-green, not the usual pea-green.

See 7.13.0 for the second issue.

7.13.0. *The Europeans*, first American edition, ninth impression, second issue, one volume, Boston and New York [n.d., 1894].

The title-page, collation, and contents are identical to those of the first edition, ninth impression, first issue, 7.12.9, except the ad on [ii] within a single rule frame headed "Henry James's Books. [in Gothic type]" lists 16 titles with dollar prices, the last dated being *The Spoils of Poynton*.

Size: 7 3/8″ x 4 7/8″.

In the last line of 227 the word "being" has a broken "b".

Binding: olive-green vertical-rib-grain cloth, with lettering and decoration in gilt on the front cover and spine. The front cover has within a single-rule border an elaborate centered cartouche within which is the title and author's name separated by a decorative rule. The spine reads: "[rule] I THE I EUROPEANS I [decorative rule] I HENRY JAMES I HOUGHTON I MIFFLIN & CO. I [rule]". The ampersand in the publisher's imprint is stylized. The back cover has a single-rule border in blind. The endpapers are of white laid paper, and the text is printed on wove paper. A binder's fly-leaf of wove paper is at the front, but none at the back. All edges are trimmed, and the top edge is stained ochre.

This binding is uniform with that of the first American edition, first impression, of *The Spoils of Poynton* (1897), 48.6.0, on which it was first used; and the fact that that title is included in the ad on [ii] also indicates that these sheets of the ninth impression were bound-up after the publication of *The Spoils of Poynton*. It is to be noted that the first issue of the ninth impression differs from this impression in the ad on [ii] and the style of the binding. Given the identical collations, and the fact that the first signatures of both are of eight leaves, this would suggest that the first signature, 1^8, or the conjugate leaves 1_1 and 1_8, with the chages to the ad on [ii], may have been reprinted for this issue.

THE EUROPEANS

7.14.0. *The Europeans*, first American edition, tenth or eleventh impression, one volume, Boston and New York [n.d., 1900 or 1905].

THE EUROPEANS. | A Sketch. [in Gothic type] | BY | HENRY JAMES, Jr. | [publisher's device of a piper under a tree within a frame] | BOSTON AND NEW YORK: | HOUGHTON, MIFFLIN AND COMPANY. | The Riverside Press, Cambridge. [in Gothic type]

The size and collation are identical to those of the first American edition, ninth impression, first issue, 7.12.9.

The contents are as identical to those of the first American edition, ninth impression, second issue, 7.13.0, except that the ad on [ii], while listing the same 16 titles in the same order as the ad on [ii] in 7.13.0, differs slightly in wording. *Confidence* is listed as available in "paper, 50 cents" as well as in cloth, *A Little Tour in France* is listed as "12mo, $1.50. Holiday Edition. With about 70 Illustrations by Joseph Pennell. Crown 8vo, $3.00.", and after the title *Daisy Miller* the line "The above thirteen 12mo volumes, in box, $22.00." is not present. In addition, on [282] there is the printer's imprint: "The Riverside Press [in Gothic type] | Electrotyped and printed by H. O. Houghton & Co. | Cambridge, Mass, U.S.A [last two lines in italic]", which imprint is not present in either issue of the ninth impression.

In the last line of 227 the word "being" has a broken "b".

Binding: brown vertical-rib-grain cloth, lettered and decorated in gilt on the front cover and spine and decorated in blind on the back cover identical to that on 7.13.0. The endpapers are of white wove paper, and the text is printed on wove paper. A binder's fly-leaf of wove paper is at the front, but none at the back. All edges are trimmed, and the top edge is stained ochre.

This binding is uniform with that of the first American edition, first impression, of *The Spoils of Poynton* (1897), 48.6.0.

The Holiday Edition of *A Little Tour in France* with illustrations by Joseph Pennell was first published in 1900; see 23.10.0.

7.15.0. *The Europeans*, first American edition, twelfth impression, one volume, Boston and New York [n.d., 1908].

The title-page is identical to that of the first American edition, tenth or eleventh impression, 7.14.0.

Size: $7\,3/8''$ x $5''$.

THE EUROPEANS

The collation is as set forth for the first American edition, ninth impression, first issue, 7.12.9.

Contents: [i–ii] blank, verso ad within a single-rule frame headed: "By Henry James [in Gothic type]", listing 17 titles without dollar prices, the last dated being *Italian Hours*; [iii–iv] title-page, verso copyright notice and reservation of rights: "COPYRIGHT 1878 BY HOUGHTON, OSGOOD & COMPANY | COPYRIGHT 1906 BY HENRY JAMES | ALL RIGHTS RESERVED"; [1]–281 text; [282] blank; [283–284] blank leaf.

Binding: glazed smooth blue cloth, lettered in gilt and decorated in black and gilt. The front cover, within a black double-rule border within which is a black single-rule frame, reads: "[decorative device of rules, dots and flowers] | THE | EUROPEANS | [small four cornered device] | HENRY [dot] JAMES | [decorative device of rules, dots and flowers]". The spine, which is lettered and decorated in gilt with an oblong frame within which are five decorative ovals in each of which is a stem of flowers, reads: "THE | EUROPEANS | [small decorative device] | HENRY | JAMES". The back cover is blank, The endpapers are of white wove paper, and the text is printed on wove paper. There are no binder's fly-leaves. The top edge is gilt, and the other edges are rough trimmed.

On the front free endpaper is blind-stamped: "BOUGHT FROM | LINDMARK'S BOOK SHOP | POUGHKEEPSIE, NEW YORK".

This impression was printed from the plates of the first American edition, first impression, with new prelims. Throughout the text there is a great deal of evidence of wear to the plates, including the broken "b" on the last line of 227. For bindings uniform with this binding see 1.11.0.

Given the 1906 copyright notice and the "and" in the publishers imprint (which was dropped in 1908) this copy is probably of the twelfth impression, printed on February 27, 1908, the first printed after 1906 and before the change in publisher's name.

7.16.0. *The Europeans*, first continental edition, first impression, one volume, Leipzig 1878.

THE EUROPEANS. | A SKETCH. | BY | HENRY JAMES, Jr., | AUTHOR OF "THE AMERICAN," ETC. | AUTHORIZED EDITION. [in italic] | LEIPZIG | BERNARD TAUCHNITZ | 1878.

Size: 6" x 4 $^{5}/_{16}$".

Collation: [1]⁸ 2–18⁸; pp. [1–4], [5]–288.

Contents: [1–2] series half-title, verso ad headed: "TAUCHNITZ EDITION. | By the same Author," listing 1 title, *The American*; [3–4] title-page, verso blank; [5]–288 text; 288 at foot printer's imprint offset to the right: "[rule] | PRINTING OFFICE OF THE PUBLISHER." No publisher's catalogue is bound in at the end.

Binding: rebound in dark green cloth. The title is lettered in gilt on the spine, there being no author's name or publisher's imprint. The endpapers are of white wove paper, and the text is printed on wove paper. All edges are trimmed and speckled red.

T&B 1792, records two editions, with one impression of each, of this title. The second edition has 13 titles listed on the half-title verso. Also noted in BAL 10750.

⁂

8. *DAISY MILLER: A STUDY*

8.1.0 *Daisy Miller: A Study*, first edition, first impression, cloth binding state, one volume, New York 1879 [1878].

DAISY MILLER | a Study [in Gothic type] | By HENRY JAMES, Jr. | [rule] | NEW YORK | HARPER & BROTHERS, PUBLISHERS | FRANKLIN SQUARE | 1879

Size: 4 $^{21}/_{32}$" x 4 $^{3}/_{32}$".

Collation: [1]⁸ 2–8⁸; pp. [1–6], [7]–116 [117–128].

Contents: [1]–4 ads, listing 79 titles (not including this title) under the heading: "HARPERS HALF-HOUR SERIES. | 32 mo, Paper."; [5–6] title-page, verso copyright notice: "Entered according to Act of Congress, in the year 1878, by | Harper & Brothers, | In the Office of the Librarian of Congress, at Washington."; [7]–116 text; [117–128] ads.

The twelve pages of ads at the end, being the last six leaves of signature 8, are headed: [117–118] "By the Author of 'John Halifax.'", [119] "By F.W. ROBINSON.", [120] "R.D. BLACKMORE'S NOVELS.", [121] "CHARLES READE'S NOVELS.", [122] "WILKIE COLLINS'S NOVELS.", [123] WILLIAM BLACK'S NOVELS.", [124] "W.M. THACKERAYS WORKS.", [125] "By VIRGINIA W. JOHNSON.", [126] "Katharine King's Novels.", and [127–128] "By Mrs. Oliphant."

DAISY MILLER: A STUDY

Binding: green diagonal fine-ribbed cloth over flexible boards. The front cover is lettered and decorated in red and black and reads: "[red decorative rule extending across the top, down the back of the front cover, and across the bottom] | HARPER'S | Half-Hour Series. [series title in red] | [in black, thick followed by a thin rule] | DAISY MILLER | A Study [in Gothic type] | By HENRY JAMES, Jr. [title and author's name in black] | [in black, thin followed by a thick rule] | [publisher's device in red] | [bottom extension of red rule] | "COPYRIGHT 1877 BY HARPER & BROTHERS. [in red]". The spine, lettered in black but not decorated, reads vertically down the spine: "DAISY MILLER". The back cover has a centered publisher's device in black. The endpapers are of cream wove paper with no ads on them, and the text is printed on wove paper. All edges are trimmed, and the top edge is stained brown.

On the front pastedown is the small leather bookplate of the English photographer, E. H. Mills (1874–1942), and the engraved bookplate of the Indiana novelist, playwright and book collector, George Barr McCutcheon (1886–1928). On the front free endpaper is the "cum grano salis" bookplate of Charles Walker Andrews (with his pencil notation on the front pastedown: "Bot of Jas F Drake Sept 1944–very rare"), and tipped on to the front free endpaper is a letter from James to Harpers dated April 18, 1887 regarding corrections to the proofs of the second half of his story "Cousin Maria", and querying the whereabouts of the other part of the proofs.[15] Tipped onto the rear free endpaper is a description of this volume and the letter by the New York bookseller James F. Drake from whom Andrews acquired this volume and the letter in 1944.

American printing history. Harper & Brothers Archive. First edition: the only record in the Archive of the printing history of the first impression of this title is in Reel 23, page 507: "3500 [copies] Daisy Miller. By Henry | James Jr. Half-Hour | Series 128 pp. [illegible] | Bourgeois. Riche Sep. 9/78 | 26 x 40 f s 60 lbs".[16] The first impression was published on No-

---

15 'Cousin Maria' first appeared in *Harper's Weekly* on the 6, 13 and 20th of August 1887. It was later retitled 'Mrs. Temperly' when it first appeared in book form in *A London Life* in 1889; see 33.1.0–33.5.0.

16 The Harper Archive through 1914 in the Butler Library is available to researchers only on microfilm of very poor quality and poorly indexed. It has been described by one researches not as the Harper Archive, but the "Harper's attic". Only three entries directly recording the printing of Henry James titles appear to have survived. The only other records of printings that have survived are in the royalty ledgers for

vember 1, 1878, as number 82 in Harper's Half-Hour Series. From the Royalty Records: Reel 33, ledger page 31 headed October 1881, records on hand on April 21, 1879, 1057 copies [remaining from the first three (?) impressions],[17] printed since [the fourth impression?] 8594 copies, and on hand on November 2, 1881, 203 copies; Reel 33, ledger page 194 headed July 1883, records on hand on November 2, 1881, 203 copies, printed since [the fifth impression?] 1905 copies, and on hand on July 13, 1883, 252 copies; Reel 33, ledger page 369 headed May 1885, records on hand on July 13, 1883, 252 copies, printed since [sixth impression?] 548 copies, and on hand on May 10, 1885, 176 copies; Reel 34, ledger page 9 headed July 1888, records on hand on November 10, 1885, 176 copies, printed since [seventh impression?] 635 copies, and on hand on July 16, 1888, 193 copies; Reel 34, ledger page 556 headed December 1893, records on hand on July 16, 1888, 193 copies, printed since [eighth impression?] 301 copies, and on hand on December 15, 1893, no copies; Reel 35, ledger page 415 headed November 1896, records "Daisy Miller H. School Classics" 520 copies printed [ninth impression?][18] between December 15, 1895, and November 15, 1896. Two hundred and thirty copies of this impression remained on hand on December 31, 1897.

Priced at $.35 in cloth and $.20 in wrappers.

This title was immensely popular, and 20,000 copies of the first edition were sold in a few weeks; see Anesko, 43. In contrast the English two-volume first edition, priced at 21s., sold only 285 copies between its publication in February 1879, and November 10, 1879; see Moore, Letter 59.

---

the period October 1881 through December 1897, which records copies on hand at the beginning of the period, copies printed since, copies sold and given away or destroyed and copies on hand at the end of the period. After 1897, the royalty records no longer reflect printings, but are merely a very sloppy record of copies sold.

17 There is no doubt that there was more than one impression of this edition between November 1878 and April 1879. Given the instant success of this title it seems highly unlikely that only 2443 copies were sold between those dates. From copies 8.1.0, with 79 titles listed in the preliminary ad, 8.2.0 (with no inscription), with 94 titles listed in the preliminary ad, 8.3.0 (inscription dated April 1879), with 100 titles listed in the preliminary ad, and 8.6.0 (inscription dated October 1879), with 120 titles listed in the preliminary ad, it would appear that there were four impressions by October 1879. It would also appear that there were two further impression in 1880 as copy 8.6.5 has 120 titles listed in the preliminary ads, but without an inscription, and 8.7.0 with an inscription dated 1880 has 145 titles listed in the preliminary ads.

18 It is possible that what is shown as the ninth impression is a separate edition, although the small number of copies printed suggests otherwise.

Second edition (which includes *An International Episode, The Diary of a Man of Fifty*, and *A Bundle of Letters*): published as part of the Franklin Square Library printed in double column format. Reel 33, ledger page 194 headed July 1883, records no copies on hand on November 2, 1881, printed since 12,746 copies, and on hand July 13, 1883, 5137 copies; Reel 33, ledger page 369 headed May 1885, records on hand on May 13, 1883, 5137 copies, none printed since, and on hand on May 10, 1885, 2705 copies; Reel 34, ledger page 9 headed July 1888, records on hand on May 10, 1885, 2705 copies, none printed since, and on hand on July 16, 1888, 1707 copies; Reel 34, ledger page 556 headed December 1893, records on hand on July 16, 1888, 1707 copies, none printed since and a notation 1450 copies destroyed, and no copies on hand on December 15, 1893. There are no further printings of this edition recorded through the end of 1897. Reel 23, ledger page 116 records: "12,500 Daisy Miller & Other Stories | By Henry James 45 [crossed out] 56 pp | in L.P. F.S. Library, 2 coll | On W Low's Machine Jan 27/82 [date of printing order?] 33 x 46 f.s. 65 lbs".

Priced at $.75.

Third edition (which includes *An International Episode* and is illustrated by Harry W. McVickar) published in December 1892: Reel 34, ledger page 556 headed December 1893, records on hand July 16, 1888, no copies, printed since 6142 copies [probably the first three impressions, trade], given away 197 copies, and on hand on December 15, 1893, 623 copies.

Reel 34, ledger page 556 also records [a separate limited impression] on hand July 16, 1888, no copies, printed since 250 copies, given away 3 copies, and on hand on December 15, 1893, 113 copies. There were no further printings of the de-luxe impression recorded, and there were only 4 copies sold between 1893 and December 1897 when 109 copies remained on hand.

Reel 34, ledger page 669 headed November 1894, records on hand on December 15, 1893, 623 copies [remaining copies of the third impression, trade], printed since none, and on hand on November 20, 1894, 250 copies; Reel 34, ledger page 215 headed December 1895, on hand on November 20, 1894, 250 copies [trade impression], printed since [fourth impression, trade] 531 copies, and on hand on December 21, 1895, 465 copies; Reel 35, ledger page 415 headed November 1896, records on hand on December 21, 1895, 465 copies [trade impression], printed since none, and on hand on November 15, 1896, 340 copies; Reel 35, ledger page 56 headed December 1896, records on hand on

DAISY MILLER: A STUDY

November 15, 1896, 340 copies [trade impression], printed since none, and on hand on December 31, 1896, 334 copies; Reel 35, ledger page 171 headed June 1897, records on hand on December 31, 1896, 334 copies [trade impression], printed since none, and on hand on June 30, 1897, 285 copies; Reel 35, ledger page 296 headed December 1897, records on hand on June 30, 1897, 285 copies [trade impression], printed since none, and on hand on December 31, 1897, 200 copies.

Priced at $15.00 for the de-luxe impression and $3.50 for the trade impressions. Both impressions were boxed.

There were later printings of the third edition (see 8.15.9 and 8.16.0), as well as at least eight later printings of *Daisy Miller* from the third edition plates printed as separate impressions of that title without *An International Episode*: see 8.11.5 (1900), 8.12.0 (1901), 8.13.0 (1904), 8.13.5 (between 1906 and 1912), 8.14.0 (1913), 8.14.5 with an introduction by W. D. Howells (1916?), 8.15.0 (probably 1919) and 8.16.0 (1920). No record of these printings has been found in the Harper Archive.

8.1.5. *Daisy Miller: A Study*, first edition, first impression, wrappered binding state, one volume, New York 1879 [1878].

The title-page, collation, and contents (including the preliminary ads, and the ads on [117–128]) are identical to those of the first edition, first impression, cloth binding state, 8.1.0.

Size: $4\,{}^{25}/_{32}''$ x $3\,{}^{3}/_{16}''$.

Binding: pale buff wrappers, cut flush. The front cover, lettered and decorated in red and black, reads: "Price Twenty Cents [in black italic] | [red decorative rule extending across the top, down the back of the front cover and across the bottom] | HARPER'S | Half-Hour Series. [series title in red] | [in black, thick followed by a thin rule] | DAISY MILLER | A Study [in Gothic type] | By HENRY JAMES Jr. [title and author's name in black] | [in black, thin followed by a thick rule] | [publisher's device in red] | [at bottom, extension of the red rule] | Copyright 1877 by Harper & Brothers". The spine, lettered in black but not decorated, reads: "82 DAISY MILLER", vertically down the spine. The back cover has an ad headed : "HARPER'S PERIODICALS." The inside front cover has an ad headed: "HARPER'S LIBRARY | OF | AMERICAN FICTION." The inside back cover has an ad headed: "HARPER'S LIBRARY | OF | SELECT NOVELS." The text is printed on wove paper.

DAISY MILLER: A STUDY

8.2.0. *Daisy Miller: A Study*, first edition, later (second?) impression, wrappered binding state, one volume, New York [n.d., 1879].

DAISY MILLER | A Study [in Gothic type] | By HENRY JAMES, Jr. | [rule] | NEW YORK | HARPER & BROTHERS, PUBLISHERS | FRANKLIN SQUARE

Size: 4 $^{25}/_{32}$" x 3 $^{3}/_{16}$".

Collation: [1]^8 2–8^8; pp. [1–6], [7]–116 [117–128].

Contents: [1]–4 ads, listing 94 titles (including this title as number 82); [5–6] title-page, verso copyright notice: "Entered according to Act of Congress, in the year 1878, by | Harper & Brothers, | In the Office of the Librarian of Congress, at Washington."; [7]–116 text; [117–128] ads.

The twelve pages of ads at the end, being the last six leaves of signature 8, are headed: [117–118] "By Mrs. Oliphant.", [119] "W. M. THACKERAY'S WORKS.", [120] "GEORGE ELIOT'S NOVELS.", [121] "WILKIE COLLINS'S NOVELS.", [122] "R. D. BLACKMORE'S NOVELS.", [123] "CHARLES READE'S NOVELS.", [124] "WILLIAM BLACK'S NOVELS.", [125] "By VIRGINIA W. JOHNSON.", [126] "By F. W. Robinson.", and [127–128] "By the Author of 'John Halifax.'".

Binding: pale buff wove paper wrappers, cut flush, with lettering and decoration in red and black on the front cover as on the first edition, first impression, wrappered binding state, 8.1.5. The back cover and the insider of the front and back covers have ads identical to those on 8.1.5. The text is printed on wove paper.

This copy has 94 titles listed in the four pages of ads preceding the title-page under the heading: "HARPER'S HALF-HOUR SERIES. | 32mo, Paper."

8.3.0. *Daisy Miller: A Study*, first edition, later (third?) impression, cloth binding state, one volume, New York [n.d., 1879].

The title-page, size, collation, and contents (except as noted below) are identical to those of the first edition, first impression, cloth binding state, 8.1.0.

The twelve pages of ads at the end, being the last six leaves of signature 8, are headed: [117–118] "By the Author of 'John Halifax.'", [119] "By VIRGINIA W. JOHNSON.", [120] "Katharine King's Novels.", [121–122] "BULWER'S WORKS.", [123] "By Mrs. Gaskell.", [124] "W. M.

DAISY MILLER: A STUDY

THACKERAY'S WORKS.", [125–126] "By Mrs. Oliphant.", [127] "WILLIAM BLACK'S NOVELS.", and [128] "R. D. BLACKMORE'S NOVELS."

This copy has 100 titles listed in the four pages of ads preceding the title-page under the heading: "HARPER'S HALF-HOUR SERIES. | 32mo, Paper."

Binding: green diagonal-fine-ribbed cloth over flexible boards, lettered and decorated identically to 8.1.0. The endpapers are of buff wove paper with no ads on them, and the text is printed on wove paper. All edges are trimmed.

On the title-page is the ink inscription: "F.L. Crawford | April 1879".

Photographs have been examined of a copy of Thomas Hardy's *Fellow Townsmen*, New York: Harper & Brothers 1880, issued as one of the titles (number 136) in Harper's Half-Hour Series, bound in green cloth over flexible boards uniform with *Daisy Miller: A Study*, 8.3.0, *An International Episode*, 9.2.0, and *The Diary of a Man of Fifty*, 14.1.0. What is striking about that particular volume is that it has a dust-jacket. This jacket is of buff wove paper, without any lettering or decoration printed on it, but to which have been applied two labels. The label toward the head of the spine is missing (but its outline can be seen), but the label at the foot has printed on it "22".

It is obviously impossible to state with any certainty whether this dust-jacket was original to the book and used by Harpers as a protective covering. It is thought that the labels might not have been original to the dust-jacket, as the number "22" seems to have no relation to this particular volume or its price (20 cents). However, it raises the possibility that all (or some) of Harper's Half-Hour Series issued in green cloth over flexible boards had similar protective coverings.

8.4.0. *Daisy Miller: A Study*, first edition, later (third?) impression, wrappered binding state, one volume, New York [n.d., 1879].

The title-page, size, collation, and contents (including the ads preceding the title-page listing 100 titles and the 12 pages of ads at the end) are identical to those of the first edition, later (second?) impression, 8.2.0.

Binding: pale buff wove paper wrappers, cut flush, with lettering and decoration identical to the first edition, first impression, wrappered binding state, 8.1.5. The text is printed on wove paper.

8.5.0. *Daisy Miller: A Study*, first edition, later (fourth?) impression, cloth binding state, one volume, New York [n.d., 1879].

The title-page, size, collation, and contents (except as noted below) are identical to those of the first edition, first impression, 8.1.0.

The twelve pages of ads at the end, being the last six leaves of signature 8, are headed: [117] "W. M.THACKERAY'S WORKS.", [118] "By VIRGINIA W. JOHNSON.", [119–120] "BULWER'S WORKS.", [121] "GEORGE ELIOT'S WORKS.", [122] "WILLIAM BLACK'S WORKS.", [123–124] "By Mrs. Oliphant.", [125–126] "Anthony Trollope's Works.", [127] "Katharine King's Novels.", and [128] "By Mrs. Gaskell."

This copy has 120 titles listed on the four pages of ads preceding the title-page under the heading: "HARPER'S HALF-HOUR SERIES | 32mo, Paper."

Binding: green diagonal-fine-ribbed cloth over flexible boards, with lettering and decoration identical to that on 8.1.0. The endpapers are of buff wove paper (with no ads on them), and the text is printed on wove paper. All edges are trimmed.

8.6.0. *Daisy Miller: A Study*, first edition, later (fourth?) impression, wrappered binding state, one volume, New York [n.d., 1879].

The title-page, size, collation, and contents (including the ads preceding the title-page listing 120 titles and the twelve pages of ads at the end) are identical to those of the first edition, later (fourth?) impression, 8.5.0.

Binding: pale buff wove paper wrappers, cut flush, with lettering and decoration identical to that of the first edition, first impression, wrapperd binding state, 8.1.5. The back cover and the inside of the front and back covers have ads identical to those on 8.5.1. The text is printed on wove paper.

On the title-page is the inscription: "Lucy from Frances | October 1879–".

8.6.5. *Daisy Miller: A Study*, first edition, later (fifth?) impression, wrappered binding state, one volume, New York [n.d., 1880?]

The title-page, size, collation, and contents (except as noted below) are identical to those of the first edition, first impression, wrapped binding state, 8.1.5.

The twelve pages of ads at the end, being the last six leaves of signature 8, are headed: [117] "CHARLES READ'S WORKS.", [118] "GEORGE ELIOT'S WORKS.", [119–120] "By Mrs. Oliphant.", [121] "By Mrs. Gaskell.", [122] "R. D. BLACKMORE'S NOVELS.", [123–124] "Bulwer's Works.", [125] "W. M. THACKERAY'S WORKS.", [126] "WILLIAM BLACK'S WORKS.", [127] "By VIRGINIA W. JOHNSON.", and [128] "Katharine King's Novels."

This copy has 130 titles on the four pages of ads preceding the title-page under the heading: "HARPER'S HALF-HOUR SERIES. | 32mo, Paper."

Binding: pale buff wove paper wrappers, cut flush with lettering and decoration in red and black on the front cover as on the first edition, first impression, wrapped binding state, 8.1.5. The back cover and the inside of the front and back covers have ads identical to those on 8.1.5. The text is printed on wove paper.

8.7.0. *Daisy Miller: A Study*, first edition, later (sixth?) impression, cloth binding state, one volume, New York [n.d., probably 1880].

The title-page, size, collation, and contents (except as noted below) are identical to those of the first edition, first impression, cloth binding state, 8.1.0.

There twelve pages of ads at the end, being the last six leaves of signature 8, are headed: [117] "CHARLES READE'S WORKS.", [118] "GEORGE ELIOT'S WORKS.", [119–120] "By Mrs. Oliphant.", [121] "By Mrs. Gaskell", [122] "R. D. BLACKMORE'S NOVELS.", [123–124] "Bulwer's Works.", [125] "W. M. THACKERAY'S WORKS.", [126] "WILLIAM BLACK'S WORKS.", [127] "By VIRGINIA W. JOHNSON.", and [128] "Katharine King's Novels."

This copy has 145 titles listed on the four pages of ads preceding the title-page under the heading: "HARPER'S HALF-HOUR SERIES." The phrase "32mo, Paper.", appearing in the first page of the ads preceding the title-page in the earlier (first through fifth) impressions under the heading "HARPER'S HALF-HOUR SERIES." is not present in the ads in this copy. It was probably removed in order to have more space for listing titles on the same four pages.

Binding: green diagonal-fine-ribbed cloth over flexible boards, with lettering and decoration identical to that on the first edition, first impression, cloth binding state, 8.1.0. The endpapers are of buff wove paper (with no ads on them), and the text is printed on wove paper. All edges are trimmed.

On the front free endpaper is the ink inscription: "Annie R. Sibhart | 1880".

8.8.0. *Daisy Miller: A Study*, third American edition, first impression (trade), one volume, New York 1892.

Daisy Miller | & An Interna- | tional Episode [all of the foregoing in orange swash italic] | BY HENRY JAMES, JR., ILLUS- | TRATED FROM DRAWINGS BY | HARRY W. McVICKAR | HARPER & BROTHERS | NEW YORK [space] MDCCCXCII [all but the title in black swash italic]

Size: 8″ x 5 7/16″.

Collation: [unsigned, 1^2 (1_1+X_1) 2^2 $3-20^8$ 21^4]; pp. [i–viii] [1–2], 3–[296] plus 2.

Contents: [i–ii] blank leaf; colored frontispiece with tissue guard tipped in and not reckoned in the pagination; [iii–iv] title-page, verso copyright notice and reservation of rights: "Copyright, 1878, by Harper & Brothers. | [rule] | Copyright, 1892, by Harper & Brothers. | [rule] | All rights reserved. [in italic]"; v-vi "List of Illustrations", verso continuation of list; [vii–viii] continuation of list, verso blank; [1–2] divisional fly-title, verso blank; 3–[296] text.

Colored frontispiece with tissue guard is not reckoned in the pagination, but three further full-page black-and-white illustrations, [93], [109] and [171], are reckoned in the pagination. The "List of Illustrations" lists 101 illustrations, ninety-seven (all black-and-white) on or within the text pages.

Binding: coarse beige buckram, decorated on the front and back covers with an overall pattern of diagonal alternate bands of beige and light green. The front cover is additionally decorated on the right side with a horizontal design of three gilt wreaths in the center of which are the letters "DM" in green, and beneath each wreath is a gilt crown beneath which are the letters "I E" in green. The spine, which is lettered and decorated in gilt, and reads: "Daisy | Miller | [elaborate scroll-like device] | An International Episode [the latter title running vertically up the spine] | Harpers [all the foregoing in swash upper and lower case]". The endpapers are of white laid paper, and the text is printed on heavy coated paper. The top edge is gilt, and the other edges are untrimmed.

This impression was issued boxed, priced at $3.50.

8.9.0. *Daisy Miller: A Study*, third American edition, second impression (limited), one volume, New York 1892.

The title-page is identical to that of the third American edition, first impression (trade), 8.8.0.

Size: $8\,^{1}/_{16}"$ x $5\,^{1}/_{2}"$.

Collation: [unsigned, 1^4 (1_1+X_1) $2-19^8$ 20^4]; pp. [i–viii][1–2], 3–[296] plus 2.

Contents: [i–ii] limitation notice: "NOTICE | [rule] | Of this edition of "Daisy Miller" and "An Inter- | national Episode" only two-hundred and fifty copies | have been printed, of which this is | No. 80 | HARPER & BROTHERS [all in italic]", verso blank; colored frontispiece with tissue guard tipped in and not reckoned in the pagination; [iii–iv] title-page, verso copyright notice and reservation of rights as in the third American edition, first impression (trade), 8.8.0; v–vi "List of Illustrations", verso continuation of list; [vii–viii] continuation of list, verso blank; [1–2] divisional fly-title, verso blank; 3–[296] text.

Colored frontispiece with tissue guard tipped in and not reckoned in the pagination. A further three full-page illustrations, [93] and [109] in gray and white, and [171] in sepia, are reckoned in the pagination. The "List of Illustrations" lists 101 illustrations, ninety-seven of them on or within the text pages. The illustrations in *Daisy Miller* are in gray and white (rather than black-and-white) and those in *An International Episode* are in sepia and white.

Binding: off-white antiqued paper simulating parchment over semi-flexible boards, with the front and back covers having yapp fore-edges. The front cover and spine are lettered and decorated in gilt identically to the lettering and decoration on 8.8.0, except that it does not have the diagonal alternate bands on the front and back covers. The back cover is neither lettered nor decorated. The endpapers are of heavy white wove paper, and the text is printed on wove paper (not coated stock), with many pages having a deckle edge. All edges are untrimmed, and the top and fore-edges are speckled brown (antiqued).

On the front free endpaper is the ink inscription: "A Merry Christmas | to my dear Kelly. | 1892." On the back pastedown is a small pink label that reads: "DOXEY | IMPORTER | San Francisco".

The printing history as well as differences in the imposition, paper and the color of the illustrations (gray-and-white the pages devoted to *Daisy Miller*, and sepia on the pages devoted to *An International Episode* in this limited impression) between the trade impression and this limited impression suggest that it was a separate impression. E&L records it, erroneously, as the limited issue of the first impression.

8.10.0. *Daisy Miller: A Study*, third American edition, third impression (trade), one volume New York 1893.

The title-page, size, collation, and contents are identical to those of the third American edition, first impression (trade), 8.8.0, except that the title-page is dated "MDCCCXCIII" at the foot. All of the illustrations (other than the frontispiece) are printed in black-and-white.

Binding: coarse beige buckram, lettered and decorated identically to 8.8.0. The endpapers are of cream laid paper, and the text is printed on a thick coated paper. The top edge is gilt, and the other edges are untrimmed.

8.11.0. *Daisy Miller: A Study*, third American edition, fourth impression (trade), one volume, New York 1895.

The title-page, size, collation, and contents are identical to those of the third American edition, first impression (trade), 8.8.0, except that the title-page is dated "MDCCCXCV" at the foot. All of the illustrations (other than the frontispiece) are printed in black-and-white.

Binding: coarse beige buckram, lettered and decorated identically to 8.8.0. The endpapers are of laid paper, and the text is printed on a thick coated paper. The top edge is gilt, and the other edges are untrimmed.

The coated paper on which this impression is printed is slightly thinner than the coated paper used for the first impression, this copy being .941" thick as against 1.124" thick for the first impression. Both measurements are without the boards.

On the recto of the first blank leaf is the inscription: "Christmas 1897 | Aunt Hg".

DAISY MILLER: A STUDY

8.11.5. *Daisy Miller: A Study*, third American edition, first separate impression, one volume, New York and London 1900.

Daisy Miller [in orange swash italic] | BY HENRY JAMES, JR., ILLUS- | TRATED FROM DRAWINGS | BY HARRY W. McVICKAR | [publisher's device] | HARPER & BROTHERS | NEW YORK AND LONDON | M-D-C-C-C-C [all but the title in black swash italic].

Size: 8" x 5 3/8".

Collation: [unsigned, 1^8 (1_1+X_1) 2–8^8 9^6], an additional leaf is inserted between [1_1] and [1_2]; pp. [i–vi][1–2], 3–[134][135–136] plus 2. The inserted leaf is the title-leaf.

Contents: [i–ii] blank, verso black-and-white frontispiece with tissue guard; [iii–iv] title-page, verso copyright notice and reservation of rights: "Copyright, 1878, by Harper & Brothers. | [rule] | Copyright, 1892, by Harper & Brothers. | [rule] | All rights reserved. [in italic]"; v–[vi] "List of Illustrations", verso list continued; [1–2] fly-title, verso blank; 3–[134] text; [135–136] blank leaf.

The frontispiece with tissue guard and two further full-page illustrations, [93] and [109], all in black-and-white, are reckoned in the pagination. The "List of Illustrations" lists 42 illustrations, 39 of which (one repeated three times), all in black-and-white, which are on or within the text pages

Binding: pearl-gray vertical-ribbed quarter cloth with lavender (faded to brown) paper over boards. The front cover, which is lettered and decorated in gilt, has on the top a row of three wreaths below which is the title in a elaborate swash script. The back cover is neither lettered nor decorated. The spine, which is also lettered and decorated in gilt, reads: "[small wreath] | Daisy | Miller | [small wreath] | Henry | James | Harpers [all the foregoing in swash script]". The endpapers are of cream laid paper, and the text is printed on thick coated paper. The top edge is gilt, and the other edges are untrimmed.

On this separate impression, see 9.6.0.

8.12.0. *Daisy Miller: A Study*, third American edition, second separate impression, one volume, New York and London 1901.

The title-page, size, collation, and contents are identical to those of the third American edition, first separate impression, 8.11.5, except that the title-page is dated "M-D-C-C-C-C-I" at the foot.

DAISY MILLER: A STUDY

Binding: pearl gray vertically-ribbed quarter cloth with lavender paper over boards, lettered and decorated identically to 8.11.5.

Dust-jacket: light brown wove paper. The front cover, which is lettered and decorated in lavender within an oblong single-rule frame offset to the left, reads: "Daisy [leaf device] | Miller | [rule] | Henry James | [dot] Illustrated [dot]". The spine, which is also lettered in lavender, reads: "DAISY | MILLER | Henry | James | $1.²⁵ | Harpers". The back cover, which is lettered in lavender within an oblong single-rule frame, reads: "By Mary E. Wilkins | [divisional rule] | [list of 11 titles with dollar prices] | [divisional rule] | HARPER & BROTHERS, PUBLISHERS | NEW YORK AND LONDON". The front and back inner flaps are blank.

On the back pastedown is a small white label lettered in red within a red single-rule frame which reads: "NEDWICKS BOOK STORE | 171 NO. MICHIGAN AVE. | CHICAGO 1, ILL. | OUT-OF-PRINT-BOOKS".

8.13.0. *Daisy Miller: A Study*, third American edition, later separate impression, one volume, New York and London 1904.

Daisy Miller [in orange swash italic] | BY HENRY JAMES, JR., ILLUS- | TRATED FROM DRAWINGS | BY HARRY W. McVICKAR | [publisher's device] | HARPER & BROTHERS | NEW YORK AND LONDON | MCMIV [all but the title in black swash italic]

Size: 8" x 5 1/8".

Collation: [unsigned, 1–9^8]; pp. [2] [i–vi] [1–2], 3–[134] [135–136].

Contents: blank leaf; [i–ii] blank, verso black-and-white frontispiece with tissue guard; [iii–iv] title-page, verso copyright notice and reservation of rights: "Copyright, 1878, by Harper & Brothers. | [rule] | Copyright, 1892, by Harper & Brothers. | [rule] | All rights reserved. [in italic]"; v–[vi] "List of Illustrations", verso list of illustrations continued; [1–2] fly-title, verso blank; 3–[134] text; [135–136] blank leaf.

The frontispiece (printed in black-and-white, with a tissue guard), and two further full-page black-and-white illustrations, [93] and [109], are reckoned in the pagination. The "List of Illustrations" lists 42 illustrations, 39 (one repeated three times), all in black-and-white, which are on or within the text pages.

Binding: green fine-diagonal-ribbed cloth. The front cover is decorated within a black double-rule frame with 26 intersecting (left and right) diagonal lines composed of black dashes, at the intersections of each of which is a white daisy with a yellow center. Superimposed on the upper right of this overall pattern is an elaborate cartouche outlined in lighter green within which is the title and author's name in gilt separated by a small gilt scroll. The spine, which is lettered in gilt, reads: "[two black rules] | DAISY | MILLER | [small gilt scroll] | HENRY | JAMES | HARPERS | [two black rules]". The endpapers are of white laid paper, and the text is printed on thick coated paper. The top edge is gilt, and the other edges are untrimmed.

8.13.5. *Daisy Miller*, third American edition, later separate impression, one volume, New York and London [n.d., between 1906 and 1912].

The title-page, size, collation, and contents are identical to those of the third American edition, later separate impression (1904), 8.13.0, except that the title-page is undated, and the title-leaf verso reads: "Copyright, 1878, 1892, by Harper & Brothers. | [rule] | Copyright, 1906, by Henry James. | [rule] | All rights reserved."

Binding: green diagonal-fine-ribbed cloth, with lettering and decoration identical to 8.13.0. The endpapers are of white wove paper, and the text is printed on thick coated paper. The top edge is gilt, and the other edges are untrimmed.

Dust-jacket: gray thick wove paper. The front cover, which is lettered and decorated in lavender within an oblong single-rule frame offset to the left, reads: "Daisy [leaf device] | Miller | [rule] | Henry James | [dot] Illustrated [dot]". The spine, which is also lettered in lavender, reads: "DAISY | MILLER | Henry | James | Harpers". The back cover, which is lettered in lavender within an oblong single-rule frame, reads: W.M. THACKERAY'S | COMPLETE WORKS | The Biographical Edition [in italic] | PREPARED BY | ANNE THACKERAY RITCHIE | The Surviving Daughter of the Great Novelist | In 13 Volumes. With Illustrations. Crown Octavo, Cloth. | Ornamental Gilt Tops . . . . Each $1.75 | Cloth . . . . . per Set $23.00 | Three-quarter Calf . . . . [per Set] $60.00 | Three-quarter Levant . . . . [per Set] $65.00 | [rule] | [followed by a list of the titles and a further blurb] | [rule] | HARPER & BROTHERS, Publishers | NEW YORK AND LONDON". The front and back inner flaps are blank.

The presence of a 1906 copyright date on the title-leaf verso and the absence of a dating code on that page (which was introduced by

Harpers in 1912), suggests that this impression was printed between those dates.

8.14.0. *Daisy Miller: A Study*, third American edition, later separate impression, one volume, New York and London [n.d., 1913].

The title-page and size are identical to those of the third American edition, later separate impression (1904), 8.13.0, except that the title-page is printed entirely in black, and it has no date at the foot.

Contents: blank leaf; [i–ii] blank, verso black-and-white frontispiece; [iii–iv] title-page, verso copyright notice, place of printing and printing code: "Copyright, 1878, 1892, By Harper & Brothers. | [rule] | Copyright, 1906, by Henry James. | [rule] | PRINTED IN THE UNITED STATES OF AMERICA | I-N"; v–[vi] "List of Illustration", verso list of illustrations continued; [1–2] fly-title, verso blank; 3–[134] text; [135–136] blank leaf.

The frontispiece (printed in black-and-white, without a tissue guard), and two further full-page black-and-white illustrations, [93] and [109], are reckoned in the pagination. The "List of Illustrations" lists 42 illustrations, 39 (one repeated three times), all in black-and-white, which are on or within the text pages.

Binding: identical to that on 8.13.0. The endpapers are of white wove paper, and the text is printed on coated paper (not as thick as the coated paper used on 8.13.0). The top edge is gilt, and the other edges are untrimmed.

Starting in 1912 Harper's began using letters on the copyright page to indicate the month and year of printing. The first such letter shown indicates the month (starting with A for January through M for December, but omitting J) and the second letter the year (starting with M for 1912 through Z for 1925, then A through Y for 1926 through 1949, but omitting J). The letters "I-N" on the copyright page of this copy indicated it was printed in September 1913 or September 1938, the latter date being, of course, unlikely. For this dating code information see Edward Myers, *A Bibliographical Check List and Price Guide for the Writings of R.C. Grey, Romer Grey and Zane Grey* (Collinsville, Ct.: [n.d.])

8.14.5. *Daisy Miller: A Study*, third American edition, later separate impression with additions, one volume, New York and London [n.d., probably 1916].

Daisy Miller | BY HENRY JAMES, JR., ILLUS- | TRATED FROM DRAWINGS | BY HARRY W. McVICKAR | [publisher's device] | HARPER & BROTHERS | NEW YORK AND LONDON [all the foregoing in black swash italic]

Size: 7 $^{13}/_{16}$″ x 5″.

Collation: [unsigned, 1–9^8 10^4]; pp. [i–xvi] [1–2], 3–134 [135–136].

Contents:[i–ii] blank, verso photographic portrait of James with his signature in facsimile beneath the portrait]; [iii–iv] title-page, verso copyright notice and country of printing: "Copyright, 1878, 1892, by Harper & Brothers. | [rule] | Copyright, 1906, by Henry James. | PRINTED IN THE UNITED STATES OF AMERICA [in sans-serif]"; v–[vi] "List of Illustrations.", verso list of illustrations continued; vii–xv "INTRODUCTION", with Howells' name on xv; [xvi] blank; [1–2] fly-title, verso blank; 3–[134] text; [135–136] blank leaf.

The frontispiece (printed in black and white, with a tissue guard), and two further full-page illustrations, [93] and [109], are reckoned in the pagination. The "List of Illustrations" list 42 illustrations, 39 (one repeated three times), all in black-and-white, which are on or within text pages.

Binding: royal-blue diagonal-fine-ribbed cloth. The front cover is decorated with a cartouche outlined in light green, within which is the title and the author's name separated by a decorative rule. The back cover is neither lettered nor decorated. The spine, which is lettered and decorated in gilt, reads: "DAISY | MILLER | [decorative device] | HENRY | JAMES | HARPERS". The endpapers are of cream wove paper, and the text is printed on coated paper. All edges are trimmed, and the top edge is stained gray.

The reference on vii in Howells' introduction to "this hour of the immeasurable loss which literature has sustained through the author's death" suggests a 1916 publication date; see BAL 9845. The introduction is new to this impression. The absence of a dating code on the title-leaf verso is curious. BAL records a copy of *Daisy Miller: A Study* with *An International Episode*, with the Howells introduction, published by Boni and Liveright in 1918.

DAISY MILLER: A STUDY

8.15.0. *Daisy Miller: A Study*, third American edition, later impression, one volume, New York [n.d., 1919?].

Daisy Miller | BY HENRY JAMES, JR., ILLUS- | TRATED FROM DRAWINGS | BY HARRY W. McVICKAR | [publisher's device] | HARPER & BROTHERS | NEW YORK AND LONDON [all the foregoing in black swash italic]

Size: 7 7/16″ x 4 5/8″.

Collation: [unsigned, 1–19^8]; pp. 1π–4π i–[iv] [1–2], 3–[134] plus [1–2], [3–162].

Contents: 1π–2π blank, verso ad: "NOVELS BY HENRY JAMES | PUBLISHED BY HARPER & BROTHERS | [list of 5 titles] | Per volume $2.50 [in italic] | The novels of Henry James published by | Houghton Mifflin Co. and Charles Scrib- | ner's Sons are issued in style uniform with | the above"; 3π–4π title-page, verso copyright notice and printing code: "Daisy Miller | [rule] Copyright, 1878, 1892 by Harper & Brothers | Copyright, 1906, by Henry James | Copyright, 1920, by Mrs. Henry James | Printed in the United States of America | L-T"; i–[ii] "List of Illustrations." [for *Daisy Miller* only], verso list continued; iii–[iv] "List of Illustrations." [for *An International Episode* only], verso list continued; [1–2] fly-title, verso "Part II."; 3–[134] text of *Daisy Miller*; [1–2] divisional fly-title, verso blank; [3–162] text of *An International Episode*.

The frontispiece to *Daisy Miller*, included in the list of illustrations for that title, is not present (and would not be called for in the collation). The frontispiece to *An International Episode*, included in the list of illustrations for that title, is in fact the half-title. The three full-page illustrations are reckoned in the pagination. The rest of the illustrations are on or within the text pages. All the illustrations are in black-and-white.

Binding: dark blue linen-grain cloth. The front cover is lettered with Henry James's facsimile signature in gilt. The back cover is neither lettered nor decorated. The spine, which is lettered and decorated in gilt, reads: "[two rules] | DAISY | MILLER | [short rule] | AN | INTER- | NATIONAL | EPISODE | HENRY | JAMES | HARPER | [two rules]". The endpapers are of cream wove paper, and the text is printed on coated paper. The top edge is trimmed, the fore-edge is untrimmed, and the bottom edge is rough trimmed.

Dust-jacket: smooth beige wove paper, lettered and decorated in black. The front cover and spine replicate the front cover and spine of the book. The back cover has within a single-rule frame three single-rule panels. The top panel reads: "Every well-read Person should Own these | Standard Classics". The larger central panel lists works by ten authors (none by James), each with a blurb. The small lower panel reads: "See them at your bookseller or order them from the Publisher | HARPER & BROTHERS: 49 East 33rd Street : NEW YORK". Below the frame is "No. 1336". The front inner flap is blank. The back inner flap, with the head of Uncle Sam with a finger across his lips, cautions not to talk about "troops, ships, war weapons [and] war production".

The printing code "L-T" on the copyright page indicates that this copy was printed in November 1919; see note on 8.14.0. However, it is to be noted that the copyright notice includes the 1920 copyright date. The dust-jacket probably was printed in 1923, or later, as Harper's did not move its offices from Franklin Square to 49 East 33rd Street until 1923, but it may have been printed from old plates (hence the war caution on the back inner flap) with a new ad for the back cover; see Eugene Exman, *The House of Harper* (New York, Evanston, and London: Harper & Row, 1967), 217.

The non-continuous pagination of the text indicates, among other things, that this copy was printed from the same plates that were used to print the separate impressions of *Daisy Miller: A Study*, 8.12.0, and *An International Episode*, 9.6.0, the only modifications being the additional copyright information and printing code on the title-leaf verso, moving the separate list of illustrations for *An International Episode* to follow the similar list for *Daisy Miller*, and omitting the frontispiece to *Daisy Miller* even though it is included in the list of illustrations for that title. There is evidence throughout of considerable wear to the plates.

As is stated in the ad on the verso of the first leaf, [1$_1$], of this copy, in 1919 or possibly as late as 1923 Harper & Brothers, Houghton, Mifflin Company and Charles Scribner's Sons, each of which owned the American copyrights to certain James titles, agreed to issue separately in a uniform style of binding 22 of James's novels. In accordance with this arrangement, Harper & Brothers issued five titles, Charles Scribner's Sons issued nine titles, and Houghton, Mifflin Company issued eight titles. For a list of the titles each publisher issued, see the description of the ad on the dust-jacket on *The Portrait of a Lady*, 16.21.0, and *The Tragic Muse*, 34.7.5.

DAISY MILLER: A STUDY

8.16.0. *Daisy Miller: A Study*, third American edition, later separate impression, one volume, New York [n.d., 1920].

The title-page is identical to that of the third American edition, later seperate impression, 8.13.0, except that it is printed entirely in black, and has no date at the foot.

Size: 8" x 5 1/4".

Collation: [unsigned, 1–9^8 10^4]; pp. [i–xvi] [1–2], 3–[134] [135–136].

Contents: [i–ii] blank, verso frontispiece photographic portrait of James with facsimile signature; [iii–iv] title-page, verso copyright notice and printing code: "DAISY MILLER | [rule] | Copyright, 1878, 1892, by Harper & Brothers | Copyright, 1906, by Henry James | Copyright, 1920, by Mrs. Henry James | Printed in the United States of America | E-U"; v–[vi] "List of Illustrations", verso list of illustrations continued; vii-xv "INTRODUCTION" with Howells' name on xv; [xvi] blank; [1–2] divisional fly-title, verso blank; 3–[134] text; [135–136] blank leaf.

The frontispiece and two further full-page illustrations, [93] and [109], all in black-and-white, are reckoned in the pagination. The "List of Illustrations" lists 42 illustrations, 39 of which (one repeated three times), all in black-and-white, which are on or within the text pages.

Binding: royal-blue diagonal-fine-ribbed cloth. The front cover is decorated with a light green cartouche outlined in light green, within which in gilt is the title and author's name separated by a decorative device. The back cover is neither lettered nor decorated. The spine, which is lettered and decorated in gilt, reads: "DAISY | MILLER | [decorative device] | HENRY JAMES | HARPERS". The endpapers are of cream wove paper, and the text is printed on coated paper. The top edge is trimmed, and the other edges are untrimmed.

The letters "E-U" on the title-leaf verso indicate that this impression was printed in May 1920; see note 8.14.0.

On the rear pastedown is a powder-blue ticket lettered in gilt reading: "BRENTANO'S | Booksellers & Stationers | New York".

DAISY MILLER: A STUDY

8.17.0. *Daisy Miller: A Study*, first English edition, first impression, two volumes, London 1879.

DAISY MILLER: A STUDY. | AN INTERNATIONAL EPISODE. | FOUR MEETINGS. | By HENRY JAMES, Jr. | IN TWO VOLUMES [in italic] | VOL. I. [II.] | LONDON [in Gothic type] | MACMILLAN AND CO. | 1879. | [Right of Translation is reserved.] [in italic within square brackets]

Size: 7 $^{1}/_{16}$" x 5 $^{13}/_{16}$".

Collation: Volume I: [A]^4 B–I K–S^8; pp. [i–viii], [1]–271 [272]. Volume II: [A]^4 B–I K–R^8 S^4; pp. [i–viii], [1]–263 [264].

Contents: Volume I: [i–ii] half-title, verso publisher's device; [iii–iv] title-page, verso printer's imprint: "Bungay [in Gothic type] | CLAY AND TAYLOR, PRINTERS"; [v–vi] "NOTE", verso blank; [vii–viii] "CONTENTS OF VOL. I", verso blank; [1]–271 text; [272] blank. Volume II: [i–ii] half-title, verso publisher's device; [iii–iv] title-page, verso printer's imprint as on Volume I title-leaf verso; [v–vi] "CONTENTS OF VOL. II", verso blank; [vii–viii] divisional fly-title, verso blank; [1]–263 text; [264] printer's imprint as on volume I title-page verso.

Binding: bright blue sand-grain cloth decorated on the front covers in black with a double-rule border, within which is a single-rule panel curved at the corners, with a similar design in blind on the back covers. The spines, which are decorated in black and lettered in gilt, read: "[rule] | [row of dots] | [rule] | DAISY | MILLER | AND OTHER | STORIES | H. JAMES Jr. | VOL. I [II] | [publisher's device] | Macmillan & Co. | [rule | [row of dots] | [rule]". The "o" in "Co" is raised above a dot. The endpapers are of brown coated paper, and the text is printed on wove paper. All edges are untrimmed. A 38-page paginated publisher's catalogue, dated November 1878, is bound in at the end of Volume II, which is followed by a two-page unpaginated ad for "MACMILLAN'S POPULAR NOVELS."

On the front pastedown of both volumes is the bookplate of the Royal Artillery Library, Woolwich, with the ink notation "Recd:12.4.80".

English printing history: Macmillan Archive. MEB, 265, records that there were two impressions of the two-volume first English edition of *Daisy Miller: A Study*, each of 250 copies, and both printed from standing type. The first impression was printed in February 1879 (published February 19, 1879), and the second in March 1879. Both were priced at 21s. for the two volumes. The distinguishing feature of the first impression is the mispagination of Volume II, page 144 as 145, which was corrected in the second impression.

MEB, 265 also records that stereotype plates were made to print the one-volume second edition, of which there were three printings. The first impression was of 500 copies in August 1879, the second was of 1,000 copies in December 1879, and the third (exclusively for the yellowback) was of 2,000 copies in January 1888. The first two impressions were priced at 6s., and the third at 2s. Macmillan destroyed the plates in March 1921.

For the third English edition see *The Collective Edition of 1883*, 20.1.0–20.5.0.

A fourth English edition was published by Thomas Nelson and Sons. EC records that it was published in May 1918, priced at 6d. net; see note following 4.21.5 and 8.23.5.

8.18.0. *Daisy Miller: A Study*, second English edition, first impression, The Times Book Club binding state, one volume, London 1879.

DAISY MILLER: A STUDY. | AN INTERNATIONAL EPISODE. | FOUR MEETINGS. | By HENRY JAMES, Jr | NEW EDITION. [in italic] | LONDON: [in Gothic type] | MACMILLAN AND CO. | 1879. | [Right of Translation is reserved.] [in italic within square brackets]

Size: $7\,^{3}/_{16}''$ x $4\,^{13}/_{16}''$.

Collation: [A]^4 B–I K–U X–Z AA–BB^8; pp. [i–viii], [1]–380 [381–384].

Contents: [i–ii] half-title, verso publisher's device; [iii–iv] title-page, verso printer's imprint: "Bungay [in Gothic type] | CLAY AND TAYLOR, PRINTERS."; [v–vi] "NOTE", verso blank; [vii–viii] "CONTENTS", verso blank; [1]–380 text; [381–384] ads. The ad on [381], headed: "WORKS BY | HENRY JAMES, Jr.", (the heading being on two lines) listing 4 titles: *The Europeans*, *The American*, *Roderick Hudson* and *French Poets and Novelists*, each with press commentary.

Binding: yellow-orange linen-grain cloth, with decorative bands in black printed (but not stamped) across the front cover and spine. The spine, which is lettered and decorated in black, reads: "[printed black band] | DAISY | MILLER | AND OTHER | STORIES | HENRY JAMES [all of the foregoing in italic] | [printed black band] | [circular Times Book Club device]". The back cover is neither lettered nor decorated. The endpapers are of white wove paper, and the text is printed on wove paper. All edges are trimmed.

This Times Book Club binding state is erroneously noted in E&L F24 as being of the "Second English edition, 1880".

E&L A8c notes : "In January 1880 Macmillan published a one-volume 'new edition', consisting of two printings before publication totaling 1500 copies at 6/-, uniform with A4c". However, E&L makes no mention of copies with an 1879 date on the title-page, such as this copy.

This copy, together with the four copies recorded below might suggest that in fact there may have been four impressions of the second English edition prior to 1888, two dated 1879 and two dated 1880, as follows:

> First impression (1879), 8.18.0: the printer's imprint on the title-leaf verso reads: "Bungay | CLAY AND TAYLOR, PRINTERS.", and the ad on [381] has the heading on two lines and lists four James titles;

> First impression (1879), 8.19.0: the printer's imprint on the title-leaf verso reads: "Bungay | CLAY AND TAYLOR, PRINTERS.", and the ad on [381] has the heading on a single line and lists five James titles;

> Second Impression (1880), 8.22.0: the printer's imprint on the title-leaf verso reads: "Bungay: | CLAY AND TAYLOR, THE CHAUCER PRESS.", and the ad on [381] has the heading on two lines and lists four James titles; and

> Second impression (1880), 8.20.0 and 8.21.0: the printer's imprint on the title-leaf verso reads: "Bungay | CLAY AND TAYLOR, THE CHAUCER PRESS.", and the ad on [381] has the heading on a single line and lists five James titles.

However, MEB, 265, and MBC, 360, records the first printing of the one-volume edition in August, 1879, the second in December, 1879, (with an 1880 date on the title-page), and the third (the yellowback) in 1888.[19] The fact that there are seemingly two states of both the

---

19 In this connection it should be noted that MBC records that the yellowback is the third impression of the second English edition. The title-leaf verso of 8.23.0 erroneously suggests that the yellowback is the first impression of the fourth edition. The "New Edition (Pott 8vo.), 1883" referred to in that printing history is a new (third) edition of this title published as part of *The Collective Edition of 1883*.

first and second impressions of the second English edition may be reconciled with the record that there were only two printings of the second English edition prior to the 1888 printing of the yellowback if one assumes that (a) the first impression (1879) lists four titles on [381] and the second (1880) lists five titles (which is logical, give that the additional title, the one volume edition of *The Madonna of the Future*, was published in 1880), and (b) that the aberrant states appear only in the much later Times Book Club binding states (c. 1905). Based on this it would appear that in binding up The Times Book Club issues, the binder used the remaining first and second impression sheets which it had on hand, and bound in the two states of signature BB^8 either without regard to the impression with which it should be associated or because it had run out of sheets of that signature of one of the two impressions.

8.19.0. *Daisy Miller: A Study*, second English edition, mixed sheets of the first and second impressions, The Times Book Club binding state, one volume, London 1879.

Size: 7 3/8″ x 4 7/8″.

The title-page (including the title-page date, 1879), size, collation and contents are identical to those of the second English edition, first impression, 8.18.0, except that the ad on [381], BB_{7r}, under the heading "WORKS BY HENRY JAMES, Jr." (the heading being on a single line) lists five (rather than four) titles: *The Madonna of the Future, The Europeans, The American, Roderick Hudson* and *French Poets and Novelists*, each with press commentary. The remaining three pages of ads on [382–384] are identical to those in 8.18.0.

Binding: light tan smooth-linen-grain cloth, with two decorative bands in black printed (but not stamped) across the front cover and spine, with lettering and decoration on the spine identical to that on 8.18.0. The endpapers are of white laid paper, and the text is printed on wove paper. All edges are trimmed.

On the front pastedown is the ink inscription: "Daisy Browning | from | Frank H D Smythe | July: 7: 06".

Illustrated Plate 32.

DAISY MILLER: A STUDY

8.20.0. *Daisy Miller: A Study*, second English edition, second impression, binding state A, one volume, London 1880.

The title-page and collation are identical to those of the second English edition, first impression, 8.18.0, except that the title-page is dated 1880.

Size: 7 3/8″ x 4 15/16″.

Contents: identical to those of 8.18.0, except that the title-leaf verso reads: "Bungay:[in Gothic type]|CLAY AND TAYLOR, THE CHAUCER PRESS.", and the ad on [381] is headed: "WORKS BY HENRY JAMES, Jr." (the heading being on a single line) and lists 5 (rather than 4) titles starting with *The Madonna of the Future*, and is identical to the ad on [381] of the second English edition, mixed sheets of the first and second impressions, 8.19.0. The ads on [382–384] are identical to those of 8.18.0.

Binding: dark blue-green pebble-grain cloth, lettered and decorated in gilt, black, and in blind uniform with the second English edition of *The American* (1879), 4.17.0. No lettering is present on the front or back covers. The spine, which is lettered in gilt, reads: "DAISY | MILLER | AND OTHER | STORIES | H. JAMES, Jr. [all the foregoing in italic] | Macmillan & Co." The "o" in "Co" is raised above a line. The endpapers are of dark-brown coated paper, and the text is printed on wove paper. The top edge is untrimmed, and the other edges are rough trimmed. Bound in at the end is a 40-page publisher's catalogue, the first 35 pages of which are paginated, dated December 1879.

8.21.0. *Daisy Miller: A Study*, second English edition, second impression, binding state B, one volume, London 1880.

The title-page is identical to that of the second English edition, first impression, 8.18.0, except that it is dated 1880.

Size: 7 1/8″ x 4 7/8″.

Collation: identical to that of 8.18.0.

Contents: identical to those of the second English edition, second impression, binding state A, 8.20.0.

Binding: dark blue-green fine-pebble-grain cloth, lettered and decorated in gilt, black, and in blind uniform with the second English edition of *The American*, 4.17.0. No lettering is present on the front or back covers. The spine, which is lettered in gilt, reads: "DAISY |

DAISY MILLER: A STUDY

MILLER | AND OTHER | STORIES | HENRY JAMES [all the foregoing in italic] | MACMILLAN & Co." The "o" in "Co." is raised above a dot. The endpapers are of dark green coated paper, and the text is printed on slightly rough wove paper. The top edge is untrimmed, and the other edges are trimmed. Four pages of unnumbered and undated ads are at the end, being the last two leaves of signature BB. Bound in at the end are 16 numbered pages of ads printed on laid paper, dated 15.9.99 on page 16.

The late-dated ads, as well as the absence of "Jr." in the author's name on the spine, indicates that this copy is a later binding-up of second impression sheets.

8.22.0. *Daisy Miller: A Study*, second English edition, mixed sheets of the first and second impressions, The Times Book Club binding state, one volume, London 1880.

Size: 7 $^{3}/_{16}$" x 4 $^{13}/_{16}$".

The title-page, size, collation, and contents are identical to those of the second English edition, first impression, the Times Book Club binding state, 8.18.0, except that the title-page is dated 1880, the title-leaf verso reads: "Bungay [in Gothic type] | CLAY AND TAYLOR, THE CHAUCER PRESS.", and the ad on [381] reads: "WORKS BY | HENRY JAMES, Jr." (the heading being on two lines) and lists 4 (rather than 5) titles starting with *The Europeans*. The ads on [382–384] are identical to those of 8.18.0.

Binding: yellow-orange smooth-linen-grain cloth, with two black bands printed (but not stamped) across the front cover and spine with lettering and decoration on the spine identical to that on 8.18.0. The endpapers are of white wove paper, and the text is printed on wove paper. All edges are trimmed.

8.23.0. *Daisy Miller: A Study*, second English edition, third impression (yellowback), one volume, London 1888.
DAISY MILLER: A STUDY. | AN INTERNATIONAL EPISODE. | FOUR MEETINGS. | By HENRY JAMES. | London: [in Gothic type] | MACMILLAN AND CO. | AND NEW YORK. | 1888. | [Right of Translation is reserved.] [in italic within square brackets]

DAISY MILLER: A STUDY

Size: 6 $^{15}/_{16}$" x 4 $^{1}/_{2}$".

Collation: [A]⁴ B–I K–U X–Z AA–BB⁸; pp. [i–viii], [1]–380 [381–384].

Contents: [i–ii] half-title, verso publisher's device; [iii–iv] title-page, verso copyright notice and printing history: "Copyright [in italic] | 1879 | By Henry James. | First Edition (2 vols. Crown 8vo.), February 1879; reprinted | March 1879; New Edition (1 vol. Crown 8vo.), August 1879; | reprinted December 1879; New Edition (Pott 8vo.), 1883; New | Edition (Globe 8vo.), 1888."; [v–vi] "NOTE.", verso blank; [vii–viii] "CONTENTS.", verso blank; [1]–380 text; 380 at foot printer's imprint: "[R. Clay & Sons, Limited, London & Bungay. [offset to the right and all in italic, the closing square bracket being absent]"; [381–384] ads, headed: [381–382] BY THE SAME AUTHOR.", [383] MACMILLAN & CO.'S PUBLICATIONS. | [rule] | The Golden Treasury Series. [in Gothic type]", and [384] "MACMILLAN'S GLOBE LIBRARY."

Binding: ivory boards with an elaborate floral design in red and black on the front and back covers, signed on the lower right of both covers "L.F. Day". The front cover also has a central red panel on which is printed in black: "Daisy | Miller". The back cover has a similar central red panel on which is printed in black, on a black outlined triangular scroll device: "Macmillan | & Co. [the "o" in "Co" is raised above a dot]". The spine of this copy is missing. The endpapers are of white wove paper, and the text is printed on wove paper. All edges are trimmed. On the front pastedown, and on the recto and verso of the front free endpaper are ads headed: "MACMILLAN & CO.'S POPULAR 6s. NOVELS.", starting on the front pastedown, continuing on to the recto of the front free endpaper, and then on to the first third of the verso of the front free endpaper, the balance of the verso of the front free endpaper being taken up with an ad headed: "MACMILLAN'S TWO-SHILLING NOVELS." On the recto of the rear free endpaper is an ad headed: "English Men of Letters [in large Gothic type]", followed by an ad headed: "Mr. John Morley's Collected Writings. [in smaller Gothic type]", and on the verso an ad for the biographical series "ENGLISH STATESMEN.", followed by an ad for "The English Citizen: [in Gothic type] | A SERIES OF SHORT BOOKS ON | HIS RIGHTS AND RESPONSIBILITIES." On the rear pastedown is an ad for "The English Illustrated Magazine. [in Gothic type]".

Blind-stamped on the front free endpaper is: "W. H. SMITH & SON | LONDON".

DAISY MILLER: A STUDY

This copy has been printed from the plates used to print the first impression of the second English edition, with a change in date on the title-page, the deletion of the printer's imprint from the verso of the title-page, and its addition on the bottom of 380, the addition of copyright notice and printing history on the verso of the title-page, and the addition of a Gothic "S" at the left foot of [1], indicating it is printed from stereotype plates. In addition, the ads on [381–384] have been changed: [381–382] each being headed: "BY THE SAME AUTHOR", [383] headed: "MACMILLAN & CO.'S PUBLICATIONS. | [rule] | The Golden Treasury Series. [in Gothic type]", and [384] headed: "MACMILLAN'S GLOBE LIBRARY." MBC, 360 confirms that the "New Edition (Globe 8vo.) 1888" referred to in the printing history on the title-leaf verso of this copy is not a new edition in the sense used in the MBC [v], that is "an impression from type set up afresh either with or without alteration and read for press by a proof-reader", but merely the third impression of the second English edition.

See Sadleir 3601.

8.23.5. *Daisy Miller: A Study*, fourth English edition, one volume, London [n.d., 1918].

DAISY MILLER: A STUDY. | AN INTERNATIONAL EPISODE. | FOUR MEETINGS. | BY | HENRY JAMES | [publisher's device] | THOMAS NELSON AND SONS, Ltd. | LONDON, EDINBURGH, AND NEW YORK

Size: 6 $^{9}/_{16}$" x 4 $^{3}/_{8}$".

Collation: [1]^{16} 2–8^{16}, also signed as π^4 1a–7a^{16} 8a^{12}; pp. [1–8], [9]–253 [254] [255–256].

Contents: [1–2] half-title for *Daisy Miller*, verso blank; [3–4] title-page, verso blank; [5–6] "NOTE | [rule] | The first two tales contained in this | volume originally appeared in the 'Cornhill | Magazine.' The other is republished from 'Scribner's Monthly.'", verso blank; [7–8] "CONTENTS.", verso blank; [9]–253 text; [254] publisher's device and imprint: "Established 1789 | [publisher's device] | T. NELSON | & SONS, Ltd. | PRINTERS AND | PUBLISHERS"; [255] ad headed: "A FEW OF THE RECENT ISSUES | IN NELSON'S EXTENSIVE LIST | OF POPULAR NOVELS. | PUBLISHED AT 1s. 6d. NET.", listing 12 titles (none by James); [256] ad headed: "NELSON'S LIBRARY | OF

DAISY MILLER: A STUDY

GENERAL LITERATURE | War Price, 1s. 6d. net", listing 12 titles (none by James).

Binding: light-blue linen-textured cloth. The front cover has a black single-rule border, within which is title and the author's name: "DAISY | MILLER | HENRY JAMES", both in black swash italic. The back cover is neither lettered nor decorated. The spine, which is lettered and decorated in black, reads: "[double decorative rule] | DAISY | MILLER | [double decorative rule] | [single decorative rule | [double decorative rule] | HENRY | JAMES | [small circular decoration] | NELSON | [double decorative rule] [all of the foregoing lettering is in swash italic]". The endpapers are of cream wove paper, and the text is printed on poor quality wove paper. The top and bottom edges are trimmed, and the fore-edge is untrimmed.

Dust-jacket: cream wove paper. The front cover has a frontal three-quarter length image of a young lady holding a pink sun shade against an overall light blue background with a balustrade behind her. Above this image, within a scroll across the top, is the title: "DAISY MILLER". Below this image, also within a scroll, is: "BY HENRY JAMES". To the right of the author's name is a circle within which, on a white background, is: "1/6 | NET". Below this circle, within a small scroll, is the name: "F. TENNYSON JESSE" in small capitals. The spine has a light gray background, and reads: "DAISY [dot] | MILLER | BY | HENRY | JAMES | [circle] in which is 1/6 | NET | [medallion suspended by a blue ribbon with a girl's face in profile]". The back cover, which has a white background has an ad listing 4 title (none by James), each with the price: "1/6 net.", each followed by a blurb. The front and back inner flaps are neither lettered nor decorated.

This dust-jacket was designed by the novelist F. Tennyson Jesse.

The poor quality of the text paper is probably due to the paper shortage during WWI.

The text of these three stories is that of the first English edition published by Macmillan in 1879, but it has been reset for this edition; see note following 4.21.5 regarding Thomas Nelson obtaining the rights to publish this and other James titles.

DAISY MILLER: A STUDY

8.24.0. *Daisy Miller: A Study*, first continental edition, second impression, one volume, Leipzig 1879.

DAISY MILLER: | A STUDY. | AN INTERNATIONAL EPISODE. | FOUR MEETINGS. | BY | HENRY JAMES, Jr. | AUTHORIZED EDITION. [in italic] | LEIPZIG | BERNHARD TAUCHNITZ | 1879.

Size: 6 $7/16''$ x 4 $9/16''$.

Collation: $[1]^8$ 2–18^8; pp. [1–6], [7]–288.

Contents: [1–2] series half-title and volume number, verso ad headed: "TAUCHNITZ EDITION. | By the same Author.", listing 13 titles, the last of which is *A Little Tour in France*; [3–4] title-page, verso James's authorization notice; [5–6] "CONTENTS.", verso blank; [7]–288 text; 288 at foot printer's imprint: "[rule] | PRINTING OFFICE OF THE PUBLISHER. [offset to the right]".

Binding: buff wove paper wrappers, cut flush, with lettering on the front cover in black within a black single-rule frame which is decorated with a flower-like device at each of the four corners, with lettering above and below the frame. The spine is also lettered in black between eight pairs of thick and thin black rules. The back cover, which is also lettered in black, reads: "December 1893. | Tauchnitz Edition. | [rule] | Latest Volumes: | [followed by a list of 24 titles, Tauchnitz volumes 2922 through 2955, the last listed being *The Brownies and other Tales* [sic], by J. H. Ewing | [long rule] | The Tauchnitz Edition is to be had at all Book- | sellers and Railway Libraries on the Continent, price | M 1, 60 or 2 francs per volume. A complete Cata- | logue of the Tauchnitz Edition is attached to this work. [all after the rule in italic]" The insides of the front and back covers are blank. A 16-page paginated publisher's catalogue, dated February 1896, is bound in at the end. It is sewn, not stapled.

T&B 1819 records copies of the second impression with wrappers dated October 1893 and September 1908, but none with the wrapper and catalogue dated as in this copy. *The Brownies and Other Tales* was first published by Tauchnitz in 1893. T&B records one edition with four impressions of this title. The first has no titles, the second has 13 titles, the third has 15 titles, and the fourth has 7 titles listed on the half-title verso.

DAISY MILLER: A STUDY

8.24.5. *Daisy Miller: A Study*, first continental edition, third impression, one volume, Leipzig, 1879.

Size: 6 7/16" x 4 3/4".

The title-page, collation, and contents are identical to those of the first continental edition, second impression, 8.24.0, except that the series half-title verso, [2], under the heading "TAUCHNITZ EDITION. | By the same Author," lists 15 titles, the last of which is *The Outcry*.

Binding: identical to the binding on 8.24.0, except that the back cover, which is lettered in black, reads: "August 1912. | Tauchnitz Edition. | [rule] | Latest Volumes: | [followed by a list of 22 titles, Tauchnitz volumes 4323 through 4350, the last listed being *Stories without Tears* [sic], by Barry Pain] | [long rule] | "The Tauchnitz Edition is sold by all Booksellers and Rail- | way Libraries on the Continent, price of each volume M 1, 60 or | francs 2,00 sewed M 2, 20 or francs 2, 75 cloth (original-Leinen- | band), M 3,00 or francs 3, 75 in elegant soft binding (Original- | Geschenkband). A complete Catalogue of the Tauchnitz Edition is | attached to this work." The insides of the front and back covers are blank. There is no publisher's catalogue bound in at the end. It is stapled not sewn.

On the series half-title is the inscription "P. Walillet | Eninghoven, | Germany, | Sept. 1919."

8.25.0. *Daisy Miller: A Study*, first continental edition, fourth impression, one volume, Leipzig [n.d.].

DAISY MILLER | A STUDY | AN INTERNATIONAL EPISODE | FOUR MEETINGS | BY | HENRY JAMES, Jr. | COPYRIGHT EDITION. [in italic] | LEIPZIG | BERNHARD TAUCHNITZ

Size: 6" x 4 5/16".

Collation: [1]^8 2–18^8; pp. [1–6], [7]–288.

Contents: [1–2] series half-title and volume number, verso ad headed: "TAUCHNITZ EDITION | By the same Author", listing 7 titles, the last listed being *A Little Tour in France*; [3–4] title-page (undated), verso James's authorization notice; [5–6] "CONTENTS", verso blank; [7]–288 text; 288 at foot printer's imprint: "[rule] PRINTING OFFICE OF THE PUBLISHER. [offset to the right]".

Binding: maroon vertical-rib-grain cloth. The front cover is decorated in blind with an oval Tauchnitz emblem with a large centered "T", and around the inner perimeter "TAUCHNITZ EDITION". The back cover is neither lettered nor decorated. The spine, which is lettered in gilt, and decorated in black and gilt, reads: "[in upper compartment] Daisy | Miller | by | Henry James | [long strapwork design] | [lower compartment] TAUCHNITZ | EDITION | [small diamond shaped gilt decoration]". The endpapers are of white wove paper, and the text is printed on wove paper. All edges are trimmed and unstained. It is sewn, not stapled.

See T&B 1819, which records the fourth impression as listing only 7 James titles in the ad on [2], and not having a date on the title-page. T&B does not record a copy of this title in boards, but does reproduce a picture of this type of binding on 583. It is characterized as the most common variant of "Gift Book" binding used in the period 1910–1915. T&B, 953–954. No other James title is recorded by T&B as being issued in other than wrappers. This is the only impression of all of Tauchnitz's James titles which T&B records as not having a date on the title-page. It is curious that the ad on [2] in this fourth impression lists fewer titles than the similar ad on [2] in the second impression; see 8.24.0.

❦

9. *AN INTERNATIONAL EPISODE*

9.1.0. *An International Episode*, first edition, first impression, wrappered binding state, one volume, New York 1879.

AN INTERNATIONAL EPISODE | By HENRY JAMES, Jr. | AUTHOR OF "DAISY MILLER" ETC. | [rule] | NEW YORK | HARPER & BROTHERS, PUBLISHERS | FRANKLIN SQUARE | 1879

Size: $4\,3/4''$ x $3\,1/8''$

Collation: [A]^8 B–I^8; pp. [1–6], [7]–136 [137–144].

Contents: [1]–4 ads listing 87 titles (but not this title) under the heading: "HARPER'S HALF-HOUR SERIES. | 32mo, Paper." ; [5–6] title-page, verso copyright notice: "Entered according to Act of Congress, in the year 1878, by | Harper & Brothers | In the Office of the Librarian of Congress, at Washington."; [7]–136, text; [137–144] ads.

AN INTERNATIONAL EPISODE

The eight pages of ads at the end, being the last four leaves of signature I, are headed: [137] "By VIRGINIA W. JOHNSON.", [138] "W. M. THACKERAY'S WORKS.", [139] "By F. W. Robinson.", [140] "WILLIAM BLACK'S NOVELS.", [141] "WILKIE COLLINS'S NOVELS.", [142] "GEORGE ELIOT'S NOVELS.", and [143–144] "By Mrs. Oliphant."

Binding: pale buff wrappers, cut flush. The front cover, lettered and decorated in red and black, reads: "Price Twenty Cents [in black italic] | [red decorative rule extending across the top, down the back of the front cover and across the bottom] | HARPER'S | Half-Hour Series. [series title in red] | [in black, thick followed by a thin rule] | AN INTERNATIONAL EPISODE | By HENRY JAMES Jr. [title and author's name in black] | [in black, thin followed by a thick rule] | [publisher's device in red] | [at bottom, extension of the red rule] | Copyright 1877 by Harper & Brothers". The spine, lettered in black but not decorated, reads: "97 AN INTERNATIONAL EPISODE", vertically down the spine. The back cover has an ad headed : "HARPER'S PERIODICALS.", the inside front cover has an ad headed: "HARPER'S LIBRARY | OF | AMERICAN FICTION." The inside back cover has an ad headed: "HARPER'S LIBRARY | OF | SELECT NOVELS.", and the back cover has an ad headed: "HARPER'S PERIODICALS." The text is printed on wove paper.

The title-page is dated 1879, and the last line of page 44 is repeated on the first line of 45.

E&L states that all copies of the first impression have ads for Bulwer's works on [137] and King's on [144]. BAL 10539 disputes this, stating: "intensive checking by BAL has failed to locate a copy of the first state [printing?] with the Bulwer advertisements on p. [137]." This copy and the cloth bound copy of the first impression, recorded below, would suggest that BAL is correct; but see 9.3.0. BAL records the first impression as having the error on 44 and 45 and the Johnson ad on [137], as is the case here. BAL records the wrappers as being "gray", but this copy and the copies of the later impressions, 9.3.0 and 9.5.0 have buff wrappers, albeit with a grayish cast.

Illustrated Plate 6.

Printing history. Harper & Brothers Archive. First edition: published January 1879 in Harper's Half-Hour Series. There are no entries in the royalty ledger through 1897 relating to *An International Episode*. The sole

AN INTERNATIONAL EPISODE

entry found is in Reel 23, page 513 and is undated: "3500 [copies] An International Episode | Henry James Jr | for H Half 136 pp. | Half Hour Series 26 x 40 | F.S. 60 lbs". This most probably refers to the first impression of the first edition. From the evidence of the books themselves there appear to have been at least three and possibly four further impressions: 9.3.0 possibly being a second impression; 9.3.5 possibly being a third impression (only the terminal ads differ from 9.3.0); 9.4.0 being possibly a fourth impression; and 9.5.0 possibly being a fifth impression. The number of copies printed in these later four impressions is unknown.

Priced at $.35 in cloth and $.20 in wrappers.

A second edition of this title was published with *Daisy Miller: A Study* in 1892; see 8.8.0, and printing history under *Daisy Miller: A Study*, 8.1.0. It was priced at $3.50 (trade impression) and $15.00 (limited impression).

A first separate impression of the second edition of this title was published in 1902 from the third edition plates of *Daisy Miller: A Study*, see 9.6.0 and 9.7.0. It was priced at $1.25.

9.2.0. *An International Episode*, first edition, first impression, cloth binding state, one volume, New York 1879.

Size: 4 5/8" x 3 3/16".

The title-page, collation, and contents are identical in all respects to the preceding copy of the first edition, first impression, wrapped binding state, 9.1.0, including the ads on [1]–4 and [137–144], and the repeated line on 44 and 45.

Binding: green diagonal fine-ribbed cloth over flexible boards. The front cover, lettered and decorated in red and black, reads: "[red decorative rule extending across the top, down the back of the front cover, and across the bottom] | HARPER'S | Half-Hour Series. [series title in red] | [in black, thick followed by a thin rule] | AN INTERNATIONAL EPISODE | By HENRY JAMES, Jr. [title and author's name in black] | [in black, thin followed by a thick rule] | [publisher's device in red] | [bottom extension of red rule] | "COPYRIGHT 1877 BY HARPER & BROTHERS. [in red]". The spine, lettered in black but not decorated, reads vertically down the spine: "AN INTERNATIONAL EPISODE". The back cover has a centered publisher's device in black. The endpapers are of cream wove paper with no ads on them, and the text is

AN INTERNATIONAL EPISODE

printed on wove paper. All edges are trimmed, and the top edge is stained brown.

Illustrated Plate 6.

9.3.0. *An International Episode*, first edition, second (?) impression, wrappered binding state, one volume, New York [n.d.].

The title-page, size, collation, contents of this copy are identical to those of the first edition, first impression, wrappered binding state, 9.1.0, except that there are 100 titles listed in the four pages of ads preceding the title-page under the heading "HARPER'S HALF-HOUR SERIES | 32mo, Paper." (the first impression has 87 such titles listed), no date appears on the title-page, the errors on pages 44 and 45 have been corrected, and as noted below the terminal ads differ.

The eight pages of ads at the end, being the last four leaves of signature I, are headed: [137] "BULWER'S WORKS", [138] Bulwer's Works.", [139] "KATHARINE KINGS NOVELS.", [140] "GEORGE ELIOT'S NOVELS.", [141] "CHARLES READE'S NOVELS.", [142] "WILLIAM BLACK'S NOVELS.", [143] "WILKIE COLLINS'S NOVELS." and [144] "W. M. THACKERAY'S WORKS."

Binding: buff wove paper wrappers, cut flush, lettered and decorated identically to 9.1.0. The text is printed on wove paper.

9.3.5. *An International Episode*, first edition, third (?) impression, cloth binding state, one volume, New York [n.d.]

The title page, size, collation, and contents are identical to those of the first edition, first impression, wrappered binding state, 9.1.0, except that there are 100 titles listed in the four pages of ads preceding the title-page under the heading "HARPERS HALF-HOUR SERIES. | 32mo. Paper.", no date appears on the title-page, the errors on pages 44 and 45 have been corrected, and as noted below the terminal ads differ.

The eight pages of ads at the end, being the last four leaves of signature I, are headed [137] "WILLIAM BLACK'S NOVELS.", [138] "CHARLES READE'S NOVELS.", [139] "By Mrs. Gaskell.", [140] "By VIRGINIA W. JOHNSON.", [141] "R. D. BLACKMORE'S NOVELS.", [142] "W. M. THACKERAY'S WORKS.", [143] "POTTERY AND PORCELAIN | OF ALL TIMES AND NATIONS.", and [144] "Holly's Modern Dwellings."

Binding: green diagonal fine-ribbed cloth lettered and decorated identically to the first edition, first impression, cloth binding state, 9.2.0. The endpapers are of cream wove paper with no ads on them, and the text is printed on wove paper. All edges are trimmed.

Note that while the initial four pages of ads in this copy are identical to those in 9.3.0, the eight pages of terminal ads differ.

9.4.0. *An International Episode*, first edition, fourth (?) impression, cloth binding state, one volume, New York [n.d.].

The title-page, size, collation, and contents are identical to those of the first edition, first impression, wrapperd binding state, 9.1.0, except that there are 107 titles listed in the four pages of ads preceding the title-page under the heading "HARPER'S HALF-HOUR SERIES.|32mo, Paper.", no date appears on the title-page, the errors on pages 44 and 45 have been corrected, and, as noted below, the terminal ads differ.

The eight pages of ads at the end, being the last four leaves of signature I, are headed: [137–8] "Bulwer's Works.", [139] "W. M. THACKERAY'S WORKS.", "[140] "R. D. BLACKMORE'S NOVELS.", [141] "By VIRGINIA W. JOHNSON.", [142] "Katharine King's Novels.", [143–144] "By Mrs. Oliphant."

Binding: green diagonal-fine-ribbed cloth, lettered and decorated identically to the first edition, first impression, cloth binding state, 9.2.0. The endpapers are of cream wove paper with no ads on them, and the text is printed on wove paper. All edges are trimmed.

9.5.0. *An International Episode*, first edition, fifth (?) impression, wrappered binding state, one volume, New York [n.d.].

The title-page, size, collation, and contents are identical to those of the first edition, first impression, wrappered binding state, 9.1. 0, except that there are 127 titles listed in the four pages of ads preceding the title-page under the heading: "HARPER'S HALF-HOUR SERIES. | 32mo, Paper.", no date appears on the title-page, the errors on pages 44 and 45 have been corrected, and, as noted below, the terminal ads differ.

The eight pages of ads at the end, being the last four leaves of signature I, are: [137] "GEORGE ELIOT'S WORKS.", [138] "W. M. THACKERAY'S WORKS.", [139] "WILLIAM BLACK'S WORKS.", [140] "By

AN INTERNATIONAL EPISODE

VIRGINIA JOHNSON.", [141] "R. D. BLACKMORE'S NOVELS.", [142] "F. W. ROBINSON'S NOVELS.", and [143–144] "By The Author of 'John Halifax'".

Binding: buff wove paper wrappers, cut flush, lettered and decorated identically to 9.1.0. The text is printed on wove paper.

The contents of this copy conform to those of the second impression (with correction of the errors on 44 and 45) as described in BAL 10539 and E&L A9, but the ads on [137–144] are not as described by either.

9.6.0. *An International Episode*, second edition, first separate impression, binding state A, one volume, New York and London 1902.

An Interna- | tional Episode [in orange italic] | BY HENRY JAMES, JR., ILLUS- | TRATED FROM DRAWINGS | BY HARRY W. McVICKAR | [publisher's device] | HARPER & BROTHERS | NEW YORK AND LONDON | M-C-M-I-I [all but the title in black italic]

Size: 7 7/8" x 6 1/4".

Collation: [unsigned, 1^2 2–11^8 12^2]; pp. [i–iv] [1–2], [3–162] [163–164]. The single full-page illustration on [37] is reckoned in the pagination. The remaining 58 illustrations are on or within the text pages. All the illustrations are in black-and-white. There is no frontispiece.

Contents: [i–ii] title-page, verso copyright notice and reservation of rights: "Copyright, 1878, by Harper & Brothers. | [rule] | Copyright, 1892, by Harper & Brothers. | [rule] | All rights reserved. [in italic]"; iii–[iv] "List of Illustrations", verso list of illustrations continued; [1–2] fly-title [called a "Frontispiece" in the list of illustrations], verso centered: "Part 1 [in Gothic type]"; [3–162] text; [163–164] blank, verso ad headed: "By HENRY JAMES", listing 13 titles with dollar prices, the last dated being *The Awkward Age*. There is no dating code on the title-leaf verso.

Binding: dark green fine-linen-grain cloth lettered and decorated in gilt. The front cover is decorated with two hearts surmounted by a crown, on each side of which are floral swags, beneath which is the title: "An International | Episode [in swash upper and lower case]". The back cover is neither lettered nor decorated. The spine reads: "An | Inter | national | Episode | Henry | James | Harpers [all in swash upper and lower case]". The endpapers are of cream laid paper, and the text and illustrations are printed on heavy coated paper. The top edge is trimmed and stained ochre, and the other edges are untrimmed.

The third American edition of *Daisy Miller: A Study*, which includes *An International Episode*, was first published by Harpers in two impressions in 1892 (see 8.8.0 and 8.9.0), with a third impression published in 1893, and a fourth in 1895; see 8.10.0 and 8.11.0. There was one later impression of these works probably published in 1919; see 8.15.0. In 1900 and later the plates of this third edition were used (with new title-pages and lists of illustrations) to print both *Daisy Miller: A Study* (see 8.11.5–8.14.5 and 8.16.0), and *An International Episode* (as recorded here), as separate volumes. While these plates are the third edition of *Daisy Miller: a Study*, they are the second edition of *An International Episode*.

9.7.0. *An International Episode*, second edition, first separate impression, binding state B, one volume, New York and London 1902.

Title-page, size, collation and contents are identical to those of the second American edition, first separate impression, binding state A, 9.6.0.

Binding: light-blue vertical-rib-grain quarter cloth with purple paper over boards. The front cover is decorated and lettered in gilt identically to the front cover of 9.6.0. The back cover is neither lettered nor decorated. The spine, which is lettered and decorated in gilt, reads: "An | Inter | national | Episode | [decorative device of a ribbon bow] | Henry | James | Harpers [all in swash upper and lower case]". The endpapers are of cream laid paper, and the text and illustrations are printed on heavy coated paper. The top edge is gilt, and the other edges are untrimmed.

On the front free endpaper is the inscription: "Euginia R. Peters | April 7, 1903 Milton".

10. *THE MADONNA OF THE FUTURE*

10.1.0. *The Madonna of the Future*, first edition, two volumes, London 1879.

THE | MADONNA OF THE FUTURE | AND OTHER TALES. | BY | HENRY JAMES, Jr. | IN TWO VOLUMES. [in italic] | VOL. I. [II.] | London: [in Gothic type] | MACMILLAN AND CO. | 1879. | The Right of Translation is Reserved. [in italic]

Size: 7 1/2″ x 4 7/8″.

Collation: Volume I: [A]⁴ B–I K–T⁸; pp. [i–viii], [1]–288. Volume II: [A]⁴ B–I K–Q⁸ R⁴; pp. [i–viii], [1]–245 [246] [247–248].

Contents: Volume I: [i–ii] half-title, verso publisher's device; [iii–iv] title-page, verso printer's imprint: "LONDON: | R. CLAY, SONS, AND TAYLOR, | BREAD STREET HILL."; [v–vi] "NOTE.", verso blank; [vii–viii] "CONTENTS OF VOL. I.", verso blank; [1]–288 text. Volume II: [i–ii] half-title, verso publisher's device; [iii–iv] title-page, verso printer's imprint as on Volume I title-leaf verso; [v–vi] "CONTENTS OF VOL. II.", verso blank; [vii–viii] divisional fly-title, verso blank; [1]–245 text; [246] printer's imprint: "LONDON: | R. CLAY, SONS, AND TAYLOR, PRINTERS, | BREAD STREET HILL."; [247] ad headed: "WORKS BY HENRY JAMES, Jr.", listing 5 titles; [248] ad headed: "MACMILLAN'S POPULAR NOVELS.", listing works by 7 authors.

Binding: dark blue fine-bead-grain cloth decorated on the front covers in black with a double-rule border within which is a single-rule panel curved at the corners, with a similar design in blind on the back cover. The spines, which are decorated in black and lettered in gilt, read: "[rule] | [row of dots] | [rule] | THE | MADONNA | OF | THE | FUTURE | AND OTHER | TALES | H. JAMES Jr | VOL. I [II] | [publisher's device] | MACMILLAN & Co. | [rule] | [row of dots] | [rule]". The "o" in "Co" is raised above a line. The endpapers are of brown coated paper, and the text is printed on wove paper. The top edges are untrimmed, and the other edges are rough trimmed.

This binding is uniform with those on the first English editions of *Roderick Hudson* (1879), 3.17.0, and *Daisy Miller: A Study* (1879), 8.17.0.

On the rear pastedown of Volume II is a diamond-shaped white binder's ticket, lettered and decorated in greenish-blue, reading: "BOUND BY | BURN | & CO". Burn was Macmillan's (probably exclusive) English binder in this period; see Ball, 105.

Printing history: Macmillan Archive. MEB 266 records that the two-volume first edition of *The Madonna of the Future* was printed from standing type in a single impression of 500 copies in September 1879. The two volumes were priced at 21s. Stereotype plates were made which were used for two impressions of the one-volume second edition: the first impression of 1,000 copies was printed in March 1880, priced at 6s., and the second of 2,000 copies (exclusively for the yellowback) was printed in June 1888, priced at 2s. Macmillan destroyed the plates in February 1921. This title was not published in America.

10.2.0. *The Madonna of the Future*, second edition, first impression, binding state A, one volume, London 1880.

THE | MADONNA OF THE FUTURE | AND OTHER TALES. | BY | HENRY JAMES, Jr. | NEW EDITION. [in italic] | London: [in Gothic type] | MACMILLAN AND CO. | 1880. | The Right of Translation is Reserved. [in italic]

Size: $7\frac{1}{2}''$ x $5''$.

Collation: $[A]^4$ B–I K–U X–Z AA–DD^8; pp. [i–viii], [1]–413 [414] [415–416]. In this copy $[A]_1$, the half-title, is missing.

Contents: [i–ii] half-title, verso publisher's device ([i–ii] missing in this copy); [iii–iv] title-page, verso printer's imprint: "LONDON: | R. CLAY, SONS, AND TAYLOR, | BREAD STREET HILL."; [v–vi] "NOTE.", verso blank; [vii–viii] "CONTENTS.", verso blank; [1]–413 text; [414] printer's imprint as on [iv]; [415] ad headed: "WORKS BY HENRY JAMES, Jr.", listing 5 titles; [416] ad headed: "MACMILLAN'S POPULAR NOVELS.", listing works by 7 authors.

Binding: dark blue-green fine-bead-grain cloth, lettered and decorated in gilt, black, and in blind uniform with the second English edition of *The American* (1879), 4.17.0. No lettering is present on the front or back covers. The spine reads: "THE | MADONNA | OF | THE FUTURE | AND OTHER | TALES | H. JAMES Jr. [all the foregoing in italic] | Macmillan & Co." The "o" in "Co" is raised above a line. The endpapers are of dark brown coated paper, and the text is printed on wove paper. The top and fore-edges are untrimmed, and the bottom edge is rough trimmed. Bound in at the end is a 38-page publisher's catalogue, the first 35 pages of which are paginated, printed on wove paper, dated October 1879.

THE MADONNA OF THE FUTURE

10.3.0. *The Madonna of the Future*, second edition, first impression, binding state B, one volume, London 1880.

Size: 7 7/16" x 4 15/16".

The title-page, collation, and contents are identical to those of the second edition, first impression, binding state A, 10.2.0, including the ads on [415–416]. In this copy [A]$_1$, the half-title, is present.

Binding: dark blue-green fine bead grain cloth, lettered and decorated in gilt, black, and in blind uniform with the second English edition of *The American*, 4.17.0, and, except as noted below for the spine lettering, is identical to the binding on 10.2.0. The spine reads: "THE | MADONNA | OF | THE FUTURE | AND OTHER | TALES | HENRY JAMES [all of the foregoing in italic] | MACMILLAN & Co." The "o" in "Co" is raised above a line. The endpapers are of greenish-black coated paper, and the text is printed on wove paper. The top edge is untrimmed, and the other edges are trimmed. Bound in at the end is a 16-page paginated (except for [16]) publisher's catalogue, printed on smooth wove paper, headed: "MACMILLAN & CO'S | SIX–SHILLING NOVELS | AUTUMN, 1902", and dated at the foot of [16] "20.9.02". No title by James is listed in this catalogue.

10.4.0. *The Madonna of the Future*, second edition, first impression, The Times Book Club binding state, one volume, London 1880.

Size: 7 3/16" x 4 15/16".

The title-page, collation, and contents (including the ads on [415–416]) are identical to those of the second edition, first impression, binding state A, 10.2.0. In this copy [A]$_1$, the half-title is present. No publisher's catalogue of ads is bound in at the end.

Binding: pale yellow linen-grain cloth with two decorative bands in black printed (but not stamped) across the front cover and spine. The spine, which is decorated and lettered in black, reads: "[decorative band] | THE | MADONNA | OF | THE FUTURE | AND OTHER | TALES | HENRY JAMES | [decorative band] | [circular Times Book Club device]". The back cover is neither lettered nor decorated. The endpapers are of white laid paper, and the text is printed on wove paper. All edges are trimmed.

[139]

10.5.0. *The Madonna of the Future*, second edition, second impression (yellowback), one volume, London and New York 1888.

THE | MADONNA OF THE FUTURE | AND OTHER TALES. | BY | HENRY JAMES, [sic] | London: [in Gothic type] | MACMILLAN AND CO. | AND NEW YORK. | 1888. | The Right of Translation is Reserved. [in italic]

Size: 6 $^{15}/_{16}$" x 4 $^{1}/_{2}$".

Collation: [A]^4 B–I K–U X–Z AA–DD^8; pp. [i–viii], [1]–413 [414] [415–416].

Contents: [i–ii] half-title, verso circular publisher's device; [iii–iv] title-page, verso printer's imprint and printing history: "Richard Clay and Sons, Limited, | LONDON AND BUNGAY. | First Edition (2 Vols. Crown 8vo.) printed 1879. | New Edition (1 Vol. Crown 8vo.) 1880. | New Edition (1 Vol. Globe 8vo.) 1888. [printing history, except numerals, all in italic]"; [v–vi] "NOTE.", verso blank; [vii–viii] "CONTENTS.", verso blank; [1]–413 text; [414] printer's imprint as on [iv]; [415–16] ads, [415] headed: "BY THE SAME AUTHOR. | Uniform with this Volume.", listing 14 titles, and further down the page under the heading: "MR. HENRY JAMES'S NOVELS AND TALES.", listing the 10 titles (14 volumes) of *The Collective Edition of 1883*; [416] headed: "By the Same Author. | [rule]", listing 5 titles, the first 4 with press opinions.

Binding: ivory boards with an elaborate floral design in red and black on the front and back covers, signed on the lower right of both covers "L. F. Day". The front cover also has a central red panel on which is printed in black: "The | Madonna | of the | Future". The back cover has a similar central red panel on which is printed in black, on a black outlined triangular scroll device: "Macmillan | & Co." The "o" in "Co" is raised above a dot. The spine of this copy is missing. The endpapers are of white wove paper, and the text is printed on wove paper. The front and rear pastedowns, and the recto and verso of the front and rear free endpapers have ads on them identical to the ads found on the endpapers of the second edition, third impression (yellowback), of *Daisy Miller: A Study* (1888), 8.23.0. All edges are trimmed.

10.6.0. *The Madonna of the Future*, first continental edition, first impression, one volume, Leipzig 1880.

THE | MADONNA OF THE FUTURE. | LONGSTAFF'S MARRIAGE. | MADAME DE MAUVES. | BY | HENRY JAMES, Jr. | AUTHORIZED EDITION. [in italic] | LEIPZIG | BERNARD TAUCHNITZ | 1880.

Size: 6 $^1/_{16}$" x 4 $^5/_{16}$".

Collation: [1]^8 2–18^8; pp.[1–6], [7]–286 [287–288].

Contents: [1–2] series half-title, verso ad headed: "TAUCHNITZ EDITION. | By the same Author," listing 4 titles, the last listed being *Daisy Miller* [A Study]; [3–4] title-page, verso blank; [5–6] "CONTENTS.", verso blank; [7]–286 text; [287] printer's imprint: "[rule] | PRINTING OFFICE OF THE PUBLISHER. | [rule]"; [288] blank.

Binding: rebound in half-leather with marbled paper over boards (together with the first continental edition, first impression, of *The American*). The endpapers are of light-blue coated paper, and the text is printed on wove paper. All edges are trimmed and red speckled.

Noted in BAL 10751. T&B 1881 records one edition with two impressions of this title. For the second impression see 10.7.0.

Tauchnitz published the six stories contained in the first English edition of *The Madonna of the Future* in two separately titled volumes, each with three of the stories. The first of these volumes, entitled *The Madonna of the Future*, contains the title story, 'Longstaff's Marriage', and 'Madame de Mauves' (see this copy and 10.7.0); the second volume, entitled *Eugene Pickering*, contains the title story, 'The Diary of a Man of Fifty', and 'Benvolio'; see 10.8.0.

10.7.0. *The Madonna of the Future*, first continental edition, second impression, one volume, Leipzig 1880.

Size: 6 $^7/_{16}$" x 4 $^{11}/_{16}$".

The title-page, collation, and contents are identical to those of the first continental edition, first impression, 10.6.0, except that the ad on the half-title verso, [2], under the heading "TAUCHNITZ EDITION. | By the same Author," lists 13 titles, the last listed being *A Little Tour in France*.

Binding: buff wove paper wrappers, cut flush, with lettering on the front cover in black within a black single-rule frame which is decorated with a flower-like device in each of the four corners with lettering above and below the frame. The spine is also lettered in black between a series of eight pairs of thick and thin black rules. The back cover, which is also lettered in black, reads: "September 1911.|Tauchnitz Edition.|[rule]|Latest Volumes:|[followed by a list of 25 titles, the last listed being *Tales of the Uneasy*, by Violet Hunt|[long rule]|[followed by, all in italic] The Tauchnitz Edition is sold by all Booksellers and Rail-|way Libraries on the Continent, price of each volume M 1, 60 or| francs 2,00 sewed, M 2, 20 or francs 2, 75 cloth (Original-Leinen-|band), M3,00 or francs 3, 75 in elegant soft binding (Original-|Geschenk-band). A complete Catalogue of Tauchnitz Edition is|attached to this work." The insides of the front and back covers are blank. A 32-page publisher's catalogue, dated July 1, 1913, is bound in at the end.

This copy has a glassine dust-jacket with no lettering or decoration on it. This dust-jacket extends over onto the inside of the top and bottom of the front and rear covers as well as inside the fore-edges of the front and rear covers. It is not known whether this dust-jacket was original to this copy when issued.

See T&B 1881, which does not record a copy with wrappers dated 1911, but does record a copy with 13 titles on the verso of the half-title, as here, with wrappers dated 1905. *A little Tour in France* was first published by Tauchnitz in 1885.

10.8.0. *Eugene Pickering*, first continental edition, one volume, Leipzig 1880.

EUGENE PICKERING. | THE DIARY OF A MAN OF FIFTY. | BENVOLIO. | BY | HENRY JAMES, Jr. | AUTHORIZED EDITION. [in italic] | LEIPZIG | BERNHARD TAUCHNITZ | 1880.

Size: 6 $^1/_{16}$″ x 4 $^3/_8$″.

Collation: [1]^8 2–17^8; pp. [1–8], [9]–270 [271–272].

Contents: [1–2] series half-title, verso ad headed: "TAUCHNITZ EDITION.|By the same Author," listing 5 titles, the last listed being *The Madonna of the Future*; [3–4] title-page, verso blank; [5–6] "CONTENTS.", verso blank; [7–8] divisional fly-title, verso blank; [9]–270 text; [271] printer's imprint: "[rule]| PRINTING OFFICE OF THE PUBLISHER. |[rule]"; [272] blank.

CONFIDENCE

Binding: rebound in dark blue cloth with an overall embossed pattern of branches and leaves (together with the first continental edition of *Yeast*, "by the Author of Alton Locke", Charles Kingsley). The endpapers are of white wove paper, and the text is printed on wove paper. All edges are trimmed, the top-edge is stained dark blue and the other edges are red speckled.

T&B 1881 records one impression of a single edition of this title.

See note following 10.6.0 regarding the contents of this volume.

✤

11. CONFIDENCE

11.1.0. *Confidence*, first edition, first impression, two volumes, London 1880 [1879].

CONFIDENCE | By HENRY JAMES Jr. | [publisher's device] | IN TWO VOLUMES | VOL. I. [II.] | London [in Gothic type] | CHATTO & WINDUS, PICCADILLY | 1880 | All Rights Reserved [in italic]

Size: 7 $^{9}/_{32}$" x 4 $^{15}/_{16}$".

Collation: Volume I: [A]² B–I K–U⁸ X⁴; pp. [i–iv], [1]–309 [310] [311–312]. Volume II: [A]² B–I K–R⁸; pp. [i–iv], [1]–253 [254] [255–256].

Contents: Volume I: [i–ii] half-title, verso within a single-rule frame ad headed: "NEW NOVELS.", listing 5 titles (none by James); [iii–iv] title-page, verso printer's imprint: "LONDON: PRINTED BY | SPOTTISWOODE AND CO., NEW-STREET SQUARE | AND PARLIAMENT STREET"; [1]–309 text; 309 at foot printer's imprint as on title-leaf verso; [310] blank; [311] publisher's device as on title-page; [312] blank. Volume II: [i–ii] half-title, verso ad as on [ii] in Volume I; [iii–iv] title-page, verso printer's imprint as on Volume I title-leaf verso; [1]–253 text; 253 at foot printer's imprint as on Volume I title-leaf verso; [254] blank; [255] publisher's device as on title-pages; [256] blank.

Binding: smooth olive-brown cloth, with the title in black on the front covers at an angle above a black patterned and bordered decorative triangular area on the lower right of the front covers, and an identical black patterned and bordered design in black on the upper left of the back covers. The spines, which are lettered in gilt, read:

"Confidence | H. James Jr [all the foregoing in sans-serif] | VOL. I [II] | CHATTO & WINDUS". The endpapers are of a blue-on-white patterned floral paper, and the text is printed on wove paper. The top edge is untrimmed, and the other edges are rough trimmed. A 32-page paginated publisher's catalogue dated "[De ember 1879." (the closing square bracket and the letter "c" in the month being missing), printed on a thinner wove paper, is bound in at the end of Volume II.

On the rear pastedown of volume I is a diamond-shaped pink binder's ticket, lettered and decorated in orange-red, reading: "BOUND BY | BURN | & CO".

In Volume I the half-title is inscribed: "from the Author. Jany. 1880", and the title-page is inscribed: "from the Author". Both inscriptions, which are in pencil, appear to be in James's hand.

Both BAL and E&L record this impression as also being issued in green cloth.

A Note on The English Editions of *Confidence*

James confided the first sketch of what was to become *Confidence* to his notebook under an entry headed "3 Bolton St., W., November 7, 1878", but it does not appear that he started to write the novel until March 1879, when he wrote his brother, William, that he was "immediately getting to work upon it" as a serial for Scribner's. CWJ, Volume I, 310. It was probably finished by the end of August 1879 when he travelled to Paris, and it ran in *Scribner's Monthly* from August 1879 to January 1880. It was not serialized in England.

Macmillan clearly expected to publish it in book form in England; see Moore, Letter 60. However, the poor sales of his prior four works that Macmillan had published in England puzzled James. On September 28, 1879, he wrote to Frederick Macmillan: "I received yesterday my account of the Sales of my books, from your people. The results are not brilliant – on the contrary – & I grieve that the books should not do better. It seems to me an anomaly that they don't, as they have on the whole largely & favourably noticed, & apparently a good deal talked about"; Moore, Letter 54. Or, as he more forcefully wrote to his brother, William, in June, 1879: "The Macmillans are everything that's friendly – caressing – old Macmillan physically hugs me; but

CONFIDENCE

the delicious ring of the sovereign is conspicuous in our intercourse by its absence"; CWJ, I, 315. It was in this context that James decided in September 1879 to offer *Confidence* to Chatto & Windus, who agreed to pay James £100 for a licence to publish it for three years. Macmillan acknowledged to James that he felt "hurt" about James's defection to Chatto, adding: "I am sorry that you should have gone elsewhere merely because you wanted some ready money"; Moore, Letter 61. James thereafter returned to the Macmillan fold until an almost final parting in 1890; see note following 34.8.0.

English printing history. Chatto & Windus Archive. Ledger CW B/2/14, p. 305. First edition, two volumes: *first impression*, 500 copies ordered from Spottiswood & Co., printer, November 12, 1879, 500 copies delivered to Burne & Co, binders, December 4, 1879. Published December 1879, priced at 21s. *Second impression* 250 copies ordered from Spottiswood & Co. January 20, 1880, 252 [sic] copies delivered, 150 to Burne & Co. on January 27, 1880, and 102 copies to "selves" on February 5, 1880.

Second edition, one volume, entitled the "2/- Ed.": *first (and sole?) impression*, 2500 copies ordered from Spottiswood & Co. May 11, 1880, 2,000 copies delivered to "Pen" or "Psw"" [?] June 8, 1880, and 525 [sic] to "selves" June 8, 1880, with the further notation under the heading "Binder": "2,000 June of 80 Pen [or "Psw"] and "545 June 2/83 [illegible] [total] 2545". Published July 1880, priced at 2s.

Third (?) edition, one volume, entitled the "3/6 Edit.": *first impression*, 500 copies ordered from Spottiswood & Co. September 29, [1880], 505 [sic] copies delivered to "LW" on October 12 [1880]. Published November 1880, priced at 3s. 6d.

On the same page, under the caption "Remarks", are the notations: "July 2/86 Spotts sent us the stereos for melting"; "June 21/80 Evans ptd. 3,000 covers [for] 2/- [edition]"; and "July 8/83 do [Evans printed] 1,000 covers Rooke".

It would appear that the 545 (or 525) copies of the 2s. edition delivered to '"selves" in June 1880 were issued in June 1883, perhaps in a different format.

There appears to be some confusion in the record as to the dates of publication of the two later editions, and whether they were separate editions or two impressions of a single edition. BAL records that the one-volume second edition was published by Chatto in June or July

1880, and seems to imply that it was reprinted in November 1880 as a volume in the "Piccadilly Novels series". E&L A11c records that the first of these one-volume editions was published in October 1880 at 3s. 6d.; and that the second one-volume edition was published in August 1881 at 2s. as a yellowback, that was made up of remainder sheets of the October 1880 edition. E&L also notes that there was a further printing from the plates of the one-volume edition in September 1882 as part of the Piccadilly Library series. However, E&L's dating of the first two one-volume editions is in conflict with the announcements that appear in PC during 1880. In the issue of July 15, 1880, under the heading of "NEW WORKS | PUBLISHED FROM JULY 1 TO 14." there appears the announcement: "James (H.) – Confidence, New edit. 12mo. pp. 316, boards, 2s. Chatto"; and in the issue of November 15, 1880, 1003, under the heading "NEW WORKS | PUBLISHED FROM NOVEMBER 1 TO 15." there appears the announcement "James (H.) – Confidence. New edit. post 8vo. pp 310, 3s. 6d. Chatto". The fact that both are characterized as "new editions", and that the paginations differ would suggest that they are separate editions, and that the cheaper 2s. edition, illogically, was published before the 3s. 6d. edition.

There is no record in EC of editions of *Confidence* published by Chatto & Windus subsequent to 1880.

The fourth (?) English edition of *Confidence* was published by Macmillan in 1883 as part of *The Collective Edition of 1883*, 20.1.0 (reprinted in 1886, 20.5.0). Although Chatto's three-year licence to publish *Confidence* had expired by then, in August 1883 Macmillan asked James to request Chatto to stop selling *Confidence*, which they continued to advertise among their 2s. novels; Moore, Letter 100. *Confidence* was not included in *The Novels and Tales of Henry James* (the New York Edition 1907–1909), but it was included in Percy Lubbock's edition of *The Novels and Stories of Henry James* (1921–1923), 86.1.0– 86.2.0.

11.2.0. *Confidence*, first edition, second impression, two volumes, London 1880.

The title-pages are identical to those of the first edition, first impression, 11.1.0, except that this impression has "SECOND EDITION [in italic]" between "VOL. I. [II.]" and the publisher's imprint.

Size: $7\,3/8''$ x $4\,7/8''$.

CONFIDENCE

Collation: identical to that of 11.1.0.

Contents: identical to those of 11.1.0, except that the ad on [ii] in both volumes lists 7 rather than 5 titles (none by James).

Binding: lettered and decorated identically to 11.1.0. The endpapers are of a blue-on-white floral patterned paper, and the text is printed on wove paper. The top edges are untrimmed, the fore-edges are rough trimmed, and the bottom edges are trimmed. Bound in at the end of Volume II is a 32-page paginated publisher's catalogue dated October, 1879.

On the rear pastedown of Volume II is a diamond-shaped white binder's ticket, lettered and decorated in powder-blue, reading: "BOUND BY | BURN | & CO".

11.3.0 *Confidence*, first American edition, first impression, first binding state, one volume, Boston 1880.

CONFIDENCE. | By HENRY JAMES, Jr. | [shield-shaped publisher's device] | BOSTON: | HOUGHTON, OSGOOD AND COMPANY. | The Riverside Press, Cambridge. [in Gothic type] | 1880.

Size: 7 $7/16''$ x 4 $7/8''$.

Collation: [1–14^{12} 15^{6}], signed as [1]^{8} 2–21^{8} 22^{6}; pp. [1–4], [5]–347 [348].

Contents: [1–2] blank leaf; [3–4] title-page, verso copyright notice and printer's imprint: "Copyright, [in italic] 1880, | By Henry James, Jr. | University Press: | John Wilson and Son, Cambridge."; [5]–347 text; 347 at foot beneath a rule printer's imprint: "University Press: John Wilson & Son, Cambridge."; [348] blank.

The errors on pages 171, line 9 ("like me call" for "like me to call"), [323], line 7 ("to place, as" for "to place it, as") and 345, line 1 ("chance" for "change") recorded in BAL 10549 are present.

Binding: terra-cotta sand-grain cloth over bevelled boards, with the front and back covers decorated in blind with a single-rule frame within a wider single-rule border. The spine, which is lettered and decorated in gilt, reads: "[thick followed by a thin rule] | Confidence | [rule] | H. James Jr. | Houghton, Osgood & Co. | [thin followed by a thick rule]". The endpapers are of chocolate-brown coated paper, and the text is printed on wove paper. A binder's fly-leaf of wove paper is

[147]

at the back, but none at the front. All edges are trimmed, and the top edge is stained brown.

E&L 11b records the cloth as fine-cross-ribbed, but, as BAL records the cloth as C cloth (sand-grain), E&L must be in error.

On the recto of the front binder's fly-leaf is the ink signature "James Laurence".

American printing history. Houghton Mifflin Archive. First edition: Ms Am 2030(16), 129: *first* [Houghton, Osgood] *impression* February 6, 1880, 1526 copies, 1506 bound between February 11, 1880, and March 13, 1880; *second impression* February 27, 1880, 1014 copies, 1015 [*sic*] bound between February 28 and March 1, 1880; *third impression* March 9, 1880, 1016 copies, 1008 bound between March 11, 1880, and January 26, 1881, with 243 copies "rebound" in six batches between June 3, 1882, and October 9, 1884. Ms Am 2030(17), 117: *fourth* [first Houghton, Mifflin] *impression* July 31, 1885, 156 copies, 157 [*sic*] bound between August 24, 1885, and September 22, 1888. Ms Am 2030(19), 153: *fifth impression* April 20, 1889, 160 copies, 75 of which were bound on May 3, 1889, and June 23, 1890; undated notation: "Trans 75"; *sixth impression* June 5, 1890, 158 copies, 150 bound between August 18, 1891, and May 21, 1897 (the 25 copies bound on that latter dated noted as "N[ew] S[tyle]"). Ms Am 2030(21), 220: *seventh impression* November 2, 1898, 156 copies, 236 [*sic*] bound between November 17, 1898, and January 2, 1908.[20] Ms Am 2030(22), 220: *eighth impression* May 5, 1909, 158 copies, 155 bound June 2, 1909, and February 27, 1917; notation: "[total copies] 4344".

Priced at $1.50, which price was unchanged through 1905. In 1901 and 1905 copies in "paper" were advertised at $.50.

11.4.0. *Confidence*, first American edition, first impression, first binding state, one volume, Boston 1880.

This copy is identical to the first American edition, first impression, first binding state, 11.3.0, except that it is bound in dark green sand-grain cloth.

E&L records the cloth as being fine cross-ribbed, but as indicated above, this must be an error. BAL records the first binding state of the

---

20 This binding-up of 236 copies may have included both the 156 printed on November 2, 1898, plus the 75 copies "Trans[ferred]".

CONFIDENCE

first American edition as being in green and terra-cotta only. E&L, in addition to dark green, records two other cloth colors: red-brown and orange-brown. The difference in these two colors may possibly be due to fading.

11.5.0. *Confidence*, first American edition, third impression, second binding state, one volume, Boston 1880.

The title-page, size, collation, and contents (including the typographical errors) are identical to the first American edition, first impression, first binding state, 11.3.0.

Binding: tan diagonal-fine-ribbed cloth with lettering in red-brown, and decoration in tan, red-brown, and gilt on the front cover and spine. The gilt panel carrying the title on the front cover has a pronounced maze-like background pattern. The publisher's imprint at the foot of the spine reads: "Houghton Mifflin & Co." The ampersand has a flat rather than a rounded top. The endpapers are of a tan floral design on white coated paper, and the text is printed on wove paper. A binder's fly-leaf of wove paper is at both the front and the back. All edges are trimmed.

This is a copy is one of the 243 copies of the third impression which were "rebound" by Houghton, Mifflin between June 3, 1882, and October 9, 1884; see American printing history. This binding is uniform with that on the first American impression of the second edition of *The Portrait of a Lady* (1881), 16.5.0.

11.6.0. *Confidence*, first American edition, sixth impression, one volume, Boston and New York [n.d., 1890].

CONFIDENCE. | By HENRY JAMES, Jr. | Sixth Edition. [in italic] | [oblong publisher's device of a piper under a tree within a frame] | BOSTON: | HOUGHTON, MIFFLIN AND COMPANY. | New York: 11 East Seventeenth Street. [in sans-serif] | The Riverside Press, Cambridge. [in Gothic type]

Size: 7 $^{11}/_{32}$" x 4 $^{13}/_{16}$".

Collation: [1]^8 2–21^8 22^6; pp. [1–4], [5]–347 [348].

Contents: [1–2] blank, verso ad within a single-rule frame headed: "Henry James's Books. [in Gothic type]", listing 8 titles, after the first 7 of which it reads: "The set, 7 vols. 12mo, $12.00."[21]; [3–4] title-page, verso copyright notice: "Copyright, [in italic] 1880, | By Henry James, Jr."; [5]–347 text; 347 at the foot no printer's imprint; [348] blank.

Binding: chocolate-brown diagonal-fine ribbed cloth, with lettering in red-brown and decoration in chocolate-brown, red-brown, and gilt on the front cover and spine. The gilt panel carrying the title on the front cover has a pronounced maze-like background pattern. The publisher's imprint at the foot of the spine reads: "HOUGHTON | MIFFLIN [dot] & [dot] CO." The ampersand in the publisher's imprint is stylized and is like a figure "8". The endpapers are of white laid paper, and the text is printed on wove paper. A binder's fly-leaf of wove paper is at both the front and the back. All edges are trimmed, and the top edge is stained brown.

This binding is uniform with that of the first American impression of the second edition of *The Portrait of a Lady* (1881), 16.5.0.

11.7.0. *Confidence*, first American edition, sixth impression, one volume, Boston and New York [n.d., 1890].

The title-page, size, collation, and contents are identical to those of the first American edition, sixth impression, 11.6.0.

Binding: pea-green diagonal-fine ribbed cloth, lettered and decorated identically to 11.6.0. The title on the front cover and spine is within a gilt panel with a pronounced maze-like background pattern. It has endpapers of white laid paper, and the text is printed on wove paper. A binder's fly-leaf of wove paper is at both the front and the back. All edges are trimmed, and the top edge is stained greenish-brown.

On the front binder's fly-leaf is the inscription "C. K. Barry. | 1895."

11.7.5. *Confidence*, first American edition, sixth impression, one volume, Boston and New York [n.d., 1890].

The title-page, size, collation, and contents are identical to those of the first American edition, sixth impression, 11.6.0.

---

21 This set, uniformly bound with the second edition, first American impression of *The Portrait of a Lady*, consists of *A Passionate Pilgrim*, *Transatlantic Sketches*, *Roderick Hudson*, *The American*, *The Europeans*, *Confidence* and *The Portrait of a Lady*.

CONFIDENCE

Binding: tan diagonal-fine-ribbed cloth, lettered and decorated identically to 11.6.0. The title on the front cover and spine is within a gilt panel with a pronounced maze-like background pattern. The endpapers are of white laid paper, and the text is printed on wove paper. A binder's fly-leaf of wove paper is at both the front and the back. All edges are trimmed and the top edge is stained dark ochre.

On the front free endpaper is the bold signature: "Henry James", underscored.

11.8.0. *Confidence*, first continental edition, first impression, Leipzig, 1880.

CONFIDENCE | BY | HENRY JAMES, Jr. | AUTHORIZED EDITION. [in italic] | LEIPZIG | BERNHARD TAUCHNITZ | 1880.

Size: 6 $^{1}/_{8}$″ x 4 $^{3}/_{16}$″.

Collation: [1]^8 2–18^8; pp. [1–4], [5]–287 [288].

Contents: [1–2] series half-title, verso ad headed: "TAUCHNITZ EDITION." | By the same Author" listing 6 titles, the last listed being *Eugene Pickering*; [3–4] title-page, verso blank; [5]–287 text; [288] printer's imprint centered: "[rule] | PRINTING OFFICE OF THE PUBLISHER. | [rule]".

Binding: rebound in black quarter imitation leather, with black cloth over boards, with no lettering or decoration on the front or back covers. The spine, lettered and decorated in gilt, reads: "[rule] | [rule] JAMES | [short rule] | [rule] | [spaced double rules]". The endpapers are of shiny off-white wove paper, and the text is printed on wove paper, All edges are trimmed. There is no catalogue of ads bound in at the end.

On the front pastedown is a small rectangular orange label printed in black, reading "Boyveau & Chevillet | Livres en toutes Langues | 23, Rue de la Banque, PARIS".

T&B 1901 lists one edition with two impressions of this title, the first listing 6 James titles on the series half-title verso, and the second listing 13 such titles.

12. *HAWTHORNE*

12.1.0. *Hawthorne*, first edition, first impression, first state ads, one volume, London 1879.

HAWTHORNE | BY | HENRY JAMES, Junr. | London [in Gothic type] | MACMILLAN AND CO | 1879 | The Right of Translation and Reproduction is Reserved [in italic]

Size: 7 $5/16$" x 4 $13/16$".

Collation: [A]^4 B^8 [C]^8 D–I K–M^8 N^4; pp. [i–viii], [1]–183 [184]. As noted in BAL 10544 the signature mark "C" is absent in some copies, as is the case here.

Contents: [i–ii] series half-title, verso blank; [iii–iv] title-page, verso printer's imprint: LONDON: | R. CLAY, SONS, AND TAYLOR, | BREAD STREET HILL."; [v]–vi "CONTENTS.", continued on verso; [vii–viii] fly-title, verso blank; [1]–183 text; [184] printer's imprint as on [iv].

There is no period after "CO" on the title-page and "Junr." appears after the author's name. Page 3, line 12 reads "talents", page 47, line 4 from the bottom reads "expresss", and page 137, line 1 reads "Blithdale". Also the page number on page 83 has the numeral "3" $3/32$" higher than the numeral "8".

Binding: crimson smooth-linen-grain cloth lettered and decorated in the cloth color and black on the front and back covers, and lettered and decorated in black on the spine. The front cover reads: "[black rule] | ENGLISH MEN OF LETTERS | Edited by [in italic slightly to the right of center] | John Morley [further to the right of center] | HAWTHORNE [centered in cloth color within a black panel] | HENRY JAMES Jr | [publisher's monogram]". The back cover reads: "[black rule] | [publisher's device in cloth color on a black panel background with two sets of rules extending horizontally from the panel]". The spine, which is lettered vertically upwards, reads: "HAWTHORNE | [two double rules] | H. JAMES Jr | [single rule]". The endpapers are of black coated paper, and the text is printed on wove paper. All edges are trimmed. Bound in at the end are 4 pages of paginated ads, [1]–2 of which are devoted to the English Men of Letters series, listing 11 titles as issued (four of them on 2) and 13 titles (including *Hawthorne*) "IN PREPARATION". The first title so listed, *Milton*, has opposite it the printed comment "[Shortly. [in italic]" (*sic*). Pages 3 and 4 of the ads are devoted to "MACMILLAN'S GLOBE LIBRARY." The ads are printed on wove paper appreciably thinner than the text paper. This is the first state of the ads recorded by BAL.

This binding is BAL's binding variant C. Of the three binding variants described in BAL 10544 (without priority) this variant is the most commonly seen.[22]

English printing history: Macmillan Archive. MEB, 168, records the following impressions of the first and only English edition of *Hawthorne* in the English Men of Letters series: *first impression* December 1879, 6,000 copies; *second impression* January 1883, 2,000 copies; *third impression* July 1887, 5,000 copies, with a title-leaf cancel printed in December 1887; *fourth impression* May 1902, 1,000 copies, with an index added; and *fifth and final impression* April 1909, of 3,000 copies. All were printed from electrotype plates. The first impression was published on December 12, 1879. The first and second impressions were priced at 2s. 6d. The third was priced at 1s. 6d. in cloth, and 1s. in salmon wrappers. The fourth (with an index) was priced at 2s. net, and the fifth impression was priced at 1s. net. The last two impressions were designated as "net books" pursuant to the Net Book Agreement.

MEB, 173, also records that in 1894 and 1895 the English Men of Letters series was published in a 13-volume format (3 biographies in each volume), the first volume being published in 1894, and the remaining 12 in 1895. They were priced at 3s. 6d. per volume. Volume 8 contains James's *Hawthorne*; see 12.8.7. There was not a separate printing of *Hawthorne* for this format, it being made up from sheets of the second impression Macmillan had on hand.

Macmillan (New York) also published this edition in 12 rather than 13 volumes in America, with the difference that *Hawthorne* (and two other authors) were not included among the 36 titles it contained. Exactly when this was first published is uncertain, but in the first American edition, later impression of *Hawthorne* dated 1899, 12.16.5, the ad on [179] refers to this 12-volume edition as the "People's Edition", and in

22 Professor Anesko suggests that close analysis of James's Hawthorne reveals that "in composing his critical biography, Henry James was, if not an outright plagiarist then at least a transparently deceptive appropriator of another distinguished critic's work." See Michael Anesko, 'Is James's Hawthorne really James's Hawthorne?', *The Henry James Review*, 29 (2008) 36. The critic whose ideas James appropriated was Émile Montégur (1825–1895).

the first impression of the first edition of Leslie Stephen's *George Eliot* (The Macmillan Company, 1902), an ad on [208] lists the 12 volumes and their contents (omitting *Hawthorne*) of "three biographies in each volume" listing the price as "$1.00 each" in cloth. An ad in that volume on [207] indicates, the individual biographies published in America by Macmillan (omitting *Hawthorne*) were priced at "40 cents, each" in cloth. The omission of *Hawthorne* was undoubtedly due to the fact that its American copyright was owned by Harpers.

John Morley, as the general editor of the English Men of Letters series was paid by Macmillan a £250 up-front payment, a second payment of £250 to be deducted from future royalty payments (but not refundable), and a royalty of "five (5) per cent. of the nominal selling price on all copies published under his Editorship and sold in England." Memorandum of Agreement (undated, but endorsed "Nov. 1877"), Macmillan Archive, Mss 55055, Vol. cclxx, f. 80.

12.2.0. *Hawthorne*, first edition, first impression, first state ads, one volume, London 1879.

This copy is identical to the first edition, first impression, first state ads, 12.1.0, except that the signature mark "C" on page 17 is present and the page number on page 83 has the numeral "3" slightly lower than the numeral "8". The first state of the ads is present at the end, which on 2 lists *Hawthorne* as one of 13 titles "IN PREPARATION". The first title so listed, *Milton*, has opposite it the printed comment "[Shortly. [*sic*, in italic]". The ads are printed on wove paper appreciably thinner than the text paper.

12.3.0. *Hawthorne*, first edition, first impression, first state ads, one volume, London 1879.

Size: 7 $^{9}/_{16}$" x 5".

The title-page, collation, and contents are identical to the first edition, first impression, first state ads, 12.1.0.

The title-page has no period after "CO" and has "Junr." after the author's name. Signature mark "C" is not present. The three typographical errors described in the preceding copies are present, as well as the only slightly lower "3" in the pagination of page 83.

Binding: unbleached linen, with no lettering or decoration on the front or back covers. The spine has a small paper label which reads: "[rule] | Hawthorne [in Gothic type] | H. James, Jr. | [rule]". The endpapers are of white wove paper, and the text is printed on wove paper. All edges are untrimmed. The first state of the ads is present at the end, which on 2 lists *Hawthorne* as one of 13 titles "IN PREPARATION". The first title so listed, *Milton*, has opposite it the printed comment "[Shortly. [sic, in italic]". These ads are printed on wove paper appreciably thinner than the text paper.

This copy is as described in BAL 10544, binding variant A, ad state a.

12.4.0. *Hawthorne*, first edition, first impression, first state ads, one volume, London 1879.

This copy is identical to the first edition, first impression, 12.3.0 (including the typographical errors and the ads), except that signature mark C is present.

12.5.0. *Hawthorne*, first edition, first impression, second state ads, one volume, London 1879.

This copy is identical to the first edition, first impression, 12.3.0 (including the typographical errors), except that signature mark "C" is present, and the ads at the end on 2 list five titles published with extracts from reviews, four further titles (including *Hawthorne*) published without any reviewers' comments, and eight titles under the heading "IN PREPARATION." One of the titles listed as in preparation, *Cowper*, has opposite it the printed comment "[Shortly." [sic, in italic]. These ads are printed on paper slightly thicker than the text paper. In this copy the ad pages have been reversed, that is 3 and 4 precede 1 and 2.

On the half-title is the brown ink signature "James A. Purchas", and on [184] is the notation, also in brown ink, "4.5.80".

This copy is as described in BAL 10544, binding variant A, ad state b.

12.6.0. *Hawthorne*, first edition, first impression, third state ads, one volume, London 1879.

The title-page, size, collation, and contents (including the typographical errors) are identical to those of the first edition, first impression, first state ads, 12.1.0.

The title-page has no period after "CO" and has "Junr." after the author's name. Signature mark "C" is absent. The three typographical errors described above are present, and the slightly lower "3" in the pagination of page 83.

Binding: bright crimson fine-linen-grain cloth, with lettered and decorated identically to 12.1.0. The endpapers are of dark blue-green coated paper, and the text is printed on wove paper. All edges are trimmed. Inserted at the end are four pages of ads printed on thick wove paper, pages [1]–3 being devoted to the English Men of Letters series, listing 21 titles (including *Hawthorne*) as issued and 5 "IN PREPARATION." The last page of the ads, which is not paginated, is headed "MACMILLAN'S GLOBE LIBRARY." None of the 5 titles listed as "IN PREPARATION" is noted as being issued "Shortly". These ads are printed on wove paper slightly thicker than the text pages.

This third state of the ads is not recorded in E&L or BAL.

12.7.0. *Hawthorne*, first edition, first impression, third state ads, one volume, London 1879.

This copy is identical to the first edition, first impression, third state ads, 12.6.0 (including the typographical errors and the ads), except that the "3" in the pagination of page 83 is appreciably higher than the "8", and the ads are printed on wove paper slightly thinner than the paper used in the body of the book.

On the title-page is the ink inscription "Mary L. Hay | T.W. June '81." On the rear free end-paper is blind-stamped, within two concentric blind-stamped ovals, "PELTON TUNBRIDGE WELLS | BOOKSELLERS".

12.8.0. *Hawthorne*, first edition, first impression, one volume, London 1879.

This copy is identical to the first edition, first impression, first state ads, 12.1.0 (including the typographical errors), except that the page number on page 83 has the numeral "3" slightly lower than the numeral "8", and no ads are bound in at the end.

12.8.5. *Hawthorne*, first edition, second impression, first issue, one volume, London 1883.

The title-page is identical to that of the first edition, first impression, first state ads, 12.1.0, except it is dated 1883 at the foot.

Size: 7 1/4" x 4 3/4".

Collation: identical to that of 12.1.0. Signature mark "C" is present.

Contents: identical (including the typographical errors on 3, 47, and 137) to those of 12.1.0, except that on the title-leaf verso under the printer's imprint there is added "SEVENTH THOUSAND. [in italic]", and the printer's imprints on the title-leaf verso and on [184] read: "LONDON: | R. CLAY, SONS, AND TAYLOR, | BREAD STREET HILL, E.C."

Binding: crimson smooth linen-grain cloth, with lettered and decorated identically to 12.1.0. The endpapers are of black coated paper, and the text is printed on wove paper. All edges are trimmed, and the top edge is stained black. Bound in at the end are four pages of ads, paginated [1]–4. These ads are: [1] ad for the English Men of Letters series, listing 33 titles in two columns, the last title being "SHERIDAN. | By Mrs. Oliphant. | [Just ready [sic, in italic]", with none noted in preparation; [2] ad headed: "MACMILLAN'S 4s. 6d. SERIES."; 3 ad headed: "MACMILLAN'S GLOBE LIBRARY. [in sans-serif]"; and 4 an ad for "THE ENGLISH CITIZEN."

12.8.7. *Hawthorne*, first edition, second impression, second issue, (1883) sheets bound with two other titles in the same series, one volume, London 1895.

DEFOE | By W. MINTO | STERNE | By H. D. TRAILL | HAWTHORNE | By HENRY JAMES | London [in Gothic type] | MACMILLAN AND CO. | AND NEW YORK | 1895.

Size: 7 3/8" x 5 15/16".

Collation: π^2 [A]⁴ B–I K–L⁸ M⁸ (–M$_{7,8}$); [A]⁴ B–I K–M⁸; [A]⁴ B–I K–M⁸ N⁴; pp. [i–xii], [1]–171 [172]; [i–viii], [1]–176; [i–viii], [1]–183 [184].

Contents: [i–ii] series half-title headed: "English Men of Letters [in Gothic type] | EDITED BY JOHN MORLEY | VOLUME VIII", verso publisher's device; [iii–iv] title-page, verso blank; [v–vi] half-title for *Daniel Defoe*, verso blank; [vii–viii] title-page for *Daniel Defoe*, dated 1885, verso printing history and printer's imprint: "NINTH THOUSAND. | LONDON: R. CLAY, SONS, AND TAYLOR."; [ix–x] "PREFACE", [x] paginated vi; [xi–xii] "CONTENTS", [xii] paginated viii; [1]–171 text; 171 at foot printer's imprint: "R. CLAY, SONS, AND TAYLOR, PRINTERS." [172] blank; [i–ii] half-title for *Sterne*, verso blank; [iii–iv] title-page for *Stern*, dated 1882, verso blank, [v]–vi "PREFATORY NOTE."; [vii]–viii "CONTENTS."; [1]–176 text; [i–ii] half-title for *Hawthorne*, verso blank; [iii–iv] title-page for *Hawthorne*, identical to that on the first edition, first impression, 12.1.0, except that it is dated 1883 at the foot, verso printer's imprint and printing history: "LONDON: | R. CLAY, SONS, AND TAYLOR, | BREAD STREET HILL, E. C. | EIGHTH THOUSAND."; [iii–iv] "CONTENTS.", [iv] paginated vi; [vii–viii] fly-title, verso blank; [1]–183 text; [184] printer's imprint: "LONDON: | R. CLAY, SONS, AND TAYLOR, | BREAD STREET HILL, E. C."

Binding: dark-blue diaper cloth. The front cover has centered a small oval cartouche with a gilt outline and gilt central panel with the letters "[dot] E [dot] M [dot] L [dot]" in the cloth color. The back cover is neither lettered nor decorated. The spine, which is lettered and decorated in gilt, reads: "[thin followed by thicker rule] | DEFOE | W. MINTO | STERN | H. D. TRAILL | HAWTHORNE | HENRY JAMES | English | Men | of | Letters [series-title in Gothic type] | [thick rule] | MACMILLAN & CO. | [thin rule]". The end papers are of cream wove paper, and the texts are printed on wove paper. The top edge is untrimmed, the bottom edge is rough-trimmed, and the fore-edge is untrimmed.

The errors on 3, 47 and 137 of *Hawthorne* are present.

This copy, consisting of earlier sheets of the three titles, constituting what is a multi-volume set of the English Men of Letters series, of which this is Volume VIII. As MBC records only one printing (in 1883) of James's *Hawthorne* between 1879 (the first impression) and 1887 (third impression), these sheets must be of the sheets of the second impression, with a change made to the title-leaf verso (i.e. "EIGHTH THOUSAND") during the press run. The fourth impression was printed in 1902. Why the 1883 sheets rather than those of the third impression (1887) were used for this volume is unknown.

These sheets with "Eighth Thousand" on the title-leaf verso suggests that 1,000 sets of sheets of the second impression of *Hawthorne* were published as a stand alone volume, and that the second 1,000 printed (with "Eighth Thousand") were published in the 13-volume format.

12.9.0. *Hawthorne*, first edition, third impression, second state, one volume, London 1887.

HAWTHORNE | BY | HENRY JAMES | London [in Gothic type] | MACMILLAN AND CO. | AND NEW YORK | 1887 | The Right of Translation and Reproduction is Reserved [in italic].

Size: 7 3/16″ x 4 3/4″.

Collation: [A]⁴ (±[A]₂) B–I K–M⁸ N⁴; pp. [i–viii], [1]–183 [184]. [A]₂, the title-leaf, is a cancel.

Contents: [i–ii] series half-title, verso blank; [iii–iv] title-page, verso printer's imprint and printing history: "Printed by Richard Clay and Sons, 1879. | Reprinted 1883, 1887."; [v]–vi "CONTENTS", verso continuation of contents; [vii–viii] fly-title, verso blank; [1]–183 text; [184] printer's imprint: "Richard Clay and Sons, London and Bungay."

Binding: beige smooth-linen-grain cloth, lettered and decorated in dark blue. The front cover reads: "English Men of Letters [in a modified Gothic type, underscored] | EDITED BY JOHN MORLEY | HAWTHORNE | HENRY JAMES | [publisher's device]". The spine reads: "HAWTHORNE [dot] HENRY JAMES [up the spine vertically]. At the foot of the spine is the series title: "English | Men | of | Letters. [horizontally]". The endpapers are of white wove paper. The back free endpaper has ads on the recto for the English Men of Letters series, and on the verso for the works of Emerson, Macmillan's Globe Library and The English Illustrated Magazine. The text is printed on wove paper. All edges are trimmed. There are no ads inserted at the end.

The errors on 3, 47 and 127 are present.

MBC, 358 records that the third impression was printed in July 1887, and the cancel added in December 1887. The cancelled title-leaf was in response to James's request that the "Junʳ" after his name be eliminated. However, as the fourth and fifth impressions, below, show, this request was subsequently ignored.

On the front pastedown is the library label of Rev. James L. Murray.

12.10.0. *Hawthorne*, first edition, fourth impression, one volume, London 1902.

[All within a red single-rule frame divided by two horizontal red rules into three compartments] ENGLISH MEN OF LETTERS [in italic] | HAWTHORNE | BY | HENRY JAMES, Junʳ. | LONDON: MACMILLAN & CO., LIMITED | NINETEEN HUNDRED AND TWO

Size: $7\,^{5}/_{16}''$ x $4\,^{13}/_{16}''$.

Collation: $[A]^4$ B–I K–N^8; pp. [2] [i]–vi, [1]–183 [184] [185–192].

Contents: blank leaf; [i–ii] series half-title, verso publisher's device; [iii–iv] title-page, verso printing history: "First published 1879 [in italic]"; [v]–vi "CONTENTS.", continued on verso; [1]–183 text; [184] blank; [185]–191 "INDEX"; [192] printer's imprint: "Richard Clay and Sons, Limited. | LONDON AND BUNGAY."

Binding: crimson smooth-linen-grain cloth. The front and back covers are neither lettered nor decorated. The spine, which is lettered and decorated in gilt, reads: "HAWTHORNE|[square floral device]|HENRY |JAMES| ENGLISH [dot] MEN | OF [dot] LETTERS." The endpapers are of white wove paper, and the text is printed on wove paper. The top edge is gilt, and the other edges are trimmed. The back is flat rather than rounded. Bound in at the end are four pages of unpaginated ads, [1] of which is headed: "English Men of Letters [in Gothic type] | NEW SERIES. | Crown 8vo. Gilt tops. Flat backs. 2s. net per vol. [in italic]", and [4] of which is headed: "English Men of Letters [in Gothic type] | Edited by JOHN MORLEY. | RE-ISSUE OF THE ORIGINAL SERIES. | Library Edition. Uniform with the New Series." Below the heading are listed in two columns the 39 titles of the original English Men of Letters series. These ads are dated "5.8.07" at the foot of [4].

The text of this impression was printed from the corrected plates of the first impression with, for the first time, the addition of an index. However, curiously, the printing history on the title-leaf verso refers to the first printing only rather than expanding on that found in the third impression, second state. This reissue of the original English Men of Letters series with additional titles in the New Series was called the "Library Edition" by the publisher.

12.11.0. *Hawthorne*, first edition, fifth impression, one volume, London 1909.

[All within a black single-rule frame divided by two horizontal black rules into three compartments] ENGLISH MEN OF LETTERS [in italic] | HAWTHORNE | BY | HENRY JAMES Jun. | MACMILLAN AND CO., LIMITED | ST. MARTIN'S STREET, LONDON | 1909

Size: 6 $^{13}/_{16}$" x 4 $^{1}/_{4}$".

Collation: [A]⁴ B–I K–N⁸; pp. [2] [i]–vi, [1]–183, [184] [185–186] [187]–191 [192].

Contents: blank leaf; [i–ii] series half-title and half-title, verso publisher's device followed by list of affiliated companies; [iii–iv] title-page, verso printer's imprint and printing history: "Richard Clay and Sons, Limited, | BREAD STREET HILL, E.C., AND | BUNGAY, SUFFOLK. | First Edition, 1879. Reprinted 1883, 1887. | Library Edition, 1902. | Pocket Edition, 1909. [printing history in italic]"; [v]–vi "CONTENTS.", continued on verso; [1]–183 text; [184] blank; [185] "INDEX" divisional fly-title; [186] blank; [187]–191 index; [192] printer's imprint as on [iv].

Binding: dark green sand-grain cloth. On the front cover the series title is lettered in blind within a blind frame and the title is lettered in gilt, and on the spine the series title is lettered in blind and the title and author's name are lettered in gilt. The front cover and spine are also elaborately decorated in blind. The back cover is neither lettered nor decorated. The endpapers are of white wove paper, and the text is printed on wove paper. All edges are trimmed, and the top edge appears brown stained. Bound in at the end is a single leaf of ads headed (recto): "NEW POCKET EDITION | English Men of Letters", listing 39 titles, and (verso) "English Men of Letters | NEW SERIES", listing 23 titles with a further 2 titles "In the Press". These ads are dated "10.5.09" at the foot of [2].

On the front free endpaper is the library slip of the Hull Subscription Library.

The text of this impression was printed from the corrected plates of the first impression with the addition of an index. This index first appeared in the so called "Library Edition" (fourth impression) of 1902; see 12.10.0.

12.12.0. *Hawthorne*, first American edition, first impression, one volume, New York 1880.

HAWTHORNE | BY | HENRY JAMES, Jr. | [publisher's device] | NEW YORK | HARPER & BROTHERS, PUBLISHERS | FRANKLIN SQUARE | 1880

Size: 7 5/16" x 4 7/8".

Collation: [1]¹² 2–8¹²; pp. [i]–viii, [1]–177 [178] [179–184].

Contents: [i–ii] blank leaf; [iii–iv] series half-title, verso blank; [v–vi] title-page, verso copyright notice and reservation of rights: "Entered according to Act of Congress, in the year 1879, by | Harper & Brothers, | In the Office of the Librarian of Congress, at Washington. | [rule] | ALL RIGHTS RESERVED."; [vii]–viii "CONTENTS.", continued on verso; [1]–177 text; [178] blank; [179–184] six pages of ads, being the last 3 leaves of signature 8, the first of which is devoted to the English Men of Letters series, and lists 12 titles as "now ready", at "75 cents a volume", followed by a rule, then lists "HAWTHORNE. By Henry James, Jr. .... 12mo, Cloth, $1 00.", followed by a further rule, then lists 12 titles as "VOLUMES IN PREPARATION". The other pages of ads are headed: [180] "By GEORGE WILLIAM CURTIS.", [181] "OLIVER GOLDSMITH.", [182] "SAMUEL JOHNSON." [183] "A NEW LIBRARY EDITION | OF | MACAULAY'S ENGLAND." and [184] "MOTLEY'S HISTORIES."

Binding: dark olive-drab linen-grain cloth. The front cover, which is lettered and decorated in red, reads: "Nathaniel Hawthorne [in Gothic type] | BY | HENRY JAMES, JR. [all but title in sans-serif] | [small rule]". The spine, which is lettered and decorated in red, reads: "ENGLISH | MEN | OF | LETTERS | [small rule] MORLEY | Hawthorne [in Gothic type] | HARPERS [all of the foregoing, except that the title, is in sans-serif]". The back cover has the publisher's monogram, centered, in red. The endpapers are of brown coated paper, and the text is printed on wove paper. A binder's fly-leaf of wove paper is at both the front and the back. All edges are trimmed.

There are variations in the text of this copy from the copy described in E&L A12b as the first impression. This copy on page 3, line 8 reads "three or four beautiful talents" (which is the same reading as the

English edition on page 3, line 12) not "three or four beautiful plants" called for by E&L. The typographical errors in the first English edition in the spelling of "express" and "Blithedale" have, on the other hand, been corrected (on 46, line 6 from the bottom, and 132, line 12 from the bottom).

It is possible that this copy, which has some but not all of the errors found in the English first edition, first impression, corrected, is in fact the first impression of the first American edition (or first state of the first impression), and that the copy with all errors corrected described by E&L as the first impression is in fact a later impression (or state).

Priced initially at $1.00, but was later reduced to $.75.

No record was found of the printing history of this title in the Harper & Brothers Archive. Anesko, 64, records that the first Harpers printing was of 2,500 copies.

12.13.0. *Hawthorne*, first American edition, second (?) impression, one volume, New York 1880.

The title-page, size, and collation of this copy are identical to the first American edition, first impression, 12.12.0.

Contents: identical to 12.12.0 (including the error on page 3, line 8), except that the 6 pages of ads at the end, being the last 3 leaves of signature 8, differ from those in the first impression, as the first page lists 15 titles in the English Men of Letters series as "now ready" at "75 cents a volume", followed by a rule, then lists "HAWTHORNE. By Henry James, Jr. ..... 12mo, Cloth, $1 00.", followed by a further rule, then lists 9 titles as "VOLUMES IN PREPARATION". The other 5 pages of ads are identical to those in 12.12.0.

Binding: smooth black cloth, lettered and decorated in red as on 12.12.0. The endpapers are of brown coated paper, and the text is printed on wove paper. A binder's fly-leaf of wove paper is at both the front and the back. All edges are trimmed.

E&L records copies in olive-drab but does not mention copies in black cloth. BAL 10544 records the cloth as linen-grain "dark green (i.e., faded black?)". Neither records the two states of the ads.

12.14.0. *Hawthorne*, first American edition, third (?) impression, one volume, New York [n.d.].

This copy is identical to the first American edition, first impression, 12.12.0, except that no date appears on the title-page, and the error on page 3, line 8 has been corrected.

The ads are in all respects identical to those in the first American edition, second (?) impression, 12.13.0.

Binding: olive-drab smooth-linen-grain cloth, lettered and decorated in red as on 12.12.0. The endpapers are of brown coated paper, and the text is printed on wove paper. A binder's fly-leaf of wove paper is at both the front and the back. All edges are trimmed.

12.15.0. *Hawthorne*, first American edition, later impression, one volume, New York [n.d.].

The title-page is identical to that of the first American edition, first impression, 12.12.0, except that there is no date at the foot.

Size: $7\,1/4''\times 4\,7/8''$.

The collation and contents are identical to those of 12.12.0, except that the error on page 3, line 8 has been corrected and, as recorded below, the contents of 2 of the 6 pages of ads at the end is different.

Of the 6 pages of ads ([179–184]), being the last 3 leaves of signature 8, all except [179] and [183] are identical to those in 12.12.0. However, the first page, [179], which is devoted to The English Men of Letters series, lists 35 titles (including *Hawthorne*) as "now ready" at "75 cents per volume", and lists none as in preparation. The fifth page, [183], which is devoted to "A NEW LIBRARY EDITION | OF | MACAULAY'S ENGLAND", has on line 4 of the text the added phrase "Sheep, $12 50; Half Calf, $21 25.", and after "OTHER EDITIONS OF MACAULAY'S ENGLAND" a change of price of the "Popular Edition" to "$2 50" (it was formerly $4.00), and a change in price of the "Cheap Edition" to "Paper, $1 00" (it was formerly $1.50) with the added phrase: "In one volume, 8vo, Cloth, $1 25."

Binding: black smooth-linen-grain cloth, lettered and decorated in red identically to 12.12.0. The endpapers are of dark brown coated paper, and the text is printed on wove paper. A binder's fly-leaf of wove paper is at both the front and the back. All edges are trimmed.

12.16.0. *Hawthorne*, first American edition, later impression, one volume, New York [n.d.].

The title-page, size, collation, and contents are identical to those of the first American edition, later impression, 12.15.0, except that the ad on [179] lists 36 titles (including *Hawthorne*) as "now ready" rather than 35. The ad on [183] is identical to the ad on that page in 12.15.0.

The additional title listed on [179] is the last, *Coleridge*, which was first published by Harpers in 1884.

Binding: light olive smooth-linen-grain cloth, lettered and decorated in black identically to the first American edition, first impression, 12.12.0. The endpapers are of chocolate-brown coated paper, and the text is printed on wove paper. A binder's fly-leaf of wove paper is at both the front and the back. All edges are trimmed, and the top edge is stained ochre.

12.16.5. *Hawthorne*, first American edition, later impression, one volume, New York 1899.

HAWTHORNE | BY | HENRY JAMES, Jr. | [publisher's device] | HARPER & BROTHERS PUBLISHERS | NEW YORK AND LONDON | 1899

Size: $7\,^5/_{16}$" x 5".

Collation: $[1]^{12}$ $2-8^{12}$, also signed $[A]^8$ B–I K–M^8; pp. [i]–viii, [1]–177 [178] [179–184].

Contents: [i–ii] blank leaf; [iii–iv] series half-title, verso blank; [v–vi] title-page, verso copyright notice and reservation of rights as in the first edition, first impression, 12.12.0; [vii]–viii "CONTENTS", continued on verso; [1]–177 text; [178] blank; [179–184] six pages of ads, being the last 3 leaves of signature 8, the first page of which is devoted to the English Men of Letters series and list 39 titles followed by: "12 mo, Cloth, 75 cents per Volume. | Also, People's Edition (36 volumes in 12), 12 mo, Cloth, $1 00 per volume. | Other Volumes in Preperation. [in italic]." The other pages of the ads are headed: [180] "By GEORGE WILLIAM CURTIS.", [181] "SAMUEL JOHNSON.", [182] "EARLY LIFE OF DEAN SWIFT.", [183] "A NEW LIBRARY EDITION | OF | MACAULEY'S ENGLAND.", and [184] "THOMAS CARLYLE"S WORKS."

Binding: olive-drab linen-grain cloth, lettered and decorated in black. The front cover reads: "Nathaniel Hawthorne [in Gothic type] | BY |

HENRY JAMES, JR. | [rule] [all but the title in sans-serif]". The spine reads: "ENGLISH | MEN | OF | LETTERS | [rule] | MORLEY [all the foregoing in sans-serif] | Hawthorne [in Gothic type] | HARPERS [in sans-serif]". The back cover has the publisher's monogram, centered. The endpapers are of brown coated paper, and the text is printed on wove paper. There are no binder's fly-leaves. All edges are trimmed, and the top edge is stained ochre.

See printing history following 12.1.0 regarding the 12 volume issue referred to in the ad on [179] as the "People's Edition".

12.17.0. *Hawthorne*, first American edition, later impression, one volume, New York 1901.

[all within a double-rule frame, divided by two long rules into three panels] Hawthorne [in Gothic type] | [long rule] | by | HENRY JAMES | AUTHOR OF | "FRENCH POETS AND NOVELISTS" "DAISY MILLER" | "THE PORTRAIT OF A LADY" ETC. | English Men of Letters [in Gothic type] | EDITED BY | JOHN MORLEY | [publisher's device] | [long rule] | HARPER & BROTHERS PUBLISHERS | NEW YORK AND LONDON | 1901

Size: 7 1/8" x 4 3/4".

Collation: [A]⁸ B–F⁸ [G]⁸ H-I⁸ [K–M]⁸, also signed [1]¹¹ 2–7¹² [8]¹³; pp. [i–vi], [1]–177 [178] [179–186]. [vi] is paginated viii. The ads on [179–186] are the last four leaves of [M]⁸.

Contents: [i–ii] series half-title; verso blank; [iii–iv] title-page, verso copyright notice and reservation of rights as on the title-leaf verso of the first American edition, first impression, 12.12.0; [v–vi] "CONTENTS", verso continuation of contents [continuation of contents paginated viii]; [1]–177 text; [178] blank; [179–186] ads.

The ads are headed: [179] "BISMARCK'S AUTOBIOGRAPHY", [180] "By SVEN HEDIN", [181] "By CHARLES DUDLEY WARNER", [182] "THE BROWNING LETTERS", [183] "By HENRY LAUREN CLINTON", [184] THE HAWORTH BRONTE", [185] "By Sir WALTER BESANT, and [186] "By THOMAS HARDY".

Binding: burgundy vertical-rib-grain cloth. The front cover, which has a black single-rule border and is lettered and decorated in silver, reads: "Nathaniel | Hawthorne [title in Gothic type] | BY | HENRY JAMES,

JR. [in sans-serif] | [publisher's device]". The spine, which is decorated in black and silver and lettered in silver, reads: "[double black rules] | ENGLISH | MEN | OF | LETTERS | [small silver rule] | MORLEY | [double black rules] [small wreath ornament] | Hawthorne [in Gothic type] | [small wreath ornament] | HARPERS | [double black rule]". The back cover is neither lettered nor decorated. The endpapers are of white laid paper, and the text is printed on heavy laid paper. All edges are trimmed.

This impression has been printed from the plates used to print the later impression, 12.14.0, with a new title-page, changed ads at the end and the error on page 3, line 8 corrected. The pagination of [vi] as viii is the result of the omission in this impression of the first blank leaf found in the first American edition, first impression, 12.12.0.

❧ † ☙

13. *A BUNDLE OF LETTERS*

13.1.0. *A Bundle of Letters*, first edition (unauthorized), first state, one volume, Boston [n.d., 1880].

A BUNDLE | OF | LETTERS. [in bold type] | BY | HENRY JAMES, Jr. | (REPRINTED FROM THE PARISIAN.) | [decorative rule] | LORING, Publisher, | Corner Bromfield & Washington Streets, | BOSTON.

Size: 6 3/4" x 5 3/8".

Collation: [unsigned, 1–4⁸]; pp. [1–2], 3–64.

Contents: [1–2] title-page, verso blank; [3]–64 text, 64 at foot printer's imprint: "[rule] | Rockwell & Churchill, Printers, 39 Arch Street."

Binding: pale cream stiff wove paper wrappers, cut flush, with a plaid-like pattern of five lines in blue (horizontal) and five in red (vertical) with lettering in black. The front cover reads: "A Bundle | of | Letters [the foregoing in a back slanting script] | BY | Henry James, Jr., | Loring, Publisher, | Corner of Bromfield and Washington streets [*sic*], | BOSTON." On the front cover the author's name is printed in wide serif letters narrowly spaced (set 1 15/16" wide), and a comma is present after "Jr.". In addition, on the front cover there is 23/32" between "Letters" and "BY", and 1 1/4" between "HENRY" and "LORING". The back cover has ads on it printed in black. The insides of the wrappers are decorated with the same plaid-like design, and have ads on them printed in black. The text is printed on wove paper. It is stapled, not sewn.

E&L, having examined "numerous early-dated copies", identifies this lettering variant as the primary state, and one of the four wrapper colors it identifies (wrapper color b). It is BAL's lettering variant A (no priority). BAL identifies only three wrapper colors: blue, cream and pink. The pale yellow-green wrapper recorded by E&L, but not by BAL, may be a copy of the pale yellow wrapper, recorded below.

The title-pages, collations and contents as well as the ads on the back covers and inside the front and back covers are identical on all seven copies here catalogued.

American printing history. No information has been found regarding the printing history of Loring's unauthorized edition of this title. It has not been, it is believed, subsequently published as a stand-alone title. However, in 1880 Harpers published it in a new edition together with *The Diary of a Man of Fifty* as number 135 in its Half-Hour Series; see 14.1.0. In 1883 Harpers published a further edition of title, together with *The Diary of a Man of Fifty* and *An International Episode* (not in the collection). On March 13, 1908 Harpers deposited two copies of a new edition of this title only in The Library of Congress for copyright purposes. This edition was printed on the recto of the leaves only, and is bound in orange wrappers. One of the two copies was deaccessioned by The Library of Congress and is now in The Carter Burden Collection at The Morgan Library and Museum. It is not known if this 1908 edition was ever published.

Priced at $.25.

13.2.0. *A Bundle of Letters*, first edition (unauthorized), first state, one volume, Boston. [n.d., 1880].

This copy is identical to the preceding copy, 13.1.0, except that it is bound in pale yellow stiff wove paper wrappers, cut flush. It is stapled, not sewn.

E&L identifies four wrapper colors, one of which, d, is pale yellowish green; see note on the previous copy. This copy is also BAL's lettering variant A.

A BUNDLE OF LETTERS

13.3.0. *A Bundle of Letters*, first edition (unauthorized), one volume, Boston. [n.d., 1880]

Size: 6 5/8″ x 5 3/8″.

Binding: pale blue stiff wove paper wrappers, cut flush. On the front cover the author's name is printed in wide serif letters narrowly spaced (set 1 15/16″ wide), but there is no comma after "Jr." In addition, on the front cover there is 31/32″ between "Letters" and "BY" and 11/32″ between "HENRY" and "LORING". It is stapled, not sewn.

Other than as identified above, this copy is identical to 13.1.0.

This copy is BAL's lettering variant B, and E&L wrapper color a. Note that the author's name on the front cover is set at the same width as in the two preceding copies of setting A, even though, unlike the two preceding copies, there is no comma after "Jr."

13.4.0. *A Bundle of Letters*, first edition (unauthorized), one volume, Boston [n.d., 1880].

Size: 6 5/8″ x 5 3/8″.

Binding: cream stiff wove paper wrappers, cut flush. On the front cover the author's name is printed in wide serif letters narrowly spaced (set 1 15/16″ wide), but no comma is present after "Jr." In addition, on the front cover there is 31/32″ between "Letters" and "BY", and 1 1/32″ between "HENRY" and "LORING". Other than the difference in color, this copy is identical to the immediately preceding copy, 13.3.0, except that it is not stapled, it is oversewn (that is sewn through the side of the signatures, rather than in their fold).

13.5.0. *A Bundle of Letters*, first edition (unauthorized), one volume, Boston [n.d., 1880].

Size: 6 1/2″ x 5 5/16″.

Binding: cream stiff wove paper wrappers, cut flush, with a plaid-like pattern of five lines in red (horizontal) and five lines in blue (vertical); however, the plaid-like pattern is not present on the insides of the wrappers. On the front cover the author's name is printed in wide serif letters narrowly spaced (set 1 15/16″ wide), but no comma is present after "Jr." In addition, on the front cover there is 28/32″ between "Letters" and "BY", and 1 1/32″ between "HENRY" and "LORING". Like the immediately preceding copy, 13.4.0, it is oversewn.

This copy is BAL's lettering variant B, and E&L wrapper color b.

On the front cover is the ink inscription "Emma L. Weber | 1879". This may be the dated copy referred to in I. R. Brussel, *Anglo-American First Editions, Part Two: West to East 1786–1930* (London: Constable & Co. Ltd., 1936), 89, note 1. E&L states: "Published 24 January 1880, at 25 cents. Brussel reports a copy with an 1879 inscription, but the Loring newspaper announcement and James family correspondence establish the later date." In fact, the James family correspondence reveals that on January 17, 1880 James's mother wrote him that Loring had told Henry James Sr. (at some previous unspecified time) that he was going to reprint his *A Bundle of Letters*; see HJL II, 268. It had first appeared in *The Parisian* on December 18, 1879.

13.6.0. *A Bundle of Letters*, first edition (unauthorized), one volume, Boston [n.d., 1880].

Size: $6\,3/4''$ x $5\,7/16''$.

Binding: pale pink stiff wove paper wrappers, cut flush, with a plaid-like pattern of five lines in blue (horizontal) and five in red (vertical); however, the plaid-like pattern is not present on the insides of the wrappers. On the front cover the author's name is printed in small serif letters more widely spaced (set 2" wide), and no comma is present after "Jr." In addition, on the front cover there is 27/32" between "Letters" and "BY" and 1 1/4" between "HENRY" and "LORING". It is stapled, not sewn.

This copy is BAL's and E&L's lettering variant C, and E&L wrapper color c.

13.7.0. *A Bundle of Letters*, first edition (unauthorized), one volume, Boston [n.d., 1880].

Size: $6\,3/4''$ x $5\,7/16''$.

Binding: pale blue stiff wove paper wrappers, cut flush, with a plaid-like pattern of five blue lines (horizontal) and five in red (vertical); however, the pattern is not present on the insides of the wrappers. On the front cover the author's name is set in small serif letters more widely spaced (2" wide) and no comma is present after "Jr." In addition on the front cover there is $27/32''$ between "Letters" and "BY" and 1 1/4" between "HENRY" and "LORING". It is stapled, not sewn.

THE DIARY OF A MAN OF FIFTY

This copy is BAL's and E&L's lettering variant C, and E&L wrapper color a.

See Appendix C for a summary of points on the above states.

❧✢❧

14. *THE DIARY OF A MAN OF FIFTY*

14.1.0. *The Diary of a Man of Fifty*, first American edition (authorized), cloth binding state, one volume, New York 1880.

THE | DIARY OF A MAN OF FIFTY | AND | A BUNDLE OF LETTERS | BY | HENRY JAMES, Jr. | AUTHOR OF | "DAISY MILLER" "AN INTERNATIONAL EPISODE" ETC. | [rule] | NEW YORK | HARPER & BROTHERS, PUBLISHERS | FRANKLIN SQUARE | 1880

Size: 4 5/8" x 3 1/8".

Collation: [1]^8 2–9^8; pp. [1–8], [9]–135 [136] [137–144].

Contents: [1–4] ads, listing 132 titles (but not this title) under the heading: "HARPER'S HALF-HOUR SERIES. | 32 mo, Paper."; [5–6] title-page, verso copyright notice and reservation of rights: "Copyright, 1880, by HENRY JAMES, Jr. | [rule] | All rights reserved. [in italic]; [7–8] divisional fly-title, verso copyright notice and reservation of rights as on [6]; [9]–135 text; [136] blank; [137–144] ads.

The 8 pages of ads at the end, being the last 4 leaves of signature 9, are headed: [137–138] "By The Author of 'John Halifax.", [139] "WILKIE COLLINS'S NOVELS.", [140] "CHARLES READE'S WORKS.", [141–142] "By Mrs. Oliphant.", [143] "GEORGE ELIOT'S WORKS.", and [144] "W. M. THACKERAY'S WORKS."

Binding: green diagonal fine-ribbed cloth over flexible boards. The front cover, lettered and decorated in red and black, reads: "[red decorative rule extending across the top, down the back of the front cover, and across the bottom] | HARPER'S | Half-Hour Series. [series title in red] | [in black, thick followed by a thin rule] | THE | DIARY OF A MAN OF FIFTY | AND | A BUNDLE OF LETTERS | By HENRY JAMES, Jr. [titles and author's name in black] | [in black, thin followed by a thick rule] | [publisher's device in red] | [bottom extension of red rule] | "COPYRIGHT 1877 BY HARPER & BROTHERS. [in red]".

THE DIARY OF A MAN OF FIFTY

The spine, lettered in black but not decorated, reads vertically down the spine: "THE DIARY OF A MAN OF FIFTY AND A BUNDLE OF LETTERS". The back cover has a centered publisher's device in black. The endpapers are of cream wove paper with no ads on them, and the text is printed on wove paper. All edges are trimmed, and the top edge is stained brown.

E&L A14 records three spine variants of the cloth issue: one with both titles in red-brown, a second with both titles in black, and a third with only the title *The Diary of a Man of Fifty*, in orange-red. BAL 10550 records being able to locate only two spine variants, both in black, the first with both titles, and the second with only one title, *The Diary of a Man of Fifty*.

Printing history. Harper & Brothers Archive. First edition (which also contains *A Bundle of Letters*) published as No. 135 in Harpers Half-Hour Series on April 9, 1880. Reel 33, page 31, headed October 1881, records on hand April 21, 1879, no copies, printed since [first and sole impression] 5186 copies, on hand November 2, 1881, 1139 copies, 248 copies having been given away. There are no further printings reflected in the royalty records through December 31, 1897, on which date 227 copies of this impression remained on hand.

Priced at $.40 in cloth and $.25 in wrappers. This title was not published in England.

On March 13, 1908, Harpers deposited two copies of a new edition of *The Diary of a Man of Fifty* (without *A Bundle of Letters*) in The Library of Congress for copyright purposes. This edition is printed on the recto of the leaves only, and is bound in orange wrappers. One of the two copies was deaccessioned by The Library of Congress, and is now in the Carter Burden Collection at The Morgan Library and Museum. it is not know if this 1908 edition was ever published.

14.2.0. *The Diary of a Man of Fifty*, first American edition (authorized), wrappered binding state, one volume, New York 1880.

The title-page, size, collation, and contents (including the ads) are identical to those of the first American edition (authorized), cloth binding state, 14.1.0.

Binding: pale buff wrappers, cut flush. The front cover, lettered and decorated in red and black, reads: "Price Twenty Cents [in black italic] | [red decorative rule extending across the top, down the back of the front cover and across the bottom] | HARPER'S | Half-Hour Series. [series title in red] | [in black, thick followed by a thin rule] | THE DIARY OF A MAN OF FIFTY | AND | A BUNDLE OF LETTERS | By HENRY JAMES Jr. [title and author's name in black] | [in black, thin followed by a thick rule] | [publisher's device in red] | [at bottom, extension of the red rule] | Copyright 1877 by Harper & Brothers". The spine, lettered in black but not decorated, reads: "135 THE DIARY OF A MAN OF FIFTY AND A BUNDLE OF LETTERS", vertically down the spine. The back cover has an ad headed : "HARPER'S PERIODICALS." The inside front cover has an ad headed: "HARPER'S LIBRARY | OF | AMERICAN FICTION." The inside back cover has an ad headed: "HARPER'S LIBRARY | OF | SELECT NOVELS." The text is printed on wove paper.

❧✠❧

15. WASHINGTON SQUARE

15.1.0. *Washington Square*, first edition, first impression, one volume, New York 1881 [1880].

WASHINGTON SQUARE | By HENRY JAMES, Jr. | AUTHOR OF | "DAISY MILLER" "AN INTERNATIONAL EPISODE" ETC. | ILLUSTRATED BY GEORGE DU MAURIER [in italic] | NEW YORK | HARPER & BROTHERS, FRANKLIN SQUARE | 1881.

Size: $6\,5/8''$ x $4\,9/16''$.

Collation: $[1]^8\ 2-17^8$; pp. [1–6], [7]–266 [267–272].

Contents: [1–2] blank, verso frontispiece with tissue guard; [3–4] title-page, verso copyright notice and reservation of rights: "Entered according to Act of Congress, in the year 1880, by | HENRY JAMES, Jr. | In the Office of the Librarian of Congress, at Washington. | [rule] | All rights reserved [in italic]"; [5–6] "ILLUSTRATIONS." (listing 6, which includes the frontispiece), verso blank; [7]–266 text; [267–272] ads paginated [1]–6 headed on [1]: "SOME POPULAR NOVELS | Published by HARPER & BROTHERS, New York." with dollar prices, and on [6] there is listed 3 James titles: *Daisy Miller*, *An International Episode*, and *The*

Diary of a Man of Fifty. The 6 full-page illustrations are reckoned in the pagination. There are 6 smaller illustrations within the text.

Binding: olive-drab diagonal-fine-ribbed cloth with an illustration on the front cover in red-brown and olive-drab of one of the streets of town houses bordering Washington Square, which illustration is framed by an elaborate border in red-brown on each side with gilt panels above and below. The front cover reads: "WASHINGTON | SQUARE | HENRY JAMES JR." The back cover is neither lettered nor decorated. The spine, which is lettered in red-brown, and decorated in red-brown and gilt, reads: "WASHINGTON [at an angle] | SQUARE | HENRY JAMES Jr. | HARPERS". The "r" in Jr." is raised above a line. The endpapers are of drab-tan-coated paper, and the text is printed on wove paper. A binder's fly-leaf of wove paper is at both the front and the back. All edges are trimmed.

American printing history. Harper & Brothers Archive. First edition: published December 1880. Reel 33, page 31, headed October 1881, records on hand on April 21, 1879, none, printed since [*first impression*, referred to as the "fine edition"] 3056 copies, and on hand on November 2, 1881, 755 copies; Reel 33, page 194, headed July 1883 records on hand on November 2, 1881, 755 copies, printed since none, and on hand on July 13, 1883, 611 copies; Reel 33, page 369, headed May 1885 records on hand on July 13, 1883, 611 copies, printed since none, and on hand on May 10, 1885, 480 copies; Reel 34, page 9, headed July 1888, records on hand May 10, 1885, 480 copies, printed since none, and on hand on July 16, 1888, 438 copies; Reel 34, page 556, headed December 1893, records on hand on July 16, 1888, 438 copies, printed since none, and on hand December 15, 1893, 368 copies; Reel 34, page 669, headed November 1894 records on hand on December 15, 1893, 368 copies, printed since none, notation: "taken from sheets of fine edition for quarterly series – 254", on hand November 20, 1894, 103 copies; Reel, 35, page 215, headed December 1895 records on hand November 20, 1894, 103 copies, printed since none, and on hand on December 31, 1895, 82 copies; Reel 35, page 215, headed December 1895 records "cheap ed." on hand November 20, 1894, none, printed since [*second impression*] 1775 copies plus 254 from "fine ed.", on hand December 31, 1895, 1085 copies; Reel 35, page 415, headed November 1896 records on hand on December 31, 1895, "fine ed." 82 copies and "cheap ed." 1085 copies, printed since [*third impression*, referred to as "H. School Classics"] 520 copies, and on hand on November 15, 1896, "fine ed." 71, "cheap ed." 1123,[23] and "H. School Classics" 404 copies, notation: "Less royalty on the following returned: 28 Wash. Square cheap"; Reel 35, page 56, headed December 1896 records on hand on November 15, 1896, "fine ed." 71, "cheap ed." 1123 and "H. School Classics" 404 copies, printed since none, on hand December 31, 1896, "fine ed." 69, "cheap ed." 1070 and "H. School Classics" 395 copies; Reel 35, page 171, headed June 1897 records on hand on December 31, 1896, "fine ed." 69, "cheap ed." 1070 and "H. School Classics" 395 copies, printed since none, on hand on June 30, 1897, "fine ed." 62, "cheap ed." 1008 and "H. School Classics" 389 copies; Reel 35, page 296, headed December 1897 records on hand June 30, 1897, "fine ed." 62, "cheap ed." 1008 and "H. School Classics" 389 copies, printed since none, and on hand December 31, 1897, "fine ed." 59, "cheap ed." 1117 "sold -109" and "109 Wash Square Cheap Ed Retnd", and "H. School Classics" 230 copies.

The "fine edition" was priced at $1.25; the "cheap edition" was priced at $.50, and the "High School Classics" was priced at $.75.

There were at least two further impressions of this edition not reflected in the Archive: a 1901 printing (see 15.2.0), and a 1926 printing (not catalogued) from Harper's first edition plates, but published by Albert and Charles Boni as part of The American Library, but with new illustrations. The number of copies printed is unknown.

The 1901 printing was priced at $.75, and the 1926 printing was priced at $1.25.

15.1.5. *Washington Square*, first edition, second impression, one volume, New York 1894.

The title-page, the title-page verso, and the collation are the same as those of the first edition, first impression, 15.1.0, except that the title-page is dated 1894 at the foot.

Size: 7 1/8" x 4 13/16".

Contents: identical to 15.1.0, except that the 6 pages of ads with dollar prices on [267–272] are headed: [267] "By HENRY JAMES.", listing 8 titles, the last dated being *Theatricals* [Second Series] listed as "Nearly

---

[23] It is apparent from adding up the number of copies sold, that the 254 sets of sheets are being counted as part of the "cheap edition" for the first time, hence augmenting the number of copies of the "cheap edition" even though none had been printed since.

Ready"; [268] "By CONSTANCE F. WOOLSON."; [269] "By MARY E. WILKINS."; [270] "By WILLIAM DEAN HOWELLS."; [271] "R. D. BLACKMORE'S NOVELS."; and [272] "By GEORGE DU MAURIER."

Binding: pea-green smooth cloth. The front and back covers are neither lettered nor decorated. The spine, which is lettered and decorated in gilt, reads: "[double rule] | WASHINGTON | SQUARE | [single rule] | HENRY JAMES | [double rule] | HARPERS". The endpapers are of white wove paper, and the text is printed on smooth wove paper. There are no binder's fly-leaves. All edges are trimmed.

The ad on [267] states that the retail price of this title was "Cloth, Ornamental, $1 25; Paper, 50 cents".

15.2.0. *Washington Square*, first edition, later impression, one volume, New York 1901.

WASHINGTON SQUARE [in red] | By Henry James | ILLUSTRATED | [publisher's device] | NEW YORK AND LONDON | HARPER & BROTHERS PUBLISHERS | 1901 [all within a single-rule frame within which are three single-rule panels].

Size: 7 3/8" x 5".

Collation: π^2 (π_1 +X$_1$)[1]^6 2–16^8 17^4; pp. [1–6], [7]–264 plus 2. The frontispiece, not reckoned in the pagination, is tipped in between π_1 and π_2.

Contents: [1–2] blank leaf; frontispiece photographic portrait of James with tissue guard tipped in; [3–4] title-page, verso copyright notice and reservation of rights: "Entered according to Act of Congress, in the year 1880, by | Henry James, Jr. | In the Office of the Librarian of Congress, at Washington. | [rule] | All rights reserved. [in italic]"; [5–6] "Illustrations" (listing 5, including the frontispiece), verso blank; [7]–264 text. Of the five listed illustrations all but the frontispiece are reckoned in the pagination.

Binding: bright red vertical-rib-grain cloth, lettered on the front cover in black within a black rule border within which are three black ruled panels. The top panel reads: "Washington | Square". The central panel has a publisher's device in black and gilt. The bottom panel reads: "Henry James [in italic]". The back cover is neither lettered nor decorated. The spine, which is lettered in gilt, reads: "Washington | Square | [rule] | James [in italic] | [flower and leaf device] | Harpers". The endpapers are of white laid paper, the frontispiece is printed on smooth wove paper, and the text is printed on laid paper. There are no binder's fly-leaves. The top edge is gilt, and the other edges are trimmed. A red ribbon marker is bound in.

In this copy, was printed from the 1880 first edition plates, the original frontispiece illustration is omitted and replaced by a photographic portrait of James. The leaf with the illustration originally appearing on 262 is also omitted, and a blank leaf, [1–2], added, thus reducing the number of text pages from 266 to 264. The remaining original 4 full-page illustrations, which are reckoned in the pagination, as well as the original 6 smaller illustrations within the text, are all present. The title-page has been reset, as has the list of illustrations on [5] and the pagination of 261–264.

15.3.0. *Washington Square*, first English edition, first impression, two volumes, London 1881.

WASHINGTON SQUARE | THE PENSION BEAUREPAS | A BUNDLE OF LETTERS | By HENRY JAMES, Jun. | VOL. I. [II.] | LONDON | MACMILLAN AND CO. | 1881.

Size: $7\,7/16''$ x $4\,7/8''$.

Collation: Volume I: [A]^4 B–I K–R^8 S^4 [T]^2; pp. [i–viii], [1]–265 [266] [267–268]. Volume II: [A]^2 B–I K–S^8; pp. [i–iv], [1]–271 [272]. Pages 268, 269, and 271 of Volume II are misnumbered 368, 369 and 371.

Contents: Volume I: [i–ii] half-title, verso publisher's device; [iii–iv] title-page, verso blank; [v–vi] "NOTE", verso blank; [vii–viii] divisional fly-title, verso blank; [1]–265 text; 265 at foot printer's imprint: "Printed by R. & R. Clark, Edinburgh. [all but printer's name in italic]"; [266] blank, [267–268] blank leaf. Volume II: [i–ii] half-title, verso publisher's device; [iii–iv] title-page, verso blank; [1]–271 (misnumbered 371) text; 271 at foot printer's imprint as on 265 of Volume I; [272] blank.

Binding: dark blue-green fine-bead-grain cloth, with a double-rule border within which is a curved-edge panel in black on the front covers, and in blind on the back covers. The spines, which are lettered in gilt, read: "[two black rules separated by a row of black dots] | WASHINGTON | SQUARE | H. JAMES Jr | VOL. I [II] | [circular publisher's device] | MACMILLAN AND Co. | [two black rules separated by a row of black dots]". The brasses used for "VOL. I" differ slightly from those used for "VOL. II", in that the letters "OL" in "VOL. I" slope slightly to the right (that is, they are in italic capitals). The initial "M" in "Macmillan" is slightly larger than the other capital letters in the imprint, and the "o" in "Co" is raised above a line. The endpapers are of white wove paper (probably not original), and the text is printed on wove paper. The top edge are untrimmed, and the other edges are trimmed. A 40-page paginated publisher's catalogue, dated December 1879, printed on a lighter wove paper, is bound in at the end of Volume II, the last page of which is blank except for the printer's imprint.

This is a copy of the first impression, with the misnumbering of pages 268, 269 and 271 of Volume II and the author's name "H. JAMES Jr" on the spines; see Sadleir 1295a.

English printing history: Macmillan Archive. MEB, 268, records that the two-volume first English edition was printed from standing type in January 1881 in an impression of 500 copies. It was published January 26, 1881, priced at 21s. A second impression was printed from the standing type in March 1881 in an impression of 250 copies. A one volume second English edition was printed from stereotype plates in August 1881 in an impression of 500 copies.[24] It was priced at 6s. A second impression was printed from these same plates in January 1889 in an impression of 2,000 copies (a yellowback). It was priced at 2s.; see MBC, 400. Macmillan destroyed these plates in March 1921.

Macmillan published a third edition of this title as part of *The Collective Edition of 1883*; see 20.1.0 and a fourth edition as Volume V of *The Novels and Stories of Henry James*; see 81.1.0–81.2,0. *Washington Square* was not included in *The Novels and Tales of Henry James* (The New York Edition), 64.1.0.

The sequence of the editions recorded in MEB in all probability masks the actual sequence of their production. Given that the same-size type is used in both editions, it is probable that the one volume second edition was the first set in type and that stereotype plates were made for printing the second edition. The type was then leaded out to fill the two volumes of the first edition, and the first edition

---

24 On the English publishing practice of publishing a cheaper second edition after the two or three-decker first edition, see Simon Eliot, "The Three-Decker Novel and its First Cheap Reprint, 1862–94", *The Library*, Sixth Series, Volume VII, (March 1985): 38–53, and Troy J. Bassett, "The Production of Three-volume Novels in Britain, 1863–97", *Papers of The Bibliographical Society of America*, Volume 102, (March 2008): 61–75.

was printed from this leaded out type. The second edition was then printed from the stereotype plates.

15.4.0. *Washington Square*, first English edition, second impression, binding state A, two volumes, London 1881.

The title-pages are identical to those of the first English edition, first impression, 15.3.0.

The size, collation and contents are identical to those 15.3.0, including the presence in Volume I of leaf $[T]_2$, except that the misnumbering of pages 268, 269, and 271 of Volume II has been corrected.

Binding: rust-brown sand-grain cloth, decorated in black on the front covers with a double-rule border within which is a curved-edge panel, with the same decoration in blind on the back covers. The spines, which are lettered in gilt, read: "[two black rules separated by a row of black dots]|WASHINGTON|SQUARE|[gilt rule]|HENRY [in italic]|JAMES, JUN [in italic]|Vol. I [II]|[circular publisher's device] |Macmillan & Co.|[two black rules separated by a row of black dots]". The initial "M" in "Macmillan" is slightly larger than the other capital letters in the imprint, and the "o" in "Co" is raised above a line. The endpapers are of pale yellow coated paper, and the text is printed on wove paper. All edges are untrimmed. No publisher's catalogue of ads is bound in at the back of Volume II (none called for).

Although the design of the binding on this second impression is very similar to that of the first impression, the curved-edge panel on the covers measures 6 3/8" x 3 5/8" as against 6 1/8" x 3 1/4" for the first impression, and the brasses used on the spines differ from those used on the first impression; see E&L Plate IV for a photograph of the spines of the two impressions. Both BAL and E&L regard this brown binding as the primary binding of the second impression of the first edition. For the possible secondary binding, see 15.4.5, below.

Illustrated Plate 7.

15.4.5. *Washington Square*, first English edition, second impression, binding state B, two volumes, London 1881.

The title-pages are identical to those of the first English edition, first impression, 15.3.0.

The size, collation and contents are identical to those of 15.3.0, including the presence in Volume I of leaf [T]$_2$, except that the misnumbering of pages 268, 269 and 271 of Volume II has been corrected.

Binding: dark blue-green fine bead-grain cloth, with a double-rule border within which is a curved-edge panel in black on the front covers and in blind on the back covers. The spines, which are lettered in gilt, read: "[two black rules separated by a row of black dots] | WASHINGTON | SQUARE | H. JAMES Jr. | VOL. I [II] | [circular publisher's device] | MACMILLAN & Co. | [two black rules separated by a row of black dots]". The brasses used on "VOL. I" and "VOL. II" on the spines are identical and the letters are upright, the initial "M" in MACMILLAN is slightly larger than the other capital letters, and the "o" in "Co" is raised above a line. The endpapers are of dark-brown coated paper, and the text is printed on wove paper. The top edge is untrimmed, and the other edges are trimmed. A 24-page paginated publisher's catalogue dated January 1881, printed on a lighter wove paper, is bound in at the end of Volume II.

The curved-edge panels on the covers of this state B of the second impression are 6 1/8" x 3 1/4", and are identical to the size of the panels on the first impression binding.

E&L A15b notes the existence of second impression sheets in a first impression binding, as this copy, and characterizes it as a "hybrid".

15.5.0. *Washington Square*, second English edition, one volume, London 1881.

WASHINGTON SQUARE | THE PENSION BEAUREPAS | A BUNDLE OF LETTERS | By HENRY JAMES, Jun. | LONDON | MACMILLAN AND CO. | 1881

Size: 7 1/2" x 4 15/16".

Collation: [A]^4 B–I K–U X–Z 2A–2C^8 [2D]^2; pp. [i–viii], [1]–401 [402] [403–404].

Contents: [i–ii] half-title, verso publisher's device; [iii–iv] title-page, verso blank; [v–vi] "NOTE" (5 lines), verso blank; [vii–viii] divisional fly-title, verso blank; [1]–401 text; 401 at the foot the printer's imprint: "Printed by R. & R. Clark, Edinburgh. [all but printer's name in italic]"; [402] blank; [403–404] blank leaf.

WASHINGTON SQUARE

Binding: dark blue-green fine-bead-grain cloth, lettered and decorated in gilt, black and in blind uniform with the second English edition of *The American* (1879), 4.17.0. No lettering is present on the front or back covers. The spine reads: "WASHINGTON | SQUARE | H. JAMES Jr. [all the foregoing in italic] | Macmillan & Co." The "o" in "Co" is raised above a line. The endpapers are of dark brown coated paper, and the text is printed on wove paper. All edges are untrimmed. A 24-page paginated publisher's catalogue, dated April 1881, printed on a lighter wove paper, is bound in at the end.

Noted but not described in E&L A15c.

15.6.0. *Washington Square*, first continental edition, first impression, two volumes, Leipzig 1881.

WASHINGTON SQUARE | THE | PENSION BEAUREPAS | A BUNDLE OF LETTERS | BY | HENRY JAMES, Jr. | AUTHORIZED EDITION. [in italic] | IN TWO VOLUMES. –VOL. I [II] | LEIPZIG | BERNHARD TAUCHNITZ | 1881.

Size: 6" x 4 3/8".

Collation: Volume I: $[1]^8$ $2-18^8$; pp. [1–8], [9]–287 [288]; Volume II: $[1]^8$ $2-18^8$; pp. [1–7], [8]–287 [288].

Contents: Volume I: [1–2] series half-title, verso ad headed "TAUCHNITZ EDITION. | By the same Author," listing 7 titles; [3–4] title-page, verso blank; [5–6] "NOTE.", verso blank [7–8] divisional fly-title, verso blank; [9]–287 text; [288] printer's imprint: "[long rule] | PRINTING OFFICE OF THE PUBLISHER. | [long rule]". Volume II: [1–2] series half title, verso blank; [3–4] title-page, verso blank; [5–6] divisional fly-title, verso blank; [7]–287 text; [288] printer's imprint as in Volume I [288].

Binding: rebound, two volumes bound in one volume in half cloth with red and black marble paper over boards. There is no lettering or decoration on the front and back covers. The spine, lettered in gilt, reads:"[two spaced rules] | JAMES | WASHINGTON | SQUARE | [three spaced rules]". The endpapers are of cream wove paper, and the text is printed on wove paper. All edges are trimmed and marbleized.

T&B 1977 records only one edition with a single impression of this title.

16. *THE PORTRAIT OF A LADY*

16.1.0. *The Portrait of a Lady*, first edition, first impression, three volumes, London 1881.

THE PORTRAIT OF A LADY | BY | HENRY JAMES, Jr., | AUTHOR OF "THE EUROPEANS," ETC., ETC. | IN THREE VOLUMES. [in italic] | VOL. I. [II] [III.] | London: [in Gothic type] | MACMILLAN AND CO. | 1881. | The Right of Translation and Reproduction is Reserved. [in italic, with a lower case initial "r" in "reserved" in Volume III]

The Volume II title-page lacks a period after both "IN THREE VOLUMES" and "VOL II".

Size: 7 1/2″ x 4 7/8″.

Collation: Volume I: [A]^2 B–I K–R^8 S^6; pp. [i–iv], [1]–266, [267–268]. Volume II: [A]^2 B–I K–Q^8 R^8 (–R$_8$) pp. [i–iv], [1]–253 [254]. Volume III: [A]^2 B–I K–Q^8 R^4; pp. [i–iv], [1]–248.

Contents: Volume I: [i–ii] half-title, verso publisher's device; [iii–iv] title-page, verso printer's imprint: "CLAY AND TAYLOR, PRINTERS, | BUNGAY, SUFFOLK."; [1]–266 text; [267–268] blank leaf. Volume II: [i–ii] half-title, verso publisher's device; [iii–iv] title-page, verso printer's imprint as on Volume I title-leaf verso; [1]–253 text; [254] printer's imprint as on Volume I title-leaf verso. Volume III: [i–ii] half-title, verso publisher's device; [iii–iv] title-page, verso printer's imprint as on Volume I title-leaf verso; [1]–248 text; 248 at the foot the printer's imprint: "[rule] | CLAY AND TAYLOR, PRINTERS, BUNGAY."

Binding: blue fine-bead-grain cloth, with a panel with curved corners within a double-rule border in black on the front covers, and in blind on the back covers. The spines, which are lettered in gilt, with a gilt publisher's device, read: "[in black, thin rule, row of dots, thick rule] | THE | PORTRAIT | OF A | LADY | H. JAMES Jr | VOL. I [II] [III] | [publisher's device] | MACMILLAN & Co. | [in black, thin rule, row of dots, thick rule]". The "o" in "Co" is raised above a line. The endpapers are of dark brown coated paper, and the text is printed on wove paper. The top edges are untrimmed, and the other edges are rough trimmed. A 24-page paginated publisher's catalogue, dated April, 1881, is bound in at the end of Volume III.

Both BAL and E&L record that the last signature of Vol. II of the first edition, first impression, of this title is R^8. However in this copy of the first edition, first impression, the last signature is $R^8(-R_8)$, the blank leaf being absent. In the second impression the last signature of Vol. II is R^8, the blank leaf is present; see 16.2.0.

See Appendix E: A Note on the Text of *The Portrait of a Lady*.

English printing history: Macmillan Archive. MEB, 266, records that the three-volume first English edition of *The Portrait of a Lady* was printed from standing type in two impressions: the *first impression*, printed in October 1881, was of 750 copies with the title-page dated 1881; and the *second impression*, printed in January 1882, was of 250 copies with the title-page dated 1882. The first impression was published on November 8, 1881, at 31s. 6d. A second English edition in one volume was printed in a single impression of 1,000 copies from stereotype plates in June 1882. It was priced at 6s. The plates were destroyed in February 1921. Macmillan published a third English edition as a part of *The Collective Edition of 1883*, 20.1.0, reprinted in 1886, 21.5.0, and a fourth English edition as volumes [V] and [VI] of *The Novels and Stories of Henry James*, 86.1.0–86.2.0.

16.2.0. *The Portrait of a Lady*, first edition, second impression, three volumes, London 1882.

THE PORTRAIT OF A LADY | BY | HENRY JAMES, Jr., | AUTHOR OF "THE EUROPEANS," ETC., ETC. | IN THREE VOLUMES. [in italic] | VOL. I. [II] [III.] | London: [in Gothic type] | MACMILLAN AND CO. | 1882. | The Right of Translation and reproduction is reserved. [in italic, with an upper case initial "R" in "Reserved" in Volume II only]".

Size: $7\,^7/_{16}$" x $4\,^7/_8$".

Collation: as in the first edition, first impression, 16.1.0, except that in this impression R_8 in Volume II, a blank leaf, is present.

Contents: as in 16.1.0, except that in this impression pages [255–256] in Volume II, a blank leaf, are present.

Binding: dark blue fine-bead-grain cloth, with a panel with curved corners within a double-rule border in black on the front covers and in blind on the back covers. The spines, which are lettered in gilt, with a gilt publisher's device, read: "[in black, thin rule, row of dots, thick rule] | THE | PORTRAIT | OF A | LADY | H. JAMES Jr | VOL. I [II] [III] | [publisher's device] | Macmillan & Co. | [in black, thin rule, row of dots, thick rule]". The "o" in "Co" is raised above a dot. The endpapers are of dark brown coated paper, and the text is printed on wove paper. The top edges are untrimmed, and the other edges are rough trimmed. A 24-page paginated publisher's catalogue, dated December 1881, is bound in at the end of Volume III.

Note no period appears after "VOL. II" on the Volume II title-page. Also, on that page the period after "IN THREE VOLUMES" is very faint.

BAL 10553 records: "A copy [of the first impression] has been reported (not seen by BAL) with catalogue dated *December, 1881*." It is possible that the copy so reported was of the second impression.

16.3.0. *The Portrait of a Lady*, first edition, second impression, sheets of the three volumes bound in one volume, London 1882.

THE PORTRAIT OF A LADY | BY | HENRY JAMES, Jr., | AUTHOR OF "THE EUROPEANS," ETC., ETC. | IN THREE VOLUMES. [in italic] | VOL. I. [II] [III.] | LONDON: [in Gothic type] | MACMILLAN AND CO. | 1882. | The Right of Translation and Reproduction is reserved. [in italic]".

Note that no period appears after "VOL. II" on the volume II title-page. Also on that page the period after "IN THREE VOLUMES" is very faint. The word "reserved" has a lower case "r" on the Volume I and III title-pages, and an upper case "R" on the Volume II title-page.

Size: $7\,3/16'' \times 4\,13/16''$.

Collation: Volume I sheets: $[A]^2$ B–I K–R^8 S^6 (–S$_6$); pp. [i–iv], [1]–266. Volume II sheets: $[A]^2$ B–I K–Q^8 R^8 (–R$_8$); pp. [i–iv], [1]–253 [254]. Volume III sheets: $[A]^2$ B–I K–Q^8 R^4; pp. [i–iv], [1]–248.

Contents: Volume I sheets: [i–ii] half-title, verso publisher's device; [iii–iv] title-page, verso printer's imprint: "CLAY AND TAYLOR, PRINTERS, | BUNGAY, SUFFOLK."; [1]–266 text. Volume II sheets: [i–ii] half-title, verso publisher's device; [iii–iv] title-page, verso printer's imprint as on verso of Volume I title-leaf; [1]–253 text; [254] printer's imprint as on verso of Volume I title-leaf. Volume III sheets: [i–ii] half-title, verso publisher's device; [iii–iv] title-page, verso printer's imprint as on verso of Volume I title-leaf; [1]–248 text; 248 at the foot the printer's imprint: "[rule] | CLAY AND TAYLOR, PRINTERS, BUNGAY."

Binding: bright red fine-diagonal-ribbed cloth. The front cover is lettered and decorated in black, with the title and author's name placed between wide decorative borders at the top and the bottom. The rear cover is decorated with a blind stamped border and a centered blind stamped decorative device. The spine is lettered in gilt, with the title within a rectangular gilt rule border, and with one plus three gilt rules at the head and three plus one gilt rules at the foot of the spine (the spine has neither the author's name nor the publisher's imprint). The endpapers are of pale yellow-coated paper, and the text is printed on wove paper. All edges are trimmed. No catalogue of ads is bound in at the end.

Illustrated Plate 8.

Noted but not described in E&L A16a. The rather anonymous type of binding on this copy, with the absence of the author's name and the publisher's imprint on the spine, would suggest that it is a remainder binding of the second impression.

16.4.0. *The Portrait of a Lady*, second edition, binding state A, one volume, London 1882.

THE | PORTRAIT OF A LADY | BY | HENRY JAMES, Jr. | A NEW EDITION. [in italic] | London: [in Gothic type] | MACMILLAN AND CO. | 1882. | The Right of Translation and Reproduction is Reserved [in italic]

Size: 7 ½" x 5".

Collation: [A]² B–I K–U X–Z AA–II KK⁸ LL⁶; pp. [i–iv], [1]–520 [521–524].

Contents: [i–ii] half-title, verso publisher's device; [iii–iv] title-page, verso printer's imprint: "LONDON: | R. Clay, Sons, and Taylor, | BREAD STREET HILL, E.C."; [1]–520 text; [521–524] ads.

The ads are headed: [521] "BY THE SAME AUTHOR.", listing 7 titles, [522 and 523]: "MACMILLAN'S POPULAR SIX–SHILLING NOVELS.", and [524]: "MACMILLAN & CO'S PUBLICATIONS."

Binding: dark green fine-bead-grain cloth, lettered and decorated in gilt, black and in blind uniform with the second English edition of *The American* (1879), 4.17.0. There is no lettering on the front or back covers. The spine reads: "THE | PORTRAIT | OF A | LADY | H. JAMES Jr. [all the foregoing in italic] | Macmillan & Co." The "o" in "Co" is raised above a dot. The endpapers are of dark brown coated paper, and the text is printed on thin wove paper. The top edge is untrimmed, and the other edges are rough trimmed. A 24-page paginated publisher's catalogue, dated May 1882, is bound in at the end.

16.4.1. *The Portrait of a Lady*, second edition, binding state B, one volume, London 1882.

Size: 7 $^{15}/_{16}$″ x 4 $^{7}/_{8}$″.

The title-page, collation, and contents (including the ads on [521–524]) are identical to those in the second edition, binding state A, 16.4.0.

Binding: dark green fine-bead-grain cloth, lettered and decorated in gilt, black and in blind uniform with the second English edition of *The American* (1879), 4.17.0. No lettering is present on the front or back covers. The spine reads: "THE | PORTRAIT | OF A | LADY | HENRY JAMES | MACMILLAN & Co." The "o" in "Co" is raised above a dot. The endpapers are of dark green coated paper, and the text is printed on thin wove paper. The top edge is untrimmed, and the other edges are trimmed. A 16-page unpaginated publisher's catalogue headed: "SUMMER SEASON, 1901 | EIGHT NEW & NOTABLE | SIX–SHIL-LING NOVELS" is bound in at the end.

This copy is a later binding up of first impression sheets. On this binding, and the binding on 16.4.0, see the note following 4.17.0.

16.5.0. *The Portrait of a Lady*, second edition, first American impression, binding state A, one volume, Boston and New York 1882. [1881].

THE | PORTRAIT OF A LADY. | BY | HENRY JAMES, JR. | [shield-shaped publisher's device] | BOSTON: | HOUGHTON, MIFFLIN AND COMPANY. | NEW YORK: 11 EAST SEVENTEENTH STREET. | The Riverside Press, Cambridge. [in Gothic type] | 1882.

The title-leaf of this copy is a separate leaf, [1¹]. The dimensions of the type on the title-page of this copy, from the top of "THE" to the bottom of "1882", is 5.956″. The verso of the title-leaf reads: "Copyright, 1881. | By HENRY JAMES, JR.", with a period after the date.

Size: 7 $^{3}/_{8}$″ x 3 $^{3}/_{4}$″.

Collation: [1¹ 2–22¹² 23⁸], signed as [A]¹ B–I K–U X–Z AA–II KK⁸ LL⁴; pp. [i–ii], [1]–520.

Contents: [i–ii] title-page, verso copyright notice: "Copyright, 1881. | By HENRY JAMES, JR."; [1]–520 text.

Binding: chocolate-brown diagonal-fine-ribbed cloth, lettered in red-brown, and decorated in chocolate-brown, red-brown, and gilt, on the front cover and spine. The gilt panel carrying the title on the front cover has a less pronounced maze-like background pattern than the copy of the first edition, first impression, binding state B, 16.8.0. The publisher's imprint at the foot of the spine reads: "Houghton Mifflin & Co.", and is on one line rather than the two lines on 16.8.0. The ampersand in the publisher's imprint has a flat rather than a rounded top. The endpapers are of brown coated paper, and the text is printed on wove paper. A binder's fly-leaf of wove paper is at both the front and the back. All edges are trimmed. It is stapled, not sewn.

On the title-page is the brown ink inscription: "L.E. Opdycke | 19 Nov. 1881. | '59 Kirkland Street'". On the recto of the rear binder's fly-leaf is the following commentary: "At a dinner 2 Mch. 1883 (at the St Botolph Club, Boston ?) I heard Mr. James say that Henrietta's "just you wait" [on page 520, line 9 of the text] was meant only to suggest that something might turn up favorable to Goodwood, if he were more patient. L.E.O. N.Y., 13 Oct. 1889." Pasted on the endpapers and binder's fly-leaves of this copy are clippings of several contemporaneous reviews.

For a discussion of James titles published by Houghton, Mifflin & Co. in bindings uniform with the binding on this copy, see 1.7.0.

It should be stressed that the contention of E&L A16b that the first impression is identifiable by a period after the copyright imprint on the title-page verso is incorrect. The first impression is identifiable from the fact that the title-leaf is a singleton and that the dimensions of the type on the title-page from the top of "THE" to the bottom of "1882" is 5.596″ (or roughly $5\,{}^{31}/_{32}$″); see footnote 25.

Illustrated Plate 9.

E&L A 16b designates this second edition of *The Portrait of a Lady* as the "American issue". Strictly speaking it is not an "issue" but a separate impression as it was printed in America from plates created in and exported from England. As Bowers at 408 points out, "issue can have no precise significance as a differentiating term unless it is applied within an impression." On the other hand if the sheets had been imported rather than the plates, then it would be appropriate to designate it as an "issue".

American printing history. Houghton Mifflin Archive. Second edition (and first American edition): Ms Am 2030(16), 130: *first impression* October 27, 1881, 1520 copies, all bound between November 15 and 23, 1881; notation "[no date, but possibly November 11] 18 sewn"; *second impression* November 22, 1881, 1012 copies, all bound between November 23 and December 12, 1881; *third impression* December 9, 1881, 1020 copies, 986 bound between December 12, 1881, and January 4, 1882. Ms Am 2030(17), 116: *fourth impression* January 24, 1882, 1005 copies, 996 bound between January 24, 1882, and February 9, 1882; *fifth impression* March 7, 1882, 1020 copies, 912 bound between March 7, 1882, and August 11, 1882; *sixth impression* August 26, 1882, 516 copies, 533 [sic] bound between September 4, 1882, and February 15, 1883; *seventh impression* February 24, 1883, 276 copies, all bound between February 28, 1883, and July 3, 1883; *eighth impression* July 24, 1883, 280 copies, 278 bound between July 30, 1883, and February 5, 1884; *ninth impression* April 14, 1884, 278 copies, all bound between April 25, 1884, and March 5, 1885; notation: "[April] 25 rebound 23"; *tenth impression* May 27, 1885, 156 copies, 162 [sic] bound between June 6, 1885, and February 22, 1886. Ms Am 2030(18), 136: *eleventh impression* May 13, 1886, 156 copies, 151 bound between May 24, 1886, and January 7, 1887; *twelfth impression* October 14, 1887, 158 copies, 154 bound between October 20, 1887, and January 30, 1889. Ms Am 2030(19), 153: *thirteenth impression* August 13, 1889, 158 copies, 153 bound on September 27, 1889, and April 21, 1890; *fourteenth impression* May 28, 1891, 160 copies, 137 bound between June 4, 1891, and March 17, 1893; *fifteenth impression* March 28, 1892, 160 copies, 174 [sic] bound between April 1, 1892, and March 17, 1893. Ms Am 2030(20), 173: sixteenth *impression* May 1, 1894, 274 copies, 269 bound between May 9, 1894, and January 23, 1896. Ms Am 2030(21), 221: *seventeenth impression* February 2, 1897, 270 copies, 256 bound between February 23, 1897, and November 9, 1897; *eighteenth impression* March 15, 1899, 274 copies, 267 bound between March 25, 1899, and July 8, 1900. Ms Am 2030(22), 218: *nineteenth impression* November 23, 1900, 266 copies, all bound between December 5, 1900, and October 28, 1902; *twentieth impression* January 14, 1903, 264 copies, all bound between January 19, 1903, and November 28, 1903; *twenty-first impression* June 22, 1904, 271 copies, 273 [sic] bound between July 1, 1904, and January 31, 1905; *twenty-second impression* April 12, 1905, 273 copies, 272 bound between April 15, 1905, and August 31, 1905; *twenty-third impression* December 28, 1905, 273 copies, 277 [sic] bound between January 4, 1906, and March 20, 1906; *twenty-fourth impression* October 16, 1906, 270 copies, 277 [sic] bound between October 24, 1906, and December 31, 1906; *twenty-fifth impression* April 22, 1907, 499 copies, 500 [sic] bound between April 27, 1907, and August 29, 1907; *twenty-sixth impression* May 14, 1908, 509 copies, all bound between May 20, 1908, and February 4, 1909; *twenty-seventh impression* April 21, 1909, 499 copies, 503 [sic] bound between May 6, 1909, and April 30, 1910. Ms Am 2030(23), 213: *twenty- eighth impression* June 25, 1910, 501 copies, all bound between July 8, 1910, and August 2, 1912; notation dated August 2, 1912, "¹/₂ levant and 1 spec"; *twenty-ninth impression* December 1, 1911, 517 copies, 518 [sic] bound between December 8, 1911, and May 4, 1913; *thirtieth impression* May 13, 1913, 520 copies, 505 bound between May 21, 1913, and December 4, 1913; *thirty-first impression* May 6, 1914, 525 copies, 514 bound between June 5, 1914, and May 17, 1915; *thirty-second* impression January 8, 1916, 526 copies, 518 bound between February 18, 1916, and January 4, 1917; notations: "plates melted Mar. 9, 1920" and total number of copies printed 14, 421.[25]

Priced at $2.00, which price was unchanged through 1905.

For the second American edition, see *The Novels and Tales of Henry James* (the New York Edition), 64.1.0.

On June 29, 1916, Ferris Greenslet of Houghton Mifflin wrote to Charles Scribner that "after thirty-five years' of constant use, our plates of ...'[The] Portrait of a Lady' have become so battered that we are forced to make an entirely new set. In view of this ... we are proposing to change the format of the book somewhat and issue it in two handsome library volumes", and requested permission "to use in the reprinting the revised text which was prepared for your subscription [The New York] edition." Scribner's gave its consent by letter dated July 5, 1916, but stipulated "that you do not make an advertising point of its use; and of course...you will not use the preface prepared for our edition." Then realizing it might be able to use the plates of the New York edition rather than create a new set, Houghton, Mifflin asked for permission to make a duplicate set of plates from those plates (which were in two volumes, and were stored at The Riverside Press). Permission to do so was granted, subject to a payment of $350.00, which, it was noted, was half of the cost Scribner's originally paid to Houghton, Mifflin for creating the plates. Houghton, Mifflin

---

25 For a detailed discussion of the first seven impressions of the American edition of *The Portrait of a Lady*, see David J. Supino and Richard S. Loomis, Jr., 'The True First Impression of the American Edition of The Portrait of a Lady', *The Book Collector*, Vol. 55, No. 1 (Spring 2006), pp. 29–46.

THE PORTRAIT OF A LADY

and Company Contracts, Houghton Archive, MS Am 2346(1151), 39.

Second American edition, two volumes, separate impressions printed from the plates of The New York Edition. Ms Am 2030(23), 212: *first impression* October 4, 1916, Vol. I 1028 and Vol. II 1044 copies, 1,000 bound between November 29, 1916, and April 20, 1917; notation: "10/24/16 pad. 1020 1–steel plate [and] 1179 tissues"; *second impression* January 12, 1918, Vol. I 527 and Vol. II 526 copies, 509 bound between February 13, 1918, and December 4, 1918; notation: "1/24/18 pad. 624 1 p. tissues [and] 510 1–steel plate"; *third impression* January 31 (for Vol. I) and February 2 (for Vol. II), 1919, Vol. I 534 and Vol. II 506 copies, 519 bound between April 1, 1919, and December 23, 1920; notation: "1/3/19 pad. 710 tissues [and] 525 1–steel plate"; *fourth impression* June 10, 1920, 1043 copies of both Volumes, 1008 bound between November 10, 1920, and [illegible], 1921; notation: "6/10/20 1269 tissues [and] 1020 1–steel plate"; *fifth impression* April 22, 1922, Vol. I 1050 and Vol. II 1057 copies, 1010 bound between June 5, 1922, and [illegible], 1923; notations: "3/16/22 1058 jackets, 4/22/22 1246 1–tissue [and] 1020 1–photo Vol I" and "[total copies] 4143". There is no mention in these entries of jackets being printed, except in connection with the 1922 printing; see 16.20.5 and 16.21.0.

16.6.0. *The Portrait of a Lady*, second edition, first American impression, binding state A, one volume, Boston and New York 1882. [1881].

This copy is identical to the second edition, first American impression, 16.5.0, except that it is bound in tan diagonal-fine-ribbed cloth, with lettering in red-brown and decoration in tan, red-brown, and gilt on the front cover and spine.

Illustrated Plate 9.

16.7.0. *The Portrait of a Lady*, second edition, first American impression, binding state A, one volume, Boston and New York 1882. [1881].

This copy is identical to the second edition, first American impression, 16.5.0, except that it is bound in pea-green diagonal-fine-ribbed cloth, with lettering in red-brown and decoration in pea-green, red-brown, and gilt on the front cover and spine.

On the recto of the rear free endpaper is the inscription: "[Illegible] H. Miller | Forrest-Glen | Maryland".

Illustrated Plate 9.

THE PORTRAIT OF A LADY

16.8.0. *The Portrait of a Lady*, second edition, first American impression, binding state B, one volume, Boston and New York 1882. [1881].

The title-page (including its type dimension and the period after the copyright date on the verso), the size, collation (including the fact that the title-page is a singleton, and the last signature is 23^8), and contents are identical to those of the preceding copies of the second edition, first American impression, binding state A, 16.5.0–16.7.0.

Binding: chocolate-brown diagonal-fine-ribbed cloth, lettered in red-brown, and decorated in chocolate-brown, red- brown, and gilt on the front cover and spine. The gilt panel carrying the title on the front cover has a more pronounced maze-like background pattern than that on the copies of the first American impression, binding state A, above. The publisher's imprint at the foot of the spine reads: "HOUGHTON | MIFFLIN [dot] & [dot] CO", and is on two lines rather than one on 16.5.0. The ampersand is like a figure "8", and is larger than the rest of the letters in the imprint. The endpapers are of olive-gray-green coated paper, and the text is printed on wove paper. A binder's fly-leaf of wove paper is at both the front and the back. All edges are trimmed. It is stapled, not sewn.

Illustrated Plate 9

It is unclear why E&L A16b characterizes dark-brown and grey-green bindings on this title as "secondary" binding states, and regards the tan and forest-green bindings as the only primary bindings. Dark brown or chocolate-brown bindings were used by Houghton, Mifflin (along with green and tan, with slight variations of shade) on this title and on subsequent editions and impressions of James titles continuously from 1881 until 1897, when Houghton, Mifflin changed its binding style on James bindings, starting with *The Spoils of Poynton* (1879). Differences in the shades of brown, green and tan can be accounted for by variations in bookcloth dye lots.

16.9.0. *The Portrait of a Lady*, second edition, second American impression, one volume, Boston and New York 1882 [1881].

THE | PORTRAIT OF A LADY. | BY | HENRY JAMES, JR. | [shield-shaped publisher's device] | BOSTON: | HOUGHTON, MIFFLIN AND COMPANY. | NEW YORK: 11 EAST SEVENTEENTH STREET. | The Riverside Press, Cambridge. [in Gothic type] | 1882.

The title-leaf, [1₁], is conjugate with leaf [1₁₂], and is not a singleton. The dimension of the type on the title-page of this copy, from the top of "THE" to the bottom of "1882", is 5.872″ or .084″ less than on the copies of the second edition, first American impression. The title-leaf verso reads: "Copyright, 1881. | By HENRY JAMES Jr." with a period after the year.

Size: 7 3/8‴″ x 4 3/4″.

Collation: [1–21¹² 22¹² (–22₁₁, ₁₂)], signed as [A]¹ B–I K–U X–Z AA–II KK⁸ LL⁵; pp. [i–ii], [1]–520 [521–522].

Contents: [i–ii] title-page, verso copyright notice: "Copyright 1881. | By HENRY JAMES, Jr."; [1]–520 text; [521–522] blank leaf.

Binding: pea-green diagonal-fine-ribbed cloth, lettered in pea-green, and decorated in pea-green, red-brown, and gilt on the front cover and spine identical to that on the preceding copies of the first American impression. The gilt panel carrying the title on the front cover has a very faint maze-like background pattern. The publisher's imprint at the foot of the spine reads: "Houghton Mifflin & Co." The ampersand has a flat rather than a rounded top. The endpapers are of brown coated paper, and the text is printed on wove paper. A binder's fly-leaf of wove paper is at both the front and the back. All edges are trimmed. It is stapled, not sewn.

This copy is inscribed in ink on the recto of the front binder's leaf: "H. J. Osgood | Dec. 14 | 1881." H. J. Osgood was a professor at Columbia University.

16.10.0. *The Portrait of a Lady*, second edition, second American impression, one volume, Boston and New York 1882 [1881].

The title-page, title-page type dimensions, size, collation, and contents are identical to the second edition, second American impression, 16.9.0, including the title leaf, [1₁], being conjugate with [1₁₂]. The title-leaf verso reads: "Copyright 1881. | By HENRY JAMES, JR.", with a period after the date.

Binding: tan diagonal-fine-ribbed cloth, lettered in red-brown, and decorated in tan, red-brown, and gilt on the front cover and the spine. The gilt panel carrying the title on the front cover has no discernible maze-like background pattern The publisher's imprint at the foot of the spine reads: "Houghton Mifflin & Co." The ampersand has a flat rather than a rounded top. The endpapers are of brown coated paper, and the text is printed on wove paper. A binder's fly-leaf of wove paper is at both the front and back. All edges are trimmed. It is stapled not sewn.

16.11.0. *The Portrait of a Lady*, second edition, second or third American impression, one volume, Boston and New York 1882 [1881].

The title-leaf, title-page type dimension, size, collation and contents of this copy are identical to those of the second edition, second American impression, 16.9.0, including the title-leaf, [1_1], being conjugate with [1_{12}]. However, the verso of the title-leaf reads: "Copyright 1881 | By HENRY JAMES, JR.", with no period after the year.

Binding: tan diagonal-fine-ribbed cloth, lettered in red-brown, and decorated in tan, red-brown, and gilt on the front cover and spine. The gilt panel carrying the title on the front cover has a pronounced maze-like background pattern. The publisher's imprint at the foot of the spine reads: "Houghton Mifflin & Co." The ampersand has a flat rather than a rounded top. The endpapers are of brown coated paper, and the text is printed on wove paper. A binder's fly-leaf of wove paper is at both the front and the back. All edges are trimmed. It is stapled, not sewn.

16.11.1. *The Portrait of a Lady*, second edition, second or third American impression, one volume, Boston and New York 1882 [1881].

The title-leaf, title-page type dimension, size, collation, and contents are identical to those of the second edition, second American impression, 16.9.0, including the title-leaf, [1_1], being conjugate with [1_{12}]. However, the title-leaf verso reads: "Copyright 1881 | By HENRY JAMES, JR.", with no period after the year.

Binding: chocolate-brown diagonal-fine-ribbed cloth, lettered in red-brown, and decorated in chocolate-brown, red-brown, and gilt on the front cover and spine. The gilt panel carrying the title on the front cover has a pronounced maze-like background pattern. The publisher's imprint at the foot of the spine reads: "Houghton Mifflin & Co." The ampersand has a flat rather than a rounded top. The endpapers are of brown coated paper, and the text is printed on wove paper. A binder's fly-leaf of wove paper is at both the front and the back. All edges are trimmed, the top edge is stained brown. It is stapled not sewn.

16.11.2. *The Portrait of a Lady*, second edition, second or third American impression, one volume, Boston and New York 1882 [1881].

The title-page, title-page type dimension, size, collation, and contents are identical to those of the second edition, second American impression, 16.9.0, including the title-leaf, [1_1], being conjugate with [1_{12}]. However, the title-leaf verso reads: "Copyright 1881 | By HENRY JAMES, JR.", with no period after the year.

Binding: pea-green diagonal-fine-ribbed cloth, lettered in red-brown, and decorated in pea-green, red-brown, and gilt on the front cover and spine. The gilt panel carrying the title on the front cover has a pronounced maze-like pattern The publisher's imprint at the foot of the spine reads: "Houghton Mifflin & Co." The ampersand has a flat rather than a rounded top. The endpapers are of brown coated paper, and the text is printed on wove paper. A binder's fly-leaf of wove paper is at both the front and the back. All edges are trimmed, the top edge is stained brown. It is stapled not sewn.

16.12.0. *The Portrait of a Lady*, second edition, fourth (?) American impression, one volume, Boston and New York 1882.

The title-page is identical to that on the second edition, second American impression, 16.9.0, except that the title-page type dimension is 5.901". The title-leaf verso reads: "Copyright, 1881 | By HENRY JAMES, JR.", with no period after the year.

Size: 7 3/8" x 4 3/4".

Collation: [1–21^{12} 22^{12} (–22$_{12}$)], signed as [A]^1 B–I K–U X–Z AA–II KK^8 LL^6; pp. [i–ii], [1]–520 [521–524].

Contents: [i–ii] title-page, verso copyright notice: "Copyright, 1881 | By HENRY JAMES, JR."; [1]–520 text; [521–524] two blank leaves.

Binding: tan diagonal-fine-ribbed cloth, lettered in red-brown, and decorated in tan, red-brown, and gilt on the front cover and spine. The gilt panel carrying the title on the front cover has a pronounced maze-like background pattern. The publisher's imprint at the foot of the spine reads: "Houghton Mifflin & Co." The ampersand has a flat rather than a rounded top. The endpapers are of a tan floral design on white coated paper, and the text is printed on wove paper. A binder's fly-leaf of wove paper is at the front, but none is at the back. All edges are trimmed, and it is sewn, not stapled.

16.12.1. *The Portrait of a Lady*, second edition, fourth (?) American impression, one volume, Boston and New York 1882.

The title-page is identical to that on the second edition, second American impression, 16.9.0, except that the title-page type dimension is 5.901". However, the title-leaf verso reads: "Copyright, 1881 | By HENRY JAMES, JR.", with no period after the year.

The size, collation, and contents are identical to those of second edition, fourth (?) impression, 16.12.0.

Binding: chocolate-brown diagonal-fine-ribbed cloth, lettered in red-brown, and decorated in chocolate-brown, red-brown, and gilt on the front cover and spine. The gilt panel carrying the title on the front cover has a pronounced maze-like background pattern. The publisher's imprint at the foot of the spine reads: "Houghton Mifflin & Co." The ampersand has a flat rather than a rounded top. The endpapers are of a tan floral design on white coated paper, and the text is printed on wove paper. A binder's fly-leaf of wove paper is at the front, but none at the back. All edges are trimmed. It is sewn, not stapled.

16.13.0. *The Portrait of a Lady*, second edition, fifth American impression, one volume, Boston and New York 1882.

THE | PORTRAIT OF A LADY. | BY | HENRY JAMES, JR. | [shield shaped publisher's device] | BOSTON: | HOUGHTON, MIFFLIN & COMPANY. | NEW YORK: 11 EAST SEVENTEENTH STREET. | The Riverside Press, Cambridge. [in Gothic type] | 1882.

The title-leaf, $[1_1]$, is conjugate with $[1_{12}]$, and is not a singleton. The dimension of the type on the title-page from the top of "THE" to the bottom of "1882" is 5.940". The verso of the title-leaf reads: "Copyright, 1881 | By HENRY JAMES, JR.", with no period after the year.

Size: 7 3/8" x 4 3/4".

Collation: $[1-22^{12}\ 23^6\ (-23_6)]$, signed as $[A^1]$ B–I K–U X–Z AA–II KK–LL^8 [MM]^4; pp. [i–ii], 1–520 [521–536].

THE PORTRAIT OF A LADY

Contents: [i–ii] title-page, verso copyright notice: "Copyright, 1881 | By HENRY JAMES, JR."; [1]–520 text; [521–536] ads paginates [1–3] 4–16. The ads on [1] are headed: "STANDARD AND POPULAR | Library Books [in Gothic type] | SELECTED FROM THE CATALOGUE OF [in italic] | HOUGHTON, MIFFLIN & CO." The ads are not an inserted publisher's catalogue, but consist of the last three leaves of signature [22] and the entire signature [23^6 (-23_6)]. On 4 of the ads under the series title "American Statesmen | Edited by John T. Morse, Jr." all 10 titles are listed under the heading "(In Preparation)", and none is listed as issued; on 10 under the author's name G. P. Lathrop only 1 title is listed; and on the same page under the author's name H. W. Longfellow the last title listed is *Translation of the Divina Commedia of Dante*. In the above respects these ads differ from those in the second edition, seventh American impression, 16.16.0.

Binding: dull olive-green linen-grain cloth, lettered in red-brown, and decorated in red-brown, olive-gree, and gilt on the front cover and spine. The gilt panel carrying the title on the front cover has a pronounced maze-like background pattern. The publisher's imprint at the foot of the spine reads: "Houghton Mifflin & Co." The ampersand has a flat rather than a rounded top. The endpapers are of a gray floral design on white coated paper, and the text is printed on wove paper. A binder's fly-leaf of wove paper is at both the front and the back. All edges are trimmed. It is sewn, not stapled.

On the front binder's fly-leaf is the inscription: "With Love | to Papa on his | 42 nd Birthday | July 21 st 1882". The fifth impression was printed on March 7, 1882 and the sixth on August 26, 1882.

Note that the cloth on this copy is linen-grain, not the diagonal fine-ribbed found on other copies.

16.13.1. *The Portrait of a Lady*, second edition, fifth American impression, one volume, Boston and New York 1882.

The title-leaf, title-page type dimension, size, collation, and contents (including the ads) are identical to those of the second edition, fifth American impression, 16.13.0.

Binding: tan diagonal fine-ribbed cloth, lettered in red-brown, and decorated in tan, red-brown, and gilt on the front cover and the spine. The gilt panel carrying the title on the front cover has a discernable maze-like background pattern. The publisher's imprint at the foot of the spine reads: "Houghton Mifflin & Co." The ampersand has a flat rather than a rounded top. The endpapers are of a gray floral design on white coated paper, and the text is printed on wove paper. A binder's fly-leaf of wove paper is at the front, but none at the back. All edges are trimmed, and the top edge is stained brown. It is sewn, not stapled.

On the first page of the text is the ink inscription "Mary E. Eaton | May 10th. 1882". On the back pastedown is a white bookseller's ticket printed in black reading: "ARTHUR S. ALLEN, | BOOKSELLER AND | STATIONER, | 454 Fulton Street, | Troy, N. Y."

16.13.2. *The Portrait of a Lady*, second edition, fifth American impression, one volume, Boston and New York 1882.

The title-leaf, title-page type dimension, size, collation, and contents (including the ads) are identical to those of the second edition, fifth American impression, 16.13.0.

Binding: chocolate-brown diagonal fine-ribbed cloth, lettered in red-brown, and decorated in tan, red-brown, and gilt on the front cover and the spine. The gilt panel carrying the title on the front cover has a discernable maze-like background pattern. The publisher's imprint at the foot of the spine reads: "Houghton Mifflin & Co." The ampersand has a flat rather than a rounded top. The endpapers are of a gray floral design on white coated paper, and the text is printed on wove paper. A binder's fly-leaf of wove paper is at the front, but none at the back. All edges are trimmed, and the top edge is stained ochre. It is sewn, not stapled.

On the binder's fly-leaf is the ink inscription "Jessie M. Brooks | June 1882 | Cincinnati".

16.14.0. *The Portrait of a Lady*, second edition, fifth or sixth (?) American impression, one volume, Boston and New York 1882.

THE | PORTRAIT OF A LADY. | BY | HENRY JAMES, JR. | [shield-shaped publisher's device] | BOSTON: | HOUGHTON, MIFFLIN AND COMPANY. | NEW YORK: 11 EAST SEVENTEENTH STREET. | The Riverside Press, Cambridge. [in Gothic type] | 1882.

The title-leaf, [1₁], is conjugate with [1₁₂], and is not a singleton. The dimension of the type on the title-page from the top of "THE" to the bottom of "1882" is 5.940″. The title-leaf verso reads: "Copyright 1881 | By HENRY JAMES Jr.", with no period after the year.

Size: 7 ¹³/₃₂″ x 4 ¾″.

Collation: [1–22¹² 23⁶ (–23₆)], signed as [A]¹ B–I K–U X–Z AA–II KK–LL⁸ [MM]⁴; pp. [i–ii], [1]–520 [521–536].

Contents: [i–ii] title-page, verso copyright notice: "Copyright, 1881 | By HENRY JAMES, JR."; [1]–520 text; [521–536] ads paginated [1–3] 4–16. These ads are not an inserted publisher's catalogue, but consist of the last three leaves of signature [22] and the entire signature [23⁶ (–23₆)]. These ads are identical to those in 16.13.0, and differ slightly from those in 16.16.0.

Binding: chocolate-brown diagonal-fine-ribbed cloth, lettered in chocolate-brown, and decorated in chocolate-brown, dark brown, and gilt on the front cover and spine. The gilt panel carrying the title on the front cover has a pronounced maze-like background pattern. The publisher's imprint at the foot of the spine reads: "Houghton Mifflin & Co." The ampersand has a flat rather than a rounded top. The endpapers are of a tan floral design on white-coated paper, and the text is printed on wove paper. A binder's fly-leaf of wove paper is at both the front and the back. All edges are trimmed. It is sewn, not stapled.

16.15.0. *The Portrait of a Lady*, second edition, fifth or sixth (?) American impression, one volume, Boston and New York 1882.

The title-page, size, collation, and contents (including the ads) are identical to those of the second edition, fifth or sixth American impression, 16.14.0, except that the title-page type dimension from the top of "THE" to the bottom of "1882" is 5.963″.

Binding: pea-green diagonal-fine-ribbed cloth, lettered in pea-green, and decorated in pea-green, red-brown, and gilt on the front cover and spine. The gilt panel carrying the title on the front cover has a pronounced maze-like background pattern. The publisher's imprint at the foot of the spine reads: "Houghton Mifflin & Co." The ampersand has a flat rather than a rounded top. The endpapers are of a tan floral design on white coated paper, and the text is printed on wove paper. A binder's fly-leaf of wove paper is at both the front and the back. All edges are trimmed. It is sewn, not stapled.

16.16.0. *The Portrait of a Lady*, second edition, seventh American impression, one volume, Boston and New York 1883.

The title-page is identical to that of the second edition, fifth or sixth American impression, 16.14.0, except that it is dated 1883 at the foot, and the title-page type dimension from the top of "THE" to the bottom of "1883" is 5.934″. The title-leaf verso reads: "Copyright, 1881 | By HENRY JAMES, Jr.", with no period after the year. The title-leaf, [1₁], is conjugate with [1₁₂], and is not a singleton.

The size, collation, and contents are identical to those of the second edition, fifth American impression, 16.13.0, except that the ads on 4 under the series title "American Statesmen | by John T. Morse, Jr." lists 3 titles as published and 8 titles as "(In Preparation)"; on 10 under the author's name "G. P. Lathrop" 2 titles are listed; and on the same page under the author's name "H. W. Longfellow" the last title listed is *Poets and Poetry of Europe*. Note these ads differ from those in 16.13.0–16.15.0.

Binding: chocolate-brown diagonal-fine-ribbed cloth, lettered in chocolate-brown, and decorated in chocolate-brown, red-brown, and gilt on the front cover and spine. The gilt panel carrying the title on the front cover has a pronounced maze-like background pattern. The publisher's imprint at the foot of the spine reads: "Houghton Mifflin Co." The ampersand has a flat rather than a rounded top. The endpapers are of a tan floral design on white coated paper, and the text is printed on wove paper. A binder's fly-leaf of wove paper is at both the front and the back. All edges are trimmed, and the top edge is stained light-brown. It is sewn, not stapled.

On the recto of the front binder's fly-leaf is the inscription: "Augusta D. Coolbaugh. | Wilkes-Barre, | Pa. | June 29, 1883."

16.16.1. *The Portrait of a Lady*, second edition, seventh American impression, one volume, Boston and New York 1883.

The title-page, size, collation, and contents (including the title-page type dimension and the ads) are identical to those of the second edition, seventh American impression, 16.16.0.

Binding: pea-green diagonal-fine-ribbed cloth, lettered in red-brown, and decorated in pea-green, red-brown, and gilt on the front cover and spine. The gilt panel carrying the title on the front cover has a pronounced maze-like background pattern. The publisher's imprint at the foot of the spine reads: "Houghton Mifflin & Co." The ampersand has a flat rather than a rounded top. The endpapers are of a tan floral design on white coated paper, and the text is printed on wove paper. A binder's fly-leaf of wove paper is at both the front and the back. All edges are trimmed, and the top edge is stained ocher. It is sewn, not stapled.

On the recto of the front binder's fly leaf is the inscription: "To | Mrs J. A. Hubbard | From her Husband | Jan 1883". The dating of this inscription is curious as the date of printing of the seventh impression is February 24, 1883; see printing history, 16.5.0.

16.16.5. *The Portrait of a Lady*, second edition, twelfth American impression, one volume, Boston and New York 1887.

The title-page is identical to that of the second edition, first American impression, 16.5.0, except that it has "TWELFTH EDITION." between the author's name and the publisher's device, is dated 1887 at the foot and the type dimension from the top of "THE" to the bottom of "1887" is 5.877". The title-leaf, $[1_1]$, is conjugate with $[1_{12}]$, and is not a singleton.

Size: 7 3/8" x 4 7/8".

Collation[1–22^{12} 23^6], signed as [A]² B–I K–U X–Z AA–FF⁸ [GG]⁸ HH- II KK–LL⁸ [MM]⁴; pp. [i–iv], [1]–520 [521–522] [523–534] [535–536].

Contents: [i–ii] blank, verso ad within a single-rule frame headed "MR. JAMES'S WRITINGS.", listing 8 titles with dollar prices, the last dated being this title; [iii–iv] title-page, verso copyright notice: "Copyright, 1881 | By HENRY JAMES JR."; [1]–520 text; [521–522] blank leaf; [523–534] ads, paginated [1] 2–12, headed on [523] "Works of Fiction [in Gothic type] | PUBLISHED BY | HOUGHTON, MIFFLIN AND COMPANY, | 4 Park St., Boston; 11 E. 17TH St., New York."; [535–536] blank leaf.

Binding: tan diagonal-fine ribbed cloth, lettered and decorated identically to the second edition, first American impression, binding state B, 16.8.0, including the publisher's imprint at the foot of the spine with the ampersand like a figure "8" that is larger than the other letters in the imprint. The gilt panel carrying the title on the front cover has a pronounced maze-like background pattern. The endpapers are of a tan floral design on white coated paper, and the text is printed on wove paper. A binder's fly-leaf of wove paper is at both the front and the back. All edges are trimmed, and the top edge is stained light brown. It is sewn, not stapled.

In this and all subsequent impressions from the second edition, American impression plates, signature mark GG is missing.

16.16.7. *The Portrait of a Lady*, second edition, eighteenth American impression, one volume, Boston and New York 1899.

THE | PORTRAIT OF A LADY. | BY | HENRY JAMES, JR. | NINE-TEENTH IMPRESSION. [sic] | [oblong publisher's device of a piper under a tree within a frame] | BOSTON: HOUGHTON, MIFFLIN AND COMPANY. | NEW YORK: 11 EAST SEVENTEENTH STREET. | The Riverside Press, Cambridge. | 1899

Size: 7 7/16" x 4 15/16".

Collation: [1–21^{12} 22^{10}], signed as [A]^2 B–I K–U X–Z AA–FF^8 [GG]^8 HH-II KK^8 LL^4; pp. [i–iv], [1]–520.

Contents: [i–ii] blank, verso ad within a single-rule frame headed "Henry James's Books. [in Gothic type]" listing 16 titles with dollar prices, the last dated being *The Spoils of Poynton*; [iii–iv] title-page, verso copyright notice: "Copyright, 1881 | By HENRY JAMES, JR."; [1]–520 text.

Binding: green vertical-rib grain cloth, lettered and decorated in gilt on the front cover and spine. The front cover has within a single-rule border an elaborate centered cartouche within which are the title and the author's name separated by an ornamental rule. The spine reads: "[rule] | THE PORTRAIT | OF A LADY | [ornamental rule] | HENRY JAMES | HOUGHTON | MIFFLIN & CO." The ampersand in the publisher's imprint is stylized. The back cover has a single-rule border on blind. The endpapers are of cream laid paper, and the text is printed on wove paper. A binder's fly-leaf of laid paper is at the front and of wove paper at the back. All edges are trimmed, and the top edge is stained light brown. It is sewn, not stapled.

On the front free endpaper is the inscription "C.K. Barry | 1901".

This impression was printed from second edition plates, with new prelims. There is evidence of wear to the plates throughout. Despite the fact that the title-page denominates it as the nineteenth impression, that impression was not printed until November 23, 1900. The eighteenth impression was printed on March 15, 1899; see printing history, 16.5.0.

This binding is uniform with that on the first American edition, first impression, of *The Spoils of Poynton* (1897), 48.6.0.

16.17.0. *The Portrait of a Lady*, second edition, twenty-third or later American impression, one volume, Boston and New York, [n.d., 1905 or later].

THE | PORTRAIT OF A LADY. | BY | HENRY JAMES, Jr. | [oblong publisher's device of a piper under a tree within a frame] | BOSTON AND NEW YORK | HOUGHTON MIFFLIN COMPANY | The Riverside Press Cambridge [in Gothic type]

Size: 7 3/8" x 4 7/8".

Collation: [1–21^{12} 22^{10}], signed as [A]^2 B–I K–U X–Z AA–FF^8 [GG]^8 HH-II KK^8 LL^4; pp. [i–iv], [1]–520.

Contents: [i–ii] blank, verso ad within a single-rule frame headed "By Henry James [in Gothic type]", listing 18 titles with dollar prices, the last dated being *English Hours*; [iii–iv] title-page, verso copyright notice and reservation of rights: "Copyright, 1881 | By HENRY JAMES, JR."; [1]–520 text.

Binding: green vertical-rib-grain cloth, lettered and decorated in gilt on the front cover and spine. The front cover has within a single-rule border an elaborate centered cartouche within which are the title and author's name separated by an ornamental rule. The spine reads: "[rule] | THE PORTRAIT | OF A LADY | [ornamental rule] | HENRY JAMES | HOUGHTON | MIFFLIN CO. | [rule]". The back cover has a single-rule border in blind. The endpapers are of cream laid paper, and the text is printed on wove paper. There are no binder's fly-leaves. All edges are trimmed, and the top edge is stained yellowish-green. It is sewn, not stapled.

This binding is uniform with that on the first American edition, first impression of *The Spoils of Poynton* (1897), 48.6.0. *English Hours* was published by Houghton, Mifflin in October 1905. The twenty-third impression was printed in December 1905; see American printing history, 16.5.0.

16.18.0. *The Portrait of a Lady*, second edition, twenty-third or later American impression, one volume, Boston and New York [n.d., 1905 or later].

The title-page, size, collation, and contents (including the ads on [ii]) are identical to those of the second edition, twenty-third or later American impression, 16.17.0.

Binding: brown vertical-rib-grain cloth, lettered and decorated on the front cover and spine, and decorated in blind on the back cover identically to 16.17.0. It has endpapers of cream wove paper, and the text is printed on wove paper. There are no binder's fly-leaves. All edges are trimmed and the top edge is stained light brown. It is sewn, not stapled.

This binding is uniform with that on the first American edition, first impression of *The Spoils of Poynton* (1897), 48.6.0.

16.19.0. *The Portrait of a Lady*, second edition, twenty-seventh or later American impression, one volume, Boston and New York [n.d., 1909 or later].

The title-page, size, and collation are identical to those of the second edition, twenty second or later American impression, 16.17.0.

The contents (including the ad on [ii]) are identical to those of 16.17.0, except that the title-leaf verso reads: "COPYRIGHT, 1881, BY HENRY JAMES, JR. | COPYRIGHT, 1909, BY HENRY JAMES | ALL RIGHTS RESERVED".

Binding: brown vertical-rib-grain cloth, lettered and decorated in gilt on the front cover and spine, and decorated in blind on the back, cover identically to 16.17.0. It has endpapers of cream wove paper, and the text is printed on wove paper. There are no binder's fly-leaves. All edges are trimmed, and the top edge is stained brown. It is sewn, not stapled.

This binding is uniform with that on the first American edition, first impression of *The Spoils of Poynton* (1897), 48.6.0.

16.20.0. *The Portrait of a Lady*, second edition, twenty-seventh or later American impression, one volume, Boston and New York [n.d., 1909 or later].

The title-page, size, and collation are identical to those of the second edition, twenty-third or later American impression, 16.17.0.

The contents are identical to those of 16.17.0, except that the ad on [ii] within a single-rule frame headed: "By Henry James [in Gothic type]", lists 17 rather than 18 James titles, omitting *The Author of Beltraffio* and *Watch and Ward*, and adding the last dated title *Italian Hours*. In addition, it differs from the ad on [ii] in 16.17.0 in that no dollar prices are given. The title-page verso copyright information is identical to that on 16.19.0.

Binding: green vertical-rib-grain cloth, lettered and decorated in gilt on the front cover and spine, and decorated in blind on the back cover, identically to 16.17.0. The endpapers are of white wove paper, and the text is printed on wove paper. There are no binder's fly-leaves. All edges are trimmed, and the top edge is stained ochre. It is sewn, not stapled.

On the front free endpaper is a small rectangular yellow label, framed and lettered in brown, which reads: "Book Shop | 319 Essex Street. | Salem".

This binding is uniform with that on the first American edition, first impression of *The Spoils of Poynton* (1897), 46.

16.20.5. *The Portrait of a Lady*, second American edition, first separate impression, two volumes, Boston and New York, 1916.

THE PORTRAIT | OF A LADY | BY | HENRY JAMES | VOLUME I [II] | [oval publisher's device of a piper under a tree] | BOSTON AND NEW YORK | HOUGHTON MIFFLIN COMPANY | The University Press Cambridge [in Gothic type] | 1916

Size: 7 ½" x 5".

Collation: Volume I: [unsigned, 1^8 (1_1+X_1) 2–26^8 27^{10}]; pp. [i–vi], 1–[428] [429–430] plus 2; frontispiece with printed tissue guard tipped in between [1_1] and [1_2] and not reckoned in the pagination; Volume II: [unsigned, 1–28^8]; pp. [i–vi], 1–[438][439–440][441–442].

Contents: Volume I: [i–ii] half-title, verso blank; frontispiece portrait of James, with facsimile signature, with printed tissue guard tipped in, and not reckoned in the pagination; [iii–iv] title-page, verso copyright notice and reservation of rights: "COPYRIGHT, 1881, BY HENRY JAMES, JR. | COPYRIGHT, 1909, BY HENRY JAMES | ALL RIGHTS RESERVED"; [v–vi] fly-title, verso blank; 1–428 text; [429–430] blank leaf. Volume II: [i–ii] half-title, verso blank; [iii–iv] title-page, verso copyright notice and reservation of rights as in Volume I title-leaf verso; [v–vi] fly-title, verso blank; 1–[438] text; [439–440] blank, verso printer's imprint: "The Riverside Press [in Gothic type] | CAMBRIDGE [dot] MASSACHUSETTS | U [dot] S [dot] A"; [441–442] blank leaf.

Binding: glazed smooth blue cloth, lettered and decorated in black and gilt. The front cover, within a black double-rule border within which is a gilt single-rule frame, is lettered and decorated in gilt, and reads: "[horizontal decorative device of rules, dots and flowers] | THE | PORTRAIT | OF A | LADY | [small four-cornered device] | HENRY [dot] JAMES | [horizontal decorative device of rules, dots and flowers]". The spine, which is lettered in gilt, and decorated in gilt with an oblong frame within which are five decorative ovals in each of which is a stem of flowers, reads: "THE | PORTRAIT | OF A | LADY | [small decorative device] | HENRY | JAMES". The back cover is neither lettered nor decorated. The endpapers are of white wove paper, and the text is printed on wove paper. There are no binder's fly-leaves in either volume. The top edge is gilt, and the other edges are untrimmed.

This copy was printed from the plates of Volumes III and IV of *The Novels and Tales of Henry James* (The New York Edition), 64.1.0 (which is the first impression of the second American edition) but without James's Preface. On the control of these plates, see 3.16.0 and Appendix G; also see American printing history following 16.5.0

For bindings uniform with this binding see 1.11.0.

16.21.0. *The Portrait of a Lady*, second American edition, fourth or fifth separate impression, two volumes, Boston and New York [n.d., probably 1920 or 1922].

THE PORTRAIT | OF A LADY | BY | HENRY JAMES | VOLUME I [II] | [oval publisher's device of a piper under a tree] | BOSTON AND NEW YORK | HOUGHTON MIFFLIN COMPANY | The Riverside Press Cambridge [in Gothic type].

Size: $7\,7/16''$ x $5''$.

Collation: Volume I: [unsigned, 1^{16} (1_1+X_1) $2-13^{16}$ 14^{10}]; pp. [i–vi], 1–[428] [429–430] plus 2. Volume II: [unsigned, $1-13^{16}$ 14^{14}]; pp. [i–vi], 1–[438].

Contents: Volume I: [i–ii] I half-title, verso blank; frontispiece portrait of James with facsimile signature and over-printed tissue guard tipped in, and not reckoned in the pagination; [iii–iv] title-page, verso copyright notice and reservation of rights: "COPYRIGHT, 1881, BY HENRY JAMES JR. | COPYRIGHT, 1909, BY HENRY JAMES | ALL RIGHTS RESERVED"; [v–vi] fly-title, verso blank; 1–[428] text, [429–430] blank leaf. Volume II: [i–ii] half-title, verso blank; [iii–iv] title-page, verso copyright notice and reservation of rights as on Volume I title-leaf verso; [v–vi] fly-title, verso blank; 1–[438] text.

Binding: dark blue vertical-rib-grain cloth. The front covers are lettered with Henry James's facsimile signature in gilt. The back covers are neither lettered nor decorated. The spines, which are lettered and decorated in gilt, read: "[two rules] | THE | POR- | TRAIT | OF A | LADY | [one star [two stars] on Volume I [II]] | HENRY | JAMES | HOUGHTON | MIFFLIN CO. | [two rules]". The endpapers are of white wove paper, and the text is printed on wove paper. There are no binder's fly-leaves in either volume. The top and bottom edges are trimmed, and the fore-edges are rough trimmed.

Dust-jackets: beige wove paper, lettered and decorated in green. The front covers and spines replicate the front covers and spines of the books, except that on the spines between the author's name and the publisher's imprint there is "VOLUME | ONE [TWO]" instead of one or two stars. The back covers each have within a double-rule border an identical ad that reads: "NOVELS BY | HENRY JAMES | Issued in Uniform Style [in italic] | [rule] | What Maisie Knew The Finer Grain | The Wings of the Dove, 2 vols. The Outcry | The Better Sort The Ivory Tower | The Golden Bowl, 2 vols. The Sense of the Past | The Sacred Fount | Per Volume, $2.50 [in italic] | Published by CHARLES SCRIBNER'S SONS | The Portrait of a Lady, 2 vols. The American | Roderick Hudson The Europeans | A Passionate Pilgrim, and The Siege of London | Other Tales The Spoils of Poynton | The Tragic Muse, 2 vols. | Published by HOUGHTON MIFFLIN COMPANY | The Awkward Age Daisy Miller | The Ambassadors An International Episode | Washington Square | Published by HARPER & BROTHERS". The front inner flaps have the price "$2.50". The front and back inner flaps are blank.

Tipped into Volume I is a press cutting that reads as follows: "The publishers of separate volumes of Henry James' immortal works have decided to issue the James novels in uniform bindings. Anyone who has tried lately to get a complete set of James from the three publishers who do him – Harpers, Scribner's and Houghton Mifflin

– has found himself the possessor of volumes of variegated shapes and colors, and never the possessor of all of them. Some were always out of print. Everything is now to be in print and to look alike." The clipping is dated in pencil "10-6-23".

See also *Daisy Miller: A Study*, 8.15.0, and *The Tragic Muse* 34.7.5 for similar bindings.

❦

17. *THE POINT OF VIEW*

No copy in the collection.

E&L records that only one copy is known to be extant. BAL 10557 records that the printer was instructed by Macmillan to print six proof copies.

❦

18. *DAISY MILLER: A COMEDY*

18.1.0. *Daisy Miller: A Comedy*, first published edition, first impression, first binding state, one volume, Boston 1883.

HENRY JAMES | [rule] | DAISY MILLER | A Comedy [in Gothic type] | IN THREE ACTS [in italic] | [publisher's device] | BOSTON | JAMES R. OSGOOD AND COMPANY [in sans-serif] | [rule] | 1883

Size: $7\,^{5}/_{16}"$ x $4\,^{3}/_{4}"$.

Collation: $[1-16^6]$, signed as $[1]^9\ 2-11^8\ 12^7$; pp. [i–ii] [1–6], [7]–189 [190].

Contents: [i–ii] half-title, verso blank; [1–2] blank, verso within a single-rule frame ad headed: "By the Same Author. [in italic]" listing 1 title, *The Siege of London*, with press opinions [3–4] title-page, verso copyright notice, reservation of rights and printer's imprint: "Copyright, 1883, [in italic] | By Houghton, Mifflin and Company, | and | James R. Osgood and Company. | [rule] | All rights reserved. [in italic] | Cambridge: [in Gothic type] | PRINTED BY JOHN WILSON AND SON, | UNIVERSITY PRESS."; [5–6] "Dramatis Personae. [in Gothic type]", verso blank; [7]–189 text; 189 at foot printer's imprint: "[rule] | Cambridge: University Press, John Wilson & Son."; [190] blank.

DAISY MILLER: A COMEDY

Binding: dark blue diagonal-fine-ribbed cloth. The front and back covers are decorated in blind with a single-rule frame within a wider single-rule rule border. The spine, which is lettered and decorated in gilt, reads: "Daisy | Miller | a | Comedy | [rule] | Henry James | [J. R. Osgood monogram]". The endpapers are of white laid paper, and the text is printed on laid paper. The chain lines of the paper run horizontally across the printed page. There are no binder's fly-leaves. All edges are trimmed.

BAL records six cloth colors for the first binding state of this impression: blue, blue-green, brown, green, purple and red. E&L records one additional color, rose, but does not record a copy in green other than blue-green. It may be that the copy that E&L records as rose is merely a faded copy of the red cloth, which it records as wine, and that the copy that both record as purple or purple-brown may be the red copy which is purple-red.

This is the first appearance of the elaborate "JRO" monogram on the spine of a James title. The monogram was designed for Osgood in 1869 by Mary ("Kate") Field (1838–1896) for use on his personal stationery.

It is curious that the verso of the title-leaf reads: "Copyright, 1883, | By Houghton, Mifflin and Company, | and | James R. Osgood and Company. | [rule] | All rights reserved." It is possible that Houghton, Mifflin's interest in the copyright arose from the fact that the first published appearance of this play was in the *Atlantic Monthly*, April–June 1883. The *Atlantic Monthly* had been acquired by Hurd & Houghton (Houghton, Mifflin's predecessor) from Osgood in December 1873. James had offered the publication of the play in book form to Houghton, Mifflin but they declined the offer, at which point James "transferred the opportunity" to Osgood.

Printing history. Houghton Mifflin Archive. First edition: Ms Am 2030.3(9), 9 and Ms Am 2030.3(14), 70: *first* [and sole Osgood] *impression* August 17, 1883, 1016 copies, 768 bound between August 21 and 24, 1883, and a further 130 bound [by Ticknor & Co.] on March 30, 1888; notation "binding of only 50 paid for". Ms Am 2030(19), 157: "rcvd from T[icknor] & Co. 4/11/89 90 copies", 88 bound between December 3, 1889, and March 7, 1891; [*second* [and first Houghton, Mifflin] *impression*, but not specified] March 14, 1892, 160 copies, 138 bound between March 26, 1892, and February 1, 1893. Ms Am 2030(20), 174: [*third impression*, but not specified] May 29, 1893, 158 copies, 156 bound between June 3, 1893, and February 15, 1894; [*fourth impression*, but not specified] May 9, 1894, 276 copies, 269 bound between May 16, 1894, and November 13, 1895; Ms Am 2030(21), 221: [*fifth impression*, but not specified] April 18, 1896, 276 copies, all bound between April 25, 1896, and May 14, 1898; [*sixth impression*, but not specified] September 6, 1899, 274 copies, 271 bound between December 8, 1899, and July 29, 1902. Ms Am 2030(22), 219 [*seventh impression*, but not specified] November 21, 1904, 158 copies, all bound on January 16, 1905, and January 17, 1906; [*eighth impression*, but not specified] January 28, 1907, 157 copies, 155 bound between February 14, 1907, and March 25, 1908; [*ninth impression*, but not specified] February 1, 1909, 161 copies, 155 bound between March 31, 1909, and December 2, 1913; [*tenth impression*, but not specified] January 30, 1912, 286 copies, 285 bound between February 7, 1912, and December 26, 1917; [*eleventh impression*, but not specified] April 21, 1916, 278 copies, all bound between May 2, 1916, and April 20, 1917; notation: "18/8/17 275 jackets". Ms Am 2030(23), 213: [*twelfth impression*, but not specified] July 17, 1919, 282 copies, 275 bound between February 2 and August 5, 1920; notations: "7/18/19 ptd. 308 jackets" and "2/23/22 To be dropped when stock is exhausted – see Mr. Scaife". "[in a different hand] I questioned this matter but got no different reply." Mr. Scaife was Roger Livingstone Scaife who was Houghton, Mifflin's production manager.

Priced at $1.50, reduced to $1.25 in 1905.

This title was not published in England. However, Macmillan & Co. printed in England two small impressions of this title for James, clearly labeled "Not Published", in June (6 copies) and July (12 copies), 1882. Although they were possibly printed for English copyright purposes, this seems unlikely as there is no record of their deposit in the Copyright Offices or the British Museum (now the British Library); see BAL 10556. Also, see letter of James to Isabel Gardner dated June 5, 1882, in Rosella Mamoli Zorzi (Ed.), *Henry James Letters to Isabel Stewart Gardner* (London, Pushkin Press, 2009), Letters XVI, XXI and XXII.

18.2.0. *Daisy Miller: A Comedy*, first published edition, first impression, first binding state, one volume, Boston 1883.

This copy is identical to the first published edition, first impression, first binding state, 18.1.0, except that it is bound in purple-red diagonal-fine-ribbed cloth. The endpapers are of white laid paper,

DAISY MILLER: A COMEDY

and the text is printed on laid paper. The chain lines of the paper run horizontally across the printed page. There are no binder's fly-leaves. All edges are trimmed.

18.3.0. *Daisy Miller: A Comedy*, first published edition, first impression, first binding state, one volume, Boston 1883.

This copy is identical to the first published edition, first impression, first binding state, 18.1.0, except that it is bound in dark brown diagonal-fine-ribbed cloth. The endpapers are of white laid paper, and the text is printed on laid paper. The chain lines of the paper run horizontally across the printed page. There are no binder's fly-leaves. All edges are trimmed.

18.4.0. *Daisy Miller: A Comedy*, first published edition, first impression, first binding state, one volume, Boston 1883.

This copy is identical to the first published edition, first impression, first binding state, 18.1.0, except that it is bound in forest-green diagonal-fine-ribbed cloth. The endpapers are of white laid paper, and the text is printed on laid paper. The chain lines of the paper run horizontally across the printed page. There are no binder's fly-leaves. All edges are trimmed.

This cloth color is not noted in E&L.

This copy is from the library of George Godfrey (1840–1897), who was a partner of Ticknor & Co. from 1885 (when it bought out the second Osgood firm) until 1889, when Ticknor & Co. was acquired by Houghton, Mifflin.

18.5.0. *Daisy Miller: A Comedy*, first published edition, first impression, third binding state, one volume, Boston 1883.

Size: 7 3/8″ x 4 3/4″.

The title-page, collation, and contents are identical to those of the first published edition, first impression, first binding state, 18.1.0.

Binding: olive-green smooth cloth. The front and back covers are neither lettered nor decorated. The spine, which is lettered and decorated in gilt, reads: "Daisy | Miller | a | Comedy | [rule] | Henry James. | HOUGHTON | MIFFLIN [dot] & [dot] CO". The ampersand is like a figure "8". The endpapers are of white laid paper, and the text is printed on laid paper. The chain lines of the paper run horizontally across the printed page. A binder's fly-leaf of wove paper is at both the front and the back. All edges are trimmed.

This binding of first edition, first impression, sheets is uniform with (but not the same size as) the binding of the first published edition, second (?) impression, 18.6.0.

On the front free endpaper is the inscription: "Edward [illegible] | Dec. '92."

Houghton, Mifflin acquired first edition, first impression sheets of this title when it acquired the assets of Ticknor & Company in April 1889 (Ticknor having previously acquired these same sheets from James R. Osgood & Co. in 1885). One hundred and thirty copies of the first edition, first impression sheets were bound with the Ticknor & Company monogram at the foot of the spine on March 30, 1888. A photograph of such a copy has been examined, bound in brown cloth the spine reading: "Daisy | Miller | A | Comedy | [rule] | Henry James [the "J" is a drop-cap] | TCO [intertwined Ticknor & Co. monogram]". This would indicate that copies of the first edition, first impression, sheets bound with the Houghton, Mifflin imprint on the spine, as this copy, are of the third binding state. These were bound between December 1889 and March 1891. This title was first reprinted by Houghton, Mifflin in March 1892; see 18.6.0.

18.6.0. *Daisy Miller: A Comedy*, first published edition, second impression, one volume, Boston 1892.

HENRY JAMES | [rule] | DAISY MILLER | A Comedy [in Gothic type] | IN THREE ACTS [in italic] | [publisher's device of a piper under a tree within a frame] | BOSTON AND NEW YORK | HOUGHTON, MIFFLIN AND COMPANY | The Riverside Press, Cambridge [in Gothic type] | 1892.

Size: $6\,^{29}/_{32}$" x $4\,^{9}/_{16}$".

Collation: $[1]^8$ $2-12^8$; pp. [1–6], [7]–189 [190] [191–192].

Contents: [1–2] half-title, verso blank; [3–4] title-page, verso copyright notice, reservation of rights and printer's imprint: "Copyright, 1883, | By Houghton, Mifflin and Company, | and | James R. Osgood and

Company. | [rule] | All rights reserved. [in italic] | The Riverside Press, Cambridge, Mass., U [sic] S.A. [in italic] | Printed by H. O. Houghton & Company."; [5–6] "Dramatis Personae [in Gothic type]", verso blank; [7]–189 text; 189 no printer's imprint; [190] blank; [191–192] blank leaf.

Binding: olive-green smooth cloth. The front and back covers are neither lettered nor decorated. The spine, which is lettered and decorated in gilt, reads: "DAISY | MILLER | A | COMEDY | [rule] | Henry James | HOUGHTON | MIFFLIN [dot] & [dot] CO." The ampersand is like a figure "8". The spine lettering is slightly too wide for the width of the spine. The endpapers are of white laid paper, and the text is printed on wove paper. A binder's fly-leaf of wove paper is at the front, but none at the back. All edges are trimmed.

On the front pastedown is an Andover Public Library label which reads: "Andover Public Library | From the J.P. Whitney Fund | March first 1893 | Shelf 898 Accession No. 574". An Andover Public Library label is on the front free endpaper.

18.7.0. *Daisy Miller*: A Comedy, first published edition, fourth impression, one volume, Boston and New York 1894.

The title-page is identical to that of the first published edition, second impression, 18.6.0, except that it is dated 1894 at the foot.

The size, collation and contents are identical to those of 18.6.0.

Binding: olive-green smooth cloth. The front and back covers are neither lettered nor decorated. The spine, which is lettered and decorated in gilt, is identical to the spine of 18.6.0, except that the publisher's imprint at the foot reads: "HOUGHTON | MIFFLIN & CO". The ampersand is stylized, not like a figure "8", but like a Greek π. The endpapers are of white laid paper, and the text is printed on wove paper. A binder's fly-leaf of wove paper is at the front, but none at the back. All edges are trimmed.

18.8.0. *Daisy Miller: A Comedy*, first published edition, sixth or seventh impression, one volume Boston and New York [n.d., 1899 or 1904].

The title-page is identical to that of the first published edition, second impression, 18.6.0, except that there is no date at the foot.

Size: $7\,1/8''$ x $4\,3/4''$.

DAISY MILLER: A COMEDY

Collation: [1–12⁸], signed as [1]⁹ 2–11⁸ 12⁷; pp. [i–ii] [1–6], [7]–189 [190].

Contents: [i–ii] blank, verso ad within a single-rule frame headed: "Henry James [in Gothic type]", listing 16 titles with dollar prices, the last dated being *The Spoils of Poynton*; [1–2] half-title, verso blank; [3–4] title-page, verso copyright notice, reservation of rights and printer's imprint as on [4] in 18.6.0; [5–6] "Dramatis Personae [in Gothic type]", verso blank; [7]–189 text; 189 no printer's imprint; [190] blank.

Binding: brown vertical-rib-grain cloth, lettered and decorated in gilt on the front cover and spine. The front cover has within a single-rule border an elaborate centered cartouche within which is the title and author's name separated by an ornamental rule. The spine which is lettered and decorated in gilt, reads: "[rule] | DAISY | MILLER | [ornamental rule] | HENRY JAMES | HOUGHTON | MIFFLIN & CO. | [rule]". The ampersand at the foot of the spine is not stylized. The back cover has a single-rule border in blind. The endpapers are of white laid paper, and the text is printed on wove paper. A binder's fly-leaf of smooth wove paper is at both the front and the back. The top edge is trimmed, the fore-edge is untrimmed, and the bottom edge is rough trimmed.

This binding is uniform with that on the first American edition of *The Spoils of Poynton* (1897), 48.6.0. The ad on [2], listing *The Spoils of Poynton*, suggests that this impression was printed in 1899 or 1904, but probably prior to 1905.

18.9.0. *Daisy Miller: A Comedy*, first published edition, impression later than the seventh, one volume, Boston [n.d., 1907 or later].

The title-page is identical to that of the first published edition, second impression, 18.6.0, except that there is no comma between "The Riverside Press" and "Cambridge", and there is no date at the foot.

Size: 7 1/8" x 4 5/8".

Collation: [1–12⁸], signed as [1]⁹ 2–11⁸ 12⁷; pp. [i–ii] [1–6], [7]–189 [190].

Contents: [i–ii] blank, verso ad within a single-rule frame headed: "By Henry James [in Gothic type]", listing 18 titles with dollar prices, the last dated being *The Question of Our Speech*, and *English Hours*; [1–2] half-title, verso blank; [3–4] title-page, verso copyright notice and reservation of rights: "Copyright, 1883, [in italic] | By Houghton, Mifflin and

Company, | and | James R. Osgood and Company. | [rule] | All rights reserved. [in italic]"; [5–6] "Dramatis Personae" [in Gothic type], verso blank; [7]–189 text; 189 no printer's imprint; [190] blank.

Binding: brown vertical-rib-grain cloth, lettered and decorated in gilt on the front cover and spine. The front cover has within a single-rule border an elaborate centered cartouche within which is the title and author's name separated by an ornamental rule. The spine, which is lettered and decorated in gilt, reads: "[rule] | DAISY | MILLER | [ornamental rule] | HENRY JAMES | HOUGHTON | MIFFLIN CO. | [rule]". The title and author's name on the spine are too wide for the width of the spine. The back cover has a single-rule border in blind. The endpapers are of white wove paper, and the text is printed on wove paper. There are no binder's fly-leaves. The top edge is trimmed and stained brown, the fore-edge is trimmed, and the bottom edge is untrimmed.

This binding is uniform with that on the first American edition of *The Spoils of Poynton* (1897), 48.6.0. The ad on [ii], listing *The Question of Our Speech* (1905) suggests that this impression was printed in 1907 or later, but probably prior to 1909.

18.10.0. *Daisy Miller: A Comedy*, first published edition, tenth (?) impression, one volume, Boston [n.d., 1912?].

The title-page is identical to that of the first published edition, second impression 18.6.0, except that at the foot there is no comma between "The Riverside Press" and "Cambridge", and there is no date at the foot.

The size and collation are identical to those of the first published edition, impression later than the seventh, 18.9.0.

The contents are identical to those of 18.9.0 including the ad on [ii], except that the title-page verso reads: "COPYRIGHT, 1883, BY HOUGHTON, MIFFLIN AND COMPANY | AND JAMES R. OSGOOD AND COMPANY | COPYRIGHT, 1911, BY HENRY JAMES | ALL RIGHTS RESERVED".

Binding: olive-green vertical-rib-grain cloth lettered and decorated on the front cover and spine in gilt, and decorated in blind on the back cover, identically to 18.9.0. The endpapers are of white wove paper, and the text is printed on wove paper. There are no binder's fly-leaves. All edges are trimmed, and the top edge is stained ochre.

The tenth impression was printed on January 30, 1912, and the eleventh on April 21, 1916.

18.11.0. *Daisy Miller: A Comedy*, first published edition, eleventh or twelfth impression, one volume, Boston [n.d., 1916 or 1919].

The title-page is identical to that of the first published edition, second impression, 18.6.0, except there is no comma between "The Riverside Press" and "Cambridge", and there is no date at the foot.

Size: 7 7/16" x 5".

The collation and contents are identical to those of the first published edition, impression later than the seventh, 18.9.0, except that the ad on [ii] lists 17 titles, the last dated being *Italian Hours* (1909), and omits dollar prices.

Lines 4, 5, 7 and 8 on 127 show damaged type. The damaged type suggests that it is not a reissue of the sheets of an earlier impression.

Binding: glazed smooth blue cloth, lettered and decorated in black and gilt. The front cover, within a black double-rule border, within which is a black single-rule frame, is lettered and decorated in gilt and reads: "[horizontal decorative device of rules, dots and flowers] | DAISY | MILLER | [small four-cornered device] | HENRY [dot] JAMES | [horizontal decorative device of rules, dots and flowers]". The spine, which is lettered in gilt and decorated with an elaborate floral strapwork device in gilt, reads: "DAISY | MILLER | [small decorative device] | HENRY | JAMES". The back cover is neither lettered nor decorated. The endpapers are of white wove paper, and the text is printed on wove paper. There are no binder's fly leaves. The top edge is gilt, and the other edges are untrimmed.

For bindings uniform with this binding see 1.11.0.

19. *THE SIEGE OF LONDON*

19.1.0. *The Siege of London*, first edition, first impression, one volume, Boston 1883.

THE SIEGE OF LONDON, | THE PENSION BEAUREPAS, | AND | THE POINT OF VIEW. | BY | HENRY JAMES, Jr. | AUTHOR OF "DAISY MILLER," "THE AMERICAN," | "THE PORTRAIT OF A LADY," ETC. | [publisher's device of J. R. Osgood] | BOSTON: | JAMES R. OSGOOD AND COMPANY. | 1883.

Size: 7 3/8" x 4 13/16".

Collation: $[1-25^6]$, signed as $[1]^{15}$ $2-12^{12}$ 13^3; pp. [2] [i–iv] [1–2], [3]–294.

Contents: blank leaf; [i–ii] title-page, verso copyright notice, reservation of rights and printer's imprint: "Copyright, [in italic] | 1879, by Houghton, Osgood, & Co.; | 1882, by The Century Company and H. James, Jr. | [rule] | All rights reserved. [in italic] | University Press: | John Wilson and Son, Cambridge."; [iii–iv] "CONTENTS.", verso blank; [1–2] divisional fly-title, verso blank; [3]–294 text.

Binding: light chocolate-brown diagonal-fine-ribbed cloth. The front and back covers are decorated in blind with a single-rule frame within a thicker single-rule border. The spine, which is lettered and decorated in gilt, reads: "The | Siege | of | London | Etc. | [rule] | Henry James Jr. | [J. R. Osgood monogram]". The endpapers are of white laid paper, and the text is printed on wove paper. There are no binder's fly-leaves. All edges are trimmed.

On the front free endpaper is the inscription: "M. B. Burt | June 1884"

American printing history. Houghton Mifflin Archive. First edition: Ms Am 2030.3(8), 253 and Ms Am 2030.3(14), 70: *first* [Osgood] *impression* January 19, 1883, 1528 copies, 1520 bound between January 29 and February 27, 1883; *second impression* March 12, 1883, 1038 copies, 698 bound between March 16, 1883, and March 30, 1885; Ms Am 2030(19), 157: notation: "rcvd from T[icknor] & Co. 4/11/89 300 copies",[26] 340 [*sic*]

---

[26] Probably 340 copies, not 300, were received by Houghton, Mifflin from Ticknor & Co., since the 1038 copies of the second impression only 698 were bound by Osgood (500 copies on March 16, 1883, 100 on March 4, 1884, and 98 copies on March 30, 1885). No copies were bound by Ticknor & Co., which acquired these

THE SEIGE OF LONDON

bound between April 26, 1890, and December 5, 1895 [this is not a separate impression]. Ms Am 2030(22) 219: [*third* [and first Houghton, Mifflin] *impression*, but not specified] February 4, 1901, 146 copies, 144 bound between February 26, 1901, and October 14, 1906; [*fourth impression*, but not specified] March 4, 1908, 153 copies, 146 bound between March 30, 1908, and November 9, 1916; [*fifth impression*, but not specified] August 2, 1919, 285 copies, 276 bound between August 4, 1920, and October 25, 1923.

Priced at $1.50, which price was increased to $2.00 in 1919.

The title was not published in England, but the title story in this collection was published in England along with another story, "Madame de Mauves", as part of *The Collective Edition of 1883*; see 20.1.0 – 20.5.0.

19.2.0. *The Siege of London*, first edition, first impression, one volume, Boston 1883.

This copy is identical to the first edition, first impression, 19.1.0, except that it is bound in olive-green diagonal-fine-ribbed cloth.

E&L describes this binding, one of four primary binding colors recorded, as green without noting the shade.

19.3.0. *The Siege of London*, first edition, first impression, one volume, Boston 1883.

This copy is identical to the first edition, first impression, 19.1.0, except that it is bound in royal-blue diagonal-fine-ribbed cloth.

This cloth color is not noted in E&L. BAL 10558 does record copies in blue S (diagonal-fine-ribbed) cloth.

19.4.0. *The Siege of London*, first edition, first impression, one volume, Boston 1883.

This copy is identical to the first edition, first impression, 19.1.0, except that it is bound in forest-green diagonal-fine-ribbed cloth.

---

sheets from Osgood in May 1885, and which in turn Houghton, Mifflin acquired from Ticknor & Co. in April 1899.

19.5.0. *The Siege of London*, first edition, first impression, one volume, Boston 1883.

This copy is identical to the first edition, first impression, 19.1.0, except that it is bound in terra-cotta sand-grain cloth.

E&L records a terra-cotta binding in diagonal-fine-ribbed cloth, but not sand-grain as on this copy. BAL 10558 records a copy in terra-cotta C (sand-grain) cloth.

19.6.0. *The Siege of London*, first edition, first impression, one volume, Boston 1883.

This copy is identical to the first edition, first impression, 19.1.0, except that it is bound in dark purple (plum) diagonal-fine-ribbed cloth.

On the title-page is the inscription "C. K. Griffin | 208 East 15th St-".

E&L A19a records a copy in dark purple-brown, and BAL 10558 records a copy in mottled purple.

19.7.0. *The Siege of London*, first edition, first impression, one volume, Boston 1883.

This copy is identical to the first edition, first impression, 19.1.0, except that it is bound in dark brown diagonal-fine-ribbed cloth.

19.8.0. *The Siege of London*, first edition, second impression, first binding state, one volume, Boston 1883.

The title-page, size, collation, and contents are identical to those of the first edition, first impression, 19.1.0, except that the title-page has printed on it between the publisher's monogram and the publisher's imprint "SECOND EDITION."

Binding: dark brown diagonal-fine-ribbed cloth, decorated in blind on the front and back covers, and lettered in gilt on the spine, identically to 19.1.0, including the J. R. Osgood monogram in gilt at the foot of the spine. The endpapers are of white wove paper, and the text is printed on wove paper. There are no binder's fly-leaves. All edges are trimmed.

As the title-page type dimension of this copy (from the top of the title to the bottom of the date) is 5.334" and that of the first edition, first impression is 5.215″, this title-page is not an overprinted copy of the first edition, first impression title-page.

19.9.0. *The Siege of London*, first edition, second impression, first binding state, one volume, Boston 1883.

This copy is identical to first edition, second impression, 19.8.0, except that it is bound in light chocolate-brown diagonal-fine-ribbed cloth.

On the front free endpaper is a small pink bookseller's ticket that reads: "W. B. CLARK & CARRUTH, | Booksellers, | BOSTON, MASS. [all within a thin single-rule frame]" On the recto of the initial blank leaf is the inscription: "Harry Bruce Scott - | Christmas 1883 -".

The second binding state (a Houghton, Miffling binding) was of the 300 [340?] second impression sheets that Houghton, Mifflin acquired from Ticknor & Co. in April 1889. The Houghton, Mifflin records do not indicate that any copies of the second impression were bound by Ticknor & Co.

19.10.0. *The Siege of London*, first edition, third impression, one volume, Boston and New York [n.d., 1901].

THE SIEGE OF LONDON, | THE PENSION BEAUREPAS, | AND | THE POINT OF VIEW. | BY | HENRY JAMES, Jr. | AUTHOR OF "DAISY MILLER," "THE AMERICAN," | "THE PORTRAIT OF A LADY," ETC. | [publisher's device of a piper under a tree within a frame] | BOSTON AND NEW YORK | HOUGHTON, MIFFLIN AND COMPANY | The Riverside Press, Cambridge [in Gothic type]

Size: $7\,7/16''$ x $4\,15/16''$.

Collation: $[1-25^6]$, signed as $[1]^{14}$ $2-12^{12}$ 13^4; pp. [i–iv] [1–2], [3]–294 [295–296].

Contents: [i–ii] title-page, verso copyright notice, reservation of rights and printing history: "Copyright, [in italic] | 1879, by Houghton, Osgood, & Co.; | 1882, by The Century Company and H. James, Jr. | [rule] | All rights reserved. [in italic] | THIRD IMPRESSION"; [iii–iv] "CONTENTS.", verso blank; [1–2] divisional fly-title, verso blank; [3]–294 text; [295–296] blank, verso printer's imprint: "The Riverside Press [in Gothic type] | PRINTED BY H. O. HOUGHTON & CO. | CAMBRIDGE, MASS. | U.S.A."

Binding: brown vertical-rib-grain cloth, with lettering and decoration in gilt on the front cover and spine. The front cover has within a single-rule border an elaborate centered cartouche within which is the title and author's name separated by a decorative rule. The spine reads: "[rule] | THE SIEGE OF | LONDON ETC. | [decorative rule] | HENRY JAMES | HOUGHTON | MIFFLIN & CO. | [rule]". The ampersand in the publisher's imprint is stylized. The back cover has a single-rule border in blind. The endpapers are of white laid paper, and the text is printed on wove paper. A binder's fly-leaf of white coated paper is at the front, but none is at the back. The top edge is trimmed and stained light brown, and the other edges are rough trimmed.

This binding is uniform with that on the first American edition, first impression, of *The Spoils of Poynton* (1897), 48.6.0, on which it first appeared.

19.11.0. *The Siege of London*, first edition, third impression, one volume, Boston and New York [n.d., 1901].

The title-page, size, collation, and contents are identical to those of the first edition, third impression, 19.10.0.

Binding: olive-green vertical-rib-grain cloth, lettered and decorated identically to 19.10.0. The endpapers are of white laid paper, and the text is printed on wove paper. A binder's fly-leaf of wove paper (not coated) is at the front, but none is at the back. The top edge is trimmed and stained light brown, and the other edges are rough trimmed.

19.12.0. *The Siege of London*, first edition, fifth impression, one volume, Boston and New York [n.d., 1919].

The title-page is identical to that of the first edition, third impression, 19.10.0.

Size: $7\,^{7}/_{16}''$ x $5''$.

Collation: [1–18^8 19^6], signed as [1]^{14} 2–12^{12} 13^4; pp. [i–iv] [1–2], [3]–294 [295–296].

Contents: [i–ii] title-page, verso copyright notice, reservation of rights and printing history: "COPYRIGHT, 1882 AND 1910, BY HENRY JAMES, JR. | COPYRIGHT, 1882 and 1910, BY THE CENTURY COMPANY | ALL RIGHTS RESERVED | FOURTH IMPRESSION [*sic*]";

THE SEIGE OF LONDON

[iii–iv] "CONTENTS.", verso blank; [1–2] divisional fly-title, verso blank; [3]–294 text; [295] blank; [296] printer's imprint: "The Riverside Press [in Gothic type] | CAMBRIDGE . MASSACHUSETTS | U . S . A [sic]".

Binding: glazed smooth blue cloth lettered in gilt, and decorated in black and gilt. The front cover, within a black double-rule border within which is a black single-rule frame, reads: "[horizontal decorative device of rules, dots and flowers] | THE SIEGE OF | LONDON ETC. | [small four-cornered device] | HENRY [dot] JAMES | [horizontal decorative device of rules, dots and flowers]". The spine, which is lettered in gilt, and decorated in gilt within an oblong frame within which are five decorative ovals in each of which is a stem of flowers, reads: "THE | SIEGE OF | LONDON | ETC. | [small decorative device] | HENRY | JAMES". The back cover is neither lettered nor decorated. The endpapers are of white wove paper, and the text is printed on wove paper. There are no binder's fly-leaves. The top and fore-edges are trimmed, and the bottom edge is untrimmed.

Dust-jacket: tan wove paper, lettered and decorated in green. The front has an elaborate centered cartouche within which is the title and author's name separated by a decorative rule. The spine reads: "THE SIEGE OF | LONDON ETC. | [decorative rule] | HENRY JAMES | [rectangular publisher's device] | $2.00 net [in italic] | HOUGHTON | MIFFLIN CO." The back cover has within a single-rule border an ad for 11 James titles under the heading: "Novels and Stories", and 5 further James titles under the heading: "Travel".

This impression was printed from the first edition plates, with a new title-leaf, changes on [ii] to reflect more recent copyright information and printing history, as well as the addition of the printer's imprint on [296]. Although denominated the fourth impression, which was printed on March 4, 1908, it is clearly not given the copyright date 1910 on [ii]. The only printing after 1908 was the fifth impression in August 1919.

For bindings uniform with this binding see 1.11.0.

The dust-jacket, while probably not "married" to this book (given the pristine condition of the binding), is curious because its front cover and spine are lettered and decorated identically (except for the publisher's device and price on the spine) to the front cover and spine of the first edition, third impression, of this title, 19.10.0.

THE SEIGE OF LONDON

19.13.0 *The Siege of London*, first continental edition, first impression, one volume, Leipzig 1884.

THE SIEGE OF LONDON; | THE POINT OF VIEW; | A PASSIONATE PILGRIM. | BY | HENRY JAMES, | AUTHOR OF "DAISY MILLER," "THE AMERICAN," ETC. | AUTHORIZED EDITION [in italic] | LEIPZIG | BERNHARD TAUCHNITZ | 1884.

Size: 6 3/16" x 4 7/16".

Collation: [1]⁸ 2–18⁸ 19⁴; pp. [1–10], [11]–294 [295–296].

Contents: [1–2] series half-title, verso ad headed: "TAUCHNITZ EDITION. | By the same Author," listing 11 titles, the last dated being *French Poets and Novelists*; [3–4] title-page, verso blank; [5–6] authorization notice signed by James, verso "NOTE" reading: "It is proper to state that the last of the three tales | contained in this volume, a story originally published | in Boston in 1872, has been, in matters of language, | much altered and amended for reproduction here. | H.J. | December 1883."; [7–8] "CONTENTS.", verso blank; [9–10] divisional fly-title, verso blank; [11]–294 text; [295] printer's imprint centered: "[rule] | PRINTING OFFICE OF THE PUBLISHER. | [rule]"; [296] blank.

Binding: rebound in red diagonal-grain quarter cloth with marbled paper over boards, with no lettering or decoration on the front or back covers. The spine has a small brown leather label, lettered and decorated in gilt, that reads: "[double rule] | H. James | [rule] | THE SIEGE | OF LONDON | [double rule]". Beneath the label is a floral ornament and at the foot "1884 | [double rule]". The endpapers are of white wove paper, and the text is printed on wove paper. All edges are trimmed and speckled brown. There is no catalogue of ads at the end.

T&B 2234, records one edition with one impression of this title

20. THE COLLECTIVE EDITION OF 1883

The Collective Edition of 1883
An Overview

The project for a collected edition of Henry James's fictional works, that became known as *The Collective Edition of 1883*[27] (but was referred to in MBC, 438, as *The Novels and Tales by Henry James*, and in Macmillan ads as the "Popular Editions"), was suggested to James by Frederick Macmillan in April 1883; see Moore, Letter 96. It was designed to be an attractive and inexpensive collection of six of his novels (*Watch and Ward* was excluded), and four volumes of his tales, in all comprising 14 volumes. The tales included were determined by James (see Moore, Letter 98), some of which James revised for this edition. All of the titles in this edition were completely reset, and were not re-impressions of prior editions.

The first impression of *The Collective Edition* was published in uniform bindings on November 13, 1883. All 14 volumes were issued both in blue smooth cloth, lettered and decorated in gilt, (20.1.0), which is regarded as the primary binding, and in paper wrappers, lettered and decorated in red (20.2.0). Two secondary bindings of the first impression, slightly smaller in size, were also issued: one in salmon smooth cloth, (20.3.0), and the other in light-green cloth, (20.4.0), both in flexible boards, lettered and decorated in red-brown; see illustration Plate 10. The 14 volumes were sold separately, but they were also sold as a boxed set at 21s.; see 20.4.5, Moore, Letter 108, and MEB, 265. E&L record that variant bindings were also issued in ochre and cream cloth. No such copies have been seen.

The title-pages of the first impression are all dated 1883, and the volumes (except for the three multi-volume titles: *The Portrait of a Lady*, three volumes, *Roderick Hudson*, two volumes, and *The American*, two volumes) were not numbered or otherwise identified as being part of a set. This was probably a conscious decision by Macmillan to facilitate their sale as individual titles. MBC list the titles in the following order: [1–3] *The Portrait of a Lady*; [4–5] *Roderick Hudson*; [6–7] *The American*; [8] *Washington Square*; [9] *The Europeans*; [10] *Daisy Miller*;

---

27 This title was given to this edition by E&L. James, in correspondence, occasionally referred to the New York edition of his *Novels and Tales* (64.1.0) as a "collective" edition.

THE COLLECTIVE EDITION OF 1883

[11] *An International Episode*; [12] *The Siege of London*; [13] *The Madonna of the Future*; and, [14] *Confidence*.

Within the first impression (primary binding) there are variations in the publisher's imprints on the spines as well as the presence of ads at the end. This is probably a consequence of batch binding of the sheets. MCB, 438 records two pages of ads at the end of all of the volumes except: Volume I of *The Portrait of a Lady*, *The America* (two volumes), *Washington Square* (one volume), and *The Madonna of the Future* (one volume). The ads, when present, are all identical.

Printing history: Macmillan Archive. MEB, at 265, records that the sheets of the first impression of the 14 volumes of *The Novels and Tales of Henry James* were printed from electrotype plates, were received by Macmillan in November 1883, and were published on November 13 of that same year. Also recorded are that the titles were sold in sets at 21s. and separately at "1/6d [in cloth] & 1/ [in paper] per vol., [and increased to] 2/ each in 1888". The electrotype plates of this edition were destroyed in March 1921.

The number of copies of the first impression printed is recorded as 5,000, but no mention of the number of copies of the second impression published in 1886 (referred to in MBC) was found in MEB. However, the number of copies of the first impression recorded is in conflict with the notation in the same entry of the reams of paper used to print each title. In the case of *Washington Square*, for example, 6 ½ reams of "D Pott 8vo" were used to print that title, which has (including prelims) 208 pages, or 104 leaves, which calculates out at a mere 500 copies.[28]

---

28 I am indebted to Nicolas Barker for this calculation, which is as follows: "Double Pott produces 32pp 8vo. 32 x 6 ½ = 208 pages. 500 sheets to the ream, so 500 copies printed." The recorded amount of paper used for the other volumes conforms to this calculation. However, it is not out of the realm of possibility that there were other "hidden" printings indistinguishable from the 1883 first impression. It should be recalled that the first impression of *The Collective Edition* was published in four different bindings: blue, salmon-coloured, light-green and lastly paper wrappers; it seems unlikely that 500 sets of sheets were spread out over the four bindings, especially in view of the fact that the blue bindings are the most commonly seen today. Also, the edition was printed from electrotype plates, rather than stereos. Electros were favoured over stereos, because they wore out less rapidly, which would imply that large print runs were anticipated. Finally, it should be noted that there is no record of the 1886 "second" impression in the MEB; it is, however, recorded in MBC, which does not record print runs, such information being, undoubtedly, a "trade" secret.

THE COLLECTIVE EDITION OF 1883

A second impression of *The Collective Edition of 1883* was published in 1886 and 1887, the titles being issued at intervals. All the title-pages of this impression are dated 1886, except *Daisy Miller*, which is dated 1887. All are bound in blue smooth cloth, lettered and decorated in gilt identically to the first impression. There are variations in the presence of ads (which ads are identical to the first impression ads) at the end, and also variations in the publisher's imprint at the foot of the spines. Again, this was probably the result of batch binding. No variant bindings of this impression have been seen, but the ads in the second impression state that it was also issued in paper wrappers, priced at 1s. per volume. No copies of the wrapped second impression have been found.

Both the impressions in smooth blue cloth, as well as the first impression, wrappered binding are sewn, not stapled. The two secondary bindings of the first impression are stapled, not sewn. BAL 10757 records that the sheets of the primary binding occur either stapled or sewn, but the copies here catalogued indicate that the primary and wrappered binding states are sewn and the secondary binding states are stapled. No stapled copies of the primary binding have been seen.

The first Catalogue (1905) of the Times Book Club lists for sale to subscribers 6 James titles, which were undoubtedly copies of these titles in *The Collective Edition of 1883*. These 6 titles are *The American* (2 volumes), *The Europeans*, *An International Episode*, *The Portrait of a Lady* (3 volumes) and *The Siege of London*. All are advertised as having a publisher's retail price of 2s. per volume. Clearly the only multi-volume edition of both *The American* and *The Portrait of a Lady* with such a low retail price is the *Collective Edition*. Similarly the only single-volume titles with such a low price are from that same edition. Also listed is *The Madonna of the Future* with a publisher's price of 2s. This may be either from *The Collective Edition of 1883* or sheets of the yellow-back (10.5.0).

In entries 20.1.0 to 20.5.0 a full description is given of *The Portrait of a Lady*, and summary descriptions of the 11 other volumes (to the extent in the collection) in the order recorded in MBC; however, in the case of the wrappered binding of the first impression, as only one title (*Confidence*) is in the collection, it, instead of *The Portrait of a Lady*, is fully described

* * *

THE COLLECTIVE EDITION OF 1883

20.1.0. *The Collective Edition of 1883*, first collective edition, first impression, primary binding state, 14 volumes, London 1883.

The Portrait of a Lady, three volumes.

THE | PORTRAIT OF A LADY | BY | HENRY JAMES | IN THREE VOLUMES | VOL. I. [II.] [III.] | London [in Gothic type] | MACMILLAN AND CO. | 1883

Size: 6 5/16″ x 4 1/8″.

Collation: Volume I: [A]² B–I K–Q⁸; pp.[i–iv], [1]–239 [240]. Volume II: [A]² B–I K–P⁸ Q⁴; pp. [i–iv], [1]–229 [230] [231–232]. Volume III: [A]² B–I K–P⁸ [Q]²; pp. [i–iv], [1]–225 [226] [227–228].

Contents: Volume I: [i–ii] half-title, verso publisher's device; [iii–iv] title-page, verso printer's imprint: "Printed by R. & R. Clark, Edinburgh. [all except printer's name in italic]"; [1]–239 text; 239 at foot printer's imprint as on Volume I title-leaf verso; [240] blank. Volume II: [i–ii] half-title, verso publisher's device; [iii–iv] title-page, verso printer's imprint as on Volume I title-leaf verso; [1]–229 text; [230] blank; [231–232] ads. Volume III: [i–ii] half-title, verso publisher's device; [iii–iv] title-page, verso printer's imprint as on Volume I title-leaf verso; [1]–225 text; 225 at foot printer's imprint as on Volume I title-leaf verso; [226] blank; [227–228] ads.

The ads, [227–228], on the recto list the 14 volumes comprising *The Collective Edition* under the heading: "WORKS BY | HENRY JAMES | In 18mo, Paper covers 1s. each volume. | Cloth binding 1s. 6d. each volume. [all after author's name in italic]". On the verso under the heading : "Now Publishing in Crown 8vo, Price 2s. 6d. each, [in italic] | English Men of Letters. [in Gothic type] | Edited by JOHN MORLEY.", listing 33 titles in this series in two columns.

Binding: royal-blue smooth cloth. The front covers are decorated with two gilt single-rule borders, the outer thicker than the inner, and the back covers are similarly decorated in blind. The spines which are lettered and decorated in gilt, read: "[thick rule followed by thin rule] | THE | PORTRAIT | OF A | LADY | HENRY | JAMES | Vol. I [II] [III] | MACMILLAN | [thin followed by a thick rule]". The publisher's imprints on the spines are in uniform capitals 1/8″ high. The endpapers are of white wove paper, and the texts are printed on wove paper. All edges are untrimmed. They are sewn, not stapled.

THE COLLECTIVE EDITION OF 1883

This title was also published in an identical binding (except for the spine imprint), without ads at the end of Volumes II and III, Q_4 in Volume II and Q_2 in Volume III having being excised.

On this copy the publisher's imprints on the spines read "MAC-MILLAN" in uniform capitals $5/32''$ high.

The remaining eleven volumes are uniformly bound and decorated. The title-page of each volume is dated 1883. The endpapers are of white wove paper, and the texts are printed on wove paper. All edges are untrimmed. They are sewn, not stapled.

They are:

> *Roderick Hudson*, two volumes. Collation: Volume I: [A]² B–I K–O⁸; pp. [i–iv], [1]–206 [207–208]. Volume II: [A]² B–I K–N⁸ O²; pp. [i–iv], [1]–193 [194] [195–196]. The last leaf of both signature O in Volume I and signature O in Volume II are identical ads, which are the same ads as appear at the end of Volumes II and III of the primary binding of this impression of *The Portrait of a Lady*, above. The publisher's imprint on the spine reads: "MACMIL-LAN" in uniform capitals a scant $1/8''$ high.
>
> This title also issued in an identical binding, but without ads at the end of both volumes, O_4 in Volume I and O_2 in Volume II having been excised.
>
> *The American*, two volumes. Collation: Volume I: [A]² B–I K–N⁸ O⁶; pp. [i–iv], [1]–203 [204]. Volume II: [A]² B–I K–O⁸; pp. [i–iv], [1]–208. There are no ads present in either volume. The publisher's imprint on the spines reads: "MACMILLAN" in uniform capitals $5/32''$ high.
>
> *Washington Square*, one volume. Collation: [A]² B–I K–N⁸ O⁶; pp. [i–iv], [1]–204. There are no ads present. The publisher's imprint on the spine reads: "MACMILLAN" in uniform capitals $1/8''$ high.
>
> *The Europeans*, one volume. Collation: [A]² B–I K–N⁸; pp. [i–iv], [1]–190 [191–192]. On the last leaf of signature N are the same ads as appear at the end of Volumes II and III of the primary binding of this impression of *The Portrait of a Lady*. The publisher's imprint on the spine reads: "MACMILLAN & Co.", with all the letters except the "o" being in uniform capitals $3/16''$ high.

THE COLLECTIVE EDITION OF 1883

Also issued in an identical binding (except for the publisher's imprint on the spine), but without ads at the end, N_8 having been excised. On that copy the publisher's imprint on the spine reads: "MACMILLAN" in uniform capitals $1/8''$ high.

Daisy Miller, one volume. Collation: [A]^4 B–I K–N^8 O^4 O2^2(–O2$_2$); pp. [2] [i–vi] [1–2], [3]–202. There are no ads present. The publisher's imprint on the spine reads: "MACMILLAN" in uniform capitals $5/32''$ high.

An International Episode, one volume. Collation: [A]^4 B–I K–O^8 P^4; pp. [2] [i–vi] [1–2], [3]–214 [215–216]. On the last leaf of signature P are the same ads as appear at the end of Volumes II and III of the primary binding of this impression of *The Portrait of a Lady*. The publisher's imprint on the spine reads "MACMILLAN" in uniform capitals $1/8''$ high.

This title also issued in an identical binding, but without ads at the end, P_4 having been excised.

The Siege of London, one volume. Collation: [A]^4 B–I K–N^8 O^4 (–O$_4$); pp. [2] [i–vi] [1–2], [3]–197 [198]. There are no ads present. The publisher's imprint on the spine reads: "MACMILLAN" in uniform capitals $5/32''$ high.

The Madonna of the Future, one volume. Collation: [A]^4 B–I K–M^8 N^4,N2^2; pp. [2] [i–vi] [1–2], [3]–187 [188]. There are no ads present. The publisher's imprint on the spine reads: "MACMILLAN" in uniform capitals $1/8''$ high.

Confidence, one volume. Collation: [A]^2 B–I K–Q^8; pp. [i–iv], [1]–237 [238] [239–240]. On the last leaf of signature Q are the same ads as appear at the end of Volumes II and III of the primary binding of this impression of *The Portrait of a Lady*. The publisher's imprint on the spine reads: "MACMILLAN" in uniform capitals $5/32''$ high.

Illustrated Plate 10.

THE COLLECTIVE EDITION OF 1883

20.2.0. *The Collective Edition of 1883*, first collective edition, first impression, wrapped binding state, 14 volumes, London 1883.

Confidence, one volume.

CONFIDENCE | BY | HENRY JAMES | London [in Gothic type] | MACMILLAN AND CO. | 1883

Size: 5 ⁷/₈" x 4".

Collation: [A]² B–I K–Q⁸; pp. [i–iv], [1]–237 [238] [239–240].

Contents: [i–ii] half-title, verso publisher's device; [iii–iv] title-page, verso printer's imprint: "Printed by R. & R. Clark, Edinburgh. [all except printer's name in italic]"; [1]–237 text; 237 at foot printer's imprint as on title-leaf verso; [238] blank; [239] ad for this *Collective Edition*, listing 10 titles (14 volumes); [240] ad for "English Men of Letters [in Gothic type] | Edited by JOHN MORLEY", listing 33 titles in two columns.

Binding: light tan stiff wove paper wrappers, cut flush, lettered and decorated in red. The front cover, within two single-rule borders (the outer thicker than the inner), reads: "CONFIDENCE | BY | HENRY JAMES | London [in Gothic type] | MACMILLAN AND CO. | 1883". Below the outer border at the foot reads: "ONE SHILLING [in italic]". On the back cover within a single-rule frame is an ad that replicates the ad on [239]. The spine reads: "HENRY | JAMES | [rule] | CONFIDENCE | MACMILLAN". The insides of the front and back covers are blank. The text is printed on wove paper of the same type as that used in the primary binding, 20.1.0. All edges are trimmed. It is sewn, not stapled.

Illustrated Plate 10.

No other titles in the collection.

20.3.0. *The Collective Edition of 1883*, first collective edition, first impression, secondary binding state A, 14 volumes, London 1883.

The Portrait of a Lady, three volumes.

The title-pages are identical to those of this title in the first collective edition, first impression, primary binding state, 20.1.0.

Size: 6 ¹/₃₂" x 4".

Collation: Volume I: [A]² B–I K–Q⁸; pp. [i–iv], [1]–239 [240]. Volume II: [A]² B–I K–P⁸ Q⁴; pp. [i–iv], [1]–229 [230] [231–232]. Volume III: [A]², B–I,

THE COLLECTIVE EDITION OF 1883

K–P^8 [Q]^2; pp. [i–iv], [1]–225 [226] [227–228].

Contents: as in 20.1.0. In Volume II leaf Q$_4$, pages [231–232], and in volume III leaf [Q]$_2$, pages [227–228], are present. These two leaves, which are identical, have on the recto an ad for *The Collective Edition*, listing 10 titles (14 volumes), and on the verso an ad for the "English Men of Letters. [in Gothic type] | Edited by JOHN MORLEY", listing 33 titles in two columns.

Binding: salmon-colored smooth cloth over flexible boards, lettered and decorated in red-brown. The front covers read: "[thin followed by a thick rule] | HENRY | JAMES | [single rule] | THE PORTRAIT OF A LADY | [publisher's device] | thick followed by a thin rule]". The rules on the front covers extend across the spines and the back covers. The spines read: "[thin followed by a thick rule] | HENRY | JAMES | [rule] | THE | PORTRAIT | OF A | LADY | Vol. I [II] [III] | [thick followed by a thin rule] MACMILLAN & Co. [the "o" is raised above a dot]". On the back covers, centered, is a circular publisher's device. The endpapers are of white wove paper, and the texts are printed on wove paper of the same type as that used in the primary binding, 20.1.0. All edges are trimmed. They are stapled, not sewn.

The remaining eleven volumes are uniformly bound and decorated. The title-page of each volume is dated 1883. The endpapers are of white wove paper, and the texts are printed on wove paper. All edges are trimmed. They are stapled, not sewn. They are:

Roderick Hudson, two volumes. Collation: Volume I: [A]^2 B–I K–O^8 (–O$_8$); pp. [i–iv], [1]–206. Volume II: [A]^2 B–I K–N^8 O^2 (–O^2); pp. [i–iv], [1]–193 [194]. No ads are present in either volume.

The American, two volumes. Collation: Volume I: [A]^2 B–I K–N^8 O^6; pp. [i–iv], [1]–203 [204]. Volume II: [A]^2 B–I K–O^8; pp. [i–iv], [1]–208. No ads are present in either volume.

Washington Square, one volume. Collation: [A]^2 B–I K–N^8, O^6; pp. [i–iv], [1]–204. No ads are present.

The Europeans, one volume. Collation: [A]^2 B–I K–N^8; pp. [i–iv], [1]–190 [191–192]. On the last leaf of signature N are the same ads as appear at the end of Volumes II and III of the primary binding of the first impression of this edition of *The Portrait of a Lady*.

[230]

THE COLLECTIVE EDITION OF 1883

Daisy Miller: A Study, one volume. Collation: [A]⁴ B–I K–N⁸ O⁴ O2²; pp. [2] [i–vi] [1–2], [3]–202 [203–204]. On the last leaf of signature O are the same ads as appeared at the end of Volumes II and III of the primary binding of the first impression of this edition of *The Portrait of a Lady*.

An International Episode, one volume. Collation: [A]⁴ B–I K–O⁸ P⁴; pp. [2] [i–vi] [1–2], [3]–214 [215–216]. On the last leaf of signature P are the same ads as appear at the end of Volumes II and II of the primary binding of the first impression of this edition of *The Portrait of a Lady*.

The Siege of London, one volume. Collation: [A]⁴ B–I K–N⁸ O⁴; pp. [2] [i–vi] [1–2], [3]–197 [198] [199–200]. On the last leaf of signature O are the same ads as appeared at the end of Volumes II and III of the primary binding of the first impression of this edition of *The Portrait of a Lady*.

The Madonna of the Future, one volume. Collation: [A]⁴ B–I K–M⁸ N⁶; pp. [2] [i–vi] [1–2], [3]–187 [188]. No ads are present.

Confidence, one volume. Collation: [A]² B–I K–Q⁸; pp. [i–iv], [1]–237 [238] [239–240]. On the last leaf of signature Q are the same ads as appear at the end of Volumes II and III of the primary binding of the first impression of this edition of *The Portrait of a Lady*.

Illustrated Plate 10.

20.4.0. *The Collective Edition of 1883*, first collective edition, first impression, secondary binding state B, 14 volumes, London 1883.

The Portrait of a Lady, three volumes.

The title-pages are identical to those of this title in the first collective edition, first impression, primary binding state, 20.1.0.

Size: 6" x 3 ¹⁵/₁₆".

Collation: Volume I: [A]² B–I K–Q⁸; pp. [i–iv], [1]–239 [240]. Volume II: [A]² B–I K–P⁸ Q⁴; pp. [i–iv], [1]–229 [230] [231–232]. Volume III: [A]² B–I K–P⁸ [Q]²; pp. [i–iv], [1]–225 [226] [227–228].

Contents: as in 20.1.0. In Volume II leaf Q₄, pages [231–232], and in Volume III leaf [Q]₂, pages [227–228], are present. These two leaves, which are identical, have on the recto an ad for *The Collective Edition*, listing 10 titles (14 volumes), and on the verso an ad for "English Men of Letters. [in Gothic type] | Edited by JOHN MORLEY", listing 33 titles in two columns.

Binding: light green smooth cloth over flexible boards, lettered and decorated in red-brown. The front covers read: "[thin followed by a thick rule] | HENRY JAMES | [single rule] | THE PORTRAIT OF A LADY | [publisher's device] | [thick followed by thin rule]". The rules on the front covers extend across the spines and the back covers. The spines read: "[thin followed by a thick rule] | HENRY | JAMES | [rule] | THE | PORTRAIT | OF A | LADY | Vol. I [II] [III] | [thick followed by a thin rule] | MACMILLAN & Co. [the "o" is raised above a dot]". On the back covers, centered, is a circular publisher's device. The endpapers are of white wove paper, and the texts are printed on wove paper of the same type as that used on the primary binding, 20.1.0. All edges are trimmed. They are stapled, not sewn.

The remaining eleven volumes are uniformly bound and decorated. The title-page of

each volume is dated 1883. The endpapers are of white wove paper, and the texts are printed on wove paper. They are stapled, not sewn. Titles that are in the collection are:

> *Roderick Hudson*, two volumes. Collation: Volume I: [A]² B–I K–O⁸; pp. [i–iv], [1]–206 [207–208]. Volume II: [A]² B–I K–N⁸ O²; pp. [i–iv], [1]–193 [194] [195–196]. On the last leaf of signature O in both volumes are the same ads as appeared at the end of Volumes II and III of the primary binding of the first impression of this edition of *The Portrait of a Lady*.

> *The American*, two volumes. Collation: Volume I: [A]² B–I K–N⁸ O⁶; pp. [i–iv], [1]–203 [204]. Volume II: [A]² B–I K–O⁸; pp. [i–iv], [1]–208. There are no ads present in either volume.

> *Washington Square*, one volume. Collation: [A]² B–I K–N⁸ O⁶; pp. [i–iv], [1]–204. No ads present.

> *The Europeans*, one volume. Collation: [A]² B–I K–N⁸; pp. [i–iv], [1]–190 [191–192]. On the last leaf of signature N are the same ads as appeared at the end of Volumes II and III of the primary binding of the first impression of this edition of *The Portrait of a Lady*.

THE COLLECTIVE EDITION OF 1883

Daisy Miller: A Study, one volume. Collation: [A]⁴ B–I K–N⁸ O⁴ O2²; pp. [2] [i–vi] [1–2], [3]–202 [203–204]. On the last leaf of signature O are the same ads as appeared at the end of Volumes II and III of the primary binding of the first impression of this edition of *The Portrait of a Lady*.

An International Episode, one volume. Collation: [A]⁴ B–I K–O⁸ P⁴; pp. [2] [i–vi] [1–2], [3]–214 [215–216]. On the last leaf of signature P are the same ads as appear at the end of Volumes II and III of the primary binding of the first impression of this edition of *The Portrait of a Lady*.

The Siege of London, one volume. Collation: [A]⁴ B–I K–N⁸ O⁴; pp. [2] [i–vi] [1–2], [3]–197 [198] [199–200]. On the last leaf of signature O are the same ads as appeared at the end of Volumes II and II of the primary binding of the first impression of this edition of *The Portrait of a Lady*.

The Madonna of the Future, one volume. Collation: [A]⁴ B–I K–M⁸ N⁶; pp. [2] [i–vi] [1–2], [3]–187 [188]. No ads present.

Confidence, one volume. Collation: [A]² B–I K–Q⁸; pp. [i–iv], [1]–237 [238] [239–240]. On the last leaf of signature Q are the same ads as appeared at the end of Volumes II and III of the primary binding of the first impression of this edition of *The Portrait of a Lady*.

Illustrated Plate 10.

20.4.5. *The Collective Edition of 1883*, first collective edition, first impression, secondary binding state B, 12 volumes, boxed set, 1883.

This boxed set contains 12 of the 14 volumes, lacking *The Europeans* and *Confidence*. The title-pages, sizes, collations, contents, and bindings are identical to those of 20.4.0. On the front free endpaper of the volume *Daisy Miller* is the inscription: "Charles C Rofus | Fʳ Harrie | [rule] | Stanan Park | Christmas 1884 | [rule]".

The box containing the volumes is constructed of cardboard ³/₃₂″ thick, and measures 4 ½″ high, 8 ½″ wide and 6 ³/₈″ deep. It has a top lid, hinged at the rear, and a front flap which extends ½″ over the front side of the box. Both the inside and outside of the box are covered in

THE COLLECTIVE EDITION OF 1883

brown diagonal fine-ribbed cloth. The top lid, lettered in gilt, reads: "NOVELS AND TALES | BY | HENRY JAMES [all centered]".

Curiously, the box has room for only 12 of the 14 volumes of this edition. The box certainly seems to be contemporaneous with the 1884 inscription, and it is likely the type of box referred to in the Macmillan printing history. It is possible that the box was constructed to contain only 12 volumes because the other two volumes were out of print in this style of binding.

20.5.0. *The Collective Edition of 1883*, first collective edition, second impression, 14 volumes, London 1886–1887.

The Portrait of a Lady, three volumes.

The title-pages are identical to those of this title in the first collective edition, first impression, primary binding state, 20.1.0, except that they are dated 1886 or 1887 at the foot.

Size: 6 $^{11}/_{32}$″ x 4 $^{1}/_{8}$″.

Collation and contents are identical to those of this title in 20.1.0. There are no ads present in any of the volumes.

Binding: royal-blue smooth cloth. The lettering and decoration are identical to those on this title in 20.1.0, except that the publisher's imprints at the foot of the spines read "Macmillan". The endpapers are of white wove paper, and the texts are printed on wove paper. All edges are untrimmed. They are sewn, not stapled.

The remaining eleven volumes are uniformly bound and decorated The publisher's imprint at the foot of the spines is uniform and reads: "Macmillan". The end-papers are of white wove paper, and the texts are printed on wove paper. All edges are untrimmed. They are sewn, not stapled. They are:

Roderick Hudson, two volumes, 1886. Collation: Volume I: [A]^2 B–I K–N^8 O^8 (–O$_8$); pp. [i–iv], [1]–206. Volume II: [A]^2 B–I K–N^8 O^2 (–O$_2$); pp. [i–iv], [1]–193 [194]. No ads are present in either volume.

The American, two volumes, 1886. Collation: Volume I: [A]^2 B–I K–N^8 O^6; pp. [i–iv], [1]–203 [204]. Volume II: [A]^2, B–I, K–O^8; pp. [i–iv], [1]–208. No ads are present in either volume.

Washington Square, one volume, 1886. Collation: [A]² B–I K–N⁸ O⁶; pp. [i–iv], [1]–204. No ads are present.

The Europeans, one volume, 1886. Collation: [A]⁴ B–I K–N⁸; pp. [i–iv], [1]–190 [191–192]. The last leaf of signature of N⁸ is the same two pages of ads as appear at the end of Volumes II and III of the primary binding of the first impression of this edition of *The Portrait of a Lady*.

Daisy Miller, one volume, 1887. Collation: [A]⁴ B–I K–N⁸ O⁴ O2²; pp. [2] [i–vi] [1–2], [3]–202 [203–204]. The last leaf of signature O2² is the same two pages of ads as appeared at the end of Volumes II and III of the primary binding of the first impression of this edition of *The Portrait of a Lady*.

An International Episode, one volume, 1886. Collation: [A]⁴ B–I K–O⁸ P⁴ (–P$_4$); pp. [2] [i–vi] [1–2], [3]–214. No ads are present.

The Siege of London, one volume, 1886. Collation: [A]⁴ B–I K–N⁸ O⁴(–O$_4$); pp. [2] [i–vi] [1–2], [3]–197 [198]. No ads are present.

The Madonna of the Future, one volume, 1886. Collation: [A]⁴ B–I K– M⁸ N⁴ N2²; pp. [2] [i–vi] [1–2], [3]–187 [188]. No ads are present.

Confidence, one volume, 1886. Collation: [A]² B–I K–P⁸ Q⁸ (–Q$_8$); pp. [i–iv], [1]–237 [238]. No ads are present.

❧✢❧

21. PORTRAITS OF PLACES

21.1.0. *Portraits of Places*, first edition, first issue, binding state A, one volume, London 1883.

PORTRAITS OF PLACES | BY | HENRY JAMES | London [in Gothic type] | MACMILLAN AND CO. | 1883

Size: 7 $^{7}/_{16}$" x 4 $^{15}/_{16}$".

Collation: [A]⁴ B–I K–U X–Z 2A⁸, 2B⁴; pp. [i–viii], [1]–376.

Contents: [i–ii] half-title, verso publisher's device; [iii–iv] title-page, verso printer's imprint: "Printed by R. & R. Clark, Edinburgh. [all but printer's name in italic]"; [v]–vi "NOTE TO THE ENGLISH EDITION", verso note continued; [vii–viii] "CONTENTS.", verso blank; [1]–376 text; 376 at foot printer's imprint as on title-leaf verso.

Binding: greenish-blue smooth cloth with a shiny surface. The front and back covers are neither lettered nor decorated. The spine, which is lettered in gilt, reads: "PORTRAITS | OF | PLACES | HENRY | JAMES | Macmillan & Co." The author's surname on the spine is printed in uniform capitals as is his given name, but the latter capitals are slightly smaller than those of the surname. The publisher's imprint at the foot of the spine has an initial "M", "&" and final "C" in letters slightly larger than the rest. The endpapers are of white wove paper, and the text is printed on smooth wove paper. The bottom edge is rough trimmed, and the other edges are untrimmed.

This is a copy of binding A, the first of the two binding states recorded in BAL 10562.

English printing history: Macmillan Archive. MEB, 267, records only one English edition, with one impression, of this title. That impression was of 1,000 copies printed from stereotype plates in December 1883. It was published on December 18, 1883, priced at 7s. 6d. Macmillan destroyed the plates in March 1921.

21.2.0. *Portraits of Places*, first edition, first issue, binding state A, one volume, London 1883.

This copy is identical to the first edition, first issue, binding state A, 21.1.0, including the lettering on the spine, except that it is bound in dark blue-black smooth cloth with a less shiny surface. The endpapers are of white wove paper, and the text is printed on wove paper. The bottom edge is rough trimmed, and the other edges are untrimmed.

E&L A21a notes first issue copies in both shiny and dull cloth, but does not note copies in blue-black cloth. This cloth color and texture is not noted in BAL.

This is a copy of binding A, the first of the two binding states recorded in BAL 10562

PORTRAITS OF PLACES

21.3.0. *Portraits of Places*, first edition, first issue, binding state B, one volume, London 1883.

This copy is identical to the copies of the first edition, first issue, binding state A, 21.1.0 and 21.2.0, including the lettering on the spine, except that the publisher's imprint at the foot of the spine is in letters of uniform size with the exception of the "o" in "Co." which is raised above a dot.

This is a copy of binding B, the second of two binding states recorded in BAL 10562.

Percy H. Muir, *Points 1874–1930* (London: Constable & Co. Ltd., 1931), 132, states that the distinction between this and the previous copies of the first issue of this title "is clearly a difference of state. Macmillan will have had several brasses in use at the same time and the binders will have used them indifferently."

21.4.0. *Portraits of Places*, first edition, second issue, one volume, London 1883.

This copy is identical to the three copies of the first edition, first issue, 21.1.0–21.3.0, except that the brasses on the spine differ in that they are thicker and slightly differently placed on the binding (Muir makes the point that they are later in style), the "J" in the author's surname is a drop-cap, and the initial letters in "Macmillan"and "Co." in the publisher's imprint are significantly larger than the remaining letters.

Muir, *Points*, 132, characterizes this second issue as a remainder. Muir has a reproduction of the first and second issue bindings facing 132.

21.5.0. *Portraits of Places*, first American edition, first impression, one volume, Boston 1884.

HENRY JAMES | [rule] | PORTRAITS OF PLACES | [monogram publisher's device] | BOSTON | JAMES R. OSGOOD AND COMPANY [in sans-serif] | [rule] | 1884

Size: $7\,5/16''$ x $4\,7/8''$.

Collation: $[1-32^6]$, signed as $[A]^4$ B–I [K] L–U X–Z $2A^8$ $2B^4$; pp. [i–viii], [1]–376.

Contents: [i–ii] half-title, verso ad within a single-rule frame headed: "By the Same Author. [in italic]", listing *Daisy Miller: A Comedy* and *The Siege of London*, with dollar prices and press opinions; [iii–iv] title-page, verso copyright notice, reservation of rights and printer's imprint: "Copyright, 1883, [in italic] | By James R. Osgood and Company. | [rule] | All rights reserved. [in italic] | University Press: [in Gothic type] | John Wilson and Son, Cambridge."; [v–vi] "NOTE.", verso blank; [vii–viii] "CONTENTS.", verso blank; [1]–376 text.

Binding: chocolate-brown diagonal-fine-ribbed cloth. The front and back covers are decorated in blind with a single-rule border within a thicker single-rule frame. The spine, which is lettered and decorated in gilt, reads: "PORTRAITS | OF | PLACES | [rule] | Henry James | [J. R. Osgood monogram]". The endpapers are of white laid paper, and the text is printed on wove paper. There are no binder's fly leaves. All edges are trimmed.

American printing history. Houghton Mifflin Archive. First edition: Ms Am 2030.3(9), 39 and Ms Am 2030.3(14), 70: *first* [Osgood] *impression* January 3, 1884, 1524 copies, 1513 bound between January 21 and November 4, 1884; *second impression* January 30, 1885, 280 copies, 76 bound on February 14 and March 9, 1885. Ms Am 2030(19), 157: notation: "rcvd from T[icknor] & Co. 4/11/89 200 copies", 194 bound between June 1, 1889, and July 5, 1892. Ms Am 2030(20), 174: [*third* [first Houghton, Mifflin] *impression*, but not specified] August 1, 1893, 156 copies, 154 bound between August 7, 1893, and January 10, 1896. Ms Am 2030(21), 221: [*fourth impression*, but not specified] June 15, 1897, 152 copies, 150 bound between July 12, 1897, and June 28, 1900. Ms Am 2030(22), 219: [*fifth impression*, but not specified] July 2, 1901, 268 copies, 263 bound between July 23, 1901, and April 16, 1906; [*sixth impression*, but not specified] December 27, 1907, 156 copies, 152 bound on January 7, 1908, and July 13, 1910; [*seventh impression*, but not specified] August 13, 1912, 159 copies, 152 bound between September 25, 1912, and March 6, 1917.

The first impression was priced at $1.50, and was advertised at that price in 1906.

Ms Am 2030.3(9), 39 (cost records) records that the plates used by Osgood to print the first impression were "Plates from Macmillan & Co. £40.5.0 say [$]200.00". A comparison of the American and English first impressions shows that, except for the preliminaries, they were printed from the same plates. The entry "new pages [$] 6.50", probably refers to the preliminaries.

21.6.0. *Portraits of Places*, first American edition, first impression, one volume, Boston 1884.

This copy is identical to the first American edition, first impression, 21.5.0, except that it is bound in light gray-brown diagonal-fine-ribbed cloth (definitely not a faded brown or maroon). The endpapers are of white laid paper, and the text is printed on wove paper. There are no binder's fly-leaves. All edges are trimmed.

21.7.0. *Portraits of Places*, first American edition, first impression, one volume, Boston 1884.

This copy is identical to the first American edition, first impression, 21.5.0, except that it is bound in ochre pebble-grain cloth. The endpapers are of white laid paper, and the text is printed on wove paper. There are no binder's fly-leaves. All edges are trimmed.

BAL 10563 records mustard colored copies in both sand-grain (C cloth) and pebble-grain (P cloth) cloth. E&L records ochre colored copies in fine-ribbed or sand-grain cloth, but does not record ochre (or any color) copies in pebble-grain cloth.

21.8.0. *Portraits of Places*, first American edition, first impression, one volume, Boston 1884.

This copy is identical to the first American edition, first impression, 21.5.0, except that it is bound in blue diagonal-fine-ribbed cloth. The endpapers are of white wove paper rather than the laid paper of the preceding copies of the first American edition. The text is printed on wove paper. There are no binder's fly leaves. All edges are trimmed.

This binding is not noted in BAL 10563 (which records copies in, among other colors, green-blue in sand-grain cloth, and gray-blue in diagonal-fine-ribbed cloth). E&L A21b records copies in, among other colors, dark blue-green and light blue-gray diagonal-fine-ribbed or sand-grain cloth.

PORTRAITS OF PLACES

21.9.0. *Portraits of Places*, first American edition, first impression, one volume, Boston 1884.

This copy is identical to the first American edition, first impression, 21.5.0, except that it is bound in maroon diagonal-fine-ribbed cloth. The endpapers are of white laid paper, and the text is printed on wove paper. There are no binder's fly-leaves. All edges are trimmed.

This cloth color is recorded in E&L A22b, but not in BAL 10563.

21.10.0. *Portraits of Places*, first American edition, first impression, one volume, Boston 1884.

This copy is identical to the first American edition, first impression, 21.5.0, except that it is bound in light gray-blue diagonal-fine-ribbed cloth. The endpapers are of white laid paper, and the text is printed on wove paper. There are no binder's fly-leaves. All edges are trimmed.

21.10.5. *Portraits of Places*, first American edition, second impression, second binding state, one volume, Boston 1885.

The title-page and size are identical to the first American edition, first impression, 21.5.0, except that the title-page has "SECOND EDITION" between the publisher's device and the publisher's imprint, and is dated 1885 at the foot.

The collation and signing is identical to that of the first impression, except that the signature mark P is missing on 209.

The contents are identical to those of 21.5.0, except that the ad on [ii] within a single rule frame headed: "Henry James's Latest Works" lists 7 titles (six with dollar prices), the last dated being *The Bostonians* under the heading: "In Press. [in italic]" .

Binding: dark brown diagonal-fine-ribbed cloth, lettered in red-brown with decoration in red-brown, dark brown, and gilt on the front cover and spine. The title on the front cover and spine is in red-brown within a gilt panel with a pronounced maze-like background pattern. The publisher's imprint at the foot of the spine reads: "HOUGHTON | MIFFLIN [dot] & [dot] CO." The ampersand in the publisher's imprint is stylized and like a figure "8". The endpapers are of white laid paper, and the text is printed on wove paper. A binder's fly-leaf of wove paper is at both the front and the back. All edges are trimmed, and the top edge is stained brown.

This binding is uniform with that on the second edition, first American impression of *The Portrait of a Lady* (1881), 16.5.0.

This copy is one of 280 sets of sheets of the second impression printed on January 30, 1885, 76 copies of which were bound by James R. Osgood & Co. (the first binding state), and 200 copies of which were acquired by Houghton, Mifflin from Ticknor & Co. on April 11, 1889, and which Ticknor had acquired from Osgood in May 1885. Of these 200 copies, 194 (the second binding state) were bound by Houghton, Mifflin between between June 1, 1889 and July 5, 1892. No copies of the second impression were bound by Ticknor & Co.

21.11.0. *Portraits of Places*, first American edition, third impression, one volume, Boston and New York 1893.

HENRY JAMES | [rule] | PORTRAITS OF PLACES | THIRD EDITION | [oblong publisher's device of a piper under a tree within a frame] | BOSTON AND NEW YORK | HOUGHTON, MIFFLIN AND COMPANY | The Riverside Press, Cambridge [in Gothic type] | 1893

Size: 7 $^{5}/_{16}$" x 4 $^{3}/_{4}$".

Collation: [1–24^8], signed as: [A]^4 B–I^8 [K]^8 L-U X–Y [Z]^8 2A^8 2B^4; pp. [i–viii], [1]–376.

Contents: [i–ii] half-title, verso ad within a single-rule frame headed: "Henry James's Books. [in Gothic type]" listing 15 titles with dollar prices, the last dated being *The Tragic Muse* ; [iii–iv] title-page, verso copyright, reservation of rights and printer's imprint: "Copyright, 1883, [in italic] | By James R. Osgood and Company. | [rule] | All rights reserved. [in italic] | The Riverside Press, Cambridge, Mass., U.S.A. [in italic] | Printed by H. O. Houghton & Company."; [v–vi] "NOTE.", verso blank; [vii–viii] "CONTENTS.", verso blank; [1]–376 text.

Binding: dark brown diagonal-fine-ribbed cloth, lettered in red-brown with decoration in red-brown, dark brown, and gilt on the front cover and spine. The title on the front cover and spine is in red-brown within a gilt panel with a pronounced maze-like background pattern. The publisher's imprint at the foot of the spine reads: "HOUGHTON | MIFFLIN [dot] & [dot] CO." The ampersand in the publisher's imprint is stylized and like a figure "8". The endpapers are of white laid paper, and the text is printed on wove paper. A binder's fly-leaf of wove paper is at both the front and the back. All edges are trimmed, and the top edge is stained ochre.

This binding is uniform with that on the second edition, first American impression of *The Portrait of a Lady* (1881), 16.5.0.

21.12.0. *Portraits of Places*, first American edition, fifth impression, one volume, Boston and New York [n.d., 1901].

HENRY JAMES | [rule] | PORTRAITS OF PLACES | [oblong publisher's device of a piper under a tree within a frame] | BOSTON AND NEW YORK | HOUGHTON, MIFFLIN AND COMPANY | The Riverside Press, Cambridge [in Gothic type]

Size: 7 3/8" x 4 7/8".

Collation: identical to that of the first American edition, third impression, 22.11.0.

Contents: [i–ii] half-title, verso ad within a single-rule frame headed: "Henry James [in Gothic type]" listing 16 titles, the last dated being *The Spoils of Poynton*; [iii–iv] title-page, verso copyright, reservation of rights, printing history and printer's imprint: "Copyright, 1883, [in italic] | By James R. Osgood and Company. | [rule] | All rights reserved. [in italic] | FIFTH IMPRESSION | The Riverside Press, Cambridge, Mass., U.S.A. [in italic] | Printed by H. O. Houghton & Company."; [v–vi] "NOTE.", verso blank; [vii–viii] "CONTENTS.", verso blank; [1]–376 text.

Binding: brown vertical-rib-grain cloth, with lettering and decoration in gilt on the front cover and spine. The front cover has within a single-rule border an elaborate centered cartouche within which is the title and author's name separated by a decorative rule. The spine reads: "[rule] | PORTRAITS | OF PLACES | [decorative rule] | HENRY JAMES | HOUGHTON | MIFFLIN & CO." The ampersand in the printer's imprint is stylized. The back cover has a single-rule border in blind. The endpapers are of white laid paper, and the text is printed on wove paper. A binder's fly-leaf of wove paper is at both the front and the back. All edges are trimmed.

This binding is uniform with that on the first American edition of *The Spoils of Poynton* (1897), 48.6.0.

21.13.0. *Portraits of Places*, first continental edition, first impression, one volume, Leipzig 1884.

PORTRAITS OF | PLACES. | BY | HENRY JAMES, | AUTHOR OF "DAISY MILLER," "THE AMERICAN," ETC. | AUTHORIZED EDITION. [in italic] | LEIPZIG | BERNHARD TAUCHNITZ | 1884.

Size: 6 $7/16$" x 4 $11/16$".

Collation: $[1]^8$ 2–19^8; pp. [1–8], [9]–303 [304].

Contents: [1–2] series title and half-title, verso ad headed: "TAUCHNITZ EDITION. | By the same Author", listing 12 titles, the last of which is *The Siege of London*; [3–4] title-page, verso blank; [5–6] James's authorization note, verso blank; [7–8] "CONTENTS.", verso blank; [9]–303 text; [304] centered printer's imprint: "[rule] | PRINTING OFFICE OF THE PUBLISHER. | [rule]".

Binding: buff wove paper wrappers, cut flush, with lettering on the front cover in black within a black single-rule frame which is decorated with a flower-like device at each of the four corners with lettering above and below the frame. The spine is also lettered in black between a series of eight pairs of thick and thin black rules. The back cover, which is also lettered in black, reads: "August 1884. | TAUCHNITZ EDITION. | [rule] | Forthcoming Volumes: [followed by a list of 16 works, the last of which is *A new [sic] Story* by F. Marion Crawford] | A complete Catalogue of the Tauchnitz | Edition is attached to this work. | [rule] | Bernhard Tauchnitz, Leipzig; | And sold by all booksellers." The inside of the front and back covers are blank. A 16-page paginated publisher's catalogue, dated August 1884, is bound in at the end.

Illustrated Plate 11.

See T&B 2276, which notes: "text as for London first edition, except that chapters XV–XX are eliminated." T&B records the earliest wrapper and catalogue date as August 1884, as in this copy. However, the absence of ads inside the back wrapper may indicate that it is a copy of the second binding state of the first impression; see, Appendix B: A Note on Tauchnitz's James Editions. T&B records one edition with two impressions of this title. The first has 12 titles listed on the half-title verso and the second has 15.

21.14.0. *Portraits of Places*, first continental edition, second impression, one volume, Leipzig 1884.

Size: 6 ½″ x 4 ⅝″.

The title-page and collation are identical to those of the first continental edition, first impression, 21.13.0.

Contents: identical to those of 21.13.0, except that the ad on [2] under the heading "TAUCHNITZ EDITION. | By the same Author," lists 15 titles, the last dated being *The Outcry*.

Binding: buff wove paper wrappers, cut flush with lettering on the front cover in black within a double rule frame, the outer rule being wider than the inner, which frames are divided into three panels by thin double rules. The lettering in the upper panel reads: "TAUCHNITZ EDITION | COLLECTION OF BRITISH AND AMERICAN AUTHORS | VOL. 2276". The middle panel reads: "PORTRAITS OF PLACES | BY | HENRY JAMES [all the foregoing in sans-serif] | IN ONE VOLUME | LEIPZIG: BERNARD TAUCHNITZ | PARIS: LIBRAIRIE HENRY GAULON, 39, RUE MADAME". The lower panel reads: "The copyright of this Collection is purchased for Continental Circulation | only and the volumes may not therefore be introduced into Great Britain | or her Colonies. (See also pp. 3–6 of Larger Catalogue)". Below the frame reads "EACH VOLUME SOLD SEPERATELY". The spine, also lettered in black between a series of eight pairs of thin and thick black rules, between the sixth and the seventh reads: "PRICE | M 1.60". The back cover, also lettered in black, reads at the top: "TAUCHNITZ EDITION | Latest Volumes | 4–6 new volumes are published regularly every month [in italic] | May 1925", followed by a list of volumes 4687 to 4669 in descending numerical order. Bound in at the end is a 32 page paginated publisher's catalogue, dated on [1] "September 1927".

The Outcry was published by Tauchnitz in 1912.

22. *NOTES ON DRAWINGS BY GEORGE DU MAURIER*

No copy in the collection.

23. *A LITTLE TOUR IN FRANCE*

23.1.0. *A Little Tour in France*, first edition, first impression, first binding state, one volume, Boston 1885 [1884].

HENRY JAMES | [rule] | A Little Tour in France | [monogram publisher's device] | BOSTON | JAMES R. OSGOOD AND COMPANY | [rule] | 1885

Size: 7 3/8″ x 4 7/8″.

Collation: $[1-20^6\ 21^{10}]$, signed as $\pi^2\ 1-16^8$; pp. [i–iv], [1]–255 [256].

Contents: [i–ii] blank, verso ad headed: "Henry James's Latest Works.", listing 5 Titles, four with press opinions, and the fifth, *Tales of Three Cities*, as "In Press."; [iii–iv] title-page, verso copyright notice, reservation of rights and printer's imprint: "Copyright, 1884, [in italic] | By Henry James. | [rule] | All rights reserved. [in italic] | University Press: [in Gothic type] | John Wilson and Son, Cambridge."; [1]–255 text; 255 at foot printer's imprint: "[rule] | University Press, Cambridge: John Wilson & Son."; [256] blank.

Binding: light chocolate-brown diagonal-fine-ribbed cloth. The front and back coves are decorated in blind with a single-rule border within a thicker single-rule frame. The spine, which is lettered and decorated in gilt, reads: "A | LITTLE TOUR | IN | FRANCE | [rule] | Henry James | [J. R. Osgood monogram]". The endpapers are of white wove paper, and the text is printed on laid paper. There are no binder's fly-leaves. All edges are trimmed.

On 205, line 1 there is the misprint "chapell ede Sainte-Croix". This misprint is present in all subsequent impressions of the first edition.

BAL 10570 states that all copies of the first edition, first impression, first binding state, have no binder's fly-leaves and that all have blind-stamped frames and borders on the covers. E&L A23a records that some copies have no binder's fly-leaves and no frames and borders on the covers. This copy, and those described below, would indicate that BAL is correct.

American printing history. Houghton Mifflin Archive. First edition: Ms Am 2030.3, 91 and Ms Am 2030.3(14), 70: *first* [and sole Osgood] *impression* August 14, 1884, 1528 copies, 1168 of which bound between August 21, 1884, and April 10, 1885. Ms Am 2030(19), 157: notation: "rcvd from

T[icknor] & Co. 4/11/89 350 copies", 192 bound between September 13, 1889, and December 24, 1891, and 175 copies were pulped on October 26, 1890[29]; [*second* [first Houghton, Mifflin] *impression*, but not specified] July 2, 1892, 158 copies, 154 bound July 8, 1892, and August 2, 1893. Ms Am 2030(20), 174: [*third impression*, but not specified] July 30, 1894, 150 copies, 147 bound between August 3, 1894, and November 13, 1895. Ms Am 2030(21), 221: [*fourth impression*, but not specified] October 30, 1895, 154 copies, 142 bound between November 13, 1895, and February 4, 1897; [*fifth impression*, but not specified] March 2, 1897, 264 copies, 272 [*sic*] bound between March 13, 1897, and April 26, 1898; [*sixth impression*, but not specified] May 18, 1899, 272 copies, 270 bound between June 7, 1899, and December 5, 1900. Ms Am 2030(22), 218: notation "12mo"; [*seventh impression*, but not specified] January 14, 1901, 276 copies, 274 bound between January 27, 1901, and August 19, 1901; notation on seventh through the eleventh impressions "12mo"; [*eighth impression*, but not specified] June 20, 1902, 270 copies, 269 bound between July 16, 1902, and June 11, 1904; [*ninth impression*, but not specified] January 7, 1905, 275 copies, 273 bound between January 12, 1905, and April 25, 1905; [*tenth impression*, but not specified] December 16, 1905, 270 copies, 268 bound between January 2, 1906, and August 7, 1906; [*eleventh impression*, but not specified] [illegible] 6, 1907, 277 copies, 267 bound between June 13, 1907, and May 15, 1908; [*twelfth impression*, but not specified] April 9, 1909, 274 copies [binding data off sheet]. Ms Am 2030(23), 214: notation on thirteenth through fifteenth impressions "12mo" [*thirteenth impression*, but not specified] July 1, 1912, 285 copies, 271 bound between September 20, 1912, and April 24, 1918; [*fourteenth impression*, but not specified] December 11, 1918, 289 copies, 286 bound between March 6, 1919, and December 7, 1920; [*fifteenth impression*, but

---

29 The figures do not quite add up. Since Osgood printed a first impression of 1528 copies, and bound 1168 copies, that would leave 360 unbound copies that would eventually be acquired by Houghton Mifflin from Ticknor & Co., which is close to the 350 copies it recorded as having received, and is also close to the 367 aggregate copies Houghton Mifflin recorded as being bound (192) and pulped (175). However, BAL 10570 records that Ticknor & Co. bound on April 10, 1888, 50 sets of the sheets of the first impression it received from Osgood (although BAL concedes it has not seen a copy thus). No record of such a binding-up appears in the Houghton Mifflin records. But if Ticknor and Co. did bind 50 copies that would leave only 310 copies available to Houghton Mifflin to bind or pulp, unless one assumes that the Ticknor copies were rebound by Houghton Mifflin or were among the copies that were pulped.

not specified] July 26, 1922, 524 copies, 514 bound between December 11, 1922, and September 19, 1925.

The first edition was priced at $1.50, which price was unchanged through 1905.

Second edition. Ms Am 2030(22), 219: *first impression* October 15, 1900, 2030 copies, 1990 bound between October 19, 1900, and May 25, 1901; notation on first and third through the seventh impressions "Hol[iday Edition]"; [*second impression*, but not specified] November 19, 1900, 265 copies "L[arge] P[aper]", 260 bound between November 21, 1900, and December 1, 1900 (on November 1, 1900, one copy was bound for "author" and on November 9 one for "artist"); *second* [i.e. third] *impression* July 26, 1901, 512 copies, 506 bound between August 23, 1901, and October 12, 1904; *third* [i.e. fourth] *impression* February 10, 1905, 520 copies, 517 bound between February 16, 1905, and May 6, 1907; *fourth* [i.e. fifth] *impression* April 27, 1907, 283 copies, 277 bound between May 16, 1907, and August 22, 1908 (of which 18 copies bound in "½ mar[occo]". Ms Am 2030(23), 215: *fifth* [i.e. sixth] *impression* October 29, 1908, 518 copies, 487 bound between December 8, 1908, and March 31, 1920, some bindings, May 1910 and later, noted in levant, ½ levant and ½ morocco; notation: "10/29/08 ptd. 606 titles"; *sixth* [i.e. seventh] *impression* May 20, 1912, 277 copies, 248 bound between June 2, 1913, and November 15, 1918; notations: "5/20/12 ptd. 360 titles" and "[total copies of Holiday edition] 4405".

The "Holiday Edition" (trade) was priced at $3.00. The "Large Paper" (limited) was priced at $5.00.

Third (?) edition. Ms Am 2030(23), 215: notation: "Pocket Edition"; *first* (and sole) *impression* August 3, 1914, 1061 copies, 1013 bound between September 16, 1914, and October 22, 1923, 10 copies bound in ½ levant and 10 in ½ morocco; notation: "5/3/14 ptd. 1048 1–cut 1275 4 pp. titles".

23.2.0. *A Little Tour in France*, first edition, first impression, first binding state, one volume, Boston 1885 [1884].

This copy is identical to the first edition, first impression, first binding state, 23.1.0, except that it is bound in royal-blue diagonal-fine-ribbed cloth. It has endpapers of white laid paper, and the text is printed on wove paper. There are no binder's fly-leaves. All edges are trimmed.

23.3.0. *A Little Tour in France*, first edition, first impression, first binding state, one volume, Boston 1885 [1884].

This copy is identical to the first edition, first impression, first binding state, 23.1.0, except that it is bound in terra-cotta fine sand-grain cloth. The endpapers are of white laid paper, and the text is printed on laid paper. There are no binder's fly-leaves. All edges are trimmed.

E&L A23a records this binding color as red-brown.

23.4.0. *A Little Tour in France*, first edition, first impression, third binding state A, one volume, Boston 1885 [1884].

The title-page, size, collation, and contents are identical to those of the first edition, first impression, first binding state, 23.1.0, including the ad on [ii].

Binding: smooth chocolate-brown cloth. The front and back covers are neither lettered nor decorated. The spine, which is lettered and decorated in gilt, reads: "A | LITTLE TOUR | IN | FRANCE | [rule] | Henry James | HOUGHTON | MIFFLIN & CO." The ampersand is stylized. The endpapers are of white laid paper, and the text is printed on laid paper. A binder's fly-leaf of laid paper is at both the front and the back. All edges are trimmed.

This binding is uniform with that of the first edition, second binding state A, of *The Author of Beltraffio* (1885), 26.6.0, except for the stylized ampersand.

This copy is one of the 350 (or 360) sets of sheets acquired by Houghton, Mifflin from Ticknor & Co. on April 11, 1889, when Ticknor was dissolved. The second binding state is the Ticknor & Co. binding.

23.5.0. *A Little Tour in France*, first edition, first impression, third binding state B, one volume, Boston 1885 [1884].

This copy is identical to the first edition, first impression, third binding state, 23.4.0, except that it is bound in smooth olive-green cloth, and the publisher's imprint at the foot of the spine reads: "HOUGHTON | MIFFLIN [dot] & [dot] CO". The ampersand is stylized. The endpapers are of white laid paper, and the text is printed on wove paper. A binder's fly-leaf of wove (rather than laid) paper is at the back, but not at the front. All edges are trimmed.

23.5.5. *A Little Tour in France*, first edition, second impression, one-volume, Boston and New York 1892.

HENRY JAMES | A Little Tour in France | [oblong publisher's device of a piper under a tree within a single-rule frame] | BOSTON AND NEW YORK | HOUGHTON, MIFFLIN AND COMPANY | The Riverside Press, Cambridge [in Gothic type] | 1892

Size: 7 $^{5}/_{16}$" x 4 $^{13}/_{16}$".

Collation: [1–15^8 16^{10}], signed as π^2 1–16^8; pp. [i–iv], [1]–255 [256].

Contents: [i–ii] blank, verso ad within a single-rule frame headed: "Henry James's Books. [in Gothic type]", listing 15 James titles with dollar prices, the last dated being *The Tragic Muse*; following *A Little Tour in France*, it reads: "12mo, $1.50"; and following the title *Daisy Miller*, it reads: "A Comedy. 12mo, $1.25. | The above thirteen 12mo volumes, in box, $22.00."; [iii–iv] title-page, verso copyright notice and reservation of rights: "Copyright, 1884. [in italic] | By Henry James. | [rule] | All rights reserved. [in italic] | The Riverside Press, Cambridge, Mass., U.S.A. [in italic] | Printed by H. O. Houghton & Company."; [1]–255 text; no printer's imprint on 255; [256] blank.

Binding: pea-green smooth cloth. The front and back covers are neither lettered nor decorated. The spine, which is lettered and decorated in gilt, reads: "A | LITTLE TOUR | IN | FRANCE | [rule] | Henry James | HOUGHTON | MIFFLIN [dot] & [dot] CO." The publisher's imprint is in sans-serif, and the ampersand is stylized like a figure "8". It has endpapers of cream laid paper, and the text is printed on wove paper. A binder's fly-leaf of wove paper is at both the front and the back. All edges are trimmed, and the top edge is stained brown.

The ad on [ii] states that 13 (of the 15) James titles listed, including this one, were sold as a boxed set for $22.00, and were presumably bound uniformly.[30]

---

30 These titles are: *A Passionate Pilgrim, Transatlantic Sketches, Roderick Hudson, The American, The Europeans, Confidence, The Portrait of a Lady, The Author of Beltraffio, The Siege of London, Tales of Three Cities, A Little Tour in France, Portraits of Places,* and *Daisy Miller*. Not included were *The Tragic Muse* and *Watch and Ward*, and James' works the copyrights of which were owned by other publishers, Macmillan and Harpers. This is an example of Houghton, Mifflin capitalizing on its backlist.

23.5.6 *A Little Tour in France*, first edition, second impression, one volume, Boston and New York 1892.

This copy is identical to the first edition, second impression, 23.5.5, except that it is bound in brown smooth cloth. The endpapers are of cream laid paper, and the text is printed on wove paper. A binder's fly-leaf of wove paper is at both the front and the back. All edges are trimmed, and the top edge is stained ochre.

23.6.0. *A Little Tour in France*, first edition, third impression, one volume, Boston 1894.

HENRY JAMES | [rule] | A Little Tour in France | [publisher's device of a piper under a tree within a single-rule frame] | BOSTON AND NEW YORK | HOUGHTON, MIFFLIN AND COMPANY | The Riverside Press, Cambridge [in Gothic type] | 1894

Size: $7\,^{5}/_{16}''$ x $4\,^{3}/_{4}''$.

Collation: $[1-16^8\ 17^2]$, signed as $\pi^2\ 1-16^8$; pp. [i–iv], [1]–255 [256].

Contents: identical to those of the first edition, second impression, 23.5.5.

Binding: brown smooth cloth. The front and back covers are neither lettered nor decorated. The spine, which is lettered and decorated in gilt, reads: "A | LITTLE TOUR | IN | FRANCE | [rule] | Henry James | HOUGHTON | MIFFLIN & CO." The ampersand in the publisher's imprint is stylized and is like a Greek π. The endpapers are of cream laid paper, and the text is printed on wove paper. A binder's fly-leaf of wove paper is at both the front and the back. All edges are trimmed, and the top edge is stained brown.

Another copy has been examined, which is identical in all respects to this copy, except that it is bound in green smooth cloth, and the publisher's imprint at the foot of the spine reads: "HOUGHTON | MIFFLIN & [dot] CO." The ampersand is stylized and is like a figure "8" rather than a Greek π. There is no dot before the ampersand.

23.7.0. *A Little Tour in France*, first edition, sixth impression, one volume, Boston 1899.

HENRY JAMES | [rule] | A Little Tour in France | [publisher's device of a piper under a tree within a frame] | BOSTON AND NEW YORK | HOUGHTON, MIFFLIN AND COMPANY | The Riverside Press, Cambridge [in Gothic type] | 1899

Size: 7 3/8" x 4 15/16".

Collation: $[1\text{–}20^6\ 21^{10}]$, signed as $\pi^2\ 1\text{–}16^8$; pp. [i–iv], [1]–255 [256].

Contents: [i–ii] blank, verso an ad within a single-rule frame headed: "Henry James's Books. [in Gothic type]", listing 16 James titles with dollar prices, the last dated being *The Spoils of Poynton*; following the title *A Little Tour in France*, it reads: "12mo, $1.50."; and following the title *Daisy Miller*, it reads: "A Comedy. 12mo, $1.25. | The above thirteen 12mo volumes, in box, $22.00."; [iii–iv] title-page, verso copyright notice, reservation of rights and printer's imprint: "Copyright, 1884, | By Henry James. | [rule] | All rights reserved. [in italic] | The Riverside Press, Cambridge, Mass., U.S.A. [in italic] | Printed by H. O. Houghton & Company."; [1]–255 text; no printer's imprint on 255; [256] blank.

Binding: green vertical-rib-grain, lettered and decorated in gilt on the front cover and spine. The front cover has within a single-rule border an elaborate centered cartouche within which is the title and author's name separated by an ornamental rule. The spine, reads: "[rule] | A LITTLE TOUR | IN FRANCE | [ornamental rule] | HENRY JAMES | HOUGHTON | MIFFLIN & CO. | [rule]". The ampersand in the publisher's imprint is stylized. The back cover has a single-rule border in blind. The endpapers are of white laid paper, and the text is printed on wove paper. A binder's fly-leaf of wove paper is at both the front and the back. All edges are trimmed.

This binding is uniform with that of the first American edition, first impression, of *The Spoils of Poynton* (1897), 48.6.0.

23.8.0. *A Little Tour in France*, first edition, sixth impression, one volume, Boston 1899.

The title-page, size, collation, and contents are identical to the first edition, sixth impression, 23.7.0.

Binding: chocolate-brown vertical-rib-grain cloth decorated and lettered identically to 23.7.0. The endpapers are of white laid paper, and the text is printed on wove paper. A binder's fly-leaf of wove paper is at both the front and the back. All edges are trimmed.

Dust-jacket: tan wove paper lettered in black. The front and rear covers, as well as the front and rear inner flaps, are blank. The spine, which is lettered and ornamented in black, reads: "A LITTLE TOUR | IN FRANCE | [ornamental rule] | HENRY JAMES | HOUGHTON | MIFFLIN & CO." The ampersand is stylized, and the lettering and decoration on the spine of the dust-jacket are identical to those on the spine of the book.

Tanselle dust-jacket 99.67 and plate 12.

23.9.0. *A Little Tour in France*, first edition, seventh (?) impression, one volume, Boston [n.d., 1901].

The title-page, size, collation, and contents are identical to those of the first edition, sixth impression, 23.7.0, except that there is no date on the title-page, the ad on [ii], which lists the same 16 James titles in the same order and with the same dollar prices, is headed "Henry James [in Gothic type]" rather than "Henry James's Books. [in Gothic type]"; following the title *A Little Tour in France*, it reads: "12mo, $1.50; Holiday | Edition. With about 70 Illustrations by Joseph Pennell. | Crown 8vo, $3.00."; and following the title *Daisy Miller*, it reads: "A Comedy. 12mo, $1.25.", with no reference made to the 13 James titles sold as a boxed set.

Binding: green vertical-rib-grain cloth lettered and decorated identically to 23.7.0. The endpapers are of cream wove paper and the text is printed on a grade of wove paper inferior to 23.7.0 and 23.8.0. A binder's fly-leaf of smooth wove paper is at both the front and the back. All edges are trimmed.

Evidence of wear to the plates can be seen throughout the volume. However, the reference in the ad on [ii] to the "Holiday Edition" illustrated by Joseph Pennell, which was first published in 1900, 23.10.0, indicates that this copy must have been published subsequent to 1900; see printing history following 23.1.0.

23.9.3. *A Little Tour in France*, first edition, tenth or eleventh impression, one volume, Boston and New York [n.d., 1905 or 1907].

The title-page and size are identical to those of the first edition, sixth impression, 23.7.0, except that the title-page has no date at the foot.

Collation: $[1-16^8\ 17^2]$, signed as $\pi^2\ 1-16^8$; pp. [i–iv], [1]–255 [256].

Contents: identical to 23.7.0, except that the ad on [ii] within a single-rule frame is headed: "By Henry James [in Gothic type]", and lists 18 James titles with dollar prices, but with no reference to a boxed set, the last dated being *English Hours*, and on [256] there is the printer's imprint: "The Riverside Press [in Gothic type] | Electrotyped and printed by H. O. Houghton & Co. | Cambridge, Mass., U.S.A. [last two lines in italic].

Binding: green vertical rib-grain cloth with lettering and decoration identical to 23.7.0. The endpapers are of cream wove paper, and the text is printed on wove paper of a quality similar to 23.7.0. A binder's fly-leaf of wove paper is at both the front and back. The top edge is trimmed and stained brown, the bottom edge is trimmed, and the fore-edge is rough trimmed.

The fact that English Hours published in October 1905 is advertised on [ii] and the publisher's imprint on the title-page reads: "Houghton, Mifflin and Company", which imprint was changed to "Houghton Mifflin Company" in 1908, suggests that this copy is of the tenth or eleventh impression.

23.9.5. *A Little Tour in France*, first edition, thirteenth or later impression, one volume, Boston and New York [n.d., 1912 or later].

HENRY JAMES | [rule] | A Little Tour in France | [publisher's device of a piper under a tree within a single-rule frame] | BOSTON AND NEW YORK | HOUGHTON MIFFLIN COMPANY | The Riverside Press Cambridge [in Gothic type]

Size: $7\frac{1}{2}$" x 5".

Collation: [unsigned, $1-15^8\ 16^{10}$]; pp. [i–iv], 1–255 [256].

Contents: [i–ii] blank, verso ad within a single-rule frame headed: "By Henry James", listing 17 titles without dollar prices, the last dated being *Italian Hours*; [iii–iv] title-page, verso copyright notice, reservation of rights and printer's imprint: "COPYRIGHT, 1884 AND 1912, BY HENRY JAMES | ALL RIGHTS RESERVED"; 1–255 text; [256] blank.

Binding: glazed smooth blue cloth, lettered and decorated in black and gilt. The front cover, within a black double-rule border within which is a black single-rule frame, reads: "[horizontal decorative device of rules, dots and flowers] | A LITTLE TOUR | IN FRANCE | [small four cornered device] | HENRY [dot] JAMES | [horizontal decorative device of rules, dots and flowers]". The spine, which is lettered in gilt, and decorated in gilt within an oblong frame within which are five decorative ovals in each of which is a stem of flowers, reads: "A LITTLE | TOUR IN | FRANCE | [small decorative device] | HENRY | JAMES". The back cover is blank. The endpapers are of white wove paper, and the text is printed on wove paper. There are no binder's fly-leaves. All edges are trimmed, and the top edge is stained light brown.

The ad on [ii] differs from the ad on [ii] in the first edition seventh (?) impression, 23.9.0 as it is slightly smaller in size, drops the dollar prices and two titles, *The Author of Beltraffio* and *Watch and Ward*, and adds three titles, *The Question of Our Speech*, *Italian Hours* and *English Hours* (1909). It also mentions the "Holiday Edition" of this title, with illustrations by Joseph Pennell, first published in 1900.

The text block is 1″ thick. For bindings uniform with this binding, see 1.11.0.

23.9.7. *A Little Tour in France*, first edition, sixteenth impression, one volume. Boston and New York [n.d., later than 1922].

The title-page, size, collation, and contents are identical to those of the first edition, thirteenth or later impression, 23.9.5, except that the title-leaf verso has on it between the reservation of rights and the printer's imprint: "SIXTEENTH IMPRESSION".

Binding: glazed smooth blue cloth. The front and back covers are neither lettered nor decorated. The spine lettered and decorated in gilt, is identical to the spine on 23.9.5. The endpapers are of cream wove paper, and the text is printed on wove paper. There are no binder's fly-leaves. All edges are trimmed, and the top edge is stained brown.

A LITTLE TOUR IN FRANCE

The text block is $^{27}/_{32}''$ of an inch thick. For bindings uniform with this binding, see 1.11.0.

23.10.0. *A Little Tour in France*, second edition, first impression (trade), binding state A, one volume, Boston 1900.

A LITTLE TOUR | IN FRANCE [all the foregoing in red] | BY HENRY | JAMES | WITH ILLUSTRATIONS | BY JOSEPH PENNELL | [device in red of The Riverside Press] | BOSTON AND NEW YORK | HOUGHTON, MIFFLIN AND COMPANY | The Riverside Press, Cambridge [in red Gothic type] | MDCCCC.

Size: 7 3/4" x 5 1/8".

Collation: [unsigned, 1^2 (1_1+X_1) 2^6 $3-24^8$]; pp. $1\pi-4\pi$ [i–xiv], [1]–345 [346] [347–352]. Half-title not tipped in, but not included in the pagination. Frontispiece, X_1, and 43 additional leaves with full-page illustrations (on the rectos only) tipped in and not reckoned in the pagination.

Contents: $1\pi-2\pi$ half-title, verso blank; $3\pi-4\pi$ blank, verso frontispiece with tissue guard tipped in and not reckoned in the pagination; [i–ii] title-page, verso copyright notice: "COPYRIGHT, 1884 AND 1900, BY HENRY JAMES | COPYRIGHT, 1900, BY HOUGHTON, MIFFLIN & CO."; [iii]–vii "PREFACE"; [viii] blank; [ix]–x "CONTENTS"; [xi]–xiii "LIST OF ILLUSTRATIONS"; [xiv] blank; [1]–345 text; [346] blank; [347]–350 "INDEX"; [351–352] blank, verso printer's imprint: "The Riverside Press [in Gothic type] | Electrotyped and Printed by H. O. Houghton & Co. | Cambridge, Mass., U.S.A. [last two lines in italic]".

Binding: dark green smooth-linen-grain cloth. The front cover is lettered in cream-green and decorated in red, cream-green and gilt, which lettering and decoration are enclosed within a single-rule cream-green border subdivided into five further panels with cream-green borders, and reads: "A LITTLE | TOUR IN | FRANCE | [illustration of a castle with cream-green walls and ramparts, red roofs and gilt sky] | by [in swash italic] | HENRY JAMES". The back cover is neither lettered nor decorated. The spine, which is lettered in gilt and decorated in cream-green reads: "[within a cream-green frame] A LITTLE | TOUR IN | FRANCE | By | HENRY | JAMES | Illustrated | By | Joseph Pennell | [two vertical fleurs de lys] | [within a small cream-green frame] HOUGHTON | MIFFLIN & CO." The publisher's imprint at the foot of the spine has a stylized ampersand and a period after the "O" in "CO". The endpapers are of white laid paper, and the text is printed on smooth wove paper. A binder's fly-leaf of wove paper is at the front, but none at the back. The top edge is gilt, the fore-edge untrimmed, and the bottom edge rough trimmed.

23.11.0. *A Little Tour in France*, second edition, first impression (trade), binding state B, one volume, Boston 1900.

This copy is identical to the second edition, first impression (trade), 23.10.0, except that the lettering and panels on the front cover and spine, and the castle walls and ramparts on the front cover, are cream-yellow rather than cream-green.

23.11.5. *A Little Tour in France*, second edition, first impression (trade), "de-luxe" binding state, one volume, Boston and New York 1900.

Size; 7 3/4" x 5".

The title-page, collation, and contents are identical to those of the second edition, first trade impression (trade), 23.10.0.

Binding: bright-red polished half-morocco, with red marble paper over boards and red morocco fore-corners. The front and rear covers are decorated with a gilt fillet where the leather meets the marble paper. The spine, which is lettered in gilt, reads: "[gilt ornament with leaves and a flower canted to the right] | [false raised band] | A LITTLE | TOUR IN | FRANCE | [false raised band] | [gilt ornament with leaves and a flower canted to the left] | [false raised band] | HENRY | JAMES | [false raised band] | [gilt ornament with leaves and a flower canted to the right] | [false raised band] | [larger gilt ornament with leaves and a flower canted to the left]". The endpapers are of red marble paper (the same as the marble paper covering the boards), and the text is printed on smooth wove paper. Two binder's fly-leaves of wove paper are at both the front and the back. The top edge is gilt, and the other edges are rough trimmed. A red ribbon marker is bound in.

Noted in E&L A23b. For a similar binding see 23.17.5.

23.12.0. *A Little Tour in France*, second edition, second impression (limited), one volume, Cambridge 1900.

[continuous rule composed of fleurs-de-lys in red] | A Little Tour | in France | by | HENRY JAMES | [red rule] | WITH ILLUSTRATIONS BY JOSEPH PENNELL | [red rule] | [publisher's device in black of a piper under a tree within a frame] | CAMBRIDGE | Printed at The Riverside Press [in red Gothic type] | MDCCCC

Size: 8 ¹³⁄₁₆″ x 6″.

Collation and contents identical to those of the second edition, first impression (trade), 23.10.0, except that on the title-leaf verso, in addition to the copyright notice, there is a limitation notice which reads: "Two Hundred and Fifty Copies | Printed. Number 234 [all but numerals in Gothic type]".

Binding: white half buckram with light gray-blue paper over boards with small white paper fore-corners. The front and back covers are neither lettered nor decorated. The spine has a paper label which reads: "[five red fleurs-de-lys in a row] | A LITTLE | TOUR | IN | FRANCE | [red rule] | HENRY JAMES | [red rule] | Large Paper [in Gothic type] | [five red fleurs-de-lys in a row]". The endpapers are of white laid paper, and the text is printed on laid paper. A binder's fly-leaf of laid paper is at the front, but none at the back. All edges are untrimmed.

This limited impression was originally issued in a slipcase box, which is not present on this copy.

23.13.0. *A Little Tour in France*, second edition, third impression, one volume, Boston 1901.

The title-page is identical to that of the second edition, first impression (trade), 23.10.0, except that it is dated MDCCCCI at the foot.

The size, collation, and contents are identical to those of 23.10.0.

The binding is identical to that on 23.10.0, including the lettering on the front cover and spine, except that the castle walls and ramparts on the front cover are in cream-yellow rather than cream-green. The endpapers are of white laid paper, and the text is printed on smooth wove paper. A binder's fly-leaf of wove paper is at the front, but none at the back. The top edge is gilt, and the other edges are rough trimmed On the front free endpaper is the inscription: "J. L. H. | from | E. W. H. | Xmas. 1903."

23.14.0. *A Little Tour in France*, second edition, fifth or sixth impression, one volume, Boston [n.d., 1907 or 1908].

The title-page, size, collation, and contents are identical to those of the second edition, first impression (trade), 23.10.0, except that the title-page is undated.

The binding on this copy is identical to that on 23.10.0, including the lettering and panels on the front cover and spine, and the castle walls and ramparts on the front cover in cream-green. The endpapers are of white laid paper, and the text is printed on smooth wove paper. A binder's fly-leaf of wove paper is at the front, but none at the back. The top edge is gilt, and the other edges are untrimmed.

On the front pastedown is the bookplate of Diane Maxwell, and on the front free end-paper is the inscription: "To dear Addie from [illegible] | in memory of our | "little tour" in 1908. | Xmas."

23.15.0. *A Little Tour in France*, second edition, fifth impression, The Atlantic Monthly Library of Travel binding state A, one volume, Boston 1907.

[Within a red frame] | THE ATLANTIC MONTHLY | [red rule] | LIBRARY OF TRAVEL | [red rule] | VOLUME THREE | [red rule] | A LITTLE TOUR | IN FRANCE | BY | HENRY JAMES | WITH ILLUS-TRATIONS | BY JOSEPH PENNELL | [oval publisher's device in red] | [red rule] | BOSTON AND NEW YORK | HOUGHTON MIFFLIN & COMPANY | THE RIVERSIDE PRESS | CAMBRIDGE | [red rule] | 1907

Size: $7\,3/4''$ x $4\,15/16''$.

Collation: [unsigned, 1–28^8 29^4]; pp. 1π–4π [i–xiv], [1]–345 [346] [347]–350 [352–352] plus 86. Series half-tithe leaf, [1$_1$], frontispiece, [1$_2$], and a further 43 additional leaves with full page illustrations (on the rectos only), not tipped in, but not reckoned in the pagination.

Contents: 1π–2π series half-title, verso blank; 3π–4π blank, verso frontispiece with tissue guard; [i–ii] title-page, verso "COPYRIGHT, 1884 AND 1900, BY HENRY JAMES | COPYRIGHT, 1900, BY HOUGHTON, MIFFLIN & CO."; [iii]–vii "PREFACE"; [viii] blank; [ix]–x "CONTENTS" [xi]–xiii "LIST OF ILLUSTRATIONS"; [xiv] blank; [1]–345 text; [346] blank; [347]–350 "INDEX"; [351–352] blank leaf. The series half-title, 1π–2π, and frontispiece, 3π–4π, and a further 43 full-page illustrations

[258]

not tipped in, but not reckoned in the pagination. These 43 illustrations are printed on the recto of each of their leaves, the verso being blank. The reverse is the case for the frontispiece. Leaf [29$_4$], [351–352], of this impression lacks on the verso the printer's imprint present in the second edition, first impression (trade), 23.10.0.

Binding: bright red smooth cloth, decorated on the front and back covers with a double-rule border in blind with small quarter circles in blind at the four corners of the ruled border. The spine, which is elaborately decorated in gilt with three panels and three circular decorations of a tree in fruit, reads: "The | Atlantic | Monthly | Library | of | Travel | [circular tree ornament] | III | A Little Tour | In France | Henry | James Jr. | [two circular tree ornaments] | Houghton | Mifflin & Co". The endpapers are of white laid paper, and the text and illustrations are printed on smooth wove paper. A binder's fly-leaf of wove paper is at both the front and the back. The top edge is gilt, and the other edges are rough trimmed.

It should be noted that the series half-title leaf, the frontispiece, and the 43 leaves with full-page illustrations, although not reckoned in the pagination, are in this copy printed on book stock and are an integral part of the signatures of the book rather than being tipped in as they were (with the exception of the series half-title leaf) in the second edition, first impression, (trade), 23.10.0.

Noted but not described in E&L A23b.

23.16.0. *A Little Tour in France*, second edition, fifth impression, The Atlantic Monthly Library of Travel binding state B, one volume, Boston 1907.

The title-page, size, collation, and contents of this copy are identical to those of the second edition, fifth impression, 23.15.0, (including the wording "THE ATLANTIC MONTHLY LIBRARY | OF TRAVEL" on the series half-title).

Binding: identical to that on 23.15.0, except that the spine reads: "A | Little Tour | In France | by | Henry | James Jr. | The | Atlantic | Library | of | Travel | Houghton | Mifflin & Co". The word "Monthly" is not present in the series title on the spine.

A LITTLE TOUR IN FRANCE

23.17.0. *A Little Tour in France*, second edition, later impression, one volume, Boston [n.d.].

The title-page, size, collation, and contents are identical to those of the second edition, first impression (trade), 23.10.0, except that the title-page is undated.

Binding: identical to that on 23.10.0, including the lettering and panels on the front cover and spine, and the castle walls on the front cover are in cream-yellow. However, the publisher's imprint on the spine reads: "HOUGHTON | MIFFLIN & CO", with a stylized ampersand but with no period after the "O" in "CO". The endpapers are of thick white wove paper, and the text is printed on smooth wove paper. A binder's fly-leaf of wove paper is at the front, but none at the back. The top edge is gilt, and the other edges are untrimmed.

Dust-jacket: beige wove paper, with all lettering and decoration in red. On the front cover lettering within two horizontal rectangular panels which are separated by three vertical panels, all of which are within a ruled border, and on the spine lettering within two single-rule panels separated by two fleurs-de-lys, all within a single-rule border. The front cover reads: "A LITTLE | TOUR IN | FRANCE | [three rectangular panels] | by [in swash italic] | HENRY JAMES". The spine reads: "A LITTLE | TOUR IN | FRANCE | By [in swash italic] | HENRY | JAMES | Illustrated | By | Joseph | Pennell [all after the author's name in swash italic] | [two fleurs-de-lys] | HOUGHTON | MIFFLIN & CO." The ampersand in the publisher's imprint is stylized. The back cover and the front and back inner flaps are blank.

23.17.5. *A Little Tour in France*, second edition, later impression, "de-luxe" binding state, one volume, Boston [n.d., 1908 or later].

A LITTLE TOUR | IN FRANCE [all the foregoing in red] | BY HENRY | JAMES | WITH ILLUSTRATIONS | BY JOSEPH PENNELL | [publisher's device in red] | BOSTON AND NEW YORK | HOUGHTON MIFFLIN COMPANY | The Riverside Press, Cambridge [in red Gothic type]

Collation: [unsigned, 1^{10} (-1_{10}) $2-8^8$ 9^{10} (-9_{10}) $10-27^8$ 28^{10} (-28_{10})]; pp. $1\pi-4\pi$ [i–xiv], [1–345] [346] [347]–350 plus 86. This collation is conjectural as it is not possible to ascertain the exact composition of $[1^{10}]$ and $[28^{10}]$, except to record that they are of nine leaves each, because these signatures are tightly machine side-sewn. Forty-three leaves with full-page illustrations (on the recto only) are an integral part of the signatures of the book and are not tipped in, but not reckoned in the pagination.

Contents: 1π–2π half-title, verso blank; 3π–4π blank, verso frontispiece with tissue guard not tipped in, but not reckoned in the pagination; [i–ii] title-page, verso copyright notice: "COPYRIGHT, 1884 AND 1900, BY HENRY JAMES | COPYRIGHT, 1900, BY HOUGHTON, MIFFLIN & CO."; [iii]–vii "PREFACE"; [viii] blank; [ix]–x "CONTENTS"; [xi]–xiii "LIST OF ILLUSTRATIONS"; [xiv] blank; [1]–345 text; [346] blank; [347]–350 "INDEX".

Binding: red half-leather, with red marble paper over boards and red leather fore-corners. The front and rear covers are decorated with a gilt fillet where the leather meets the marble paper. The spine, which is lettered and decorated in gilt, reads: "[square gilt ornament] | [false raised band] | A LITTLE | TOUR IN | FRANCE | [false raised band] | [square gilt ornament] | [false raised band] | HENRY JAMES | [false raised band] | [square gilt ornament] | [false raised band] | [square gilt ornament followed by small oblong gilt ornament]". The endpapers are of red marble paper, and the text is printed on smooth wove paper. There are two binder's fly-leaves of rougher wove paper at both the front and the back. The top edge is gilt, and the other edges are rough trimmed. A red ribbon marker is bound in.

For a similar binding, see 23.11.5.

23.17.7. *A Little Tour in France*, second edition, seventh impression, one volume, Boston and New York [n.d., 1912].

The title-page is identical to that of the second edition, later impression, 23.17.5, except it is printed entirely in black.

Size: 7 3/8" x 4 7/16".

Collation: [unsigned, 1^8 (1_1+X_1) 2–22^8 23^6]; pp. 1π–4π [i]–x, [1]–345 [346] [347]–350 [351–352] plus 2.

Contents: 1π–2π series half-title and half-title, verso blank, not reckoned in the pagination; 3π–4π blank, verso frontispiece tipped in, not reckoned in the pagination; [i–ii] title-page, verso copyright notice and printer's imprint: "COPYRIGHT, 1SS4 [sic], 1900, AND 1912, BY HENRY JAMES | COPYRIGHT, 1900, BY HOUGHTON, MIFFLIN & CO. | The Riverside Press [in Gothic type] | CAMBRIDGE [dot]

MASSACHUSETTS | PRINTED IN THE U. S. A."; [iii]–vii "PREFACE"; [viii] blank; [ix]–x "CONTENTS", verso continuation of contents; [1]–345 text; [346] blank; [347]–350 "INDEX"; [351–352] blank leaf.

The only full-page illustrations in 23.17.5 present in this copy is the frontispiece, X_1. The illustrations on or within text pages are identical to those in 23.17.5

Binding: red linen-grain cloth. The front cover has a centered gilt floral crown-like cartouche within which, lettered in gilt, is: "The | Park Street Library". The spine, lettered and decorated in gilt, reads: "[rule] | [small horizontal leaf and vine design] | A LITTLE | TOUR | IN FRANCE | [rule] | HENRY | JAMES | [decoration of an old coach] | HOUGHTON | MIFFLIN CO. | [small horizontal leaf and vine design] | [rule]". The back cover is neither lettered nor decorated. The endpapers are of cream heavy wove paper, and the text is printed on smooth wove paper. There are no binder's fly-leaves. All edges are trimmed.

The seventh impression of the second edition was printed on May 20, 1912. It is the last recorded impression of this edition.

E&L A23b records that: "sheets of the second edition were later issued, with unaltered title-page date [1900], in the uniform binding of the Park Street Library." This copy indicates that not all copies contain a title-page date, which would suggest more than one printing of this title was used for the Park Street Library series.

See *English Hours*, 62.11.0, for another James title in The Park Street Library of Travel.

23.18.0. *A Little Tour in France*, first English edition, first impression (trade), one volume, London 1900.

A LITTLE | TOUR IN FRANCE | BY | HENRY JAMES | [illustration of a street and church] | WITH NINETY-FOUR ILLUSTRATIONS BY | JOSEPH PENNELL | LONDON | WILLIAM HEINEMANN | 1900

Size: $8^{1}/_{16}''$ x 6".

Collation: $\pi^8(\pi_1+X_1)$ A–I K–R^8; pp. [i]–xvi, 1–270 [271–272] plus 2. Frontispiece, X_1, and 43 further illustrations tipped in and not reckoned in the pagination. A further 50 illustrations are on or within the text pages.

Contents: [i–ii] half-title, verso ad headed: "NOVELS BY | HENRY JAMES", listing 7 titles; frontispiece with tissue guard tipped in not reckoned in the pagination; [iii–iv] title-page, verso copyright notice: "[all in italic] This Edition enjoys Copyright in all | Countries Signatory to the Berne | Treaty, and is not to be imported | into the United States of America."; v-viii "Preface"; ix–xi "Contents"; [xii] small illustration centered on the page; xiii–xvi "List of Illustrations"; 1–270 text; 270 at foot printer's imprint: "Printed by Ballantyne, Hanson & Co. | London & Edinburgh"; [271–272] blank leaf.

Binding: gray linen-grain cloth, lettered and decorated on the front cover and spine in black and gilt, and lettered on the back cover in black. The front cover reads: "A : LITTLE : TOUR : IN | FRANCE : BY : HENRY | JAMES : ILLUSTRATED | BY : JOSEPH : PENNELL | W [windmill] H". The spine reads: "A : LITTLE | TOUR : IN | FRANCE | HENRY [small flower design] | JAMES [small flower design] | HEINEMANN [in gilt]". The back cover is the same as the front cover, except that it lacks the windmill device and "W" and "H". The endpapers are of white wove paper, and the text is printed on smooth wove paper. The top edge is gilt, and the other edges are untrimmed. This binding has a rounded back.

English printing history: There is no information in the Heinemann Archive regarding the printing history of this title, as the Ledger for the period 1898 to 1905 is missing. From secondary sources and the books themselves the following information is available: the first impression (trade) of 1500 copies was published in 1900, priced at 10s. The second impression (limited) of 150 copies was also published in 1900, priced at £2.00. A third impression was published in 1901 (repaginated, but clearly printed from the first English edition plates). The number of copies printed of the third impressions is unknown. A fourth impression, known as the "New and Cheaper Edition" (also repaginated, but clearly printed from the first English edition plates), was published in 1907 and reprinted in 1922 and 1924. The number of copies printed and the price are unknown.

23.19.0. *A Little Tour in France*, first English edition, second impression (limited), one volume, London 1900.

Size: 9 7/8″ x 6 3/8″.

The title-page, collation, and contents are identical to those of the first English edition, first impression (trade), 23.18.0, except that the illustration on the title-page is in sepia, and the addition of the limitation notice on the verso of the half-title-leaf which reads: "This Edition on Japanese Vellum consists | of One Hundred and Fifty Copies Only, | of which this is No. 48".

Binding: white vellum lettered and decorated in gilt on the front and back covers and spine. The front and back covers are lettered identically to 28.18.0, but having both the windmill device and "W" and "H" within a small single-rule gilt frame, beneath which is "HEINEMANN". The spine is lettered and decorated identically to that of 23.18.0. The text is printed on a heavy Japanese vellum, and the endpapers are of the same stock. The top edge is gilt, and the other edges are untrimmed.

Dust-jacket: cream laid paper, lettered on the front cover and spine in brown. The lettering, publisher's device and other decorative elements on the front cover and spine of the dust jacket are identical to those on the front cover and spine of the book, except that the spine of the dust-jacket has printed on it between the title and author's name: "£2/0/0 | NET". The back cover is blank, as are the inner front and rear flaps, which have deckle edges.

Tanselle dust-jacket 1900.61.

23.20.0. *A Little Tour in France*, first English edition, third impression, one volume, London 1901.

The title-page is identical to that of the first English edition, first impression (trade), 23.18.0, except that it is dated 1901 at the foot.

Size : 8″ x 5 13/16″.

Collation: $\pi^8(\pi_1+X_1)$ A–I K–U X^8; pp. [i–xvi], 1–[334] [335–336] plus 2. Frontispiece, X_1, with tissue guard and a further 11 illustrations with tissue guards, are tipped in and not reckoned in the pagination. However, 32 full-page illustrations, which in the first impression, above, were also tipped in and not reckoned in the pagination, in this impression are printed as part of the signatures of the text and are reckoned in the pagination. In each case the illustration is on the recto of the leaf, and the verso is blank. These full-page illustrations that are not tipped in account for the fact that this impression has sixty-four more pages than 23.18.0.

Contents: [i–ii] half-title, verso ad for Howells's *Italian Journeys*; frontispiece with tissue guard tipped in not reckoned in the pagination; [iii–iv] title-page, verso printing history and copyright notice: "First Impression, 1900 | Second [*sic*, actually the third] Impression, 1901 | This Edition enjoys Copyright in all | Countries signatory to the Berne | Treaty, and is not to be imported | into the United States of America [all the foregoing in italic, but with no period at the end]"; v–viii "Preface"; ix–xi "Contents"; [xii] small centered illustration; xiii–xv "List of Illustrations"; [xvi] small centered illustration; 1–[334] text; [334] at foot printer's imprint: "Printed by Ballantyne, Hanson & Co. | London & Edinburgh; [335–6] blank leaf.

Binding: identical to that on the first English edition, first impression (trade), 23.18.0, except that it has a square rather than a rounded back. The endpapers are of white wove paper, and the text is printed on smooth wove paper. The top edge is gilt, the fore-edge is trimmed and the bottom edge is untrimmed.

The "Contents" and "List of Illustrations" have been reset.

The verso of the title-leaf of Heinemann's 1924 impression of this title states that a new "edition" was published by Heinemann in 1907, and was reprinted in 1922 and 1924; see 23.21.0.

23.21.0. *A Little Tour in France*, first English edition, fourth impression, one volume, London 1907.

The title-page is identical to that of the first English edition, first impression (trade), 23.18.0, except that it is dated 1907 at the foot.

Size: $7\,1/2''$ x $4\,7/8''$.

Collation: $1\pi^8\ 2\pi^2$ A–I K–U X–Y^8 [Z]^2; pp. [i–xviii], 1–[334] plus 24. The frontispiece and eleven further leaves, illustrated on the recto, with the verso blank, are not tipped in, but are not reckoned in the pagination.

Contents: [i–ii] blank leaf; [iii–iv] half-title, verso ad headed: "Delightful Books of Travel [in Gothic type]", listing 9 titles, one (*English

Hours) by James; frontispiece with tissue guard not tipped in, but not reckoned in the pagination; [v–vi] title-page, verso printing history and copyright notice: "First Printed, 1900 | Second [*sic*, actually the third] Impression, 1901 | New and Cheaper Edition, 1907 | This Edition enjoys Copyright in all | Countries signatory to the Berne | Treaty, and is not to be imported | into the United States of America [all the foregoing in italic, but with no period at the end]"; vii-x "Preface"; xi–xiii "Contents", [xiv] small centered illustration ; xv-xviii "List of Illustrations"; 1–2 "Introductory"; 3–[334] text; [334] at foot printer's imprint: "Printed by Ballantyne & Co. Limited | Tavistock Street, London".

Binding: blue linen-grain cloth over semi-flexible boards. The front cover, lettered and decorated in gilt, reads: "[in upper left, scrollwork decorative arm from which hangs a shield with an oval townscape centered on it] | A LITTLE TOUR | IN FRANCE". The back cover has in the lower right a circular publisher's device in blind. The spine, lettered and decorated in gilt, reads: "[shield-shaped scroll hanging from a decorative bar within which is] A Little | Tour in | France | [dot] | Henry James | [at the foot within a scroll] Heinemann [all the foregoing lettering in swash italic]". The endpapers are of white wove paper, and the text is printed on coated paper. The top edge is trimmed and stained dark blue, the fore-edge is trimmed, and the bottom edge is rough trimmed.

23.22.0. *A Little Tour in France*, first continental edition, first impression, one volume, Leipzig 1885.

A LITTLE TOUR | IN | FRANCE. | BY HENRY JAMES, | AUTHOR OF "DAISY MILLER," "THE AMERICAN," ETC. | AUTHORIZED EDITION. [in italic] | LEIPZIG | BERNHARD TAUCHNITZ | 1885.

Size: $6\,5/8''$ x $4\,3/4''$.

Collation: $[1]^8$ $2-17^8$ 18^4; pp. [1–4], [5]–279 [280].

Contents: [1–2] series half-title and volume number, verso ad headed: "Tauchnitz edition. | By the same Author", listing 13 titles, the last of which is *Portraits of Places*; [3–4] title-page, verso James's authorization note dated May, 1885; [5]–279 text; [280] centered printer's imprint: "[rule] | PRINTING OFFICE OF THE PUBLISHER. | [rule]".

Binding: buff wove paper wrappers, cut flush, with lettering on the front cover in black within a black single-rule frame which is decorated with a flower-like device at each of the four corners with lettering above and below the frame. Within the frame the title and author's name are on one line. The spine is also lettered in black between a series of eight pairs of thick and thin black rules. The back cover, which is also lettered in black, reads: "October 1895. | TAUCHNITZ EDITION. | [rule] | Latest volumes: | [followed by a list of 25 Tauchnitz titles (six being two volumes), volumes 3054 to 3084, the last of which is *At Heart a Rake* by Florence Marryat] | [long rule] | The Tauchnitz Edition is to be had at all Book- | sellers and Railway Libraries on the Continent, price | M 1, 60. or 2 francs per volume. A complete Cata- | logue of the Tauchnitz Edition is attached to this work." The insides of the front and back covers are blank. A 16-page paginated publisher's catalogue, dated October 1895, is bound in at the end.

See T&B 2334a. T&B does not record a copy of the first impression with wrappers dated October 1895, but notes the first impression with wrappers dated June 1885, March 1894, July 1901, May 1909, and March and September 1910. T&B 3083 records that *At Heart a Rake* was first published by Tauchnitz in 1895.

23.23.0. *A Little Tour in France*, first continental edition, first impression, one volume, Leipzig 1885.

The title-page, size, collation, and contents are identical to those of the first continental edition, first impression, 23.22.0.

Binding: identical to the binding on 23.22.0, except as noted below. The title and author's name on the front cover are on three lines rather than one, reading "A LITTLE TOUR IN FRANCE. | BY | HENRY JAMES. [in sans-serif]". The addresses below the publisher's imprint on the front cover are on two lines rather than three and read: "PARIS: LIBRAIRIE H. GAULON & Cie, 39, RUE MADAME; | THE GALIGNANI LIBRARY, 224, RUE DE RIVOLI." Below the frame a notice reads: "The Copyright of this Collection | is purchased for Continental Circulation only, and the volumes may | therefore not be introduced into Great Britain or her Colonies. | (See also pp. 3–6 of Larger Catalogue.)". The back cover is dated at the top "May 1909.", and lists Tauchnitz volumes 4080 to 4109/10, the last of which is *An Incompleat Etonian* by Frank Damby. At the foot of the back cover is the legend: "The Tauchnitz Edition is to be had at all Book- | sellers and Railway Libraries on the Continent, price | M 1, 60. or 2 francs per volume. A complete Cata-|logue of the Tauchnitz Edition is attached to this work." The spine is identical to that of 23.22.0. The insides of the front and back covers are blank. A 32-page paginated catalogue, dated February 1, 1910, is bound in at the end.

T&B 4109–4910 records that *An Incompleat Etonian* was first published by Tauchnitz in 1909.

Illustrated Plate 11.

23.24.0. *A Little Tour in France*, first continental edition, second impression, one volume, Leipzig 1885 [1913].

The title-page, size, collation, and contents are identical to those of the first continental edition, first impression, 23.22.0, except that the half-title verso lists 15 titles, the last dated being *The Outcry*, rather than the 13 titles listed in the first impression.

Binding: identical to the binding on 23.22.0, except as noted below. The title and the author's name on the front cover are on three lines rather than one, reading: "A LITTLE TOUR IN FRANCE.|BY|HENRY JAMES.[in sans-serif]". The addresses below the publisher's imprint on the front cover read: "PARIS: LIBRARIE HENRI GAULON, 39, RUE MADAME;|THE GALIGNANI LIBRARY, 224, RUE DE RIVOLI." The notice below the frame on the front cover reads as in 23.23.0. The back cover is dated at the top "February 1913", and lists Tauchnitz volumes 4357 to 4386, the last of which is *The Procession of Life*, by Horace Annesley Vachell. Following a long rule at the foot of the back cover is the legend: "The Tauchnitz Edition is sold by all Booksellers and Rail-|way Libraries on the Continent, price of each volume M 1, 60 or|francs 2,00 sewed, M 2, 20 or francs 2, 75 cloth (Original –Leinen-| band), M 3,00 or francs 3, 75 in elegant soft binding (Original -|Geschenkband). A complete Catalogue of the Tauchnitz Edition is | attached to this work." The spine is identical to that of 23.22.0. The insides of the front and back covers are blank. A 32-page paginated publisher's catalogue, dated April 1, 1914, is bound in at the end.

T&B 2334b records copies with wrappers and catalogue dated as above, as the second impression. *The Procession of Life* was first published by Tauchnitz in 1913. T&B records one edition with three impressions of this title prior to 1921. The first has 13, the second has 15 and the third has 16 titles listed on the half-title verso.

A LITTLE TOUR IN FRANCE

23.25.0. *A Little Tour in France*, first continental edition, third impression, one volume, Leipzig, 1885.

Title-page, size, collation, and contents are identical to those of the first continental edition, first impression, 23.22.0, except that the half-title verso lists 16 titles, the last dated being *The Outcry*, rather than the 13 titles listed in the first impression and 15 in the second impression, on [4], below the authorization note, is centered the printer's imprint: "PRINTED BY BERNHARD TAUCHNITZ, LEIPZIG", and on [280] the printer's imprint reads: "[rule] | PRINTED BY BERNHARD TAUCHNITZ, LEIPZIG | [rule]".

Binding: buff wove paper wrappers, cut flush, with lettering on the front cover in black within a double-rule frame, the outer being wider than the inner, which frames are divided into three sections by thin double rules. The lettering in the upper panel reads: :TAUCHNITZ EDITION | COLLECTION OF BRITISH AND AMERICAN AUTHORS | VOL. 2334". The middle panel reads: "A LITTLE TOUR | IN FRANCE | BY | HENRY JAMES [all the foregoing in sans-serif] | IN ONE VOLUME | LEIPZIG: BERNHARD TAUCHNITZPARIS: LIBRAIRIE HENRY GAULON, 39, RUE MADAME". The lower panel reads: "The Copyright of this Collection is purchased for Continental Circulation | only and the volumes may not be introduced into Great Britain | or her Colonies. (See also pp. 3–6 of Larger Catalogue.)" Below the frame reads: "EACH VOLUME SOLD SEPERATELY".The spine, also lettered in black between a series of eight pairs of thick and thin rules, between rules six and seven reads: "PRICE | M 1.60". The back cover, also lettered in black, reads at the top: "TAUCHNITZION | Latest volumes | 4–6 new volumes are published regularly every month [in italic] | March 1925", followed by a list of volumes 4677 to 4647, in descending numerical order. There is no catalogue of ads bound in at the end.

23.26.0. *A Little Tour in France*, first continental edition, fourth impression, one volume, Leipzig 1885.

Title-page, size, collation, and contents are identical to those of the first continental edition, third impression, 23.25.0, except that on [280] the printer's imprint is absent.

Binding: identical to the binding on the first continental edition, third impression, except that the back cover reads: "TAUCHNITZION |

Latest Volumes | 4–6 new volumes are published regularly every month [in italic] | July 1925", followed by a list of volumes 4693 to 4665, in descending numerical order. Bound in at the end is a 4 page publisher's catalogue of ads dated January 1926.

❧✢❧

24. TALES OF THREE CITIES

24.1.0. *Tales of Three Cities*, first edition, first impression, first binding state, one volume, Boston 1884.

HENRY JAMES | [rule] | TALES OF THREE CITIES | [monogram publisher's device] | BOSTON | JAMES R. OSGOOD AND COMPANY | [rule] | 1884

Size: $7\,5/16''$ x $4\,13/16''$.

Collation: $[1^2\ 2\text{–}31^6]$, signed as $[1]^{10}\ 2\text{–}4^8\ [5]^8\ 6\text{–}16^8\ [17]^8\ 18\text{–}22^8\ 23^4$; pp. [2] [i–ii] [1–2], [3]–359 [360].

Contents: blank leaf; [i–ii] title-page, verso copyright notice, reservation of rights and printer's imprint: "Copyright, 1883 and 1884, [in italic] | By Henry James. | [rule] | All rights reserved. [in italic] | University Press: [in Gothic type] | John Wilson and Son, Cambridge."; [1–2] divisional fly-title, verso blank; [3]–359 text; [360] blank.

Binding: ochre diagonal-fine-ribbed cloth. The front and back covers are decorated in blind with a single-rule border within a thicker single-rule frame. The spine, lettered and decorated in gilt, reads: "TALES | OF | THREE CITIES | [rule] | Henry James | [J. R. Osgood monogram]". The endpapers are of white wove paper, and the text is printed on wove paper. There are no binder's fly-leaves. All edges are trimmed, and the top-edge is stained light brown.

The text block of this copy is $1\,1/4''$ thick.

BAL 10569 records four cloth colors for the first binding state of this impression: blue, brown, green and mustard. E&L records three colors, omitting green. Both record copies in diagonal-fine-ribbed cloth only.

American printing history. Houghton Mifflin Archive. First edition: Ms Am 2030.3(9), 26 and Ms Am 2030.3(14), 70: *first* [Osgood] *impression* June 24, 1884, 1508 copies, 1102 bound between October 11, 1884, and February 14, 1885; Ms Am 2030.3(14), 222: *second* [first Ticknor & Co.] *impression* July 6, 1887, 3018 copies, 2967 bound between July 18, 1887, and July 22, 1887; Ms Am 2030(19), 157: notation: "rcvd from T[icknor] & Co. 4/11/89 400 copies", 282 bound between May 19, 1890, and September 23, 1898.[31] Ms Am 2030(20), 220: notation "March 31, 1899 bal. 113 copies", 97 bound between March 7, 1901, and March 24, 1905. Ms Am 2030(22), 219: *third* [first Houghton, Mifflin] *impression*, but not specified, March 31, 1906, 154 copies, 150 bound between March 31, 1906, and August 2, 1910; *fourth impression*, but not specified, November 27, 1912, 156 copies, 150 bound between March 7, 1913, and October 4, 1915.

Priced (in cloth) at $1.50. In 1892, 1897, and 1901 copies of this title in paper were advertised at $.50.

24.2.0. *Tales of Three Cities*, first edition, first impression, first binding state, one volume, Boston 1884.

This copy is identical to first edition, first impression, first binding state, 24.1.0, except that it is bound in blue diagonal-fine-ribbed cloth. The endpapers are of white wove paper, and the text is printed on wove paper. There are no binder's fly-leaves. All edges are trimmed, and the top edge is stained light-brown.

24.3.0. *Tales of Three Cities*, first edition, first impression, first binding state, one volume, Boston 1884.

This copy is identical to first edition, first impression, first binding state, 24.1.0, except that it is bound in light chocolate-brown diagonal-fine-ribbed cloth. The endpapers are of white wove paper, and the text is printed on wove paper. There are no binder's fly-leaves. All edges are trimmed, and the top edge is stained light-brown.

E&L A24a calls this binding color dull violet-brown.

---

31 The 400 copies received by Houghton, Mifflin from Ticknor & Co. were of the first not the second impression. See David J. Supino, "Henry James' Tales of Three Cities: A Correction", *The Papers of the Bibliographical Society of America*, Volume 104, Number 3 (September 2010), 361–364.

TALES OF THREE CITIES

24.4.0. *Tales of Three Cities*, first edition, first impression, first binding state, one volume, Boston 1884.

This copy is identical to the first edition, first impression, first binding state, 24.1.0, except that it is bound in forest-green diagonal-fine-ribbed cloth. The endpapers are of white wove paper, and the text is printed on wove paper. There are no binder's fly-leaves. All edges are trimmed.

This cloth color is not recorded in E&L.

This copy is from the library of George Godfrey (1840–1897), who was a partner of Ticknor & Co. from 1885 (when it bought out the second Osgood firm) until 1889, when Ticknor & Co. was acquired by Houghton, Mifflin.

24.5.0. *Tales of Three Cities*, first edition, first impression, second binding state, one volume, Boston 1884.

The title-page, collation, and contents of this copy are identical to those of the first edition, first impression, first binding state, 24.1.0.

Size: 7 3/8″ x 4 13/16″.

Binding: smooth olive-green cloth. The front and back covers are neither lettered nor decorated. The spine, which is lettered in gilt, reads: "TALES | OF | THREE CITIES | [rule] | Henry James | HOUGHTON | MIFFLIN [dot] & [dot] CO." The ampersand is like a figure "8", but is the same size as the other letters in the imprint. The endpapers are of cream laid paper, and the text is printed on wove paper. A binder's fly-leaf of wove paper is at the back, but none at the front. All edges are trimmed.

The text block is 1 1/4″ thick, as is the case with 24.5.5 and 24.6.0. This copy and the one below (24.5.5) were bound by Houghton, Mifflin between May 1890 and March 1905.

Noted in Wolff 3585.

24.5.5. *Tales of Three Cities*, first edition, first impression, second binding state, one volume, Boston 1884.

The title-page, collation, and contents of this copy are identical to those of the first edition, first impression, first binding state, 24.1.0.

Size: 7 5/16″ x 4 13/16″″

TALES OF THREE CITIES

Binding: smooth brown cloth. The front and back covers are neither lettered nor decorated. The spine is lettered and decorated in gilt identically (including the publisher's imprint) to that of the first edition, first impression, second binding state, 24.5.0. The endpapers are of cream laid paper, and the text is printed on wove paper. A binder's fly-leaf of wove paper is at the back, but none at the front. All edges are trimmed, and the top edge is stained brown.

On the recto of the first leaf is the inscription "C K Barry.|1895."

24.6.0. *Tales of Three Cities*, first edition, first impression, third binding state, one volume, Boston and New York 1891.

TALES OF THREE CITIES | BY | HENRY JAMES | [oblong publisher's devise of of a piper under a tree within in a frame] | BOSTON AND NEW YORK | HOUGHTON, MIFFLIN AND COMPANY | The Riverside Press, Cambridge [in Gothic type] | 1891

Size: 7 3/8" x 4 7/8".

Collation: $[1^1\ 2\text{--}31^6]$, signed as $[1]^9\ 2\text{--}4^8\ [5]^8\ 6\text{--}16^8\ [17]^8\ 18\text{--}22^8\ 23^4$; pp. [i–ii] [1–2], [3]–359 [360].

Contents: [i–ii] title-page, verso copyright notice and reservation of rights as in first edition, first impression, first binding state, 24.1.0, except that there is no printer's imprint present; [1–2] divisional fly-title, verso blank; [3]–359 text; [360] blank.

Binding: brown vertical-rib-grain cloth, lettered and decorated in gilt on the front cover and spine. The front cover has within a single-rule border an elaborate cartouche within which is the title and author's name separated by a decorative rule. The spine reads: "[rule] | TALES OF | THREE CITIES | [decorative rule] | HENRY JAMES | HOUGHTON | MIFFLIN & CO. | [rule]". The ampersand in the publisher's imprint is stylized. The back cover has a single-rule border in blind. The endpapers are of white laid paper, and the text is printed on wove paper. A binder's fly-leaf of thin wove paper is at both the front and the back. All edges are trimmed, and the top edge is stained brown.

On the front free endpaper is the pencil inscription "M E Robinson | Aug. 1. 1903."

This copy is bound up from the first edition, first impression sheets (printed for James R. Osgood and Co.) which were acquired in April

TALES OF THREE CITIES

1889 by Houghton, Mifflin from Ticknor & Company, and issued with a new title-leaf.

This binding is uniform with that on the first impression of the first edition of *The Spoils of Poynton* (1897), 48.6.0.

24.7.0. *Tales of Three Cities*, first edition, second impression, one volume, Boston 1887.

TALES OF THREE CITIES | BY | HENRY JAMES | AUTHOR OF "DAISY MILLER: A COMEDY," "THE SIEGE OF LONDON," | "PORTRAITS OF PLACES," ETC. | FIFTH EDITION [*sic*] [in italic] | [publisher's device of a scroll and pendant shield] | BOSTON | TICKNOR AND COMPANY | 1887

Size: $6\,7/8''$ x $4\,5/8''$.

Collation: $[1-11^{16}\ 12^{8}]$, signed as $[1]^{10}\ 2-4^{8}\ [5]^{8}\ 6-16^{8}\ [17]^{8}\ 18-22^{8}\ 23^{6}$; pp. [i–iv] [1–2], [3]–359 [360] [361–364].

Contents: [i–ii] title-page, verso copyright notice and printer's imprint, as in the first edition, first impression, first binding state, 24.1.0; [iii–iv] "CONTENTS", verso blank; [1–2] divisional fly-title, verso blank; [3]–359 text; [360] blank; [361–364] ads, the first three pages of which are devoted to works by James with dollar prices and press opinions, and the last to "MR. HOWELL'S LATEST NOVELS."

Binding: gray wove paper wrappers, cut flush, decorated and printed in red and a darker gray. The front cover, which is lettered in red, reads: "NUMBER 12 [space] JULY 23, 1887 | [dot] TICKNOR'S [dot] PAPER [dot] SERIES [dot] | [dash] OF [dash] | [dot] CHOICE [dot] READING [dot] | [long rule of closely placed dots] | [three dots in triangle] ISSUED [three dots in triangle] WEEKLY [three dots in a triangle] | ENTERED AT THE POST OFFICE AT BOSTON AS SECOND CLASS MATTER [each word has a dot between it] | [dot] TALES OF [dot] | [dot] THREE CITIES [dot] | [dot] BY [dot] | [dot] HENRY JAMES [dot] | [dot] BOSTON [dot] | [within an elaborate scroll] TICKNOR AND COMPANY | SINGLE NUMBERS 50 CTS [each word with a dot between it] | [dot] QUARTERLY [dot] SUBSCRIPTION [dot] $6.50". A large scroll and cartouche publisher's device printed in gray is centered on the front cover over which the red lettering is in part superimposed. The spine, which is lettered and decorated in red, reads: "[rule of closely spaced dots] | [dot] TICKNOR'S [dot] | [dot] PAPER [dot] | [dot] SERIES [dot] |

[rule of closely spaced dots] | [decorative rule] | TALES | [dot] OF [dot] | THREE | CITIES | [rule of less closely spaced dots] | [dot] BY [dot] | HENRY | JAMES | [decorative rule] | [at the foot all within a decorative frame] TICKNOR | [three dots in a triangle] & [three dots in a triangle] | COMPANY | [rule of closely spaced dots] | BOSTON". The back cover, which is lettered and decorated in red and gray, is headed "Ticknor's Paper Series | For The Summer of 1887 | [short rule] | [followed by a five-line blurb] | The following are the titles of the first numbers: [followed by a list of 14 titles, the twelfth of which is this title] | Price per volume, FIFTY CENTS. Sub- | scription price, post paid, $6.50 a | quarter. Subscriptions received | by the Publishers. | [decorative thin scrolls in red and gray over the bottom]". Inside the front and back covers are ads printed in red within a red beaded frame. There are no endpapers. The text is printed on thin wove paper.

The text block is $3/4$" thick.

Although this copy is stated to be of the "fifth edition" on the title-page, the Ticknor & Co. imprint and the 1887 date would indicate that it is composed of second impression sheets.

The Houghton, Mifflin printing records note that on April 11, 1889, Houghton, Mifflin received 400 sets of sheets of the first edition from Ticknor & Company. BAL 10569 notes that "the record indicates that no copies [of the first impression] were bound by Ticknor & Co." The thickness of the text block ($3/4$") as compared to that issued in Houghton, Mifflin bindings (1 $1/4$") indicate that BAL is correct, that is, the later Houghton, Mifflin bindings-up were of sheets of the first impression.[32]

Paperbacks books, such as this copy, were published in America in so-called periodical form to allow publishers to take advantage of lower postal rates for periodicals (second-class matter) than for books (third-class matter). The difference in rates was significant: in 1885 and continuing until at least 1904, second-class postage was one cent a *pound* or a fraction thereof, whereas third-class postage was one cent for *two ounces* or a fraction thereof. American publishers published books in this periodical format from at least 1879, when these postal classifications were formulated by the United States postmaster. However, in 1902 a newly appointed postmaster sought

---

32 See American printing history following 24.1.0.

to revoke the second-class mail certificate of Houghton, Mifflin & Co. which had been used by them since 1885 to mail their Riverside Literature Series as periodicals, the postmaster contending that the publications in this series were books not periodicals. In that same year Houghton, Mifflin sued the postmaster to enjoin him from revoking their certificate, and prevailed in the lower court. However, this victory was reversed by the D.C. Court of Appeals in *Payne v. Houghton*, 22 App. D.C. 234 (1903), and that reversal was upheld by the U.S. Supreme Court in *Houghton v. Payne*, 194 U.S. 88 (1904), thus ending this practice.

Illustrated plate 12.

24.7.5. *Tales of Three Cities*, first edition, fourth impression, one volume, Boston and New York [n.d., 1912].

TALES OF THREE CITIES | BY | HENRY JAMES | [oblong publisher's device of a piper under a tree within a frame] | BOSTON AND NEW YORK | HOUGHTON MIFFLIN COMPANY | The Riverside Press Cambridge

Size: 7 3/8" x 5".

Collation: [1–22^8 23^6], signed as 1^9 2–4^8 [5]^8 6–16^8 [17]^8 18–22^8 23^5; pp. [i–ii] [1–2], [3]–359 [360] [361–362].

Contents: [i–ii] title-page, verso copyright notice and reservation of rights: "COPYRIGHT, 1883, 1884, 1911 AND 1912, BY THE CENTURY CO. | COPYRIGHT, 1884 AND 1912, BY HENRY JAMES | ALL RIGHTS RESERVED"; [1–2] divisional fly-title, verso blank; [3]–359 text; [360] blank, [361–362] blank leaf.

Binding: brown vertical rib-grain cloth, with lettering and decoration in gilt on the front cover and spine. The front cover has within a blind single-rule border an elaborate cartouche within which is the title and author's name separated by a decorative rule. The spine reads: "[rule] | TALES OF | THREE CITIES | [decorative rule] | HENRY JAMES | HOUGHTON | MIFFLIN CO. | [rule]". The back cover is neither lettered nor decorated. The endpapers are of white wove paper, and the text is printed on wove paper. There are no binder's fly-leaves. All edges are trimmed, and the top edge is stained light brown.

This impression was printed from the same plates used to print the first impression, with changes to the prelims, [i–ii]. The Houghton, Mifflin printing records indicate that the last impression (the fourth) of this edition was printed on November 27, 1912.

This binding is uniform with that of the first American edition, first impression, of *The Spoils of Poynton* (1897), 48.6.0

24.8.0. *Tales of Three Cities*, first English edition, first binding state, one volume, London 1884.

TALES | OF | THREE CITIES | BY | HENRY JAMES | London [in Gothic type] | MACMILLAN AND CO. | 1884

Size: 7 7/16" x 4 15/16".

Collation: [A]⁴ B–I K–U⁸ X⁴; pp. [2] [i–vi] [1–2], [3]–309 [310] [311–312].

Contents: blank leaf; [i–ii] half-title, verso publisher's device; [iii–iv] title-page, verso blank; [v–vi] "CONTENTS", verso blank; [1–2] divisional fly-title, verso blank; [3]–309 text; 309 at foot printer's imprint: "Printed by R. & R. Clark, Edinburgh. [all but printer's name in italic]"; [310] blank; [311–312] ads, headed on [311]: "MACMILLAN AND CO's PUBLICATIONS. [in sans-serif] | [rule] | BY THE SAME AUTHOR.", listing 7 titles, and on [312]: "MACMILLAN'S 4s. 6d. SERIES."

Binding: dark green smooth cloth. The front and back covers have a single-rule border in blind. The spine, which is lettered and decorated in gilt, reads: "[rule] | Tales | of | Three | Cities | Henry | James | Macmillan & Co. | [rule]". The "o" in "Co" is raised above a dot. The endpapers are of white wove paper, and the text is printed on wove paper. The top edge is untrimmed, and the other edges are trimmed.

English printing history. Macmillan Archive. MEB, 267, records only one English edition with one impression of *Tales of Three Cities*. That was an impression of 1,500 copies printed from stereotype plates in October 1884. It was published on November 18, 1884, priced at 4s. 6d. MEB, 324, records under the heading: "Colonial Library" two further impressions from the same plates as those used to print the English edition: the first in April 1886 of 1,000 copies, and the second in September 1886, also of 1,000 copies. These two later impressions were exclusively for colonial publication. Macmillan destroyed the plates in March 1921.

24.9.0. *Tales of Three Cities*, first English edition, second binding state, one volume, London 1884.

Size: 7″ x 4 ¹¹/₁₆″.

The title-page, collation, and contents, including the ads on [311–312], are identical to those of the first English edition, first binding state, 24.8.0.

Binding: maroon (claret) smooth cloth. There is no lettering or decoration on the front or back covers. The spine, which is lettered in gilt, reads: "TALES OF | THREE | CITIES | H. JAMES | MACMILLAN". The publisher's imprint at the foot of the spine is in uniform sans-serif capitals. There are no rules at the top or foot of the spine. The endpapers are of white wove paper, and the text is printed on wove paper. All edges are trimmed.

This binding is not the possible variant binding referred to in E&L A24b, and described in Sadleir 1291 as being in cheap quality smooth dark-green cloth with squatter more heavily serif spine lettering.

24.10.0. *Tales of Three Cities*, first English edition, The Times Book Club binding state, one volume, 1884.

Size: 7 ¼″ x 4 ¾″.

The title-page, collation, and contents, including the ads on [311–312], are identical those of the first English edition, first binding state, 24.8.0.

Binding: rust-brown smooth-linen-grain cloth. The front cover has a single-rule border in black. The back cover is neither lettered nor decorated. The spine, which is lettered and decorated in black, reads: "[rule] | Tales | of | Three | Cities | Henry | James | [rule]". No publisher's imprint is present at the foot of the spine. The endpapers are of white wove paper, and the text is printed on wove paper. All edges are trimmed. On the rear pastedown is a small burgundy-colored label which reads: "THE [Times device] TIMES | (Book Club) | 376–384 Oxford Street | London."

24.11.0. *Tales of Three Cities*, first English edition, first or second colonial impression, one volume. London 1886.

Macmillan's Colonial Library [in Gothic type, underscored] | TALES | OF | THREE CITIES | BY | HENRY JAMES | London [in gothic type] MACMILLAN AND CO. | 1886

Size: $7\frac{1}{2}''$ x $5''$.

Collation: [A]^4 B–I K–U^8 X^4; pp. [2] [i–vi] [1–2], [3]–309, [310] [311–312].

Contents: blank leaf, [i–ii] half-title, verso "This Edition is intended for circulation only in India | and the British Colonies. [all in italic]"; [iii–iv] title-page, verso blank; [v–vi] "CONTENTS", verso blank; [1–2] divisional fly-title, verso blank; [3]–309 text; [310] blank; [311–312] ads headed on [311]: "Macmillan's Colonial Library [in Gothic type]", and on [312]: "A MAGAZINE FOR EVERY HOUSEHOLD."

Binding: dark greenish-blue smooth cloth. The front and back covers have a single-rule border in blind. The spine, which is lettered and decorated in gilt, reads: "[rule] | TALES | OF | THREE | CITIES | HENRY | JAMES | Macmillan & Co." The "o" in "Co. is raised above a dash. The endpapers are of cream wove paper, and the text is printed on wove paper. All edges are trimmed.

This volume is $^{35}/_{64}''$ thick (excluding boards) as against $^{27}/_{32}''$ for the first English edition, first impression, 24.8.0.

25. THE ART OF FICTION

25.1.0. *The Art of Fiction*, first edition, first impression, one volume, Boston 1885.

WALTER BESANT | [rule] | THE | ART OF FICTION | BOSTON | CUPPLES, UPHAM AND COMPANY | 1885

Size: $6\frac{3}{4}''$ x $4\frac{7}{8}''$.

Collation: [unsigned, 1–5^8 6^6]; pp. [1–2], 3–85 [86] [87–92].

Contents: [1–2] title-page, verso blank; 3–85 text; 85 no printer's imprint; [86] blank; [87–91] ads dated October, 1884, headed on [87]: "A | LIST OF NEW BOOKS | PUBLISHED BY | CUPPLES, UPHAM &

THE ART OF FICTION

COMPANY, | 283 WASHINGTON STREET, BOSTON."; [92] blank, as noted in BAL 10572.

Binding: canary-yellow smooth-linen-grain cloth. The front cover, lettered and decorated in black, reads: WALTER BESANT | AND | HENRY JAMES | [rule] | THE | ART OF FICTION | Cupples, Upham & Co." The back cover is blank. The spine, which is also lettered in black, reads vertically: "ART OF FICTION". The endpapers are of smooth white wove paper, and the text is printed on wove paper. All edges are trimmed.

Priced at $.50.

This title was not published in England, but "The Art of Fiction" was included as the last essay in *Partial Portrait*, 30.1.0–30.6.0.

25.2.0. *The Art of Fiction*, first edition, second impression, one volume, Boston [n.d., 1887 or 1888].

WALTER BESANT | AND | HENRY JAMES | [rule] | THE | ART OF FICTION | BOSTON | CUPPLES AND HURD | The Algonquin Press [in Gothic type]

Size: 7 3/8" x 4 13/16".

Collation: [unsigned, 1–4^{12}]; pp. [1–2], 3–85 [86] [87–96].

Contents: [1–2] title-page, verso blank; 3–85 text; 85 at the foot the printer's imprint: "CUPPLES & HURD, THE ALGONQUIN PRESS, BOSTON. [in sans-serif]"; [86] blank; [87–96] undated ads. The 10 pages of undated ads, which are the last five leaves of signature [4], are headed on [87]: "Extracts from | Cupples & Hurd's List | The Algonquin Press | Boston."

Binding: canary-yellow diagonal-fine-ribbed cloth. The front cover, lettered and decorated in black, reads: "WALTER BESANT | AND | HENRY JAMES | [rule] | THE | ART OF FICTION". The spine, which is also lettered in black, reads vertically: "ART OF FICTION". The back cover is blank. The endpapers are of off-white wove paper, and the text is printed on wove paper. All edges are trimmed.

This is the printing from the original plates with a new title-page and ads noted in E&L A25. E&L and BAL disagree slightly as to its probable date of publication. BAL 10572 states: "Reprinted not before 1889". E&L, on the other hand, states: "the volume was reissued in 1887 or 1888."

The fact that De Wolfe, Fiske & Co. bought the plates from Cupples & Hurd (which was dissolved in 1889) and reissued the volume in 1889 or 1890 under its own name (see 25.3.0), would seem to indicate that E&L is correct.

25.3.0. *The Art of Fiction*, first edition, third impression, one volume, Boston [n.d., 1889 or 1890].

WALTER BESANT | AND | HENRY JAMES | [rule] | THE | ART OF FICTION | BOSTON | DE WOLFE, FISKE & CO. | 361 and 365 Washington Street

Size: 6 ¾" x 4 ¾".

Collation: [unsigned, 1–5^8 6^4]; pp. [1–2], 3–85 [86] [87–88].

Contents: [1–2] title-page, verso blank; 3–85 text; 85 no printer's imprint; [86] blank; [87–88] blank leaf.

Binding: mustard-yellow linen-grain cloth. The front cover, lettered and decorated in black, reads: "WALTER BESANT | AND | HENRY JAMES | [rule] | THE | ART OF FICTION". The spine, which is also lettered in black, reads vertically: "ART OF FICTION". The back cover is blank. The endpapers are of white wove paper, and the text is printed on a slightly rough wove paper. All edges are trimmed.

This impression was printed from the original first edition plates, with a new title-page.

25.4.0. *The Art of Fiction*, first edition, fourth (?) impression, one volume, Boston [n.d.].

The title-page is identical to that of the first edition, third impression, 25.3.0, except that the "e" in "De" in the publisher's imprint is in lower case, and the address "361 and 365 Washington Street" beneath that imprint is not present.

The size, collation, and contents are identical to those of 25.3.0.

Binding: cream diagonal-fine-ribbed cloth, with lettering and a rule in black on the front cover and lettering in black on the spine identically to 25.3.0. The endpapers are of white wove paper, and the text is printed on smooth wove paper (smoother and heavier than that used in the third impression). All edges are trimmed.

The difference between the title-page of this copy and that of the third impression (both of which are an integral part of the first signatures), and the different text paper make it likely that this copy is of a separate impression.

25.5.0. *The Art of Fiction*, first edition, fifth (?) impression, one volume, Boston [n.d.].

WALTER BESANT | AND | HENRY JAMES | THE | ART OF FICTION | BOSTON | De WOLFE & FISKE CO.

Size: $6\,^{13}/_{16}''$ x $4\,^{5}/_{8}''$.

Collation: [unsigned, $1-5^8\ 6^6$]; pp. [2] [1–2], 3–85 [86] [87–90]. Leaf $[6_5]$ serves as the rear free endpaper, and leaf $[6_6]$ as the rear pastedown.

Contents: blank leaf; [1–2] title-page, verso blank; 3–85 text; 85 no printer's imprint; [86] blank; [87–88] blank leaf serving as the rear free endpaper; [89–90] blank leaf serving as the rear pastedown.

Binding: dark blue vertical-rib-grain cloth. The front cover, lettered in gilt within a single-rule border in blind, reads: "ART OF FICTION". The authors' names are not present. The spine and the back cover are neither lettered nor decorated. The front endpapers are of wove paper, and the text is printed on slightly rough wove paper. All edges are trimmed.

On the front free endpaper is a pencil inscription dated "Jan. 1925". Note that the publisher's imprint on the title-page (De Wolf & Fisk Co.) differs from that on the title-page of the third and fourth impressions (De Wolf, Fisk & Co.).

26. *THE AUTHOR OF BELTRAFFIO*

26.1.0. *The Author of Beltraffio*, first edition, first binding state, one volume, Boston 1885.

HENRY JAMES | [rule] | The Author of Beltraffio | PANDORA * GEORGINA'S REASONS | THE PATH OF DUTY | FOUR MEETINGS | [publisher's device] | BOSTON | JAMES R. OSGOOD AND COMPANY | [rule] | 1885

Size: 7 ³/₁₆″ x 4 ¹³/₁₆″.

Collation: [1–30⁶ 31²], signed as π¹ 1–22⁸ 23⁵; pp. [i–ii] [1–6], [7]–362.

Contents: [i–ii] blank, verso ad headed: "Henry James's Latest Works.", listing 7 titles with dollar prices; [1–2] title-page, verso copyright notice, reservation of rights, and printer's imprint: "Copyright, 1884 and 1885, [in italic] | By Henry James. | [rule] | All rights reserved. [in italic] | University Press: [in Gothic type] | John Wilson and Son, Cambridge."; [3–4] "CONTENTS.", verso blank; [5–6] divisional fly-title, verso blank; [7]–362 text; 362 at foot printer's imprint: "[rule] | University Press: John Wilson and Son, Cambridge."

Binding: dark brown (with a purple cast) diagonal-fine-ribbed cloth. The front and back covers are decorated in blind with a single-rule border within a thicker single-rule frame. The spine, which is lettered and decorated in gilt, reads: "THE AUTHOR | OF | BELTRAFFIO | [rule] | Henry James | [J. R. Osgood monogram]". The endpapers are of white wove paper, and the text is printed on wove paper. There are no binder's fly-leaves. All edges are trimmed.

Printing history. Houghton Mifflin Archive. First edition: Ms Am 2030.3(9), 133 and Ms Am 2030.3(14), 70: *first* (and sole) *impression* January 26, 1885, 1508 copies, 810 bound between January 29, 1885, and October 14, 1885. Ms Am 2030(19), 157: notation: "rcvd from T[icknor] & Co. 4/11/89 700 copies", 692 bound between October 26, 1889, (on which date 500 copies were bound) and October 21, 1898. No copies were bound by Ticknor & Co. This title was not published in England.

Priced at $1.50, which price was unchanged through 1905.

26.2.0. *The Author of Beltraffio*, first edition, first binding state, one volume, Boston 1885.

This copy is identical in all respects to the first edition, first binding state, 26.1.0, except that it is bound in chocolate-brown diagonal-fine-ribbed cloth. The endpapers are of white wove paper, and the text is printed on wove paper. There are no binder's fly-leaves. All edges are trimmed.

The cloth on this copy is considerably lighter than that on the preceding copy. Not noted in E&L. BAL 10571 notes brown cloth without noting the shade.

26.3.0. *The Author of Beltraffio*, first edition, first binding state, one volume, Boston 1885.

This copy is identical in all respects to the first edition, first binding state, 26.1.0, except that it is bound in dull olive-green diagonal-fine-ribbed cloth. The endpapers are of white wove paper, and the text is printed on wove paper. There are no binder's fly-leaves. All edges are trimmed.

26.4.0. *The Author of Beltraffio*, first edition, first binding state, one volume, Boston 1885.

This copy is identical in all respects to the first edition, first binding state, 26.1.0, except that it is bound in forest-green diagonal-fine-ribbed cloth. The endpapers are of white wove paper, and the text is printed on wove paper. There are no binder's fly-leaves. All edges are trimmed.

E&L does not note a forest-green binding, the only green binding noted being the above copy in olive-green. BAL 10571 describes three binding colors, only one being green, but does not specify the shade of green.

26.5.0. *The Author of Beltraffio*, first edition, first binding state, one volume, Boston 1885.

This copy is identical in all respects to the first edition, first binding state, 26.1.0, except that it is bound in ochre diagonal-fine-ribbed cloth. The endpapers are of white wove paper and the text is printed on wove paper. There are no binder's fly-leaves. All edges are trimmed.

On the front pastedown is the bookplate of John Quinn. This copy is catalogued as #4669 in the Quinn Collection catalogue.

26.6.0 *The Author of Beltraffio*, first edition, second binding state A, one volume, Boston 1885.

The title-page, size, collation, and contents are identical to those of the first edition, first binding state, 26.1.0, including the ad on [ii].

Binding: chocolate-brown smooth cloth, with no lettering or decoration on the front or back covers. The spine, lettered and decorated in gilt, reads: "THE AUTHOR | OF | BELTRAFFIO | [rule] | Henry James

STORIES REVIVED

| HOUGHTON | MIFFLIN [dot] & [dot absent] Co." The ampersand in the publisher's imprint is not stylized. The endpapers are of white laid paper, and the text is printed on wove paper. A binder's fly-leaf of wove paper is at both the front and the back. All edges are trimmed.

This binding is uniform with that of the first edition, first impression, third binding state B, of *A Little Tour in France* (1885), 23.5.0 (and variant A, 23.4.0, except, in the latter case, for the ampersand in the publisher's imprint at the foot of the spine, which in this copy is not stylized). See BAL 10571 which notes: "no copy thus distinguished [with the Houghton Mifflin imprint] located".

As is the case with the first edition, first impression, third binding state, of *A Little Tour in France*, 23.4.0 and 23.5.0, there are two variants of the spine imprint on this binding state. For the second variant see 26.7.0.

26.7.0. *The Author of Beltraffio*, first edition, second binding state B, one volume, Boston 1885.

The title-page, size, collation, and contents are identical to those of the first edition, first binding state, 26.1.0, including the ad on [ii].

Binding: olive-green smooth cloth, with no lettering or decoration on the front or back covers. The spine, lettered and decorated in gilt, reads: "THE AUTHOR | OF | BELTRAFFIO | [rule] | Henry James | HOUGHTON | MIFFLIN [dot] & [dot] CO." The ampersand in the publisher's imprint is stylized. The endpapers are of cream laid paper, and the text is printed on wove paper. A binder's fly-leaf of wove paper is at both the front and the back. All edges are trimmed.

On the front free endpaper is the inscription "Elizabeth C. Bailey | 1897."

27. STORIES REVIVED

27.1.0. *Stories Revived*, first edition, binding state A, three volumes, London 1885.

Size: 7 1/2″ x 4 15/16″.

STORIES REVIVED | IN THREE VOLUMES | VOL. I. | THE AUTHOR OF 'BELTRAFFIO'. PANDORA. | THE PATH OF DUTY. | A DAY OF DAYS. A LIGHT MAN. | BY | HENRY JAMES | London [in Gothic type] | MACMILLAN AND CO. | 1885

Collation: Volume I: [A]⁴ B–I K–S⁸ T⁴; pp. [i–viii], [1]–280.

Contents: Volume I: [i–ii] half-title, verso publisher's device; [iii–iv] title-page, verso printer's imprint: "Printed by R. &. R. Clark, Edinburgh. [all except printer's name in italic]"; [v–vi] "NOTICE.", dated February 1885, verso blank; [vii–viii] "CONTENTS OF VOL. I.", verso blank; [1]–280 text; 280 at foot printer's imprint: "Printed by R. & R. Clark, Edinburgh. [all except printer's name in italic]".

STORIES REVIVED | IN THREE VOLUMES | VOL. II. | GEORGINA'S REASONS. A PASSIONATE | PILGRIM. A LANDSCAPE-PAINTER. | ROSE-AGATHE. | BY | HENRY JAMES | London [in Gothic type] | MACMILLAN AND CO. | 1885

Collation: Volume II: [A]⁴ B–I K–S⁸ T⁴; pp. [2] [i–vi], [1]–280.

Contents: Volume II: blank leaf; [i–ii] half-title, verso publisher's device; [iii–iv] title-page, verso printer's imprint as on Volume I title-leaf verso, except without a period after the ampersand; [v–vi] "CONTENTS OF VOL. II.", verso blank; [1]–280 text; 280 at foot printer's imprint as on Volume I, 280.

STORIES REVIVED | IN THREE VOLUMES | VOL. III. | POOR RICHARD. THE LAST OF THE VALERII. | MASTER EUSTACE. | THE ROMANCE OF CERTAIN OLD CLOTHES. | A MOST EXTRAORDINARY CASE. | BY | HENRY JAMES | London [in Gothic type] | MACMILLAN AND CO. | 1885

Collation: Volume III: [A]⁴ B–I K–S⁸; pp. [2] [i–vi], [1]–269 [270] [271–272].

Contents: Volume III: blank leaf; [i–ii] half-title, verso publisher's device; [iii–iv] title-page, verso printer's imprint as on Volume I title-leaf verso, except without a period after the ampersand; [v–vi]

STORIES REVIVED

"CONTENTS OF VOL. III.", verso blank; [1]–269 text; 269 at foot printer's imprint as on Volume I, 280; [270] blank; [271–272] ads headed: [271] "WORKS BY THE SAME AUTHOR. [in italic]", and [272]: "MESSERS. MACMILLAN & CO's | NEW NOVELS."

Volume I has a period after the ampersand in the printer's imprint at the bottom of page [iv], which is as called for.

Binding: dark blue fine bead-grain cloth, with a panel with curved corners within a double-rule border in black on the front covers and in blind on the back covers. The spines, which are lettered in gilt with a gilt publisher's device, read: "[in black: thin rule, row of dots, thick rule] | STORIES | REVIVED | HENRY | JAMES | VOL. I [II] [III] | [publisher's device] | Macmillan & Co. | [in black: thin rule, row of dots, thick rule]". The "o" in "Co" is raised above a line. The endpapers are of brown coated paper, and the text is printed on wove paper. All edges are untrimmed. The brasses on the spine correspond to those shown in E&L, Plate V, figure (a) with "VOL" in letters of uniform size.

This binding variant corresponds to binding A (of three binding styles noted, without priority) in BAL 10573.

On the front pastedown of each volume is the bookplate of Michael Sadlier, and another bookplate reading "LMV de W". Recorded in Sadlier 1290.

Printing history. Macmillan Archive. MEB, 267, records that the first edition in three volumes was printed from standing type in a single impression of 500 copies in May 1885. It was published on May 15, 1885, priced at 31s. 6. A second edition in two volumes, printed from stereotyped plates, was printed in a single impression of 1,000 copies in November 1885. It was priced at 6s. per volume. That entry also records under "Remarks" that in the case of this second edition "each 2 vols. sold separately". This title was not listed in the 1905 Times Book Club Catalogue, even though copies of the second edition were bound and sold by the Club; see 27.4.0 and 27.5.0. Macmillan destroyed the plates in March 1921. This title was not published in America.

27.2.0. *Stories Revived*, first edition, binding state B, three volumes, London 1885.

Size: 7 ½" x 5".

The title-pages, collations, and contents are identical to those of the first edition, binding state A, 27.1.0, including the period after the ampersand in the printer's imprint on page [iv] of two of the three volumes, and the ads on [271–272] in Volume III.

Binding: dark blue-green diagonal-fine-ribbed cloth. It is decorated in black on the front and in blind on the back covers, and decorated in black with lettering and publisher's device in gilt on the spines identically to 27.1.0, except that the brasses on the spines correspond to those shown in E&L, Plate V, figure (b), with the "V" in "Vol." being larger than the other letters. The endpapers are of wove paper with an overall blue mosaic pattern. All edges are untrimmed.

On the title-page of Volume I is written in ink: "Adele Kelley | Bournemouth | Feb. 1889.", with similar inscriptions on the title-pages of Volumes II and III. On the recto of the front free endpaper of Volume I is the circular blind-stamp of W. H. Smith, and on the verso is the pencil notation: "Pub @ 31/6 | Reduced to 5/-".

This binding variant corresponds to binding B (of three binding styles noted, without priority) in BAL 10573. The third binding variant recorded in BAL is in sand-grain (C) cloth. It is not noted in E&L (no mention is made of copies in diagonal-fine-ribbed cloth).

27.3.0. *Stories Revived*, second edition, two volumes, London 1885.

Size: 7 ⅜" x 4 ¹⁵⁄₁₆".

Volume I: STORIES REVIVED | First Series [in Gothic type] | THE AUTHOR OF 'BELTRAFFIO'. PANDORA. | A LIGHT MAN. A DAY OF DAYS. | THE PATH OF DUTY. GEORGINA'S REASONS. | A LANDSCAPE-PAINTER. | BY | HENRY JAMES | London [in Gothic type] | MACMILLAN AND CO. | 1885

Collation: Volume I : [A]⁴ B–I K–U X–Z 2A–2D⁸ 2E⁶; pp.[i–viii], [1]–428.

Contents: Volume I: [i–ii] half-title, verso publisher's device; [iii–iv] title-page, verso printer's imprint: "Printed by R. & R. Clark, Edinburgh. [all except the printer's name in italic]"; [v–vi] "NOTICE.", dated "February 1885", verso blank; [vii–viii] "CONTENTS OF FIRST SERIES", verso blank; [1]–428 text; 428 at foot printer's imprint as on Volume I title-leaf verso.

Volume II: STORIES REVIVED | Second Series [in Gothic type] | A PASSIONATE PILGRIM. ROSE-AGATHE. | POOR RICHARD. THE LAST OF THE VALERII. | MASTER EUSTACE. | THE ROMANCE OF CERTAIN OLD CLOTHES. | A MOST EXTRAORDINARY CASE. | BY | HENRY JAMES | London [in Gothic type] | MACMILLAN AND CO. | 1885

Collation: Volume II: [A]^4 B–I K–U X–Z 2A–2C^8 [2D]^2; pp. [2] [i–vi], [1]–401 [402] [403–404].

Contents: Volume II: blank leaf; [i–ii] half-title, verso publisher's device; [iii–iv] title-page, verso printer's imprint as on Volume I title-leaf verso; [v–vi] "CONTENTS OF SECOND SERIES", verso blank; [1]–401 text; 401 at foot printer's imprint as on Volume I title-leaf verso; [402] blank; [403–404] ads. The two pages of ads at the end of Volume II are headed: [403] "WORKS BY THE SAME AUTHOR. [in italic]", and [404] "MESSRS. MACMILLAN & CO.'S | NEW NOVELS."

Binding: dark blue-green bead-grain cloth, lettered and decorated in gilt, black and in blind uniform with the second English edition of *The American*, 4.17.0. There is no lettering on the front or back covers. The spines read: "STORIES | REVIVED | FIRST SERIES [SECOND SERIES] | HENRY JAMES [all the foregoing in italic] | Macmillan & Co." The "o" in "Co" is raised above a line. The endpapers are of dark brown coated paper, and the texts are printed on wove paper. The top and fore-edges are untrimmed, and the bottom edges are trimmed.

27.4.0. *Stories Revived*, second edition, The Times Book Club binding state, two volumes, London 1885.

Size: 7 ¼" x 4 ¾".

The title-pages, collations, and contents (including the ads on [403–404] of Volume II) are identical to those of the second edition, 27.3.0.

Binding: lemon-yellow (faded to lemon-orange?) fine-linen-grain cloth with decorative bands printed (but not stamped) in black across the front covers and spines, with lettering in black between the printed bands on the spines that reads: "STORIES | REVIVED | FIRST

SERIES [SECOND SERIES] | HENRY JAMES [all the foregoing in italic] | [circular Times Book Club device]". The words "FIRST [SECOND] SERIES" are in letters 1/8" high. The back covers are neither lettered nor decorated. The endpapers are of white laid paper, and the text is printed on smooth wove paper. All edges are trimmed. There are two pages of ads at the end of Volume II, being the last leaf of signature [2D]. These are the same as the ads at the end of Volume II of 27.3.0.

Illustrated Plate 32.

27.5.0. *Stories Revived*, second edition, The Times Book Club binding state, two volumes, London 1885.

The title-page, size, collation, and contents (including the ads on [403–404] of Volume II) are identical to those of the second edition, 27.3.0.

Binding: maroon fine-linen-grain cloth lettered and decorated in black identically to 27.4.0, except that on the spines the words "FIRST SERIES" and "SECOND SERIES" are in letters 3/32" high. It has endpapers of white wove paper, and the text is printed on wove paper. All edges are trimmed, and the top edge is stained ochre.

❧✛❧

28. *THE BOSTONIANS*

28.1.0. *The Bostonians*, first edition, first (?) impression, three volumes, London 1886.

THE | BOSTONIANS | A Novel [in Gothic type] | BY | HENRY JAMES | IN THREE VOLUMES [in italic] | VOL I [VOL. II.] [VOL. III.] | LONDON | MACMILLAN AND CO. | 1886

Size: 7 9/16" x 4 15/16".

Collation: Volume I: [A]² B–I K–Q⁸ R²; pp. [i–iv] [1–2], [3]–244. Volume II: [A]² B–I K–P⁸ Q²; pp. [i–iv] [1–2], [3]–226 [227–228]. Volume III: [A]² B–I K–P⁸ Q⁴ R²; pp. [i–iv], [1]–232 [233–236].

Contents: Volume I: [i–ii] half-title, verso publisher's device; [iii–iv] title-page, verso copyright notice: "COPYRIGHT | 1886 | By HENRY JAMES"; [1–2] divisional fly-title, verso blank; [3]–244 text; 244 at foot printer's imprint: "Printed by R. & R. Clark, Edinburgh. [all but printer's name in italic]". Volume II: [i–ii] half-title, verso publisher's device; [iii–iv] title-page, verso copyright notice as on Volume I title-leaf verso; [1–2] divisional fly-title, verso blank; [3]–226 text; 226 at foot printer's imprint as in Volume I, foot of 244; [227–228] ads headed: [227] "WORKS BY THE SAME AUTHOR [in italic]", and [228] "MESSERS. MACMILLAN & CO'S | NEW NOVELS." Volume III: [i–ii] half-title, verso publisher's device; [iii–iv] title-page, verso copyright notice as on Volume I title-leaf verso; [1]–232 text; 232 at foot printer's imprint as in Volume I, foot of 244; [233–236] ads headed: [233] as on [227] in Volume II, [234–235]: "MACMILLAN & Co's 6s. POPULAR NOVELS", and on [226] as on [228] in Volume II.

Binding: dark greenish-blue fine-bead-grain cloth. The front covers are decorated in black with a double rule border within which is a single-rule panel curved at the corners, with a similar border and panel in blind on the back covers. The spines, which are lettered in gilt and decorated in black and gilt, read: "[in black, thin rule, row of dots, thicker rule] | THE | BOSTONIANS | HENRY | JAMES | VOL. I [II] [III] | [round publisher's device] | Macmillan & Co. | [in black, thin rule, row of dots, thicker rule]". The "o" in "Co" is raised above a line. The endpapers are of brown coated paper, and the text is printed on wove paper. All edges are untrimmed.

In this copy the running head in Volume I on page 31 has the (incorrect) chapter number II rather than III. Note that on the Volume I title-page "VOL" lacks the period present in "VOL." on the Volumes II and III title-pages.

On the front pastedown of each volume is the bookplate of Scofield Thayer.

Printing history. Macmillan Archive. MEB, 265, records two impressions of the three-volume English first edition: the first in February 1886 of 500 copies, and the second in March 1886 of 100 copies. It was published on February 16, 1886. They were printed from standing type and priced at 31s. 6d. BAL 10575 records the two printings of the first edition, but was unable to distinguish between them, pointing out, however, that a possible distinguishing characteristic is the error in the running head on 31 of Volume I, noted above.

The second English edition (one volume) was printed in a single impression of 5,000 copies from stereotype plates in February 1886. The second English edition was priced at 6s. Three thousand of the 5,000 copies from this single impression were exported to America for use by Macmillan (New York) for the American issue; see 28.5.0 and 28.6.0. The American issue was priced at $1.75. This was the sole edition and impression of this title published in America through 1921. Macmillan destroyed the plates in March 1921.

MBC, 493 records that the second edition was printed in February, 1886, the same month as the three-volume first edition, first impression, was printed. The second impression of the first edition was printed one month later in March 1886. Both the first and second editions were set in long primer, at 35 and 40 lines per full-page, respectively.

The essentially simultaneous printing of the first and second editions was probably to have sheets of the one volume edition available for export to America, and to avoid the expense of a second setting of type to produce sheets for the one volume English edition. What probably occurred (as with *The Portrait of a Lady*) is that the type was set for the one-volume edition and plates made, from which it was printed. In order to fill three volumes, this standing type was then leaded-out, and in this process in a few instances the type was slightly redistributed along the lines by spacing out or reducing the spacing. The first edition, first impression, was printed from this leaded-out standing type. The second impression of the first edition was also printed from this same standing type, but after the second edition was printed from the stereotype plates.

For the third English edition, see *Novels and Stories of Henry James*, 86.1.0–86.2.0.

28.2.0. *The Bostonians*, first edition, first (?) impression, variant or trial binding, three volumes, London 1886.

The title-pages, size, collations, and contents (including the absence of a period after "VOL" on the Volume I title-page, the incorrect running head on 31 of Volume I, and the ads at the end of Volumes II and III) are identical to those of the first edition, first impression, 28.1.0.

Binding: light blue diagonal-fine-ribbed cloth. The front and back covers are decorated with a single-rule border in blind within which is a double-rule panel curved at the corners, also in blind. The spines, which are decorated in blind and lettered in gilt, read: "[thick followed by a thin rule in blind] | THE | BOSTONIANS [title in sans-serif] | HENRY | JAMES | VOL. I. [II] [III.] | [thin followed by a thick rule in blind]". There is no publisher's imprint on the spines. The endpapers are of dark brown coated paper, and the text is printed on wove paper. The top edge is trimmed, and the other edges are untrimmed.

Note titles on the spines are in sans-serif. This variant binding, possibly a trial binding, is not recorded in E&L or BAL.

Illustrated Plate 13.

28.3.0. *The Bostonians*, first edition, second (?) impression, three volumes, London 1886.

This copy is identical in all respects to that of the first edition, first impression, 28.1.0, including the absence of the period after "VOL" on the Volume I title-page, except that the chapter heading in running head on 31 of Volume I is correct (that is "III" rather than "II").

28.4.0. *The Bostonians*, second edition, first (sole) impression, English issue, one volume, London and New York 1886.

THE | BOSTONIANS | A Novel [in Gothic type] | BY | HENRY JAMES | London and New York [in Gothic type] | MACMILLAN AND CO. | 1886

Size: 6 3/8" x 4 7/8".

Collation: [A]² B–I K–U X–Z 2A–2F⁸ [2G]² (–[2G]₂); pp. [i–iv] [1–2], [3]–449 [450].

Contents: [i–ii] half-title, verso publisher's device; [iii–iv] title-page, verso copyright notice: "COPYRIGHT | 1886 | By HENRY JAMES"; [1–2] divisional fly-title, verso blank; [3]–449 text; 449 at foot printer's imprint: "Printed by R. & R. Clark, Edinburgh. [all but printer's name in italic]"; [450] blank.

Binding: dark greenish-blue bead-grain cloth, lettered and decorated in gilt, black and in blind uniform with the second English edition of *The American* (1879), 4.17.0. There is no lettering the front or back covers. The spine reads: "THE | BOSTONIANS | HENRY JAMES [all the foregoing in italic] | MACMILLAN & Co." "MACMILLAN" is in uniform capitals ³/₁₆″ high and the "o" in "Co" is raised above a dot. The endpapers are of dark green coated paper, and the text is printed on wove paper. The top edge is untrimmed, and the fore and bottom edges are trimmed.

Nowell-Smith, 66, states that the two preliminary leaves are cancels, the original leaves not having the copyright notice in the prescribed American form.

28.5.0. *The Bostonians*, second edition, first (sole) impression, American issue, binding state A, one volume, London and New York 1886.

The title-page, size, collation, and contents are identical to those of the second edition, first (sole) impression, English issue, 28.4.0, except that the complete signature [2G]² is present, the last leaf of which, [451–452], is two pages of dollar ads.

Binding: dark greenish-blue bead-grain cloth, which binding is identical in all respects (including lettering and decoration) to that on 28.4.0, except that the publisher's imprint at the foot of the spine is in uniform capitals ⅛″ high. This binding is uniform with the second English edition of *The American* (1879), 4.17.0. The endpapers are of white wove paper (rather than the coated paper of 28.4.0 and 28.6.0), and the text is printed on wove paper. The top edge is untrimmed, and the bottom and fore-edges are trimmed.

BAL 10576 records that copies of this binding state were issued with either blue-black coated or white wove endpapers.

On the front pastedown is the bookplate of Paul Lemperly.

Illustrated Plate 13

The presence of the dollar ads, leaf [2G]₂, is the only difference between the contents of the American and English issues of the second edition.

28.6.0. *The Bostonians*, second edition, first (sole) impression, American issue, binding state B, one volume, London and New York 1886.

The title-page is identical to that of second edition, first (sole) impression, English issue, 28.4.0.

Size: 6 ³/₈″ x 4 ⁷/₈″.

Collation and contents are identical to those of 28.4.0, except that the complete signature [2G]² is present, the last leaf of which, [451–452], is two pages of dollar ads.

Binding: maroon linen-grain quarter cloth with orange-pink linen-grain cloth boards. The front and back covers are neither lettered nor decorated. The spine, which is lettered and decorated in gilt, reads: "[within a single-rule frame] THE | BOSTONIANS | HENRY JAMES | [within a second smaller single-rule frame] Macmillan & Co." The "o" in "Co" is raised above a line. The endpapers are of dark-green coated paper, and the text is printed on wove paper. All edges are trimmed.

Illustrated Plate 13.

Simon Nowell-Smith, 80, states: "the first binding of [the first impression of the second edition, American issue of] *The Bostonians* was judged ugly and in bad taste by American booksellers and in response to an urgent appeal from their New York house Macmillan's adopted another for later consignments." Unfortunately Nowell-Smith does not identify these two bindings. One of them is no doubt the dark greenish-blue fine-bead-grain binding recorded by E&L as the "likely ... American issue", but which BAL records as "probable second binding", and the other is this maroon linen-grain quarter cloth binding, which BAL records as "probable first binding". Both BAL and E&L record that the leaf [2G]₂ of dollar ads is present in both the bindings of the second edition, first impression, American issue.

In determining the possible priority of these two binding states, it should be noted that *The Bostonians* was the first James title Macmillan published in America. Of the 11 James titles which Macmillan subsequently published in America, 10 had more colorful (if subdued) bindings, the exception being the second edition, American issue, of *The Princess Casamassima*, which was issued in two binding states; see 29.6.0 and 29.7.0. Even in England, Macmillan used this style of dark-green cloth binding on only two later James works, the second impression of second edition, English issue, of *The Princess Casamassima*, 29.3.0, also published in 1886, and one of the two binding states of the second impression of the second edition, of *The Reverberator* (31.2.0), published in 1888. It is probable that the binding deemed ugly to American eyes was the dark green binding.

29. *THE PRINCESS CASAMASSIMA*

29.1.0. *The Princess Casamassima*, first edition, binding state A, three volumes, London 1886.

THE | PRINCESS CASAMASSIMA | A Novel [in Gothic type] | BY | HENRY JAMES | IN THREE VOLUMES [in italic] | VOL. I. [II.] [III.] | London [in Gothic type] | MACMILLAN AND CO. | AND NEW YORK | 1886

Size: $7\,7/16''$ x $5''$.

Collation : Volume I: $[A]^2$ B–I K–Q^8 R^6; pp. [i–iv] [1–2], [3]–252. Volume II: $[A]^2$ B–I K–R^8 S^2; pp. [i–iv], [1]–257 [258] [259–260]. Volume III: $[A]^2$ B–I K–Q^8 R^2; pp. [i–iv], [1]–242 [243–244].

Contents: Volume I: [i–ii] half-title, verso publisher's device; [iii–iv] title-page, verso copyright notice: "COPYRIGHT | 1886 | By HENRY JAMES"; [1–2] divisional fly-title, verso blank; [3]–252 text; 252 at foot printer's imprint: "Printed by R. & R. Clark, Edinburgh. [all but printer's name in italic]". Volume II: [i–ii] half-title, verso publisher's device; [iii–iv] title-page, verso copyright notice as on Volume I title-leaf verso; [1]–257 text; 257 at foot printer's imprint as in Volume I, foot of 252; [258] blank; [259–260] ads headed: [259]: "WORKS BY THE SAME AUTHOR. [in italic]", and [260] : "NEW NOVELS." Volume III: [i–ii] half-title, verso publisher's device; [iii–iv] title-page, verso copyright notice as on Volume I title-leaf verso; [1]–242 text; 242 at foot printer's imprint as in Volume I, at foot of 252; [243–244] ads identical to those at end of Volume II.

The running heads on 33–35 of Volume I are incorrectly printed III rather than II.

Binding: blue-green fine-bead-grain cloth, with a panel with curved corners within a double-rule border in black on the front covers, and in blind on the back covers. The spines, which are lettered in gilt with a gilt publisher's device, read: "[in black: thin rule, row of dots, thick rule] | THE | PRINCESS | CASAMASSIMA | HENRY | JAMES | VOL. I [II] [III] | [publisher's device] | Macmillan & Co. | [in black: thin rule, row of dots, thick rule]". The "o" in "Co" is raised above a dot. The endpapers are of brown coated paper, and the text is printed on wove paper. All edges are untrimmed.

THE PRINCESS CASAMASSIMA

In the publisher's imprints at the foot of the spines of this copy the letters "ACMILLAN" are $^3/_{32}''$ high.

Illustrated Plate 14.

BAL 10577 records both brown and green coated endpapers, and two states of this binding, this copy being BAL's state A (no priority), the other state having green coated endpapers, and in the spine imprint the letters "ACMILLAN" being $^1/_8''$ high, with the "o" in "Co." raised above a dot; see 29.2.0 for state B. Wolff 3576 records a copy with dark green, not chocolate endpapers.

Printing history. Macmillan Archive. MEB, 267 records one printing of the three-volume English first edition, an impression of 750 copies printed from standing type in October 1886. It was priced at 31s.6d.

MEB, 267 records that the first impression of the one-volume second edition was printed in October 1886 from stereotype plates in an impression of 3,000 copies. There is no indication in this entry that a portion of this impression was exported to Macmillan, N.Y. for use as the American issue, but the unusually large press run (for a James title) certainly suggests this, and both E&L and BAL generally seem to agree that copies of the second edition with an 1886 date on the title-page are of the American issue (see 29.7.0 and 29.8.0), and those with an 1887 date and "All Rights Reserved" on the title-page are of an English issue (see 29.4.0). However, as E&L suggests, some copies with an 1886 date were diverted to the English market (see 29.2.0. and 29.3.5) and bound in both the usual trade binding and as a yellowback. First impression sheets of the second edition with a cancel title-page dated 1887 and "All Rights Reserved" were published in England and constitute the English issue of the first impression, but it is possible that some of the first impression sheets with the cancelled 1887 title-page were also issued in America (see 29.4.0, which has an American bookplate). The American issue was priced at $1.75, but in 1893 it was advertised at $1.25. The English one-volume second edition was priced at 6s.

A second impression of the one-volume second edition of 2,000 copies, was printed in May 1888, and a third impression, also of 2,000 copies, was printed in December 1888 with a title-page dated 1889. Both the second and third impressions were published only in England, and only as yellowbacks, priced at 2s.; see 29.5.0 and 29.6.0. Macmillan destroyed the plates in March 1921.

29.2.0. *The Princess Casamassima*, first edition, binding state B, three volumes, London 1886.

The title-pages, size, collations, and contents are identical to those of the first edition, binding state A, 29.1.0, including the error in the running heads on 33–35 of Volume I. The ads present at the end of Volumes II and III are identical to those found at the ends of Volumes II and III of 29.1.0.

Binding: identical to that on 29.1.0, except that in the imprints on the spines the letters "ACMILLAN" are in letters $1/8''$ high (as against $3/32''$ high on binding A), and the "o" in Co" is raised above a dot. The endpapers are of dark green coated rather than brown coated paper. All edges are untrimmed.

29.3.0. *The Princess Casamassima*, second edition, first impression, sheets of the American issue diverted to the English market, one volume, London and New York 1886.

THE | PRINCESS CASAMASSIMA | A Novel [in Gothic type] | BY | HENRY JAMES | London [in Gothic type] | MACMILLAN AND CO. | AND NEW YORK | 1886

Size: $7\ 3/8''$ x $4\ 15/16''$.

Collation: [A]² B–I K–U X–Z 2A–2I 2K–2P⁸ 2Q²; pp [i–iv] [1–2], [3]–596.

Contents: [i–ii] half-title, verso publisher's device; [iii–iv] title-page, verso copyright notice: "COPYRIGHT | 1886 | By HENRY JAMES"; [1–2] divisional fly-title, verso blank; [3]–596 text; 596 at foot printer's imprint: "Printed by R. & R. Clark, Edinburgh. [all except the printer's name in italic]".

Binding: dark greenish-blue bead-grain cloth, lettered and decorated in gilt, black and in blind uniform with the second English edition of *The American* (1879), 4.17.0. There is no lettering on the front or back covers. The spine reads: "THE | PRINCESS | CASAMASSIMA | HENRY JAMES [all the foregoing in italic] | MACMILLAN & Co." The publisher's imprint at the foot of the spine is in uniform capitals $1/8''$ high, except that the "o" in "Co" is raised above a dot. The endpapers are of white wove paper, and the text is printed on wove paper. The top edge is untrimmed, and the other edges are trimmed. There is no catalogue of ads bound in at the end.

Noted but not described in E&L A29b and BAL 10577.

Given the fact that the cloth on this binding and the binding on 29.4.0 (dark greenish-blue bead-grain) differs from the cloth that BAL identifies as the type used for the American issue (blue-green diagonal-fine-ribbed), and the line format of author's name on the spine as well as the publisher's imprint differ from those seen on the binding of the American issue, state A, 29.7.0, this copy has been tentatively identified as an English issue. Further study is clearly indicated.

29.3.5. *The Princess Casamassima*, second edition, first impression sheets of the American issue diverted to the English market, yellowback binding state, one volume, London and New York 1886.

Size: 6 7/8" x 4 1/2".

The title-page (dated 1886), collation, and contents are identical to those of the second edition, first impression sheets of the American issue diverted to the English market, 29.3.0.

Binding: buff paper over boards with an elaborate floral design in orange-red and black on the front and back covers, both of which are signed "L.F. Day" in the lower right hand corner. The spine of this copy is missing. This binding is identical to the binding on the second edition, second impression (yellowback), 29.5.0. The endpapers are of white wove paper (with no ads on them), and the text is printed on wove paper. All edges are trimmed, and the top edge is stained ochre.

The 1886 date and the absence of "All rights reserved" on the title-page indicates that these sheets were printed in England for the American market; see commentary 29.3.0 and copies of the second edition, American issue, 28.7.0 and 28.8.0. However, not all of the sheets printed for this purpose were exported. Some were diverted by Macmillan for use in the second edition, first impression, 29.3.0. This copy indicates that other of these American issue sheets were also bound up as part of the second edition, second impression (1888 yellowback).

29.4.0. *The Princess Casamassima*, second edition, first impression, English issue, one volume, London and New York 1887.

The title-page is identical to that of the second edition, first impression, 29.3.0, except that it is dated 1887 at the foot, and below the date is the phrase "All rights reserved [in italic]".

The size, collation, and contents are identical to those of 29.3.0.

Binding: dark greenish-blue bead grain cloth, lettered and decorated in gilt, black and in blind uniform with the second English edition of *The American* (1879), 4.17.0. There is no lettering on the front or back covers. The spine reads: THE | PRINCESS | CASAMASSIMA | HENRY | JAMES [all the foregoing in italic] | Macmillan & Co." The publisher's imprint at the foot of the spine is in upper and lower case letters, the "M" "&" and "C" being $^5/_{32}$″, high and the other letters are $^1/_8$″ high. The "o" in "Co" is raised above a line. The endpapers are of dark brown coated paper, and the text is printed on wove paper. The top edge is untrimmed, and the other edges are trimmed. There is no catalogue of ads is bound in at the end.

On the front pastedown is a bookplate which reads: "LIBRARY | OF THE | SUPREME COUNCIL 33° | A∴A∴S∴R∴ | Southern Jurisdiction, U.S.A. | Washington D.C. | Class No. Fiction".

29.5.0. *The Princess Casamassima*, second edition, second impression (yellowback), one volume, London and New York 1888.

THE | PRINCESS CASAMASSIMA | A Novel [in gothic type] | BY | HENRY JAMES | London [in Gothic type] | MACMILLAN AND CO. | AND NEW YORK | 1888 | [All rights reserved] [in italic within square brackets]

Size: 6 $^{13}/_{16}$″ x 4 $^1/_2$″.

Collation: [A]² B–I K–U X–Z 2A–2I 2K–2P⁸ 2Q²; pp. [i–iv] [1–2], [3]–596.

Contents: [i–ii] half-title, verso publisher's device; [iii–iv] title-page, verso copyright notice and printing history: "COPYRIGHT | 1886 | By HENRY JAMES | First edition (3 Vols., Crown 8vo) 1886 | Issued (1 Vol., Crown 8vo) 1887 | New Edition (Globe 8vo) 1888 [the printing history all in italic]"; [1–2] divisional fly-title, verso blank; [3]–596 text; 596 at foot printer's imprint: "Printed by R. & R. Clark, Edinburgh. [all except the printer's name in italic]".

Binding: buff paper over boards with an elaborate overall floral design in orange-red and black on the front and back covers. The front cover also has a central orange-red panel on which is printed in black: "The | Princess | Casamassima". The back cover has a similar central orange-red panel on which is printed in black, within an elaborate triangular scroll also printed in black: "Macmillan | & Co." The spine has at the top an oblong orange-red panel, framed in black on which is printed in black: "The | Princess | Casamassima | HENRY JAMES [in sans-serif]". Beneath this is a longer oblong floral panel on which vertically lettered in buff is "M | M | & | Co [the "o" being within the "C"]". At the foot of the spine within a small vertical black panel is the publisher's imprint in buff: "MACMILLAN & Co". The endpapers are of white wove paper, and the text is printed on wove paper. The endpapers have ads printed on them in black as follows: on the front pastedown, continuing on to the recto and verso of the front free endpaper, an ad headed: "MACMILLAN & CO.'S POPULAR 6s. NOVELS."; on the recto of the rear free endpaper an ad headed: "English Men of Letters [in Gothic type]" followed by an ad headed: "Mr. John Morley's Collected Writings. [in Gothic type]"; on the verso of the rear free endpaper an ad headed: "ENGLISH STATESMEN", followed by an ad for "The English Citizen: [in Gothic type]"; and on the rear pastedown an ad for "The English Illustrated Magazine. [in Gothic type]". The top-edge is trimmed and stained ochre, the fore-edge is trimmed, and the bottom edge is rough trimmed.

The cover design is the standard Macmillan design for two-shilling yellowbacks signed on the lower right of both the front and back covers "L.F. Day". This is the first impression of the yellowback.

Illustrated Plate 15.

29.6.0. *The Princess Casamassima*, second edition, third impression (yellowback), one volume, London and New York 1889.

The title-page is identical to that of the second edition, second impression (yellowback), 29.5.0, except that it is dated 1889, and the reservation of rights at the foot is not within square brackets. The verso of the title-leaf reads: "COPYRIGHT | 1886 | by HENRY JAMES | first edition (3 Vols., Crown 8vo) 1886 | New Edition (1 Vol., Crown 8vo) 1887 | New Edition (Globe 8vo) 1888 | Reprinted 1889 [printing history all in italic]".

The size, collation, and contents are identical to those of 29.5.0, except that the title-leaf is as noted above.

Binding: buff paper boards with an elaborate floral design in bright red and black on the front and back covers. The design of this binding is similar to that on 29.5.0, but is coarser in design (see below). The endpapers are of white wove paper, and the text is printed on wove paper. No ads are printed on the endpapers. All edges are trimmed.

The standard design for the covers of the Macmillan two-shilling issues is signed on the lower right of both the front and back covers "L.F. Day"; see 29.5.0. This cover, however, is unsigned. In addition, the covers of this copy are more coarsely printed than other signed Macmillan yellowback issues (e.g. the 1888 yellowback of this title, *Roderick Hudson*, *The Madonna of the Future* and *Daisy Miller: A Study*). Finally, this copy differs from the copies in the standard signed bindings of this title, *The Madonna of the Future* and *Daisy Miller: A Study*, in that its endpapers have no ads printed on them.

E&L A29b states: "in 1888 Macmillan published a yellowback issue, Globe 8vo., consisting of two printings of 2,000 copies each at 2/-. Sadleir 3601 records this as 1889." As this copy, dated 1889, indicates, E&L did not appreciate the fact that the title-page of the second impression of the second edition (the first printing of the yellowback) is dated 1888 and that of the third impression (the second printing of the yellowback) is dated 1889. However, MBC, 493 records the second printing of the yellowback as December 1888. It was no doubt printed in December 1888 with an title-page dated 1889.

Illustrated Plate 15.

29.6.5. *The Princess Casamassima*, second edition, third impression, remainder binding, one volume, London and New York 1889.

Size: 6 $^{15}/_{16}$" x 4 $^{1}/_{2}$".

The title-page is identical to that of the second edition, second impression (yellowback), 29.5.0, except that it is dated 1889, and the reservation of right at the foot is not within square brackets. The verso of the title-leaf reads: "COPYRIGHT | 1886 | By Henry James | first edition (3 Vols., Crown 8vo) 1886 | New Edition (1 Vol., Crown 8vo) 1887 | New Edition (Globe 8vo) 1888 | Reprinted 1889 [printing history all in italic]".

Collation and contents, except as noted above for the title-leaf, are identical to those of 29.5.0.

Binding: brown linen-grain cloth. The front and back covers are neither lettered nor decorated. The spine, lettered and decorated in gilt, reads: "[band of five triangular decorative devices in a row] | THE | PRINCESS | CASA- | MASSIMA | H. JAMES [in sans-serif] | [band of five decorative devices in a row] | [band of five decorative devices in a row]". The endpapers are of smooth cream wove paper (no ads printed on them), and the text is printed on the same wove paper as 29.6.0. All edges are trimmed.

On the front free endpaper is an inscription "C. Pouwens | London April 1921".

This is a remainder binding of third impression sheets, not a re-casing or rebinding. Note the slightly larger size of this volume. For a similar binding, see the first edition, first impression, remainder binding, of *The Golden Bowl*, 60.3.5.

29.7.0. *The Princess Casamassima*, second edition, first impression, American issue, binding state A, one volume, London and New York 1886.

Size: 7 $9/16$" x 4 $13/16$".

The title-page, title-leaf verso, collation, and contents are identical to those of the second edition, first impression, sheets of the American issue diverted to the English market, 29.3.0.

Binding: dark green diagonal-fine-ribbed cloth, lettered and decorated in gilt, black and in blind uniform with the second English edition of *The American* (1879), 4.17.0. There is no lettering on the front or back covers. The spine reads: "THE | PRINCESS | CASAMASSIMA | HENRY | JAMES [all the foregoing in italic] | Macmillan & Co." The publisher's imprint at the foot of the spine is in upper and lower case letters, the "M", "&," "C" being $5/32$" high and the other letters are $1/8$" high. The "o" in "Co" is raised above a line. The endpapers are of white wove paper, and the text is printed on wove paper. There are no binder's fly-leaves at the front or the back, and no catalogue of ads is bound in at the end. All edges are trimmed.

An oval library stamp on the front free endpaper reads: "[illegible] Hills | Public Library".

29.8.0. *The Princess Casamassima*, second edition, first impression, American issue, binding state B, one volume, London and New York 1886.

Size: 7 $5/16$" x 4 $7/8$".

The title-page, title-leaf verso, collation, and contents are identical to those of the second edition, first impression, sheets of the American issue diverted to the English market, 29.3.0.

Binding: royal-blue diagonal-ribbed cloth, decorated in gilt across the top of the front cover with a vine and leaf design with two rules above and two rules below in gilt, which design and rules extend across the top of the spine. On the bottom of the front cover are three rules in blind which extend across the foot of the spine in gilt. All these rules extend across the back cover in blind. The spine, lettered in gilt, reads: "THE | PRINCESS | CASAMASSIMA | HENRY | JAMES" (centered). The publisher's imprint in gilt at the foot of the spine (which is between two gilt rules) has an initial capital "M", a capital "&" and "C" in "Co", followed by a small "o" set above a dot. The letters "ACMILLAN" are $^1/_8''$ high. There is no lettering on the front or back covers. The endpapers are of olive-coated paper, and the text is printed on wove paper. A binder's fly-leaf of wove paper is at both the front and the back. All edges are trimmed. No publisher's catalogue is bound in at the end.

This binding variant is not noted in E&L or BAL.

❧+❧

30. *PARTIAL PORTRAITS*

30.1.0. *Partial Portraits*, first edition, first impression, one volume, London and New York 1888.

PARTIAL PORTRAITS | BY | HENRY JAMES | London [in Gothic type] | MACMILLAN AND CO. | AND NEW YORK | 1888 | All rights reserved [in italic]

Size: 7" x 4 ¾".

Collation: [A]⁶ B–I K–U X–Z 2A–2C⁸ 2D⁴; pp. [2] [i–x], [1]–408.

Contents: blank leaf; [i–ii] half-title, verso publisher's monogram; [iii–iv] title-page, verso copyright notice: "COPYRIGHT | BY | HENRY JAMES | 1888"; [v–vi] "NOTICE", verso blank; [vii–viii] "CONTENTS", verso blank; [ix–x] divisional fly-title, verso blank; [1]–408 text; 408 at foot printer's imprint: "Printed by R. & R. Clark, Edinburgh. [all but printer's name in italic]".

Binding: dark green smooth cloth, with a single-rule border in blind on the front and back covers. The spine, which is lettered and decorated in gilt, reads: "[rule] | Partial | Portraits | HENRY | JAMES | Macmillan

& Co. | [rule]". The "o" in "Co" is raised above a dot. The endpapers are of white wove paper, and the text is printed on wove paper. All edges are untrimmed. There are four pages of unpaginated and undated ads inserted at the end. These ads are: [1–2] headed on both pages: "BY THE SAME AUTHOR [in italic]", [3] headed: "MESSRS. MACMILLAN AND CO.'S PUBLICATIONS", and [4] headed: "TWELVE ENGLISH STATESMEN."

On the front free endpaper is a small white ticket reading "W. B. Clark & Co. | Booksellers & Stationers | Boston." On the front pastedown is the bookplate of Walter Leon Sawyer, dated "Boston MDCCCXCVIII".

Printing history. Macmillan Archive. MEB, at 266, records that there were six separate impressions of the first and only English edition of this title. They were all printed from stereotype plates. These printings are: a first impression of 2,000 copies in April 1888; a second of 500 copies in January 1894; a third of 500 copies in June 1899; a fourth of 500 copies in December 1905; a fifth of 500 copies in February 1911; and a sixth of 500 copies in August 1919. The first impression was priced at 6s., the second at 5s., the third through the fifth, published as part of the Eversley Series, at 4s., and the sixth, also part of the Eversley Series, at 5s. Macmillan destroyed the plates in 1932. In the remarks column opposite the first impression is the entry "revised 1894" that has been crossed out.

MPL 55909, at 37, records a print and paper order of 500 copies on December 8, 1893; MPL 55912, at 62, records a similar order on May 25, 1899; MPL 55916, at 62, records a similar order with 525 "envelopes" on September 11, 1905; MPL 55919, at 51, records a similar order on December 9, 1910, with 525 "envelopes", with the additional notation "(Eversley)"; and MPL 55923 records a similar order on July 10, 1919, with 550 "envelopes", also with the notation "Eversley".

BAL 10581 questions the assertion in E&L A30b that there was a separate American issue of this edition with terminal ads in dollars which was distributed in the United States, stating: "the publisher's records show but one printing in 1888; distributed in both Great Britain and the United States." The bookplate and bookseller's ticket in this copy supports BAL's contention that this impression, as well as the third impression, 30.3.0, which also has an American bookseller's ticket, were distributed, but not published, in the United States. In 1893, it was advertised at $1.75.

30.2.0. *Partial Portraits*, first edition, second impression, one volume, London and New York 1894.

The title-page is identical to that of the first edition, first impression, 30.1.0, except that it is dated 1894 at the foot.

Size: 7 1/16″ x 4 3/4″.

Collation: [A]⁶ B–I K–U X–Z 2A–2C⁸ 2D⁶; pp. [2] [i–x], [1]–408 [409–412].

Contents: blank leaf; [i–ii] half-title, verso publisher's monogram; [iii–iv] title-page, verso copyright notice and printing history: "COPYRIGHT | BY | HENRY JAMES | 1888 | First Edition 1888. Reprinted 1894 [printing history, except dates, in italic]"; [v–vi] "NOTICE", verso blank; [vii–viii] "CONTENTS", verso blank; [ix–x] divisional fly-title, verso blank; [1]–408 text; [409–412] ads headed: [409–411] "NOVELS AND TALES BY HENRY JAMES.", [412] "A SELECTION FROM | MACMILLAN'S THREE & SIXPENNY SERIES".

The ads on [409–412] are an integral part of signature 2D; see below for additional inserted ads.

Binding: smooth maroon cloth, lettered and decorated identically to the first edition, first impression (including the printer's imprint at the foot of the spine), 30.1.0. The endpapers are of white wove paper, and the text is printed on wove paper. The top and fore-edges are untrimmed, and the bottom edge is rough trimmed. There are two pages of unpaginated ads inserted at the end dated on [2] "10.12.93". These ads are for The Eversley Series, listing *French Poets and Novelists* but not *Partial Portraits*.

On the title-page is blind-stamped "PRESENTATION COPY".

30.3.0. *Partial Portraits*, first edition, third impression, one volume, London and New York 1899.

The title-page is identical to that of the first edition, first impression, 30.1.0, except that at the foot the publisher's imprint reads: "London [in Gothic type] | MACMILLAN AND CO., Limited | NEW YORK: THE MACMILLAN COMPANY | 1899 | All rights reserved [in italic]".

Size: 7″ x 4 3/4″.

Collation: [A]⁶ (–[A]₁) B–I K–U X–Z 2A–2C⁸ 2D⁶; pp.[i–x], [1]–408 [409–412].

Contents: [i–ii] half-title, verso publisher's monogram; [iii–iv] title-page, verso copyright notice and printing history: "COPYRIGHT | BY | HENRY JAMES | 1888 | First Edition 1888. Reprinted 1894, 1899 [printing history, except dates, in italic]"; [v–vi] "NOTICE", verso blank; [vii–viii] "CONTENTS", verso blank; [ix–x] divisional fly-title, verso blank; [1]–408 text; 408 at foot printer's imprint: "Printed by R. & R. Clark, Limited, Edinburgh. [all but printer's name in italic]"; [409] ad headed: "NOVELS AND TALES | By HENRY JAMES.", [410–411] ads headed on both pages: "NOVELS AND TALES BY HENRY JAMES.", and [412] ad headed: "BY RUDYARD KIPLING."

The ads on [409–412] are an integral part of signature 2D; see below for additional inserted ads.

Binding: smooth maroon cloth, lettered and decorated identically to 30.1.0, except that the publisher's imprint at the foot of the spine is in uniform capitals, and the "o" in "Co" is raised above a dot. The endpapers are of white wove paper, and the text is printed on wove paper. A binder's fly-leaf of wove paper is at the front, but none at the back. The top edge is untrimmed, and the other edges are rough trimmed. There are two pages of unpaginated ads inserted at the end dated on [2] "10.7.02". These ads are for The Eversley Series, listing both *Partial Portraits* and *French Poets and Novelists*.

On the rear pastedown is a small pink bookseller's ticket reading: "BRENTANO'S | Booksellers & Stationers, | Washington, D.C."

30.4.0. *Partial Portraits*, first edition, fourth impression, London and New York 1905.

The title-page is identical to that of the first edition, first impression, 30.1.0, except that at the foot the publisher's imprint reads: "London [in Gothic type] | MACMILLAN AND CO. Limited | NEW YORK: THE MACMILLAN COMPANY | 1905 | All rights reserved [in italic]".

Size: 7 1/16" x 4 3/4".

Collation; [A]⁶ B–I K–U X–Z 2A–2C⁸ 2D⁴; pp. [2] [i–x], [1]–408.

Contents: blank–leaf; [i–ii] half-title, verso publisher's monogram, [iii–iv] title-page, copyright notice and printing history: "COPYRIGHT |

PARTIAL PORTRAITS

BY | HENRY JAMES | 1888 | First Edition, 1888. Reprinted 1894, 1899, 1905 [printing history, except dates, in italic]"; [v–vi] "NOTICE", verso blank; [vii–viii] "CONTENTS", verso blank; [ix–x] divisional fly-title, verso blank; [1]–408 text; 408 at foot printer's imprint: "Printed by R. & R. Clark, Limited, Edinburgh. [all but printer's name in italic]".

Binding: smooth maroon cloth, lettered and decorated identically to 30.1.0, except that the publisher's imprint at the foot of the spine is in uniform capitals, and the "o" in "Co" is raised above a dot. The endpapers are of white wove paper, and the text is printed on wove paper. The top edge is untrimmed, and the other edges are rough trimmed. There are four pages of undated and unpaginated ads inserted at the end, headed: on [1] and [2] "The Eversley Series", on [3] "MACMILLAN'S LIBRARY | OF | ENGLISH CLASSICS", and on [4] "English Men of Letters. [in Gothic type]".

30.5.0. *Partial Portraits*, first edition, fifth impression, one volume, London 1911.

The title-page is identical to that of the first edition, first impression, 30.1.0, except that at the foot the publisher's imprint reads: "MACMILLAN AND CO., LIMITED | ST. MARTIN'S STREET, LONDON | 1911".

Size: 7 $^{1}/_{16}$" x 4 $^{5}/_{8}$".

Collation: [A]^6 B–I K–U X–Z 2A–2C^8 2D^6; pp. [2] [i–x], [1]–408 [409–412].

Contents: blank leaf; [i–ii] half-title, verso publisher's monogram followed by list of three Macmillan companies; [iii–iv] title-page, verso copyright notice and printing history: "COPYRIGHT | BY | HENRY JAMES | 1888 | First Edition, 1888. Reprinted 1894, 1899, 1905, 1911 [printing history, except dates, in italic]"; [v–vi] "NOTICE", verso blank; [vii–viii] "CONTENTS", verso blank; [ix–x] divisional fly-title, verso blank; [1]–408 text; 408 at foot printer's imprint: "Printed by R. & R. Clark, Edinburgh. [all but in printer's name in italic]"; [409–412] ads (paginated 1–4, but undated) for The Eversley Series.

The ads on [409–412] are an integral part of signature 2D.

Binding: smooth maroon cloth, lettered and decorated, identically to 30.1.0, except that the publisher's imprint at the foot of the spine is in uniform capitals, and the "o" in "Co" is raised above a dot. The endpapers are of white wove paper, and the text is printed on wove paper. The top and bottom edges are untrimmed, and the fore-edge is rough trimmed. There are no ads bound in at the end.

30.6.0. *Partial Portraits*, first edition, sixth impression, one volume, London 1919.

The title-page is identical to that of the first edition, first impression, 30.1.0, except that at the foot the publisher's imprint reads: "MACMILLAN & CO., LIMITED | ST. MARTIN'S STREET, LONDON | 1919".

Size: 7 $\frac{1}{8}$" x 4 $\frac{5}{8}$".

Collation: [A]^6(–[A]$_1$) B–I K–U X–Z 2A–2C^8 2D^6; pp. [i–x], [1]–408 [409–412].

Contents: [i–ii] half-title, verso publisher's monogram followed by a list of three Macmillan companies; [iii–iv] title-page, verso copyright notice and printing history: "COPYRIGHT | BY | HENRY JAMES | first edition 1888. Reprinted 1894, 1899, 1905, 1911, 1919. [printing history, except dates, in italic]"; [v–vi] "NOTICE", verso blank; [vii–viii] "CONTENTS", verso blank; [ix–x] divisional fly-title, verso blank; [1]–408 text; 408 at foot printer's imprint: "Printed by R. & R. Clark, Limited, Edinburgh. [all but printer's name in italic]"; [409–412] ads (paginated 1–4 but undated) for the Eversley Series.

The ads on [409–412] are an integral part of signature 2D.

Binding: smooth maroon cloth, decorated in blind on the front and back covers identically to 30.1.0. The spine, which is lettered and decorated in gilt, reads: "PARTIAL | PORTRAITS | HENRY | JAMES | MACMILLAN & Co." The "o" in "Co" is raised above a dot. The endpapers are of white wove paper, and the text is printed on wove paper. There are no ads inserted at the end. The top edge is untrimmed, and the bottom and fore-edges are rough trimmed.

31. *THE REVERBERATOR*

31.1.0. *The Reverberator*, first edition, two volumes, London and New York 1888.

THE | REVERBERATOR | BY | HENRY JAMES | IN TWO VOLUMES [in italic] | VOL. I [II] | London [in Gothic type] | MACMILLAN AND CO. | AND NEW YORK | 1888 | All Rights Reserved [in italic]

Size: 7 1/16″ x 4 3/4″.

Collation: Volume I: $[A]^2$ B–I K–N^8; pp. [i–iv], [1]–190 [191–192]. Volume II: $[A]^2$ B–I K–O^8; pp. [i–iv], [1]–207 [208].

Contents: Volume I: [i–ii] half-title, verso publisher's device; [iii–iv] title-page, verso copyright notice: "Copyright, [in italic] | 1888, | By HENRY JAMES"; [1]–190 text; 190 at foot printer's imprint: "RICHARD CLAY AND SONS, LIMITED, LONDON AND BUNGAY."; [191–192] ads for James's works headed: [191] "BY THE SAME AUTHOR." and [192]: "By the Same Author." Volume II: [i–ii] half-title, verso publisher's device; [iii–iv] title-page, verso copyright notice as on Volume I title-leaf verso; [1]–207 text; [208] printer's imprint: "Richard Clay and Sons, Limited, | LONDON AND BUNGAY."

Binding: blue-green smooth cloth. The front covers are decorated with five rules in gilt across both the top and bottom. The back covers have centered the publisher's device in blind. The spines, which are lettered and decorated in gilt, read: "[five rules] | The | Reverberator | Henry | James | VOL. I [II] | [four rules] | Macmillan & Co. | [rule]". The "o" in "Co" is raised above a dot. The endpapers are of black coated paper, and the text is printed on wove paper. All edges are untrimmed.

Printing history. Macmillan Archive. MEB, at 267, records that the first edition in two volumes was printed from standing type in a single impression of 500 copies in May 1888. The two volumes were priced at 12s., and were published on June 5, 1888. Electrotype plates were made from a second setting of type for the one-volume second edition, and were used in May 1888 to print a first impression of 3,000 copies, all of which were exported to America. The American impression was priced at $1.25, later reduced to $1.00. The printing sequence of the first edition and the second edition (American impression) is not clear, that is, whether the first edition was in fact the first book printing of this title. It is possible that the second edition was printed before the first edition in order to secure the American copyright (the English copyright had been secured through the serial publication from February through June 1888 in *Macmillan's Magazine*). The second impression of the second edition was printed from these same plates in August 1888 in an impression of 1,000 copies for publication only in England. It was priced at 6s. Macmillan destroyed the plates in February 1921.

31.2.0. *The Reverberator*, second edition, second impression (English), binding state A, one volume, London and New York 1888.

THE | REVERBERATOR | BY | HENRY JAMES | London [in Gothic type] | MACMILLAN AND CO. | AND NEW YORK | 1888 | The Right of Translation and Reproduction is Reserved [in italic]

Size: $7 \frac{1}{4}'' \times 4 \frac{7}{8}''$.

Collation: [A]² B–I K–P⁸ Q⁴; pp. [i–iv], [1]–229 [230] [231–232].

Contents: [i–ii] half-title, verso publisher's device; [iii–iv] title-page, verso copyright notice and printing history: "Copyright, [in italic] | 1888, | By Henry James. | First Edition (2 vols. Globe 8vo) June 1888. | New Edition 1 vol. Crown 8vo, August 1888. ["First Edition" and "New Edition" are in italic]"; [1]–229 text; [230] printer's imprint: "Richard Clay and Sons, Limited, | LONDON AND BUNGAY."; [231–232] blank leaf.

Binding: dark blue-green pebble-grain cloth lettered and decorated in gilt, black, and in blind uniform with the second English edition of *The American* (1879), 4.17.0. No lettering is present on the front or back covers, and no publisher's device is present on the back cover. The spine reads: "THE | REVERBERATOR | HENRY | JAMES [all the foregoing in italic] | Macmillan & Co." The "o" in "Co" is raised above a dot. The endpapers are of black coated paper, and the text is printed on wove paper. The top edge is untrimmed, and the other edges are trimmed. A 32-page paginated publisher's catalogue, dated April 1888, printed on thin wove paper, is bound in at the end.

Illustrated Plate 16.

E&L A31c records the primary binding as being in dark blue diagonal-fine-ribbed cloth, with an April 1888 catalogue, and this binding as a variant. However, the presence of an April 1888 catalogue and black coated endpapers in this copy, the and the presence of The Times Book Club ticket, the absence of a catalogue, and the use of green coated endpapers in what E&L records as the primary binding (31.3.0 which is, however, in diaper-grain not diagonal-fine-ribbed cloth) suggest that this copy is in the primary binding.

31.3.0. *The Reverberator*, second edition, second impression (English), binding state B, one volume, London and New York 1888.

The title-page, size, collation, and contents are identical to the second edition, second impression (English), 31.2.0.

Binding: royal-blue diaper-grain cloth. The front cover is decorated with an elaborate frieze design in gilt across the top, and two sets of rules between each of which is a line of dots, all in blind, across the bottom. The back cover is decorated in blind with a centered publisher's device. The spine, which is lettered in gilt, and decorated in gilt and in blind, reads: "[frieze design as on the front cover] | THE | REVERBERATOR | HENRY | JAMES | [two rules separated by a line of dots, all in blind] | MACMILLAN & Co. | [two rules separated by a line of dots, all in blind]". The "o" in "Co" is raised above a dot. The endpapers are of green coated paper, and the text is printed on wove paper. The top and fore-edges are untrimmed, and the bottom edge is trimmed. There are no ads bound in at the end.

On the rear pastedown is a small green ticket reading: "The [Times device] Times | (Book Club) | 376–384 Oxford Street | London."

Illustrated Plate 16.

31.4.0. *The Reverberator*, second edition, first impression (American), variant A, one volume, London and New York 1888.

The page size is: 6 $^7/_8$″ x 4 $^3/_4$″; the volume size is: 7 $^1/_8$″ x 4 $^7/_8$″.

The title-page, collation, and contents are identical to those of the second edition, second impression (English), 31.2.0, except that the verso of the title-leaf differs in that the printing history is omitted, and reads: "Copyright, | 1888, | By Henry James".

Binding: blue diagonal-fine-ribbed cloth. The front cover is decorated with an elaborate frieze design in gilt at the top and three rules in blind at the bottom. The back cover is decorated with four rules in blind across the top and three rules in blind across the bottom. The spine, which is lettered and decorated in gilt, reads: "[frieze design as on the front cover] | THE | REVERBERATOR | HENRY | JAMES | [gilt rule] MACMILLAN & Co. | [two rules]". The "o" in "Co" is raised above a dot. The endpapers are of black coated paper, and the text is printed on wove paper. All edges are trimmed.

BAL 10583 notes that the American impression "bears only ... 'Copyright, | 1888, | By HENRY JAMES'" on [iv], whereas the English one-volume impression has the full printing history. BAL records two variants in size, of which this is one, the other being the immediately following copy, 31.5.0. BAL also records both being in the same diagonal-fine-ribbed cloth (S cloth) which is the case here. BAL queries: "does the variation in size represent two binding orders separated by time?" These size variants are not noted in E&L.

Illustrated Plate 16.

31.5.0. *The Reverberator*, second edition, first impression (American), variant B, one volume, London and New York 1888.

Size: $7\,^{5}/_{16}''$ x $4\,^{7}/_{8}''$; the volume size is: $7\,^{5}/_{8}''$ x $5\,^{1}/_{8}''$.

The title-page, collation, and contents are identical to those of the second edition, first impression (American), variant A, 31.4.0.

Binding: blue diagonal-fine-ribbed cloth, lettered and decorated in gilt identically to 31.4.0.

This is the second variant in size noted in BAL 10583.

Illustrated Plate 16.

❧☩❧

32. THE ASPERN PAPERS

32.1.0. *The Aspern Papers*, first edition, two volumes, London and New York 1888.

THE ASPERN PAPERS | LOUISA PALLANT | THE MODERN WARNING | BY | HENRY JAMES | IN TWO VOLUMES – VOL. I [II] | London [in Gothic type] | MACMILLAN AND CO. | AND NEW YORK | 1888 | All rights reserved [in italic]

Size: $7\,^{1}/_{8}''$ x $4\,^{3}/_{4}''$.

Collation: Volume I: [A]⁴ B–I K–Q⁸; pp. [2] [i–vi], [1]–239 [240]. Volume II: [A]⁴ B–I K–R⁸ S⁴; pp. [i–viii] [1–2], [3]–258 [259–264].

Contents: Volume I: blank leaf; [i–ii] half-title, verso publisher's device; [iii–iv] title-page, verso copyright notice: "COPYRIGHT 1888 | BY | HENRY JAMES [the "1" in 1888 being smaller than the "888"]"; [v–vi] divisional fly-title, verso blank; [1]–239 text; 239 at foot printer's imprint: "Printed by R. & R. Clark, Edinburgh. [all except the printer's name in italic]"; [240] blank. Volume II: [i–ii] half-title, verso publisher's device; [iii–iv] title-page, verso copyright notice as on Volume I title-leaf verso; [v–vi] "CONTENTS", verso blank; [vii–viii] "NOTE | The second of the following Tales originally appeared in *Harper's Magazine* under a different title.",[33] verso blank; [1–2] divisional fly-title, verso blank; [3]–258 text; 258 at foot printer's imprint as on 239 of Volume I; [259–264] ads, headed: [259–260] "BY THE SAME AUTHOR.", [261] "MACMILLAN AND CO.'S POPULAR 6s. NOVELS.", [262] "CHEAP EDITIONS OF THE WORKS | OF | CHARLES KINGSLEY" [263] "CHEAP EDITIONS OF THE WORKS | OF | CHARLOTTE M. YONGE", [264] "NEW NOVELS."

Binding: dark blue smooth cloth. The front covers are decorated with five rules in gilt across both the top and bottom. The back covers have a centered publisher's device in blind. The spines, which are lettered and decorated in gilt, read: "[five rules] | The | Aspern | Papers | Henry | James | VOL. I [II] | [four rules] | Macmillan & Co. | [rule]". The "o" in "Co" is raised above a dot. The endpapers are of black coated paper, and the text is printed on thick wove paper. All edges are untrimmed.

This binding is uniform with that on the first edition of *The Reverberator* (1888), 31.1.0.

Printing history. Macmillan Archive. MEB, at 265, records that the first English edition in two volumes was printed from standing type in a single impression of 650 copies in September 1888. The two volumes were priced at 21s. Stereotype plates were made from a second setting of type for the one volume second edition and were used on a date unspecified in 1888 to print a first impression of 2,000 copies, all of which were exported to America; see 3.2.5. The placement of this entry in MEB is before the entry for the second impression (English).

33 It is the third title, "Modern Warning", not the second title, "Louisa Pallant", that first appeared under the title "Two Countries" in *Harper's New Monthly Magazine* in June 1888.

It was priced at $1.50, later reduced to $1.00. A second impression of the second edition of 2,000 copies was printed from these same plates in September 1890 for publication only in England; see 33.3.0 and 33.4.0. It was priced at 3s. 6d. Macmillan destroyed the plates in March 1921. Given the destruction of the plates in 1921, the assertion in E&L A32c that there was a second English impression in 1939 appears to be incorrect.

In 1924 Albert & Charles Boni published an edition of *The Aspern Papers* as number 8 in their American Library series.

32.2.0. *The Aspern Papers*, second edition, second impression (English), one volume, London and New York 1890.

THE ASPERN PAPERS | LOUISA PALLANT | THE MODERN WARNING | BY | HENRY JAMES | LONDON [in Gothic type] | MACMILLAN AND CO. | AND NEW YORK | 1890 | All rights reserved [in italic]

Size: $7\,^{5}/_{16}''$ x $4\,^{15}/_{16}''$.

Collation: [A]⁴ B–I K–T⁸ U²; pp. [i–viii], [1]–290 [291–292].

Contents: [i–ii] half-title, verso blank; [iii–iv] "CONTENTS", verso "NOTE" as in the first edition, 32.1.0; [v–vi] title-page, verso copyright notice and printing history: "COPYRIGHT 1888 | BY | HENRY JAMES | First Edition (2 Vols. Globe 8vo) 1888 | New Edition (1 Vol. Crown 8vo) 1890 [printing history in italic]; [vii–viii] divisional fly-title, verso publisher's device; [1]–290 text; 290 at foot printer's imprint: "Printed by R. & R. Clark, Edinburgh. [all except the printer's name in italic]"; [291–292] ads headed on both pages: "BY THE SAME AUTHOR", the first page an ad for *The Tragic Muse*, with extensive press commentary, and the second page listing 19 James titles, the last dated being *A London Life*.

Binding: bright red diaper-grain cloth. The front cover has a thin followed by a thick rule in blind across the top, and a thick followed by a more widely spaced thin rule in blind across the bottom. Centered on the front cover is a small gilt cartouche within which is the publisher's device, "& M Cº" [sic]. The rules on the front cover extend across the spine in gilt, and the back cover in blind. Centered on the back cover is the publisher's device in blind within a cartouche similar to but larger than the device on the front cover. The spine, which is lettered and decorated in gilt, reads: "[thin followed by a thick rule] | THE | ASPERN | PAPERS | HENRY | JAMES | [thick rule] | MACMILLAN & Co. | [thin rule]". The "o" in "Co" is raised above a dot. The endpapers are of white wove paper, and the text is printed on wove paper. The top edge is untrimmed, and the other edges are rough trimmed. Inserted at the end is a 60-page paginated publisher's catalogue dated August 1890.

The order of the four leaves, [A]⁴, pages [i–viii], is obviously incorrect. It should have been the half-title-leaf, [A]$_4$, the title-leaf, [A]$_3$, the contents leaf, [A]$_2$, and the divisional fly-title-leaf, [A]$_1$, as that is the normal order of prelims, and the order followed in the copy of this edition catalogued below. This appears to have been an error committed in the process of binding, as by reversing the two sheets constituting the conjugate pairs, [A]$_4$–[A]$_1$ and [A]$_2$–[A]$_3$ so that [A]$_{4r}$ becomes in effect [A]$_{1r}$ and [A]$_{3r}$ becomes [A]$_{2r}$, the error is corrected. This binding is uniform with that on the second English edition of *A London Life* (1889) and the second English edition of *The Tragic Muse* (1891), 33.2.0 and 34.10.0.

Illustrated Plate 17.

32.3.0. *The Aspern Papers*, second edition, second impression (English), The Times Book Club binding state, one volume, London and New York 1890.

The title-page, collation, and contents are identical to those of the second edition, second impression (English), 32.2.0, except that the preliminaries are in the correct order.

Binding: orange smooth-linen-grain cloth, with a single-rule black border on the front cover, and with no lettering or decoration on the back cover. The spine, which is lettered and decorated in black, reads: "[rule] | THE | ASPERN | PAPERS | HENRY | JAMES | [circular Times Book Club device] | [rule]". The endpapers are of white wove paper, and the text is printed on smooth wove paper. All edges are trimmed.

The ad on [292] lists *Novels and Tales* as one of the titles. This is a reference to the *Collective Edition of 1883*.

Illustrated Plate 32.

32.4.0. *The Aspern Papers*, second edition, second impression (English), The Times Book Club binding state, one volume, London and New York 1890.

The title-page, size, collation, and contents are identical to those of the second edition, second impression (English), 32.2.0, except that the preliminaries are in the correct order.

Binding: pale rose linen-grain cloth, lettered and decorated as 32.3.0, but it lacks the circular Times Book Club device at the foot of the spine. On the back pastedown is a small burgundy-colored ticket which reads: "THE [Times device] | (Book Club) | 376–384 Oxford Street | London."

Illustrated Plate 32.

32.5.0. *The Aspern Papers*, second edition, first impression (American), one volume, London and New York 1888.

THE ASPERN PAPERS | LOUISA PALLANT | THE MODERN WARNING | BY | HENRY JAMES | London [in Gothic type] | MACMILLAN AND CO. | AND NEW YORK | 1888 | All rights reserved [in italic]

Size: $7\,5/16''$ x $4\,3/4''$.

Collation: [A]⁴ B–I K–T⁸ U²; pp. [i–viii], [1]–290 [291–292].

Contents: [i–ii] half-title, verso publisher's device; [iii–iv] title-page, verso copyright notice: "COPYRIGHT 1888 | By | HENRY JAMES"; [v–vi] "CONTENTS", verso "NOTE" as in the first English edition, 32.1.0; [vii–viii] divisional fly-title, verso blank; [1]–290 text; 290 at foot printer's imprint: "Printed by R. & R. Clark, Edinburgh. [all except printer's name in italic]"; [291–292] blank leaf.

Binding: blue diagonal-fine-ribbed cloth. The front cover is decorated with an elaborate frieze design in gilt at the top and three rules in blind at the bottom. The back cover is decorated with four rules in blind across the top and three rules in blind across the bottom. The spine, which is lettered and decorated in gilt, reads: "[frieze design as on front cover] | THE | ASPERN | PAPERS | HENRY | JAMES | [rule] | MACMILLAN & Co. | [two rules]". The "o" in "Co" is raised above a dot. The endpapers are of black coated paper, and the text is printed on wove paper. All edges are trimmed.

A LONDON LIFE

Note that the title-leaf is dated 1888 and that there is no printing history on the title-leaf verso. The first impression of the second edition was only issued in America.

The binding of this copy is uniform with the binding of the second edition, first impression (American), variant A, of *The Reverberator* (1888), 31.4.0.

⚜

33. *A LONDON LIFE*

33.1.0. *A London Life*, first edition, two volumes, London and New York 1889.

A LONDON LIFE | THE PATAGONIA | THE LIAR | MRS. TEMPERLY | BY | HENRY JAMES | IN TWO VOLUMES - VOL. I [II] | London [in Gothic type] | MACMILLAN AND CO. | AND NEW YORK | 1889 | All rights reserved [in italic]

Size: 7 1/8" x 4 3/4".

Collation: Volume I: [A]^4 B–I K–S^8 T^4 [U]^2; pp. [i–viii], [1]–281 [282] [283–284].

Volume II: [A]^4 B–I K–U X–Z^8 2A^4 [2B]^2; pp. [2] [i–vi] [1–2], [3]–361 [362] [363–364]. The ads on leaves [U]$_2$ in Volume I, and [2B]$_2$ in Volume II are identical ads for James's works.

Contents: Volume I: [i–ii] half-title, verso publisher's device; [iii–iv] title-page, verso copyright notice: "COPYRIGHT 1889 [the "1" in 1889 being smaller than "889"] | BY | HENRY JAMES"; [v–vi] "CONTENTS", verso "NOTE | The last of the following Tales originally | appeared under a different name."; [vii–viii] divisional fly-title, verso blank; [1]–281 text; 281 at foot printer's imprint: "Printed by R. & R. Clark, Edinburgh. [all except printer's name in italic]"; [282] blank; [283–284] ads headed: "BY THE SAME AUTHOR.", [283], listing 17 James titles and the "pocket edition" of "MR. HENRY JAMES'S NOVELS AND TALES", and [284] listing 5 James titles, four with press opinions. Volume II: blank leaf; [i–ii] half-title, verso publisher's device; [iii–iv] title-page, verso copyright notice as on Volume I title-leaf verso; [v–vi] "CONTENTS", verso blank; [1–2] divisional fly-title, verso blank;

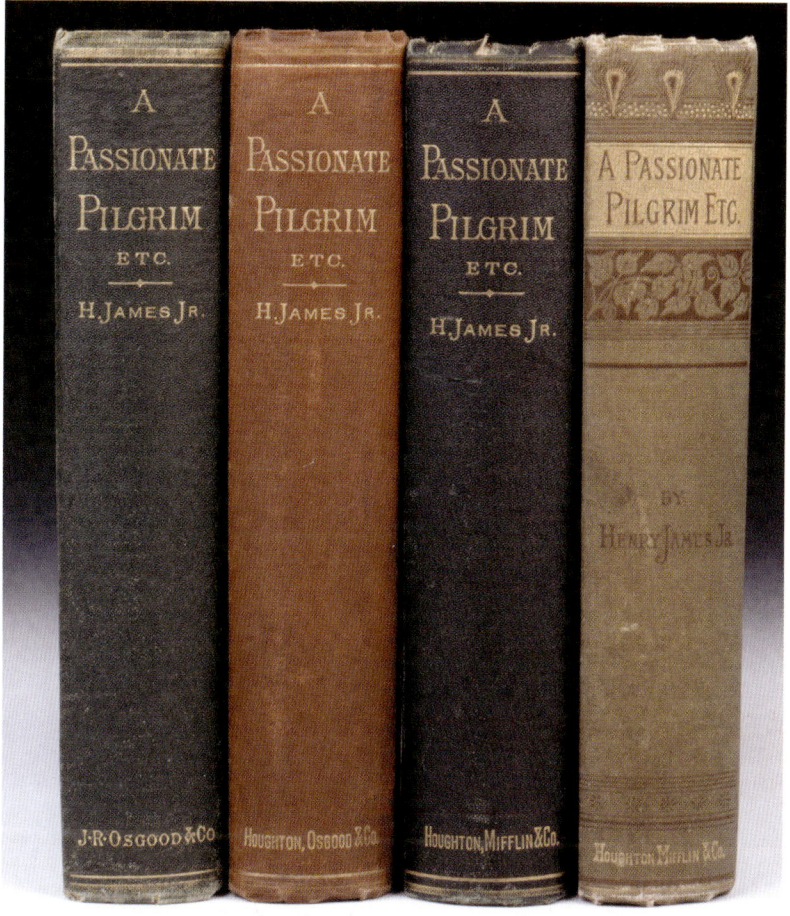

1. A Passionate Pilgrim: the four binding states of the first edition, first impression, 1.1.0, 1.5.0, 1.6.0 and 1.7.0.

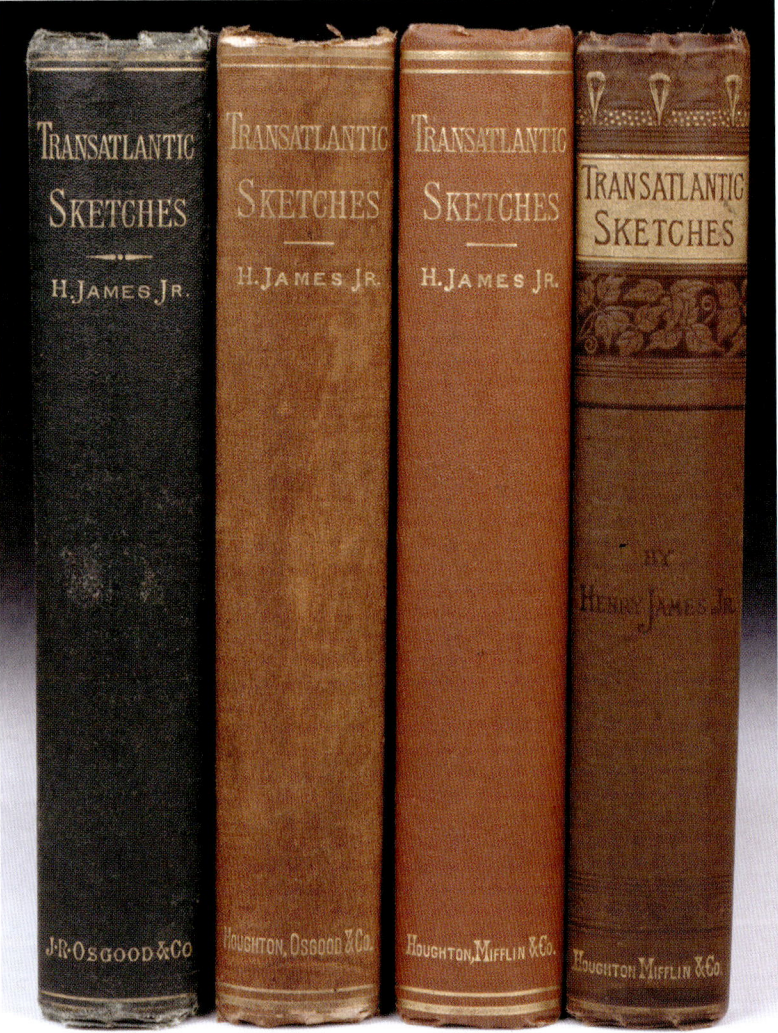

2. Transatlantic Sketches: the four binding states of the first edition, first impression, 2.2.0, 2.7.0, 2.8.0 and 2.9.0.

3. The American: two binding states of the first English edition (unauthorized), 4.15.0 and 4.16.0.

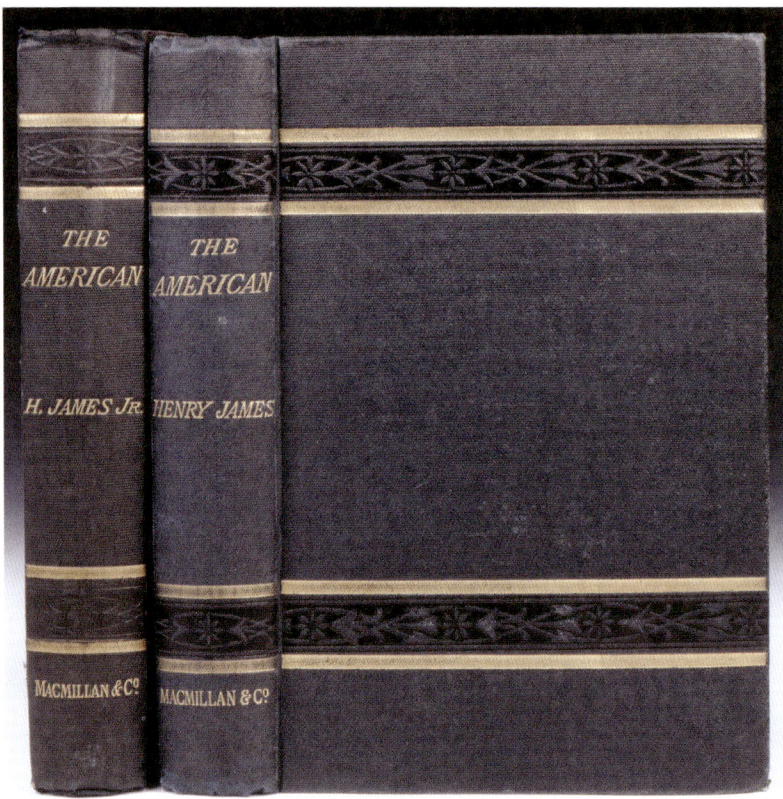

4. The American: the two binding states of the second English edition (authorized), 4.17.0 and 4.20.0. They are the styles of binding used by Macmillan on its second (one-volume) editions of 11 James titles.

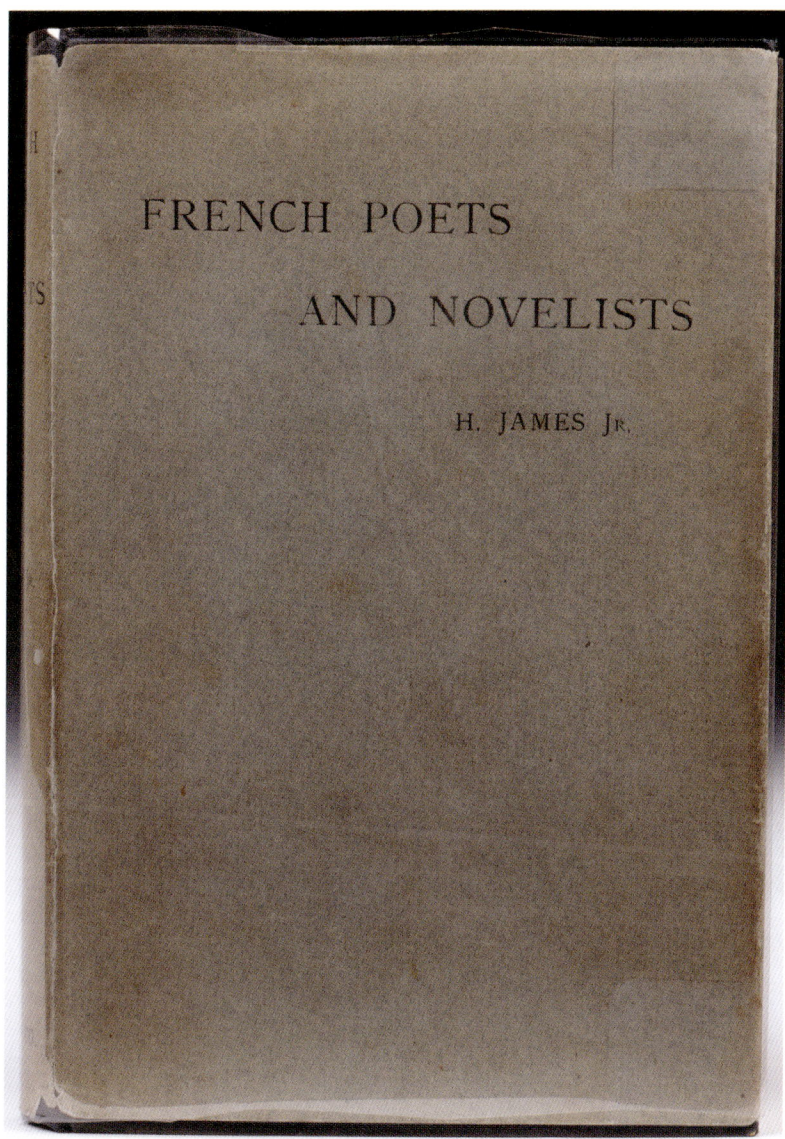

5. French Poets and Novelists: the dust-jacket of the first edition, 5.1.0.

6. An International Episode: cloth and paper bindings of the first edition, first impression, 9.2.0 and 9.1.0.

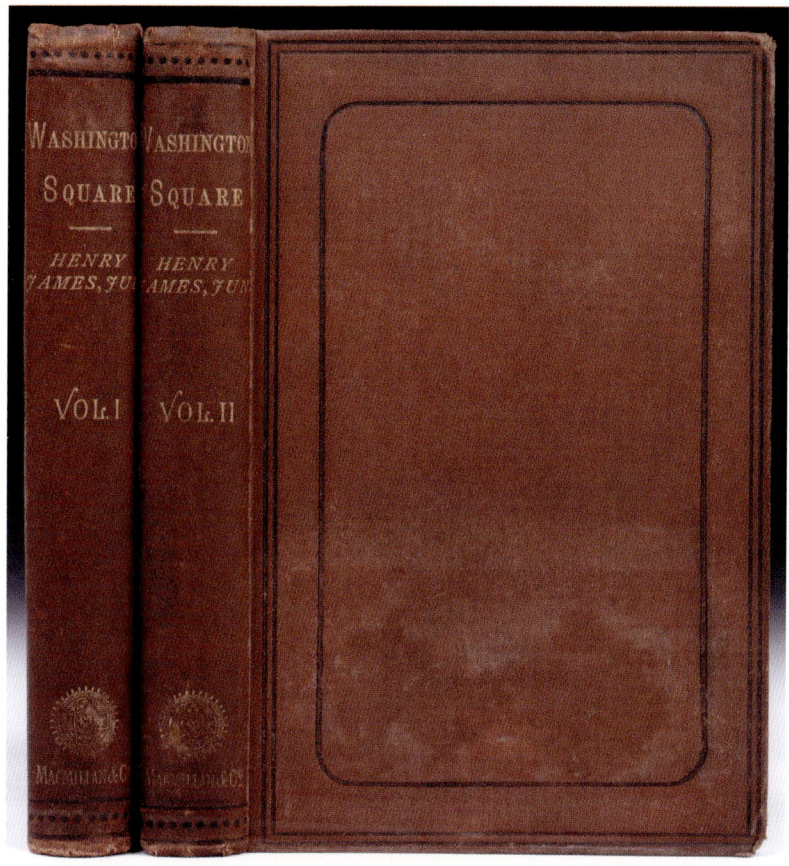

7. Washington Square: the first English edition, second impression, 15.4.0, unusual for a multi-volume Macmillan binding because of the rust-colored cloth used.

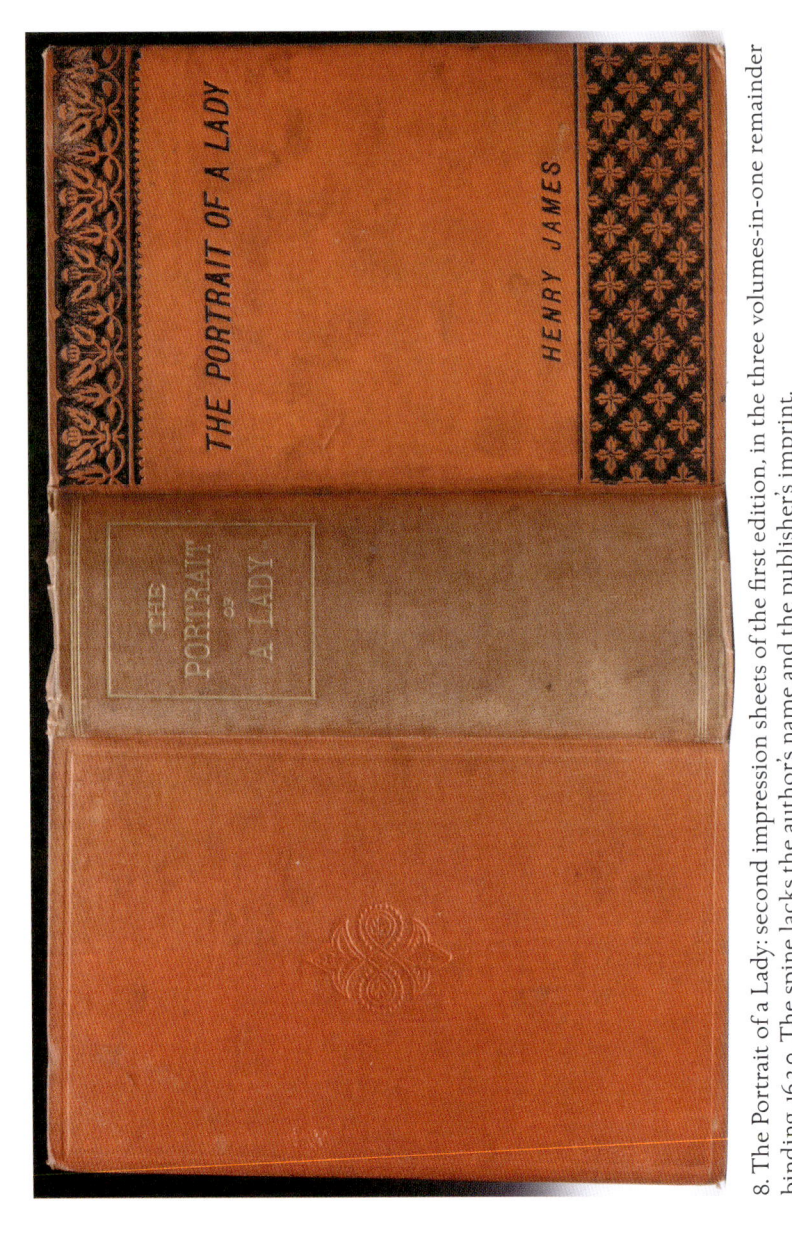

8. The Portrait of a Lady: second impression sheets of the first edition, in the three volumes-in-one remainder binding, 163.0. The spine lacks the author's name and the publisher's imprint.

9. The Portrait of a Lady: the three colors and two states of the bindings on the second edition, American issue, 16.5.0, 16.8.0, 16.6.0 and 16.7.0. This style of binding was also used by Houghton, Mifflin on six other James titles.

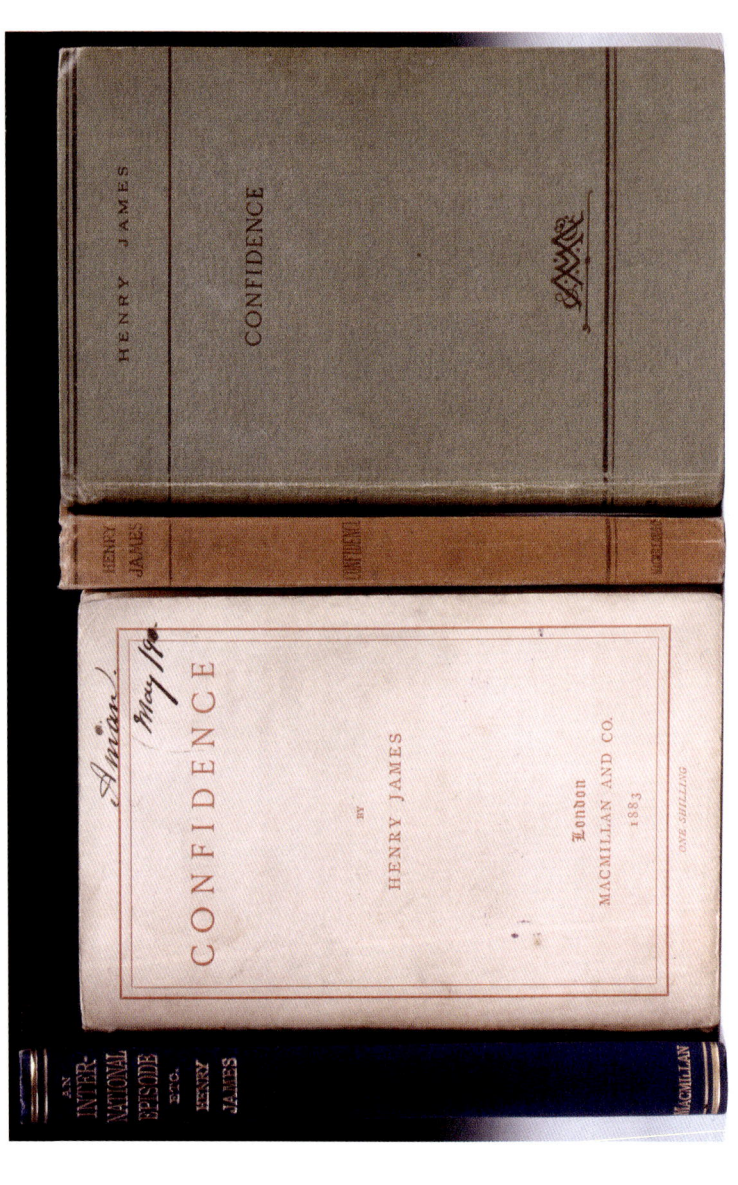

10. The Collective Edition of 1883: the four types of bindings in which the first impression was published. 20.1.0, 20.2.0, 20.3.0 and 20.4.0.

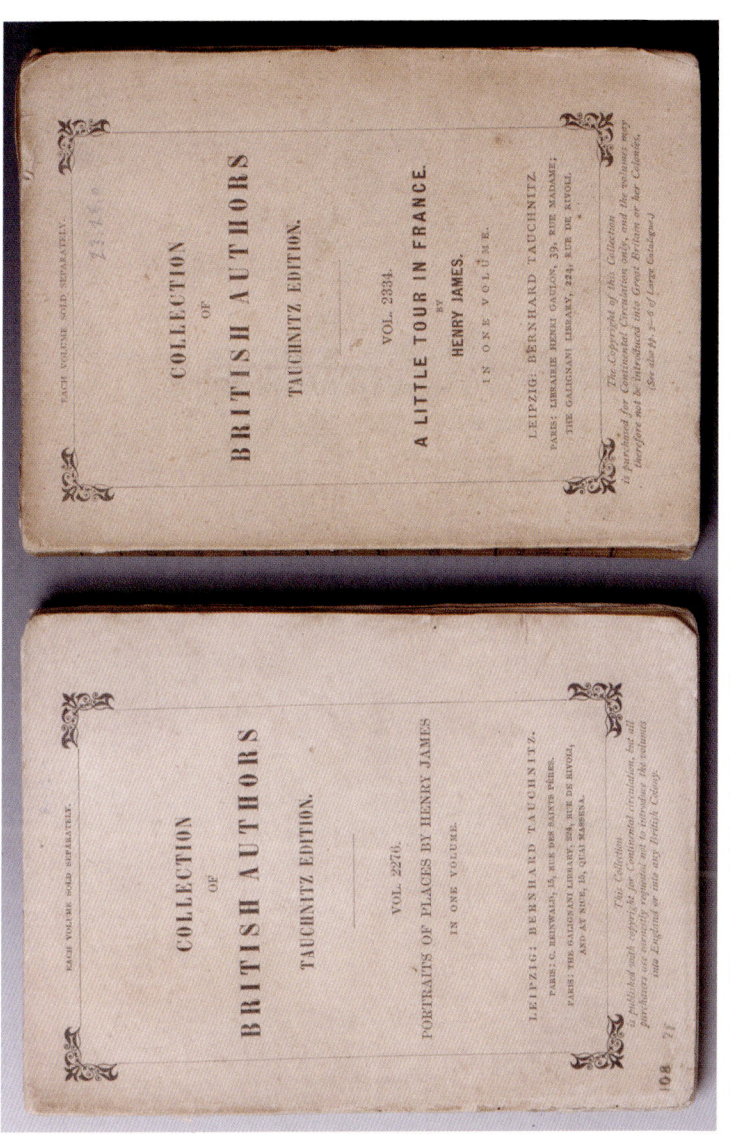

11. Portraits of Places and A Little Tour in France: the Tauchnitz editions in wrappers, 21.13.0 and 23. 23.0, typical of the wrappers used by Tauchnitz on the 16 James titles it published.

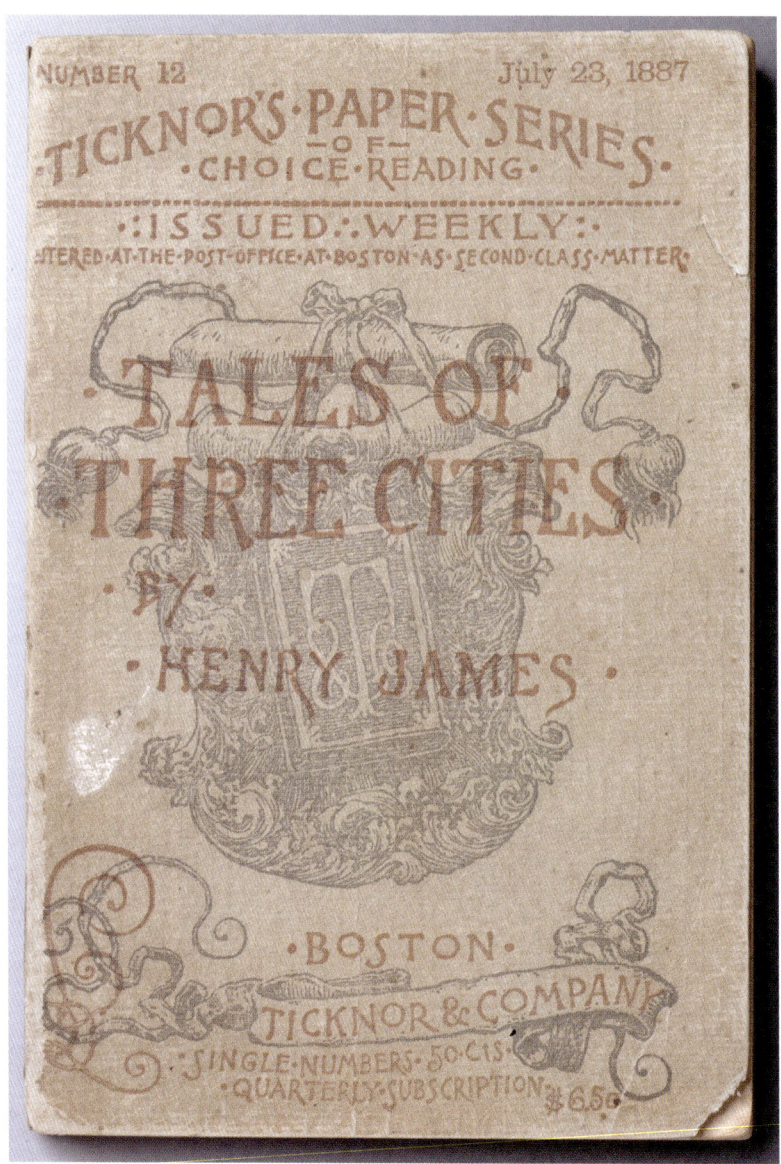

12. Tales of Three Cities: first edition, fifth impression, wrappered binding, 24.7.0.

13. The Bostonians: first edition (English), first impression, previously unrecorded variant binding, 28.2.0, and the two variants bindings of the second edition, first impression, American issue, 28.5.0 and 28.6.0.

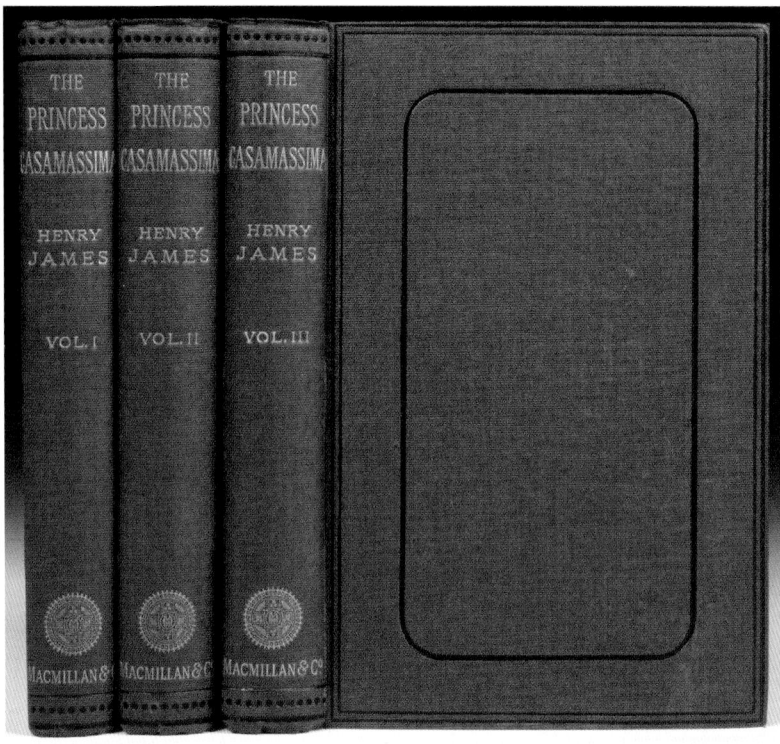

14. The Princess Casamassima: first edition, first impression binding, 29.1.0, typical of the bindings on many of James's multi-volume works published by Macmillan in England.

15. The Princess Casamassima: the yellowback bindings of the second and third impressions of the second English edition, 29.5.0 and 29.6.0. The design of the cover on the third impression is significantly coarser than that on the second.

16. The Reverberator: the two size variants of the second edition, American issue, 31.4.0 and 31.5.0, and the two binding variants of the second English edition, 31.2.0 and 31.3.0.

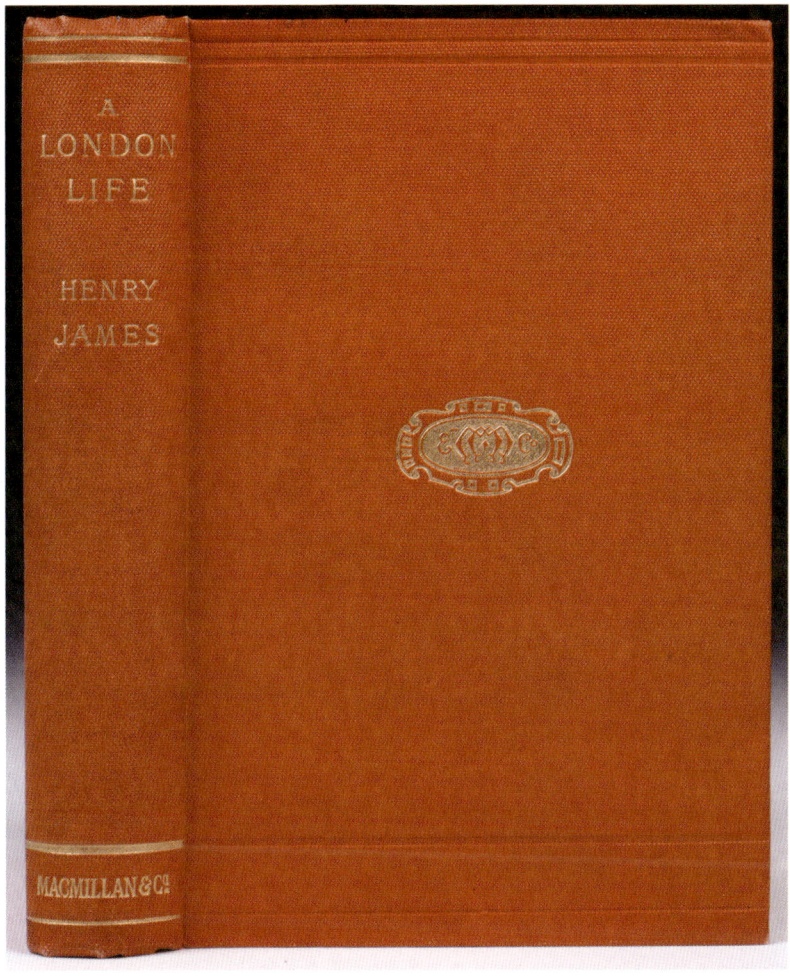

17. A London Life: the binding of the second English edition, 33.2.0.

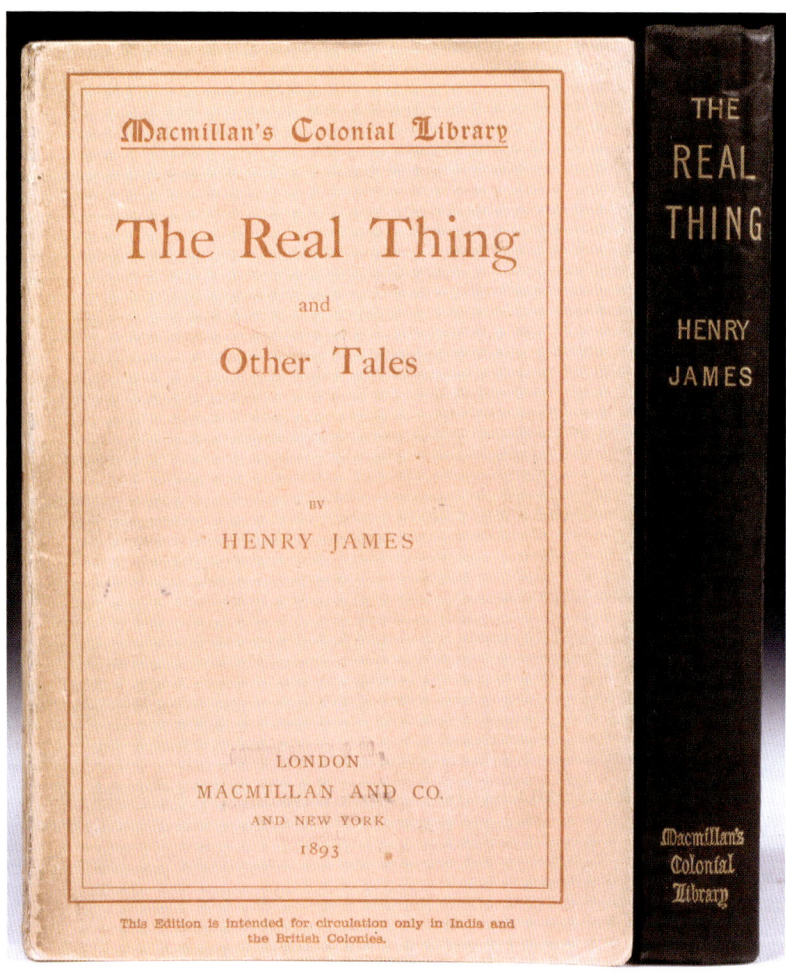

18. The Real Thing: the cloth and paper bindings of the colonial issue, 37.5.0 and 37.6.0, typical of Macmillan bindings on its James colonial issues.

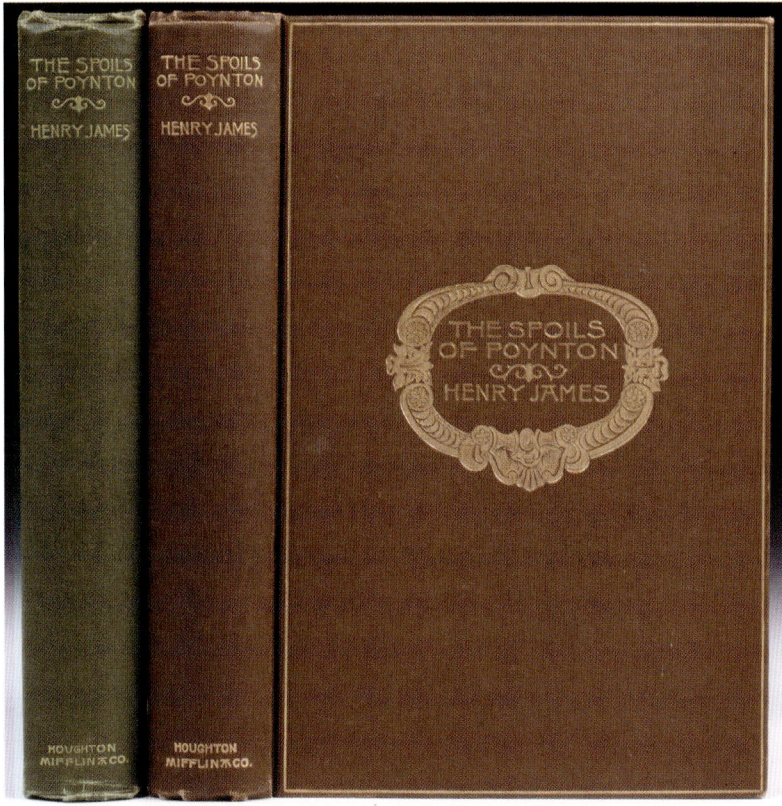

19. The Spoils of Poynton: the two bindings of the first American edition, first impression, 48.7.0 and 48.6.0, which were also used by Houghton, Mifflin on 14 other James titles.

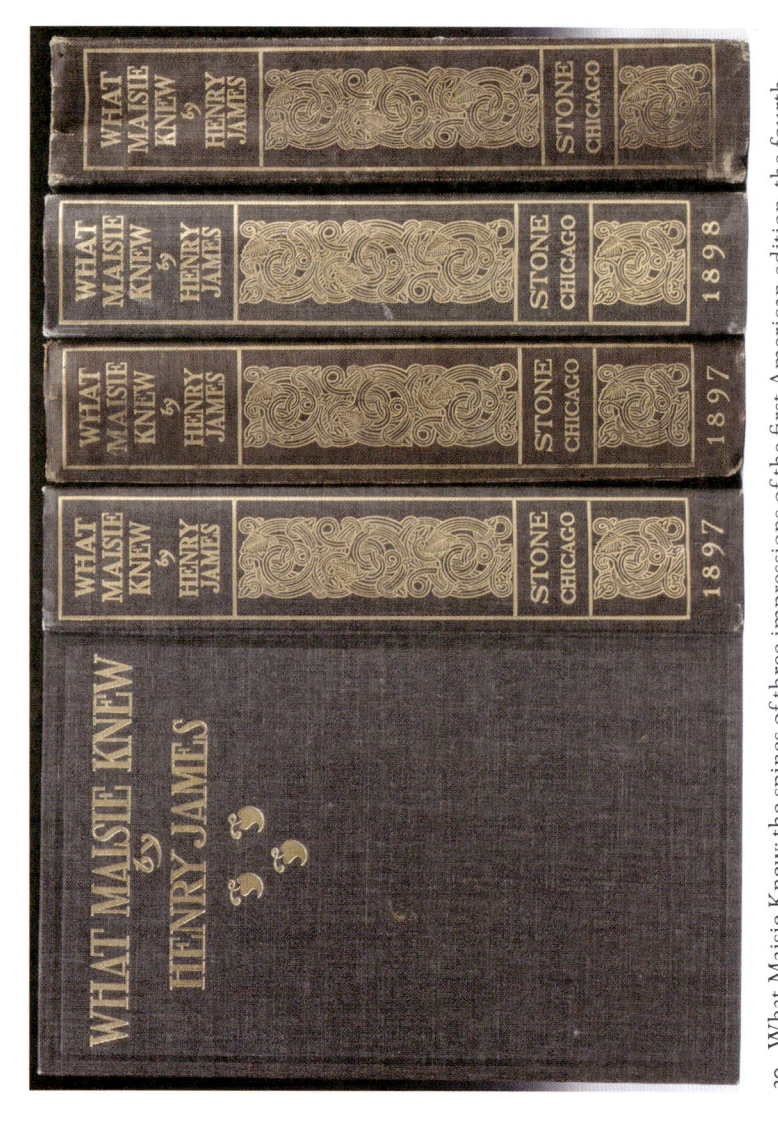

20. What Maisie Knew: the spines of three impressions of the first American edition, the fourth (undated) copy being, probably, a later binding-up of third impression sheets. 49.6.0-49.9.0.

21. In the Cage: the two states of the binding of the first edition, first impression, 51.1.o and 51.2.o, the second a previously unrecorded variant.

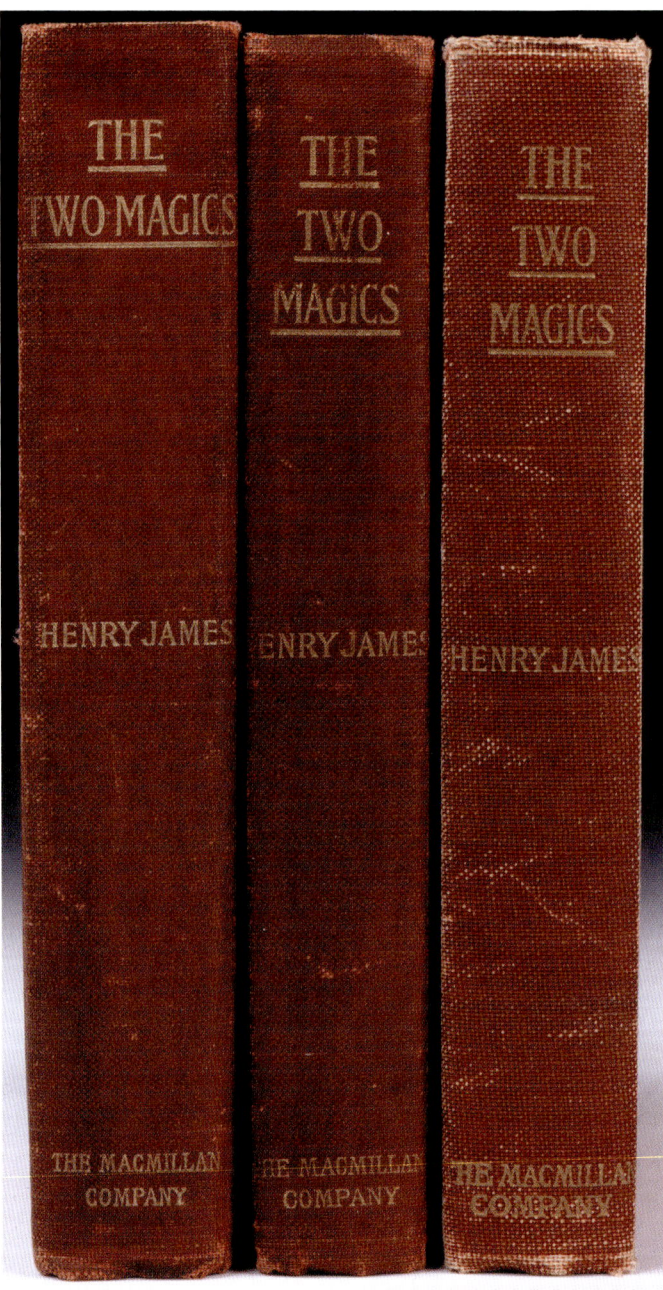

22. The Two Magics: the spines of the first American edition, first, fifth and eighth impressions, 52.6.0, 52.10.0 and 52.12.0.

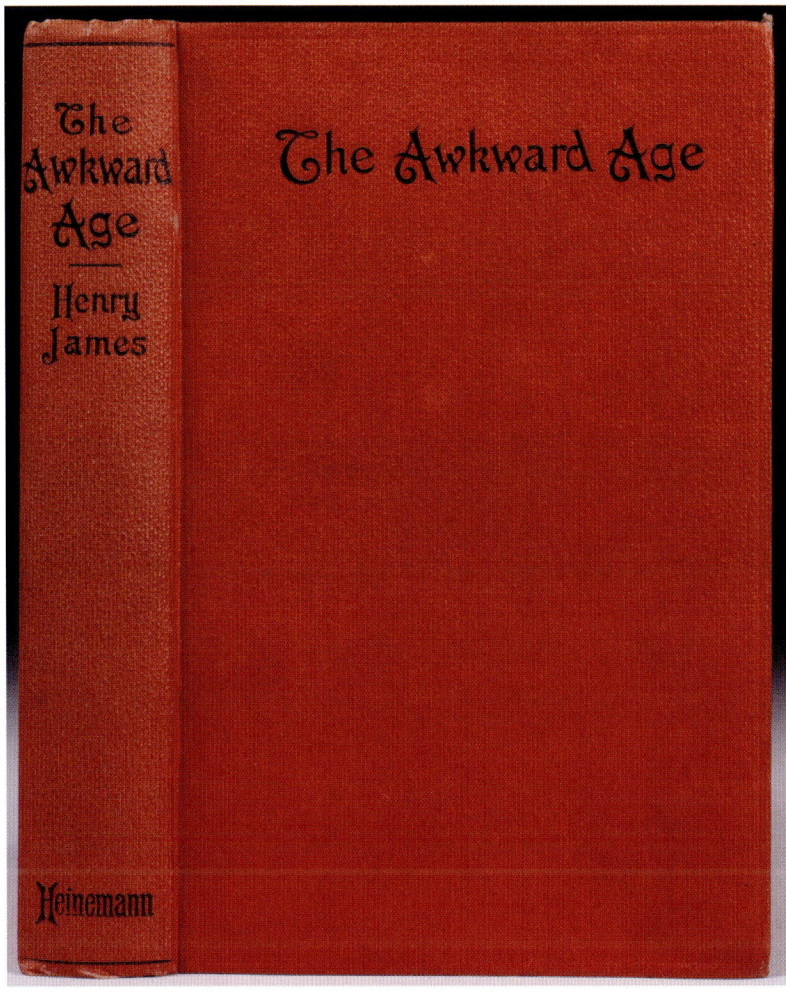

23. The Awkward Age: the cloth binding of the colonial issue, 53.2.0, typical of Heinemann's cloth bindings on its James colonial issues.

24. The Awkward Age: the first two impressions of the first American edition (priority not determined), 53.6.0 and 53.7.0.

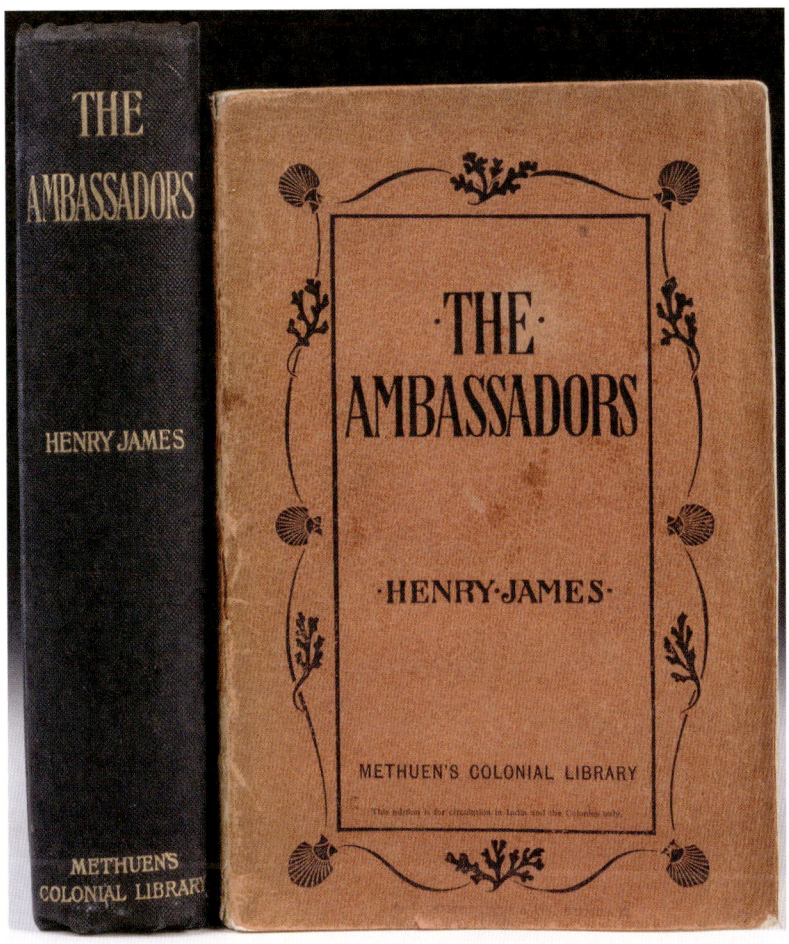

25. The Ambassadors: the cloth and paper bindings of the colonial issue, 58.4.0 and 58.5.0, typical of Methuen's bindings on its James colonial issues.

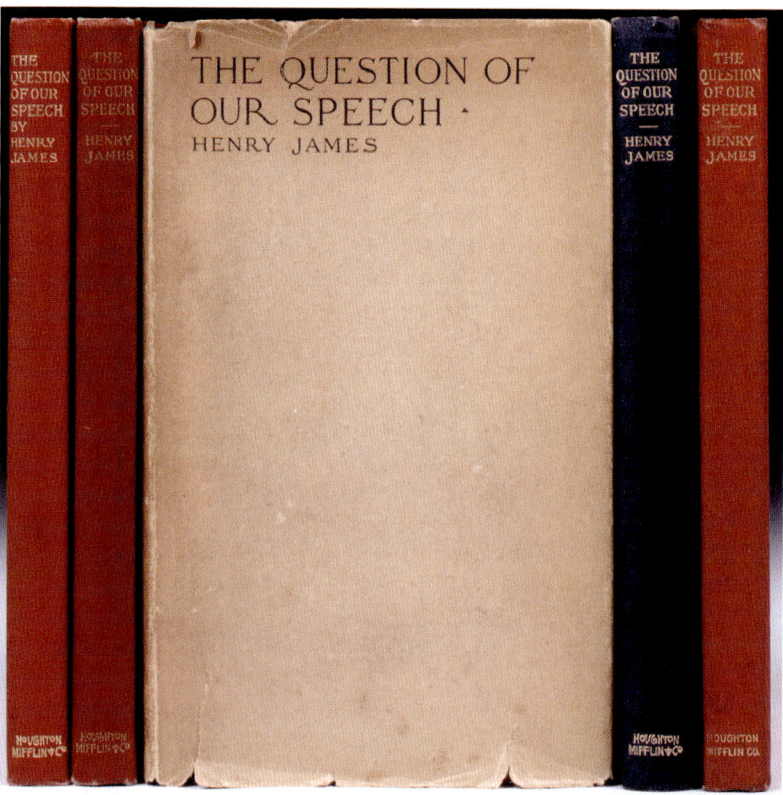

26. The Question of Our Speech: the two variant bindings of each of the first and second impressions, 61.1.0, 61.4.0 and 61.7.0, 61.8.0, and the dust-jacket on the second impression, 61.7.0.

27. Julia Bride: the dust-jacket on one of the variant bindings of the first impression, first separate edition, 66.2.0, and two previously unrecorded variant bindings, 66.5.0 and 66.6.0.

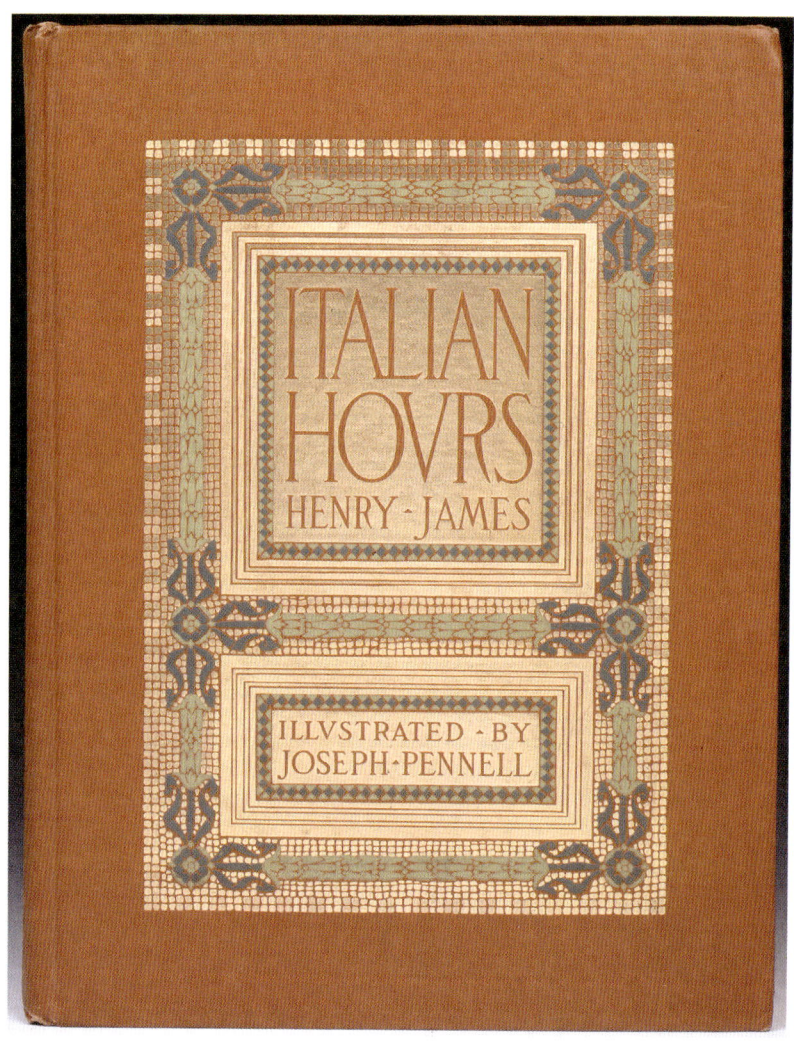

28. Italian Hours: the first American Edition, first impression, 67.3.0.

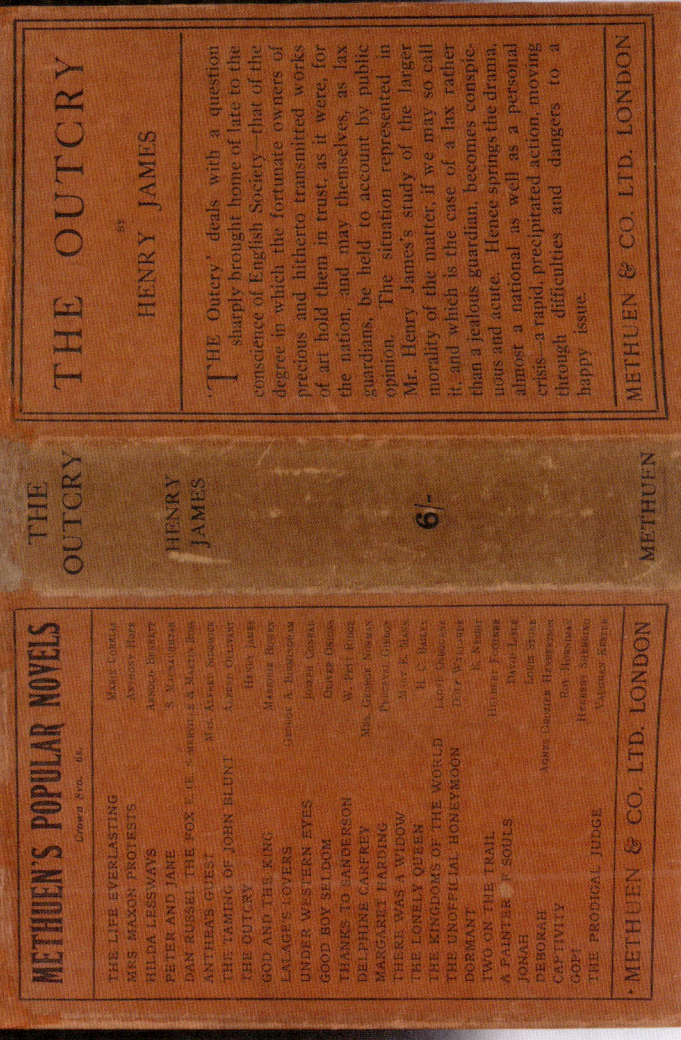

29. The Outcry: the dust-jacket on the first English edition, first impression, 70.1.0.

30. Gabrielle De Bergerac: the dust jackets on the first impression, 80.1.0, and the variant of the dust-jacket on the second impression, 80.3.0.

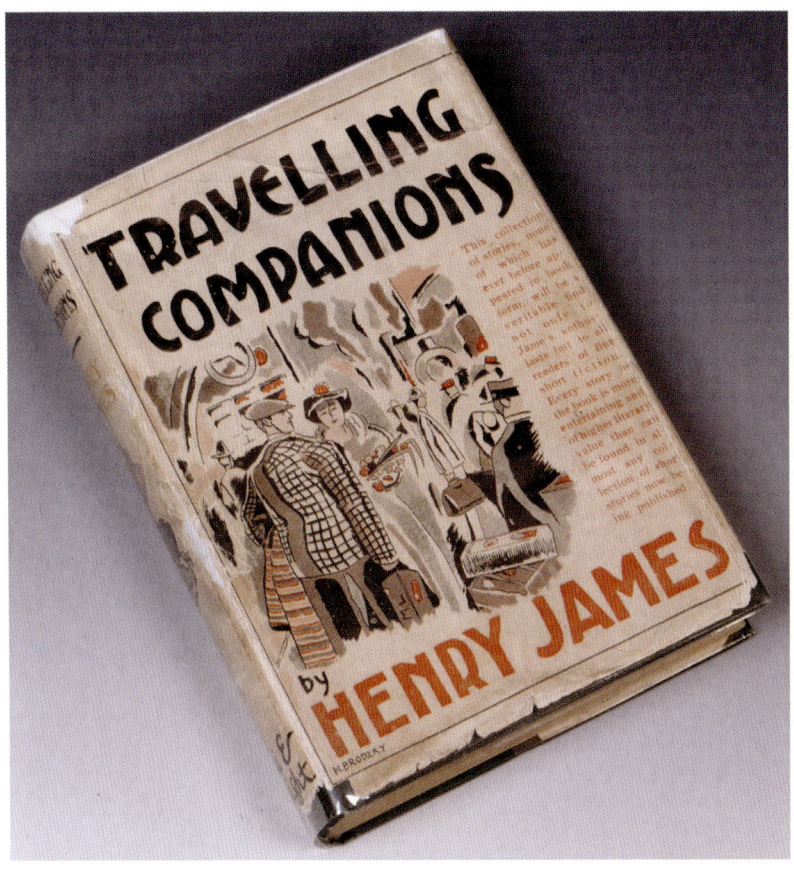

31. Travelling Companions: the dust-jacket on the first edition, first binding state, 82.1.o.

32. Representative Times Book Club bindings: Stories Revived, 27.4.0; Daisy Miller, 8.19.0; The Aspern Papers, 32.3.0 and 32.4.0; The Lesson of the Master, 36.4.0; and The Real Thing, 37.4.0.

A LONDON LIFE

[3]–361 text; 361 at foot printer's imprint as on 281 of Volume I; [362] blank; [363–364] ads as at end of Volume I.

Binding: dark blue-green smooth cloth. The front covers are decorated with five rules in gilt across both the top and bottom. The back covers have centered a publisher's device in blind. The spines, which are lettered and decorated in gilt, read: "[five rules] | A | London | Life | Henry | James | VOL. I [II] | [four rules] Macmillan & Co. | [rule]". The "o" in "Co" is raised above a short line. The endpapers are of black coated paper, and the text is printed on wove paper. All edges are untrimmed.

This binding is uniform with the binding on the first editions of *The Reverberator* (1888) and *The Aspern Papers* (1888), 31.1.0 and 32.1.0.

E&L A33a records two binding states, one in dark blue-green and the other in steel-blue. BAL 10586 records only "greenish-blue" smooth cloth.

Printing history. Macmillan Archive. MEB, at 266, records that the first English edition in two volumes was printed from standing type in a single impression of 500 copies in May [April?] 1889. The two volumes were priced at 12s. Stereotype plates were made from a second setting of type for the one-volume second edition, and were used in June [May?] 1889 to print a first impression of 2,000 copies, all of which were exported to America for publication there; see 34.4.0. It was priced at $1.50, later reduced to $1.00. The second impression of the second edition was printed from these same plates at about the same time that the first impression was printed in an impression of 2,000 copies for publication only in England; see 34.2.0 and 34.3.0. It was priced at 3s. 6d. Macmillan destroyed the plates in March 1921.

33.2.0. *A London Life*, second edition, second impression (English), one volume, London and New York 1889.

A LONDON LIFE | THE PATAGONIA | THE LIAR | MRS. TEMPERLY | BY | HENRY JAMES | London [in Gothic type] | MACMILLAN AND CO. | AND NEW YORK | 1889 | All rights reserved [in italic]

Size: 7 3/8" x 4 15/16".

Collation: [A]^4 B–I K–U X–Z 2A^8; pp. [i–viii], [1]–366 [367–368].

Contents: [i–ii] divisional fly-title, verso blank; [iii–iv] "CONTENTS", verso "NOTE" as in Volume I of the first edition, 33.1.0; [v–vi] title-page, verso copyright notice and printing history: "COPYRIGHT 1889 | BY | HENRY JAMES | First Edition (2 Vols. Globe 8vo) published April 1889 | New Edition (1 Vol. Crown 8vo) May 1889 [printing history in italic]"; [vii–viii] half-title, verso publisher's device; [1]–366 text; 366 at the foot the printer's imprint: "Printed by R. & R. Clark, Edinburgh [all except printer's name in italic]"; [367–368] ads, headed on both pages: "BY THE SAME AUTHOR.", priced in sterling. See below for a comment on the pagination.

Binding: bright red diaper-grain cloth. The front cover has a thin followed by a thick rule in blind across the top, and a thick followed by a more widely spaced thin rule in blind across the bottom. Centered on the front cover is a small gilt cartouche within which is the publisher's device, "& M Cº" [sic]. The rules on the front cover extend across the spine in gilt and the back cover in blind. Centered on the back cover is the publisher's device within a cartouche in blind, similar but larger than such device on the front cover. The spine, which is lettered and decorated in gilt, reads: "[thin followed by a thick rule] A | LONDON | LIFE | HENRY | JAMES | [thick rule] | MACMILLAN & Co. | [thin rule]." The "o" in "Co" is raised above a dot. The endpapers are of white wove paper, and the text is printed on wove paper. The top edge is untrimmed, and the other edges are rough trimmed. Inserted at the end are four pages of unpaginated ads on thinner wove paper, headed on [1]: "MACMILLAN'S THREE-AND-SIXPENNY | LIBRARY OF WORKS BY POPULAR | AUTHORS", dated on [4] "10.7.02".

The order of the four leaves, [A]^4, pages [i–viii], is obviously incorrect. This is the same binder's error as is seen in the second edition, English issue, of *The Aspern Papers*, 32.2.0

This binding is uniform with that on the second English edition of *The Aspern Papers* (1890), and second English edition of *The Tragic Muse* (1891), 32.2.0 and 34.10.0.

This impression is noted in both BAL 10586 and E&L A33c, but the binding is described in neither.

Illustrated Plate 17.

33.3.0. *A London Life*, second edition, second impression (English), one volume, London and New York 1889.

This copy is identical to the second edition, second impression (English), 33.2.0, except that the prelims, [A]⁴, are in the correct order, and this copy lacks the four pages of ads inserted at the end, having only the ads on leaf 2A$_8$ headed: "BY THE SAME AUTHOR."

33.4.0. *A London Life*, second edition, first impression (American), one volume, London and New York 1889.

A LONDON LIFE | THE PATAGONIA | THE LIAR | MRS. TEMPERLY | BY | HENRY JAMES | London [in Gothic type] | MACMILLAN AND CO. | AND NEW YORK | 1889 |

All rights reserved [in italic]

Size: 7 $^5/_{16}$" x 4 $^3/_4$".

Collation: [A]⁴ B–I K–U X–Z 2A⁸; pp. [i–viii], [1]–366 [367–368]. The last leaf, 2A$_8$, is two pages of unpaginated ads.

Contents: [i–ii] half-title, verso publisher's device; [iii–iv] title-page, verso copyright notice: "COPYRIGHT 1889 | BY | HENRY JAMES"; [v–vi] "CONTENTS", verso "NOTE" as in Volume I of the first edition, 33.1.0; [vii–viii] divisional fly-title, verso blank; [1]–366 text; 366 at foot printer's imprint: "Printed by R. & R. Clark, Edinburgh [all except printer's name in italic]"; [367–368] ads priced in dollars headed on both pages: "MACMILLAN AND CO.'S PUBLICATIONS." (these ads differ from those on the similar leaf of the second edition, second impression (English)).

Binding: blue diagonal-fine-ribbed cloth. The front cover is decorated with an elaborate frieze design in gilt across the top which extends across the top of the spine. Across the bottom, in blind, are two bands of two rules each separated by a band of dots, which extend across the foot of the spine. The back cover has a centered publisher's device in blind. The spine, which is lettered and decorated in gilt and in blind, reads: "[frieze design] | A | LONDON | LIFE | HENRY | JAMES | [two rules separated by a line of dots, in blind] | MACMILLAN & CO. | [two rules separated by a line of dots, in blind]". The "o" in "Co" is raised above a dot. The endpapers are of black coated paper, and the text is printed on wove paper. All edges are trimmed. The inserted ads present in the second edition, second impression (English), 33.2.0, are not present here.

33.5.0. *A London Life*, first continental edition, one volume, Leipzig 1891.

A London Life | BY | HENRY JAMES | AUTHOR OF | "DAISY MILLER," "THE PORTRAIT OF A LADY," "THE AMERICAN," ETC. [in italic] | LEIPZIG | HEINEMANN AND BALESTIER | LIMITED, LONDON [in italic] | 1891

Size: 5 7/8" x 4 1/4".

Collation: [A]⁴(–[A]₁) B–I K–S⁸ T⁶ (–T₆); pp. [i–vi], [1]–282.

Contents: [i–ii] series half-title and half-title, verso copyright notice: "Copyright Edition [in italic]"; [iii–iv] title-page, verso blank; [v–vi] "CONTENTS", verso blank; [1]–282 text; 282 at foot printer's imprint: "PRINTED BY F. A. BROCKHAUS, LEIPZIG."

Binding: rebound in green half-buckram with brown mottled paper boards and green buckram fore-corners. The front and back covers are neither lettered nor decorated. The spine, which is lettered and decorated in gilt, reads: "[four decorative rules] | A | LONDON | LIFE | [seven decorative rules]". The endpapers are of green coated paper with a floral and ribbon design, and the text is printed on wove paper. All edges are trimmed and speckled.

The firm of Heinemann and Balestier was a short-lived publishing venture whose partners were the English publisher William Heinemann and an American, Charles Wolcott Balestier. The firm was established to produce a continental library of cheap reprints in competition with Tauchnitz, which Tauchnitz regarded as "its most dangerous rival thus far"; see T&B 193–194. The firm was dissolved after Balestier died of typhoid fever in Dresden in December 1891. Charles Wolcott Balestier (1861–1891) was a close friend of James's. James wrote a tribute to him that was published in the May 1892 issue of *Cosmopolitan Magazine*, reprinted in *Henry James American Essays*. ed. Leon Edel (Princeton, N.J.: Princeton University Press, 1989), 175–185; see also C. E. Carrington, *The Life of Rudyard Kipling* (Garden City, N.Y., 1956), 147–152. The firm issued only two James titles, this one and *The Lesson of the Master*, 36.6.0, both published in the series entitled The English Library.

THE TRAGIC MUSE

34. *THE TRAGIC MUSE*

34.1.0. *The Tragic Muse*, first edition, first impression, binding state A, two volumes, Boston and New York 1890.

THE TRAGIC MUSE | BY | HENRY JAMES | IN TWO VOLUMES | VOL. I. [II.] | [oblong publisher's devise of a piper under a tree within a frame] | BOSTON AND NEW YORK | HOUGHTON, MIFFLIN AND COMPANY | The Riverside Press, Cambridge [in Gothic type] | 1890

Size: 7" x 4 5/8".

Collation: Volume I: [unsigned, 1^2 $2-27^8$ 28^4]; pp. [i–iv], [1]–422 [423–424]. Volume II: [unsigned, 1^2 $2-29^8$ 30^6]; pp. [2] [i–ii], [423]–882. The pagination of the two volumes overlap because no account was taken of the blank leaf, [28_4], [423–424].

The title-page of both volumes is part of the first signature of two leaves, as noted in BAL 10590 for the first of two impressions.

Contents: Volume I: [i–ii] blank, verso within a single-rule frame ad headed: "Henry James's Books. [in Gothic type]", listing 15 titles with dollar prices; [iii–iv] title-page, verso copyright notice, reservation of rights and printer's imprint: "Copyright, 1890, | By HENRY JAMES. | All rights reserved. [in italic] | The Riverside Press, Cambridge, Mass., U.S.A. [in italic] | Electrotyped and Printed by H. O. Houghton & Company."; [1]–422 text; [423–424] blank leaf. Volume II: blank leaf, [i–ii] title-page, verso copyright notice, reservation of rights and printer's imprint as on Volume I title-leaf verso; [423]–882 text.

Binding: dark-green smooth-linen-grain cloth. The front covers, lettered and decorated in gilt, have at the top nine closely spaced thin rules followed by a rectangular frame within which is the title and author's name separated by a small clover leaf. On each side of the rectangular frame is a similar small clover leaf, and immediately beneath the frame nine closely spaced thin rules. The back covers are neither lettered nor decorated. The spines, which are also lettered and decorated in gilt, read: "[nine thin rules] | THE | TRAGIC | MUSE | [small rule] | JAMES [title and author's name are within a small frame] | [nine thin rules] | [small floral device] | I [II] | [four thin rules] | [within a small frame] HOUGHTON, MIFFLIN & CO. | [four thin rules]". The endpapers are of white laid paper, and the text is printed on wove paper. A binder's fly-leaf of wove paper is at the front of Volume I, and at the back of Volume II. The top and fore-edges are trimmed, and the bottom edge is rough trimmed.

On the front free endpaper of each volume is a small bookseller's label reading: "W. B. CLARK & CO. | BOOKSELLERS & STATIONERS | BOSTON."

American printing history. Houghton Mifflin Archive. First Edition: Ms Am 2030(19), 153: *first impression* (two volumes) June 3, 1890, Vol. I 1014 copies and Vol. II 1020, 988 bound between June 4 and July 2, 1890; *second impression* November 8, 1890, 278 copies of both Volumes, 270 bound between November 18, 1890, and April 30, 1891; *third impression* Vol. I April 14 and Vol. II April 16, 1892, Vol. I 276 copies and Vol. II 278, 280 [sic] bound between April 20, 1892, and August 1, 1895; notation: "Apr. 1/91 944 1d I | 914 3 bdg + 1d II". Ms Am 2030(20), 220: *fourth impression* September 11, 1897, Vol. I 156 copies and Vol. II 154, 149 bound between September 25, 1897, and April 10, 1900. Ms Am 2030(22), 219: *fifth impression* December 10, 1900, Vol. I 158 copies and Vol. II 160, 156 bound between January 15, 1901, and April 7, 1904; *sixth impression* April 14, 1905, Vol. I 156 copies and Vol. II 159, 153 bound between April 21, 1905, and March 20, 1906; *seventh impression* February 14, 1908, Vol. I 150 copies and Vol. II 145, 130 bound between February 20, 1908, and September 19, 1908; *eighth impression* November 11, 1910, 184 copies of Vols. I and II, 165 bound between November 30, 1910, and June 29, 1912; *ninth impression* April 6, 1916, Vol. I 278 copies and Vol. II 280, 279 [sic] bound between April 28, 1916, and November 1, 1918. Notation: "[total printed] 2612".

Priced at $2.50 for the two volumes, which price was maintained for subsequent impressions through 1906.

A further impression in two volumes was printed from the first edition plates, probably in 1922 or 1923, priced at $5.00 for the two volumes; see 34.7.5.

For the second American edition, see Volumes VII and VIII of *The Novels and Tales of Henry James*, 64.1.0.

34.2.0. *The Tragic Muse*, first edition, first impression, binding state B, two volumes, Boston and New York 1890.

The title-pages, size, collations, and contents are identical to those of the first edition, first impression, 34.1.0.

Binding: bright red smooth-linen-grain cloth, with lettering and decoration in gilt identical to those on 34.1.0. The endpapers are of white wove paper, and the text is printed on wove paper. A binder's fly-leaf of wove paper is at the front of Volume I, and the back of Volume II. The top edge is trimmed, and the fore and bottom edges are rough trimmed.

On the front pastedown of both volumes is a small bookseller's ticket reading: "Eyrich's | Book Store | 130 | Canal St. | New Orleans".

BAL 10590 records copies of the first impression in both red and green "V" (smooth-linen-grain) cloth. E&L A34a also records copies in dark blue linen-grain cloth, but no such copy has been found, and the dark-green could easily be mistaken for dark blue. No priority of the binding states is implied.

34.3.0. *The Tragic Muse*, first edition, second impression, two volumes, Boston and New York 1890.

The title-pages, size and contents are identical to those of the first edition, first impression, 34.1.0, except that there is a blank leaf at the end but not at the beginning of Volume II.

Collation: Volume I: [unsigned, 1–26^8 27^6]; pp. [i–iv], [1]–422 [423–424]. Volume II: [unsigned, 1–29^8]; pp. [i–ii], [423]–882 [883–884]. These collations are as noted in BAL 10590 for the second impression.

Binding: dark-green smooth-linen-grain cloth, with lettering and decoration identical to that of 34.1.0. The endpapers are of white laid paper, and the text is printed on wove paper. There are no binder's fly-leaves in Volume I. A binder's fly-leaf of wove paper is at the front, but none at the back of Volume II. All edges are trimmed.

On the front free endpapers of both volumes is an inscription (Volume I): "Mclintock | Washington | Dec. '91."; (Volume II): "Mclintock | Washington | Dec. 1891."

34.3.5. *The Tragic Muse*, first edition, mixed set of the first and second impressions, two volumes, Boston and New York 1890.

The title-page, size, and contents are identical to those of the first edition, first and second impressions, 34.1.0–34.3.0

Collation: Volume I: [unsigned, 1^2 2–27^8 28^4]; pp. [i–iv], [1]–422 [423–424]; Volume II: [unsigned, 1–29^8]; pp. [i–ii], [423]–882 [883–884].

Binding: dark-green smooth linen-grain cloth, lettered and decorated identically to the first edition, first impression, 33.1.0. The endpapers are of white laid paper, and the text is printed on wove paper. The are no binder's fly-leaves in Volume I, but there is a binder's fly-leaf at the back of Volume II. The top edges of both volumes are trimmed, and the other edges are rough trimmed.

On the front free endpaper of each volume is the inscription "Mary L. Best | 1890".

The collations indicate that this set is a mixed one, made up of the first impression of Volume I and the second impression of Volume II. The inscription on the endpapers indicate that it was sold as a mixed set, and that in all probability Houghton, Mifflin did not keep the two printings separate as they sold sets late in 1890.

34.4.0. *The Tragic Muse*, first edition, third impression, two volumes, Boston and New York 1892.

The title-pages, size and contents are identical to those of the first edition, first impression, 34.1.0, except that there is a blank leaf at the end but not at the beginning of Volume II, and that the title-pages are dated 1892.

The collations are identical to those of the first edition, second impression, 34.3.0.

Binding: dark-green smooth-linen-grain cloth, with lettering and decoration identical to that of 34.1.0. The endpapers are of white laid paper, and the text is printed on wove paper. The top and bottom edges are trimmed, and the fore-edge is rough trimmed. A binder's fly-leaf of wove paper is at the front of both volumes, but none at the back.

34.4.5. *The Tragic Muse*, first edition, fourth impression, two volumes, Boston 1897.

THE TRAGIC MUSE | BY | HENRY JAMES | IN TWO VOLUMES | VOL. I. [II.] | [oblong publisher's device of a piper under a tree within a frame] | BOSTON and New YORK | HOUGHTON, MIFFLIN AND COMPANY | The Riverside Press, Cambridge [in Gothic type] | 1897

Size: $7\,3/8''$ x $4\,15/16''$.

THE TRAGIC MUSE

Collation: Volume I: [unsigned, 1–26^8 27^6]; pp. [i–iv], [1]–422 [423–424]. Volume II: [unsigned, 1–29^8]; pp. [i–ii], [423]–882 [883–884]. These collations are the same as those of the second impression.

Contents: Volume I: [i–ii] blank, verso ad headed: "Henry James's Books. [in Gothic type]", listing 16 James titles with dollar prices, the last dated being *The Spoils of Poynton*, and after the thirteenth title listed (*Daisy Miller: A Comedy*), the notation: "The above thirteen 12mo volumes, in box, $22.00."; [iii–iv] title-page, verso copyright notice, reservation of rights and printer's imprint: "Copyright, 1890, | By HENRY JAMES. | All rights reserved. [in italic] | The Riverside Press, Cambridge, Mass., U.S.A. [in italic] | Electrotyped and Printed by H. O. Houghton & Company."; [1]–422 text; [423–424] blank leaf. Volume II: [i–ii] title-page, verso copyright notice, reservation of rights and printer's imprint as on Volume I title-leaf verso; [423]–882 text; [883–884] blank leaf.

Binding: brown vertical-rib-grain cloth, with lettering and decoration in gilt on the front covers and spines. The front covers have within a single-rule border an elaborate centered cartouche within which are the title and author's name separated by a decorative rule. The back covers have a single-rule border in blind. The spines, which are lettered and decorated in gilt, read: "[rule] | THE TRAGIC | MUSE | [decorative rule] | HENRY JAMES | I [II] | HOUGHTON | MIFFLIN & CO. | [rule]". The ampersands in the spine imprints are stylized, and are like a Greek π. The endpapers are of white laid paper, and the text is printed on smooth wove paper. A binder's fly-leaf of wove paper is at the front of both volumes, but none at the back. All edges are trimmed.

This binding is uniform with that of the first American edition of *The Spoils of Poynton* (1897), 48.6.0.

34.5.0. *The Tragic Muse*, first edition, fifth impression, two volumes, Boston an*d* New York 1901.

The title-pages, size, collations, and contents are identical to those of the first edition, fourth impression, 34.4.5, except that the title-pages are dated 1901 and the ad on [ii] in Volume I is headed: "Henry James [in Gothic type]", rather than "Henry James's Books. [in Gothic type]", and the reference to thirteen volumes, boxed, is absent.

Binding: olive-green vertical-rib-grain cloth, lettered and decorated in gilt and in blind identically to 34.4.5. The endpapers are of white wove paper, and the texts are printed on smooth wove paper. A binder's fly-leaf of wove paper is at the front of both volumes, but none at the back. The top edges are trimmed and stained light brown, the fore-edges are rough trimmed, and the bottom edges are trimmed.

On the front free endpaper of both volumes is the inscription: "Lilian V. Sampson | 1902."

The fifth impression was printed on December 10, 1900, and the sixth in in 1905, which would indicate that this copy is of the fifth impression.

34.6.0. *The Tragic Muse*, first edition, sixth (?) impression, two volumes, Boston and New York [n.d., 1905].

Size: 7 3/8" x 4 15/16".

The title-page, collation, and contents are identical to those of the first edition, fourth impression, 34.4.5, except that the title-pages have no date at the foot, and the ad on [ii] in Volume I is headed: "Henry James [in Gothic type]", rather than "Henry James's Books. [in Gothic type]", and the reference to thirteen volumes, boxed, is absent, and the illustrated Holiday Edition of *A Little Tour in France* is added.

Binding: brown vertical-rib-grain cloth, with lettering and decoration in gilt and in blind identically to those on 34.4.5. The endpapers are of white laid paper, and the text is printed on wove paper not as smooth as the paper used for all prior impressions. A binder's fly-leaf of wove paper is at the front of both volumes, but none at the back. The top edges are trimmed and stained brown, the fore-edges are rough trimmed, and the bottom edges are trimmed.

The binding is uniform with that of the first American edition of *The Spoils of Poynton* (1897), 48.6.0.

34.7.0. *The Tragic Muse*, first edition, seventh or later impression, two volumes, Boston and New York [n.d., 1908 or later].

The title-page, size, collation, and contents are identical to those of the first edition, fourth impression, 34.4.5, except that the title-pages have no date at the foot and the ad on [ii] in Volume I, headed: "By Henry James [in Gothic type]", lists 18 James titles with dollar prices, the last dated being *The Question of Our Speech* and *English Hours*.

Binding: olive-green vertical-rib-grain cloth, lettered and decorated in gilt and in blind identically to 34.4.5, except that the publisher's imprints on the spines read: "HOUGHTON | MIFFLIN CO." The endpapers are of white wove paper, and the text is printed on smooth wove paper. There are no binder's fly-leaves. The top and bottom edges are trimmed, and the fore-edges are rough trimmed. The top edges are stained brown.

The sixth impression was printed on April 14, 1905, and the seventh was printed on February 14, 1908. *The Question of Our Speech* and *English Hours* were first published in America in October 1905. Houghton, Mifflin & Co. changed its name to Houghton Mifflin Co. in 1908.

34.7.5. *The Tragic Muse*, first edition, impression later than the ninth, two volumes, Boston and New York [n.d., probably 1922 or 1923]
THE TRAGIC MUSE | BY | HENRY JAMES | IN TWO VOLUMES | VOL. I. [II.] | [oblong publisher's device of a piper under a tree within a frame] | BOSTON AND NEW YORK | HOUGHTON MIFFLIN COMPANY | The Riverside Press Cambridge [in gothic type]
Size: 7 3/8" x 4 7/8".

The collations and contents are identical to those of the first edition, fourth impression, 34.4.5, except that in Vol. I, on [ii] the ad is headed: "By Henry James [in Gothic type]", and lists 17 titles without dollar prices, the last dated being *Italian Hours*, the publisher's name at the foot of the ad reads: "HOUGHTON MIFFLIN COMPANY", and the title-page versos of both Volumes read: "COPYRIGHT, 1890, BY HENRY JAMES | COPYRIGHT, 1918, BY HENRY JAMES | ALL RIGHTS RESERVED | The Riverside Press [in Gothic type] | CAMBRIDGE [dot] MASSACHUSETTS | PRINTED IN U.S.A."

Binding: dark blue vertical-rib-grain cloth. The front covers are lettered with Henry James's facsimile signature in gilt. The back covers are neither lettered nor decorated. The spines, which are lettered and decorated in gilt, read: "[two rules] | THE | TRAGIC | MUSE | [one star [two stars] on Volume I [II]] | HENRY | JAMES | HOUGHTON | MIFFLIN CO. | [two rules]". The endpapers are of light cream wove paper, and the text is printed on wove paper. There are no binder's fly-leaves in either volume. The top and bottom edges are trimmed, and the fore-edges are rough trimmed.

THE TRAGIC MUSE

Dust-jackets: beige wove paper, lettered and decorated in green. The front covers and spines replicate the front covers and spines of the books, except that on the spines between the author's name and the publisher's imprint there is "VOLUME | ONE [TWO]" instead of one or two stars. The back covers each have within a double-rule border an identical ad that reads: "NOVELS BY | HENRY JAMES | Issued in Uniform Style [in italic] | [rule] | What Maisie Knew The Finer Grain | The Wings of the Dove, 2 vols. The Outcry | The Better Sort The Ivory Tower | The Golden Bowl, 2 vols. The Sense of the Past | The Sacred Fount | Per Volume, $2.50 [in italic] | Published by CHARLES SCRIBNER'S SONS | The Portrait of a Lady, 2 vols. The American | Roderick Hudson The Europeans | A Passionate Pilgrim, and The Siege of London | Other Tales The Spoils of Poynton | The Tragic Muse, 2 vols. | Published by HOUGHTON MIFFLIN COMPANY | The Awkward Age Daisy Miller | The Ambassadors An International Episode | Washington Square | Published by HARPER & BROTHERS". The front inner flaps have at the top the price "$2.50". The back inner flaps are blank. The ad on the back cover of the dust-jackets is identical to the ad on 16.21.0.

On the probable dating of this impression and for similar bindings, see *Daisy Miller; A Study*, 8.15.0, and *The Portrait of a Lady*, 16.21.0.

34.8.0. *The Tragic Muse*, first English edition, three volumes, London and New York 1890.

THE TRAGIC MUSE | BY | HENRY JAMES | IN THREE VOLUMES [in italic] | VOL. I. [II.] [III.] | London [in Gothic type] | MACMILLAN AND CO. | AND NEW YORK | 1890 | The Right of Translation and Reproduction is Reserved [in italic]

Size: 7 1/8″ x 4 3/4″.

Collation: Volume I: $[A]^2$ B–I K–Q^8 R^4; pp. [i–iv], [1]–248. Volume II: $[A]^2$ B–I K–Q^8 R^6; pp. [i–iv], [1]–252. Volume III: $[A]^2$ B–I K–R^8 S^2; pp. [i–iv], [1]–258 [259–260].

Contents: Volume I: [i–ii] half-title, verso publisher's device; [iii–iv] title-page, verso printer's imprint: "Richard Clay & Sons, Limited, | London & Bungay."; [1]–248 text; 248 at foot printer's imprint: "[rule] | Richard Clay & Sons, Limited, London & Bungay. [in italic]". Volume II: [i–ii] half-title, verso publisher's device; [iii–iv] title-page, verso printer's imprint as on Volume I title-leaf verso; [1]–252 text; 252 at foot printer's imprint as on 248 of Volume I. Volume III: [i–ii] half-title, verso publisher's device; [iii–iv] title-page, verso printer's imprint as on Volume I title-leaf verso; [1]–258 text; 258 at foot printer's imprint as on 248 of Volume I; [259–260] blank leaf.

Binding: blue diaper-grain cloth. The front covers have a single-rule border in blind, with the title and author's name lettered in gilt. The back covers have a single rule border in blind. The spines, which are lettered and decorated in gilt, read: "[two rules] | The | Tragic | Muse | VOL. I [II] [III] [in sans-serif] | Henry | James | [publisher's device] | [rule] | Macmillan & Co. | [rule]". The "o" in "Co" is raised above a dot. The endpapers are of black coated paper, and the text is printed on wove paper. All edges are trimmed, and the top edges are stained brown.

English printing history. Macmillan Archive. MEB, at 599, records that the three-volume first English edition of *The Tragic Muse* was printed from standing type in June 1890 in a single impression of 500 copies. It was published in June 1890, priced at 31s. 6d. Electrotype plates were produced from a second setting of type for the one-volume second English edition, from which a single impression was printed in January 1891 of 2,000 copies. It was published in February 1891, priced at 3s. 6d.

The printing record, however, seems to be incomplete. There appears to be no record in MEB or MPL of the August 1890 colonial impression which preceded the domestic impression of the second English edition, which was published in February 1891; see Nowell-Smith, 12. Further, differences in the thickness of the text blocks of the colonial impression (34.9.0, $^{3}/_{4}$″) the domestic one-volume impression (34.10.0, 1″) and The Times Book Club binding states (34.11.0 and 34.12.0, both $^{7}/_{8}$″) would suggest that there were three impressions rather than one from the second English edition plates. This suggestion is reinforced by the fact that the title-pages of both the colonial and the domestic impressions have the number "109" at the bottom left, but this number is lacking on the title-pages of The Times Book Club binding states. Macmillan destroyed the plates in February 1921.

In 1920 Thomas Nelson and Sons published and edition of *The Tragic Muse* priced at 2s. (the second English edition); see note following 4.21.5.

THE TRAGIC MUSE

For the third English edition, see *The Novels and Stories of Henry James*, 86.1.0–86.2.0.

* * *

The publication of the English edition of *The Tragic Muse* in 1890 resulted in a break in James's long relationship with his English publisher, Macmillan & Company. Starting with James's first not pirated published work in England (*French Poets and Novelists*, in 1878) Macmillan – with the single exception of *Confidence* in 1879 – had been James's exclusive English publisher. But long before the publication of *The Tragic Muse*, James had become dissatisfied with his treatment by Macmillan. The source of his dissatisfaction was Macmillan's insistence on the half-profits contract (that is no cash advance and a percentage of the profits when and if the costs of production were met), Macmillan's absence of accountability, its elastic definition of costs, and its habit of remitting profits on a yearly rather than on a more frequent basis; see Anesko, 51.

As early as 1879, James fired a warning shot across Macmillan's bow by selling the rights to *Confidence* (for a limited three-year period) to Chatto & Windus; see Moore, 46–50; Anesko, 54–57. However, matters were patched up, and Macmillan continued thereafter as James's exclusive English publisher. When it came, however, to negotiating for the English publication of *The Tragic Muse* in 1890, Macmillan, citing disappointing sales of James's recent works, offered only a half-profits contract. James, in an eloquent letter to Macmillan, refused these terms, preferring instead to forsake publishing in England. Through the intervention of the literary agent A.P. Watt, an accommodation on a flat sum was reached – £250 for the exclusive rights to publish this title in England and the colonies for a period of 5 years and 2 months; Horne, 219–221; Moore, 155–162. But the die was cast, and except for the publication of two volumes of short stories, *The Lesson of the Master* in 1892 (which had been promised to Macmillan as early as 1888) and *The Real Thing* in 1893, Macmillan published nothing of James's in England until almost the end of his life other than the English issue of *The Novels and Tales* (New York Edition, 1909), the sheets of which were printed for Scribner's in America.

See Appendix E for a chronological list of James's publishers.

34.9.0. *The Tragic Muse*, second English edition, first impression (colonial), one volume, London and New York 1890.

Macmillan's Colonial Library [in Gothic type, underscored] | THE TRAGIC MUSE | BY | HENRY JAMES | London [in Gothic type] | MACMILLAN AND CO. | AND NEW YORK | 1890 | No.109 The Right of Translation and Reproduction is Reserved [reservation of rights in italic]

Size: 7 3/16" x 4 3/4".

Collation: [A]² B–I K–U X–Z AA–HH⁸ II⁶; pp. [i–iv], [1]–488 [489–492]. Leaves II$_{5,6}$ are ads.

Contents: [i–ii] half-title, verso: "This Edition is intended for circulation only in India and | the British Colonies. [all the foregoing in italic]"; [iii–iv] title-page, verso printer's imprint: "Richard Clay and Sons, Limited, | LONDON AND BUNGAY."; [1]–488, text; [489–492] ads, headed on both [489] and [490]: "BY THE SAME AUTHOR"; [491] ad for works by Kingsley, Hughes, Craik, and Yonge; [492] double-column list headed: "Macmillan's Colonial Library. [in Gothic type]" listing 116 titles, and this title as 109. The four pages of ads, undated, are paginated 1–4.

Binding: greenish-black smooth-linen-grain cloth over thin semi-flexible boards. The front and back covers are neither lettered nor decorated. The spine, which is lettered in gilt, reads: "THE | TRAGIC | MUSE | HENRY | JAMES [all of the foregoing in sans-serif] | Macmillan's | Colonial | Library [series title in Gothic type]". The endpapers are of white wove paper, and the text is printed on thin wove paper. All edges are trimmed. There are no ads on the front or rear pastedowns or on the front and rear free endpapers.

The text block is 3/4" thick.

On the importance of colonial sales (particularly to Australia) to English publishers during the last quarter of the nineteenth century, see Alexis Weedon, *Victorian Publishing: The Economics of Book Production for a Mass Market, 1836–1916* (Aldershot: Ashgate Publishing Ltd., 2003), 38–45.

34.10.0. *The Tragic Muse*, second English edition, second impression (domestic), one volume, London and New York 1891.

THE TRAGIC MUSE | BY | HENRY JAMES | London [in Gothic type] | MACMILLAN AND CO. | AND NEW YORK | 1891 | No. 109. The Right of Translation and Reproduction is Reserved [reservation of rights in italic]

Size: 7 5/16″ x 4 7/8″.

Collation: [A]² B–I K–U X–Z AA–HH⁸ II⁶; [i–iv], [1]–488 [489–492]. Leaves II$_{5,6}$ are ads.

Contents: [i–ii] half-title, verso publisher's device; [iii–iv] title-page, verso printer's imprint and publishing history: "Richard Clay and Sons, Limited, | LONDON AND BUNGAY. | First Edition (3 Vols., Crown 8vo), 1890. | Second Edition (1 vol., Crown 8vo), 1891. [in the printing history all but matter in parenthesis in italic]"; [1]–488 text; [489–492] ads, headed: [489–490] :"BY THE SAME AUTHOR."; [491]: "MACMILLAN'S THREE-AND-SIXPENNY EDITION | OF COPY-RIGHT NOVELS."; and [492] ad for works by Kingsley, Hughes, Craik, and Yonge. The four pages of ads, undated, are paginated 1–4.

Binding: bright red diaper-grain-cloth. The front cover has a thin followed by a thick rule in blind across the top and a thick followed by a more widely spaced thin rule in blind across the bottom. Centered on the front cover is a small gilt cartouche within which is the publisher's device, "& M C°" [sic]. The rules on the front cover extend across the spine in gilt and the back cover in blind. Centered on the back cover is the publisher's device within a cartouche in blind similar to, but larger, than such device on the front cover. The spine, which is lettered and decorated in gilt, reads: "[thin followed by a thick rule] | THE | TRAGIC | MUSE | HENRY | JAMES | [thick rule] | MACMILLAN & Co. | [thin rule]". The "o" in "Co" is raised above a dot. The endpapers are of white wove paper, and the text is printed on wove paper (thicker than the paper used for the colonial impression, 34.9.0). The top edge is untrimmed, and the other edges are trimmed. Bound in at the end is a 64-page paginated publisher's catalogue dated January, 1891.

On the front free endpaper is the ink inscription: "For dear Florrie | with the loving wishes | of H. H. Lewis | June 25th. 97."

The text block is 1″ thick.

THE LESSON OF THE MASTER

This binding is uniform with that on the second English edition of *The Aspern Papers* (1890), and *A London Life* (1889), 32.2.0 and 33.2.0.

34.11.0. *The Tragic Muse*, second English edition, third (?) impression, The Times Book Club binding state, one volume, London 1891.

THE TRAGIC MUSE | BY | HENRY JAMES | London [in Gothic script] | MACMILLAN AND CO. | AND NEW YORK | 1891 | The Right of Translation and Reproduction is Reserved [reservation of rights in italic]

Size: $7\,1/4''$ x $4\,7/8''$.

Collation: $[A]^2$ B–I K–U X–Z AA–HH^8 II^6; pp. [i–iv], [1]–488 [489–492]. Leaves II$_{5,6}$ are ads.

Contents: [i–ii] half-title, verso publisher's device; [iii–iv] title-page, verso printer's imprint and printing history: "Richard Clay and Sons, Limited, | LONDON AND BUNGAY. | First Edition [in italic] (3 Vols., Crown 8vo), 1890. | Second Edition [in italic] (1 Vol., Crown 8vo) 1891. [in the printing history all but matter in parenthesis in italic]"; [1]–488 text; [489–492] ads headed: [489–490]: "BY THE SAME AUTHOR."; [491]: "MACMILLAN'S THREE-AND-SIXPENNY EDITION | OF | COPYRIGHT NOVELS."; and [492] ad for works by Kingsley, Hughes, Craik, and Yonge. The four pages of ads, undated, are paginated 1–4.

Binding: rose smooth-linen-grain cloth, with a single black rule border on the front cover, and with no lettering or decoration on the back cover. The spine, which is lettered and decorated in black, reads: "[rule] | THE | TRAGIC | MUSE | HENRY | JAMES | [circular Times Book Club device] | [rule]". The endpapers are of white wove paper, and the text is printed on wove paper. All edges are trimmed, and the top edge appears to be stained ochre.

The text blocks of this copy and of 34.12.0 are $7/8''$ thick.

34.12.0. *The Tragic Muse*, second English edition, third impression, The Times Book Club binding state, one volume, London 1891.

The title-page, size, collation, and contents are identical to those of the second English edition, third impression, The Times Book Club binding state, 34.11.0.

THE LESSON OF THE MASTER

Binding: light blue linen-grain cloth, with a single black rule border on the front cover, and no lettering or decoration on the back cover. The spine, which is lettered and decorated in black, reads: "[rule] | THE | TRAGIC | MUSE | HENRY | JAMES". There is neither a publisher's imprint nor a circular Times Book Club device at the foot of the spine. The endpapers are of white wove paper, and the text is printed on wove paper. The top edge is trimmed and stained ochre, and the other edges are rough trimmed.

On the rear pastedown is a Times Book Club maroon sticker, which has been partially removed.

The second impression of the second English edition of this title, 34.10.0, has the number "No. 109." at the left foot of the title-page, whereas that is lacking in this and the previous copy (34.11.0) of The Times Book Club binding state.

❧✛❧

35. THE AMERICAN: A COMEDY

No copy in the collection.

E&L A35 records that only eight copies are known to be extant. These are acting copies that were privately printed; see BAL 10595.

❧✛❧

36. THE LESSON OF THE MASTER

36.1.0. *The Lesson of the Master*, first edition, first impression (American), one volume, New York and London 1892.

THE LESSON OF THE MASTER | THE MARRIAGES THE PUPIL | BROOKSMITH | THE SOLUTION SIR EDMUND ORME | BY | HENRY JAMES | New York [in Gothic type] | MACMILLAN AND CO. | AND LONDON | 1892 | All rights reserved [in italic]

Size: $7\,7/16''$ x $5''$.

Collation: $[1\text{--}20^8]$, signed as π^3 A–I K–T^8 [U]^5; pp. [i–vi], 1–302 [303–314]. The collation recorded in E&L A36a would appear to be incorrect.

THE LESSON OF THE MASTER

Contents: [i–ii] half-title, verso publisher's device; [iii–iv] title-page, verso copyright notice and printer's imprint: "Copyright, 1891, | By MACMILLAN AND CO. | Typography by J. S. Cushing & Co., Boston, U.S.A. | [rule] | Presswork by Berwick & Smith, Boston, U.S.A."; v–[vi] "CONTENTS", verso blank; 1–302 text; [303–314] ads. The ads, which are not paginated, are: [303] sixteen titles in Macmillan's "Dollar Novels" series; [304] two titles by James; [305] three further titles by James; [306] two further titles by James; [307] thirteen titles by, and a picture of, Crawford; [308] five titles by Ward; [309] six titles by Shorthouse; [310] five titles by Boldrewood; [311] three titles by Kipling; [312] "WORKS OF CHARLES KINGSLEY."; [313] "WORKS OF CHARLOTTE M. YONGE,"; and [314] "THE ADVENTURE SERIES." The ads are priced in dollars.

Binding: dull blue smooth cloth. The front cover is lettered in black with a long vertical rule in red to the left of which are seven wreath ornaments in red, centered within six of which is a red open book, and in one of which is the publisher's device in black. To the right of the vertical red rule the front cover is lettered in black: "THE LESSON | OF THE [five dots under these last two words] MASTER | BY | HENRY JAMES". The spine, lettered in gilt and decorated in red, reads: "[red wreath within which is a red book] | THE | LESSON | OF THE | MASTER | [gilt leaf device] | HENRY | JAMES | [publisher's imprint within a red wreath]". The publisher's imprint reads: "MACMILLAN" between two concentric circles, and within the center circle "& | CO." The back cover is neither lettered nor decorated. The endpapers are of white wove paper, and the text is printed on wove paper. All edges are trimmed. This copy lacks the binder's fly-leaves at both the front and the back recorded by E&L; however, BAL 10596 does not note the presence of binder's fly-leaves.

Printing history. In order to conform to the new American copyright legislation, the Chase Act of 1891, this edition had to be set in type (and plates made) and printed in the United States. This was duly done by Macmillan New York, and for obvious economic reasons both the American and English issues were printed in America from these same plates. MEB at 599 records only that "James' Lesson of the Master | Feb. 1892 Received Cr 8vo N.Y. 6/-". No information regarding the printing history of this title was found in the Macmillan (NY) Archives. The printing history recorded on the title-page verso of the colonial impression states that there were three impressions of the first edition: the first in January 1892 (ostensibly encompassing both the English and American issues, given the February receipt of sheets by Macmillan London), a second in October 1892, and a third in November 1892 for the colonial market. No information was found in the Macmillan records to indicate the size of the impressions. E&L partially confirms this interpretation, recording: "the first printing consisting of 2900 copies, divided between domestic and English issues." Copies for the American market were priced at $1.00, and copies for the English market were priced at 6s. The price of the colonial impression is unknown.

However, what E&L describes as the first impression was in fact two separate impressions, the first of the American sheets and the second of the sheets exported to England. As Nowell-Smith, 79–82, explains, the American impression was printed on standard American size paper (23˝ x 41˝), while the English impression was printed on American paper made to English specifications (30˝ x 40˝). The consequent difference in the imposition of the plates (to accommodate the different sized paper) resulted in the signature mark falling on the first leaf of each gathering of the English impression , while in the American impression it falls on the fourth leaf of each gathering. Accordingly, in this Catalogue the January 1892 American impression (36.1.0) is denominated the first, the January 1892 English impression is denominated the second (36.3.0 and 36.3.5), the October 1892 impression for the American market (36.2.0) is denominated the third, and the colonial impression of November 1892 (36.5.0) is denominated the fourth. In summary, the first and third impressions were published only in America, the second impression was published only in England, and the fourth impression was sold only in the colonies.

36.2.0. *The Lesson of the Master*, first edition, third impression (American), New York and London 1892.

The title-page and size are identical to those of the first edition, first impression (American), 36.1.0.

Collation: [1–19^8 20^6], signed as π^3 A–I K–T^8 [U]^3; pp. [i–vi], 1–302 [303–310].

Contents: [i–ii] half-title, verso publisher's device; [iii–iv] title-page, verso copyright notice, printing history and printer's imprint:

"Copyright, 1891. | By MACMILLAN AND CO. | [rule] | Set up and electrotyped January, 1892. | Reprinted October, 1892. [the foregoing below the rule in italic] | Typography by J.S. Cushing & Co., Boston, U.S.A. | [rule] | Presswork by Berwick & Smith, Boston, U.S.A."; v–[vi] "CONTENTS", verso blank; 1–302 text; [303–310] ads. The ads, which are paginated 1–8, are: [303] fourteen titles by Crawford and eleven by Dickens; [304] eight titles by Kingsley, four by James, five by Keary, three by Murray, and ten by Oliphant; [305] six titles by Shorthouse, four by Craik, three by Ward, two by Kipling, and one each by Levy and McLennan; [306] two titles by Hughes, three by Boldrewood, and one each by Cunningham, Gissing, Russell, and Lawless; [307] one title by "A NEW AUTHOR", one by Falconer, three by Church, and "STORIES FROM THE | GREEK COMEDIANS."; [308] thirty titles in two columns by Miss Yonge; and, [309] an ad for the "GOLDEN TREASURY SERIES", continuing on to [310]. The ads are priced in dollars.

Binding: identical to that on 36.1.0. The endpapers are of white wove paper, and the text is printed on wove paper. There are no binder's fly-leaves. All edges are trimmed.

For the second impression see 36.3.0.

36.3.0. *The Lesson of the Master*, first edition, second impression (English), one volume, London and New York 1892.

The title-page is identical to that of the first edition, first impression (American), 36.1.0, except that in the publisher's imprint at the foot the positions of "London" and "New York" have been reversed, and "London" is in Gothic type.

Size: $7\,{}^{5}/_{16}$" x 5".

Collation: π^4 A–I K–T^8; pp. [2] [i–vi], 1–302 [303–304].

Contents: blank leaf; [i–ii] half-title, verso publisher's device; [iii–iv] title-page, verso copyright notice and printer's imprint as in, 36.1.0; v–[vi] "CONTENTS", verso blank; 1–302 text; [303–304] blank leaf.

Binding: royal blue diaper-grain cloth. The front cover is decorated with an elaborate frieze design in gilt across the top which extends across the top of spine, and across the bottom two bands of two rules each separated by a band of dots in blind, which extend across the foot of the spine. The spine, lettered in gilt and decorated in gilt and in blind, reads: "[frieze] | THE | LESSON | OF THE | MASTER | HENRY | JAMES | [two rules separated by a line of dots] | MACMILLAN & Co. | [two rules separated by a line of dots]". The "o" in "Co" is raised above a dot. The endpapers are of green coated paper, and the text is printed on wove paper. The bottom edge is trimmed, and the other edges are untrimmed. Bound in at the end are four pages of ads for "MACMILLAN and CO.'S | RECENT PUBLICATIONS", dated 20.2.92 (which BAL 10596 notes is present in some copies), followed by a 44-page paginated publisher's catalogue, dated December 1891, both of which are printed on thin wove paper.

This binding is uniform with that on the second edition, first impression (American), of *A London Life* (1889), 33.4.0.

36.3.5. *The Lesson of the Master*, first edition, second impression (English), one volume, London and New York 1892.

Size: 7 3/8" x 4 15/16".

The title-page, collation, and contents are identical to those of the first edition, second impression (English), 36.3.0.

Binding: identical to that on 36.3.0. The endpapers are of green coated paper, and the text is printed on wove paper. The top edge is untrimmed, the fore-edge is rough trimmed, and the bottom edge is trimmed. Bound in at the end is a 44-page paginated catalogue, dated December 1891, printed on thin wove paper. The four pages of ads inserted at the end of 36.3.0 prior to the inserted catalogue, are not present in this copy.

On the front pastedown is the library label of Ballarat Public Library.

36.4.0. *The Lesson of the Master*, first edition, second impression (English), The Times Book Club binding state, London and New York 1892.

The title-page is identical to that of the first edition, first impression (American), 36.1.0, except that in the publisher's imprint at the foot the position of "London" and "New York" have been reversed, and "London" is in Gothic type.

Size: 7 1/4" x 4 7/8".

Collation: π^4 ($-\pi_1$) A–I K–S^8 T^8 ($-T_8$); pp. [i–vi], 1–302. The excised leaves, π_1 and T$_8$, are blank in the first edition, second impression (English), 36.3.0.

The contents (including the title-leaf verso), with the exception of the excised blank leaves noted above, are identical to those of 36.3.0.

Binding: bright red smooth-linen-grain cloth. The front cover has a single-rule black border. The back cover is neither lettered nor decorated. The spine, lettered and decorated in black, reads: "[rule] | THE | LESSON | OF THE | MASTER | HENRY | JAMES | [circular The Times Book Club device] | [rule]". The endpapers are of white laid paper, and the text is printed on smooth wove paper. All edges are trimmed. There are no ads bound in at the end.

36.5.0. *The Lesson of the Master*, first edition, fourth impression (colonial), London and New York 1893 [1892].

Macmillan's Colonial Library [in Gothic type, underscored] | THE LESSON OF THE MASTER | THE MARRIAGES THE PUPIL | BROOKSMITH | THE SOLUTION SIR EDMUND ORME | BY | HENRY JAMES | London [in Gothic type] | MACMILLAN AND CO. | AND NEW YORK | 1893 | All rights reserved [in italic]

Size: 7 $^{15}/_{32}$" x 4 $^{15}/_{16}$".

Collation: π^4 A–I K–T^8; pp. [2] [i–vi], 1–302 [303–304].

Contents: blank leaf, [i–ii] half-title, verso: "This Edition is intended for circulation only in India | and the British Colonies. [in italic]; [iii–iv] title-page, verso copyright notice, printing history and printer's imprint: "Copyright, 1891, | By MACMILLAN AND CO. | [rule] | Set up and electrotyped January, 1892. [in italic] | Reprinted October, 1892. [in italic] | Colonial Library Edition, printed November, 1892 | Typography by J. S. Cushing & Co., Boston, U.S.A. | [long rule] | Presswork by Berwick & Smith, Boston U.S.A."; v–[vi] "CONTENTS", verso blank; 1–302 text; [303–304] blank leaf.

Binding: dark blue-green smooth cloth. The front and back covers are decorated with a single-rule border in blind. The spine, lettered and decorated in gilt, reads: "[single rule] | THE | LESSON | OF THE | MASTER | HENRY | JAMES [the title and author's name in sans-serif] | MACMILLAN & Co. | [rule]". The publisher's imprint on the spine is in uniform capitals, except that the "o" in "Co" is raised above a dot. The endpapers are of white wove paper, and the text is printed on smooth wove paper. The top edge is untrimmed, the fore-edge is rough trimmed, and the bottom edge is trimmed. Bound in at the end is a paginated 8-page catalogue dated "10.2.93" (without prices) of Macmillan's Colonial Library, printed on thin wove paper.

As noted on the title-leaf verso of this copy, the colonial impression was printed in November, 1892 but may have been given an 1893 title-page date, as in this copy, because of the time it took to ship the copies to the Colonies.

On the front pastedown is the bookplate of Horace Morgan.

36.6.0. *The Lesson of the Master*, first continental edition, one volume, Leipzig 1892.

THE | Lesson of the Master | THE MARRIAGES THE PUPIL | BROOK-SMITH | THE SOLUTION SIR EDMUND ORME | BY | HENRY JAMES | LEIPZIG | HEINEMANN AND BALESTIER | (Ltd. London) [in italic] | 1892

Size: 6 $^{3}/_{16}$" x 4 $^{7}/_{16}$".

Collation: 1π¹ 2π² A–I K–R⁸ S¹; pp. [i–vi], [1]–273 [274].

Contents: [i–ii] series title and half-title, verso blank; [iii–iv] title-page, verso blank; [v–vi] "CONTENTS", verso blank; [1]–273 text; [274] printer's imprint: "[rule] | Printed by T. and A. Constable, Printers to Her Majesty, | at the Edinburgh University Press."

Binding: light brown wove paper wrappers cut flush, lettered and decorated in dark brown. The front cover reads: "The English Library [in Gothic type] | [rule] | The Lesson | of the Master | by | Henry James | AUTHOR OF | "THE AMERICAN," "DAISY MILLER," "A LONDON LIFE," | ETC. ETC. [this and the preceding line in italic] | LEIPZIG [in italic] | HEINEMANN AND BALESTIER | (Ltd. London) [in italic] | PARIS [in italic] | HACHETTE ET CIE | The Volumes of the English Library are published by arrangements with the Authors, and | enjoy Copyright in all Continental countries, but may not be intro- | duced | into Great Britain, Ireland, or the British Colonies [this and the preceding two lines are in italic] | [rule] | COMPLETE IN ONE VOLUME". The spine reads: "[rule] | HENRY | JAMES | [rule] | THE |

LESSON | OF THE | MASTER | [rule] | Price | M.1, 60 | or | 2 Francs | [rule] | The | English | Library [this and the preceding two lines in Gothic type] | 135 | [rule]". The back cover is headed "The English Library [in Gothic type]" followed by a list of the volumes numbered 115 to 152, followed by a long rule, under which is an ad for "THE REVIEW OF REVIEWS", followed by a further long rule under which is: "Aug. 1892. Wholesale Agents of The English Library: | Leipzig, Berlin, Vienna – F.A. BROCKHAUS. | Paris – HACHETTE ET CIE. | AND SOLD BY EVERY BOOKSELLER ON THE CONTINENT. | Price M 1, 60, or 2 Francs." Inside the front cover under the heading: "The English Library [in Gothic type]" is a list of volumes 1 to 55, which continues on to the inside of the back cover with a list of volumes 56 to 114, and on the outside of the back cover with a list of volumes 115 to 152. The text is printed on wove paper. An undated 8-page paginated publisher's catalogue is bound in at the end.

The only other James title listed in The English Library ad in this volume is *A London Life*, listed as volume 30; see 33.5.0.

❧✠❧

37. *THE REAL THING*

37.1.0. *The Real Thing*, first edition, first impression, American issue, second state, one volume, New York and London 1893.

THE REAL THING | AND OTHER TALES | BY | HENRY JAMES | New York [in Gothic type] | MACMILLAN AND CO. | AND LONDON | 1893 | All rights reserved [in italic]

Size: 7 3/8" x 4 15/16".

Collation: [unsigned, $1^8(\pm 1_2)$ 2–18^8]; pp. [i–x], 1–275 [276] [277–278].

Contents: [i–ii] half-title, verso publisher's device; [iii–iv] title-page, verso copyright notice and printer's imprint: "Copyright, 1893, | By MACMILLAN & CO. | Norwood Press: [in Gothic type] | J. S. Cushing & Co.– Berwick & Smith. | Boston, Mass, U.S.A."; [v–vi] "NOTE. | The second of the following tales bore, on its first | appearance, in *The Cosmopolitan*, a different title.", verso blank; vii–[viii] "CONTENTS.", verso blank; [ix–x] divisional fly-title, verso blank; 1–275 text; [276] blank; [277–278] two pages of ads each headed: "WORKS BY HENRY

JAMES." At the end of the text on 275 "THE END" is not present. Note: the pagination of 1 appears on the lower right.

Binding: dull blue smooth cloth. The front cover is lettered in black with a long vertical rule in red to the left of which are seven wreath ornaments in red, centered within six of which is a red open book, and in one of which is the publisher's device in black. To the right of the red rule the front cover is lettered in black: "THE | REAL THING | BY | HENRY JAMES". The spine, lettered in gilt and decorated in red, reads: "[red wreath within which there is a red book] | THE REAL | THING | [gilt leaf device] | HENRY | JAMES | [publisher's imprint within a red wreath]". The publisher's imprint, which is framed by a wreath, reads: "MACMILLAN" between two concentric circles, the inner circle having "& | CO." within it. The endpapers are of white wove paper, and the text is printed on thick wove paper. All edges are trimmed.

This binding is uniform with that on the first edition, first impression, of *The Lesson of the Master* (1892), 36.1.0.

The title-leaf is a cancel, with the copyright date 1893 on the verso, indicative of the second state of the first edition, first impression.

Both E&L A37a and BAL 10600 state that there is known only one copy of the first state without a cancelled title-leaf, that is with the 1892 copyright date. It is likely that the cancel was issued because there was a risk that the American copyright would be lost if the title-leaf verso did not have the correct copyright date. As there was no English requirement at that time that the title-page verso had to have a copyright notice, there was no necessity for a similar cancel for the English issue, below, which retained its 1892 copyright date.

Printing history: There is no information Macmillan (N.Y.) Archive regarding the printing history of this title. What is clear is that there were at least three impressions, all of which were printed in America in 1893: the first impression printed in early 1893 for the American and also the English issues, the second impression printed in July 1893 solely for publication in America, and the third impression, printed on much thinner paper, for the colonial market. A fourth impression was printed in 1922 published only in America. Nothing has been found in the Macmillan (N.Y.) records as to the size of the printings. The copies for the American market were priced at $1.00 (other than the 1922 impression), and copies for the English market were priced at 6s.

THE REAL THING

What is not entirely clear is whether, as E&L states: "the first printing consisting of 1500 copies, divided between the domestic and English issues", or whether the English sheets were of a separate impression. The only mention of this title in the printing records of Macmillan (London) is in MEB, 599: "James' Real Thing | 1893 copies bought Cr 8vo The Macm. Co. [New York] 6/-". However, the fact that the first printing for American publication, 37.1.0, has a cancelled title-leaf while the English issue, 37.3.0, retains the original cancellandum with the incorrect copyright date suggests, as E&L records, that they are both part of a single impression.

37.2.0. *The Real Thing*, first edition, second impression (American), one volume, New York and London 1893.

Size: 7 3/8" x 5".

The title-page and collation are identical to those of the first edition, first impression, American issue, 37.1.0, except that the title-leaf is not a cancel.

The contents (including the ads on [277–278]) are identical to those of 37.1.0, except that the title-leaf verso reads: "Copyright, 1893, | By MACMILLAN & CO. | Reprinted, July, 1893. | Norwood Press: [in Gothic type] | J. S. Cushing & Co. – Berwick & Smith. | Boston, Mass, U.S.A.", and on page 275 at the end of the text "THE END." is present.

Binding: olive-green smooth cloth. The lettering and decoration on the front cover and spine is identical to that on the binding of 37.1.0, except that the publisher's imprint on the spine in gilt is not framed by a red wreath, and reads: "THE MACMILLAN COMPANY", between two concentric circles, the inner circle having a Maltese cross within it.

37.2.5. *The Real Thing*, first edition, fourth impression (American), one volume, New York, 1922.

THE REAL THING | AND OTHER TALES | BY | HENRY JAMES | NEW YORK [in Gothic type] | THE MACMILLAN COMPANY | 1922 | All rights reserved [in italic]

Size: 7 7/16" x 4 5/8".

Collation: [unsigned 1–18^8]; pp. [i–x], 1–275 [276] [277–278].

Contents: [i–ii] half-title, verso publisher's device and list of 3 subsidiary companies; [iii–iv] title-page, verso copyright notice and reservation of rights: "Copyright, 1893, | By MACMILLAN & CO. | Copyright, 1921, | By HENRY JAMES | [rule] | Reprinted July, 1893."; [v–vi] "NOTE" as in 37.1.0, verso blank; vii–[viii] "CONTENTS."; [ix–x] divisional fly-title, verso blank; 1–275 text; [276] blank; [277–278] blank leaf. On 275 at the end of the text "THE END." is present. Note: the pagination of page 1 appears on the lower right.

Binding: olive vertical rib-grain cloth. The lettering and decoration on the front cover and spine is identical to that on the first edition, first impression American issue, 37.1.0, except that the publisher's imprint in gilt on the spine is framed by a red wreath and reads: "THE MACMILLAN COMPANY" between two concentric circles, the inner circle having within it a Maltese cross. The back cover is neither lettered or decorated. The endpapers are of smooth white wove paper, and the text is printed on a slightly rougher wove paper. All edges are trimmed, and the top edge is stained light-brown.

37.3.0. *The Real Thing*, first edition, first impression, English issue, one volume, London and New York 1893.

THE REAL THING | AND OTHER TALES | BY | HENRY JAMES | London [in Gothic type] | MACMILLAN AND CO. | AND NEW YORK | 1893 | All rights reserved [in italic]

Size: 7 3/8″ x 5″.

Collation: [unsigned, 1–18^8]; pp. [i–x], 1–275 [276] [277–278].

Contents: [i–ii] half-title, verso publisher's device; [iii–iv] title-page, verso copyright notice and printer's imprint: "Copyright, 1892, | By MACMILLAN & CO. | Norwood Press: [in Gothic type] | J. S. Cushing & Co. – Berwick & Smith. | Boston, Mass, U.S.A."; [v–vi] "NOTE." As in 37.1.0, verso blank; vii–[viii] "CONTENTS." verso blank; [ix–x] divisional fly-title, verso blank; 1–275 text; [276] blank; [277–278] blank leaf. On 275 at the end of the text "THE END." is not present. Note that the pagination of 1 of the text appears on the lower right.

The title-leaf of this issue is an integral part of signature [1], rather than being a cancel. The copyright notice on the verso of the title-leaf is dated 1892.

Binding: royal-blue diaper cloth. The front cover is decorated with an elaborate frieze design in gilt across the top which extends across the top of the spine, and across the bottom are two bands of two rules each separated by a band of dots in blind which extend across the foot of the spine. The spine, lettered and decorated in gilt and in blind, reads: "[frieze] | THE | REAL | THING | HENRY | JAMES | [two rules separated by a line of dots] | MACMILLAN & Co. | [two rules separated by line of dots]". The "o" in "Co" is raised above a dot. The endpapers are of dark green coated paper, and the text is printed on heavy wove paper. The bottom edge is trimmed, and the other edges are untrimmed. A 48-page paginated publisher's catalogue ([48] being blank), dated January, 1893, printed on thin wove paper, is bound in at the end.

This issue was printed in Boston from the American plates of the first edition. However, the title-leaf differs from that of the first edition, first impression, American issue, second state, 37.1.0, in that on the recto the positions of "New York" and "London" have been reversed in the publisher's imprint at the foot, and the verso reads: "Copyright, 1892, | By Macmillan & CO. | Norwood Press: | J. S. Cushing & Co. – Berwick & Smith. | Boston, Mass, U.S.A.". Also, the ads that appeared on the recto and verso of the last leaf of signature [18], pages [227–228], in the first edition, first impression, have been suppressed and that leaf is blank.

37.4.0. *The Real Thing*, first edition, first impression, English issue, The Times Book Club binding state, one volume, London and New York 1893.

Size: 7 $^3/_{16}$" x 5 $^{13}/_{16}$".

The title-page, collation, and contents (including the title-leaf verso and the absence of "THE END." on 275) are identical to those of the first edition, first impression, English issue, 37.3.0, except that the first leaf of signature [1], the half-title, has been excised.

Binding: salmon linen-grain cloth. The front cover is decorated with a single-rule border in black. The back cover is neither lettered nor decorated. The spine, lettered and decorated in black, reads: "[single rule] | THE | REAL | THING | HENRY | JAMES | [circular Times Book Club device] | [single rule]". The endpapers are of white wove paper,

THE REAL THING

and the text is printed on heavy wove paper. All edges are trimmed. No publisher's catalogue is bound in at the end.

Illustrated Plate 32.

37.5.0. *The Real Thing*, first edition, third impression (colonial), cloth binding state, one volume, London and New York 1893.

Macmillan's Colonial Library [in Gothic type underscored] | THE REAL THING | AND OTHER TALES | BY | HENRY JAMES | London [in Gothic type] | MACMILLAN AND CO. | AND NEW YORK | 1893 | No. 149 [at lower left]

Size: 7 $^{3}/_{16}$" x 4 $^{13}/_{16}$".

Collation: [unsigned, 1–18^8]; pp. [i–x], 1–275 [276] [277–278].

Contents: [i–ii] half-title, verso: "This Edition is intended for circulation only in India | and the British Colonies [all the foregoing in italic]"; [iii–iv] title-page, verso copyright notice and printer's imprint: "Copyright, 1892, | By MACMILLAN AND CO. | Norwood Press: [in Gothic type] | J. S. Cushing & Co. – Berwick & Smith. | Boston, Mass., U.S.A."; [v–vi] "NOTE.", verso blank; vii–[viii] "CONTENTS.", verso blank; [ix–x] divisional fly-title, verso blank; 1–275 text; 275 "THE END." is not present; [276] blank; [277–278] blank leaf. Note that the pagination of 1 of the text appears on the lower right.

Binding: smooth black cloth (with a green cast). The front and back covers are neither lettered nor decorated. The spine, lettered in gilt, reads: "THE | REAL | THING | HENRY | JAMES [all of the foregoing in sans-serif] | Macmillan's | Colonial | Library [the imprint in Gothic type]". The endpapers are of white wove paper, and the text is printed on thin wove paper. All edges are trimmed. A four-page, unpaginated and unpriced catalogue headed "Macmillan's Colonial Library [in Gothic type]", dated "10.11.92" on [4], is bound in at the end. The endpapers have no ads on them.

The catalogue on [3] lists four James titles, one of them being #149 entitled *Collection of Short Stories*. However, #149 in the ads on the endpapers of the wrapped colonial impression, 37.6.0, is entitled *The Real Thing*, so *Collection of Short Stories* is no doubt the publisher's provisional title.

Illustrated Plate 18.

PICTURE AND TEXT

37.6.0. *The Real Thing*, first edition, third impression (colonial), wrappered binding state, one volume, London and New York 1893.

Size: 7 1/4″ x 4 5/8″.

The title-page, collation, and contents are identical to those of the first edition, third impression, (colonial), cloth binding state, 37.5.0.

Binding: tan stiff wrappers cut flush, with lettering and decoration in red. The front cover, within a double rule frame, reads: "Macmillan's Colonial Library [in Gothic type, underscored] | The Real Thing | and | Other Tales | BY | HENRY JAMES | LONDON | MACMILLAN AND CO. | AND NEW YORK | 1893". On the front cover, beneath the double rule frame, is the legend: "This Edition is intended for circulation only in India and | the British Colonies." On the back cover, within a similar double rule frame, are ads for: "LORD TENNYSON'S LAST WORK.", "By JOHN LOCKWOOD KIPLING, C.I.E.", and "By RUDYARD KIPLING." The spine reads: "[one thick and one thin rule] | The Real | Thing | and | Other Tales | HENRY | JAMES | No. 149 | Macmillan's Colonial Library [publisher's imprint in Gothic type] | [one thin and one thick rule]". The end papers are of white wove paper, and the text is printed on thin wove paper. The front pastedown, and the recto and verso of the front free endpaper, have ads on them listing titles in Macmillan's Colonial Library in alphabetical order by author, not volume number, which list continues on to the recto and verso of the rear free endpaper and the rear pastedown, on which is the date "10.9.94".

The list of the Colonial Library on the endpapers states that "All the volumes are issued in paper covers and in cloth."

On the front cover, over the publisher's imprint, there has been ink stamped: "GORDON BROWN & CO. | BOOKSELLERS & STATIONERS | [illegible]".

Illustrated Plate 18.

PICTURE AND TEXT

38. *PICTURE AND TEXT*

38.1.0. *Picture and Text*, first edition, trade issue, one volume, New York 1893.

PICTURE | AND TEXT [all the foregoing in red] | BY | HENRY JAMES | [publisher's device in black on a cream background] | NEW YORK | HARPER AND BROTHERS [in red] | MDCCCXCIII

Size: 5 $^{29}/_{32}$" x 3 $^{1}/_{2}$".

Collation: π^4 (π_1+$X_{1,2}$) 1–11^8. pp. [2] [i–x], [1]–175 [176]. There are two conjugate leaves of coated paper inserted between π_1 and π_2. There are also seven full-page illustrations, printed on the recto on coated paper, tipped in and not included in the pagination.

Contents: blank leaf; [i–ii] blank, verso frontispiece with tissue guard with a facsimile signature of James in red; [iii–iv] title-page, verso copyright notice and reservation of rights: "Copyright, 1893, by Harper and Brothers. | [rule] | All rights reserved [in italic]"; [v–vi] "NOTE", verso blank; [vii–viii] "CONTENTS", verso blank; [ix–x] "ILLUSTRATIONS", verso blank; [1]–175 text; [176] blank.

The frontispiece and the conjugate title-leaf are an integral part of the first signature and are reckoned in the pagination.

Binding: dark green smooth cloth. The front cover is lettered in swash italic with the title and author's name within a decorative cartouche, and is decorated with all-over torch devices, all in gilt. The back cover is neither lettered nor decorated. The spine, lettered in gilt swash italic and decorated in gilt, reads: "[the title within a decorative torch cartouche] PICTURE | and | TEXT | Henry | James | HARPERS". The publisher's imprint at the foot of the spine is in sloping ornamental swash italic with one leg of the "A" and one leg of both the "R"s extending below the bottom of the other letters (that is, drop-caps). The endpapers are of white laid paper, and the text is printed on wove paper (except for the inserts on coated paper noted above). There are no binder's fly-leaves. The top edge is trimmed and stained ochre, the fore-edge is trimmed, and the bottom edge is untrimmed.

This copy is the primary binding state of the trade binding. It is possible that this binding, and that on 38.2.0, was designed by Alice C. Morse; see Mindell Dubansky, *The Proper Decoration of Book Covers:*

PICTURE AND TEXT

The Life and Work of Alice C. Morse (New York: The Grolier Club of New York, 2008), Attrib. 95.1.

Printing history. Harper & Brothers Archive. First edition published June 2, 1893, in Harper's American Essayists series. Reel 34, ledger page 556 headed December 1893 records on hand on July 16, 1888, none, printed since [first and sole (?) impression] 3050 copies, and on hand on December 15, 1893, 1381 copies. There are no further impressions reflected in the royalty records through December 31, 1897, on which date 1020 copies remained on hand. There is no mention in the Archive of the "de-luxe" binding, but given the identity of the collations and the paper used for the text it is likely that that the trade and the de-luxe issues are of a single impression. Given the number of copies on hand in 1897 and the number of secondary (remainder?) bindings, it is unlikely that this edition was subsequently reprinted.

Priced at $1.00 (trade) "in Cloth, Ornamental" and $1.25 (de-luxe). This title was not published in England.

38.2.0. *Picture and Text*, first edition, "de luxe" issue, one volume, New York 1893.

Size: 5 $^{15}/_{16}$" x 3 $^{11}/_{16}$".

The title-page, collation, and contents are identical to those of the first edition, trade issue, 38.1.0.

Binding: white smooth cloth, with lettering and decoration in gilt identical to that on 38.1.0. The publisher's imprint "HARPERS" at the foot of the spine is in the same slightly sloping ornamental swash italic as appear on 38.1.0. The endpapers are of white laid paper, and the text is printed on wove paper (except for the insert on coated paper). There are no binder's fly-leaves. The top edge is gilt, and the other edges are untrimmed.

38.3.0. *Picture and Text*, first edition, secondary binding state A, one volume, New York 1893.

Size: 5 $^{25}/_{32}$" x 3 $^{17}/_{32}$".

The title-page, collation, and contents are identical to those of the first edition, trade issue, 38.1.0.

THE PRIVATE LIFE

Binding: red linen-grain cloth, with lettering and decoration on the front cover and spine identical to that on 38.1.0, but in black rather than gilt. The publisher's imprint "HARPERS" at the foot of the spine is in uniform sans-serif (not swash italic) capitals $^3/_{32}$" high. The endpapers are of white laid paper, and the text is printed on wove paper (except for the insert on coated paper). All edges are trimmed, and the top edge is stained light brown.

This copy is in one of the three secondary bindings described in E&L A38 (a further binding, not previously recorded, is described in 38.6.0). However, E&L states that the publisher's imprint on these secondary bindings is $^3/_{16}$" high, which is probably an error given the small size of these bindings, and is clearly not the case on this or the other copies recorded here. BAL 10601 characterizes these bindings as remainders.

38.4.0. *Picture and Text*, first edition, secondary binding state B, one volume, New York 1893.

Size: $5\,^7/_8$" x $3\,^1/_2$".

The title-page, collation, and contents are identical to those of the first edition, trade issue, 38.1.0.

Binding: blue-gray linen-grain cloth with lettering and decoration on the front cover and spine identical to that on 38.1.0, but in black rather than gilt. The publisher's imprint "HARPERS" at the foot of the spine is in the same slightly sloping ornamental swash italic as appear on 38.1.0. The endpapers are of white laid paper, and the text is printed on wove paper (except for the insert on coated paper). All edges are trimmed, and the top edge is stained brown.

Because of the distinctly blue cast to the binding cloth of this copy, it is possible that it is not in the gray secondary binding described in E&L A38, or that the binding there described as gray has faded to that color.

38.5.0. *Picture and Text*, first edition, secondary binding C, one volume, New York 1893.

Size: $5\,^7/_8$" x $3\,^1/_2$".

The title-page, collation, and contents are identical to those of the first edition, trade issue, 38.1.0.

Binding: dull green linen-grain cloth, with lettering in red and decoration in gray on the front cover and spine identical to that on 38.1.0. The publisher's imprint "HARPERS" at the foot of the spine is in uniform serif (not swash italic) capitals $3/32''$ high. The endpapers are of white laid paper, and the text is printed on wove paper (except for the insert on coated paper). All edges are trimmed, and the top edge is stained brown.

38.6.0. *Picture and Text*, first edition, secondary binding D, one volume, New York 1893.

Size: $5\ {}^{27}/_{32}''$ x $3\ {}^{17}/_{32}''$.

The title-page, collation, and contents are identical to those of the first edition, trade issue, 38.1.0.

Binding: light brown linen-grain cloth. The lettering and decoration on the front cover and spine are identical to that on 38.1.0, but in black rather than gilt. The publisher's imprint "HARPERS" at the foot of the spine is in the same slightly sloping ornamental swash italic as appears on 38.1.0. The endpapers are of white laid paper, and the text is printed on wove paper (except for the insert on coated paper). All edges are trimmed, and the top edge is stained brown.

This binding variant is not noted in E&L.

※✝※

39. THE PRIVATE LIFE

39.1.0. *The Private Life*, first edition, one volume, London 1893.

THE PRIVATE LIFE | THE WHEEL OF TIME LORD BEAUPRÉ | THE VISITS THE COLLABORATION | OWEN WINGRAVE | BY | HENRY JAMES | LONDON | JAMES R. OSGOOD, McILVAINE & CO. | 45, Albermarle Street, W. | 1893

Size: $7\ {}^{1}/_{2}''$ x $5''$.

Collation: A^4 B–I K– X^8 Y^6; pp. [2] [i–vi] [1–2], [3]–331 [332].

Contents: blank leaf with signature mark "A" on the recto; [i–ii] half-title, verso blank; [iii–iv] title-page, verso blank; [v–vi] "CONTENTS.", verso blank; [1–2] divisional fly-title, verso blank; [3]–331 text; [332] printer's device and imprint: "[device of lion, dolphin and anchor] | CHISWICK PRESS: – C. WHITTINGHAM AND CO., TOOKS COURT, | CHANCERY LANE."

Binding: blue vertical-rib-grain cloth. The front cover is lettered and decorated in gilt, with a long vertical column of joined lily flowers topped by three lily buds. To the right of this design, lettered in gilt, is: "THE | PRIVATE | LIFE | HENRY | JAMES". The back cover is neither lettered nor decorated. The spine, also lettered and decorated in gilt, reads: "THE | PRIVATE | LIFE | [lily flower] | HENRY | JAMES | [lily buds] | OSGOOD, | McILVAINE & Co. [the first "c" and the "o" are each raised above a line] | [lily bulb and root]". The endpapers are of white laid paper, and the text is printed on laid paper. The top edge is untrimmed, and the other edges are rough trimmed.

On the recto of the front blank leaf is the inscription: "Beatrice W. Gibson | 25th. Aug 1893 | SWG". On the rear pastedown is a small yellow bookseller's ticket that reads: "J. G. BRIGHAM | Modern and Old Bookseller [in Gothic type] | Coniscliffe-Road, DARLINGTON."

Priced at 5s. E&L A40a records only one impression of this edition of which 1,000 copies were printed.

39.2.0. The Private Life, first American edition, primary binding state, one volume, New York 1893.

The Private Life | Lord Beaupré | The Visits | BY | HENRY JAMES | [oval publisher's device] | NEW YORK | HARPER AND BROTHERS PUBLISHERS | 1893

Size: 6 $7/8''$ x 4 $1/2''$.

Collation: 1π^2 2π^1 [1]^8 2–14^8 15^6; pp. [2] [i–iv] [1–2], [3]–232 [233–236].

Contents: blank leaf; [i–ii] title-page, verso copyright notice and reservation of rights: "Copyright, 1893, by Harper & Brothers. | [rule] | All rights reserved. [in italic]"; [iii–iv] "CONTENTS", verso blank; [1–2] divisional fly-title, verso blank; [3]–232 text; [233–236] ads. The ads are headed: [233] "By HENRY JAMES.", listing 6 titles; [234] "By GEORGE WILLIAM CURTIS.", listing 10 titles; [235] "By BRANDER MATTHEWS.", listing 4 titles; and [236] "THE ODD NUMBER SERIES." All ads are with dollar prices.

THE PRIVATE LIFE

Binding: bluish-green linen-grain cloth. The front cover has an overall symmetrical grill-work design in silver within a silver triple-rule frame, centered on which is the publisher's device in gilt and above which, also in gilt, is the title and below which, also in gilt, is the author's name. The back cover is neither lettered nor decorated. The spine has a triple-rule border in silver within which are four panels of grill-work design, also in silver, creating three spaces lettered in gilt, reading: "THE | PRIVATE LIFE | AND | OTHER STORIES", "HENRY | JAMES", and "HARPERS". The endpapers are of white laid paper, and the text is printed on heavy wove paper. The top edge is trimmed and stained ochre, and the other edges are untrimmed.

The ad on [233] erroneously lists the price of this title as "$1 25″ rather than $1.00.

The front free endpaper has the inscription: "Mary P. Lathrop. | Dec. 25, 93. | HJM".

This copy is in the primary binding. This binding is uniform with the bluish-green primary binding on the first American edition of *The Wheel of Time* (1893), 41.1.0.

E&L A39b does not record a copy with the grillwork in silver on the front cover and spine, as is present on this copy, in other than in olive green and dark green linen-grain cloth. BAL 10604 records three bindings stamped in gilt and silver, green with the top edge gilt, gray-blue with the top edge yellow, and blue with the top edge plain. Note that the silver used on late nineteenth century bindings is not silver, which rapidly tarnishes, but aluminum; see Ball, 51–52.

American Printing History. Harper & Brothers Archive. First edition published August 15, 1893. Reel 34, ledger page 669 headed November 1894 records on hand December 15, 1893, none, printed since [first and sole (?) impression] 3002 copies, and on hand November 20, 1894, 1662 copies. There are no further impressions reflected in the royalty ledger through December 31, 1897, on which date 1568 copies remained on hand. Given the number of copies on hand in 1897, and the number of secondary (remainder?) bindings, it is unlikely that this edition was subsequently reprinted.

Priced at $1.00.

THE PRIVATE LIFE

39.3.0. *The Private Life*, first American edition, secondary binding state A, one volume, New York 1893.

The title-page, size, collation, and contents of this copy are identical to those of the first American edition, primary binding state, 39.2.0.

Binding: olive-green vertical-rib-grain cloth. The lettering and decoration on the front cover and spine are identical to those of 39.2.0, except that the lettering on the spine, and the lettering and centered torch device on the front cover, are in red (rather than gilt), and the triple-rule border and grillwork design on the front cover and spine are in blind. The back cover is neither lettered nor decorated. The endpapers are of white laid paper, and the text is printed on heavy wove paper. The top edge is trimmed and stained ochre, and the other edges are untrimmed. The same four pages of ads are at the end (with erroneous price of "$1 25″ for this title) are present as are present in 39.2.0.

This is recorded as secondary binding state C in E&L A39b, although E&L states: "in all these secondary issues top edge is trimmed but unstained", which is not the case with this copy. This binding is not noted in BAL 10604. BAL characterizes these secondary bindings as "almost surely" remainder bindings. However, the number of copies on hand at Harpers in December 1897, and the presence of a dust-jacket with the Harpers imprint on a copy in a secondary binding, 39.7.0, might suggest otherwise.

39.4.0. *The Private Life*, first American edition, one volume, secondary binding state B, New York 1893.

The title-page, size, collation, and contents of this copy are identical to those of the first American edition, primary binding state, 39.2.0.

Binding: a bright green linen-grain cloth, lighter and less blue than the cloth on 39.2.0. No lettering or decoration is present on the front and back covers. However, the spine, with its triple-rule border and grillwork design in silver and lettering in gilt, is identical to the spine of 39.2.0. The endpapers are of white laid paper, and the text is printed on heavy wove paper. The top edge is trimmed and stained ochre, the other edges are untrimmed. The same four pages of ads are at the end (with the erroneous price of "$1 25″ for this title) are present as are present in 39.2.0.

This binding state is not recorded in E&L or BAL.

39.5.0. *The Private Life*, first American edition, secondary binding state C, one volume, New York 1893.

Size: 6 5/8″ x 4 1/4″ (as against 6 5/8″ x 4 1/2″ for the first American edition, primary binding state, 39.2.0).

The title-page, collation, and contents are identical to those of 39.2.0.

Binding: ochre linen-grain cloth. The front cover is decorated with a triple-rule border and grillwork design (but no lettering, torch device or author's name), and the spine is lettered and decorated with a triple-rule border, grillwork design and lettering, identical to that on the spine of 39.2.0, but all in black rather than gilt and silver. The back cover is neither lettered nor decorated. The endpapers are of white laid paper, and the text is printed on thick wove paper. All edges are trimmed, and the top edge appears to be stained ochre. The same four pages of ads are at the end (with the erroneous price of "$1 25″ for this title) are present as are present in 39.2.0.

This is recorded as secondary binding state D in E&L A39b, and binding F in BAL 10604, which records the cloth color as tan.

39.6.0. *The Private Life*, first American edition, secondary binding state D, one volume, New York 1893.

Size: 6 5/8″ x 4 1/4″ (as against 6 5/8″ x 4 1/2″ for the first American edition, primary binding state, 39.2.0).

The title-page, collation, and contents are identical to those of 39.2.0.

Binding: red linen-grain cloth, with decoration on the front cover, and lettering and decoration on the spine identical to those on the first American edition, secondary binding state C, 39.5.0. The back cover is neither lettered nor decorated. The endpapers are of white wove paper, and the text is printed on wove paper. All edges are trimmed, and the top edge appears to be stained ochre. The same four pages of ads are at the end (with the erroneous price of "$1 25″ for this title) are present as are present in 39.2.0.

This is also recorded as secondary binding state D in E&L A39b. Not noted in BAL.

39.7.0. *The Private Life*, first American edition, secondary binding state E, one volume, New York 1893.

The title-page, size, collation, and contents of this copy are identical to those of the first American edition, primary binding state, 39.2.0.

Binding: maroon embossed calico-grain cloth with no lettering or decoration on the front or back covers, but with gilt lettering, and the grillwork design and triple-rule border in blind on the spine identical to that on the spine of 39.2.0, but in blind not silver. The endpapers are of coarse white wove paper, and the text is printed on heavy wove paper. The top edge is trimmed (but not stained), and the other edges are untrimmed. The same four pages of ads are at the end (with the erroneous price of "$1.25" for this title) are present as are present in 39.2.0.

Dust-jacket: thin beige wove paper with no lettering or decoration on the front or back covers, or on the front and back inner flaps. The spine of the dust-jacket, which is printed in black, reads: "THE | PRIVATE LIFE | AND | OTHER STORIES | HENRY | JAMES | HARPERS [lightly serifed]" (all centered).

This binding is noted as secondary binding state B in E&L A39b, and binding E in BAL 10604, except that the cloth on this binding is not the "T cloth" (vertical-rib-grain) recorded by both E&L and BAL but "B" cloth (embossed calico-grain cloth). Neither E&L or BAL records a variant bound in "B" cloth.

Tanselle dust-jacket 93.46.

40. ESSAYS IN LONDON AND ELSEWHERE

40.1.0. *Essays in London and Elsewhere*, first edition, one volume, London 1893.

ESSAYS IN LONDON | AND ELSEWHERE | BY | HENRY JAMES | London | JAMES R. OSGOOD, McILVAINE & CO. | 45 ALBEMARLE STREET, W. | MDCCCXCIII | All rights reserved [in italic]

Size: $7\,7/8''$ x $5\,1/4''$.

Collation: [A]^4 B–I K–U X^8; pp. [i–viii], [1]–320.

Contents: [i–ii] half-title, verso blank; [iii–iv] title-page, verso blank; [v–vi] "NOTE", verso blank; [vii–viii] "CONTENTS", verso blank; [1]–320 text; 320 at foot printer's imprint: "Printed by R. & R. Clark, Edinburgh. [all except printer's name in italic]".

Binding: vertical-rib-grain cloth, originally salmon pink but now faded to tan with a faint pinkish tinge. The front cover is lettered and decorated in gilt with a long decorative device consisting of a vertical double-rule with a four-petal flower at each end extending the length of the cover, to the right of which is lettered: "ESSAYS | IN | LONDON | HENRY | JAMES". The back cover is neither lettered nor decorated. The spine, lettered in gilt, reads: "ESSAYS | IN | LONDON | HENRY | JAMES | OSGOOD | McILVAINE & Co [the first "c" and the "o" are each raised above a line]". The endpapers are of white laid paper, and the text is printed on laid paper. The top and fore-edges are untrimmed, and the bottom edge is trimmed. There are no ads bound in at the end (none called for).

On the rear pastedown is a small cream square binder's ticket, lettered and decorated in black, reading: "Bound | by | Leighton | Son and Hodge". On the front free endpaper is the inscription: "A. L. Leonard | Aug. 1903".

Priced at 7s. 6d. E&L 40a records only one impression of this edition of which 1,000 copies were printed.

Leighton Son & Hodge were at this time among the five largest edition binders in England. They, and their predecessor firms, Leighton & Eeles and Leighton & Son, had for many years also engaged in the manufacture of bookcloth. In the early to mid-1820s Archibald Leighton was one of the pioneers in the development of bookcloth (cotton fabric sized with dyed starch filling), gold blocking of casings (about 1832), and cloth graining (during the 1830s), although by the 1890s the bookcloth trade was dominated by The Winterbottom Book Cloth Company; see Tomlinson & Masters, *passim* and Ball, *passim*.

40.2.0. *Essays in London and Elsewhere*, first American edition, one volume, New York 1893.

Essays in London | and | Elsewhere | BY | HENRY JAMES | [oval publisher's device] | NEW YORK | HARPER & BROTHERS PUBLISHERS | 1893

Size: 7 7/16" x 5".

Collation: π⁴ 1–19⁸ [20]⁴; pp. [2] [i–vi], [1]–305 [306] [307–312].

Contents: blank leaf; [i–ii] title-page, verso copyright notice and reservation of rights: "Copyright, 1893, by Harper & Brothers. | [rule] | All rights reserved. [in italic]"; [iii–iv] "NOTE", verso blank; [v–vi] "CONTENTS", verso blank; [1]–305 text; [306] blank; [307–312] ads headed: [307] "By HENRY JAMES.", listing 7 titles; [308] "By GEORGE WILLIAM CURTIS."; [309] "HARPER'S AMERICAN ESSAYISTS."; [310] "MOTLEY'S CORRESPONDENCE."; [311] "BOSWELL'S JOHNSON."; and [312] "SCOTT'S JOURNAL." All the ads are with dollar prices.

Binding: blue diagonal-fine-ribbed cloth. The front cover, which is not lettered, is decorated in each of the four corners with a triangular filigree ornament in silver. The back cover is decorated with similar ornaments in each corner in blind. The spine, which is lettered in gilt and decorated in silver, reads: "[oblong filigree ornament] | ESSAYS | IN | LONDON | & | ELSEWHERE | HENRY | JAMES | HARPERS | [oblong filigree ornament]". The endpapers are of white laid paper, and the text is printed on smooth wove paper. The top edge is trimmed and appears to be ochre stained, and the other edges are untrimmed.

American printing history. Harper & Brothers Archive. First edition published September 12, 1893. Reel 34, ledger page 669 headed November 1894 records on hand December 15, 1893, no copies, printed since [first and sole (?) impression] 2006 copies, and on hand on November 20, 1894, 410 copies. There are no further impressions reflected in the royalty ledger through December 31, 1897, on which date 313 copies remained on hand. The number of copies on hand in 1897 make it unlikely that this edition was reprinted.

Priced at $1.25.

❦

41. *THE WHEEL OF TIME*

41.1.0. *The Wheel of Time*, first edition, primary binding state, one volume, New York 1893.

The Wheel of Time | Collaboration | Owen Wingrave | BY | HENRY JAMES | [oval publisher's device] | NEW YORK | HARPER & BROTHERS PUBLISHERS | 1893

THE WHEEL OF TIME

Size: 6 13/16" x 4 3/8".

Collation: π^2 [1]^8 2–6^8 [7]^8 8–9^8 [10]^8 11–13^8 14^6; pp. [i–iv] [1–2], [3]–220. The inferred numerical signature marks, after the first, coincide with divisional fly-titles.

Contents: [i–ii] title-page, verso copyright notice and reservation of rights: "Copyright, 1893, by Harper & Brothers. | [rule] | All rights reserved. [in italic]"; [iii–iv] "CONTENTS", verso blank; [1–2] divisional fly-title, verso blank; [3]–220 text.

Binding: blueish-green linen-grain cloth. The front cover has an overall symmetrical grillwork design in silver within a triple-rule border, also in silver, centered on which is the publisher's device in gilt and above which is the title, also in gilt, and below which, also in gilt, is the author's name. The back cover is neither lettered nor decorated. The spine within a triple-rule border in silver is lettered in gilt and reads: "[small silver grillwork panel] | THE | WHEEL OF TIME | AND | OTHER STORIES | [long silver grillwork panel] | HENRY | JAMES [author's name in sans-serif] | [long silver grillwork panel] | HARPERS | [small silver grillwork panel]". The endpapers are of white wove paper, and the text is printed on heavy wove paper. The top edge is trimmed and stained ochre, and the other edges are untrimmed.

This copy is of the primary binding. E&L A41b describes this binding color as green. BAL 10606 records the primary binding as blue-green.

This binding is uniform with the blueish-green primary binding of the first edition of *The Private Life* (1893), 39.2.0.

Printing history. Harper & Brother Archive. First edition published September 26, 1893. Reel 34, ledger page 669 headed November 1894 records on hand on December 15, 1893, none, printed since [first and sole (?) impression] 2972 copies, and on hand on November 20, 1894, 1851 copies; Reel 35, ledger page 215 headed December 1895 records on hand on November 20, 1894, 2972 copies, printed since none, and on hand on December 31, 1895, 1709 copies; Reel 35, ledger page 415 headed November 1896 records on hand on December 31, 1895, 1709 copies, printed since none, and on hand on November 15, 1896, 1752 copies, notation "Less royalty on following returned: 43 Wheel of Time"; Reel 35, ledger page 56 headed December 1896 records on hand on

November 15, 1896, 1752 copies, printed since none, and on hand on December 31, 1896, 1742 copies; Reel 35, ledger page 171 headed June 1897 records on hand on December 31, 1896, 1742 copies, printed since none, and on hand June 30, 1897, 1740 copies; Reel 35, ledger page 296 headed December 1897 records on hand on June 30, 1897, 1740 copies, printed since none, and on hand on December 31, 1897, 1728 copies. The number of copies on hand in 1897, and the number of secondary (remainder?) bindings, make it unlikely that this edition was subsequently reprinted.

Priced at $1.00. This title was not published in England.

41.2.0. *The Wheel of Time*, first edition, secondary binding state A, one volume, New York 1893.

The title-page, size, collation, and contents are identical to those of the first edition, primary binding state, 41.1.0.

Binding: maroon linen-grain cloth. The front cover is decorated with the same triple-rule border and grillwork design as that on 41.1.0, but in blind rather than silver, with the publisher's device, centered, in blind, above which is the title in gilt and below which, also in gilt, is the author's name. The spine is lettered in gilt with a triple-rule border and decoration identical to that on 41.1.0, but in blind rather than silver. The back cover is neither lettered nor decorated. The endpapers are of white laid paper, and the text is printed on smooth wove paper. The top edge is trimmed and stained ochre, and the other edges are untrimmed

On the rear pastedown is a small blue bookseller's ticket reading: "BRENTANO'S | Booksellers & Stationers, | New York".

This copy is in E&L's secondary binding state A (of two noted), although the cloth is there recorded as red and the top edge as unstained. BAL 10606, citing E&L's description of this copy, disclaims having seen a copy thus, but records a variant in maroon cloth with sides *unstamped*; see 41.4.0.

THEATRICALS

41.3.0. *The Wheel of Time*, first edition, secondary binding state B, one volume, New York 1893.

The title-page, size, collation, and contents are identical to those of first edition, primary binding state, 41.1.0.

Binding: dark green linen-grain cloth. The front and back covers are neither lettered nor decorated. The spine is lettered in red within a grillwork design identical to that on 41.1.0, but in blind. The endpapers are of white laid paper, and the text is printed on smooth wove paper. The top edge is trimmed and stained ochre, and the other edges are untrimmed.

This binding is noted in E&L A41b as secondary binding state B and in BAL 10606 as variant A. Both record the top edge as unstained.

41.4.0. *The Wheel of Time*, first edition, secondary binding state C, one volume, New York 1893.

The title-page, size, collation, and contents are identical to those of the first edition, primary binding state, 41.1.0.

Binding: maroon sand-grain cloth. The front and back covers are neither lettered nor decorated. The spine is lettered in gilt within a grillwork design identical to that on 41.1.0, but in blind. The endpapers are of white laid paper, and the text is printed on smooth wove paper. The top edge is trimmed (but not stained), the fore- and bottom edges are untrimmed.

This binding is recorded in BAL 10606 as variant B. Not recorded in E&L.

42. THEATRICALS

42.1.0. *Theatricals*, first edition, English issue, one volume, London 1894.

THEATRICALS | [rule] | TWO COMEDIES | TENANTS DISEN-GAGED | BY | HENRY JAMES | LONDON | OSGOOD, McILVAINE & CO. [the first "c" is raised with two dots under it] | 45 ALBEMARLE STREET | 1894 | All rights reserved [in italic]

Size: $7\,3/8''$ x $5''$.

THEATRICALS: SECOND SERIES

Collation: [A]⁴ B–I K–U X⁸ Y⁴; pp. [i–viii] [1–2], [3]–325 [326] [327–328].

Contents: [i–ii] half-title, verso blank; [iii–iv] title-page, verso ad: "In the Press [in italic] | [rule] THEATRICALS | SECOND SERIES | THE ALBUM THE REPROBATE"; [v]–vi "NOTE", verso continuation of note; [vii–viii] "CONTENTS", verso blank; [1–2] divisional fly-title, verso "CHARACTERS"; [3]–325 text; [325] at the foot the printer's imprint: "Printed by R. & R. Clark, Edinburgh. [all except printer's name in italic]"; [326] blank; [327] ad headed "BY THE SAME AUTHOR. [in italic]", listing 2 titles, *Essays in London and Elsewhere* and *The Private Life*, with press opinions; [328] blank.

Binding: light pea-green buckram. The front cover, lettered and decorated in gilt, with a vertical ornamental device on the left side of the front cover, to the right of which is: "THEATRICALS | TENANTS | [dot] | DISENGAGED | HENRY JAMES". The back cover is neither lettered nor decorated. The spine, lettered and decorated in gilt, reads: "THEATRICALS | TENANTS | DISENGAGED | [stylized floral device] | HENRY JAMES | OSGOOD | McILVAINE & CO." In the publisher's imprint the first "c" is raised above a dot. The endpapers are of white laid paper, and the text is printed on smooth wove paper. The top and fore-edges are untrimmed, and the bottom edge is rough trimmed.

Priced at 6s.

42.2.0. *Theatricals*, first edition, American issue, one volume, New York 1894.

The title-page is identical to that of the first edition, English issue, 42.1.0, except that the publisher's imprint at the foot reads: "NEW YORK | HARPER & BROTHERS, Publishers | 1894 | All rights reserved [in italic]".

The size, collation, and contents are identical to those of 42.1.0, except that no ad is present on [327], [327–328] being a blank leaf.

Binding: light pea-green buckram, lettered and decorated identically to 42.1.0, except that the publisher's imprint at the foot of the spine reads: "HARPERS". The endpapers are of white laid paper, and the text is printed on smooth wove paper. The top and fore-edges are untrimmed, and the bottom edge is rough trimmed.

Dust-jacket: thin wove paper, the front and back covers of which are blank, as are the front and back inner flaps. The spine, lettered in red, reads: "THEATRICALS | [short rule] | HENRY JAMES | TENANTS | DISENGAGED [all the foregoing centered]".

Priced at $1.75.

Both the English and American issues of this title were printed by R. & R. Clark of Edinburgh. Because the bookcloth used on both issues and the decoration on the casings are identical (except for the publisher's imprint on the spine), it is likely that both issues were bound in England, and that the American issue was shipped to America as bound volumes rather than as sheets.

43. *GUY DOMVILLE*

No copy in the collection.

E&L A43 records that only five copies are known to be extant. It was printed for private circulation only; see BAL 10609

44. *THEATRICALS: SECOND SERIES*

44.1.0. *Theatricals: Second Series*, first edition, English issue, one volume, London 1895 [1894].

THEATRICALS | SECOND SERIES | THE ALBUM THE REPROBATE | BY | HENRY JAMES | LONDON | OSGOOD, McILVAINE & CO. [the first "c" is raised above two dots] | 45 ALBEMARLE STREET | 1895 | All rights reserved. [in italic]

Size: 7 ½" x 5".

Collation: [A]⁸ B–I K–U X–Z 2A– 2D⁸ [2E]¹; pp. [i–xvi] [1–2], [3]–416 [417–418].

Contents: [i–ii] half-title, verso blank; [iii–iv] title-page, verso blank; [v]–xiv "NOTE"; [xv-xvi] "CONTENTS", verso blank; [1–2] divisional fly-title, verso "CHARACTERS"; [3]–416 text; [416] at the foot printer's imprint: "Printed by R. & R. Clark, Edinburgh. [all except printer's name in italic]"; [417] ad headed ; "BY THE SAME AUTHOR. [in italic]" for "THEATRICALS, I", with press opinions ; [418] ad similarly headed, listing 2 titles, *Essays in London and Elsewhere* and *The Private Life*, also with press opinions.

Binding: light pea-green buckram, lettered and decorated identically to the first edition, English issue, 42.1.0, except that the names of the plays on the front cover and spine are: "The Album" and "The Reprobate". The endpapers are of white laid paper, and the text is printed on smooth wove paper. The top and fore-edges are untrimmed, and the bottom edge is rough trimmed.

Priced at 6s.

BAL 10610 and 10611 and E&L A44a record the publication date of both the English and American issues of this title as December 1894.

44.2.0. *Theatricals: Second Series*, first edition, American issue, one volume, New York 1895 [1894].

The title-page is identical to that of the first edition, English issue, 44.1.0, except that the publisher's imprint at the foot reads: "NEW YORK | HARPER & BROTHERS, Publishers | 1895 | All rights reserved. [in italic]".

The size, collation, and contents are identical to those of 44.1.0, except that the final leaf of ads, [2E]$_1$, [417–418], is not present, those pages being blank.

Binding: light pea-green buckram, lettered and decorated identically to 44.1.0, except that the publisher's imprint at the foot of the spine reads: "HARPERS". The endpapers are of white laid paper, and the text is printed on smooth wove paper. The top and fore-edges are untrimmed, and the bottom edge is rough trimmed.

Dust-jacket: thin wove paper uniform with that on *Theatricals*, 42.2.0, with red lettering on the spine only, which reads: "THEATRICALS | [short rule] | HENRY JAMES | THE ALBUM | THE REPROBATE" (all centered).

Priced at $1.75. Tansell dust-jacket 95.43 and plate 13a.

45. TERMINATIONS

45.1.0. *Terminations*, first edition, first impression, one volume, London 1895.

TERMINATIONS [in red] | THE DEATH OF THE | LION..THE COXON | FUND..THE MIDDLE | YEARS..THE ALTAR | OF THE DEAD..... | By Henry James | [small acorn device] | LONDON: WILLIAM HEINE-MANN [in red] | MDCCCXCV

Size: 7 $\frac{1}{2}$" x 5".

Collation: π^4 A–I K–Q^8 R^2; pp. [i–viii] [1–2], [3]–260.

Contents: [i–ii] half-title, verso ad headed: "SHORT STORIES IN ONE VOLUME" [in italic], listing 5 titles, none by James; [iii–iv] title-page, verso reservation of rights: "All rights reserved [in italic]"; [v–vi] "NOTE [all in italic]", verso blank; [vii–viii] "CONTENTS [all in italic]", verso blank; [1–2] divisional fly-title, verso blank; [3]–260 text; 260 at foot printer's imprint: "Printed by Ballantyne, Hanson & Co. | London and Edinburgh. [all except printer's name in italic]".

Binding: light blue diagonal-fine-ribbed cloth with four irises in blind on the front cover, and publisher's device in blind on the back cover. The title, "TERMINATIONS", in gilt on the front cover is 1 $\frac{3}{4}$" wide. The spine, lettered in gilt but not decorated, reads: "TERMINA-TIONS | HENRY | JAMES | HEINEMANN". The publisher's imprint at the foot of the spine is in uniform capitals $\frac{3}{16}$" high. The endpapers are of white laid paper, and the text is printed on laid paper. All edges are untrimmed. A 16-page undated and unpaginated publisher's catalogue of ads, printed on a slightly lighter wove paper, is bound in at the end, each page of which is devoted to a single title (none by James), with extensive press opinions.

English printing history. Heinemann Archive. First edition, one volume: first impression, 1,000 copies, published May 15, 1895, priced at 6s. A second impression of 500 copies was printed on August 31, 1895, also priced at 6s. On November 15, 1895, a colonial impression of 1,000 copies was printed (the third impression), and it appears that all were bound in cloth. A second colonial impression (the fourth impression) was printed on September 3, 1896 (number copies not specified), and it appears that all were bound in paper wrappers. The record states that the cloth bound copies were priced at "1/9 net" and the wrappered copies at "1/5 net". It is assumed that these prices were the discount prices to colonial distributors, as the nominal retail prices were 3s. 6d. for cloth copies, and 2s. 6d. for wrappered copies. One hundred sets of sheets of the colonial impressions were diverted for use in the domestic market.

45.2.0. *Terminations*, first edition, second impression, state A, one volume, London 1895.

The title-page and size are identical to those of the first edition, first impression, 45.1.0.

Collation: π⁶ [A]⁸ B–I K–Q⁸ R²; pp. [2] [i–x] [1–2], [3]–260. Note that signature [A] is unsigned.

Contents: blank leaf; [i–ii] ad headed: "TERMINATIONS | [rule] | Some Press Opinions [in Gothic type]", continuing on verso; [iii–iv] half-title, verso ad headed: "SHORT STORIES IN ONE VOLUME [in italic]" listing 5 titles, none by James; [v–vi] title-page, verso printing history and reservation of rights: "SECOND EDITION | [rule] | First Edition, May 1895 | All rights reserved [all the foregoing in italic]"; [vii–viii] "NOTE [all in italic]", verso blank; [ix–x] "CONTENTS [all in italic]", verso blank; [1–2] divisional fly-title, verso blank; [3]–260 text; 260 at foot printer's imprint: "Printed by Ballantyne, Hanson & Co. | London and Edinburgh. [all except printer's name in italic]".

Binding: light blue diagonal-fine-ribbed cloth, with four irises in blind on the front cover and publisher's device in blind on the back cover, identical to the binding on 45.1.0. The endpapers are of white laid paper, and the text is printed on laid paper. All edges are untrimmed. A 16-page undated and unpaginated publisher's catalogue of ads printed on wove paper is bound in at the end, which is identical to the publisher's catalogue in 45.1.0.

45.3.0. *Terminations*, first edition, second impression, state B, one volume, London 1895.

The title-page and size are identical to those of the first edition, first impression, 45.1.0.

Collation: π⁴ [A]⁸ B–I K–Q⁸ R²; pp. [2] [i–vi] [1–2], [3]–260.

Contents: blank leaf; [i–ii] half-title, verso blank; [iii–iv] title-page, verso printing history and reservation of rights: "SECOND EDITION

|[rule]| First Edition, May 1895 | All rights reserved [all the foregoing in italic]"; [v–vi] "CONTENTS [all in italic]", verso blank; [1–2] divisional fly-title, verso blank; [3]–260 text; 260 at foot printer's imprint as on 260 of 45.2.0.

Note that the prelims differ from those of the first edition, second impression, state A, 45.2.0, in that the two leaves with the ad and the "NOTE" are not present.

Binding: light blue diagonal-fine-ribbed cloth, with nine tulips in blind on the front cover and publisher's device in blind on the back cover. The title, "TERMINATIONS", in gilt on the front cover is 2 3/8" wide. On the spine, which reads identically to 45.1.0, the author's name is slightly off-centered to the right. The publisher's imprint at the foot of the spine is in uniform capitals 1/8" high. The endpapers are of white laid paper, and the text is printed on laid paper. All edges are untrimmed. There are no ads bound in at the end.

The light blue cloth on this binding is of a lighter shade than that used on 45.1.0 and 45.2.0.

45.4.0. *Terminations*, first edition, third impression (colonial), cloth binding state, one volume, London 1895.

TERMINATIONS | BY | HENRY JAMES | LONDON | WILLIAM HEINEMANN | 1895 [all the foregoing in black]

Size: 7 5/16" x 4 3/4".

Collation: π^4 [A]^8 B–I K–Q^8 R^2; pp. [i–viii] [1–2], [3]–260.

Contents: [i–ii] "Heinemann's Colonial Library of Popular Fiction. [in gothic type, underscored] | VOLUME XLI. [in italic] | Issued for sale in the British | Colonies and India, and not | to be imported into Europe or | the United States of America [sale limitation all in italic]", verso ad headed: "TERMINATIONS. | SOME PRESS OPINIONS [in italic]"; [iii–iv] title-page, verso "All rights reserved. [in italic]"; [v–vi] "NOTE [all in italic]", verso blank; [vii–viii] "CONTENTS [all in italic]", verso blank; [1–2] divisional fly-title, verso blank; [3]–260 text; 260 at foot printer's imprint: "Printed by Ballantyne, Hanson & Co. | London and Edinburgh. [all except printer's name in italic]".

Binding: bright red pebble-grain cloth. On the front cover the title is lettered in black within a single-rule border in blind. On the back cover the publisher's device in black is within a single-rule border in blind. The spine, lettered and decorated in black, reads: "[rule] | Terminations | [short rule] Henry | James | Heinemann | [rule]". The endpapers are of cream wove paper, and the text is printed on smooth fairly heavy wove paper. All edges are trimmed. An 8 page undated and unpaginated publisher's catalogue is bound in at the end. The front and rear pastedowns have ads printed on them, as do the recto and verso of the front and rear free endpapers.

On the front free endpaper is the inscription: "Rachael [illegible] Simons | from Mama Christmas 1925".

45.5.0. *Terminations*, first edition, third or fourth impression, colonial sheets bound for the domestic market, one volume, 1895.

TERMINATIONS | BY | HENRY JAMES | LONDON | WILLIAM HEINEMANN | 1895 [all the foregoing in black]

Size: $7\,^1/_2$" x $5\,^1/_{16}$".

Collation: $\pi^4(\pi_2 +X_1)[A]^8$ B–I K–Q^8 R^2; pp. [4][i–vi][1–2],[3]–260. Signature π^4 has a single additional sheet inserted between π_2 and π_3, the recto of which is the title-page, and on the verso of which is: "All rights reserved."

Contents: two blank leaves; [i–ii] title-page, verso reservation of rights: "All rights reserved. [in italic]"; [iii–iv] "NOTE [all in italic]", verso blank; [v–vi] "CONTENTS [all in italic]", verso blank; [1–2] divisional fly-title, verso blank; [3]–260 text; 260 at foot printer's imprint: "Printed by Ballantyne, Hanson & Co. | London and Edinburgh. [all except printer's name in italic]".

Binding: light blue diagonal-fine-ribbed cloth, with nine tulips in blind on the front cover and publisher's device in blind on the back cover. The title, "TERMINATIONS", in gilt on the front cover is $2\,^1/_2$" wide, and the author's name on the spine is slightly off-centered to the right. The publisher's imprint at the foot of the spine is in uniform capitals $^3/_{16}$" high. The endpapers are of white wove paper, and the text is printed on a smooth fairly heavy wove paper (heavier than that used in most Heinemann colonial editions, but much smoother than the paper used for the first and second impressions, 45.1.0–45.3.0). All edges are untrimmed. There are no ads bound in at the end.

TERMINATIONS

The light blue cloth on this binding is of a lighter shade than that used on 45.1.0 and 45.2.0.

45.6.0. *Terminations*, first American edition, binding state A, one volume, New York 1895.

TERMINATIONS | The Death of the Lion | The Coxon Fund | The Middle Years | The Altar of the Dead [this and three prior lines in italic] | BY | HENRY JAMES | AUTHOR OF "DAISY MILLER" ETC. | [oval publisher's device] | NEW YORK | HARPER & BROTHERS PUBLISHERS | 1895

Size: $7\,^{1}/_{4}''$ x $4\,^{13}/_{16}''$.

Collation: π^4 1–15^8 16^4; pp. [2] [i–vi], [1]–242 [243–248]. The collation recorded in BAL 10613 would appear to be incorrect.

Contents: blank leaf; [i–ii] title-page, verso within a single-rule frame ad headed: "By HENRY JAMES", listing 8 titles with dollar prices, and below which is the copyright notice and reservation of rights: "Copyright, 1895, By Harper & Brothers. | [rule] | All rights reserved. [in italic]"; [iii–iv] "NOTE", verso blank; [v–vi] "CONTENTS", verso blank; [1]–242 text; [243–248] ads headed: [243] "By GEORGE DU MAURIER"; [244] "By THOMAS HARDY"; [245] "By CHARLES DUDLEY WARNER"; [246] "R. D. BLACKMORE'S NOVELS."; [247] "WALTER BESANT'S WORKS."; and [248] "HARPER'S AMERICAN ESSAYISTS", all with dollar prices.

Binding: pale green-on-white linen-grain cloth. The front cover, lettered in gilt and decorated with three flowers on long stems in green with gilt accents, reads: "TERMINATIONS | BY | HENRY | JAMES". The back cover is neither lettered nor decorated. The spine, lettered in gilt and decorated with one flower on a long stem in green with gilt accents, reads: "TERMINATIONS | [small gilt leaf] | HENRY | JAMES | [long stemmed flower] | HARPERS". The publisher's imprint is in lightly serif lettering $^{1}/_{8}''$ high. The endpapers are of white laid paper, and the text is printed on a heavy smooth wove paper. All edges are trimmed, and the top edge is stained brown.

On the front pastedown is an inscription dated "September 1895".

American printing history, Harper & Brother Archive. First edition published June 18, 1895. Reel 35, ledger page 215, headed December 1895 records copies on hand November 1894, none, printed since 2050

EMBARRASSMENTS

copies, and on hand December 31, 1895, 479 copies (146 given away, 1400 sold); Reel 35, ledger page 415, headed November 1896, records on hand December 31, 1895, 479 copies, printed since none, and on hand on November 15, 1896, 397 copies (82 sold). Reel 35, ledger page 56 [?], headed December 1896, records on hand on November 15, 1896, 397 copies, and on hand December 31, 1896, 381 copies (16 sold). Reel 35, ledger page 171, headed June 1897, records on hand December 31, 1896, 381 copies and on hand June 30, 1897, 380 copies (1 sold). Reel 35, ledger page 296, headed December 1897, records 380 copies on hand both on June 30, 1897, and December 31 1897 (none sold).

Priced at $1.25

45.7.0. *Terminations*, first American edition, binding state B, one volume, New York 1895.

The title-page, size, collation, and contents are identical to those of the first American edition, binding state A, 45.6.0.

Binding: green-on-white linen-grain cloth. The front cover is identical to that on 45.6.0. The back cover is neither lettered nor decorated. The spine, lettered and decorated in gilt, reads: "TERMINATIONS | [small gilt leaf] | HENRY | JAMES | HARPERS". The publisher's imprint at the foot of the spine is ever so slightly more heavily serifed than the first American edition, binding state A, and is in letters 3/32″ high. The long floral ornament in dark green and gilt present on the spine of 45.6.0 is not present om this copy. The endpapers are of white wove paper, and the text is printed on a heavy smooth wove paper. All edges are trimmed, and the top edge is stained brown.

On the front free endpaper is an ink inscription dated "June 1908".

The cloth color of binding state B is darker than the cloth color on binding state A, but not as dark as what would normally be characterized as pea-green.

BAL 10615 records that: "all copies examined by BAL have two ornaments on the spine." E&L A45b records a secondary binding in pea-green linen-grain cloth lettered and blocked as this copy, but without the leaf ornament on the spine. It is possible that E&L, while correct as to the existence of this secondary binding not seen by BAL, overlooked or disregarded the small gilt leaf between the title and the author's name on the spine of this copy.

46. *EMBARRASSMENTS*

46.1.0. *Embarrassments*, first edition, first impression, one volume, London 1896.

EMBARRASSMENTS [in red] | THE FIGURE IN THE | CARPET .. GLASSES. | THE NEXT TIME .. | THE WAY IT CAME .. | By Henry James | [small acorn device] | LONDON: WILLIAM HEINEMANN [in red] | MCCCXCVI

Size: 7 $\frac{1}{2}$" x 5".

Collation: π^4 A–I K–Q^8 R^4; pp. [i–viii] [1–2], [3]–263 [264].

Contents: [i–ii] half-title, verso a small ad in italic headed: "BY THE SAME AUTHOR", listing *Terminations* with press opinions; [iii–iv] title-page, verso reservation of rights: "All rights reserved [in italic]"; [v–vi] "NOTE" [all in italic], verso blank; [vii–viii] "CONTENTS" [all in italic]; [1–2] divisional fly-title, verso blank; [3]–263 text; 263 at foot printer's imprint: "Printed by Ballantyne, Hanson & Co. | London and Edinburgh [all except printer's name in italic]"; [264] blank.

Binding: light blue diagonal-fine-ribbed cloth with four irises in blind on the front cover, and the publisher's device in blind on the back cover. The title, "EMBARRASMENTS" in gilt on the front cover is 1 $^{13}/_{16}$" wide. The spine, lettered in gilt but undecorated, reads: "EMBARRASSMENTS | HENRY | JAMES | HEINEMANN". The publisher's imprint at the foot of the spine is in uniform capitals $^{5}/_{32}$" high. The endpapers are of white laid paper, and the text is printed on laid paper. All edges are untrimmed. A 32-page unpaginated and undated publisher's catalogue of ads, printed on a lighter wove paper, is bound in at the end. The recto of the first leaf advertises Caine's *The Manxman*, and each page is devoted to a single title with press opinions.

In this copy a full signature of eight leaves had been bound in between the end of signature P and the start of signature Q, that is between 240 and [241], which leaves have been cut off leaving the stubs bound in.

English printing history. Heinemann Archive. First edition, one volume: first impression, 1250 copies, published June 12, 1896, priced at 6s. A second impression for the colonial market, was published on March 31, 1897 (number of copies not specified), bound in both cloth and paper wrappers, but it was probably printed in 1896 at about the same time as the first domestic impression was printed. The record states that the colonial copies were priced at "1/9 net" in cloth and "1/5 net" in wrappers. It is assumes that these prices were the discount prices to colonial distributors, as the nominal retail prices were 3s. 6d. for cloth copies and 2s. 6d. for wrapped copies.

From the books themselves it is clear that there was a second impression for the domestic market (the third impression), printed in March 1897; see 46.2.0. E&L records that this impression was of 250 copies. An unknown number of sheets of the colonial impression were diverted for use in the domestic market; see 46.4.0.

46.1.5. *Embarrassments*, first edition, first impression, one volume, London 1896.

The title-page, size, collation, and contents are identical to those of the first edition, first impression, 46.1.0.

Binding: light blue diagonal-fine-ribbed cloth lettered and decorated identically to 46.1.0. Bound in at the end is the same 32-page unpaginated and undated publisher's catalogue as is present in 46.1.0.

This copy does not have the extra signature of eight leaves bound between the end of signature P and the start of signature Q, the stub of which is present in 46.1.0.

46.2.0. *Embarrassments*, first edition, third impression, one volume, London 1897.

The title-page is identical to the title-page of the first edition, first impression, 46.1.0, except that at the foot it is dated "MDCCCXCVII".

The size, and collation are identical to those of 46.1.0.

The contents are identical to those of 46.1.0, except that the ad on [ii] lists *Terminations*, *The Spoils of Poynton* and *The Other House* with press opinions under the heading: "BY THE SAME AUTHOR", and the verso of the title-leaf, [iv], reads: "First Edition, June 1896; Reprinted March 1897 | All rights reserved [all the foregoing in italic]".

Binding: light blue diagonal-fine-ribbed cloth, with nine tulips in blind on the front cover, but without the publisher's device in blind on the back cover. The title, "EMBARRASSMENTS", in gilt on the front cover is 2 $^{13}/_{16}$" wide. The spine, lettered in gilt but undecorated, reads: "EMBARRASSMENTS | HENRY | JAMES | HEINEMANN". The publisher's imprint at the foot of the spine is in uniform capitals $^{1}/_{8}$" high. The endpapers are of white wove paper, and the text is printed on laid paper. All edges are untrimmed. No publisher's catalogue of ads is bound in at the end.

46.3.0. *Embarrassments*, first edition, second (?) impression (colonial), cloth binding state, one volume, London 1897.

EMBARRASSMENTS | BY | HENRY JAMES | LONDON | WILLIAM HEINEMANN | 1897 [all the foregoing in black]

Size: 7 $^{5}/_{16}$" x 4 $^{3}/_{4}$".

Collation: π^4 A–I K–Q^8 R^4; pp. [i–viii] [1–2], [3]–263 [264].

Contents: [i–ii] "Heinemann's Colonial Library of Popular Fiction. [in Gothic type, underscored] | Issued for sale in the British Colonies | and India, and not to be imported | into Europe or the United States | of America. [sale limitation all in italic]", verso ad headed: "BY THE SAME AUTHOR", listing 3 titles with press opinions; [iii–iv] title-page, verso reservation of rights: "All rights reserved [in italic]"; [v–vi] "NOTE [all in italic]", verso blank; [vii–viii] "CONTENTS [all in italic]", verso blank; [1–2] divisional fly-title, verso blank; [3]–263 text; [263] at foot printer's imprint as on [263] of the first edition, first impression, 46.1.0; [264] blank.

Binding: bright red pebble-grain cloth. On the front cover the title is lettered in black within a single-rule border in blind. On the back cover the publisher's device in black is within a single-rule border in blind. The spine, decorated and lettered in black, reads: "[rule] | Embarrassments | [short rule] | Henry James | Heinemann | [rule]". The endpapers are of light cream wove paper, and the text is printed on smooth fairly heavy wove paper. All edges are trimmed. An 8-page unpaginated and undated publisher's catalogue of ads printed on wove paper is bound in at the end. The front and rear pastedowns have ads on them, as do the recto and verso of the front and rear free endpapers.

E&L F41 notes "*Embarrassments* (1896 [1897])", which would presumably mean an 1896 title-page date but an 1897 publication date. Also Sadleir

EMBARRASSMENTS

1269 records a copy with "the title (black only) of the secondary issue [which] does not carry the names of the four stories" with an 1896 date on the title-page. The 1897 date on the title-page of this copy may possibly mean that it is a copy of the second colonial impression.

46.4.0. *Embarrassments*, first edition, second (?) impression, colonial sheets bound for the domestic market, one volume, London 1897 [1896?].

EMBARRASSMENTS | BY | HENRY JAMES | LONDON | WILLIAM HEINEMANN | 1897 [all the foregoing in black]

Size: $7 \frac{1}{2}"$ x $5 \frac{1}{16}"$.

The collation is the same as that of the first edition, first impression, 46.1.0, except that leaf π_1, the colonial half-title leaf, has been excised.

Contents: [i–ii] title-page, verso reservation of rights: "All rights reserved [in italic]"; [iii–iv] "NOTE [all in italic]", verso blank; [v–vi] "CONTENTS [all in italic]", verso blank; [1–2] divisional fly-title, verso blank; [3]–263 text; 263 at foot printer's imprint: "Printed by Ballantyne, Hanson & Co. | London & Edinburgh [all except printer's name in italic]"; [264] blank.

Binding: light blue diagonal-fine-ribbed cloth, with nine tulips in blind on the front cover, and the publisher's device in blind on the back cover. The title, "EMBARRASSMENTS", on the front cover is $2 \frac{3}{4}"$ wide. The spine, lettered in gilt but not decorated, reads: "EMBARRASS- | MENTS" rather than "EMBARRASSMENTS", as it appears on the first and the third impressions of the first edition, 46.1.0, 46.1.5 and 46.2.0. The publisher's imprint at the foot of the spine is in uniform capitals $\frac{1}{8}"$ high. The endpapers are of white wove paper, and the text is printed on wove paper. The top and fore-edges are untrimmed, and the bottom edge is rough trimmed. There are no ads bound in at the end.

46.5.0. *Embarrassments*, first American edition, first impression, binding state A, one volume, New York and London 1896.

EMBARRASSMENTS | BY | HENRY JAMES | AUTHOR OF "DAISY MILLER," "THE EUROPEANS" | ETC., ETC. | New York [in Gothic type] | THE MACMILLAN COMPANY | LONDON: MACMILLAN & CO., Ltd. | 1896 | All rights reserved [in italic]

THE OTHER HOUSE

Size: 7 3/4" x 5 1/8".

Collation: [1–20⁸ 21⁴], signed as [A]³ [B]⁸ C-I K–U X⁸ [Y]¹; pp. [i–vi] [1–2], 3–320 [321–322].

Contents: [i–ii] half-title, verso publisher's device; [iii–iv] title-page, verso copyright notice and printer's imprint: "Copyright, 1896, | By THE MACMILLAN COMPANY. | Norwood Press [in Gothic type] | J. S. Cushing & Co.– Berwick & Smith | Norwood Mass. U.S.A."; v–[vi] "CONTENTS", verso blank; [1–2] divisional fly-title, verso blank; 3–320 text; [321–322] ads headed: [321] "WORKS BY HENRY JAMES.", listing 7 titles; and [322] "WORKS BY HENRY JAMES.", listing 2 titles, with press opinions and dollar prices on both pages.

Binding: maroon linen-grain cloth. The front and back covers are not lettered, but are decorated with a single-rule border in blind. The spine, lettered in gilt and decorated in gilt and in blind, reads: "[rule in blind] | EMBARRASSMENTS [underscored] | HENRY JAMES | MACMILLAN & Co. | [rule in blind]". The publisher's imprint at the foot of the spine is in capitals of uniform size, except that the "o" is raised above a double dot. The endpapers are of white laid paper, and the text and the two pages of ads at the end, leaf [21₄], are printed on laid paper. There are no binder's fly-leaves. The top edge is gilt, and the other edges are untrimmed.

Both E&L and BAL describe two binding states of this first impression. This copy is described in BAL 10618 as binding A. It differs slightly from the description in E&L A46b, in that it lacks the fly-leaves. However, BAL 10618 notes that this variant has no flyleaves. See the copy recorded below for the second of the two states. No priority is assigned by either BAL or E&L to the two binding states.

American printing history. There is no information in the Macmillan & Co. (N.Y.) Archive as to the American printing history of this title, however the title-page verso of 46.7.0 indicates that there were two impressions of the first American edition, the first in June 1896 and the second in December 1896. E&L records that 1600 copies of the first impression were printed.

Priced at $1.50 (both impressions).

46.6.0. *Embarrassments*, first American edition, first impression, binding state B, one volume, New York and London 1896.

This copy is identical in all respects (including the ads at the end) to the first edition, first impression, binding state A, 46.5.0, except that there is a binder's fly-leaf of white laid paper at the front, but none at the back, and the printer's imprint at the foot of the spine reads: "THE MACMILLAN | COMPANY" in capitals of uniform size.

This copy conforms to the description of binding B in BAL 10618, the second of the two binding variants.

46.7.0. *Embarrassments*, first American edition, second impression, one volume, New York and London 1897.

The title-page, size, collation, and contents of this copy (including the ads at the end) are identical to the first edition, first impression, binding states A and B, 46.5.0 and 46.6.0, except that the title-page is dated 1897, and the verso of the title-page reads: "Copyright, 1896, | By THE MACMILLAN COMPANY. | [rule] | Set up and electrotyped June, 1896. Reprinted December, | 1896. | Norwood Press [in Gothic type] | J. S. Cushing & Co.-Berwick & Smith | Norwood Mass. U.S.A."

Binding: identical to that on the first impression, binding state B, 46.6.0. The endpapers are of white wove paper, and the text (and ads) are printed on laid paper. There are no binder's fly-leaves. The top edge is gilt, and the other edges are untrimmed.

※✦※

47. THE OTHER HOUSE

47.1.0. *The Other House*, first edition, first impression, two volumes, London 1896.

The Other House | By | Henry James | In Two Volumes | Vol. i [ii] | London | William Heinemann | 1896

The last "n" in the printer's imprint at the foot of the title-pages is spaced more widely than the other letters.

Size: $7 \frac{1}{4}''$ x $4 \frac{3}{4}''$.

Collation: Volume I: π^2 A–I K–N^8; pp. [i–iv] [1–2], [3]–206 [207–208]. Volume II: π^2 A–I K–M^8 N^6; pp. [i–iv], [1] -202 [203–204].

THE OTHER HOUSE

Contents: Volume I: [i–ii] half-title, verso ad headed: "By the Same Author, 6s. each. [in italic]", listing *Terminations* and *Embarrassments*, with press opinions; [iii–iv] title-page, verso reservation of rights: "All rights reserved [in italic]"; [1–2] divisional fly-title with signature mark "A" at the foot, verso blank; [3]–206 text; 206 at foot printer's imprint: "Printed by Ballantyne, Hanson & Co. | London and Edinburgh [all except printer's name in italic]"; [207–208] blank leaf. Volume II: [i–ii] half-title, verso ad identical to that on [ii] in Volume I; [iii–iv] title-page, verso reservation of rights as on [iv] in Volume I; [1]–202 text; 202 at the foot, printer's imprint as on 206 in Volume I; [203–204] blank leaf.

Binding: light blue diagonal-fine-ribbed cloth. The front covers have a large (1 ¹³⁄₁₆″ diameter) circular ornament in blind to the left of the title in gilt with no other lettering or decoration. The back covers have a small publisher's device in blind. The spines, lettered in gilt but not decorated, read: "The | Other | House | Vol. I [II] | Henry | James | Heinemann". The endpapers are of white laid paper, and the text is printed on a thicker laid paper. All edges are trimmed, and the top edge appears to be stained ochre. At the end of each volume is an identical 32 pages of undated and unpaginated ads printed on wove paper, the first leaf advertising Caine's *The Manxman*, and each page devoted to a single title with press opinions. These are the same ads that appear at the end of the first edition, first impression, of *Embarrassments*, 46.1.0.

Volume II has blind-stamped on both the title-page and the following first page of the text: "Presentation | Copy".

Wolff, at 3570, records, as does BAL 10620, a copy of this edition in which the undated 32-page catalogue of ads at the end of Volume I differs from the 32-page catalogue at the end of Volume II, and that the latter is dated August 1896; see 47.2.0. E&L A47a records both volumes as having ads dated August 1896, but also notes copies of the first impression with undated ads as in this copy.

BAL disputes E&L's assertion that some copies lack the circular ornament in blind on the front cover.

English printing history. Heinemann Archive. First edition, two volumes: first impression, 1,000 copies, published October 1, 1896, priced at 10s. A second edition in one volume (number of copies not specified) was published on July 16, 1897, priced at 6s. On June 25, 1897, a one-volume colonial impression of the second edition was printed (number of copies not specified), bound in both cloth and in wrappers. The record states that the cloth bound copies were priced at "1/9 net" and the wrappered copies at "1/5 net". It is assumed that these prices were the discounted prices to colonial distributors, as the nominal retail prices were 3s. 6d. for cloth copies and 2s. 6d. for wrappered copies.

From the books themselves, it is clear that there were not one but two impression of the two-volume first edition, the second impression being printed in the same month as the first; see 47.1.0–47.4.0 and E&L A47a. The two impressions of the first edition aggregated 1,000 copies, and the first impression of the one-volume second edition was of 1500 copies for the domestic market. One hundred and fifty sets of sheets of the colonial impression were diverted for use in the domestic market.

47.2.0 *The Other House*, first edition, first impression, two volumes, London 1896.

The title-pages, size, collations, and contents are identical to those of the first edition, first impression, 47.1.0.

Binding: light blue diagonal-fine-ribbed cloth, lettered and decorated in gilt and in blind identically to 47.1.0. The endpapers are of white laid paper and the text is printed on thicker laid paper. All edges are trimmed, and the top edges appears to be stained ochre. At the end of Volume I is 32 pages of undated and unpaginated ads printed on wove paper, the first page advertising Caine's *The Manxman*, and each page devoted to a single title with press opinions. At the end of volume II is a 32-page paginated catalogue of ads entitled "A List of | Mr. William Heinemann's | Publications and | Announcements", dated August 1896. The ads inserted at the end of Volume I are the same as those in both Volumes of 47.1.0, and those at the end of the first edition, first impression, of *Embarrassments*, 46.1.0.

On the title-page of both volumes is blind-stamped "PRESENTATION | COPY".

The cloth on this copy and on 47.3.0, is slightly darker than the cloth on 47.1.0.

THE OTHER HOUSE

47.3.0. *The Other House*, first edition, second impression, two volumes, London 1896.

The title-pages, size, collation, and contents (including the ad on [ii]) are identical to those of the first edition, first impression, 47.1.0, except that the title-pages have on them "Second Edition" between "Vol. i [ii]" and the publisher's imprint.

Binding: light blue diagonal-fine-ribbed cloth, lettered and decorated identically to 47.1.0. The endpapers are of white wove paper, and the text is printed on laid paper. All edges are trimmed, and the top edges appear to be stained ochre. Bound in at the end of each Volume is an identical 32-page unpaginated and undated catalogue of ads printed on wove paper, which are the same ads as appear at the end of each Volume of 47.1.0.

47.4.0. *The Other House*, second edition, first impression, one volume, London 1897.

THE OTHER HOUSE [in red] | By Henry James | [small acorn device] | LONDON: WILLIAM HEINEMANN [in red] | MDCCCXCVII

Size: 7 ½″ x 5″.

Collation: π^2 A–I K–T^8 U^6; pp. [i–iv] [1–2], [3]–316.

Contents: [i–ii] half-title, verso ad headed: "By the Same Author, 6s. each.", listing *The Spoils of Poynton*, *Terminations* and *Embarrassments*, with press opinions; [iii–iv] title-page, verso printing history and reservation of rights: "First Edition, 2 vols., October 1896 | All rights reserved [all of the foregoing except the year in italic]"; [1–2] divisional fly-title with signature mark "A" at the foot, verso blank; [3]–316 text; 316 at foot printer's imprint: "Printed by Ballantyne, Hanson & Co. | London & Edinburgh".

Binding: light blue diagonal-fine-ribbed cloth, with four irises in blind on the front cover, and publisher's device in blind on the back cover. The title, "THE OTHER HOUSE", in gilt on the front cover is 2 ½″ wide. The spine, lettered in gilt but undecorated, reads: "THE OTHER | HOUSE | HENRY | JAMES | HEINEMANN". The publisher's imprint at the foot of the spine is in uniform serif capitals $^3/_{16}$″ high. The endpapers are of white laid paper, and the text is printed on thicker laid paper. All edges are untrimmed. Bound at the end is a

THE OTHER HOUSE

32-page catalogue of unpaginated and undated ads printed on light wove paper, each page of which is devoted to either one or two titles with press opinions, beginning with Harold Frederic's *Illumination*.

E&L A47c records copies with either 16 or 32 pages of unpaginated and undated ads at the end.

47.5.0 *The Other House*, second edition, first impression, one volume, London 1897.

The title-page (and the ad on [ii] and the title-leaf verso), size, collation, and contents are identical to those of the second edition, first impression, 47.4.0.

Binding: light blue diagonal-fine-ribbed cloth, with nine tulips in blind on the front cover, and publisher's device in blind on the back cover. The title, "THE OTHER HOUSE", in gilt on the front cover is 3″ wide. The spine, lettered in gilt but undecorated, reads: "THE OTHER | HOUSE | HENRY | JAMES | HEINEMANN". The publisher's imprint at the foot of the spine is in uniform sans-serif capitals $^1/_8$″ high. The endpapers are of white wove paper, and the text is printed on thick laid paper. All edges are untrimmed. There are no ads bound in at the end.

47.6.0. *The Other House*, second edition, first impression, one volume, London 1897.

The title-page (the ad on [ii] and the title-leaf verso), size, collation, and contents are identical to those of the second edition, first impression, 47.4.0.

Binding: light blue diagonal-fine-ribbed cloth, with nine tulips in blind on the front cover, but *without* the publisher's device in blind on the back cover. The title, "THE OTHER HOUSE", in gilt on the front cover is 3″ wide. The spine, lettered in gilt but undecorated, reads: "THE OTHER | HOUSE | HENRY | JAMES | HEINEMANN". The publisher's imprint on the spine is in uniform serif capitals $^3/_{16}$″ high. The endpapers are of white wove paper, and the text is printed on thick laid paper. All edges are untrimmed. There are no ads bound in at the end.

THE OTHER HOUSE

47.7.0. *The Other House*, second edition, second impression (colonial), cloth binding state, one volume, London 1897.

THE OTHER HOUSE | BY | HENRY JAMES | LONDON | WILLIAM HEINEMANN | 1897 [all the foregoing in black]

Size: 7 1/4" x 4 3/4".

Collation: π^2 A–I K–T^8 U^6; pp. [i–iv] [1–2], [3]–316.

Contents: [i–ii] "Heinemann's Colonial Library of Popular Fiction. [in Gothic type, underscored] | Issued for sale in the British Colonies | and India, and not to be imported | into Europe or the United States | of America [sale limitation all in italic]", verso ad headed: "By the same Author, uniform | with this Volume [all in italic]", listing *The Spoils of Poynton*, *Terminations* and *Embarrassments*, with press opinions; [iii–iv] title-page, verso reservation of rights: "All rights reserved [in italic]"; [1–2] divisional fly-title with signature mark "A" at the foot, verso blank; [3]–316 text; 316 at foot printer's imprint: "Printed by Ballantyne, Hanson & Co. | London & Edinburgh".

Binding: bright red pebble-grain cloth. On the front cover the title is lettered in black within a single-rule border in blind. On the back cover the publisher's device in black is within a single-rule border in blind. The spine, lettered and decorated in black, reads: "[rule] | The | Other | House | [short rule] | Henry | James | Heinemann | [rule]". The endpapers are of light cream wove paper, and the text is printed on wove paper. The front and rear pastedowns have ads printed on them, as do the recto and verso of the front and rear free endpapers. All edges are trimmed. An 8-page unpaginated and undated catalogue of ads printed on thin wove paper is bound in at the end.

47.8.0. *The Other House*, second edition, second impression, colonial sheets bound for the domestic market, one volume, London 1897.

THE OTHER HOUSE | BY | HENRY JAMES | LONDON | WILLIAM HEINEMANN | 1897 [all the foregoing in black]

Size: 7 3/16" x 4 3/4".

Collation: π^1 A–I K–T^8 U^6; pp. [i–ii] [1–2], [3]–316.

Contents: [i–ii] title-page, verso reservation of rights: "All rights reserved [in italic]"; [1–2] divisional fly-title with signature mark "A" at the foot, verso blank (except for the stamp: "Printed in Great Britain");

THE OTHER HOUSE

[3]–316 text; 316 at foot printer's imprint: "Printed by Ballantyne, Hanson & Co. | London & Edinburgh".

Binding: light blue diagonal-fine-ribbed cloth, with nine tulips in blind on the front cover, and the publisher's device in blind on the back cover. The title, "THE OTHER HOUSE", in gilt on the front cover is 2 $^{11}/_{16}''$ wide. The spine, lettered in gilt but undecorated, reads: "THE | OTHER | HOUSE | HENRY | JAMES | HEINEMANN". The publisher's imprint at the foot of the spine is in serif capitals $^{1}/_{8}''$ high. The end-papers are of white wove paper, and the text is printed on wove paper. All edges are trimmed. There are no ads bound in at the end.

47.9.0. *The Other House*, second edition, colonial sheets bound for the domestic market, one volume, London 1897.

This copy is identical to the second edition, second impression, 47.8.0, except that it does not have stamped on [2] "Printed in Great Britain".

47.10.0. *The Other House*, first American edition, first impression, one volume, New York and London 1896.

THE OTHER HOUSE | BY | HENRY JAMES | AUTHOR OF "DAISY MILLER," "THE EUROPEANS" | ETC., ETC. | New York [in Gothic type] | THE MACMILLAN COMPANY | LONDON: MACMILLAN & CO., Ltd. | 1896 | All rights reserved [in italic]

Size: 7 $^{1}/_{2}''$ x 5 $^{1}/_{8}''$.

Collation: [1–24^8 25^6], signed as [A]^2 [B]^8 C-I K–U X–Z 2A–2B^8 2C^4; pp. [i–iv] [1–2], 3–388 [389–392].

Contents: [i–ii] half-title, verso publisher's device; [iii–iv] title-page, verso copyright notice and printer's imprint: "Copyright, 1896, | By THE MACMILLAN COMPANY. | Norwood Press [in Gothic type] | J. S. Cushing & Co. – Berwick & Smith | Norwood Mass. U.S.A."; [1–2] divisional fly-title, verso blank; 3–388 text; [389–391] ads; [392] blank. The ads are headed: [389] "EMBARRASSMENTS.", with a full page of press opinions; [390] "WORKS BY HENRY JAMES.", listing 7 titles, 6 with press opinions; and [391] "WORKS BY HENRY JAMES.", listing 2 titles with press opinion; [392] blank. All the ads have dollar prices.

THE OTHER HOUSE

Binding: claret linen-grain cloth. The front and back covers have a single-rule border in blind, with no lettering or other decoration. The spine, lettered in gilt and decorated in gilt and in blind, reads: "[rule in blind] | THE | OTHER | HOUSE [title on three lines, underscored with gilt rules] | HENRY JAMES | THE MACMILLAN | COMPANY | [rule in blind]". The publisher's imprint at the foot of the spine is in capitals of uniform size $1/8''$ high. The endpapers are of smooth white wove paper, and the text and the three pages of undated ads at the end, which are on the last two leaves of signature [25], are printed on laid paper. The top edge is gilt, and the other edges are untrimmed.

BAL 10621 records the bindings as red and also maroon, linen. E&L A47b records a claret but not a maroon binding.

BAL also records that the copyright deposit copies have the title on the spine (underscored) on two lines rather than the three lines for the first published copies, and have white laid rather than white wove endpapers. It characterizes these bindings on the deposit copies as variant or possibly trial bindings. However, in view of the fact that the second impression of the first American edition has the same spine lettering and the same laid endpapers as the deposit copies (see 47.11.0), and was printed only a month after the first impression, it is possible that the deposit copies were of the second impression. The second and third impressions were printed on a thicker paper than the first, and it is the width of the spine which determines whether the title could be accommodated on two rather than three lines.

American printing history. There is no information in the Macmillan & Co. (N.Y.) Archive as to the printing history of this title; however, the title-page verso of 47.12.0 indicates that there were three impressions, the first in October 1896, the second in November 1896 and the third in January 1897. E&L A47b records that 2150 copies of the first impression were printed, but erroneously records that there was only one printing of the first American edition.

Priced at $1.50 (all impressions).

THE SPOILS OF POYNTON

47.11.0. *The Other House*, first American edition, second impression, one volume, New York and London 1896.

The title-page, size, and collation are identical to those of the first American edition, first impression, 47.10.0.

The contents (including the three pages of ads at the end) are identical to those of 47.10.0, except that the title-leaf verso reads: "Copyright, 1896, | By THE MACMILLAN COMPANY. | [rule] | Set up and electrotyped October, 1896. Reprinted November, | 1896. | Norwood Press [in Gothic type] | J. S. Cushing & Co.– Berwick & Smith | Norwood Mass. U.S.A."

Binding: claret linen-grain cloth identical to the binding on 47.10.0, except that the spine reads: "[rule in blind] | THE | OTHER HOUSE [title on two lines, underscored with gilt rules] | HENRY JAMES | THE MACMILLAN | COMPANY | [rule in blind]". The publisher's imprint at the foot of the spine is in uniform capitals $1/8''$ high. The endpapers are of white laid paper, and the text and the three pages of ads at the end, which are the last two leaves of signature [25], are printed on laid paper. The top edge is gilt and the other edges are untrimmed.

This copy is printed on thicker paper than that used for 47.10.0, this volume being 1.25″ thick as against 1.03″ thick for the first impression. These measurements are of the text pages without the boards. The thicker paper used in this copy permitted the spine to accommodate the title in two rather than three lines; see 47.10.0.

On the recto of the front free endpaper is an inscription dated "Feby 1897".

47.12.0. *The Other House*, first American edition, third impression, one volume, New York and London 1897.

The title-page is identical to that of the first American edition, first impression, 47.10.0, except that it is dated 1897.

Size: $7\,7/16''$ x $5''$.

The collation is identical to that of 47.10.0.

The contents (including the three pages of ads at the end) are identical to those of 47.10.0, except that the title-leaf verso reads: "Copyright, 1896, | By THE MACMILLAN COMPANY. | [rule] | Set up and electrotyped October, 1896. Reprinted November, | 1896; January, 1897.

| Norwood Press [in Gothic type] | J. S. Cushing & Co. – Berwick & Smith | Norwood Mass. U.S.A."

Binding: claret linen-grain cloth, identical to the binding on 47.10.0, except that the spine reads: "[rule in blind] | THE | OTHER HOUSE [title on two lines underscored with gilt rules] | HENRY JAMES | THE MACMILLAN | COMPANY | [rule in blind]". The publisher's imprint at the foot of the spine is in uniform capitals $^{1}/_{8}$" high. The endpapers are of white laid paper, and the text and the three pages of ads at the end, which are the last two leaves of signature [25], are printed on laid paper. The top edge is gilt, and the other edges are untrimmed.

This impression is printed on thicker paper than the paper used for the first American edition, first impression. This impression, like the second impression, is 1.25" thick a against 1.03" thick for the first impression. The measurements are of the text pages without the boards.

48. *THE SPOILS OF POYNTON*

48.1.0. *The Spoils of Poynton*, first edition, first impression, one volume, London 1897.

THE | SPOILS OF POYNTON [in red] | By Henry James | AUTHOR OF | "TERMINATIONS," "EMBARRASSMENTS" | [small acorn device] | LONDON: WILLIAM HEINEMANN [in red] | MDCCCXCVII

Size: $7\,^{7}/_{16}$" x 5".

Collation: [A]^2 B–I K–T^8; pp. [i–iv], [1]–286 [287–288].

Contents: [i–ii] half-title, verso ad headed: "By the Same Author, 6s. each.", listing *Terminations* and *Embarrassments*, with press opinions; [iii–iv] title-page, verso reservation of rights: "All rights reserved. [in italic]"; [1]–286 text; 286 at foot printer's imprint: "[rule] | Richard Clay & Sons, Limited, London & Bungay. [all in italic]"; [287] ad for *Embarrassments*, with a full-page of press opinions; [288] blank.

Binding: light blue diagonal-fine-ribbed cloth, with four irises in blind on the front cover, and publisher's device in blind on the back cover. The title, "THE SPOILS OF POYNTON", in gilt on the front cover is in uniform capitals 3 1/8" wide. The spine, lettered in gilt but undecorated, reads: "THE SPOILS | OF | POYNTON | HENRY | JAMES | HEINEMANN". The word "OF" in the title on the spine is in a font 1/8" high, while the rest of the title is in a font 3/16" high. The publisher's imprint at the foot of the spine is in uniform capitals 3/16" high. The endpapers are of white laid paper, and the text is printed on laid paper. The top edge is untrimmed, and the other edges are rough trimmed. Bound in at the end is a 32-page undated and unpaginated catalogue of ads printed on wove paper, the first page devoted to Caine's *The Manxman*, and each page devoted to a single title, with press opinions. These are the same ads as are bound in at the end of the first editions, first impressions, of *Embarrassments*, 46.1.0, and *The Other House*, 47.1.0.

English printing history. Heinemann Archive. First edition, one volume: first impression, 2,000 copies, published February 6, 1897, priced at 6s. The record indicates that moulds were made. On an unspecified date in 1897 a colonial impression of 1,000 copies was printed. There is no information as to price; however, as was the case with all other James titles published by Heinemann in the colonies, the nominal retail price was 3s.6d. for copies in cloth and 2s. 6d. for wrappered copies. Three hundred sets of colonial sheets were diverted for use in the domestic market.

A second English edition was published by Macmillan as part of Volume XV of *The Novels and Stories of Henry James*, see 86.1.0–86.2.0.

48.2.0. *The Spoils of Poynton*, first edition, first impression, one volume, London 1897.

The title-page, size, collation, and contents (including the ad on [287]) are identical to those of the first edition, first impression, 48.1.0.

Binding: light blue diagonal-fine-ribbed cloth, with nine tulips in blind on the front cover, and the publisher's device in blind on the back cover. The title, "The SPOILS of POYNTON", in gilt on the front cover is in uniform capitals 3 5/32" wide, with the exception of the words "The" and "of" which are all or partly in lower case letters. The spine, lettered in gilt but undecorated, reads: "THE SPOILS | OF | POYNTON | HENRY | JAMES | HEINEMANN". The word "OF" in the title on the spine is in a font 1/8" high, while the rest of the title is in

THE SPOILS OF POYNTON

a font ³⁄₁₆″ high. The publisher's imprint at the foot of the spine is in uniform capitals ⅛″ high. The endpapers are of white wove paper, and the text is printed on laid paper. All edges are untrimmed. No ads are bound in at the end.

See E&L Plates VI (ii) and VII (ii a).

48.3.0. *The Spoils of Poynton*, first edition, second impression (colonial), cloth binding state, one volume, London 1897.

THE SPOILS OF POYNTON | BY | HENRY JAMES | AUTHOR OF "TERMINATIONS," "EMBARRASSMENTS, ETC. | LONDON | WILLIAM HEINEMANN | 1897 [all the foregoing in black]

Size: 7 ³⁄₁₆″ x 4 ⅝″.

Collation: [A]² B–I K–T⁸; pp. [i–iv], [1]–286 [287–288].

Contents: [i–ii] "Heinemann's Colonial Library of Popular Fiction. [in Gothic type, underscored] | Issued for sale in the British | Colonies and India, and not | to be imported into Europe or | the United States of America. [sale limitation all in italic]", verso ad headed: "By the Same Author, uniform with this volume. [in italic]", listing *Terminations*, and *Embarrassments*, with press opinions; [iii–iv] title-page, verso reservation of rights: "All rights reserved. [in italic]"; [1]–286 text; 286 at foot printer's imprint: "[rule] | Richard Clay & Sons, Limited, London & Bungay. [in italic]"; [287] ad for *Embarrassments*, with a full page of press opinions; [288] blank.

Binding: bright red pebble-grain cloth. On the front cover the title is lettered in black within a single-rule border in blind. On the back cover the publisher's device in black is within a single-rule border in blind. The spine, lettered and decorated in black, reads: "[rule] | The | Spoils | of | Poynton | [short rule] | Henry | James | Heinemann | [rule]". The endpapers are of light cream wove paper, and the text is printed on wove paper. The front and rear pastedowns have ads printed on them, as do the recto and verso of the front and rear free endpapers. All edges are trimmed. An 8-page unpaginated and undated publisher's catalogue of ads, printed on wove paper, is bound in at the end.

48.4.0. *The Spoils of Poynton*, first edition, mixed colonial and domestic sheets bound for the domestic market, one volume, London 1897.

THE SPOILS OF POYNTON | BY | HENRY JAMES | AUTHOR OF | "TERMINATIONS," "EMBARRASSMENTS," ETC. | LONDON | WILLIAM HEINEMANN | 1897 [all the foregoing in black]

Size: 7 1/2" x 5".

Collation: [A]¹ B–I K–T⁸; pp. [i–ii], [1]–286 [287–288]. Signatures [A] and B are of colonial sheets, and the balance of the volume is of domestic sheets.

Contents: [i–ii] title-page, verso reservation of rights: "All rights reserved. [in italic]"; [1]–286 text; 286 at foot printer's imprint: "[rule] | Richard Clay & Sons, Limited, London & Bungay. [all in italic]"; [287] ad for *Embarrassments*, with press opinions; [288] blank.

Binding: light blue diagonal-fine-ribbed cloth (lighter and with a more greenish cast than 48.1.0 and 48.2.0), with nine tulips in blind on the front cover, and the publisher's device in blind on the back cover. The title, "The SPOILS of POYNTON", in gilt on the front cover is in uniform capitals 3 1/4" wide, with the exception of the words "The" and "of" which are all or partly in lower case letters. The spine, lettered in gilt but undecorated, reads: "THE SPOILS | OF | POYNTON | HENRY | JAMES | HEINEMANN". The word "OF" in the title on the spine is in a font 1/8" high, while the rest of the title is in a font 3/16" high. The publisher's imprint at the foot of the spine is in uniform capitals 1/8" high. The endpapers are of white wove paper, signatures [A] and B are printed on wove paper (sheets of the colonial impression), and the balance of the signatures are printed on laid paper (sheets of the domestic impression). All edges are untrimmed. There are no ads bound in at the end.

48.5.0. *The Spoils of Poynton*, first edition, second impression, colonial sheets bound for the domestic market, one volume, London 1897.

The title-page, printed in black, is identical to that of the first edition, second impression (colonial), 48.3.0.

Size: 7 9/16" x 5".

The collation and contents (including the ad on [287]) are identical to those of 48.3.0, except that the first signature is [A]¹ rather than [A]², the colonial series half-title having been excised.

THE SPOILS OF POYNTON

Binding: light blue diagonal-fine-ribbed cloth, with nine tulips in blind on the front cover, and the publisher's device in blind on the back cover. The title, "THE SPOILS of POYNTON", in gilt on the front cover is in uniform capitals 3 $^{11}/_{32}$" wide, with the exception of the word "of" which is in lower case letters. The spine, lettered in gilt but undecorated, reads: "THE | SPOILS | OF | POYNTON | HENRY | JAMES | HEINEMANN". The word "OF" in the title on the spine is in a font $^1/_8$" high, while the rest of the title is in a font $^3/_{16}$" high. The publisher's imprint at the foot of the spine is in uniform capitals $^1/_8$" high. The endpapers are of white wove paper, and the text is printed entirely on wove paper. All edges are untrimmed. No catalogue of ads is bound in at the end.

Dust-jacket: semi-transparent onion-skin paper with no lettering or decoration on it.

48.6.0. *The Spoils of Poynton*, first American edition, first impression, one volume, Boston and New York 1897.

The Spoils of Poynton | By | Henry James | [oblong publisher's device of a piper under a tree not within a frame] | BOSTON AND NEW YORK | HOUGHTON, MIFFLIN AND COMPANY | The Riverside Press, Cambridge [in Gothic type] | 1897

Size: 7 $^3/_8$" x 5".

Collation: [unsigned, 1–20^8 21^4]; pp. [i–iv], [1]–323 [324].

Contents: [i–ii] blank, verso, within a single-rule frame, ad headed: "Henry James's Books. [in Gothic type]", listing 16 titles with dollar prices, the last listed being this title; [iii–iv] title-page, verso copyright notice, reservation of rights and printer's imprint: "Copyright, 1896, | By HENRY JAMES. | All rights reserved. [in italic] | The Riverside Press, Cambridge, Mass., U.S.A. [in italic] | Electrotyped and Printed by H. O. Houghton & Company."; [1]–323 text; [324] blank.

Binding: brown vertical-rib-grain cloth, with lettering and decoration in gilt on the front cover and spine. The front cover has within a single-rule border an elaborate centered cartouche within which are the title and author's name separated by a decorative rule. The spine reads: "[rule] | THE SPOILS | OF POYNTON | [decorative rule] | HENRY JAMES | HOUGHTON | MIFFLIN & CO. | [rule]". The ampersand in the publisher's imprint on the spine is stylized. The back cover has a single-rule border in blind. The endpapers are of white laid paper, and the text is printed on laid paper. A binder's fly-leaf of laid paper is at both the front and back. The top edge is trimmed and appears to be stained brown, the bottom edge is rough trimmed, and the fore-edge is untrimmed.

This is a copy in one of the two primary binding states described by E&L.

Illustrated Plate 19.

This style of binding, in brown (as above) and in olive-green (as in 48.7.0) vertical-rib-grain cloth with uniform lettering and decoration, was used by Houghton, Mifflin on James's works (principally reprints of titles issued earlier) from 1897 until at least 1910. Its first appearance on a James title was on the first American edition, first impression, of *The Spoils of Poynton*. In all 15 James titles were issued in this binding. Thirteen of these titles, uniformly bound, were advertised as being sold boxed for $22.00; see the ad on [ii] in this copy.[34] This style of binding was also used on post-1897 bindings-up of sheets printed prior to 1897; see e.g. *Roderick Hudson*, 3.11.5.

American printing history. Houghton Mifflin Archive. First edition: Ms Am 2030(21), 221: *first impression* January 25, 1897, 1554 copies, 1527 bound between January 27 and February 24, 1897; *second impression* March 10, 1897, 508 copies, 518 [sic] bound between March 26, 1897, and March 14, 1904. Ms Am 2030(22), 219: *third impression* May 25, 1905, 150 copies, all bound between June 7, 1905, and April 18, 1906; *fourth impression* January 25, 1909, 158 copies, 150 bound between February 24, 1909, and March 28, 1912; *fifth impression* May 21, 1914, 159 copies, 153 bound on November 14, 1914, and August 18, 1916; *sixth impression* May 22, 1918, 286 copies all of which were bound between October 16, 1918, and February 4, 1921; *seventh impression* June 14, 1922, 284 copies, 268 bound between August 29, 1922, and October 26, 1923; notation: "[total copies printed] 3099".

A second American edition was published as Volume X of *The Novels and Tales of Henry James*; see 64.1.0.

---

34 These thirteen titles are: *A Passionate Pilgrim, Transatlantic Sketches, Roderick Hudson, The American, The Europeans, Confidence, The Portrait of A Lady, The Author of Beltraffio, The Siege of London, Tales of Three Cities, A Little Tour in France, Portraits of Places,* and *Daisy Miller. The Tragic Muse* and *The Spoils of Poynton* were also issued in this uniform binding but were not included in this boxed set presumably because these two titles had recent first publication.

48.7.0. *The Spoils of Poynton*, first American edition, first impression, one volume, Boston and New York 1897.

The title-page, size, collation, and contents (including the verso of the title-leaf and the ad on [ii]) are identical to those of the first American edition, first impression, 48.6.0.

Binding: olive-green vertical-rib-grain cloth, with lettering and decoration on the front cover and spine, and in blind on the back cover identical to those on 48.6.0. The endpapers are of white laid paper, and the text is printed on laid paper. A binder's fly-leaf of laid paper is at both the front and the back. The top edge is trimmed and appears to be stained brown, the bottom edge is rough trimmed and the fore-edge is untrimmed.

This binding state is the second of the two primary binding states, which is described as "dark green" in E&L A48b. BAL 10623 records the two states as "brown" and "green".

Illustrated Plate 19.

48.8.0. *The Spoils of Poynton*, first American edition, second (?) impression, one volume, Boston and New York 1897.

The title-page, collation, and contents (including the ad on [ii] and the verso of the title-leaf) are identical to those of the first American edition, first impression, 48.6.0.

Size: $7\,^{3}/_{8}''$ x $4\,^{15}/_{16}''$.

Binding: maroon fine-diaper cloth, with decoration and lettering in gilt on the front cover and spine identical to (including the publisher's imprint with a stylized ampersand at the foot of the spine), 48.6.0, except that the single-rule border on the front cover, and the rule at the head and foot of the spine, are in blind rather than gilt. The endpapers are of white laid paper, and the text is printed on laid paper. A binder's fly-leaf of laid paper is at both the front and the back. The top edge is trimmed and appears to be stained brown, and the other edges are rough trimmed.

48.9.0. *The Spoils of Poynton*, first American edition, fifth or later impression, one volume, Boston and New York [n.d., 1914 or later].

The Spoils of Poynton | By | Henry James | [oblong publisher's device of a piper under a tree not within a frame] | BOSTON AND NEW YORK | HOUGHTON MIFFLIN COMPANY | The Riverside Press Cambridge

Size: 7 7/16" x 5".

The collation and contents are identical to those of the first American edition, first impression, 48.6.0, except that the ad on [ii] is headed: "By Henry James [in Gothic type]", lists 17 titles without dollar prices, the first 3 of which are *The Question of Our Speech, English Hours* and *Italian Hours* (none of these titles are present in the ad on [ii] in the first American edition, first impression), and drops two titles, *The Author of Beltraffio* and *Watch and Ward*; the title-leaf verso reads: "Copyright, 1896, | By HENRY JAMES | All rights reserved. [in italic]", but without a printer's imprint.

Binding: smooth blue glazed cloth, lettered and decorated in black and gilt. The front cover, within a double-rule black border within which is a black single-rule frame, is lettered and decorated in gilt, and reads: "[decorative device of rules, dots and flowers] | THE SPOILS | OF POYNTON | [small four-cornered device] | HENRY [dot] JAMES". The spine, lettered in gilt, and decorated in gilt with an oblong frame within which are five decorative ovals in each of which is a stem of flowers, reads: "THE | SPOILS OF | POYNTON | [small decorative device] | HENRY | JAMES". The back cover is blank. The endpapers are of white wove paper, and the text is printed on wove paper. There are no binder's fly-leaves. The top edge is gilt, and the other edges are rough trimmed.

The presence of the title *Italian Hours* (published November 1909) in the ad shows that this impression was printed no earlier than the fifth impression, printed in May 1914, as the prior impression was printed in January 1909.

For bindings uniform with this binding see 1.11.0.

49. *WHAT MAISIE KNEW*

49.1.0. *What Maisie Knew*, first edition, first impression, one volume, London 1898 [1897].

WHAT MAISIE KNEW [in red] | By Henry James | [small acorn device] | LONDON: WILLIAM HEINEMANN [in red] | MDCCCXCVIII

Size: 7 ½" x 5".

Collation : π^2 A–I K–T^8; pp. [i–iv], [1]–304.

Contents: [i–ii] half-title, verso ad headed: "By the Same Author, 6s. each. [in italic]", listing *The Spoils of Poynton, The Other House, Terminations* and *Embarrassments* with press opinions; [iii–iv] title-page, verso reservation of rights: "All rights reserved [in italic]"; [1]–304 text; 304 at foot printer's imprint: "Printed by Ballantyne, Hanson & Co. | London & Edinburgh".

Binding: light blue diagonal-fine-ribbed cloth, with four irises in blind on the front cover, and the publisher's device in blind on the back cover. The title, "WHAT MAISIE KNEW", in gilt on the front cover is in uniform capitals 2 9/16" wide. The spine, lettered in gilt but undecorated, reads: "WHAT MAISIE | KNEW | HENRY | JAMES | HEINEMANN". The publisher's imprint at the foot of the spine is in uniform capitals 3/32" high. The endpapers are of white laid paper, and the text is printed on laid paper. The top and fore-edges are untrimmed, and the bottom edge is rough trimmed. Bound in at the end are 32 pages of unpaginated and undated ads, signed A and A2, on a fairly heavy wove paper, each page of which is devoted to one or two titles with press opinions, the first to Harold Frederic's *Illumination*. These ads are the same as those at the end of the second edition, first impression, of *Embarrassments*, 46.1.0, and *The Other House*, 47.4.0.

BAL 10625 and E&L A49a both record the first edition, first impression, of this title as being published in 1897. This is corroborated by the printing history on [iv] of the third impression which records that the first impression was printed in September 1897, and that there were two further printing in that year.

English printing history. Heinemann Archive. First edition, one volume: first impression, an unspecified number of copies, published September 17, 1897, priced at 6s. A further impression for the colonial market was printed in August 1897 (the second impression), but not published until March 23, 1898, bound in both cloth and paper wrappers. It was priced at 3s. 6d. in cloth and 2s. 6d. in paper wrappers.

From the books themselves it is clear that there were two further domestic impression printed in October 1897 (the third impression) and December 1897 (the fourth impression), respectively; see 49.2.0–49.3.0. E&L A49 records that 2,000 copies of the first impression were printed. The number of copies printed of the two further domestic impressions or the colonial impression are unknown. E&L also records that 125 sets of sheets of the colonial impression were diverted for use in the domestic market; see 49.5.0.

49.2.0. *What Maisie Knew*, first edition, third impression, one volume, London 1898 [1897].

The title-page, size, and collation are identical to those of the first edition, first impression, 49.1.0.

The contents are identical to those of 49.1.0, except that the verso of the title-leaf reads: "First Edition, September 1897 | Reprinted, October 1897 | All rights reserved [all of the foregoing in italic]".

Binding: light blue diagonal-fine-ribbed cloth, with four irises in blind on the front cover, and publisher's device in blind on the back cover. The lettering in gilt on the front cover and spine are identical to that on 49.1.0. The endpapers are of white laid paper, and the text is printed on laid paper. The top edge is untrimmed, and the other edges are rough trimmed. Bound in at the end is a 16-page paginated publisher's catalogue printed on wove paper, the first page of which reads: "Mr. William Heinemann's | Autumn Announcements | mdcccxcvii | [publisher's square device with windmill and W. H.] | THE BOOKS MENTIONED IN THIS LIST MAY | BE OBTAINED THROUGH ANY | BOOKSELLER [the last three lines in italic, and all of the foregoing within a large thin single-rule rule border]".

The publisher's catalogue bound in at the end of this copy differs from the ads bound in at the end of the copy of the first impression and the fourth impression.

WHAT MAISIE KNEW

49.3.0. *What Maisie Knew*, first edition, fourth impression, one volume, London 1898.

Size: 7 9/16" x 5".

The title-page and collation are identical to those of the first edition, first impression, 49.1.0.

The contents are identical to those of 49.1.0, except that the verso of the title-leaf reads: "First Edition, September 1897 | Reprinted, October 1897 | Reprinted, December 1897 | All rights reserved [all of the foregoing in italic]".

Binding: light blue diagonal-fine-ribbed cloth, with four irises in blind on the front cover, and publisher's device in blind on the back cover. The lettering in gilt on the front cover and spine is identical to that on 49.1.0. The endpapers are of white laid paper, and the text is printed on laid paper. The top edge is untrimmed, and the other edges are rough trimmed. Bound in at the end are 32 pages of undated and unpaginated ads, signed A and A2, printed on a lighter wove paper, each page is devoted to one or two titles with press opinions, the first page to Harold Frederic's *Illumination*. These ads are the same as those which appear at the end of the first impression of this title and the second English edition of *The Other House*, 47.4.0.

E&L A49b records the third impression (actually the fourth impression, as the colonial impression preceded it) as being bound in the second standard binding (nine tulips), which is not the case with this copy which is in the first standard binding (four irises). Given the December 1897 printing of this impression, it may have been published in 1898 rather than 1897.

49.4.0. *What Maisie Knew*, first edition, second impression (colonial), cloth binding state, one volume, London 1897 [1898].

WHAT MAISIE KNEW | BY | HENRY JAMES | LONDON | WILLIAM HEINEMANN | 1897 [all the foregoing in black]

Size: 7 1/4" x 4 3/4".

Collation: π^2 A–I K–T^8; [i–iv], [1]–304.

Contents: [i–ii] "Heinemann's Colonial Library of Popular Fiction. [in Gothic type underscored] | Issued for sale in the British Colonies | and India, and not to be imported | into Europe or the United States

| of America. [sale limitation in italic]", verso ad for work "BY THE SAME AUTHOR [in italic]", listing 4 titles; [iii–iv] title-page, verso reservation of rights: "All rights reserved [in italic]"; [1]–304 text; 304 at foot printer's imprint: "Printed by Ballantyne, Hanson & Co. | London & Edinburgh."

Binding: bright red pebble-grain cloth. On the front cover the title is lettered in black within a single-rule border in blind. On the back cover the publisher's device in black is within a single-rule border in blind. The spine, lettered and decorated in black, reads: "[rule] | What | Maisie | Knew | [short rule] | Henry | James | Heinemann | [rule]". The endpapers are of light cream wove paper, and the text is printed on wove paper. The front and rear pastedowns have ads on them, as do the recto and verso of the front and rear free endpapers. All edges are trimmed. A 12-page undated and unpaginated publisher's catalogue of ads headed on each page "MR. WILLIAM HEINEMANN'S LIST", printed on thin wove paper, is bound in at the end.

Noted but not described in E&L A49a. The sequence of the printing of the first domestic impression, 49.1.0, and this colonial impression is not entirely clear; see the English printing history following 49.1.0 as to what is known of the dates of printing and publication.

49.5.0. *What Maisie Knew*, first edition, colonial sheets bound for the domestic market, one volume, London 1897 [1898].

WHAT MAISIE KNEW | BY | HENRY JAMES | LONDON | WILLIAM HEINEMANN | 1897 [all the foregoing in black]

Size: $7\frac{1}{4}"$ x $4\frac{3}{4}"$.

Collation: $\pi^2(-\pi_1)$ A–I K–T^8; [i–ii], [1]–304. The colonial series half-title leaf, π_1 in the first edition, second impression (colonial), 49.4.0, has been excised.

Contents: [i–ii] title-page, verso reservation of rights: "All rights reserved [in italic]"; [1]–304 text; 304 at the foot printer's imprint: "Printed by Ballantyne, Hanson & Co. | London & Edinburgh."

Binding: light blue diagonal-fine-ribbed cloth, with nine tulips in blind on the front cover, and the publisher's device in blind on the back cover. The title, "WHAT MAISIE KNEW", in gilt on the front cover is in large ($\frac{1}{4}"$ high) uniform capitals 4" wide. The spine, lettered in gilt but undecorated, reads: "WHAT | MAISIE | KNEW | HENRY | JAMES | HEINEMANN". The title on the spine is in uniform capitals $^3/_{16}$" high. The publisher's imprint at the foot is in uniform capitals $^1/_8$" high. The endpapers are of white wove paper, and the text is printed on wove paper. All edges are trimmed. A 10-page undated and unpaginated catalogue of ads, headed on each page: "MR. WILLIAM HEINEMANN'S LIST", printed on thin wove paper, is bound in at the end.

49.6.0. *What Maisie Knew*, first American edition, first impression, one volume, Chicago and New York 1897.

What Maisie Knew | BY | HENRY JAMES | [publisher's device in red] | HERBERT S. STONE & CO. | CHICAGO & NEW YORK | MDCCCXCVII [all of the foregoing within a black double-rule frame]

Size: $7 \frac{1}{2}$" x $4 \frac{3}{4}$".

Collation: $\pi^2 [1]^8 \, 2\text{--}29^8 \, 30^4$; pp. [i–iv], [1]–470 [471–472].

Contents: [i–ii] half-title, verso blank; [iii–iv] title-page, verso copyright notice: "COPYRIGHT 1897 BY | HERBERT S. STONE & CO."; [1]–470 text; [471] rectangular printer's device of John Wilson & Son; [472] blank.

Binding: dark olive-green linen-grain cloth. The front and back covers are identically lettered and decorated in gilt within a thick single-rule border in blind, and read: "WHAT MAISIE KNEW | by [in swash italic] | HENRY JAMES | [three leaf devices]". The spine, lettered and decorated in gilt, reads within a gilt single-rule border: "WHAT | MAISIE | KNEW | by [in swash italic] | HENRY | JAMES | [rule connecting both sides of the border] | [long strapwork design] | [rule connecting both sides of the border] | STONE | CHICAGO | [rule connecting both sides of the border] | [smaller strapwork design] | 1897 [below the border]". The endpapers are of, and the text is printed on, laid paper watermarked "Stone & Kimball | New York". Double binder's fly-leaves of laid paper are at both the front and the back. The top edge is gilt, and the other edges are untrimmed.

This book was designed by Frank Hazen; see Sue Allen and Charles Gullans, *Decorated Cloth In America: Publishers' Bindings 1840–1910* (Center for 17th and 18th Century Studies, UCLA, Williams Andrews Clark Memorial Library, 1994), 75–91 and Plate 39.

Illustrated Plate 20.

BAL 10627 queries whether the Stone & Kimball watermark might be a distinguishing feature of the first printing, noting that Herbert S. Stone & Company succeeded Stone & Kimball in 1896. E&L A49b disputes this, stating: "we have noted both watermarks in first impression copies." However, E&L does not state what other features might distinguish the second from the first printing. Kramer at [138] records that a second impression was printed, so marked, and was printed not by John Wilson & Son but by the Lakeside Press in Chicago on laid paper with the watermark "H. S. Stone & Company | Chicago | The Chap Book". As both this copy and 49.7.0 were printed by John Wilson & Son, and neither indicates it is a second impression, it could be concluded that they are part of a single impression. However, other differences (type of paper and collation) indicate that they may represent two impressions. No copy marked "second impression" has been found. The differences between this copy and 49.7.0 indicate that further study is warranted.

American Printing History. Kramer [138]. First edition: the first impression of the first edition was published November 1897 (the number of copies printed is unknown). It was priced at $1.50. Kramer records that a second impression was printed in 1898, but makes no mention of a third impression and also a possible fourth impression, both printed in 1898; see 49.8.0 and 49.9.0.

A second edition was published by Scribner's as part of Volumes XI of *The Novels and Tales of Henry James* (the New York Edition); see 64.1.0.

A single impression of 510 copies of a first separate impression of the second edition (the New York Edition) of this title, in one volume, was printed by Scribner's on September 28, 1923. All the sheets of this impression were bound between September 22, 1923 and August 4, 1924. It was published by Scribner's on September 28, 1923, priced at $2.50; see 49.10.0.

49.7.0. *What Maisie Knew*, first American edition, second (?) impression, one volume, Chicago and New York 1897.

The title-page and size are identical to those of the first American edition, first impression, 49.6.0.

The collation of this copy differs from that of the first impression, in that the first signature is $\pi^2(-\pi_1)$, the half-title being excised.

The contents (including the title-leaf verso and the printer's device on [471]) are identical to those of 49.6.0, except that the half-title is not present.

Binding: identical to that of the first impression, including the date "1897" in gilt at the foot of the spine. However, the endpapers are of, and the text is printed on, laid paper watermarked "H.S. Stone & Company | Chicago | The Chap Book". There are no binder's fly-leaves. The top edge is gilt, and the other edges are untrimmed.

Illustrated Plate 20.

49.8.0. *What Maisie Knew*, first American edition, third impression, one volume, Chicago and New York 1898.

The title-page is identical to that of the first American edition, first impression, 49.6.0, except that it is dated 1898 at the foot.

The size and collation are identical to those of the first impression, except that the first signature is π^4.

Contents: identical to those of the first impression, except that the half-title is preceded by two blank leaves, the title-leaf verso reads: "COPYRIGHT 1897 BY | HERBERT S. STONE & CO. | THIRD | IMPRESSION", on [471] no printer's device is present, and on that page the printer's imprint reads: "PRINTED AT THE LAKESIDE PRESS | BY R. R. DONNELLEY & SONS CO. | CHICAGO, ILLINOIS, MDCCCXCVIII"; [472] blank.

Binding: identical to those of the first and second impressions, except that the date in gilt at the foot of the spine is "1898". The endpapers are of, and the text is printed on, laid paper watermarked "H.S. Stone & Company | Chicago | The Chap Book". There are double binder's fly-leaves of laid paper at the back, but none at the front. The top edge is gilt, and the other edges are untrimmed.

Not recorded in Kramer.

Illustrated Plate 20.

49.9.0. *What Maisie Knew*, first American edition, third or fourth impression, one volume, Chicago and New York, [1898].

The title-page is missing.

IN THE CAGE

Size: 7 7/16″ x 4 13/16″.

Collation: π^2 [1]^8 2–29^8 30^4. pp. [i–iv], [1]–470 [471–472]. π_2, the title-leaf, is missing.

Contents: [i–ii] half-title, verso blank, [iii–iv] the title-leaf is missing; [1]–470 text; [471] printer's imprint: "PRINTED AT THE LAKESIDE PRESS | BY R. R. DONNELLEY & SONS CO. | CHICAGO, ILLINOIS, MDCCCXCVIII"; [472] blank.

Binding: dark olive-green linen-grain cloth. The front and back covers are lettered and decorated in gilt identically to that on the first American edition, first impression, 49.6.0. The spine, which is also lettered and decorated in gilt, is identical to the spine of 49.6.0, except that there is no date at the foot. It has endpapers of white laid paper, and the text is printed on laid paper watermarked "H. S. Stone & Company | Chicago | The Chap Book". A single binder's fly-leaf is at the front and a double binder's fly-leaf at the back, all of laid paper. The top edge is gilt, and the other edges are untrimmed.

This copy is either a later binding-up of the third impression sheets (which is suggested by the printer's imprint on [471]), or a fourth impression.

Illustrated Plate 20.

49.10.0. *What Maisie Knew*, second American edition, first separate impression, one volume, New York 1923.

What Maisie Knew | By [in swash italic] | Henry James | [small flower device] | New York | Charles Scribner's Sons | 1923 [all the foregoing within a double-rule frame]

Size: 7 1/2″ x 4 7/8″.

Collation: [unsigned, 1–23^8]; pp. [i–iv] 1–2, 3–[363] [364].

Contents: [i–ii] half-title, verso ad headed: "NOVELS BY HENRY JAMES | PUBLISHED BY CHARLES SCRIBNER'S SONS", listing 9 titles, "Per volume $2.50 [in italic] | The novels of Henry James, published by | Houghton, Mifflin Co., and Harper Brothers | are issued in a style uniform with the above | rule | NOVELS AND TALES OF HENRY JAMES | NEW YORK EDITION | Sold by subscription only | 26 volumes, $91.00 [in italic]"; [iii–iv] title-page, verso copyright notice and printer's imprint: "COPYRIGHT, 1897, BY | HERBERT S. STONE

IN THE CAGE

& CO.|[rule]|COPYRIGHT, 1908, BY|CHARLES SCRIBNER'S SONS|[rule]|printed in the United States of America"; [1–2] fly-title, verso blank; 3–[363] text; [364] blank.

Binding: dark blue vertical rib-grain cloth. The front cover is lettered with Henry James's facsimile signature in gilt. The back cover is neither lettered nor decorated. The spine, which is lettered and decorated in gilt, reads: "[two rules]|WHAT|MAISIE|KNEW|HENRY|JAMES|SCRIBNERS|[two rules]". The endpapers are of white wove paper, and the text is printed on rough wove paper. There are no binder's fly-leaves. The top edge is trimmed and stained light brown, and the fore and the bottom edges are rough-trimmed.

This copy is printed from the plates of this title from *The Novels and Tales of Henry James*, The New York Edition; see 64.1.0, Volume XI, which also contains 'In the Cage' and 'The Pupil', not included in this impression.

※✢※

50. JOHN DELAVOY

No copy in the collection.

E&L A50 records that only two copies are known to be extant. It was printed for copyright purposes only.

※✢※

51. IN THE CAGE

51.1.0. *In the Cage*, first edition, first impression, binding state A, one volume, London 1898.

IN THE CAGE|BY|HENRY JAMES|[publisher's device]|LONDON|DUCKWORTH AND CO.|3 HENRIETTA STREET, W.C.|1898

Size: 7 3/8" x 4 15/16".

Collation: π^2 A–I K–M^8 N^6; pp. [i–iv], [1]–187 [188] [189–204]. This collation is as noted in BAL 10631 for the first of the two impressions recorded.

Contents: [i–ii] half-title, verso reservation of rights and copyright notice: "All rights reserved | Copyright in America [all in italic]"; [iii–iv] title-page, verso printer's imprint: "Edinburgh: T. and A. Constable, Printers to Her Majesty"; [1]–187 text; 187 at foot printer's imprint: "[rule] | Printed by T. and A. Constable, Printers to Her Majesty | at the Edinburgh University Press"; [188] blank; [189–204] undated and unpaginated ads. These ads are the last two leaves of signature M, and the entire signature N.

Binding: light buff buckram, decorated in dark-brown with two telegraph poles and wires on the front cover, and the publisher's device in dark-brown on the back cover. The front cover, which is lettered in dark-brown, reads: "[on the left side] IN | THE | CAGE", and "[on the right side] BY | HENRY | JAMES". The spine, also lettered in dark-brown but undecorated, reads: "IN | THE | CAGE | BY | HENRY | JAMES | DUCKWORTH & CO." The endpapers are of white laid paper, and the text is printed on thick rough wove paper. The top and fore-edges are untrimmed, and the bottom edge is rough trimmed.

Priced at 3s. 6d.

Illustrated Plate 21.

E&L A51a records that there are copies in this cloth color without the publisher's device on the back cover. But see 51.2.0, which suggests that E&L did not distinguish between the two binding states of the first impression.

51.2.0. *In the Cage*, first edition, first impression, binding state B, one volume, London 1898.

The title-page, size, collation, and contents (including the ads at the end) are identical to those of the first edition, first impression, binding state A, 51.1.0.

Binding: identical to that on 51.1.0 (including the lettering and decoration on the front cover and spine), except that it is bound in bright yellow rather than buff buckram, is lettered and decorated in a lighter brown rather than dark-brown, and has no publisher's device on the back cover. The endpapers are of white laid paper, and the text is printed on the same thick rough paper as 51.1.0. The top edge is untrimmed, and the other edges are rough trimmed.

This variant binding of the first impression is not noted in E&L or BAL. BAL 10631 states: "all examined copies have the publisher's device stamped in black [sic] on the back cover, Edel-Laurence (p. 112) report 'some copies lack publisher's device on back cover'; no copy thus seen by BAL." BAL's findings would appear to be true only of the more commonly seen binding in buff buckram (binding state A).

Illustrated Plate 21.

51.3.0. *In the Cage*, first edition, second impression, The Times Book Club binding state, one volume, London 1898.

The title-page is identical to that of the first edition, first impression, binding state A, 51.1.0.

Size: $7\,^5/_{16}$" x $4\,^7/_8$".

Collation: π^2 A–I K–L^8 M^6; pp. [i–iv], [1]–187 [188]. This collation is as noted in BAL 10631 for the second of two impressions recorded, which notes this collation is seen only in The Times Book Club binding.

Contents: identical to those of 51.1.0, except that the ads that appear on [189–204], the last two leaves of signature M^8 and the entire signature N^6, present in the first impression, are not present here, those pages having been omitted.

Binding: smooth blue cloth, lettered in black within a black single-rule frame on the front cover, and lettered and decorated in black on the spine. The front cover reads: "IN | THE | CAGE | BY | HENRY | JAMES [all justified on the left side of the front cover]". The spine reads: "[rule] | IN | THE | CAGE | BY | HENRY | JAMES | [circular device of The Times Book Club] | [rule]". The back cover is neither lettered nor decorated. The endpapers are of white wove paper, and the text is printed throughout on wove paper somewhat thinner than that used for the first impression. All edges are trimmed.

BAL 10631 queries whether the second impression is of signature M only. However, the difference in paper on which the text is printed in the first and this second impression, and the use of the same paper throughout the text of this second impression, would suggest that BAL's surmise that the second impression was of signature M only is probably not correct.

E&L A51a records, erroneously, that there was only one impression.

IN THE CAGE

51.4.0. *In the Cage*, first edition, second impression, The Times Book Club binding state, one volume, London 1898.

The title-page, size, collation, and contents are identical to those of the first edition, second impression, The Times Book Club binding state, 51.3.0.

Binding: smooth tan cloth lettered and decorated in black identically to 51.3.0. The endpapers are of white wove paper, and the text is printed on wove paper somewhat thinner than that used for the first impression, 51.1.0, but of the same thickness as that used for the second impression, 51.3.0. All edges are trimmed, and the top-edge is stained brown.

51.5.0. *In the Cage*, first American edition, first impression, one volume, Chicago and New York 1898.

IN THE CAGE | BY | HENRY JAMES | [publisher's device in red] | HERBERT S. STONE & COMPANY | CHICAGO & NEW YORK | MDCCCXCVIII [all the foregoing within a black double-rule frame]

Size: 7 1/2" x 4 5/8".

Collation: [unsigned, 1^4 2–15^8 16^4]; pp. [4] [i–iv], 1–229 [230] [231–232]. The pagination of the first page of each chapter is at the foot of the page.

Contents: two blank leaves; [i–ii] half-title, verso blank; [iii–iv] title-page, verso copyright notice: "COPYRIGHT 1898, BY | HERBERT S. STONE & CO."; 1–229 text; [230] blank; [231] printer's imprint: "PRINTED BY R. R. DONNELLEY | AND SONS COMPANY AT THE | LAKESIDE PRESS, CHICAGO, ILL.", [332] blank.

Binding: dark olive-green linen-grain cloth. The front and back covers are identically lettered and decorated in gilt, within a thick single-rule border in blind, and read: "IN THE CAGE | by [in swash italic] | HENRY JAMES | [three leaf devices]". The spine, lettered and decorated in gilt, reads: "[rule] | IN | THE | CAGE | by [in swash italic] | HENRY | JAMES | [rule] | [long strapwork design] | [rule] | STONE | CHICAGO | [smaller strapwork design] | [rule] | 1898". The endpapers are of laid paper, and the text is printed on laid paper watermarked: "H.S. Stone & Company | Chicago | The Chap Book". There are double binder's fly-leaves of laid paper at the back, but none at the front. The top edge is gilt, and the other edges are untrimmed.

E&L A51b states that the last signature of the volume is [17]², preceded by [16]⁴, while BAL 10630, on the other hand, correctly states that the last signature of the volume is [16]⁴ and that the last two leaves are a "double flyleaf of book stock at [the] back."

This binding, probably designed by Frank Hazen, is similar to that on the first American edition, first impression, of *What Maisie Knew* (1897), 49.6.0.

American printing history. Kramer [159]. A single impression of this title is recorded as being printed by R.R. Donnelley & Sons for Herbert S. Stone & Co. It was published in September 1898, priced at $1.25. A second impression was printed from the first edition plates by Fox Duffield & Co. in 1906; see 51.6.0. The number of copies printed of either impression is unknown.

In 1908 Scribners published a second edition of this title as part of Volume XI of *The Novels and Tales of Henry James* (The New York Edition); see 64.1.0.

51.6.0. *In the Cage*, first American edition, second impression, one volume, New York 1906.

IN THE CAGE | BY | HENRY JAMES | [publisher's device in red] | NEW YORK | FOX DUFFIELD & COMPANY | 1906 [all of the foregoing within a black double-rule frame]

Size: 7 3/8" x 4 3/4".

Collation: [unsigned, 1⁴ 2–15⁸ 16⁴]; pp. [4] [i–iv], 1–229 [230] [231–232].

Contents: two blank leaves; [i–ii] half-title, verso blank; [iii–iv] title-page, verso copyright notice: "COPYRIGHT 1898, BY | HERBERT S. STONE & CO."; 1–229 text; [230] blank; [231] printer's imprint: "PRINTED BY R. R. DONNELLEY | AND SONS COMPANY, AT THE | LAKESIDE PRESS, CHICAGO, ILL."; [232] blank.

Binding: dark olive-green linen-grain cloth. The front and back covers are identically lettered and decorated in gilt, within a thick single-rule border in blind, and read: "IN THE CAGE | by [in swash italic] | HENRY JAMES | [three leaf devices]". The spine, lettered and decorated in gilt, reads: "[rule] | IN | THE | CAGE | by [in swash italic] | HENRY | JAMES | [rule] | [long strapwork design] | [rule] | FOX | DUFF-IELD | & COMPANY | [rule] | [smaller strap-work design] | [rule]". No date is present at the foot of the spine. The endpapers are of, and the text is printed on, unwatermarked laid paper. There are no binder's fly-leaves. The top edge is gilt, and the other edges are untrimmed.

This impression was printed from the same plates as the first edition, first impression, with changes to the title-page and the printer's imprint on [231] only. The cloth on this binding, as well as the lettering and decoration on the front and back covers, are identical to those on the first American edition, first impression, 51.5.0. The spine is similar, lacking only the date at the foot, and, of course, it has a different publisher's imprint. It would appear that the binder of this impression used the same brasses as were used in the first impression binding.

Herbert S. Stone & Company was acquired by Fox, Duffield & Company in March 1906; see Kramer, 136.

❧✢❧

52. *THE TWO MAGICS*

52.1.0. *The Two Magics*, first edition, first impression, one volume, London 1898.

THE TWO MAGICS [in red] | THE TURN OF THE SCREW | COVERING END | By Henry James | [acorn device] | LONDON: WILLIAM HEINEMANN [in red] | MDCCCXCVIII

Size: $7\,^1/_2''$ x $5''$.

Collation: π^2 A–I K–T^8 U^4; pp. [i–iv] [1–2], [3]–310 [311–312].

Contents: [i–ii] half-title, verso ad headed: "By the Same Author, 6s. each.", listing 5 titles with press opinions; [iii–iv] title-page, verso copyright notice and sale limitation: "This Edition enjoys Copyright in all Countries | Signatory to the Berne Treaty, and is not to be | imported into the United States of America. [all in italic]"; [1–2] divisional fly-title with signature mark "A" at the foot, verso blank; [3]–310 text; 310 at foot printer's imprint: "Printed by Ballantyne, Hanson & Co. | London & Edinburgh"; [311–312] blank leaf.

Binding: light blue diagonal-fine-ribbed cloth, with four irises in blind on the front cover, and the circular publisher's device in blind on the back cover. The title, "THE TWO MAGICS", in gilt on the front cover is in uniform capitals 2 ⁵/₁₆" wide. The spine, lettered in gilt but undecorated, reads: "THE TWO | MAGICS | HENRY | JAMES | HEINEMANN". The publisher's imprint at the foot of the spine is in uniform capitals ³/₁₆" high. The endpapers are of, and the text is printed on, laid paper. The top and fore-edges are untrimmed, and the bottom edge rough trimmed. Bound in at the end are 32 pages of unpaginated and undated ads printed on a lighter wove paper, signed A and A2, each page devoted to one or two titles with press opinions, the first page to Harold Frederic's *Illumination*. These are the same ads that appear at the end of the second edition, first impressions, of *The Other House*, 46.1.0, *Embarrassments*, 47.1.0, and *What Maisie Knew*, 49.1.0.

English printing history. First edition: there is no information in the Heinemann Archive regarding the English printing history of this title as the ledger for the period 1898 to 1905 is missing. However, the title-leaf verso of 52.2.0 records that a first impression of the first edition was printed in January 1898, and a further impression (the second (?) impression) was printed in November 1898 (number of copies unknown). Both impressions were priced at 6s. A separate colonial impression (the third (?) impression) was also printed in 1898 (month and number of copies unknown). It was priced at 3s. 6d. in cloth and 2s. 6d. in paper. The sequence of the printing of these latter two impressions is unclear. E&L A52a records that 1500 copies of the first impression were printed, and that 300 sets of sheets of the colonial impression were diverted for use in the domestic market.

52.2.0. *The Two Magics*, first edition, second (?) impression, one volume, London 1898.

The title-page, size, collation, and contents (including the ad on [ii]) are identical to those of the first edition, first impression, 52.1.0, except that on the title-leaf verso the printing history: reads: "First Edition [dot] January 1898. | New Impression [dot] November 1898. [all but years in italic]".

Binding: light blue diagonal-fine-ribbed cloth, with nine tulips in blind on the front cover, and the publisher's circular device in blind on the back cover. The title, "THE TWO MAGICS", in gilt on the front cover is 2 ⁷/₃₂" wide. The spine, lettered in gilt but undecorated, reads: "THE TWO | MAGICS | HENRY | JAMES | HEINEMANN". The publisher's imprint at the foot of the spine is in uniform capitals ³/₁₆" high. The endpapers are of white wove paper, and the text is printed on laid paper. The top and fore-edges are untrimmed, and the bottom edge is rough trimmed. There are no ads bound in at the end.

A copy of this impression has also been seen in a first impression (four iris) binding.

52.3.0. *The Two Magics*, first edition, third (?) impression (colonial), one volume, London 1898.

THE TWO MAGICS | THE TURN OF THE SCREW | COVERING END | BY | HENRY JAMES | AUTHOR OF | "THE SPOILS OF POYNTON" [in italic] | &c. [in italic] | LONDON | WILLIAM HEINE-MANN | 1898 [all the foregoing in black]

Size: 7 ¼" x 4 ¾".

Collation: π^2 A–I K–T^8 U^4; pp. [i–iv] [1–2], [3]–310 [311–312].

Contents: [i–ii] "Heinemann's Colonial Library of Popular Fiction. [in Gothic type, underscored] | Issued for sale in the British | Colonies and India, and not | to be imported into Europe or | the United States of America. [sale limitation in italic]", verso ad headed: "BY THE SAME AUTHOR. [in italic]", listing 4 titles without press opinions; [iii–iv] title-page, verso reservation of rights: "All rights reserved [in italic]"; [1–2] divisional fly-title with signature mark "A" at the foot, verso blank; [3]–310 text; 310 at foot printer's imprint: "Printed by Ballantyne, Hanson & Co. | London & Edinburgh"; [311–312] blank leaf.

Binding: bright red pebble-grain cloth. On the front cover the title is lettered in black within a single-rule border in blind. On the back cover the publisher's device in black is within a single-rule border in blind. The spine, lettered and decorated in black, reads: "[rule] | The | Two | Magics | [short rule] | Henry | James | Heinemann | [rule]". The endpapers are of cream wove paper, and the text is printed on smooth fairly heavy wove paper. The front and rear pastedowns have ads printed on them, as do the recto and verso of the front and rear free endpapers. All edges are trimmed. Bound in at the end is a 12-page undated and unpaginated publisher's catalogue, each page of which is headed: "MR. WILLIAM HEINEMANN'S LIST. [in italic]".

52.4.0. *The Two Magics*, first edition, mixed colonial and domestic sheets bound for the domestic market, one volume, London 1898.

THE TWO MAGICS | THE TURN OF THE SCREW | COVERING END | BY | HENRY JAMES | AUTHOR OF | "THE SPOILS OF POYN- TON"[in italic] | &c. [in italic] | LONDON | WILLIAM HEINEMANN | 1898 [all the foregoing in black]

Size: 7 9/16" x 5".

Collation: π¹ A–I K–T⁸ U⁴; pp. [i–ii] [1–2], [3]–310 [311–312].

Contents: [i–ii] title-page, verso reservation of rights: "All rights reserved [in italic]"; [1–2] divisional fly-title with signature mark "A" at the foot, verso blank; [3]–310 text; 310 at the foot printer's imprint: "Printed by Ballantyne, Hanson & Co. | London & Edinburgh"; [311–312] blank leaf.

Binding: light blue diagonal-fine-ribbed cloth, with nine tulips in blind on the front cover, and the publisher's circular device in blind on the back cover. The title, "THE TWO MAGICS", in gilt on the front cover is in uniform capitals 2 5/8" wide. The spine, which is lettered in gilt but undecorated, reads: "THE TWO | MAGICS | HENRY | JAMES | HEINEMANN". The publisher's imprint at the foot of the spine is in uniform capitals 3/16" high. The endpapers are of white wove paper, and signatures π, A, L, R, and T are printed on wove paper (sheets of the colonial edition), and the balance on laid paper (sheets of the first edition, first (or second?) impression). All edges are untrimmed. There are no ads bound in at the end.

52.5.0. *The Two Magics*, first edition, colonial sheets bound for the domestic market, one volume, London 1898.

The title-page, size, collation, and contents of this copy are identical to those of the first edition, mixed colonial and domestic sheets bound for the domestic market, 52.4.0.

Binding: light blue diagonal-fine-ribbed cloth, with four irises in blind on the front cover, and publisher's device in blind on the back cover. The lettering in gilt on the front cover and spine is identical to that on 52.4.0, except that the publisher's imprint at the foot of the spine is in uniform capitals 1/8" high. The endpapers are of white wove paper, and the text is printed entirely on wove paper (sheets of the colonial edition only). All edges are untrimmed. There are no ads bound in at the end.

THE TWO MAGICS

52.6.0. *The Two Magics*, first American edition, first impression, state A, one volume, New York and London 1898.

THE TWO MAGICS | THE TURN OF THE SCREW | COVERING END | BY | HENRY JAMES | AUTHOR OF "DAISY MILLER," "THE EUROPEANS" | ETC., ETC. | New York [in Gothic type] | THE MACMILLAN COMPANY | LONDON: MACMILLAN & CO., Ltd. | 1898 | All rights reserved [in italic]

Size: $7\,^{1}/_{2}''$ x $5\,^{1}/_{8}''$.

Collation: $[1-25^{8}\;26^{1}]$, signed as $[A]^{2}\,[B]^{8}$ C-I K-U X-Z $2A-2B^{8}\;2C^{6}\,[2D]^{1}$; pp. [i–iv] [1–2], 3–393 [394] [395–398].

Contents: [i–ii] half-title, verso publisher's device; [iii–iv] title-page, verso copyright notice and printer's imprint: "Copyright, 1898, | By THE MACMILLAN COMPANY. | Norwood Press [in Gothic type] | J. S. Cushing & Co. – Berwick & Smith | Norwood Mass. U.S.A."; [1–2] divisional fly-title, verso blank; 3–393 text; [394] blank; [395–397] ads headed on each page: "WORKS BY HENRY JAMES", with press opinions and dollar prices; [398] blank.

Binding: claret linen-grain cloth, with single-rule borders in blind on the front and back covers. The spine, lettered and decorated in gilt and in blind, reads: "[blind rule] | THE | TWO MAGICS [title underscored in gilt] | HENRY JAMES | THE MACMILLAN | COMPANY | [blind rule]". The publisher's imprint on the spine is in capitals of uniform size. The endpapers are of white wove paper, and the text is printed on laid paper. The top edge is gilt, and the other edges are untrimmed. This copy is 1.15″ thick (excluding boards).

Priced at $1.50.

BAL 10634 identifies three binding and terminal ad variants (no priority noted), of which this copy is BAL's variant B. BAL's variant A has the spine imprint in large and small capitals and three pages of ads at the end; see below for BAL's variant C.

Illustrated Plate 22.

American printing history. There is no information in the Macmillan & Co (N.Y.) Archive as to the printing history of this title. However, the title-leaf verso of 52.13.5 records that there were nine separate impressions of the first edition of this title between September 1898 and

THE TWO MAGICS

1916: September and October 1898, January, April and May 1899, March 1905, March 1907, September 1911, and February 1916. There was a tenth impression in 1918, and at least one further printing of this edition after that date; see 52.14.0. E&L records that 2250 copies of the first impression were printed.

Correspondence in the Macmillan & Co. (N.Y.) Archive suggests that at one point Macmillan contemplated publishing *The Turn of the Screw* and *The Two Magics* as separate volumes.

52.7.0. *The Two Magics*, first American edition, first impression, state B, one volume, New York and London 1898.

This copy (including the publisher's imprint at the foot of the spine being in capitals of uniform size) is identical to the first American edition, first impression, state A, 52.6.0, except that signature [26^1], pages [397–398], is not present, resulting in only two pages of ads at the end. This copy is 1.15″ thick (excluding boards).

This copy is BAL's variant C.

52.8.0. *The Two Magics*, first American edition, second impression, one volume, New York and London 1898.

The title-page and size are identical to those of the first American edition, first impression, state A, 52.6.0.

Collation: identical to that of 52.6.0, except that the last signature is [26^2], the recto of the first leaf is ads, the verso blank, and the second leaf is blank.

Contents: identical (including ads) to those of, 52.6.0, except that the title-leaf verso, reads: "Copyright, 1898, | By The Macmillan Company. | [rule] | Set up and electrotyped September, 1898. Reprinted October, | 1898. | Norwood Press [in Gothic type] | J. S. Cushing & Co. – Berwick & Smith | Norwood Mass. U.S.A.", and the ads on [395–397] are present but [398] is blank, and [399–400], which are also present, are both blank.

Binding: claret linen-grain cloth, with a single-rule border in blind on the front and back covers. It is lettered in gilt on the spine identically to that on 52.6.0, except that the publisher's imprint at the foot of the spine reads: "The Macmillan | Company". The endpapers are of

THE TWO MAGICS

white wove paper, and the text is printed on laid paper. The top edge is gilt, and the other edges are untrimmed. This copy is 1.15″ thick (excluding boards).

52.9.0. *The Two Magics*, first American edition, fourth impression, one volume, New York and London 1899.

The title-page and size are identical to those of the first American edition, first impression, state A, 52.6.0, except that the date at the foot of the title-page is 1899.

The collation and contents are identical to those of 52.6.0, except that signature [26¹], pages [397–398], is not present, and the title-leaf verso reads: "Copyright, 1898, | By THE MACMILLAN COMPANY. | [rule] | Set up and electrotyped September, 1898. Reprinted October, | 1898; January, April, 1899. | Norwood Press [in Gothic type] | J. S. Cushing & Co. – Berwick & Smith | Norwood Mass. U.S.A."

Binding: claret linen-grain cloth, with decoration in blind on the front and back covers, and in gilt on the spine identical to that on 52.6.0. The publisher's imprint at the foot of the spine reads: "THE MACMILLAN | COMPANY" in capitals of uniform size. The endpapers are of white wove paper, and the text is printed on laid paper. The top edge is gilt, and the other edges are untrimmed. This copy is 1.18″ thick (excluding boards).

52.10.0. *The Two Magics*, first American edition, fifth impression, one volume, New York and London 1899.

The title-page and size are identical to those of the first American edition, first impression, state A, 52.6.0, except that the date at the foot of the title-page is 1899.

The collation and contents are identical to those of 52.6.0, that is the ads on [395–396] are present, but signature [26¹], pages [397–398], is not present, and the title-leaf verso reads: "Copyright, 1898, | By THE MACMILLAN COMPANY.|[rule]|Set up and electrotyped September, 1898. Reprinted October, | 1898; January, April, May, 1899. | Norwood Press | J. S. Cushing & Co. – Berwick & Smith | Norwood Mass. U.S.A."

Binding: claret linen-grain cloth, with decoration in blind on the front and back covers identical to that on 52.6.0. The spine, lettered and decorated in gilt, reads: "THE | TWO | MAGICS [title underscored in gilt] | HENRY JAMES | THE MACMILLAN | COMPANY", the title being on three lines rather than the two of all the previous impressions. The publisher's imprint at the foot of the spine is in capitals of uniform size. The brasses used on the spine are too wide for the width of the binding, and as a consequence the letters "H" and "S" in the author's name are almost in the gutters of the binding. The endpapers are of white wove paper, and the text is printed on laid paper. The top edge is gilt, and the other edges are untrimmed. The text paper is lighter than the paper used for 52.6.0, and as a consequence this volume is only .93" thick (excluding boards).

On the front free endpaper is the inscription: "Francis H.B. B[illegible] | Boston | Dec.^{bre} 1900." There is also a small white booksellers ticket that reads: "W. B. CLARK CO. | Booksellers & Stationers | Park St. Church, Boston".

Illustrated Plate 22.

52.11.0. *The Two Magics*, first American edition, seventh impression, one volume, New York and London 1907.

The title-page and size are identical to those of the first American edition, first impression, state A, 52.6.0, except that the date at the foot of the title-page is 1907.

The collation and contents are identical to those of 52.6.0, including the identical ads on [395–397], and [398] blank, except that the title-leaf verso reads: "Copyright, 1898, | By THE MACMILLAN COMPANY. | [rule] | Set up and electrotyped September, 1898. Reprinted October, | 1898; January, April, May, 1899; March, 1905; March, 1907. | Norwood Press [in Gothic type] | J. S. Cushing & Co. – Berwick & Smith | Norwood Mass. U.S.A."

Binding: claret buckram, with decoration in blind on the front and back covers identical to that on 52.6.0. The spine, lettered and decorated in gilt, reads: "THE | TWO | MAGICS [title underscored in gilt] | HENRY JAMES | THE MACMILLAN | COMPANY". The publisher's imprint is in capitals of uniform size. The endpapers are of white wove paper, and the text is printed on laid paper. The top edge is gilt, and the fore- and bottom edges are rough trimmed. This copy is 1.03" thick (excluding boards).

THE TWO MAGICS

52.12.0. *The Two Magics*, first American edition, eighth impression, one volume, New York and London 1911.

The title-page, size, and collation are identical to the first American edition, first impression, state A, 52.6.0, except that the date at the foot of the title-page is 1911.

Contents: identical to those of 52.6.0, including the identical ads on [395–397], and [398] blank, except that the title-leaf verso reads: "Copyright, 1898, | By THE MACMILLAN COMPANY. | [rule] | Set up and electrotyped September, 1898. Reprinted October, | 1898; January, April, May 1899; March, 1905; March, 1907; | September, 1911. | Norwood Press [in Gothic type] | J. S. Cushing & Co. – Berwick & Smith | Norwood Mass. U.S.A."

Binding: claret buckram, with decoration in blind on the front and back covers identical to that on 52.6.0. The spine, lettered and decorated in gilt, reads: "THE | TWO | MAGICS [title underscored in gilt] | HENRY JAMES | THE MACMILLAN | COMPANY". The publisher's imprint is in capitals of uniform size. The endpapers are of white wove paper, and the text is printed on laid paper. The top edge is gilt and the other edges are untrimmed. This copy is .96″ thick (excluding boards).

On the rear pastedown is a small white bookseller's ticket with rounded corners lettered in black within a frame with rounded corners that reads: "G. F. WARFIELD & CO. | Booksellers & Stationers | Hartford, Conn."

Illustrated Plate 22.

52.13.0. *The Two Magics*, first American edition, ninth impression, one volume, New York and London 1916.

The title-page and size are identical to those of the first American edition, first impression, state A, 52.6.0, except that the date at the foot of the title-page is 1916.

The collation and contents are identical to those of 52.6.0, including identical ads on [395–397] and [398] blank, except that the title-leaf verso reads: "Copyright, 1898, | By THE MACMILLAN COMPANY. | [rule | Set up and electrotyped September, 1898. Reprinted October, | 1898; January, April, May, 1899; March, 1905; March, 1907; | September,

1911; February, 1916. | Norwood Press | J.S. Cushing & Co. – Berwick & Smith | Norwood Mass. U.S.A."; and at the foot of [393], beneath a rule, the legend: "Printed in the United States of America."

Binding: claret buckram with decoration in blind on the front and back covers identical to that on 52.6.0. The spine, lettered and decorated in gilt, reads: "THE | TWO | MAGICS [title underscored in gilt] | HENRY JAMES | THE MACMILLAN | COMPANY". The publisher's imprint is in capitals of uniform size. The endpapers are of white wove paper, and the text is printed on wove rather than laid paper. The top edge is gilt, and the other edges are untrimmed. This copy is 1.06″ thick (excluding boards).

On the rear pastedown is a small black and gold circular sticker reading: "THE NORMAN, REMINGTON CO. | BALTIMORE-TOLEDO", and the inscription "Mrs N. H. G. Belt | 613 Reservoir St."

The fact that the same ads, with the same dollar prices, appear at the end of the first impression printed in 1898, the seventh impression printed in 1907 and the ninth impression printed in 1916 is an indication of the stability of book prices in America during that period.

52.13.5. *The Two Magics*, first American edition, tenth impression, one volume, New York 1918.

The title-page and size are identical to those of first American edition, first impression, state A, 56.6.0, except that the date at the foot of the title-page is 1918.

Collation: [1–25^8 26^4], signed as [A]^2 [B]^8 C-I K–U X–Z 2A–2B^8 2C^{10}; pp. [i–iv] [1–2], 3–393 [394] [395–400] [401–404].

Contents: [i–ii] half-title, verso publisher's device; [iii–iv] title-page, verso copyright notice, printing history and printer's imprint "Copyright, 1898, | By THE MACMILLAN COMPANY. | [rule] | Set up and electrotyped September, 1898. Reprinted October, | 1898; January, April, May 1899; March, 1905; March, 1907; | September, 1911; February, 1916. | Norwood Press [in Gothic type] | J. S. Cushing & Co. – Berwick & Smith | Norwood Mass. U.S.A."; [1–2] divisional fly-title, verso blank; 3–393 text, 393 at foot "[rule] | Printed in the United States of America."; [394] blank; [395] centered within a single-rule rectangular frame: "The following pages contain advertisements of a | few of the Macmillan books on kindred subjects"; [396] blank; [397] ad headed:

"WORKS BY HENRY JAMES.", listing *Embarrassments* and *The Other House*, with press opinions; [398] ad also headed: "WORKS BY HENRY JAMES.", listing 7 titles, 6 with press opinions; [399] ad also headed: "WORKS BY HENRY JAMES.", listing *The Real Thing* and *The Lesson of the Master*, with press opinions; all the foregoing ads with dollar prices; [400] blank; [401–404] two blank leaves.

Binding: claret buckram, decorated with a single rule frame in blind on the front cover, and in gilt on the spine. The spine reads: "[rule] | THE | TWO | MAGICS [title underscored] HENRY JAMES | MACMILLAN". The publisher's imprint on the spine is in capitals 3/16" high. The back cover is neither lettered nor decorated. The endpapers are of white wove paper, and the text is printed on wove paper. The top edge is trimmed and stained light brown, the bottom edge is trimmed, and the fore-edge is rough trimmed.

52.14.0. *The Two Magics*, first American edition, eleventh or later impression, one volume, New York 1920.

The title-page is identical to that of the first American edition, first impression, state A, 52.6.0, except that it is dated 1920 at the foot.

Size: 7 $^9/_{16}$" x 5 $^1/_{16}$".

The collation is identical to that of 52.6.0, except that signature [2D^1], [397–398], is not present.

The contents are identical to those of 52.6.0, except that the title-leaf verso has after the copyright notice the following printing history only: "[rule] | Set up and electrotyped September, 1898.", on [393], beneath a rule, there is the legend "Printed in the United States of America." There are no ads at the end, [394–396] are blank.

Binding: pinkish-red linen-grain cloth. The front and back covers are decorated with a single-rule border in blind. The spine, lettered and decorated in gilt and blind, reads: "[blind rule] | THE | TWO | MAGICS [title underscored in gilt] | HENRY JAMES | MACMILLAN | [three gilt dots] | [blind rule]". The publisher's imprint at the foot of the spine is in uniform capitals 3/16" high. The endpapers are of white wove, and the text is printed on wove paper. All edges are trimmed, and the top edge is stained light yellow.

It is curious that the title-leaf verso omits most of the printing history recorded in the tenth impression.

THE AWKWARD AGE

53. *THE AWKWARD AGE*

53.1.0. *The Awkward Age*, first edition, first impression, one volume, London 1899.

THE AWKWARD AGE [in red] | By Henry James | AUTHOR OF | "THE TWO MAGICS," "WHAT MAISIE KNEW," | "THE SPOILS OF POYNTON," ETC. ETC. | [small acorn device] | LONDON: WILLIAM HEINEMANN [in red] | MDCCCXCIX

Size: $7\,^9/_{16}$" x 5".

Collation: *⁴ A–I K–U X–Z 2A–2C⁸; pp. [2] [i]–vi, [1]–414 [415–416].

Contents: blank leaf with signature mark "*" at the foot of the recto; [i–ii] half-title, verso ad headed: "Novels for 1899 [in Gothic type]", listing 15 titles (none by James); [iii–iv] title-page, verso copyright notice and sale limitation: "This Edition enjoys Copyright in all Countries | signatory to the Berne Treaty, and is not to be | imported into the United States of America. [sale limitation all in italic]"; v–vi "Contents", verso continuation of contents; [1]–414 text; 414 at foot printer's imprint: "Printed by Ballantyne, Hanson & Co. | Edinburgh & London"; [415–416] ads headed: "BY THE SAME AUTHOR [underscored]", listing 3 titles on each page with press opinions. Note that v and vi are paginated.

Binding: light blue diagonal-fine-ribbed cloth, with four irises in blind on the front cover, and the publisher's circular device in blind on the back cover. The title, "THE AWKWARD AGE", on the front cover is in uniform capitals and 2 ¾" wide. The spine, lettered in gilt but undecorated, reads: "THE | AWKWARD AGE | HENRY | JAMES | HEINEMANN". The publisher's imprint at the foot of the spine is in uniform serif capitals $^5/_{32}$" high. The endpapers are of white laid paper, and the text is printed on laid paper, somewhat lighter than that usually used in Heinemann domestic editions. The top edge is untrimmed and the other edges are rough trimmed. There are 32 pages of ads printed on wove paper bound in at the end, the first page of which is devoted to Elizabeth Robbins's *The Open Question* and Kassandra Vivaria's *Via Lucis*, and the last to Conrad's *The Nigger of the 'Narcissus'* and Davis's *Soldiers of Fortune*, all with press opinions.

Note that the printer's imprint on 414, which usually reads "London & Edinburgh", is in this copy "Edinburgh & London".

THE AWKWARD AGE

BAL 10637 identifies two variants (no priority given) of the catalogue of ads inserted at the end. The last page of the first variant has on its last page an ad for Conrad's *The Nigger of the 'Narcissus'*. The second has a last page headed: "The Latest Fiction". Sadleir 1263 plausibly argues that the catalogue with a last page which lists "without quotes" (that is, without quotations from reviewers) "The Latest Fiction" is the earlier form.

BAL disputes E&L's assertion that some copies lack the publisher's device in blind on the back cover.

English printing history. There is no information in the Heinemann Archive regarding the printing history of this title as the ledger for the period 1898 to 1905 is missing. A first impression of the first edition was printed in April 1899. It was priced at 6s. A separate colonial impression (the second impression) was also printed in 1899 (number of copies unknown). It was priced at 3s. 6d in cloth and 2s. 6d. in wrappers. E&L A53a records that 2,000 copies of the first impression were printed, and that 475 sets of sheets of the colonial impression were diverted for use in the domestic market.

A second edition, was published by Macmillan as Volume [XIV] of *The Novels and Stories of Henry James*; see 86.1.0–86.2.0.

53.2.0. *The Awkward Age*, first edition, second impression, (colonial), one volume, London 1899.

THE AWKWARD AGE | BY | HENRY JAMES | LONDON | WILLIAM HEINEMANN | 1899 [all the foregoing in black]

Size: 7 5/16" x 4 13/16".

Collation: *⁴ A–I K–U X–Z 2A–2B⁸ 2C⁸ (–2C$_8$); [2] [i]–vi, [1] 2–414. The excised leaf is two pages of ads in the first edition, first impression, 53.1.0.

Contents: blank leaf with signature mark "*" at foot of the recto; [i–ii] "Heinemann's Colonial Library of Popular Fiction [in Gothic type, underscored] | Issued for sale in the British | Colonies and India, and not | to be imported into Europe or | the United States of America. [sale limitation all in italic]", verso ad headed: "BY THE SAME AUTHOR [underscored]", listing 6 titles; [iii–iv] title-page, verso: "All rights reserved [in italic]"; v–vi "Contents", verso continuation of contents;

[420]

[1]–414 text; 414 at the foot printer's imprint: "Printed by Ballantyne, Hanson & Co. | Edinburgh & London".

Binding: bright red pebble-grain cloth. On the front cover the title, lettered in black, is within a single-rule border in blind. On the back cover the publisher's device in black is within a single-rule border in blind. The spine, lettered and decorated in black, reads: "[rule] | The | Awkward | Age | [rule] | Henry | James | Heinemann | [rule]". The endpapers are of light cream wove paper, and the text is printed on wove paper. All edges are trimmed. A 12-page undated and unpaginated publisher's catalogue of ads, headed on each page: "MR. WILLIAM HEINEMANN'S LIST [in italic]", is bound in at the end. The front and rear pastedowns have ads on them, as do the recto and verso of the front and rear free endpapers.

Illustrated Plate 23.

53.3.0. *The Awkward Age*, first edition, second impression, colonial sheets bound for the domestic market, one volume, London 1899.

THE AWKWARD AGE | BY | HENRY JAMES | LONDON | WILLIAM HEINEMANN | 1899 [all the foregoing in black]

Size: $7\,7/16''$ x $4\,15/16''$.

Collation: *^{4} (–*$_2$) A–I K–U X–Z 2A–2C^8; pp. [2][iii]–vi, 1–414 [415–416]. The excised leaf has the colonial series half-title on the recto, and an ad for 6 titles "BY THE SAME AUTHOR [underscored]" on the verso; see 53.5.0. Leaf 2C$_8$ is two pages of ads identical to those at the end of the last signature of the first edition, first impression, 53.1.0.

Contents: [i–ii] blank leaf with signature mark "*" at the foot of the recto; [iii–iv] title-page, verso, reservation of rights: "All rights reserved [in italic]"; v–vi "Contents", verso continuation of contents; [1]–414 text; 414 at the foot printer's imprint: "Printed by Ballantyne, Hanson & Co. | Edinburgh & London"; [415–6] ads headed: "BY THE SAME AUTHOR [underscored]", listing 3 titles on each page with press opinions.

Binding: light blue diagonal-fine-ribbed cloth, with nine tulips in blind on the front cover, and the circular publisher's device in blind on the back cover. The title, "THE AWKWARD AGE", on the front cover is in uniform capitals $3\,1/8''$ wide. The spine, lettered in gilt but undecorated, reads: "THE | AWKWARD AGE | HENRY | JAMES |

THE AWKWARD AGE

HEINEMANN". The publisher's imprint at the foot of the spine is in uniform sans-serif capitals $1/8''$ high. The endpapers are of white wove paper, and the text is printed on wove paper. The top edge is trimmed and stained ochre, the fore-edge is trimmed, and the bottom edge is untrimmed. There are no ads bound in at the end.

53.4.0. *The Awkward Age*, first edition, second impression, colonial sheets bound for the domestic market, one volume, London 1899.

Size: $7 1/2'' \times 5''$.

The title-page, collation, and contents are identical to those of the first edition, second impression (colonial), 53.2.0, except that: the first signature is *⁴ (−*$_{1,2}$), both leaves *$_{1,2}$ being absent. The excised leaf *$_1$ has the signature mark "*" on the recto and a blank verso; and leaf *$_2$ has the colonial series half-title on the recto, and an ad listing 6 titles under the heading: "BY THE SAME AUTHOR [underscored]" on the verso. Leaf 2C$_8$, two pages of ads, as in the first edition, first impression, 53.1.0, is present.

Binding: light blue diagonal-fine-ribbed cloth, with nine tulips in blind on the front cover, and the circular publisher's device in blind on the back cover. The title "THE AWKWARD AGE", on the front cover is in uniform capitals 3" wide. The spine, lettered in gilt but undecorated, reads: "THE | AWKWARD AGE | HENRY | JAMES | HEINEMANN". The publisher's imprint at the foot of the spine is in uniform serif capitals $1/8''$ high. The endpapers are of white wove paper, and the text is printed on wove paper. The top edge is trimmed and stained ochre, and the other edges are untrimmed.

53.5.0. *The Awkward Age*, first edition, second impression, colonial sheets bound for the domestic market, one volume, London 1899.

Size: $7 9/16'' \times 5''$.

The title-page, collation, and contents are identical to those of the first edition, second impression (colonial), 53.2.0, except that leaf 2C$_8$, two pages of ads, is present, as in the first edition, first impression, 53.1.0.

Binding: light blue diagonal-fine-ribbed cloth, with nine tulips in blind on the front cover, and the circular publisher's device in blind on the back cover. The title, "THE AWKWARD AGE", on the front cover is in uniform capitals 3″ wide. The spine which is lettered in gilt but undecorated, reads: "THE | AWKWARD AGE | HENRY | JAMES | HEINEMANN". The publisher's imprint at the foot of the spine is in uniform serif capitals $^{5}/_{32}$″ high. The endpapers are of white wove paper, and the text is printed on wove paper. All edges are untrimmed.

This copy is what E&L would call a "freak", as normally (as in the preceding copy) the colonial series half-title, with its limitation on sale, would have been removed in cases where colonial sheets were diverted to domestic use.

53.6.0. *The Awkward Age*, first American edition, impression A, one volume, New York and London 1899.

[double-rule] | THE AWKWARD AGE | [double-rule] | A Novel. By HENRY JAMES | Author of "Washington Square" | "Daisy Miller" "Picture and Text" | "Terminations" "The Private Life" [all of the foregoing except the title and the author's name in italic] | [double rule] | [publisher's device] | [double-rule] | HARPER & BROTHERS PUBLISHERS | NEW YORK AND LONDON | 1899 | [double-rule]

Size: 7 $^{3}/_{16}$″ x 4 $^{13}/_{16}$″.

Collation: π^2 [A]^8 B–F^8 [G]^8 H^8 [I]^8 K–U X–Z 2A–2E^8 2F^6; pp. [i–iv] [1–2], 3–[457] [458] [459–460]. The inferred Roman alphabetical signature marks coincide with divisional fly-titles.

Contents: [i–ii] title-page, verso within a single-rule frame ad headed: "BY THE SAME AUTHOR.", listing 13 titles with dollar prices, and below the frame copyright notice and reservation of rights: "Copyright, 1899, by Harper & Brothers. | [rule] | All rights reserved."; [iii–iv] "CONTENTS", verso blank; [1–2] divisional fly-title, verso blank; 3–[457] text; [458] blank; [459–460] ads headed: [459] "By Sir WALTER BESANT"; and [460] "By LAURENCE HUTTON".

Binding: chocolate-brown vertical-rib-grain cloth. The front and back cover, identically lettered in gilt, read: "The [in italic] | Awkward Age | Henry James". The spine, lettered in gilt, reads: "The [in italic] | Awkward | Age | Henry | James | Harpers". The publisher's imprint at the foot of the spine has an "H" that does not have pronounced feet, has a sans serif "p", an "s" that is not slanting, and is $^{7}/_{8}$″ wide. The endpapers are of white laid paper, and the text is printed on wove paper. All edges are trimmed, and the top edge appears to be stained ochre.

This copy is printed on a thicker wove paper than the copy below, and is 1.5″ thick (excluding boards).

Illustrated Plate 24.

American printing history. There is no information in the Harper & Brothers Archive regarding the printing history of this title. E&L A53b records that 1,000 copies of the first impression were printed, and that the spine imprint on 53.6.0 is indicative of the primary "issue". However, BAL 10636, recognizing these points, says that the sequence of the two impressions has not been determined, but that they (and the different weight of paper) may indicate that there were two impressions; see 53.7.0.

This copy is recorded in BAL 10636 as variant A (no priority).

53.7.0. *The Awkward Age*, first American edition, impression B, one volume, New York and London 1899.

The title-page, size, collation, and contents are identical to the first American edition, impression A, 53.6.0.

Binding: chocolate-brown vertical-rib-grain cloth, lettered identically to 53.6.0, except that the publisher's imprint at the foot of the spine has an "H" with more pronounced feet, a serif "p", an "s" which is slanted (that is in italic), and is $^{13}/_{16}$″ wide. The endpapers are of white laid paper, and the text is printed on wove paper appreciably thinner than the paper used in variant "A". As a consequence the volume is 1.26″ thick (versus 1.5″, in both cases excluding boards). All edges are trimmed, and the top edge appears to be stained ochre.

E&L A53b, which records this as "secondary issue", also states that it is bound in lighter brown cloth than impression A. However, the brown cloth on impression B is in the same shade of brown as that on impression A. BAL 10636 records both binding variants both as being "cloth: brown".

This copy is recorded in BAL 10636 as variant B (no priority).

Illustrated Plate 24.

THE SOFT SIDE

54. *THE SOFT SIDE*

54.1.0. *The Soft Side*, first edition, first impression, English issue, one volume, London 1900.

THE SOFT SIDE | BY | HENRY JAMES | METHUEN & CO. | 36 ESSEX STREET W.C. | LONDON | 1900

Size: 7 $^{7}/_{16}$" x 5".

Collation: π⁴ A–I K–U X–Z 2A⁸ 2B⁴; pp. [2] [i–vi], [1]–391 [392].

Contents: blank leaf; [i–ii] half-title, verso ad headed: "BY THE SAME AUTHOR", listing 9 titles; [iii–iv] title-page, verso blank; [v–vi] "CONTENTS", verso blank; [1]–391 text; [392] at foot printer's imprint: "Printed by T. and A. Constable, Printers to Her Majesty | at the Edinburgh University Press".

Binding: red vertical-rib-grain cloth. The front cover has an oblong gilt frame off centered to the right within which is lettered in gilt: "The | Soft | Side | BY | HENRY | JAMES". The back cover is neither lettered nor decorated. The spine has at the top a vertical oblong gilt frame within which is lettered in gilt: "THE | Soft | Side | HENRY | JAMES", and at the foot in gilt within a smaller horizontal gilt frame: "METHUEN". The endpapers are of white laid paper, and the text is printed on laid paper. The top edge is trimmed and stained ochre, the fore-edge is rough trimmed, and the bottom edge is untrimmed. A 48-page ([48] is blank) paginated publisher's catalogue printed on laid paper, dated August 1900, is bound in at the end.

This binding is uniform with that on the first edition, English issue of *The Better Sort* (1903), 57.1.0, and the first edition, first impression of *The Ambassadors* (1903), 58.1.0.

English printing history. Methuen Archive. Methuen Mss. LMC 2230. Stock Ledger, Vol. 1, p. 424. First edition: *first impression*: July 11, 1900, 3,000 copies, with 27 over, of which 2500 were bound for the English issue between July 15, 1900, and December 18, 1906 (2100 were bound in 1900), and 527 [sic] copies were bound for a portion of the colonial issue, both in cloth and paper wrappers, between December 11 and 18, 1900 (250 cloth and 450 paper wrappers, although the binding order called for 300 in cloth and 400 in paper); *second impression*, printed on December 1 and 3, 1900, 1,000 copies (received in two batches the first

950 copies with the dates "Dec 1+3" and the second "Jan 31 50 [copies]"). One hundred and seventy three of these copies were bound for the remaining portion of the colonial issue bound between December 11 and December 18, 1900. A further 140 copies of the second impression were also bound for the colonial issue (60 in cloth and 80 in paper wrappers) between July 12 and August 26, 1904 [1907?]. Also 581 copies of the second impression were bound for the domestic issue. One hundred unbound copies of this impression were pulped on September 24, 1904 [1907?]. The copies of the second impression bound and the 100 pulped total 994 copies.

Notations: "Plates melted down June 24/04" and "Lettering destroyed Feb 5/13".

The English issue was priced at 6s., the colonial at 1s. 9d. in cloth and 1s. 6d. in wrappers.

Because portions of this ledger page have been damaged, certain data regarding the second impression are somewhat obscured. Also, notations regarding colonial covers and possibly wrappers are illegible.

A Note on the English Publication of *The Soft Side*

In 1898, James began using the services of the English literary agent James B. Pinker in negotiations with magazine and book publishers. This was not James's first use of a literary agent. In 1888, he had engaged the services of Alexander P. Watt, the first of the truly professional literary agents; see CWJ, Vol. 2, 82. But the relationship faltered by 1890, and James turned to his friend Charles Wolcott Balestier until Balestier's untimely death in 1891; see note following 33.5.0.

English publishers greatly resented the intrusion of literary agents into the 'cosy' relations between authors and publishers, and none more so than the English publisher William Heinemann. Heinemann was the most vociferous spokesman for the view that literary agents were parasites who interfered with the proper relationship between author and publisher, and that by focusing on the commercial aspects of that relationship debased literature.[35]

---

35 On the rise of the literary agent and Heinemann's antipathy to them, see James Hepburn, *The Author's Empty Purse and The Rise of the Literary Agent* (London: Oxford University Press, 1968).

THE SOFT SIDE

Heinemann had been James's English publisher since the 1895 publication of *Terminations*. Previously James had broken off relations with Macmillan & Co. over a dispute concerning his fees and royalties involving *The Tragic Muse* (see note following 34.8.0), had moved to Osgood, Macilvaine & Co. in 1892, and, after the death of Osgood, had moved to Heinemann. Between 1895 and 1909, Heinemann published ten of his works; see appendix F.

On January 24, 1900, James, writing to Mrs. W. K. Clifford, noted: "a lively row (temporarily calmed) with Heinemann – over Pinker!" HJL IV, 130. The row was caused by James having entrusted the negotiations for *The Soft Side* to Pinker. Two weeks previously, in a letter to Pinker, James reported: "1st he [Heinemann] tells me that he will not even answer your letter! & 2nd I have written to him repeating that I have placed the disposal of the book in question definitely in your hands & that it must remain in them. *That* point is therefore settled [emphasis in original]." Horne, 334. Temporary calm notwhistanding, the upshot was that Heinemann did not publish *The Soft Side*, which was placed by Pinker with Methuen & Co., and in fact Heinemann published only two further James works, *English Hours* in 1905 and *Italian Hours* in 1909.[36] Pinker, remained as James's very effective and accommodating literary agent to the end of James's life, and subsequently for the literary executors of James's estate.

54.2.0. *The Soft Side*, first edition, first impression, English issue, one volume, London 1900.

This copy is identical to the first edition, first impression, English issue, 54.1.0, except that the 48-page paginated publisher's catalogue printed on laid paper bound in at the end is dated October 1900.

BAL 10640 records copies of the first edition with catalogues dated August, October and November 1900. E&L A54a records catalogues dated August and November 1900, but not October 1900.

---

36 Heinemann also published the first English edition of James's *A Little Tour in France* in November 1900. The copyright of *A Little Tour in France* was owned by Houghton, Mifflin & Company which its predecessor firm had first published in America in 1884. As a result neither James nor Pinker may have had a hand in this much later English edition published by Heinemann.

THE SOFT SIDE

54.3.0. *The Soft Side*, first edition, first impression, English issue, one volume, London 1900.

This copy is identical to the first edition, first impression, English issue, 54.1.0 and 54.2.0, except that no publisher's catalogue is bound in at the end.

E&L A54a states: "several copies examined, including James's presentation copies and the British Museum deposit copy, have no catalogue of advertisements at end. The earliest date of a catalogue, where found, is August 1900".

54.4.0. *The Soft Side*, first American edition, first impression, one volume, New York and London 1900.

THE SOFT SIDE | BY | HENRY JAMES | AUTHOR OF "THE OTHER HOUSE," "THE | TWO MAGICS," ETC. | New York [in Gothic type] | THE MACMILLAN COMPANY | LONDON: MACMILLAN & CO., Ltd. | 1900 | All rights reserved [in italic]

Size: $7 \frac{1}{2}''$ x $5 \frac{1}{8}''$.

Collation: $[1-21^8]$, signed as $[A]^3$ B–I K–U X^8 Y^5; pp. [i–vi], 1–326 [327–330].

Contents: [i–ii] half-title, verso publisher's device; [iii–iv] title-page, verso copyright notice and printer's imprint: "Copyright, 1900, | By THE MACMILLAN COMPANY. | Norwood Press [in Gothic type] | J. S. Cushing & Co. – Berwick & Smith | Norwood Mass. U.S.A."; v–[vi] "CONTENTS", verso blank; 1–326 text; [327–329] ads; [330] blank. The ads, each page devoted to one title with press opinions, are headed: [327] "A FRIEND OF CAESAR"; [328] "THE GREATEST NOVEL OF THE YEAR [underscored]"; and [329] "THE BANKER AND THE BEAR".

The running titles on pages 208 and 209 are printed in a noticeably darker ink than the running titles in the rest of the text (although the font is the same).

Binding: claret linen-grain cloth. The front and back covers have a single-rule border in blind, but no lettering or other decoration. The spine, lettered and decorated in gilt and in blind, reads: "[blind rule] | THE | SOFT SIDE [title underscored in gilt] | HENRY JAMES | THE MACMILLAN | COMPANY | [blind rule]". The publisher's imprint at

THE SOFT SIDE

the foot of the spine is in capitals of uniform size. The endpapers are of white wove paper, and the text and the three pages of ads, which are the last two leaves of the last signature, [21], are printed on laid paper. The top edge is gilt, and the other edges are untrimmed.

BAL 10639 notes: "in some copies there is a blindstamped rule at top and at bottom of spine." It is possible that such rules appear on all copies of the first impression, as the nature of this binding makes such rules hard to discern.

American printing history. There is no information in the Macmillan (N.Y.) Archive regarding the printing history of this title. However, the title-page verso of 54.6.0 indicates that there were at least two impressions, the first in August 1900 and the second in January 1901. E&L A54b records that there was only one impression of 2800 copies, which as 54.6.0 demonstrates, is clearly erroneous.

54.5.0. *The Soft Side*, first American edition, first impression, variant binding state, one volume, New York and London 1900.

The title-page (and the title-leaf verso) are identical to those of the first American edition, first impression, 54.4.0.

Size: $7\,^{3}/_{16}"$ x $4\,^{7}/_{8}"$, significantly smaller than 54.4.0.

Collation: identical to that of 54.4.0, except that leaf [21$_8$], [329–330], has been excised (the excised leaf has an ad on the recto, and the verso blank).

Contents: identical to those of 54.4.0, except that there are two pages of ads at the end, [327–328], rather than three, the last leaf with an ad for *The Banker and the Bear* on the recto having been excised.

The running titles on pages 208 and 209 are printed in a noticeably darker ink than the running titles in the rest of the text, as is also the case in the preceding copy.

Binding: maroon vertical-rib-grain cloth, decorated with a single-rule border within a single wide-rule frame in blind on the front cover, within which is centered a decorative device, also in blind. The back cover is neither lettered nor decorated. The spine, decorated and lettered in yellow, reads: "[triple-rules] | THE | SOFT SIDE | [small square device] | HENRY | JAMES [author's name in italic] | [triple-rules]". No publisher's imprint is present at the foot of the spine. The endpapers are of white laid paper, and the text is printed on laid paper of the same weight as 54.4.0. All edges are trimmed, and the top edge is stained ochre.

This variant binding is not noted in E&L or BAL. It is similar to the variant binding on the first impression, first edition of *The Sacred Fount* (1901), 55.2.0, and the variant binding on the first edition of *The Wings of the Dove* (two volumes, 1902), 56.2.0. Is it possibly a Tabard Inn Library Binding; see BAL, Volume 1, xxxii–xxxiii.

The Tabard Inn Library (as well as The Booklovers' Library) was the brainchild of Seymour Eaton, a rather unscrupulous entrepreneur. Founded in Philadelphia in 1902, it went bankrupt in 1905.

54.6.0. *The Soft Side*, first American edition, second impression, one volume, New York and London 1901.

THE SOFT SIDE | BY | HENRY JAMES | AUTHOR OF "THE OTHER HOUSE," "THE | TWO MAGICS," ETC. | New York [in Gothic type] | THE MACMILLAN COMPANY | LONDON: MACMILLAN & CO., LTD. | 1901 | All rights reserved [in italic]

The size, collation, and contents (including the ads on [327–329]) are identical to those of the first American edition, first impression, 54.4.0, except for the date on the title-page and, as noted below, for the title-leaf verso. Leaf $[21]_8$ is present. The ads are identical to those of 54.4.0. The running titles on pages 208 and 209 are in a noticeably darker ink than the running titles in the rest of the text, as is the case in both the above copies of the first impression. The title-leaf verso reads: "Copyright, 1900, | By THE MACMILLAN COMPANY. | [rule] | Set up and electrotyped August, 1900. Reprinted January, | 1901. | Norwood Press [in Gothic type] | J. S. Cushing & Co. – Berwick & Smith | Norwood Mass. U.S.A."

Binding: claret-colored buckram, with a single-rule border in blind on the front and back covers, lettered and decorated on the spine identically to 54.4.0, except that at the foot of the spine the printer's imprint reads: "MACMILLAN" in uniform capitals $^3/_{16}''$ high. The endpapers are of white wove paper, and the text is printed on laid paper. The top edge is gilt, the fore-edge is rough trimmed, and the bottom edge is untrimmed.

The paper on which this impression is printed, and the boards in which it is bound, are thicker than the paper and boards of 54.4.0 and 54.5.0. As a consequence, this volume is 1.25″ thick as compared to 1.02″ (excluding boards) for both preceding copies of the first American edition, first impression.

This impression is not noted in BAL or E&L.

※⚜※

55. THE SACRED FOUNT

55.1.0. *The Sacred Fount*, first edition, first impression, one volume, New York 1901.

THE SACRED FOUNT | BY | HENRY JAMES | NEW YORK | CHARLES SCRIBNER'S SONS | 1901

Size: 7 $^9/_{16}$″ x 5 $^1/_8$″.

Collation: [unsigned, 1² 2–21⁸]; pp. [i–iv], 1–319 [320].

Contents: [i–ii] half-title, verso blank; [iii–iv] title-page, verso copyright notice and printer's imprint: "Copyright, 1901, by | CHARLES SCRIBNER'S SONS | TROW DIRECTORY | PRINTING AND BOOK-BINDING COMPANY | NEW YORK" [printer's imprint in sans-serif]; 1–319 text; [320] blank.

The "nail heads" are present in the gutters of pages 40–41, 120–121, 184–185, 248–249 and 312–313, as noted in BAL 10644 for the first impression. No divisional half-title is present between signatures [1] and [2] that BAL notes is present in some copies of the first impression. E&L A55a also notes that presumably later issues may have both the initial blank leaf and the divisional half-title; but see 55.3.0.

Binding: tan smooth biscuit cloth. The front cover, lettered in gilt within a single-rule gilt frame, reads: "THE SACRED | FOVNT | By | HENRY JAMES". The back cover is neither lettered nor decorated. The spine, lettered and decorated in gilt, reads: "[rule] | THE | SACRED | FOVNT | [small leaf design] | HENRY | JAMES | SCRIBNERS | [rule]". The endpapers are of smooth white wove paper, and the text is printed on wove paper. The top edge is gilt, and the other edges are untrimmed.

THE SACRED FOUNT

American printing history. Scribner's Archive. Manufacturing Records, Editions Published 1880–1902, and Cards (2) Box 13: Id-J. First edition: *first impression* 3,000 copies printed January 31, 1901, all bound between February 4 and February 25, 1901; published February 8, 1901; *second impression* 1,000 copies printed March 20, 1901, all bound between June 8, 1901, and April 13, 1904; *third impression* 275 copies printed March 18, 1910, all bound between April 1, 1910, and November 16, 1916. "NEW ED[ition]" 560 copies printed June 7, 1922, all (?) bound between September 22, 1922, and October 29, 1931; notation: "Nov. 1931 Jobbed to Rock 260". It is likely that the copies jobbed were bound copies, as the balance in the bindery on October 29, 1931, was zero. Given the small print run of the "New Edition" it is probable that it was not a separate edition but is the fourth impression of the first edition.

The first two impressions of the first edition were printed on 30 $\frac{1}{2}$" x 41" Grantham 90 weight wove 6 cent paper by Trow Directory Printing and Bookbinding Company and were bound by Trow. The third impression was printed on 30 $\frac{1}{2}$" x 41" W.R. 4 $\frac{1}{2}$ 70 weight paper, and was printed and bound by Scribner's. The "New Edition" was also printed and bound by Scribner's, but the type of paper used is not recorded.

The first two impressions of the first edition and possibly the third impression were priced at $1.50. The "New Edition" was priced at $2.50.

55.2.0. *The Sacred Fount*, first edition, first impression, variant binding state, one volume, New York 1901.

Size: 7 $\frac{1}{4}$" x 4 $\frac{7}{8}$".

The title-page, collation, and contents are identical to those of the first edition, first impression, 55.1.0. The "nail heads" are present in the gutters, as recorded for 55.1.0. No divisional half-title is inserted between signatures [1] and [2], and no additional leaves are at the front or back.

Binding: maroon vertical-rib-grain cloth, decorated with a single-rule border in blind on the front and back covers. The front cover, lettered in gilt, reads: "THE SACRED | FOUNT | By HENRY JAMES". The spine, lettered and decorated in gilt, reads: "[rule] | THE | SACRED | FOUNT | [small leaf device] | JAMES | [rule]". No publisher's imprint is present at the foot of the spine. The endpapers are of white laid paper, and the text is printed on wove paper. All edges are trimmed.

The collation and presence of the "nail heads" in the gutters indicate that this copy is of first impression sheets.

This variant binding of the first impression sheets is similar to the variant bindings on the first American edition, first impression, of *The Soft Side* (1900), 54.5.0, and the first edition, first impression, of *The Wings of the Dove* (two volumes, 1902), 56.2.0. It is possibly a Tabard Inn Library binding.

This variant binding is noted in E&L A55a, but not in BAL 10644.

55.3.0. *The Sacred Fount*, first edition, second impression, binding state A, one volume, New York 1901.

The title-page is identical to that of the first edition, first impression, 55.1.0.

Size: $7\,5/16''$ x $5\,1/8''$.

Collation: [unsigned, 1^4 2–21^8]; pp. [2] [i–vi], 1–319 [320]. This collation is as noted in BAL 10644 for the second impression.

Contents: blank leaf; [i–ii] half-title, verso blank; [iii–iv] title-page, verso copyright notice and printers imprint: "Copyright, 1901, by | CHARLES SCRIBNER'S SONS | TROW DIRECTORY | PRINTING AND BOOKBINDING COMPANY | NEW YORK" [printer's imprint in sans-serif]; [v–vi] divisional half-title, verso blank; 1–319 text; [320] blank. There are no "nail heads" in the gutters.

Note that the divisional half-title is present, which BAL 10644 records as being present (as an insert) in some copies of the first impression.

Binding: tan smooth biscuit cloth, with lettering and decoration identical to that on 55.1.0. The endpapers are of smooth white wove paper, and the text is printed on wove paper. The top edge is gilt and the other edges are untrimmed.

This copy is one of two binding states (no priority) recorded in BAL 10644 for the second impression.

THE SACRED FOUNT

55.4.0. *The Sacred Fount*, first edition, second impression, binding state B, one volume, New York 1901.

The title-page, size, collation, and contents (including the presence of the divisional fly-title and the absence of nail heads) are identical to those of the second impression, binding state A, 55.3.0.

Binding: dark blue vertical-rib-grain cloth, lettered in white within a single black rule frame on the front cover, which reads: "THE SACRED | FOVNT | By | HENRY JAMES". The spine, lettered and decorated in gilt, reads: "THE | SACRED | FOVNT | [small leaf device] | HENRY | JAMES | SCRIBNERS". The back cover is neither lettered nor decorated. The publisher's imprint at the foot of the spine is in capitals of uniform size. The endpapers are of white wove paper, and the text is printed on wove paper. The top edge is trimmed and stained ochre, and the other edges are untrimmed.

This copy is the second of two binding states (no priority) that BAL 10644 records for the second impression.

55.5.0. *The Sacred Fount*, first edition, third impression, one volume, New York 1910.

THE SACRED FOUNT | BY | HENRY JAMES | NEW YORK | CHARLES SCRIBNER'S SONS | 1910

Size: $7\frac{1}{2}''$ x $5\frac{1}{8}''$.

Collation: [unsigned, 1^2, $2-21^8$]; pp. [i–iv], 1–319 [320].

Contents: [i–ii] half-title, verso ad headed: "BOOKS BY HENRY JAMES", listing 4 titles with dollar prices; [iii–iv] title-page, verso copyright notice and printer's device: "Copyright, 1901, by | CHARLES SCRIBNER'S SONS | [printer's device of the Scribner's Press]"; 1–319 text; [320] blank.

Binding: tan smooth biscuit cloth, with lettering and decoration in gilt identical to that on the first edition, first impression, binding state A, 55.1.0. The endpapers are of white wove paper, and the text is printed on wove paper. The top edge is gilt, and the other edges are untrimmed.

THE SACRED FOUNT

55.6.0. *The Sacred Fount*, first English edition, first (sole) impression, English issue, one volume, London 1901.

THE SACRED FOUNT | BY | HENRY JAMES | METHUEN & CO. | 36 ESSEX STREET W.C. | LONDON | 1901

Size: 7 $\frac{1}{2}$" x 4 $\frac{15}{16}$".

Collation: [A]² B–I K–U⁸ X⁶; pp. [i–iv], [1]–316.

Contents: [i–ii] half-title, verso ad headed: "BY THE SAME AUTHOR", listing 10 titles; [iii–iv] title-page, verso printer's imprint: "PLYMOUTH | WILLIAM BRENDON AND SON | PRINTERS"; [1]–316 text; 316 at foot printer's imprint: "[rule] | PLYMOUTH: WILLIAM BRENDON AND SON, PRINTERS."

Binding: lacquered crimson cloth. The front cover is lettered in gilt and decorated in blind, with a raised panel on which is the title and author's name in gilt separated by a gilt dot. Surrounding the panel is elaborate raised floral decoration stamped in blind. On the lower right of the front cover are the small raised initials "GAR" running vertically. The back cover is neither lettered nor decorated. The spine is also lettered in gilt and decorated in blind, with a raised panel on which is the title and author's name separated by a dot, above and below which panel are elaborate raised floral decorations stamped in blind. The publisher's imprint in gilt at the foot of the spine reads: "METHVEN [in sans-serif]". The endpapers are of white laid paper, and the text is printed on rough laid paper. The top edge is trimmed, the fore-edge is rough trimmed, and the bottom edge is untrimmed. A 48-page paginated publisher's catalogue of ads, dated November 1900, printed on thinner laid paper, is bound in at the end.

The initials "GAR" on the front cover are presumably those of the artist (unidentified) who designed it.

On the front pastedown is the armorial bookplate of Christian H. J. Head.

English printing history. Methuen Archive. Methuen Mss. LMC 2230. Stock Ledger, Vol. 1, p. 445. First edition: *first (*and sole*) impression*: February 4, 1901, 3500 copies, none over, 3500 bound, including 2102 copies for the domestic issue, bound between February 11 and June 3, 1901, and 750 copies for the colonial issue bound between March 4 and May 29, 1901 (450 were bound in paper wrappers and 300 in cloth). A

THE SACRED FOUNT

further 750 copies for the domestic issue, representing three binding orders of 250 each, were bound between May 12 and September 4, but the year or years of these bindings-up are not specified.[37] It is likely that they were bound as late as 1911 (see 55.7.0 and 55.8.0 with 1911 catalogues bound in at the end); also there is the notation at the bottom of the ledger page: "Eng [domestic issue] Titles 260 Aug 28/11". This suggests that the first signature, [A]^2, was printed on that date for the binding order (250 copies) of August 23 [1911?]. Other notation: "1000 Col Lib Covers Feb 13/01" and "Moulds destroyed Nov 23/04".

The domestic issue was priced at 6s., the colonial issue at 1s. 9d. in cloth and 1s. 6d. in wrappers.

A second English edition was published by Macmillan as Volume [XXIX] of *The Novels and Stories of Henry James*, see 86.1.0–86.2.0.

55.7.0. *The Sacred Fount*, first English edition, first (sole) impression, English issue, one volume, London 1901.

The title-page, size, collation, and contents are identical to the first English edition, first impression, English issue, 55.6.0.

Binding: lacquered crimson cloth, lettered in gilt and decorated identically to the binding on 55.6.0. The endpapers are of white wove paper, and the text is printed on rough laid paper. The top edge is trimmed and stained ochre, the fore-edge is rough trimmed, and the bottom edge is untrimmed. A 32-page (the last page of which is blank except for the printer's imprint) paginated publisher's catalogue of ads, dated March 1911, printed on thin wove paper, is bound in at the end.

55.8.0. *The Sacred Fount*, first English edition, first (sole) impression, later English issue, one volume, London 1901.

The title-page, size, collation, and contents are identical to those of the first English edition, first impression, English issue, 55.6.0, except that the printer's imprint on the title-leaf verso reads: "PRINTED BY | WILLIAM BRENDON AND SON, LTD. | PLYMOUTH". The printer's imprint at the foot of 316 reads: "[rule] | PLYMOUTH: WILLIAM BRENDON AND SON, PRINTERS.", and is the same as that on 316 of 55.6.0.

---

[37] The number of copies bound, 3602, does not tally with the number of copies printed, 3500.

THE SACRED FOUNT

Binding: identical to that on 55.6.0. The endpapers are of white wove paper, and the text is printed on rough laid paper. The top edge is trimmed and stained ochre, the fore-edge is rough trimmed, and the bottom edge is untrimmed. A 32-page paginated (the last page of which is blank except for the printer's imprint) publisher's catalogue, dated August 1911, printed on thin wove paper, is bound in at the end.

Signature [A]^2 of this issue was probably printed in August 1911; see printing history, 55.6.0.

55.9.0. *The Sacred Fount*, first English edition, first (sole) impression, colonial issue, cloth binding state, one volume, London 1901.

THE SACRED FOUNT | BY | HENRY JAMES | METHUEN & CO. | 36 ESSEX STREET W.C. | LONDON | 1901 | Colonial Library [in italic]

Size: 7 $^1\!/_2$″ x 5″.

Collation: [A]^2 B–I K–U^8 X^6; pp. [i–iv], [1]–316.

Contents: [i–ii] half-title with "Methuen's Colonial Library [in Gothic type, underscored]" at the top, verso ad headed: "BY THE SAME AUTHOR", listing 10 titles; [iii–iv] title-page, verso printer's imprint: "PLYMOUTH | WILLIAM BRENDON AND SON | PRINTERS"; [1]–316 text; 316 at foot printer's imprint: "[rule] | PLYMOUTH: WILLIAM BRENDON AND SON, PRINTERS."

Binding: greenish-blue diaper-grain cloth. The front and back covers are neither lettered nor decorated. The spine, lettered in gilt, reads: "THE | SACRED | FOUNT | HENRY JAMES | METHUEN'S | COLONIAL LIBRARY". The endpapers are of white laid paper, and the text is printed on laid paper. The top edge is trimmed, the fore-edge is rough trimmed, and the bottom is untrimmed. A 48-page paginated publisher's catalogue printed on laid paper, dated March 1901, is bound in at the end. The front pastedown starts an ad for "Methuen's Colonial Library", listing works of fiction, which list continues on the recto and verso of the front free endpaper and on the recto and verso of the rear free endpaper, followed on the verso by a list of "General Literature", which list continues on the rear pastedown.

56. *THE WINGS OF THE DOVE*

56.1.0. *The Wings of the Dove*, first edition, first impression, two volumes, New York 1902.

THE WINGS OF | THE DOVE | BY | HENRY JAMES | VOLUME I [II] | NEW YORK | CHARLES SCRIBNER'S SONS | 1902

Size: 7 9/16″ x 4 15/16″.

Collation: Volume I: π^2 [1]^8 2–7^8 [8]^8 9–14^8 [15]^8 16–20^8 21^6; pp. [i–iv] [1–2], 3–329, [330] [331–332]. Volume II: π^2 [1]^8 2–21^8 [22]^8 23–27^8 28^6; pp. [i–iv] [1–2], 3–439 [440] [441–444]. The inferred numerical signature marks coincide with divisional fly-titles.

Contents: Volume I: [i–ii] half-title, verso ad headed: "By the Same Author [in Gothic type]", listing *The Sacred Fount* with the dollar price; [iii–iv] title-page, verso copyright notice, printing history and printer's imprint: "Copyright, 1902, by | CHARLES SCRIBNER'S SONS | [rule] | Published, August, 1902 | TROW DIRECTORY | PRINTING AND BOOKBINDING COMPANY | NEW YORK [printer's imprint in sans-serif]"; [1–2] divisional fly-title, verso blank; 3–329 text; [330] blank; [331–332] blank leaf. Volume II: [i–ii] blank, verso ad as on [ii] in Volume I; [iii–iv] title-page, verso copyright notice, printing history and printer's imprint as on [iv] in Volume I; [1–2] divisional fly-title, verso blank; 3–439 text; [440] blank; [441–444] blank leaves.

Binding: smooth sateen biscuit cloth. The front and back covers are neither lettered nor decorated. The spines, which are lettered and decorated in gilt, read: "THE | WINGS OF | THE DOVE | [small leaf ornament] | HENRY | JAMES | I [II] | SCRIBNERS". The endpapers are of smooth white wove paper, and the text is printed on laid paper. A binder's fly-leaf of laid paper is at the front of both volumes, but none at the backs. The final blank leaf of Volume II, 28$_6$, is present. The top edges are gilt, and the other edges are untrimmed.

See BAL 10647, which notes that in some copies the final blank leaf of both volumes is excised, that in some copies the endpapers are of laid paper, and that fly-leaves may or may not be present.

American printing history. Scribner's Archive. Cards (2) Box 13: Id-J. First edition: *first impression* 3,000 copies of both volumes printed on August 13, 1902, all bound between August 21, 1902, and February 13,

THE WINGS OF THE DOVE

1903; published August 29, 1902; *second impression* 1,000 copies of both volumes printed December 10, 1902, all bound between May 8, 1903, and October 4, 1916; *third impression* 250 copies of both volumes printed February 15, 1917, all bound between March 13, 1917, and August 4, 1919. "NEW ED[ition]" 575 copies of both volumes printed on June 1, 1922, all bound between September 22, 1923, and November 8, 1926. Given the small print run of the "New Edition", it is possible that it is not a separate edition, but is either the fourth impression of the first edition, or the first separate impression of the second (The New York) edition.

The first two impressions were printed on 30 $^1/_2$" x 39" 90 (Volume I) and 75 (Volume II) weight Grantham laid toned 4 $^1/_2$ (for the first impression) and 4 $^5/_8$" (for the second impression) paper by Trow Directory Printing and Bookbinding Company; however, under the entry for Volume II of the first impression is the notation "2[.]o7 reams 70 weight" paper. The first two impressions were bound by Trow. The third impression and the "New Edition" were printed and bound by Scribner's, but the type of paper used is not recorded

The first two impressions, and possibly the third, were priced at $2.50 "per set". At the top of the card recording the first two impressions is the notation "Boxed". The "New Edition" was priced at $5.00.

A second American edition was published as Volumes XIX and XX of *The Novels and Tales of Henry James* (The New York Edition); see 64.1.0.

56.2.0. *The Wings of the Dove*, first edition, first impression, variant binding state, two volumes, New York 1902.

The title-pages are identical to those of the first edition, first impression, 56.1.0.

Size: 7 $^1/_{16}$" x 4 $^3/_4$".

Collation: Volume I: $\pi^2(-\pi_1)$ [1]^8 2–7^8 [8]^8 9–14^8 [15]^8 16–20^8 21^6 (-21_6); pp. [i–ii] [1–2], 3–329 [330]. Volume II: π^2 [1]^8 2–21^8 [22]^8 23–27^8 28^6 ($-28_{5,6}$); pp. [i–iv] [1–2], 3–439 [440]. The excised leaves, all of which are present in the first edition, state A, 56.1.0, are blank leaves, except π_1 in Volume I, which is the half-title, with an ad on the verso. Signature mark 25 in Volume II reflects damaged type. The inferred numerical signature marks, except the first in Volume II, coincide with divisional fly-titles.

[439]

The contents are as described in 56.1.0, except that Volume I lacks the half-title-leaf, [i–ii], and a terminal blank leaf, [331–332]; and, Volume II lacks two terminal blank leaves, [441–444].

Binding: maroon vertical-rib-grain cloth, lettered and decorated in gilt on the front covers and spines, with a widely spaced double rule in blind at the top and bottom of the front and back covers. The front covers read: "THE WINGS OF THE DOVE [underscored with a double-rule] | HENRY JAMES". The spines read: "[rule] | THE | Wings | of the [in italic] | DOVE | [short decorative rule] | JAMES | [short rule] | VOL. I [II] | [rule]". There are no publisher's imprints at the foot of the spines. There are no binder's fly-leaves. The endpapers are of smooth white wove paper, and the text is printed on laid paper. All edges are trimmed.

E&L A56a records this binding as being "russet" colored. BAL records it as being "maroon". E&L records this variant binding as being of first edition sheets sold by Scribner's to a jobber. However, given the fact that Scribner's printed two (and possibly three) further impressions, this seems unlikely. BAL 10647 queries whether this secondary binding might be a Tabard Inn Library binding. This variant binding is similar to the variant binding on the the first American edition, first impression, of *The Soft Side* (1900), 54.5.0, and on the variant binding of the first edition, first impression, of *The Sacred Fount* (1901), 55.2.0.

On the front pastedown of each Volume is the inscription: "Anna Platt | 1922".

56.3.0. *The Wings of the Dove*, first edition, third impression, two volumes, New York 1917.

THE WINGS OF | THE DOVE | BY | HENRY JAMES | VOLUME I [II] | NEW YORK | CHARLES SCRIBNER'S SONS | 1917

Size: 7 $^{7}/_{16}$" x 4 $^{15}/_{16}$".

Collation: Volume I: $[1-21^8]$, signed as $[1]^{10}$ $2-7^8$ $[8]^8$ $9-14^8$ $[15]^8$ $16-20^8$ 21^6; pp. [i–iv] [1–2], 3–329 [330] [331–332]. Volume II: $[1-27^8, 28^6]$, signed as $[1]^{10}$ $2-21^8$ $[22]^8$ $23-27^8$ 28^4; pp. [i–iv] [1–2], 3–439 [440]. The inferred signature marks, except the first in both Volumes, coincide with divisional fly-titles.

THE WINGS OF THE DOVE

Contents: Volume I: [i–ii] half-title, verso ad headed: "BOOKS BY HENRY JAMES", listing 9 titles and *The Novels and Tales* (New York Edition), all with dollar prices, the last dated being *Notes on Novelists*; [iii–iv] title-page, verso copyright notice and printer's device: "Copyright, 1902, by | CHARLES SCRIBNER'S SONS | [rule] | Published, August, 1902 | [device of the Scribner's Press]"; [1–2] divisional fly-title, verso blank, 3–329 text; [330] blank; [331–332] blank leaf. Volume II: [i–ii] half-title, verso ad as on [ii] in Volume I; [iii–iv] title-page, verso copyright notice and printer's device as on [iv] in Volume I; [1–2] divisional-fly-title, verso blank; 3–439 text; [440] blank.

Binding: smooth sateen biscuit cloth. There is no lettering or decoration on the front or back covers. The spines, lettered and decorated in gilt, read: "THE | WINGS OF | THE DOVE | [small leaf ornament] | HENRY | JAMES | I [II] | SCRIBNERS". The endpapers are of cream wove paper, and the text is printed on wove paper. There are no binder's fly-leaves. The top edges are gilt and the other edges are untrimmed.

56.4.0. *The Wings of the Dove*, first English edition, one volume, Westminster 1902.

THE | Wings of the Dove | BY | HENRY JAMES | [leaf device] | WESTMINSTER | ARCHIBALD CONSTABLE AND CO., LTD. | 2 WHITEHALL GARDENS, S.W. | 1902

Size: 7 $^{5}/_{16}$" x 4 $^{7}/_{8}$".

Collation: π^2 A–I K–U X–Z 2A–2I 2K–2N^8; pp. [i–iv] [1–2], 3–576.

Contents: [i–ii] half-title, verso blank; [iii–iv] title-page, verso printer's imprint: "Edinburgh: T. and A. Constable, (late) Printers to Her Majesty"; [1–2] divisional fly-title, verso blank; 3–576 text; 576 at foot printer's imprint: [rule] | Printed by T. and A. Constable, (late) Printers to Her Majesty | at the Edinburgh University Press".

Binding: blue vertical-rib-grain cloth. The front cover is decorated in blind with an overall stamped design of intertwined vines and leaves, and lettered in gilt within a small raised panel that reads: "THE WINGS | of [in swash italic justified on the right] | THE DOVE". The back cover is neither lettered nor decorated. The spine, lettered in gilt, reads: "THE | WINGS | OF | THE DOVE | HENRY | JAMES | CONSTABLE | WESTMINSTER [publisher's imprint in Gothic type]". The endpapers are of white wove paper, and the text is printed on coarse wove paper. All edges are trimmed. A 16-page undated paginated publisher's catalogue of ads printed on smooth wove paper is bound in at the end.

56.5.0. *The Wings of the Dove*, first English edition, one volume, Westminster 1902.

Identical to the first English edition, 56.4.0, except that there is no publisher's catalogue bound in at the end.

On the front pastedown is the label of The W. H. Smith & Sons Subscription Library.

56.6.0. *The Wings of the Dove*, first English edition, domestic sheets diverted to the colonial market (?), one volume, London 1902.

Identical to the first English edition, 56.4.0, except that the ads bound in at the end is an unpaginated and undated single leaf of thin wove paper, the recto of which is an ad for "MISS MARY JOHNSTON'S FAMOUS ROMANCES", listing 2 titles, and "PAUL LEICESTER FORD'S GREAT NOVELS", listing 3 titles, all titles with press commentary; and the verso is headed: "Constable's Colonial Library. | thin double rule" followed by a list of titles numbered 44 through 80 (in descending numerical order), and at the foot a caution that 8 of the listed titles "may not be introduced into Canada".

The presence of the leaf of ads at the end, the verso of which lists 37 titles issued in Constable's Colonial Library, suggests that sheets of the domestic issue may have been diverted to the colonial market. There is no colonial edition of this title recorded in E&L. This is the sole James title published by Constable.

57. THE BETTER SORT

57.1.0. *The Better Sort*, first edition, English issue, one volume, London 1903.

THE BETTER SORT | BY | HENRY JAMES | METHUEN & CO. | 36 ESSEX STREET W.C. | LONDON | 1903

Size: 7 7/16″ x 5″.

Collation: [A]⁴ B–I K–U⁸ X⁴; pp. [2] [i–vi], [1]–312.

Contents: blank leaf; [i–ii] half-title, verso ad headed: "BY THE SAME AUTHOR", listing 11 titles; [iii–iv] title-page, verso blank; [v–vi] "CONTENTS", verso blank; [1]–312 text; 312 at foot printer's imprint: "[rule] | Plymouth: W. Brendon and Son, Printers. [in italic]".

Binding: red vertical-rib-grain cloth. The front cover has a vertical oblong gilt frame off centered to the right within which, justified on the left, is lettered in gilt: "The | Better | Sort | BY | HENRY | JAMES". The back cover is neither lettered nor decorated. The spine has at the top an oblong gilt frame within which is lettered in gilt: "THE | Better | Sort | HENRY | JAMES", and at the foot in gilt within a smaller horizontal gilt frame: "METHUEN". The endpapers are of white wove paper, and the text is printed on coarse wove paper. The top edge is trimmed and stained brown, the fore-edge is rough trimmed, and the bottom edge is untrimmed. Bound in at the end is a 40-page paginated publisher's catalogue, dated February 1903, printed on wove paper.

This binding is uniform with those on the first edition, first impression, English issue, of *The Soft Side* (1900) and *The Ambassadors* (1903), 54.1.0 and 58.1.0.

E&L A57a records two cloth colors for the primary binding, scarlet and claret. BAL 10652 records only red for the primary binding.

English printing history. Methuen Archive. Methuen Mss. LCM 2230. Stock Ledger, Vol. 2, p. 53: First edition, *first* (and sole) *impression*, January 27, 1903, 3500 copies, with 79 over, 3190 bound between January 28, 1903, and July 10, 1909, of which 2258 were for the English issue (1849 bound in 1903), and 932 for the colonial issue (720 bound in 1903). Of the 932 copies bound for the colonial issue, 484 were bound in cloth and 448 were bound in paper wrappers. On January 22, 1908, 100 unbound copies were pulped. Notations: "2500 English 1,000 Colonial", and "Colonial Wrappers 500 5lb 6/03". Other notations: "Type distributed Apr. 4/03", "Moulds destroyed Nov 13/06", and 'Lettering destroyed 3/2/13".

The domestic issue was priced at 6s., and the colonial issues were priced at 1s. 9d. in cloth and 1s. 6d. in paper wrappers.

57.1.5. *The Better Sort*, first edition, English issue, one volume, London 1903.

This copy is identical to the first edition, English issue, 57.1.0, except that the 40-page paginated publisher's catalogue bound in at the end is dated November 1902.

57.2.0. *The Better Sort*, first edition, English issue, one volume, London 1903.

This copy is identical to the first edition, English issue, 57.1.0, except that the 40-page paginated publisher's catalogue bound in at the end is dated February 1908.

57.3.0. *The Better Sort*, first edition, English issue, one volume, London 1903.

This copy is identical to the first edition, English issue, 57.1.0, except that the 40-page paginated publisher's catalogue bound in at the end is dated June 1908.

57.4.0. *The Better Sort*, first edition, English issue, variant binding state A, one volume, London 1903.

Size: 7 7/16" x 4 7/8".

The title-page, collation, and contents are identical to those of the first edition, English issue, 57.1.0.

Binding: bright blue diagonal-fine-ribbed cloth. The front and back covers are not lettered, but are decorated with a triple-rule border in blind. The spine has triple rules in blind across the head and foot, beneath which is a vertical oblong gilt frame within which is lettered in gilt: "THE | Better | Sort | HENRY | JAMES", with the publisher's imprint, "METHUEN", in gilt at the foot (but not within a frame) in capitals of uniform size. The endpapers are of white wove paper, and the text is printed on coarse wove paper. The top and fore-edges are trimmed, and the bottom edge is untrimmed. No publisher's catalogue is bound in at the end.

This is a copy of the variant (remainder?) binding of the first edition sheets noted in E&L A57a and BAL 10652

57.5.0. *The Better Sort*, first edition, English issue, variant binding state B, one volume, London 1903

Size: 7" x 4 ⅝".

The title-page, collation, and contents are identical to those of the first edition, English issue, 57.1.0.

Binding: brownish-rose linen-grain cloth, blindstamped on the front and back covers with a geometric frame leaving a large blank central panel which is neither lettered nor decorated. The spine, lettered in gilt and stamped in blind, reads: "THE | BETTER SORT | [short rule] | JAMES [the "J" is a drop-cap] | [long blindstamped strapwork design] | [two rules]". There is no publisher's imprint at the foot of the spine. The endpapers are of cream wove paper, and the text is printed on coarse wove paper. All edges are trimmed and the top edge is stained ochre. There are no ads bound in at the end.

On the half-title is a signature and the inscription "London april [*sic*] 1921".

This is probably a remainder binding. Not noted in BAL or E&L.

57.6.0. *The Better Sort*, first edition, colonial issue, wrapped binding state, one volume, 1903.

THE BETTER SORT | BY | HENRY JAMES | METHUEN & CO. | 36 ESSEX STREET W.C. | LONDON | 1903 | Colonial Library [in italic]

Size: 7 ¼" x 5".

Collation: [A]⁴ B–I K–U⁸ X⁴; pp. [2] [i–vi], [1]–312.

Contents: blank leaf; [i–ii] half-title (with "Methuen's Colonial Library [in Gothic type, underscored]" at the top), verso ad headed: "BY THE SAME AUTHOR", listing 11 titles; [iii–iv] title-page, verso blank; [v–

vi] "CONTENTS", verso blank; [1]–312 text; 312 at foot the printer's imprint: "[rule] | Plymouth: W. Brendon and Son, Printers. [in italic]".

Binding: red paper wrappers, cut flush, lettered on the front cover in black within a single-rule black frame, with shell and branch decorations surrounding the frame, also in black. The front cover reads: "THE [dot] BETTER | [dot] SORT [dot] | HENRY [dot] JAMES | METHUEN'S COLONIAL LIBRARY [in sans-serif] | This edition is for circulation in India and the Colonies only. [in smaller type]". The back cover, also lettered in black within a double-rule black frame, reads: "METHUEN'S | COLONIAL LIBRARY." followed by a nine line description of the library, which in turn is followed by a double-column list of "AMONG THE AUTHORS CONTRIBUTING ARE–", with 16 names in the first column and 15 in the second. The spine of this volume is missing. The endpapers are of cream laid paper, and the text is printed on wove paper. A 40-page paginated publisher's catalogue printed on wove paper, dated November 1902, is bound in at the end. The front pastedown starts an ad for Methuen's Colonial Library, listing works of fiction, which list continues on the recto and verso of the front free endpaper and on the recto of the rear free endpaper. The verso of the rear free endpaper starts an ad for Methuen's Colonial Library, listing works of "General Literature", which continues onto the rear pastedown.

The title-page is stamped "WITH THE PUBLISHER'S COMPLIMENTS".

It is curious, given that the publisher's records show only one printing, that the text block of this colonial issue is slightly thicker (1.154") than that used for the domestic issue (1.107").

57.7.0. *The Better Sort*, first edition (American), first impression, binding state A, one volume, New York 1903.

THE BETTER SORT | BY | HENRY JAMES | NEW YORK | CHARLES SCRIBNER'S SONS | 1903

Size: 7 $^9/_{16}$" x 5".

Collation: [unsigned, 1⁴ 2–28⁸]; pp. [i–viii], 1–[429] [430] [431–432].

Contents: [i–ii] blank, verso ad headed: "By the Same Author [in Gothic type]", listing *The Sacred Fount* and *The Wings of the Dove*, with dollar prices; [iii–iv] half-title, verso blank; [v–vi] title-page, verso copyright notice, printing history and printer's device: "Copyright, 1903, by | CHARLES SCRIBNER'S SONS | [rule] | Published, February, 1903 | [device of the Scribner's Press]"; [vii–viii] CONTENTS", verso blank; 1–[429] text; [430] blank; [431–432] blank leaf.

Binding: faded rose sateen smooth cloth. The front cover, lettered in gilt within a single rule gilt frame, reads: "THE BETTER | SORT | By | HENRY JAMES". The back cover is neither lettered nor decorated. The spine, lettered and decorated in gilt, reads: "THE | BETTER | SORT | [small leaf device] | HENRY | JAMES | SCRIBNERS". The endpapers are of white laid paper, and the text is printed on laid paper. The top edge is gilt, and the other edges are untrimmed.

E&L A57b and BAL 10652 note two variant brasses for the publisher's imprint on the spine (no priority). The imprint on the spine of this copy is in uniform serif capitals $5/32''$ high; see 57.8.0 for the second variant binding.

American printing history. Scribner's Archive. Cards (3) Box 13: Id-J. First edition: *first impression* 3700 copies printed on February 20, 1903, all bound between February 24, 1903, and January 23, 1914; published February 26, 1903; *second impression* 260 copies printed on December 8, 1914, all bound between March 8, 1915, and April 6, 1917; *third impression* 260 copies printed on December 18, 1917, all bound between January 14, 1918, and January 27, 1921; notation opposite the second impression: "Omit gilt top, and side stamping and use a cheaper cloth". "NEW ED[ition]" 515 copies printed on June 7, 1922, all bound between September 22, 1923, and November 20, 1929; notation: "1931 Feb 1 71 [copies] destroyed".

Given the small print run it is probable that the "New Edition" is not a separate edition, but is the fourth impression of the first edition.

All impressions were printed and bound by Scribner's. The first impression of the first edition was printed on $30\frac{1}{2}''$ x 39" 80 weight Grantham laid toned 4 ½ paper. The second impression was printed on 39" x 61" 145 weight "il ni" [sic] paper. The paper used for the third impression and the "New Edition" is not recorded.

The three impressions of the first edition were price at $1.50. The "New Edition" was priced at $2.50.

THE BETTER SORT

57.8.0. *The Better Sort*, first edition (American), first impression, binding state B, one volume, New York 1903.

The title-page, size, collation, and contents are identical to those of the first edition (American), first impression, binding state A, 57.7.0.

Binding: identical to 57.7.0 , except that the cloth is a chocolate-brown smooth fine linen-grain cloth (clearly not rose sateen and less silky than that described in E&L A57b). The publisher's imprint on the spine is in uniform capitals of a finer slightly smaller type ($^3/_{32}$" high), less serifed than on 57.7.0. The endpapers are of white laid paper, and the text is printed on laid paper. The top edge is gilt, and the other edges are untrimmed.

BAL 10652 notes: "sateen: old rose; tan; the variation in color may have been caused by fading." E&L A57b records two variants of the spine brasses, but does not record the cloth color as chocolate-brown or the cloth as fine linen-grain. But the difference in cloth suggests that this binding is not just an unfaded copy of the binding described in E&L, but is a variant binding, and may in fact be the second variant recorded by E&L which was mistaken as to its cloth type.

57.9.0. *The Better Sort*, first edition (American), second impression, one volume, New York 1914.

THE BETTER SORT | BY | HENRY JAMES | NEW YORK | CHARLES SCRIBNER'S SONS | 1914

Size: 7 $^7/_{16}$" x 4 $^7/_8$".

Collation: [unsigned, 1–27^8, 28^4]; pp. [i–viii], 1–[429] [430] [431–432].

Contents: [i–ii] blank, verso ad headed: "BOOKS BY HENRY JAMES | Published By Charles Scribner's Sons", listing 9 titles with dollar prices, and "NOVELS AND TALES. NEW YORK EDITION | 24 vols., net $48.00"; [iii–iv] half-title, verso blank; [v–vi] title-page, verso copyright notice, printing history and printer's device as on the title-leaf verso of the first edition (American), first impression, 57.7.0; [vii–viii] "CONTENTS", verso blank; 1–[429] text; [430] blank; [431–432] blank leaf.

Binding: faded rose sateen smooth cloth, lettered and decorated on the front cover and spine identically to 57.7.0. The back cover is neither lettered nor decorated. The publisher's imprint at the foot of the spine is in uniform capitals 5/32″ high and is 1 5/16″ wide. The endpapers are of white wove paper, and the text is printed on wove paper. The top edge is gilt, the fore-edge is untrimmed, and the bottom edge is rough trimmed.

❧✠❦

58. THE AMBASSADORS

58.1.0. *The Ambassadors*, first edition, first impression, English issue, one volume, London 1903.

THE AMBASSADORS | BY | HENRY JAMES | METHUEN & CO. | 36 ESSEX STREET W.C. | LONDON | 1903

Size: 7 7/16″ x 4 7/8″.

Collation: [A]² B–I K–U X–Z 2A–2F⁸ 2G⁶; pp. [i–iv] [1–2], [3]–458 [459–460].

Contents: [i–ii] half-title, verso ad headed: "BY THE SAME AUTHOR", listing 13 titles; [iii–iv] title-page, verso blank; [1–2] divisional fly-title, verso blank; [3]–458 text; [459] printer's imprint: "PLYMOUTH | WILLIAM BRENDON AND SON | PRINTERS"; [460] blank.

Binding: red vertical-rib-grain cloth. The front cover has an oblong gilt frame off centered to the right within which, justified on the left, is lettered in gilt: "The | Ambassadors | BY | HENRY JAMES". The back cover is neither lettered nor decorated. The spine has at the top a vertical oblong gilt frame within which is lettered in gilt: "The | Ambassadors | HENRY | JAMES", and at the foot of the spine in gilt within a smaller horizontal gilt frame: "METHUEN". The endpapers are of white wove paper, and the text is printed on wove paper. The top edge is trimmed and stained ochre, the fore-edge is trimmed, and the bottom edge is untrimmed. A 40-page paginated publisher's catalogue, dated July 1903, printed on wove paper, is bound in at the end, the last leaf of which, [39–40], is blank.

This binding is uniform with those of the first edition, first impression, English issue, of *The Soft Side* (1900) and *The Better Sort* (1903), 54.1.0 and 57.1.0.

THE AMBASSADORS

English printing history. Methuen Mss. LMC 2230. Methuen Stock Ledger, Vol. 2, p. 234. First edition: *first impression*: September 11, 1903, 3500 copies, with 18 over, 2200 bound for the English issue between September 12 and December 7, 1903, and 799 for the colonial issue between January 11 and January 28, 1904 (399 in cloth and 400 in paper wrappers). It would appear that 501 copies of the first impression were not bound for Methuen. *Second impression*: December 24, 1903, 1500 copies, with 10 over, 491 copies were bound for the English issue between January 13, 1904, and July 13, 1907, and 210 copies for the colonial issue were bound between July 16, 1906, and August 3, 1907 (25 in cloth and 185 in paper wrappers). It would appear that 799 copies of the second impression were not bound for Methuen. The fact that 1300 copies of the two impressions, were not recorded as being bound for Methuen may be tied to an entry in red ink dated 23 November 1903: "1300 Burut". It is possible that to fulfill this order for 1300 copies, 501 copies of the first impression were used, and a second impression was printed, in part, to fulfill the 799 balance of the order. Other notations: "1000 Col[onial] 500 Eng[lish]", and "Coln[ia]l Lib. Covers 1,000 Aug. 31/03"; "Type distributed Feb. 1/04"; "Plates melted down 6/8/07"; "Letterings destroyed 5/2/13" and "M[oulds] destroyed 22/8/16".

The domestic issues were priced at 6s., and the colonial issues at 1s. 9d. in cloth and 1s. 6d. in paper wrappers.

A second English edition was published by Macmillan as Volume [XXXII and XXXIII] of *The Novels and Stories of Henry James*; see 86.1.0–86.2.0.

58.2.0. *The Ambassadors*, first edition, first impression, English issue, variant (remainder?) binding state, one volume, London 1903.

Size: $7\,^{1}/_{16}$" x $4\,^{5}/_{8}$".

The title-page, collation, and contents are identical to those of first edition, first impression, English issue, 58.1.0, except that the last leaf, $2G_6$, [459–460], has been excised, which in 58.1.0 is blank except for the printer's imprint on the recto.

Binding: poor quality light blue linen-grain cloth. The front cover has a gilt oblong single-rule frame, within which is lettered in gilt: "The | Ambassa– | dors | [rule] | H. | James". The back cover is neither lettered nor decorated. The spine, lettered in gilt, reads: "The | Ambassa– | dors

| [rule] | H. James". No publisher's imprint is present at the foot of the spine. The endpapers are of smooth white wove paper, and the text is printed on the same wove paper as that used in 58.1.0. All edges are trimmed. No publisher's catalogue is bound in at the end.

This variant (probably remainder) binding of the first edition, first impression, sheets is not noted in E&L or BAL.

58.3.0. *The Ambassadors*, first edition, second impression, English issue, one volume, London 1904.

The title-page, size, collation, and contents are identical to those of the first edition, first impression, 58.1.0, except that the title-page has on it between the author's name and the publisher's imprint "SECOND EDITION", and at the foot is dated 1904.

Binding: red vertical-rib-grain cloth lettered and decorated on the front cover and spine identically to 58.1.0. Bound in at the end is the same publisher's catalogue of ads, dated July 1903, as is bound in at the end of 58.1.0.

E&L does not record a second impression in a red or crimson binding as this copy. E&L A58a records that the second impression was bound in blue vertically-ribbed cloth, and from E&L's description of that binding it would seem that it is uniform (except as to the type of cloth) with the blue binding on the first edition, English issue, of *The Better Sort* (1903), 57.4.0, which E&L believed to be a remainder binding.

58.4.0. *The Ambassadors*, first edition, second impression, colonial issue, cloth binding state, one volume, London 1904.

THE AMBASSADORS | BY | HENRY JAMES | METHUEN & CO. | 36 ESSEX STREET W.C. | LONDON | 1904 | Colonial Library [in italic]

Size: $7\,7/16''$ x $4\,15/16''$.

Collation: $[A]^2$ (–$[A]_1$) B–I K–U X–Z 2A–2F^8 2G^6; pp. [i–ii] [1–2], [3]–458 [459–460]. The excised leaf, $[A]_1$, is the colonial half-title of which the stub is present.

Contents: [i–ii] title-page, verso blank; [1–2] divisional fly-title, verso blank; [3]–458 text; [459] printer's imprint : "PLYMOUTH | WILLIAM BRENDON AND SON | PRINTERS"; [460] blank.

THE AMBASSADORS

Binding: dark blue diaper-grain cloth, lettered in blind on the front cover: "THE | AMBASSADORS | [rule] | HENRY JAMES". No lettering or decoration is present on the back cover. The spine, lettered in gilt, reads: "THE | AMBASSADORS | HENRY JAMES | METHUEN'S | COLONIAL LIBRARY". The endpapers are of white laid paper, and the text is printed on wove paper. The top and fore-edges are trimmed, and the bottom edge is untrimmed. A 40-page paginated publisher's catalogue printed on wove paper, dated July 1903, is bound in at the end (the last leaf of which is blank). The front pastedown starts an ad for "Methuen's Colonial Library", listing works of fiction, which list continues on the recto and verso of the front free endpaper and on the recto of the rear free endpaper. The verso of the rear free endpaper starts a list of "GENERAL LITERATURE", which is continued on the rear pastedown.

The publisher's catalogue of ads bound in at the end is the same catalogue as appears at the end of the first edition, first impression, English issue, 58.1.0.

This copy is possibly an early state of the second impression (which has the same 1904 date on the title-page), although the title-page of the second impression also has on it "SECOND EDITION", which is not present here.

Illustrated Plate 25.

58.5.0. *The Ambassadors*, first edition, second impression, colonial issue, wrappered binding state, one volume, London 1904.

The title-page, which is dated 1904, is the same as that of the first edition, second impression, colonial issue, cloth binding state, 58.4.0.

Size: $7\,^{3}/_{16}"$ x $4\,^{7}/_{8}"$.

Collation: identical to that of 58.4.0, except that the first signature is [A]², the colonial half-title is present.

Contents: identical to those of 58.4.0, except that [i–ii] is the colonial half-title, verso an ad for works: "BY THE SAME AUTHOR", listing 13 titles, and [iii–iv] is the title-page, verso blank.

Binding: red wove paper wrappers, cut flush, lettered on the front cover in black within a single-rule black frame, with shell and branch decorations surrounding the frame, also in black. The front cover reads: "[dot] THE [dot] | AMBASSADORS | [dot] Henry [dot] JAMES [dot] | METHUEN'S COLONIAL LIBRARY [in sans-serif] | This edition is for circulation in India and the Colonies only. [in smaller type]". The back cover, also lettered in black within a double-rule black frame, reads: "METHUEN'S | COLONIAL LIBRARY.", followed by a nine-line description of the library, which in turn is followed by a double-column list of "AMONG THE AUTHORS CONTRIB-UTING ARE -", with 16 names in the first column and 15 in the second. The spine, lettered and decorated in black, reads: "THE | AMBASSA-DORS | [star device] | [dot] HENRY [dot] JAMES [dot] | [star device] | METHUEN". The endpapers are of white laid paper, and the text is printed on wove paper. The endpapers have the same ads as on the endpapers of the preceding copy of the colonial impression. A 40-page paginated publisher's catalogue printed on wove paper, dated July 1903, is bound in at the end.

The publisher's catalogue bound in at the end is the same as at the end of 58.1.0.

Illustrated Plate 25.

58.6.0. *The Ambassadors*, first American edition, first impression, binding state A, one volume, New York and London 1903.

THE AMBASSADORS [in red] | A NOVEL [in Gothic type] | by [in Gothic type] | HENRY JAMES | Author of "The Awkward Age" "Daisy Miller" | "An International Episode" etc. | [publisher's device] | NEW YORK AND LONDON | HARPER & BROTHERS PUBLISHERS | MCMIII

Size: 8 3/16" x 5 3/8".

Collation: π^1 [1]^8 2–27^8; pp. [i–ii] [1–2], 3–[432].

Contents: [i–ii] title-page, verso copyright notice, reservation of rights and printing history, all within a small single-rule frame: "Copyright, 1902, 1903, by Harper & Brothers. | [rule] | All rights reserved. [in italic] | Published November, 1903."; [1–2] divisional fly-title, verso blank; 3–[432] text.

Binding: greenish-blue paper over boards. The front and back covers are neither lettered nor decorated. The spine, lettered and decorated in gilt, reads: "[double rule] | THE | AMBASSADORS | [single rule]

THE AMBASSADORS

| HENRY JAMES | [double rule] | [single rule] | HARPERS | [double rule]". The publisher's imprint at the foot of the spine is in uniform capitals ³/₃₂" high. The endpapers are of white laid paper, and the text is printed on wove paper. There are no binder's fly leaves. The top edge is gilt, and the other edges are untrimmed.

Dust-jacket: dark blue diagonal-fine-ribbed stiff cloth on paper, with no lettering or decoration on the front or back covers or the front and back inner flaps. The spine is lettered and decorated in gilt identically to the spine of the book.

On the 1902 copyright date see BAL 10651.

American printing history: Nothing has been found in the surviving Harper records regarding the printing history of this title. E&L records that the first edition, first impression, was of 4,000 copies. It was published in November 1903. A second impression (number of copies unknown) was published in 1904; see 58.8.0. Two further impressions (number of copies unknown) were published in 1920 and 1923; see 58.11.0 and 58.12.0.

The first two impressions were priced at $2.00.

A second American edition was published by Scribner's as Volumes XXI and XXII of *The Novels and Tales of Henry James*; see 64.1.0.

58.7.0. *The Ambassadors*, first American edition, first impression, binding state B, one volume, New York and London 1903.

The title-page, size, collation, and contents are identical to those of first American edition, first impression, binding state A, 58.6.0.

Binding: dark blue diagonal-fine-ribbed cloth (rather than greenish-blue paper over boards of 58.6.0), which is the same cloth used for the dust-jacket on 58.6.0. The front and back covers are neither lettered nor decorated. The spine has lettering and rules in gilt identical to those on the spine of 58.6.0. The endpapers are of white laid paper, and the text is printed on wove paper. There are no binder's fly-leaves. The top edge is gilt, and the other edges are untrimmed.

On the front pastedown is the bookplate of The Booklovers Library, 1323 Walnut Street, Philadelphia.

THE AMBASSADORS

E&L A58b records this binding as being a remainder binding issued circa 1906. BAL 10656, citing E&L, states that a copy of this binding state was not located. The presence of The Booklovers Library (predecessor to The Tabard Inn Library) bookplate in this copy suggests that it is not a remainder binding but rather a library binding; see 48.8.0.

58.8.0. *The Ambassadors*, first American edition, second impression, binding state A, one volume, New York and London 1904.

The title-page, size, collation, and contents are identical to those of the first American edition, first impression, binding state A, 58.6.0 (including the title on the title-page being printed in red), except that the title-page is dated 1904 rather than 1903.

Binding: greenish-blue paper over boards identical to that on 58.6.0. The endpapers are of white laid paper, and the text is printed on wove paper. There are no binder's fly-leaves. The top edge is gilt, and the other edges are untrimmed.

Dust-jacket: identical to that on the first American edition, first impression, binding state A, 58.6.0.

Neither E&L nor BAL records a copy with a 1904 date on the title-page.

58.9.0. *The Ambassadors*, first American edition, second impression, binding state B, one volume, New York and London 1904.

The title-page, size, collation, and contents are identical to those of the first American edition, first impression, binding state A, 58.6.0 (including the title on the title-page being printed in red), except that the title-page is dated 1904 rather than 1903.

Binding: maroon vertical-rib-grain cloth, lettered and decorated in gilt on the spine identically to 58.6.0. The endpapers are of white wove paper, and the text is printed on wove paper. There are no binder's fly-leaves. The top edge is gilt, the fore-edge is untrimmed, and the bottom edge is rough trimmed.

On the front free endpaper is the inscription: "M.M.S. | From J.H.B. | 12 Nov. 1916." On the rear pastedown is a small red bookseller's ticket reading: "James Hope & Sons, | Booksellers and Stationers, | OTTAWA."

58.10.0. *The Ambassadors*, first American edition, second impression, binding state C, one volume, New York and London 1904.

Size: 8 1/4″ x 5 7/16″.

The title-page, collation, and contents are identical to those of the first American edition, first impression, binding state A, 58.6.0 (including the title on the title-page being printed in red), except that the title-page is dated 1904 rather than 1903.

Binding: blue vertical-rib-grain cloth, lettered and decorated in gilt identically to 58.6.0. The endpapers are of white wove paper, and the text is printed on wove paper. A binder's fly leaf of wove paper is at the front, but none at the back. The top edge is gilt, the fore-edge is untrimmed and the bottom edge is rough trimmed.

58.11.0. *The Ambassadors*, first American edition, later impression, one volume, New York and London [n.d., 1920].

The title-page is identical to that of the first American edition, first impression, binding state A, 58.6.0, except that it is printed entirely in black, and there is no date at the foot.

Size: 8 1/4″ x 5 3/8″.

The collation and contents are identical to those of 58.6.0, except that the title-leaf verso reads: "Copyright, 1902, 1903, by Harper & Brothers. | [rule] | All rights reserved. [in italic] | Printed in the United States of America | E-U". This is not within a single-rule frame.

Binding: maroon diaper cloth, lettered and decorated in gilt only on the spine identically to 58.6.0. The endpapers are of white wove paper, and the text is printed on wove paper. A binder's fly-leaf of wove paper is at the front, but none at the back. The top edge is trimmed and stained ochre, and the fore-edge and bottom edges are untrimmed.

This copy is 1.17″ thick (excluding boards), as against 1.31″ inches thick for all of the above copies of the first and second impressions.

The letters "E-U" on the title-leaf verso of this copy indicate that it was printed in May 1920; see 8.14.0.

58.12.0. *The Ambassadors*, first American edition, later impression, one volume, New York and London [n.d., 1923].

The title-page is identical to that of the first American edition, first impression, binding state A, 58.6.0, except that it is printed entirely in black, and there is no date at the foot.

Size: 8 1/16" x 5 7/16".

The collation and contents are identical to those of 58.6.0, except that the verso of the title-leaf reads: "Copyright, 1902, 1903, by Harper & Brothers. | [rule] | All rights reserved. [in italic] | Printed in the United States of America | A–X". This is not within a single-rule frame.

Binding: dark blue vertical-rib-grain cloth, lettered and decorated in gilt on the spine identically to 58.6.0, except that the publisher's imprint at the foot of the spine is in uniform capitals 3/16" high and is between two single gilt rules. The endpapers are of white wove paper, and the text is printed on wove paper. A binder's fly-leaf of wove paper is at the front, but none at the back. The top edge is trimmed and stained ochre, the bottom edge is trimmed and the fore-edge is rough trimmed.

This copy is 1.10" thick (excluding boards).

The letters "A–X" on the title-leaf verso indicate that this copy was printed in January 1923; see 8.14.0.

※+※

59. *WILLIAM WETMORE STORY AND HIS FRIENDS*

Shortly after the American sculptor William Wetmore Story[38] died in October 1895, Story's son and his son's wife asked James to write Story's biography from materials (letters, diaries and published works) which they would provide. James, who had known Story since 1873, agreed, albeit reluctantly. But James, recovering from four years of disastrous

---

38 William Wetmore Story (1819–1895) began his career as a lawyer practising in Boston. He wrote a number of books on the law, including *Story on Contracts* and *Story on Sales*, which were influential legal texts. He also wrote a biography on his father, Joseph Story, an associate justice of the United States Supreme Court. Story abandoned the law to pursue sculpture, first visiting Italy for instruction in sculpture in 1847, and then settling in Rome "for good" in 1856.

and unrenumerative experiments with the theatre, delayed starting work on the Story biography. The delay is entirely understandable. Not only did James need to augment his income, but the years 1896 to 1903 were for James a period of intense creativity. In that period he published five major novels: *What Maisie Knew* (1897), *The Awkward Age* (1899), *The Sacred Fount* (1901), *The Wings of the Dove* (1902), and *The Ambassadors* (1903), as well as publishing six other lesser works.

In June 1896, and again a year later, James offered to withdraw from the project, but the Storys stood firm. In October 1897, James wrote to the Edinburgh publisher William Blackwood, who had expressed through friends an interest in publishing the biography, pointing out that "my time is too valuable…for me to write Mr. Story's Life…as a mere friendly & unremunerated task." Finding it "awkward" to raise the delicate issue of money with the Story family, James suggested that Blackwood pay him "a definite fee at its completion – which should exhaust my interest in it."; Horne, Letter 158. At the time, as this letter makes clear, James thought that there was material for only one volume, and a medium-sized volume at that. James would not, however, agree to any "fixed limit of time" within which to complete the task, a condition to which the Story family agreed. Later that month James suggested to Blackwood that a fee of £250 for the British, colonial and American rights for up to (a rather optimistic) 7,000 copies would be appropriate, with a further payment of £100 for each 2,000 copies over and above the first 7,000. Blackwood accepted these terms as well as the condition of no time fixed within which to deliver the completed manuscript. As a result, James had no pecuniary interest in the success of the work, to his later regret as in America it was "much acclaimed". On December 11, 1903, James wrote to William Dean Howells:

> As for the terribly perfunctory little vols. on W. W. Story, (extorted from me by the inexorable pressure of the family, [sic]) I am sorry to say I have no material interest nor property in the American edition – having long ago, on a dark day, parted with *all* rights, for a beggarly dole, to Blackwoods here. But now I hear that the American edition is perversely *selling* – in a degree sufficient, at all events, for my confusion [emphasis in original].[39]

---

39 Quoted in Michael Anesko, *Letters, Fictions, Lives: Henry James and William Dean Howells* (Oxford: Oxford University Press, 1997), 396.

James did not actually start work on the biography until August 1902, with the preliminary copying (creating typewritten transcripts) of the letters, and probably other documents, being undertaken by his secretary, Agnes Weld. James began dictating the text to his secretary in late September 1902, and the work proceeded rapidly to his dictation. The finished manuscript was delivered to Blackwood in March 1903, and they published it in October 1903. The American issue, which consisted of imported British sheets, was published by Houghton, Mifflin & Co., also in October 1903. The British publication preceded the American in all probability by a day or two. The work went through five impressions in 1903–1905, in all 2238 copies were printed, of which 1780 [1179?] were shipped to America. James ordered 39 copies for distribution to friends. Was the large number of copies he gave away an indication of his satisfaction with what he had accomplished? The work was not reprinted again until the late 1950s, when an edition was published in Boston by the Grove Press.

59.1.0. *William Wetmore Story and His Friends*, first edition, first impression, first state, English issue, trial binding (?), two volumes, Edinburgh and London 1903.

WILLIAM WETMORE STORY | AND | HIS FRIENDS | FROM LETTERS, DIARIES, AND RECOLLECTIONS | BY | HENRY JAMES | IN TWO VOLUMES | VOL. I. [II.] | WILLIAM BLACKWOOD AND SONS | EDINBURGH AND LONDON | MCMIII | All rights reserved [in italic]

Size: 7 $^{13}/_{16}$" x 5 $^{1}/_{16}$".

Collation: Volume I: $\pi^4(-\pi_1)$ (π_2+X_1) [A]^8 B–I K–U X–Z^8 2A^2; pp. [i–vi] [1–2], [3]–371 [372] plus 2. Volume II: $\pi^4(-\pi_1)$ (π_2+X_1) [A]^8 B–I K–U X^8 Y^6(–Y$_6$); pp. [i–vi] [1–2], [3]–338 [339]–345 [346] plus 2.

Contents: [i–ii] half-title, verso blank; frontispiece with tissue guard tipped in not reckoned in the pagination; [iii–iv] title-page, verso blank; [v–vi] "CONTENTS OF THE FIRST VOLUME.", verso blank; [1–2] divisional fly-title, verso blank; [3]–371 text; 371 at foot printer's imprint: "PRINTED BY WILLIAM BLACKWOOD AND SONS"; [372] blank. Volume II: [i–ii] half-title, verso blank; frontispiece with tissue guard tipped in not reckoned in the pagination; [iii–iv] title-page, verso blank; [v–vi] "CONTENTS OF THE SECOND VOLUME.", verso blank; [1–2] divisional fly-title, verso blank; [3]–338 text; [339]–345

"INDEX."; 345 at foot printer's imprint as on 371 of Volume I; [346] blank.

The text of Volume I, signatures [A]–Q, is setting A as recorded in BAL 10655. Also, on 114, line 7 of that Volume a "slug" mark (a protruding en quadrate) is present after the first word "and".

Binding: dark blue-green diagonal-rib-grain cloth. The front and back covers are neither lettered nor decorated. The spines, lettered and decorated in gilt, read: "[single rule] | WILLIAM | WETMORE | STORY | VOL I [II] | HENRY [offset to the left] | JAMES [offset to the right] | [single rule]". There are no publisher's imprints at the foot of the spines. The endpapers are of light cream wove paper, and the text is printed on wove paper. There are no binder's fly-leaves in either volume. The top edge is trimmed and stained brown, and the other edges are trimmed.

This binding and the brasses have the "look" of a publisher's trial binding. BAL 10655 notes in his "Publication Notes" under that entry the presumptive existence of a trial binding. The off-center lettering of the author's name on the spine of this binding is the same as the style adopted for the author's name on the spine of the primary binding of the first edition, first impression, 59.2.0. This conclusion is buttressed by the fact that this copy is of setting A and it has the "slug" mark on p. 114 of Volume I.

Printing history. Blackwood and Sons Archive, Ms. 30864, Publications Ledger 1895–1907, 284. First edition, two volumes: *first impression* September (no day) 1903, 1260 copies printed, of which 520 copies on September 5, 1903, and 250 copies on October 10, 1903, were sold to Houghton Mifflin, 3 copies delivered to the author, and a further 39 copies sent at the direction of the author; *second impression* November (no day) 1903, 230 copies printed, and 250 copies (probably including some sheets of the first impression) sold to Houghton Mifflin on November 11, 1903; *third impression* December (no day) 1903, 378 copies printed, and 250 copies sold to Houghton Mifflin on December 29, 1903; notation: "250 titles Boston imprint"; *fourth impression* February (no day) 1904, 170 [150?] copies printed, and 123 copies sold to Houghton Mifflin on February 5, 1904, 127 copies on February 15, 1904, and 60 copies on November 11, 1904; *fifth impression* August (no day) 1905, 200 copies printed, all sold to Houghton Mifflin. Total copies printed 2338

[2218?]; total sold to Houghton Mifflin 1780; total to author or directed by him 42; and total sold by Blackwoods 416 [396?].

Houghton Mifflin's record of sheets imported. Houghton, Mifflin Archive. Ms Am 2030(22), 220: "rcvd from Wm Blackwood & Sons": September 5, 520/500 copies, 520 bound between September 26, 1903, and November 9, 1903; October 16, 1903 250 copies, 249 bound between November 5, 1903, and November 30, 1903; November 5 and 11, 1903, 150 and 100 copies, 251 bound between November 27, 1903, and January 20, 1904; December 29, 1903, 250 copies, all bound between January 25, 1904, and March 4, 1904; February 4, 1904, 123 copies, all bound between March 3, 1904, and March 19, 1905; February 15, 1904, 127 copies, 126 bound on March 18 and 19, 1904; November 25, 1904, 60 copies all bound between December 15, 1904, and January 18, 1905; August 21, 1905, 200 copies all bound between September 14, 1905, and March 25, 1922. Notation: "[total copies] 1760". This number tallies with the total only if one assumes the September 5, 1903, copies imported numbered 500, however, the total number bound adds up to 1779. Note that the dates of receipt are dates of the invoices, not actual delivery dates.

The English issues were priced at 24s., and the American issues were priced at $5.00.

James in a letter to William Gosse of 2 October 1903 told Gosse that the volumes of William Wetmore Story and His Friends "contain a horrid misprint somewhere ... a dreadful "causal" for "casual".... As well as the fact that there are 2 or 3 provoking little misplacements & omissions of punctuation – perpetrated after my last proofs had gone right back."[40] The "horrid misprint" "causal" has not been found. However, it is likely that the "misplacements & omissions of punctuation" were the impetus for resetting signatures [A]–Q of Volume I; see BAL 10655 which identifies changes on 32 pages of these signatures. There is a possible misprint in Volume II, 5, line 13, the last word "violet" should possibly read "violate", and on 224, line 1, the word "too" has a broken "o" and the last letter reads "c". This broken letter also appears in the third impression, 59.6.0. On 334, line 11, of Volume II one must question whether the archaic "strown" should perhaps be "strewn".

---

40 Rayburn S. Moore (ed.), *Selected Letters of Henry James to William Goss, 1882–1915* (Baton Rouge and London: Louisiana State University Press, 1988), Letter 204.

59.2.0. *William Wetmore Story and His Friends*, first edition, first impression, first state, English issue, two volumes, Edinburgh and London 1903.

WILLIAM WETMORE STORY | AND | HIS FRIENDS | FROM LETTERS, DIARIES, AND RECOLLECTIONS | BY | HENRY JAMES | IN TWO VOLUMES | VOL. I. [II.] | WILLIAM BLACKWOOD AND SONS | EDINBURGH AND LONDON | MCMIII | All rights reserved [in italic]

Size: 8 1/16″ x 5 1/4″.

Collation: Volume I: π^4 (π_2+X_1) [A]^8 B–I K–U X–Z^8 2A^2; pp. [2] [i–vi] [1–2], [3]–371 [372] plus 2. Volume II: π^4 (π_2+X_1) [A]^8 B–I K–U X^8 Y^6; pp. [2] [i–vi] [1–2], [3]–338 [339]–345 [346] [347–348] plus 2.

The collations are as set forth above for 59.1.0, except that the first signature in each Volume of this copy is π^4, and the last signature of Volume II of this copy is Y^6; consequently this copy has the initial blank leaf in both Volumes, and a final blank leaf in Volume II.

Contents: Volume I: blank leaf; [i–ii] half-title, verso blank; frontispiece with tissue guard tipped in not reckoned in the pagination; [iii–iv] title-page, verso blank; [v–vi] "CONTENTS OF THE FIRST VOLUME.", verso blank; [1–2] divisional fly-title, verso blank; [3]–371 text; 371 at foot printer's imprint: "PRINTED BY WILLIAM BLACKWOOD AND SONS."; [372] blank. Volume II: blank leaf; [i–ii] half-title, verso blank; frontispiece with tissue guard tipped in not reckoned in the pagination; [iii–iv] title-page, verso blank; [v–vi] "CONTENTS OF THE SECOND VOLUME.", verso blank; [1–2] divisional fly-title, verso blank; [3]–338 text; [339]–345 "INDEX."; 345 at foot printer's imprint as on 371 of Volume I; [346] blank; [347–348] blank leaf.

The text of Volume I, signatures [A]–Q, is setting A as recorded in BAL 10655. In addition, a "slug" mark (a protruding en quadrat) is present after the first word "and" on 114, line 7, of Volume I.

Binding: bluish-green calico-grain cloth. The front and back covers are neither lettered nor decorated. The spine, lettered and decorated in gilt, reads: "[single rule followed by two thin wavy rules] | WILLIAM | WETMORE | STORY | VOL. I. [II.] | HENRY [offset to the left] | JAMES [offset to the right] | Wm. Blackwood & Sons | Edinburgh & London | [two thin wavy rules followed by a single rule]". The "m" in the printer's imprint on the spine is raised above a dot. The endpapers are of white wove paper, and the text is printed on wove paper. There are no binder's fly-leaves in either volume. The top edge is untrimmed, and the other edges are rough trimmed.

There appear to be two variants of BAL's setting A in both the English and American first editions, first impressions, of this title, one with a "slug" mark (a protruding en quadrate) after the first word "and" on 114, line 7, of Volume I, and a second in which the "slug" mark is not present. No copy of BAL's setting B has been seen with such a "slug" mark. See comment following 59.6.0 on the possible distinguishing features of the first five impressions of the first edition of this title.

59.3.0. *William Wetmore Story and His Friends*, first edition, first impression, second state, English issue, two volumes, Edinburgh and London 1903.

This copy is identical to the first edition, first impression, first state, English issue, 59.2.0 (BAL's setting A), except that no "slug" mark is present after the first word "and" on 114, line 7, of Volume I.

There are no binder's fly-leaves in either volume.

59.4.0. *William Wetmore Story and His Friends*, first edition, second or third impression, English issue, two volumes, Edinburgh and London 1903.

This copy is identical to the first edition, first impression, first state, English issue, 59.2.0, except that the text of Volume I, signatures [A]–Q, is BAL's setting B. Also on 114, line 7, no "slug" mark is present after the first word "and".

There are no binder's fly-leaves in either volume.

On the front free endpaper is written in pencil: "Leonard Woolf's | copy with notes | by him."

59.5.0. *William Wetmore Story and His Friends*, first edition, first impression, first state, American issue, two volumes, Boston 1903.

WILLIAM WETMORE STORY | AND | HIS FRIENDS | FROM LETTERS, DIARIES, AND RECOLLECTIONS | BY | HENRY JAMES | IN TWO VOLUMES | VOL. I. [II.] | HOUGHTON, MIFFLIN & CO. | BOSTON | 1903 | All rights reserved [in italic]

Size: $7\,7/8''$ x $5\,3/16''$.

The collation and contents are identical to that of the first edition, first impression, first state, English issue, 59.2.0.

The text of Volume I, signatures [A]–Q, is BAL's setting A. Also, on 114, line 7 of that Volume a "slug" mark (a protruding en quadrate) is present after the first word "and".

Binding: dark green linen-grain cloth. The front and back covers are not lettered, but the front covers are decorated with two rules (the first thin and the second thicker) in gilt across the tops, which rules extend across the tops of the spines. The spines, lettered and decorated in gilt, read: "[two rules] | WILLIAM | WETMORE | STORY | AND HIS | FRIENDS | I [II] | HENRY JAMES | HOUGHTON | MIFFLIN & CO." The ampersand is stylized. The endpapers are of white laid paper, and the text is printed on wove paper. A binder's fly-leaf of wove paper is at the end of Volume I. There are no binder's fly-leaves in Volume II. The top edges are gilt, and the other edges are rough trimmed.

59.6.0. *William Wetmore Story and His Friends*, first edition, second or third impression, American issue, two volumes, Boston 1903.

This copy is identical to the first edition, first impression, first state, English issue, 59.2.0, except that the text of Volume I, signatures [A]–Q, is BAL's setting B. Also, on 114, line 7, of that Volume no "slug" mark is present after the first word "and".

The "Note" in BAL 10655, discussing the two settings of Volume I, is slightly ambiguous in that it is not entirely clear whether both settings are to be found in copies of the first edition, American issue, with the 1903 date on the title-page. 59.5.0 and 59.6.0 make it clear that both settings are to be so found.

59.7.0. *William Wetmore Story and His Friends*, first edition, fourth impression, American issue, two volumes, Boston 1904.

This copy is identical to the first edition, first impression, first state, English issue, 59.2.0, except that the title-page is dated 1904, the text of Volume I, signature [A]–Q is BAL's setting B, and on 114, line 7 of that volume no "slug" mark is present after the first word "and".

E&LA59 b records that impressions later than the first were printed on poorer quality paper. The above copies do not bear this out.

* * *

As a working hypothesis the following are the likely distinguishing features of the first five impressions of this title, all sheets of which were printed in England:

Copies with 1903 title-pages in BAL's setting A of Volume I, which appear in two states, one with and one without the slug mark on line 7 of page 114 of Volume I, are of the first impression of 1260 copies printed in September 1903 (of which 1,020 copies were shipped to Houghton, Mifflin & Company in America, and 39 copies were directed by James as presentation copies). The presence of the slug mark in 59.1.0 (possible trial binding) suggests that the slug mark appears in the earlier state.

Copies with 1903 title-pages in BAL's setting B of Volume I are of the second or third impressions, which are indistinguishable. BAL states that in connection with the second impression "the records suggest some resetting of the types; signatures [A]–Q?" The second impression was of 250 copies printed in November 1903. It is possible that no copies of the second impression were issued in America. The third impression was of 378 copies printed in December 1903 (of which 250 copies were shipped to America).

Copies with 1904 title-pages in BAL's setting B of Volume I are of the fourth impression printed in February 1904 (150 copies). The collation and contents are identical to those of the first edition, first impression, 59.2.0. The binding is identical to that of the first edition, first impression, American issue, 59.5.0.

Copies with 1905 title-pages in BAL's setting B of Volume I (not seen) are of the fifth impression. The fifth impression was of 200 copies printed in August 1905.

Because the American issues of this title were of imported sheets, they did not qualify for an American copyright. The Chase Act of 1891 required that to obtain an American copyright the plates had to be manufactured and the sheets printed in the United States. One can speculate that the lack of the copyright protection was not a problem because the risk of piracy was negligible.

THE GOLDEN BOWL

60. *THE GOLDEN BOWL*

60.1.0. *The Golden Bowl*, first edition, first impression, two volumes, New York 1904.

THE GOLDEN BOWL | BY | HENRY JAMES | VOLUME I [II] | NEW YORK | CHARLES SCRIBNER'S SONS | 1904

Size: $7\frac{1}{2}"$ x $4\frac{15}{16}"$.

Collation: Volume I: π^2 [1]^8 2–25^8 26^6; pp. [i–iv] [1–2], 3–412. Volume II: [1–24^8], signed as π^2 [1]^8 2–23^8 24^6; pp. [i–iv] [1–2], 3–377 [378] [379–380].

Contents: Volume I: [i–ii] half-title, verso ad headed: "BOOKS BY HENRY JAMES", listing 4 titles with dollar prices; [iii–iv] title-page, verso copyright notice, printing history and printer's imprint: "Copyright, 1904, by | CHARLES SCRIBNER'S SONS | [rule] | Published, November, 1904 | TROW DIRECTORY | PRINTING AND BOOKBINDING COMPANY | NEW YORK [printer's imprint in sans-serif]"; [1–2] divisional fly-title, verso blank; 3–412 text. Volume II: [i–ii] half-title, verso ad as on [ii] of Volume I; [iii–iv] title-page, verso copyright notice, printing history and printer's imprint as on [iv] of Volume I; [1–2] divisional fly-title, verso blank; 3–377 text; [378] blank; [379–380] blank leaf.

Binding: smooth tan sateen cloth. The front and back covers are neither lettered nor decorated. The spines, lettered and decorated in gilt, read: "THE | GOLDEN | BOWL | [small leaf device] | HENRY | JAMES | I [II] | SCRIBNERS". The endpapers are of white laid paper, the chain lines running horizontally, and the texts are printed on laid paper, the chain lines running vertically. There are no binder's fly-leaves. The top edges are gilt, and the other edges are rough trimmed.

American printing history. Scribner's Archive. Cards (2) Box 13: Id-J. First edition: *first impression* 2,000 copies of both volumes printed October 28, 1904, all bound between November 7, 1904, and December 14, 1904; published November 12, 1904; *second impression* 1,000 copies of both volumes printed December 8, 1904, all bound between December 14, 1904, and June 12, 1905; *third impression* 500 copies of both volumes printed July 26, 1905, all bound between August 7, 1905, and February 19, 1907; *fourth impression* 250 copies of both volumes printed August 20,

1907, all bound between September 13, 1907, and September 27, 1909; *fifth impression* 265 copies of both volumes printed April 29, 1910, all bound between May 18, 1910, and June 24, 1913; *sixth impression* 250 copies of both volumes printed June 15, 1914, all bound between January 8, 1915, and August 11, 1916; *seventh impression* 245 copies of both volumes printed November 9, 1916, all bound between December 7, 1916, and March 8, 1918; notation: "12/18/18 omit gilt top and use cheaper cloth omit slides [sic]"; *eighth impression* 250 copies of both volumes printed December 10, 1918, all bound between February 6, 1919, and February 11, 1920. "New Ed[ition]": *first impression* 550 copies of both volumes printed June 5, 1922, all bound between September 22, 1923, and April 2, 1925; *second impression* 570 copies of both volumes printed May 22, 1925, all copies bound between July 8, 1925, and December 20, 1927; notations: "2/19/25–540 wrappers", "5/24/27–505–wraps." and "printed 5310".

The first three impressions were printed on 30 $^1/_2$″ x 39″ [Grantham?] laid toned 4 $^1/_2$ paper with a weight of 75 for volume I and 82 for volume II, and and were printed and bound by Trow Directory Printing and Bookbinding Company. The fourth impression was printed by Trow on 33″ x 44″ 80 weight "Pickering S[5?]" paper. The first four impressions were bound by Trow. The fifth through the eighth impressions and the two impressions of the "New Edition" were printed and bound by Scribner's, but the type of paper used is not recorded.

The first impression and probably the following seven impressions of the first edition were priced at $2.50 the set. Both impressions of the "New Edition" were priced at $5.00 the set.

A second American edition was published by Scribner's as Volumes XXIII and XXIV of *The Novels and Tales of Henry James* (The New York Edition); see 64.1.0.

60.2.0. *The Golden Bowl*, first edition, mixed set, second and third impressions, two volumes, New York 1904/1905.

The title-pages (and the title-leaf versos) are identical to those of the first edition, first impression, 60.1.0, except that Volume I is dated 1905 (the third impression) at the foot and Volume II is dated 1904 (the second impression) at the foot.

The size, collations, and contents are identical to those of 60.1.0.

Binding: smooth tan sateen cloth. The front and back covers are neither lettered nor decorated. The spines are lettered and decorated in gilt identically to those of 60.1.0. Volume I has white laid endpapers at the front, the chain lines running horizontally, and white wove endpapers at the back. Volume II has white laid endpapers, the chain lines running horizontally at both the front and the back. The texts of both volumes are printed on laid paper, the chain lines running vertically. A binder's fly-leaf of wove paper is at the front of Volume I, but none at the back. There are no binder's fly-leaves in Volume II. The top edges are gilt, and the other edges are rough trimmed.

On the front free endpaper of *both* volumes is the inscription: "H.S. H. | from W.C.B., | Aguiden | Aug. '05; ['1905' in Volume II]".

60.2.5. *The Golden Bowl*, first edition, sixth impression, two volumes, New York 1914.

The title-pages are identical to those of the first edition, first impression, 60.1.0, except that both are dated 1914 at the foot.

Size: $7\,7/16''$ x $4\,7/8''$.

Collation: Volume I: $[1-26^8]$, signed as π^2 $[1]^8$ $2-25^8$ 26^6; pp. [i–iv] [1–2], 3–412. Volume II: $[1-24^8]$, signed as π^2 $[1]^8$ $2-23^8$ 24^6; pp. [i–iv] [1–2], 3–377 [378] [379–380].

Contents: identical to the first edition, first impression, 60.1.0, except that the on half-title verso, [ii], of both Volumes is an ad headed: "BOOKS BY HENRY JAMES", listing 9 titles with dollar prices, and the title-page versos, [iv], reads: "Copyright, 1904, by | CHARLES SCRIBNER'S SONS | [rule] | Published, November 1904 | [printer's device of The Scribner's Press]".

Binding: smooth tan sateen cloth. The front and back covers are neither lettered nor decorated. The spines are lettered and decorated in gilt identically to those of, 60.1.0. The endpapers are of white wove paper, and the texts are printed on wove paper. There are no binder's fly-leaves. The top edges are gilt, and the other edges are untrimmed.

On the front pastedown of both Volumes is the bookplate of Sophie Von Raelte, dated March 1916. On the rear pastedown of Volume I is a small blue bookseller's ticket printed in brown reading "BRENTANOS | Booksellers & Stationers | New York".

60.3.0. *The Golden Bowl*, first English edition, first impression, English issue, one volume, London [n.d., 1905].

THE GOLDEN BOWL | BY | HENRY JAMES | METHUEN & CO. | 36 ESSEX STREET W.C. | LONDON

Size: $7\,^1/_2''$ x $4\,^7/_8''$.

Collation: π^4 1–34^8 35^2; pp. [2] [i–vi], [1]–548.

Contents: blank leaf; [i–ii] half-title, verso ad headed: "BY THE SAME AUTHOR", listing 14 titles; [iii–iv] title-page, verso printing history: "First Published in 1905 [in italic]"; [v–vi] divisional fly-title, verso blank; [1]–548 text; 548 at foot printer's imprint: "Printed by Morrison & Gibb Limited, Edinburgh [all except printer's name in italic]".

In the ad on [iv], the third title listed is misspelled "What Mansie Knew". This error also appears in the second and third impressions.

Binding: drab blue linen-grain cloth. The front cover is decorated in gilt, with a triangular leaf and vine design in each of the two upper corners, between which is lettered in gilt: "THE | GOLDEN BOWL | HENRY JAMES". The back cover is neither lettered nor decorated. The spine, lettered and decorated in gilt, reads: "[two rules] | THE | GOLDEN | BOWL | HENRY | JAMES | [long strapwork device of intertwined vines with leaves] | METHUEN | [two rules]". The endpapers are of white wove paper, and the text is printed on laid paper. The top edge is trimmed and stained ochre, the fore-edge is trimmed, and the bottom edge is untrimmed. A 40-page paginated publisher's catalogue of ads, dated February 1905, printed on wove paper, is bound in at the end.

As noted in the Methuen letter tipped into 60.5.1, this edition was not issued in a dust-jacket.

English printing history. Methuen Archive. Mss. LMC 2230, Stock Ledger, Vol. 2, p. 413. First edition: *first impression*, January 11, 1905, 3,000 copies, with 26 over, 2389 bound for the English issue between January 31 and March 15, 1905, and 547 for the colonial issue between February 20, and March 15, 1905 (349 in cloth and 198 in paper wrappers); *second impression*, March 7–8, 1905, 1,000 copies, with 10 over, 845 bound for the English issue bound between March 9, 1905, and January 6, 1906, and 50 copies on March 27, 1905, for the colonial issue (all in paper wrappers); *third impression*, March 24, 1905, 1,000 copies, none indicated over, 704 bound for the English issue between October 15, 1908, and February 15, 1911, and 325 for the colonial issue between May 2 and October 15, 1905 (225 in cloth and 100 in paper wrappers). On September 1, 1909, it is recorded that 35 copies of the English issue of the third impression were returned "to be rebound gratis". Notations: "Colonial Covers 500 Jan 9/05", "Lettering destroyed 5/2/13", and "M[oulds] destroyed 22/8/16". Beside both the first and second impressions (but not the third) there is the notation: "Both Titles". As the number of copies of the third impression recorded as bound exceeds the number of copies printed, it is assumed that some second impression sheets were bound as part of the third impression.

All three impressions of the English issue were priced at 6s. The colonial issue is recorded as being priced at 2s. in cloth and 1s. 6d. in paper.

A second English edition was published in 1923 as Volumes [XXXIV] and [XXXXV] of *The Novels and Stories of Henry James*; see 86.1.0–86.2.0

60.3.5. *The Golden Bowl*, first English edition, first impression, English issue, remainder binding, one volume, London [n.d., 1905].

Size: 7 $^{5}/_{16}$" x 4 $^{13}/_{16}$".

The title-page, collation, and contents are identical to those of the first English edition, first impression, English issue, 60.3.0, except the first signature is π^4 ($-\pi_1$), the excised leaf being a blank.

Binding: dark-green fine diaper-grain cloth. The front and back covers are neither lettered nor decorated. The spine, which is lettered and decorated in gilt reads: "[decorative rule composed of four stem roses in a row] | THE | GOLDEN | BOWL [the title is heavily serifed] | H. JAMES [in small sans-serif] | [decorative rule, as at spine head] | [decorative rule as at spine head]". The endpapers are of smooth cream wove paper, and the text is printed on laid paper. All edges are trimmed. There are no ads bound in at the end.

On the front free endpaper is the inscription "C. Pouwens | Xmas 1920".

This is a remainder binding of first impression sheets, probably bound-up in 1919 or 1920. The binding is no doubt by the same binder which bound the second edition, third impression, of *The Princess Casamassima* (1889), 29.6.5. The heavily serifed brasses used for the title, and the small sans-serif font used for the author's name are identical to those used on 29.6.5.

60.4.0. *The Golden Bowl*, first English edition, second impression, English issue, one volume, London [n.d., 1905].

The title-page is identical to that of the first English edition, first impression, English issue, 60.3.0, except that "SECOND EDITION" is present between the author's name and the publisher's imprint.

Size, collation, and contents are identical to those of 60.3.0, except as noted above for the title-page, and the title-leaf verso on which the printing history reads: "First Published .. February 1905 | Second Edition .. [space] 1905 [all in italic]".

Binding: drab blue linen-grain cloth, with decoration and lettering in gilt on the front cover and spine identical to that of 60.3.0. The back cover is neither lettered nor decorated. The endpapers are of white wove paper, and the text is printed on laid paper. The top edge is trimmed and stained ochre, the fore-edge is trimmed, and the bottom edge is untrimmed. A 40-page paginated publisher's catalogue of ads, dated March 1905, printed on a lighter wove paper, is bound in at the end.

60.5.0. *The Golden Bowl*, first English edition, third impression, English issue, one volume, London [n.d., 1905].

The title-page is identical to that of the first English edition, first impression, English issue, 60.3.0, except that "THIRD EDITION" is present between the author's name and the publisher's imprint.

Size, collation, and contents are identical to those of 60.3.0, except as noted above for the title-page, and the verso of the title-leaf on which the printing history reads: "First Published .. February 1905 | Second Edition .. March 1905 | Third Edition .. April 1905 [all in italic]".

Binding: bright blue linen-grain cloth (distinctly brighter than the cloth on the first and second impressions), with decoration and lettering in gilt on the front cover and spine identical to that of the first and second impressions. The back cover is neither lettered nor decorated. The endpapers are of white wove paper, and the text is printed on laid paper. The top edge is trimmed and stained ochre, the fore-edge is trimmed, and the bottom edge is untrimmed. A 32-page paginated publisher's catalogue of ads, dated September 1911, printed on a lighter wove paper, is bound in at the end, [32] of which is blank except for the printer's imprint.

On the recto of the blank leaf is the inscription: "Laura Gregory | Book | –11–".

60.5.1 *The Golden Bowl*, first English edition, third impression, English issue, one volume, London [n.d. 1905].

The title-page, size, collation, and contents are identical to those of the first English edition, third impression, English issue, 60.5.0.

The binding is identical to that on 60.5.0. Bound in at the end is a 32-page paginated catalogue dated October 1910.

Tipped onto the font-free endpaper is a letter dated June 7, 1932, typed on Methuen & Co. LTD letterhead, which reads: "Andrew J. Onderdonk Esq., | 1V. Argentinier Strasse 4, | Vienna. | Dear Sir, | In reply to your card of June 4th. We regret that | Henry James, "The Golden Bowl" was not issued with a jacket. | We are, dear Sir, | Yours faithfully, | METHUEN & CO. LTD."

❧✠❧

61. THE QUESTION OF OUR SPEECH

61.1.0. *The Question of Our Speech*, first edition, first impression, trade issue, binding state A, one volume, Boston and New York, 1905.

THE QUESTION OF OUR | SPEECH | THE LESSON OF BALZAC | Two Lectures [in Gothic type] | BY HENRY JAMES | [vertical oval publisher's device in brown] | BOSTON AND NEW YORK | HOUGHTON, MIFFLIN AND COMPANY | The Riverside Press, Cambridge [in Gothic type] | 1905

Size: 7 $7/16$" x 4 $1/2$".

Collation: [unsigned, 1^8 ($1_1+X_{1,2}$) $2-7^8$ 8^4]; there are two conjugate leaves inserted between [1_1] and [1_2]; pp. [i–vi] [1–2], 3–[116] [117–118].

Contents: [i–ii] blank, verso ad headed: "By Henry James [in Gothic type]", listing 18 titles with dollar prices, the first of which is this title, and in the third line reads: "Postage extra."; [iii–iv] half-title, verso blank; [v–vi] title-page, verso copyright notice, reservation of rights and printing history: "COPYRIGHT 1905 BY HENRY JAMES | ALL RIGHTS RESERVED | Published October 1905 [in italic]"; [1–2] divisional fly-title, verso blank; 3–[116] text; [117–118] blank, verso printer's imprint: "The Riverside Press [in Gothic type] | Electrotyped and printed by H. O. Houghton & Co. | Cambridge, Mass., U.S.A. [last two lines in italic]".

Binding: maroon linen-grain cloth. The front cover, lettered and decorated in gilt, reads: "THE QUESTION OF | OUR SPEECH [small triangular device] | HENRY JAMES", and is justified on the left. The back cover is neither lettered nor decorated. The spine, which is lettered in gilt, reads: "THE | QUESTION | OF OUR | SPEECH | BY | HENRY | JAMES [all the foregoing justified on the left] | "HOUGHTON | MIFFLIN & Co". In the publisher's imprint on the spine the "o's" in "Houghton" and "Co" are raised and smaller in size than the other letters, and a stylized device is used in place of the usual ampersand. The endpapers are of cream laid paper, and the text is printed on laid paper. A binder's fly-leaf of laid paper is at the front, but none at the back. The top edge is gilt, and the other edges are untrimmed.

On the rear pastedown is stamped: "OCT 9 1905" and "120020".

This book was designed by Bruce Rogers.

Printing history. Houghton Mifflin Archive. First edition: Ms Am 2030(22), 219: *first impression* September 16, 1905, 314 [limited issue] and 1721 [trade issue] copies, all bound between September 27 and December 16, 1905; notation: "9/16/05 ptd. 1878 titles with points" and "320 titles without points";[41] *second impression* December 20, 1905, 500 copies, all bound between December 22, 1905, and March 19, 1912; *third impression* January 24, 1913, 165 copies, all bound on April 4 and 7, 1913; *fourth impression* March 10, 1919, 272 copies, all bound on November 29, 1919, and November 17, 1920; notation: "3/19/19 ptd. 306 4 pp. titles and 290 jackets". Ms Am 2030(23), 215: *fifth impression* July 29, 1926, 528 copies, all bound between August 24, 1926, and November 21, 1938. Ms Am 2030.1 (67): on December 19, 1905, under the entry "Corr. Panel" is noted "compo. Corr." $1/2$ hour and "Plate Alt" 1 hour; see 61.7.0. It also records that on December 20, 1905, there were printed 568 titles in black and brown as well as 300 jackets.

The first three trade impressions were priced at $1.00 net. This title was not published in England.

Illustrated Plate 26.

41 It is unclear what the term "points" means in this context.

THE QUESTION OF OUR SPEECH

61.2.0. *The Question of Our Speech*, first edition, first impression, trade issue, binding state A, one volume, Boston and New York 1905.

This copy is identical in every respect to the first edition, first impression, trade issue, 61.1.0, except that it is bound in dark blue linen-grain cloth.

On the front free endpaper is the pencil inscription: "Herbert Paul | from the author | Oct 1905". This inscription is not in James's hand.

61.3.0. *The Question of Our Speech*, first edition, first impression, trade issue, binding state A, one volume, Boston and New York 1905.

This copy is identical in every respect to the first edition, first impression, trade issue, 61.1.0, except that it is bound in dark greenish-black linen-grain cloth.

61.4.0. *The Question of Our Speech*, first edition, first impression, trade issue, binding state B, one volume, Boston and New York 1905.

The title-page, size, collation, and contents of this copy are identical in every respect to the first edition, first impression, trade issue, 61.1.0, including the ad on [ii] which reads: "Postage extra."

Binding: maroon linen-grain cloth, with lettering and decoration in gilt on the front cover, identical to the lettering and decoration on the front cover of 61.1.0. The back cover is neither lettered nor decorated. The spine, lettered in gilt, reads : "THE | QUESTION | OF OUR | SPEECH | [rule] | HENRY | JAMES [all of the fore-going is centered rather than being justified on the left] | HOUGHTON MIFFLIN & Co". In the publisher's imprint at the foot of the spine, the "o's" in "Houghton" and "Co" are raised and smaller in size than the rest of the letters, and a stylized device is used in place of the usual ampersand. The endpapers are of cream laid paper, and the text is printed on laid paper. A binder's fly-leaf of laid paper is at the front, but none at the back. The top edge is gilt, and the other edges are untrimmed.

The binding on this copy differs both from the bindings on the above copies of the first edition, first impression, binding state A, and from the binding on copies of the second and later impressions, catalogued below. The title and author's name on the spine of this copy are centered and the word "BY" is replaced by a rule, as in the copies of the second and later impression catalogued below. However, the printer's imprint at the foot of the spine conforms in all respects to the printer's imprint on the copies of the first impression, binding state A, and differs from the imprints on the second and the later impressions.

Illustrated Plate 26.

61.5.0. *The Question of Our Speech*, first edition, first impression, trade issue, binding state B, one volume, Boston and New York 1905.

The title-page, size, collation, and contents are identical in every respect to those of The first edition, first impression, trade issue, 61.1.0, including the ad on [ii] which reads "Postage extra."

Binding: dark greenish-black linen-grain cloth. The binding is identical in every respect (except cloth color) to that on the first edition, first impression, binding state B, 61.4.0.

61.6.0. *The Question of Our Speech*, first edition, first impression, limited issue, one volume, Boston and New York 1905.

Size: $7\,^{8}/_{16}''$ x $4\,^{1}/_{2}''$.

The title-page, collation, and contents are identical to those of the first edition, first impression, trade issue, 61.1.0, except that the title-leaf verso, [iv], has the addition of a limitation notice which reads: "OF THE FIRST EDITION THREE HUNDRED | COPIES HAVE BEEN PRINTED AND BOUND | ENTIRELY UNCUT WITH PAPER LABEL".

Binding: tan quarter cloth with sage-green paper over boards. No lettering or decoration is present on the front or back covers. The spine has a white paper label, printed in black, that reads: "[double rule] | THE | QUESTION | OF OUR | SPEECH | [short rule] | HENRY | JAMES | [double rule] First | Edition [all the foregoing centered]". No publisher's imprint is present at the foot of the spine. The endpapers are of cream laid paper, and the text is printed on laid paper. There are no binder's fly-leaves. All edges are untrimmed.

This copy has a light tan laid paper dust-jacket, $^{1}/_{4}''$ taller than the covers of the book, with lettering in black on the spine only, the lettering and layout being identical to that on the paper label on the spine of the book. The lettering on both the spine of the book and the spine of the dust-jacket is centered.

61.7.0. *The Question of Our Speech*, first edition, second impression, binding state A, one volume, Boston and New York 1905.

The title-page, size, and collation are identical to those of the first edition, first impression, trade issue, 61.1.0.

The contents are identical to those of 61.1.0 (including there being a comma after "Press" in the printer's imprint on the title-page, page [117] being blank and on [118] the printer's imprint being present), except that on the verso of the first leaf, [ii], the third line of the ad with the list of 18 titles with dollar prices "By Henry James" reads: "Postage 7 cents." rather than "Postage extra."

Binding: dark blue linen-grain cloth. The lettering and decoration in gilt on the front cover are identical to those on 61.1.0. However, the title and author's name in gilt on the spine read: "THE | QUESTION | OF OUR | SPEECH | [rule] | HENRY | JAMES", with the word "BY" replaced by a short rule, and lettering not justified on the left but centered. The publisher's imprint at the foot of the spine is not all in capitals of uniform size, but as on 61.1.0, reads: "HOUGHTON MIFFLIN & Co", the ampersand being stylized and all the "o's" being in smaller raised letters. The endpapers are of cream laid paper, and the text is printed on laid paper. A binder's fly-leaf of laid paper is at the front, but none at the back. The top edge is gilt, and the other edges are untrimmed.

Dust-jacket: light tan slightly shiny wove paper, lettered and decorated in black. The front cover reads: "THE QUESTION OF | OUR SPEECH [small triangular device] | HENRY JAMES", all justified on the left. The spine reads: "THE | QUESTION | OF OUR | SPEECH | BY | HENRY | JAMES | $1.00 | Net | HOUGHTON | MIFFLIN & Co". The "o's" in "Houghton" and "Co" are raised and smaller in size than the rest of the letters, and the ampersand is stylized. The title, "BY", and the author's name are justified on the left. The balance of the spine lettering is centered. On the back cover within a single-rule frame is an ad listing 7 titles (one by James, this title) with dollar prices, under the heading: "Essays". The front and back inner flaps are blank.

Illustrated Plate 26

Loosely inserted in the volume is a four-page unpaginated leaflet entitled "Sesame Club | 29, Dover Street, W | Programme of Literary Evenings and Debates | February to May 1906". On [2], under the heading "Literary Evenings at 8:45 p.m.", is a listing that reads: "Monday, February 12 | Lecture. 'The Lesson of Balzac.' | Mr. HENRY JAMES | (to be followed by discussion.)". At the end of the leaflet is the suggestion and admonition: "Morning or Evening Dress. No Hats or Bonnets." The Lesson of Balzac is, of course, the second of the two essays contained in *The Question of Our Speech*. The Sesame Club was a London-based philanthropic organization devoted to children's welfare.

E&L makes no mention of the differences between the first and second impressions noted above. BAL 10660, notes: "The publisher's records show that there were two printings in 1905; BAL has been unable to discover any features that might distinguish the first printing from the second. Query: was the second printing dated 1906? Or, more probably, [1905]?" The two impressions in 1905 recorded by BAL were one on September 16, 1905 and a second on December 20, 1905. On the day prior to that second impression there was a charge for alteration of the plates. It is highly likely that this alteration was the substitution of "Postage 7 cents." for "Postage extra." in the ad on [ii], as the two copies with October 1905 inscriptions recorded above have "Postage extra.", and the second impression has "Postage 7 cents." It is also possible, but has not been verified, that the second impression was bound only in the binding with the title centered on the spine.

61.8.0. *The Question of Our Speech*, first edition, second impression, binding state B, one volume, Boston and New York 1905.

The title-page, size, and collation are identical to those of the first edition, first impression, trade issue, 61.1.0.

The contents are identical to those of 61.1.0 (including there being a comma after "Press" in the printer's imprint on the title-page, page [117] being blank and on [118] the printer's imprint being present), except that on the verso of the first leaf, [ii], the third line of the ad with the list of 18 titles, headed "By Henry James", reads: "Postage 7 cents.", rather than "Postage extra."

THE QUESTION OF OUR SPEECH

Binding: maroon linen-grain cloth. The lettering in gilt on the front cover is identical to that on 61.1.0. However, the title and author's name in gilt on the spine read: "THE | QUESTION | OF OUR | SPEECH | [short rule] | HENRY | JAMES", with the word "BY" replaced by a short rule, and the lettering not justified on the left but centered. The publisher's imprint at the foot of the spine is in capitals of uniform size, and reads: "HOUGHTON | MIFFLIN CO." with no ampersand between "Mifflin" and "CO". The endpapers are of cream laid paper, and the text is printed on laid paper. A binder's fly-leaf of laid paper is at the front, but none at the back. The top edge is gilt, and the other edges are untrimmed.

Illustrated Plate 26.

61.9.0. *The Question of Our Speech*, first edition, second impression, binding state B, one volume, Boston and New York 1905.

This copy is identical in every respect to the first edition, second impression, binding state B, 61.8.0, except that it is bound in dark blue linen-grain cloth.

61.10.0. *The Question of Our Speech*, first edition, third impression, one volume, Boston and New York [n.d., 1913].

THE QUESTION OF OUR | SPEECH | THE LESSON OF BALZAC | Two Lectures [in Gothic type] | [vertical oval publisher's device in brown] | BOSTON AND NEW YORK | HOUGHTON MIFFLIN COMPANY | The Riverside Press Cambridge [in Gothic type]

The size and collation are identical to those of the first edition, first impression, trade issue, 61.1.0.

Contents: identical to those of the first edition, second impression, binding state A, 61.7.0 (including the ad [ii] with "Postage 7 cents." on the third line), except that no comma is present after "Press" in the publisher's imprint on the title-page, and no date is at the foot of the title-page. Pages [117–118] are both blank, there being no printer's imprint on [118].

Binding: maroon linen-grain cloth, lettered and decorated in gilt identically to the first edition, second impression, binding state B, 61.8.0 (including the title and author's name on the spine centered and the publisher's imprint at the foot of the spine in uniform capitals without an ampersand). The endpapers are of cream laid paper, and the text is printed on laid paper. There are no binder's fly-leaves. The top edge is gilt, and the other edges are untrimmed

61.11.0. *The Question of Our Speech*, first edition, third impression, one volume, Boston and New York [n.d., 1913].

This copy is identical in every respect to the first edition, third impression, 61.10.0, except that it is bound in dark blue linen-grain cloth.

61.12.0. *The Question of Our Speech*, first edition, fourth impression, one volume, Boston and New York [n.d., 1919].

The title-page is identical to that of the first edition, third impression, 61.10.0.

The size and collation are identical to those of the first edition, first impression, trade issue, 61.1.0.

The ad on the verso of the first leaf, [ii], listing titles "By Henry James" differs from that ad in the three prior impressions as it is smaller in size, lists 17 James titles without dollar prices (rather than 18), a number of the titles listed are different from those listed in all three prior impressions (*Italian Hours*, published in 1909, is added, and *The Author of Beltraffio* and *Watch and Ward* are omitted), and neither "Postage extra." nor "Postage 7 cents." appears on line three. No comma is present after "Press" in the publisher's imprint on the title-page, and no date is at the foot of the title-page. Pages [117–8] are both blank, there being no printer's imprint on [118].

Binding: greenish-black linen-grain cloth, lettered and decorated identically to the first edition, second impression, binding state B, 61.8.0, and the third impression (spine lettering centered and the publisher's imprint at the foot in uniform capitals without an ampersand), 61.10.0. The endpapers are of white wove paper, and the text is printed on wove paper rather than the laid paper of the three prior impressions. There are no binder's fly-leaves. The top edge is gilt, and the other edges are untrimmed.

The inclusion of *Italian Hours* in the ad on [ii] indicates that this copy was printed in 1909 or later. The fact that the text of this copy is printed on wove paper, rather than the laid paper used in the prior impressions, also suggests that this is a copy of a separate impression and not an issue of third impression sheets with only the inserted conjugate leaves, $[X_{1,2}]$, reset.

61.13.0. *The Question of Our Speech*, first edition, fifth impression, one volume, Boston and New York [n.d., 1926].

The title-page is identical to those on the first edition, third and fourth impressions, 61.10.0–69.12. o, except that the publisher's oval device is printed in black rather than brown.

Size: 7 7/16″ x 4 1/2″.

Collation: [unsigned, $1-7^8\ 8^6$]; pp. [2] [i–vi] [1–2], 3–[116].

Contents: blank leaf; [i–ii] blank, verso, ad headed: "By Henry James [in Gothic type], listing 17 titles without dollar prices (including *Italian Hours*); [iii–iv] half-title, verso blank; [v–vi] title-page, verso copyright notice, reservation of rights and printing history as in all prior impressions; [1–2] divisional fly-title, verso blank; 3–[116] text.

Binding: royal blue vertical-rib-grain cloth. The lettering and decoration on the front cover are identical to those on all of the prior impressions, except the first edition, first impression, limited issue. The back cover is neither lettered nor decorated. The spine, lettered in gilt, is identical in the lettering to the first edition, second impression, binding state B, 61.8.0 (including the title and author's name being centered and the publisher's imprint at the foot of the spine in uniform capitals without an ampersand). The endpapers are of white wove paper, and the text is printed on wove paper. There are no binder's fly-leaves. The top edge is trimmed and stained ochre, and the other edges are untrimmed.

* * *

Of the five impressions of the first edition of this title, the first two having two binding states each (ignoring the first impression, limited issue, 61.6.0), the distinguishing features are as follows:

> A) First impression, binding state A. Title-page dated 1905; ad on [ii] with "Postage Extra."; spine lettering left justified, with "BY" between the title and author's name and a stylized ampersand

in the publisher's imprint; printed on laid paper. Binding colors: maroon, dark blue and greenish-black (61.1.0–61.3.0).

B) First impression, binding state B. Title-page dated 1905; ad on [ii] with "Postage extra"; spine lettering centered, with a rule instead of "BY" between the title and author's name and a stylized ampersand in the publisher's imprint; printed on laid paper. Binding colors: maroon and greenish-black (61.4.0–61.5.0).

C) Second impression, binding state A. Title-page dated 1905; ad on [ii] with "Postage 7 cents."; spine lettering centered with a rule instead of "BY" between the title and author's name and a stylized ampersand in the printer's imprint; printed on laid paper. Binding color: dark blue (61.7.0).

D) Second impression, binding state B. Title-page dated 1905; ad on [ii] with "Postage 7 cents."; spine lettering centered, with a rule instead of "BY" between the title and the author's name and no ampersand in the publisher's imprint; printed on laid paper. Binding colors: maroon and dark blue (61.8.0–61.9.0).

E) Third impression. Title-page undated; ad on [ii] with "Postage 7 cents."; no printer's imprint on [118]; spine lettering centered, with rule instead of "BY" between the title and author's name and no ampersand in the publisher's imprint; printed on laid paper. Binding colors: maroon and dark blue (69.10.0–69.11.0).

F) Fourth impression. Title-page undated with publisher's device in brown (as is the case with all prior impressions) and no comma after "Press" in the publisher's imprint; ad on [ii] listing 17 tiles (including *Italian Hours*) with neither "Postage extra" nor "Postage 7 cents"; no printer's imprint on [118]; spine lettering centered, with a rule instead of "BY" between the title and author's name and no ampersand in the publisher's imprint; printed on wove paper. Binding color: greenish-black (61.12.0).

G) Fifth impression. Title-page undated with publisher's device in black, no comma after "Press" in the publisher's imprint; ad on [ii] listing 17 titles (including *Italian Hours*) with neither "Postage extra" nor "Postage 7 cents"; [117–118] not present; spine lettering centered, with a rule instead of "BY" between the title and the author's name and no ampersand in the publisher's imprint; printed on wove paper. The first signature is of eight leaves and the last signature is of six leaves. Binding color: royal blue (61.13.0).

62. *ENGLISH HOURS*

62.1.0. *English Hours*, first edition, one volume, London 1905.

ENGLISH HOURS | BY | HENRY JAMES | [oblong picture of a seaport] | WITH NINETY-TWO ILLUSTRATIONS BY | JOSEPH PENNELL | LONDON | WILLIAM HEINEMANN | 1905

Size: 8" x 5 7/8".

Collation: $[a]^4$ $([a]_1 + X_1)$ b^2 A–I K–T^8 U^4 X^2; pp. [i]–xii, 1–[315] [316] plus 2. Frontispiece, X_1, and 7 further full-page illustrations, each with a tissue guard, tipped in and not reckoned in the pagination. A further 84 illustrations are on or within the text pages.

Contents: [i–ii] half-title, verso ad headed: "UNIFORM WITH THIS VOLUME [in italic]", listing 3 titles, only the first by James; frontispiece with tissue guard tipped in not reckoned in the pagination; [iii–iv] title-page, verso acknowledgements, copyright notice, reservation of rights, and printing history: "The publisher desires to acknowledge the courtesy of | Messrs. Macmillan and Co., Ltd., Messrs. Harper | and Brothers, and Messrs. Sampson Low, Marston | and Company in permitting the inclusion in this | volume of various chapters of which they hold the | copyrights. | Copyright 1875, 1883 by James R. Osgood & Co. | Copyright 1893 by Harper & Brothers | Copyright 1905 by Houghton Mifflin & Co. | Copyright 1905 by William Heinemann | All rights reserved | Published October 1905 [all of the foregoing in italic]"; v–vi "Note", verso continuation of note; vii–viii "Contents", verso continuation of contents; ix–xii "List of Illustrations"; 1–[315] text; [315] at foot printer's imprint: "Printed by Ballantyne & Co. Limited | Tavistock Street, London"; [316] blank.

Binding: gray linen-grain cloth, lettered and decorated on the front cover in black and gilt, and on the back cover and spine in black. The front cover reads: "ENGLISH : HOURS | BY : HENRY : JAMES | ILLUSTRATED : BY [small fleuron] | JOSEPH : PENNELL | W [windmill decoration] H". The back cover is identical to the front cover, but without the windmill decoration and "W" and "H". The spine, which is flat rather than rounded and is lettered in black and gilt, reads: "ENGLISH | HOURS [fleuron] | HENRY [fleuron] | JAMES [fleuron] | HEINEMANN". The endpapers are of white wove paper, and the text is printed on smooth wove paper. The top edge is gilt, the fore-edge is rough trimmed, and the bottom edge is untrimmed.

ENGLISH HOURS

English printing history: There is no information in Heinemann Archive regarding the printing history of this title as the ledger for the period 1898 to 1905 is missing. E&L records that there was one impression of 2,000 copies, 1,000 of which were remaindered. It was published in October 1905, priced at 10s.

62.2.0. *English Hours*, first edition, one volume, London 1905.

Size: 8″ x 5 15/16″.

The title-page, collation, and contents are identical to those of the first edition, primary binding, 62.1.0.

Binding: rust-brown suede leather over flexible boards, with yapp edges. Around the edges of the front and back covers, and continuing on to the top and bottom of the spine, is a deeply incised continuous line in blind curving at the corners. The front cover, which is also decorated and lettered in gilt, reads: "ENGLISH HOURS | [acorn device] | HENRY JAMES". The spine, which is also lettered in gilt, reads: "ENGLISH | HOURS | HENRY | JAMES". There is no publisher's imprint. Other than the line in blind around the outer three edges, there is no lettering or decoration on the back cover. The endpapers are of pale lavender marble paper, and the text is printed on smooth wove paper. The top edge is gilt, and the other edges are untrimmed. A red ribbon marker is bound in.

This may well be a remainder binding, although its elaborateness, together with the acorn device on the front cover (often seen on the title-pages of James's works published by Heinemann) suggest that it is a publisher's presentation or "de luxe" binding. Not recorded in E&L or BAL.

62.3.0. *English Hours*, first edition, remainder binding, one volume, London 1905.

Size: 8 1/16″ x 5 15/16″.

Title-page, collation, and contents are as set forth for the first edition, primary binding, 62.1.0.

Binding: dark green quarter-buckram with lighter dull-green linen over boards. The spine, which is rounded and lettered and decorated in gilt, reads: "[double rule] | ENGLISH | HOURS | [small oval fleuron device] | HENRY | JAMES | HEINEMANN | [double rule]". The publisher's imprint at the foot of the spine is in uniform capitals $^1/_8$" high. The front and back covers are neither lettered nor decorated. The endpapers are of thin white wove paper, and the text is printed on smooth wove paper. The top edge is gilt, and the other edges are untrimmed. This copy does not have a ribbon marker.

This copy is in one of the remainder bindings.

62.4.0. *English Hours*, first edition, remainder binding, one volume, London 1905.

This copy is identical in all respects to the first edition, remainder binding, 62.3.0, except that the linen boards are of a lighter green (almost Kelly-green) linen, the device in gilt on the spine between the title and the author's name is a small leaf and branch design (rather than an oval fleuron), and the publisher's imprint at the foot of the spine is in uniform capitals $^5/_{32}$" high. The endpapers are of thin wove paper, and the text is printed on smooth wove paper. The top edge is gilt, and the other edges are untrimmed. This copy does not have a ribbon marker.

This copy is in another of the remainder bindings. Not recorded in E&L.

62.5.0. *English Hours*, first edition, remainder binding, one volume, London 1905.

Size: 8" x 5 $^{15}/_{16}$".

Title-page, collation, and contents are as set forth for the first edition, primary binding, 62.1.0.

Binding: half-vellum with greenish-blue mottled paper over boards with vellum fore-corners. The spine, which is lettered and decorated in gilt, reads: "[decorative double rule] | ENGLISH | HOURS | [small leaf and branch design] | HENRY | JAMES | [decorative double rule]". No publisher's imprint is present at the foot of the spine. The front and back covers are neither lettered nor decorated. The endpapers are of thick cream laid paper, and the text is printed on smooth wove paper. The top edge is gilt, and the other edges are untrimmed. This copy does not have a ribbon marker.

This copy is in another of the remainder bindings.

ENGLISH HOURS

62.6.0. *English Hours*, first edition, remainder binding, one volume, London 1905.

Title-page is as set forth for the first edition, primary binding, 62.1.0.

Size: 8" x 5 7/8".

Collation: as described for 62.1.0, except that the first signature is $[a]^4$ $(-[a]_1)$.

Contents: as described for 62.1.0, except that the half title-leaf is not present.

Binding: half-vellum with rust-red mottled paper boards and vellum fore-corners. The spine, which is lettered and decorated in gilt, reads: "[decorative double rule] | ENGLISH | HOURS | [small leaf and branch device] | HENRY | JAMES | [decorative double rule]". No publisher's imprint is present at the foot of the spine. The front and back covers are neither lettered nor decorated. The endpapers are of thick cream wove paper, and the text is printed on smooth wove paper. The top edge is gilt, and the other edges are untrimmed. This copy does not have a ribbon marker.

62.7.0. *English Hours*, first American edition, first impression (limited), one volume, Cambridge 1905.

English Hours [in red] | By Henry James | With Illustrations by | Joseph Pennell | [illustration of Gate House, Cambridge tipped on the page] | Cambridge [in red] | Printed at The Riverside Press | mdccccv [all of the foregoing in Gothic type]

Size: 8 3/4" x 5 7/8".

Collation: [unsigned, 1^8 $(1_4+X_{1,2})$ 2–27^8 28^4]; pp. [2] [i–iii]–vi 1π–2π [vii–xiv], [1]–330 [331]–336 [337–338] plus 88. Tipped in between $[1_4]$ and $[1_5]$ are two non-conjugate leaves on which are the "NOTE" (recto and verso) and the "PUBLISHER'S NOTE" (recto only). The Publisher's Note, the frontispiece and a further 43 leaves with full-page illustrations are not reckoned in the pagination. The leaves with the frontispiece and the 43 full-page illustrations are not tipped in but are an integral part of the signatures.

Contents: blank leaf; [i–ii] half-title, verso blank; frontispiece with tissue guard not reckoned in the pagination; [iii–iv] title-page, verso copyright notice, reservation of rights, printing history and limitation notice: "COPYRIGHT 1875 1883 BY JAMES R. OSGOOD & CO. | COPYRIGHT 1905 BY HARPER & BROTHERS | COPYRIGHT 1905 BY HOUGHTON MIFFLIN & CO. | ALL RIGHTS RESERVED | Published October 1905 [in italic] | Four Hundred Copies Printed | Number 123 [limitation notice in italic]"; [v]–vi "NOTE", verso continuation of note; 1π–2π "PUBLISHERS' NOTE", verso blank, not reckoned in the pagination; [vii]–viii "CONTENTS", verso continuation of contents; [ix]–xii "LIST OF ILLUSTRATIONS"; [xiii–xiv] divisional fly-title, verso blank; [1]–330 text; [331–332] divisional fly-title, verso blank; [333]–336 "INDEX"; [337–338] blank leaf. A printer's imprint is not present on [338].

Binding: white half-buckram with green paper boards with small white buckram fore-corners. The front and back covers are neither lettered nor decorated. The spine has a white paper label, lettered in black and decorated in red, which reads: "[red decorative band] | English Hours [in Gothic type] | [red rule] | HENRY JAMES | [red rule] | Large Paper [in Gothic type] | [red decorative band]". No publisher's imprint is present at the foot of the spine. The endpapers are of, and the text is printed on, cream laid paper watermarked with a stylized initials, "RP", within a wreath. There are no binder's fly-leaves. All edges are untrimmed.

Dust-jacket: cream laid paper, the front and back cover and the front and rear inner flaps of which are neither lettered nor decorated. The spine, lettered in black and decorated in red, replicates the paper label on the spine of the book. No publisher's imprint is present at the foot of the spine of the dust-jacket. The dust-jacket is 10 $^{3}/_{8}$" tall, 1 $^{5}/_{8}$" taller than the book, and this excess is folded over so that it covers the top and bottom edges of the book.

The volume is housed in a slipcase box covered with cream laid paper. On the spine of the box is a tan paper label lettered in black and decorated in red, which replicates the label on the spine of the book, and the lettering and decoration on the dust-jacket. At the foot of the label there is written in ink "123", the copy number of the book in the limitation notice on the title-page verso.

Loosely inserted is a four-page prospectus for the "Large Paper Edition" printed in red and black on cream laid paper, and a separate single leaf order form, also printed on cream laid paper, with the price "$5.00 net".

ENGLISH HOURS

This limited impression was printed prior to the Holiday Edition, the trade format.

American printing history. Houghton Mifflin Archive. First edition: Ms Am 2030(22), 220: *first impression* "L[arge] P[aper]" October 9, 1905, 421 copies, 411 [408?] bound between November 1 and November 14, 1905, including "bound Nov[ember] 1/05 copyright 2 | Nov[ember] 1 Publishers 3 | Nov[ember] 1 Unnumbered 4"; notation "10/9/05 ptd. 493 cuts – 504 titles"; *second impression* "Holiday [Edition]" October 20, 1905, 2034 copies, 2004 bound on October 20, 1905, and January 17, 1906; *third impression* "Holiday [Edition]" June 13, 1906, 496 copies, 498 [sic] bound between January 18, 1906, and March 15, 1907; notations: "1/10/06 ptd. 560 titles" and "11/10/06 ptd. 1055 titles"; *fourth impression* "Holiday [Edition]" November 10, 1906, 1018 copies, 1013 bound between November 30, 1906, and November 15, 1918. The records for the second through the fourth impressions show that a small number of copies were bound in half-morocco, three-quarter morocco and half-levant.

"New Edition [fifth impression of the first American edition?]". Ms Am 2030(23), 215: entry headed "Flex[ible] Leather" and "Pocket Ed."; *first* (sole) *impression* July 29, 1914, 1058 copies, 1025 bound between August 24, 1914, and March 1, 1924. Notations: "7/29/14 ptd 1263 4pp. titles" and "1043 – 1 cut". Two hundred copies bound on September 14 and 15, 1920, the only copies bound in that year, are headed "specials".

The first impression (limited format) of the first edition was priced at $5.00 net. The second impression (trade format) was priced at $3.00 in cloth. E&L records that the "new edition" was priced at $1.75, and was printed from the first edition plates; see 62.11.0.

62.8.0. *English Hours*, first American edition, second impression (trade), one volume, Boston and New York 1905.

ENGLISH HOURS [in red] | BY HENRY JAMES | WITH ILLUSTRATIONS | BY JOSEPH PENNELL | [illustration of Gate House, Cambridge] | BOSTON AND NEW YORK | HOUGHTON, MIFFLIN AND COMPANY | The Riverside Press, Cambridge [in red Gothic type] | MDCCCCV

Size: 7 $^{13}/_{16}$″ x 5 $^{1}/_{16}$″.

Collation: [unsigned, 1⁴ 2¹ 3–29⁸]; pp. 1π–2π [i]–vi 3π–4π [vii]–viii [ix]–

xii [xiii–xiv], [1]–330, [331–338] plus 86. Forty-three leaves with full-page illustrations (86 pages), are not reckoned in the pagination. These 43 leaves are not tipped in but are an integral part of the signatures. The "PUBLISHER'S NOTE", [2], is tipped in after [1], and is not reckoned in the pagination.

Contents: 1π–2π half-title, verso blank; [i–ii] blank, verso frontispiece with tissue guard; [iii–iv] title-page, verso copyright notice, reservation of rights and printing history: "COPYRIGHT 1875 1883 BY JAMES R. OSGOOD & CO. | COPYRIGHT 1893 BY HARPER & BROTHERS | COPYRIGHT 1905 BY HOUGHTON MIFFLIN & CO. | ALL RIGHTS RESERVED | Published October 1905 [in italic]"; [v]–vi "NOTE", verso continuation of note; 3π–4π "PUBLISHERS' NOTE" tipped in and not reckoned in the pagination, verso blank; [vii]–viii "CONTENTS", verso continuation of contents; [ix]–xii "LIST OF ILLUSTRATIONS"; [xiii–xiv] divisional fly-title, verso blank; [1]–330 text; [331–332] divisional fly-title, verso blank; [333]–336 "INDEX"; [337] blank; [338] printer's imprint: "The Riverside Press [in Gothic type] | Electrotyped and printed by H. O. Houghton & Co. | Cambridge, Mass., U.S.A. [last two lines in italic]".

Binding: dark green linen-grain cloth, lettered in cream-yellow within a thick double-rule border compartmentalized by horizontal and vertical thick cream-yellow rules, with a central panel in gilt, dark green and gray of a sailboat in front of St. Paul's Cathedral. The front cover reads: "ENGLISH | HOURS | [central panel] | HENRY | JAMES". The back cover is neither lettered nor decorated. The spine, lettered in gilt and decorated in cream-yellow, reads: "[thick double rules] | ENGLISH | HOURS | By [in swash italic] | HENRY | JAMES | Illustrated | By | Joseph | Pennell [all after the author's name in swash italic] | [single thick rule] | [oblong panel in cloth color outlined in cream-yellow divided internally by two thick vertical rules] | [single thick rule] | HOUGHTON | MIFFLIN & CO." The ampersand is stylized. The endpapers are of white laid paper, and the text and illustrations are printed on smooth wove paper. A binder's fly-leaf of wove paper is at the front, but none is at the back. The top edge is gilt, and the other edges are untrimmed.

This binding was designed by Thomas Watson Ball; see Richard Minsky, *The Art of American Book Covers 1875–1930* (New York: Braziller, 2005), 53.

Dust-jacket: heavy beige wove paper with lettering and decoration on the front cover and spine being the same as that on the front cover and spine of the book, but printed "negatively" in black. The back cover and the front and rear inner flaps of the dust-jacket are blank. Not only was this volume issues in a dust-jacket, but also in a slipcase box with no printing on it (not present on this copy).

62.9.0. *English Hours*, first American edition, third (?) impression, one volume, Boston and New York [n.d., 1906].

Title-page, size and contents are identical to those of the first American edition, second impression (trade), 62.8.0, except that the title-page has no date at the foot, and except as noted below.

Collation: [unsigned, 1^4, $2-28^8$]; pp. [i–xiv], [1]–[338] plus 88. The "PUBLISHER'S NOTE" present in the second impression, 62.8.0, is not present. The frontispiece and a further 43 leaves (88 pages) with full-page illustrations, are not tipped in but are an integral part of the signatures, and are not reckoned in the pagination.

Contents: [i–ii] half-title, verso blank; frontispiece not tipped in and not reckoned in the pagination; [iii–iv] title-page, verso copyright notice, reservation of rights and publication date as on [iv] in 62.8.0; [v]–vi "NOTE", verso continuation of note; [vii]–viii "CONTENTS", verso continuation of contents; [ix]–xii "LIST OF ILLUSTRATIONS"; [xiii–xiv] divisional title, verso blank; [1]–330 text; [331–332] divisional title, verso blank; [333]–336 "INDEX"; [337–338] blank, verso printer's imprint as in 62.8.0.

Binding: dark green cloth, lettered and decorated identically to 62.8.0, except that the lettering on the front cover and the decorative rule borders on the front cover and spine are in cream-green rather than cream-yellow, and the publisher's imprint at the foot of the spine reads: "HOUGHTON | MIFFLIN CO." The endpapers are of white wove paper, and the text is printed on wove paper. A binder's fly-leaf of wove paper is at the front but none is at the back. The top edge is gilt, and the other edges are untrimmed.

On the front free endpaper is the inscription: "Norman E. Boasberg | Apr. 3, 1915 | from James H. Becker".

The binding on this copy and the copy of the first American edition, second impression of this title, 62.8.0, are identical in cloth color and very similar in design to that on the second edition, ordinary issue, of *A Little Tour in France*. The first impression of the second edition, ordinary issue, state A, of *A Little Tour in France*, 23.10.0, has cream-green lettering and decorative rule borders, while the first impression, state B, and the second impression of that title have cream-yellow such elements.

62.10.0. *English Hours*, first American edition, fourth (?) impression, one volume, Boston and New York [n.d., 1906].

The title-page is identical to that of the first American edition, second impression (trade), 62.8.0, except that there is no date at the foot.

Size: 7 ¾" x 5".

The collation and contents are identical to those of the first American edition, third impression, 62.9.0.

Binding: half dark red Morocco, with red, blue and tan marble paper over boards. The front and back cover are not lettered, and are decorated with two parallel thin gilt fillets where the shelf-back and the fore-corners meet the marble paper. The spine, which is lettered in gilt and decorated in gilt with four square floral panels between the false cords, reads: "ENGLISH | HOURS | [small rule] | ILLUSTRATED | HENRY JAMES". There is no publisher's imprint at the foot of the spine. The endpapers are of marble paper (in the case of the front and rear free endpapers the marble paper is pasted to cream wove paper), and the text is printed on wove paper. There are two binder's fly-leaves of wove paper at both the front and the back. The top edge is gilt, and the fore-and bottom edges are untrimmed. There is a red ribbon marker bound in.

BAL 10662 records that 37 copies of the first American edition, first [actually the second or trade] impression, were bound in a half-morocco binding as one of the (two) bindings of that impression. Clearly, the absence of the date at the foot of the title-page of this copy indicates it is of a later impression; see printing history 62.7.0.

ENGLISH HOURS

62.11.0. *English Hours*, first American edition, fifth (?) impression, one volume, Boston and New York [n.d., 1914].

The title-page is identical to that of the first American edition, second impression (trade), 62.8.0 , except that it is printed entirely in black, the publisher's imprint reads: "HOUGHTON MIFFLIN COMPANY", and there is no date at the foot.

Size: $7\,{}^1\!/_8''$ x $4\,{}^7\!/_{16}''$.

Collation: [unsigned, 1^8 (1_1+X_1) $2-21^8$ 22^6]; pp. [i – ii] [1π–2π] [iii–x], [1]–330 [331–332] [333]–336 [337–338]. The frontispiece, X_1, is tipped in between [1_1] and [1_2] and is not reckoned in the pagination.

Contents: [i–ii] series half-title, verso blank; 1π–2π recto blank, verso frontispiece without a tissue guard tipped in and not reckoned in the pagination; [iii–iv] title-page, verso copyright notice, reservation of rights and printer's imprint: "COPYRIGHT 1875 1883 BY JAMES R. OSGOOD & CO. | COPYRIGHT 1893 BY HARPER & BROTHERS | COPYRIGHT 1905 BY HOUGHTON MIFFLIN & CO. | ALL RIGHTS RESERVED | The Riverside Press [in Gothic type] | CAMBRIDGE [dot] MASSACHUSSETS | PRINTED IN THE U.S.A."; [v]–vi "NOTE", verso continuation of note; [vii]–viii "CONTENTS", verso continuation of contents; [ix–x] divisional title, verso blank; [1]–330 text; [331–332] divisional title, verso blank; [333]–336 "INDEX"; [337–338] blank leaf.

The 43-full page illustrations present in 62.8.0 are not present in this impression. The only full-page illustration present in this impression is the frontispiece.

Binding: red linen-grain cloth. The front cover has a centered gilt floral crown-like cartouche within which, lettered in gilt, is: "The | Park Street Library". The spine, lettered and decorated in gilt, reads: "[rule] | [small horizontal leaf and vine design] | ENGLISH | HOURS | [short rule] | HENRY | JAMES | [decoration of an old coach] | HOUGHTON | MIFFLIN CO. | [small horizontal leaf and vine design] | [rule]". The back cover is neither lettered nor decorated. The endpapers are of heavy cream wove paper, and the text is printed on smooth wove paper. There are no binder's fly-leaves. All edges are trimmed.

Dust-jacket: tan wove paper lettered and decorated in brownish-red. The front cover has an overall basket-weave design, within which alternate the publisher's monogram and modes of travel (train, horse, ship, car, sailboat and steamship). Imposed on this background pattern are three single-rule tan panels. At the top is a horizontal panel which reads: "ENGLISH HOURS | By HENRY JAMES"; centered is a vertical panel which reads: "The | Park Street | Library | of | Travel [all in swash italic]"; and, at the foot is a horizontal panel which reads: "Houghton Mifflin Company [in swash italic]". The spine reads: "ENGLISH | HOURS | By | Henry James | [device of an old coach] | The Park | Street Library | of Travel [series title in swash italic] | Houghton | Mifflin | Company". The back cover is neither lettered nor decorated. The front inner flap has the price "$2.25" on the upper right, and a blurb under the heading "THE PARK STREET | LIBRARY OF TRAVEL", followed by a list of 6 titles (including 2 by James). The back inner flap has a blurb under the heading: "SO YOU'RE GOING | TO PARIS!".

A comparison of this copy with the first American edition, second impression (trade), 62.8.0, indicates that this copy was printed from the plates of the first American edition, with a number of changes, including the addition of the series half-title, a new undated title-page, the change in position of the half-title, and the elimination of the Publisher's Note, the List of Illustrations, the first divisional fly-title, 43 of the full-page illustrations, and the printer's imprint at the end. It is highly likely that it is a copy of the sole impression of the so called "new edition", and is the fifth impression of the first edition.

❧✠❧

63. THE AMERICAN SCENE

63.1.0. *The American Scene*, first edition, first impression, English issue, one volume, London 1907.

THE AMERICAN SCENE | BY | HENRY JAMES | LONDON | CHAPMAN AND HALL, Ltd | 1907

Size: 8 ½" x 5 ⁹⁄₁₆".

Collation: π^4 1–29^8 30^4; pp. [i–viii], [1]–465, [466] [467–472].

Contents: [i–ii] half-title, verso blank; [iii–iv] title-page, verso printer's imprint: "Richard Clay & Sons, Limited, | BREAD STREET HILL, E.C., AND | BUNGAY, SUFFOLK."; [v]–vi "PREFACE", verso continuation of preface; [vii–viii] "CONTENTS", verso blank; [1]–465 text; [466]

THE AMERICAN SCENE

printer's imprint as on title-leaf verso; [467–472] ads, paginated [1]–6, headed on [1]: "CHAPMAN AND HALL'S NEW BOOKS".

Binding: maroon buckram. The front cover, lettered in gilt within a double-rule border in blind, reads: "THE | AMERICAN SCENE | [gilt dot] | HENRY JAMES". The back cover is neither lettered nor decorated. The spine, lettered and decorated in gilt, reads: "[double rule]|THE|AMERICAN|SCENE|[dot]|HENRY JAMES|CHAPMAN & HALL [in sans-serif] | [double rule]". The endpapers are of white wove paper, and the text is printed on coarse wove paper. The top edge is gilt, and the other edges are trimmed.

Priced at 12s. 6d. net.

63.2.0. *The American Scene*, first edition, second (?) impression, one volume, London 1907.

The title-page, size, collation, and contents are identical to those of the first edition, first impression, English issue, 63.1.0.

Binding: bright red linen-grain cloth, with lettering in gilt and ornamentation in gilt and in blind, identical to 63.1.0, except that it has a single (rather than double) rule border in blind on the front cover, and the publisher's imprint at the foot of the spine is in uniform serif capitals. The endpapers are of white wove paper, and the text is printed on rough wove paper, thicker than the paper used in the first impression. The top edge is trimmed but not gilt, the fore-edge is rough trimmed, and the bottom edge is untrimmed. The same 6 pages of paginated ads are at the end as in 63.1.0, which are the last three leaves of signature 30.

Dust-jacket: red wove paper, with lettering in black on the spine and the front cover identical to the lettering on the book, with similar double rules in black (rather than gilt) at the head and foot of the spine, but with the addition on the spine of the dust-jacket of the price "12/6 | NET" between the author's name and the publisher's imprint. On the back cover of the dust-jacket, printed in black within a single-rule border divided into three panels, are ads for: "NEW AND IMPORTANT BOOKS FROM | CHAPMAN & HALL'S LIST", the large central panel listing 14 titles (none by James), and in the bottom panel the publisher' imprint. The front and rear inner flaps of the dust-jacket are blank.

On the front free endpaper is a small white label that reads: "CHAS. E. LAURIAT CO. | IMPORTERS AND BOOKSELLERS | 385 Wash'n St. Boston".

E&L A63a records a secondary or remainder binding in cross-grain cloth, which is clearly not the case with this copy. Cross-grain cloth is not illustrated in BAL, Sadleir or Gaskell. In addition, notwithstanding E&L's assertion that there was only one printing of the English edition, the thicker paper used in this copy (1.84″ without boards) than that used in the first impression, 63.1.0, (1.67″ without boards) suggests that this copy is of a separate impression.

63.3.0. *The American Scene*, first edition, first impression, colonial issue, one volume, London and Bombay 1907.

THE AMERICAN SCENE | BY | HENRY JAMES | [publisher's device of crossed anchor and bell] | LONDON | GEORGE BELL & SONS | AND BOMBAY | 1907

Size: 8 3/4″ x 5 5/8″.

Collation: π^4 1–29^8 30^1; pp. [i–viii], [1]–465 [466].

Contents: [i–ii] half-title: "Bell's Indian and Colonial Library [in Gothic type, underscored] | THE AMERICAN SCENE", verso "This Edition is issued for Circulation in | India and the Colonies only. [all in italic]"; [iii–iv] title-page, verso printer's imprint: "Richard Clay & Sons, Limited | BREAD STREET HILL, E. C., AND | BUNGAY, SUFFOLK."; [v]–vi "PREFACE", verso continuation of preface; [vii–viii] "CONTENTS", verso blank; [1]–465 text; [466] printer's imprint as on title-leaf verso.

Binding: red vertical-rib-grain cloth. The front cover, lettered in blind within a single-rule border in blind, reads: "THE AMERICAN SCENE". The back cover has a publisher's device in blind within a single-rule border in blind. The spine, lettered in gilt, and decorated in gilt and in blind, reads: "[ornament in blind] | THE | AMERICAN | SCENE | [rule] | HENRY JAMES | [ornament in blind] | [ornament in blind] | GEORGE BELL & SONS". The endpapers are of cream smooth wove paper, and the text is printed on rough wove paper. The top edge is trimmed, and the other edges are untrimmed. No inserted ads, or ads on the endpapers, are present.

The printer's imprint and the thickness of the paper on this issue suggest that it consists of first impression sheets with new prelims, and the last three leaves of signature 30 (ads) omitted.

63.4.0. *The American Scene*, first American edition, binding state A, one volume, New York and London 1907.

THE | AMERICAN SCENE | BY | HENRY JAMES | [oval publisher's device] | HARPER & BROTHERS PUBLISHERS | NEW YORK AND LONDON | MCMVII

Size: 8 1/8" x 5 3/8".

Collation: π^4 [1]^8 2–28^8; pp. [2] [i–viii], 1–[443] [444] [445–446].

Contents: blank leaf; [i–ii] title-page, verso within a single-rule frame copyright notice and reservation of rights: "Copyright, 1907, by Harper & Brothers. | [rule] | All rights reserved. [in italic] | Published February, 1907."; [iii–iv] "CONTENTS", verso blank; v–vi "PREFACE", verso continuation of preface; [vii–viii] divisional title, verso blank; 1–[443] text; [444] blank; [445–446] blank leaf.

Binding: dark blue vertical-rib-grain cloth. The front cover, lettered in gilt, reads: "The American Scene [in swash italic] | HENRY | JAMES [the author's name in sans-serif]". The back cover is neither lettered nor decorated. The spine, lettered and decorated in gilt, reads: "The | Amer- | ican | Scene | [small ornamental rule] | Henry | James [all the foregoing in swash italic within an ornamental frame] | Harpers [in italic outside the frame at the foot]". The endpapers are of white wove paper, and the text is printed on wove paper. The top edge is gilt, the fore-edge is untrimmed, and the bottom edge is rough trimmed.

This copy is in the primary binding.

In a letter to his agent, James B. Pinker, dated May 5, 1907, James expressed outrage at the "*mutilation* of my volume" due to the fact that Harpers suppressed the "page headlines" in this edition, which James regarded as "an essential element in the readability of the book." HJL, IV, 448. This letter also makes it clear that the American edition was set from corrected sheets of Chapman & Hall's first edition, first impression, English issue, 63.1.0.

Priced at $3.00 net.

THE AMERICAN SCENE

63.5.0. *The American Scene*, first American edition, binding state B, one volume, New York and London 1907.

Size: 7 7/8″ x 5 3/16″.

Title-page, collation, and contents are identical to those of the first American edition, binding state A, 63.4.0.

Binding: light blue calico-texture cloth, with lettering and decorative elements on the front cover and spine (including the publisher's imprint at the foot of the spine in italic with an initial capital) identical to those on 63.4.0, except in black rather than gilt. The back cover is neither lettered nor decorated. The endpapers are of white wove paper, and the text is printed on wove paper. All edges are trimmed, but the top edge is not gilt.

Dust-jacket: tan wove paper, lettered and decorated in black. The front cover reads: "The | American | Scene | By Henry James | [nine line blurb] 'THIS volume records in exquisite prose … with an eye ever keen for the picturesque.'" The spine reads: "THE | AMERICAN | SCENE | Henry | James | PRICE | $3.00 | NET | HARPERS [not in italic]". The back cover has, within a single-rule frame, an ad for: "CERTAIN DELIGHTFUL ENGLISH TOWNS | By WILLIAM DEAN HOWELLS", with a nine line blurb. The inside front flap has within a single-rule frame: "NOTICE | [double rule] | HOW | TO OPEN A | BOOK"; and the inside back flap has, within a similar frame, an ad for "THE | AMERICANISM | OF | WASHINGTON | BY | HENRY | VAN DYKE", with an eight line blurb.

E&L A63b states that the publisher's imprint at the foot of the spine of this "secondary" binding is in capitals. Such is not the case on this copy, on which the imprint is in swash italic. BAL 10663 characterizes the binding on this copy as a remainder binding. The presence of the Harpers imprint on the dust-jacket on this copy perhaps casts doubt on that characterization.

64. THE NOVELS AND TALES OF HENRY JAMES

The New York Edition:
Its Background and Aftermath

The stately 24 Volumes (later augmented to 26) of The New York Edition of *The Novels and Tales of Henry James* masks the turmoil that its coming into being entailed. The details of this turmoil also raise serious questions, as Anesko, 147–162, has shown, as to the validity of Leon Edel's argument that the "architecture" of the Edition was determined and driven from the outset by aesthetic considerations.

While James had contemplated a collected edition of his works as early as 1900, serious discussions of the idea did not start until 1904. Initially these discussions were conducted on James's behalf by his agent J. B. Pinker. A number of American publishers were considered for the Edition (Scribner's, Houghton, Mifflin and perhaps Harpers), but James "cherished" the idea of Scribner's. Horne, Letter 218. This was probably because Scribner's had published (or was in the process of publishing) collected editions of the works of Robert Louis Stevenson and George Meredith (among others), which James had admired. In addition, Scribner's was well capitalized for such a financially taxing project, having as recently as 1903 raised $2 million in capital in the process of converting to a limited liability company.

The impetus for a collected edition of his works was driven on James's part by two important considerations. First it was a "testamentary act", an "*edition definitive*", one that would (by its exclusions as well as inclusions) ensure James's place as a master of fiction on the level of Balzac. But perhaps an equally important motive was financial. James, always insecure about his income, dependant as he was from the earnings of his pen, and aware of his declining sales (and inability to sell his longer works of fiction for serialization in magazines), hoped that substantial sales of a collected edition would provide for his old age. Anesko, 141.

Scribner's, initially warm to the idea of a collected edition, by September 1904 had expressed reservations both on the general grounds of the unfavourable economic climate as well as specifically James's past poor sales. Anesko, 144–145. James scaled down his expectations, and Pinker promised Scribner's that James did not contemplate an inclusive edition, but one that was "selective" as well as "collective", and that it would comprise no more than 16 volumes. Despite Scribner's qualms, Scribner and James seem to have reached the framework of a general agreement by August 1905.

Unexpectedly, a serious obstacle reared its head and threatened to scupper the project entirely. As shown in Appendix F, in order to maximize his profits James over the years had successive recourse to a number of American publishers, notably Houghton, Mifflin, Macmillan (New York) as well as more recently Harpers. This was a practice tied in part to the rise of literary agents, such as Pinker, which George Mifflin disparagingly called "the rolling stone policy". These publishers owned the copyrights to many of James works, and their permission had to be obtained by Scribner's in order to include these works in the Edition.

Harpers, which had the least at stake, readily agreed. Macmillan (New York) wanted a lump sum up-front payment from Scribner's, but settled for a manageable royalty. Houghton, Mifflin, still smarting from James defection to other publishers, was another matter. Its demands included that the Edition be sold (at least in America) only by subscription, that the printing of the Edition was to be done at its plant, the Riverside Press, and that the plates of the Edition were to remain its property.[42] This was a blow to Scribner's, as it had recently invested considerable sums in its own printing plant, the Scribner's Press. Eventually, again through Pinker's intervention, a compromise was reached: broadly speaking it limited to three years Houghton, Mifflin's right to print from the New York Edition plates the works whose copyrights it owned, and Scribner's agreed to pay Houghton, Mifflin a 5% royalty on each volume of the Edition sold which were under a Houghton, Mifflin copyright. James, to compensate Scribner's, would receive a reduced royalty on the works the copyright of which was owned by Houghton, Mifflin. Because James received a reduced royalty on titles copyright by Houghton, Mifflin, this had the effect, as Anesko shows, of excluding those titles unless James thought that their inclusion was essential to enhance the sale of the Edition as a whole (e.g. *The American* and *The Portrait of a Lady*). Anesko, 148–149.

42 William Dean Howells had faced a similar situation with Houghton, Mifflin in connection with his collected edition a number of years before, and Howells's experience had helped James deal with Houghton, Mifflin. Michael Anesko, *Letters, Fictions, Lives: Henry James and William Dean Howells* (New York and Oxford: The Oxford University Press, 1997), 335–339.

Even by April 1906 when formal agreement was reached between Scribner's and Houghton, Mifflin, exactly what works (the shorter novels and tales) were to be included in the Edition were not fully decided. But by that time Scribner's had recognized, given the size of the type and the expansive page margins which James demanded, that 23 volumes would be needed for the Edition, a limit to which James readily agreed. In fact, the arrangements for the Edition were not finally decided until 1908, by which time a 24th volume was required, and a number of volumes of the Edition had already been published. Anesko, 155–160.

James reached agreement with Macmillan & Co., Ltd. (London) to publish the English issue on July 13, 1908. The Memorandum of Agreement between Macmillan and James provided for a royalty to James of 15% on the advertised retail price of 8s. 6d. Moore 212–213. The English issue was of imported American sheets with new prelims which Macmillan purchased from Scribner's. In MEB, at 265 there is the notation "James. Novels Edn. de Luxe 23 [struck through and over-written 24] volumes 1908–9. Copies bought from Chas. Scribner's Sons 800 [the two "oo" raised with a dot under them] 8/6 N[et]. each."

Even as these negotiations were taking place James moved ahead with the process of revising the texts of his earlier works and writing the eighteen prefaces. The heavily revised *Roderick Hudson* was sent to Scribner's in March 1906, Horne, 431, and the two volumes of that work were published in December 1907. Horne, Letter 242. This was followed by further volumes at intervals until July 1909, James having sent the revisions (proofs) of the last two volumes of the Edition (*The Golden Bowl*) in March 1909. Horne, Letter 253. During the period following the completion of *The American Scene* for Harpers in early 1906 to March 1909, when he completed his revision to *The Golden Bowl*, virtually all of James creative energies were consumed by the revisions of his works, writing the prefaces, and assisting the photographer, Alvin Langdon Coburn, with suitable frontispieces for the Edition. Moore, Letters 275, 283. Even after the publication of the Edition, James did not in his years remaining produce any major fictional work, and after a last effort (*The Bench of Desolation*) also forsook short stories. Horne, Letter 257.

It is not an exaggeration to say that the public reception of the New York Edition, which was sold in America by subscription for $48.00

the set[43] ($96.00 for the limited issue), was a financial and emotional disaster for James. James's royalties from the sales were derisory given the years of effort.

In an emotional handwritten (not dictated) letter of August 25, 1915, his last to his friend Edmund Gosse, six years after the event, James cited the complete lack of serious critical attention paid to the Edition, and the immense effort he had undertaken to produce it. He parenthetically mentioned to Gosse a further blow: that he had just heard that William Heinemann had decided to destroy the plates of four or five of his works because they had ceased to sell. He characterized the Edition "as a sort of Ozymandias of Egypt ('look on my works ye mighty & despair')", and summed up the situation darkly:

> That Edition has been, from the point of view of profit either to the publisher or to myself, practically a complete failure; vulgarly speaking, it doesn't sell – that is my annual report of what it does – the whole 25 [sic] vols. – in this country amounted to about £25 from the Macmillans; & the ditto from the Scribners in the U.S. to very little more. I am past all praying for anywhere; I remain at my age (which you know, [sic]) & after my long career, *utterly, insurmountably, unsaleable* (emphasis added).[44]

64.1.0. *The Novels And Tales of Henry James*, first edition, trade impression, (New York Edition), 26 volumes, New York 1907–1909 and 1917

I. *Roderick Hudson.*

RODERICK | HUDSON [title in red] | BY | HENRY JAMES | [square device picturing the Brooklyn Bridge and ships in orange, white and brown] | NEW YORK | CHARLES SCRIBNER'S SONS [in red] | 1907 [all the foregoing within a black double-rule frame]

Size: 8 5/16″ x 5 1/2″.

Collation: [unsigned, $1^4(1_1+X_1)$ 2–35^8]; pp. [2] [i–xxii], 1–[527] [528] plus 2.

Contents: blank leaf; [i–ii] series half-title, verso blank; frontispiece with tissue guard tipped in and not reckoned in the pagination; [iii–

---

43 In 1923 the trade issue was advertised as: "Sold by subscription only, 26 volumes, $91.00"; see 49.10.0.
44 Rayburn S. Moore, ed., *Selected Letters of Henry James to Edmund Gosse, 1882–1915* (Baton Rouge and London: Louisiana State University Press, 1988), Letter 317.

iv] title-page, verso copyright notice and arrangements notice: "Copyright, 1875, by H. O. Houghton & Co., and | James R. Osgood & Co. | Copyright, 1882, by Henry James, Jr. | Copyright, 1903, by Houghton, Mifflin & Co. | Copyright, 1907, by Charles Scribner's Sons | Published under special arrangement with | Houghton, Mifflin & Co."; v–[xx] "PREFACE"; [xxi–xxii] fly-title, verso blank; 1–[527] text; [528] centered, printer's imprint: "The Riverside Press [in Gothic type] | CAMBRIDGE [dot] MASSACHUSSETS | U [dot] S [dot] A".

Binding: smooth plum cloth.[45] The front cover, decorated in gilt, has within a single-rule gilt border a circular device within which are the stylized initials "HJ". The back cover is neither lettered nor decorated. The spine, lettered in gilt, reads: "THE NOVELS | AND TALES | OF | HENRY | JAMES | I | RODERICK | HUDSON | SCRIBNERS". The endpapers are of unwatermarked cream wove paper, and the text is printed on laid paper watermarked "HJ" throughout. A binder's fly-leaf of watermarked ("HJ") laid paper is at the back but none at the front. The top edge is gilt, and the other edges are untrimmed.

The printer's imprints in Volumes I through XI read: "U [dot] S [dot] A"; in all other volumes where a printer's imprint is present the imprints read: "U. S. A."

The other volumes, uniformly bound with Volume I, and having on the title-page the title and the publisher's imprint in red, and endpapers of unwatermarked cream wove paper, are:

> II. *The American*. The title-page is dated 1907. Collation: [unsigned, $1^2(1_1+X_1)\ 2^2,\ 3-37^8$]; pp. [i–xxiv], 1–[540] [541–542] [543–544] plus 2. Contents: [i–ii] series half-title, verso blank; frontispiece with tissue guard tipped in (not in pagination); [iii–iv] title-page, verso copyright notice and arrangements notice; v–[xxiii] "PREFACE"; [xxiv] blank; 1–[540] text; [541–542] blank, verso printer's imprint; [543–544] blank leaf. The text is printed on watermarked ("HJ") laid paper throughout. A binder's fly-leaf of unwatermarked laid paper is at the front, but none at the back.
>
> III. *The Portrait of a Lady*, Volume I. The title-page is dated 1908. Collation: [unsigned, $1^2(1_1+X_1)\ 2-29^8$]; pp. [i–xxii], 1–[428] [429–430] plus 2.

---

45 Michael Anesko states that the trade impression was also issued in a half-levant binding. Michael Anesko, "Collected Editions and the Consolidation of Cultural Authority", *Book History* 12 (2009), 198. No copies thus have been seen.

Contents: [i–ii] series half-title, verso blank; frontispiece with tissue guard tipped in (not in pagination); [iii–iv] title-page, verso copyright notice and arrangements notice; v–[xxi] "PREFACE"; [xxii] blank; 1–[428] text; [429–430] blank, verso printer's imprint. The text is printed on watermarked ("HJ") laid paper throughout. A binder's fly-leaf of unwatermarked laid paper is at the front, but none at the back.

IV. *The Portrait of a Lady*, Volume II. The title-page is dated 1908. Collation: [unsigned, 1^2 (1_1+X_1) 2–28^8 29^4]; pp. [i–iv], 1–[438][439–440] plus 2. Contents: [i–ii] series half-title, verso blank; frontispiece with tissue guard tipped in (not in pagination); [iii–iv] title-page, verso copyright notice and arrangements notice; 1–[438] text; [439–440] blank, verso printer's imprint. The text is printed on watermarked ("HJ") laid paper throughout. A binder's fly-leaf of unwatermarked laid paper is at the front, but none at the back.

V. *The Princess Casamassima*, Volume I. The title-page is dated 1908. Collation: [unsigned, 1^2 (1_1+X_1) 2–25^8]; pp. [i–xxiv] [1–2], 3–[363] [364] plus 2. Contents: [i–ii] series half-title, verso blank; frontispiece with tissue guard tipped in (not in pagination); [iii–iv] title-page, verso copyright notice and arrangements notice; v–[xxiii] "PREFACE"; [xxiv] blank; [1–2] divisional fly-title, verso blank; 3–[363] text; [364] printer's imprint. The text is printed on watermarked ("HJ") laid paper throughout. A binder's fly-leaf of unwatermarked laid paper is at the front and the back.

VI. *The Princess Casamassima*, Volume II. The title-page is dated 1908. Collation: [unsigned, 1^2 (1_1+X_1) 2–28^8]; pp. [i–iv] [1–2], 3–[431] [432] plus 2. Contents: [i–ii] series half-title, verso blank; frontispiece with tissue guard tipped in (not in pagination); [iii–iv] title-page, verso copyright notice and arrangements notice; [1–2] divisional fly-title, verso blank; 3–[431] text; [432] printer's imprint. The text is printed on watermarked ("HJ") laid paper throughout. A binder's fly-leaf of unwatermarked laid paper is at the front, and of watermarked ("HJ") laid paper at the back.

VII. *The Tragic Muse*, Volume I. The title-page is dated 1908. Collation: [unsigned, 1^2 (1_1+X_1) 2–25^8 26^6]; pp. [i–xxii] [1–2], 3–[374] [375–376] [377–378] plus 2. Contents: [i–ii] series half-title, verso blank; frontispiece with tissue guard tipped in (not in pagination); [iii–iv] title-page, verso copyright notice and arrangements notice; v–

[xxii] "PREFACE"; [1–2] divisional fly-title, verso blank; 3–[374] text; [375–376] blank, verso printer's imprint; [377–378] blank leaf. The text is printed on watermarked ("HJ") laid paper throughout. A binder's fly-leaf of unwatermarked laid paper is at the front, but none at the back.

VIII. *The Tragic Muse*, Volume II. The title-page is dated 1908. Collation: [unsigned, 1^2 (1_1+X_1) 2–28^8 29^4, 30^2]; pp. [i–iv] [1–2], 3–[441] [442] [443–444] plus 2. Contents: [i–ii] series half-title, verso blank; frontispiece with tissue guard tipped in (not in pagination); [iii–iv] title-page, verso copyright notice and arrangements notice; [1–2] divisional fly-title, verso blank; 3–[441] text; [442] printer's imprint; [443–444] blank leaf. The text is printed on watermarked ("HJ") laid paper throughout. A binder's fly-leaf of unwatermarked laid paper is at the front, but none at the back.

IX. *The Awkward Age*. The title-page is dated 1908. Collation: [unsigned, 1^2 (1_1+X_1) 2–36^8 37^4]; pp. [i–xxiv] [1–2], 3–[545] [546] [547–548] plus 2. Contents: [i–ii] series half-title, verso blank; frontispiece with tissue guard tipped in (not in pagination); [iii–iv] title-page, verso copyright notice and arrangements notice; v–[xxiv] "PREFACE"; [1–2] fly-title, verso blank; 3–[545] text; [546] printer's imprint; [547–548] blank leaf. The text is printed on watermarked ("HJ") laid paper throughout. A binder's fly-leaf of unwatermarked laid paper is at the front, but none at the back.

X. *The Spoils of Poynton*. The title-page is dated 1908. Collation: [unsigned, 1^2 (1_1+X_1) 2–33^8 34^6]; pp. [i–xxvi] [1–2], 3–[500] [501–502] plus 2. Contents: [i–ii] series half-title, verso blank; frontispiece with tissue guard tipped in (not in pagination); [iii–iv] title-page, verso copyright notice and arrangements notice; v–[xxiv] "PREFACE"; [xxv–xxvi] "CONTENTS", verso blank; [1–2] fly-title, verso blank; 3–[500] text; [501–502] blank, verso printer's imprint. The text is printed on watermarked ("HJ") laid paper throughout. A binder's fly-leaf of unwatermarked laid paper is at the front, but none at the back.

XI. *What Maisie Knew*. The title-page is dated 1908. Collation: [unsigned, 1^2 (1_1+X_1) 2–38^8 39^4]; pp. [i–xxiv] [1–2], 3–[577] [578] [579–580] plus 2. Contents: [i–ii] series half-title, verso blank; frontispiece with tissue guard tipped in (not in pagination); [iii–iv] title-page, verso copyright notice and arrangements notice; v–[xxii] "PREFACE"; [xxiii–xxiv] "CONTENTS", verso blank; [1–2] fly-title, verso blank; 3–[577] text; [578] printer's imprint; [579–580] blank leaf. Signatures [1]–[3] of the text are printed on watermarked ("HJ") laid paper, and the balance of the signatures are printed on unwatermarked laid paper. A binder's fly-leaf of watermarked ("HJ") laid paper is at the front, but none at the back.

XII. *The Aspern Papers*. The title-page is dated 1908. Collation: [unsigned, 1^2 (1_1+X_1) 2–28^8 29^2]; pp. [i–xxvi] [1–2], 3–[413] [414] plus 2. Contents: [i–ii] series half-title, verso blank; frontispiece with tissue guard tipped in (not in pagination); [iii–iv] title-page, verso copyright notice and arrangements notice; v–[xxiv] "PREFACE"; [xxv-xxvi] "CONTENTS", verso blank; [1–2] fly-title, verso blank; 3–[413] text; [414] printer's imprint. Signatures [1–3] are printed on watermarked ("HJ") laid paper, and the balance of the signatures are printed on unwatermarked laid paper. A binder's fly-leaf of watermarked ("HJ") laid paper is at the front and the back.

XIII. *The Reverberator*. The title-page is dated 1908. Collation: [unsigned, 1^2 (1_1+X_1) 2–36^8 37^6]; pp. [i–xxiv] [1–2], 3–[550] [551–552] plus 2. Contents: [i–ii] series half-title, verso blank; frontispiece with tissue guard tipped in (not in pagination); [iii–iv] title-page, verso copyright notice and arrangements notice; v–[xxi] "PREFACE"; [xxii] blank; [xxiii–xxiv] "CONTENTS", verso blank; [1–2] fly-title, verso blank; 3–[550] text; [551–552] blank, verso printer's imprint. Signatures [1–3] are printed on watermarked ("HJ") laid paper, and the balance of the signatures are printed on unwatermarked laid paper. A binder's fly-leaf of watermarked ("HJ") laid paper is at the front, but none at the back.

XIV. *Lady Barbarina*. The title-page is dated 1908. Collation: [unsigned, 1^2 (1_1+X_1) 2–40^8 41^2]; pp. [i–xxiv] [1–2], 3–[607] [608] plus 2. Contents: [i–ii] series half-title, verso blank; frontispiece with tissue guard tipped in (not in pagination); [iii–iv] title-page, verso copyright notice and arrangements notice; v–[xxii] "PREFACE"; [xxiii–xxiv] "CONTENTS", verso blank; [1–2] fly-title, verso blank; 3–[607] text; [608] printer's imprint. Signatures [1–3] are printed on watermarked ("HJ") laid paper, and the balance of the signatures are printed on unwatermarked laid paper. A binder's fly-leaf of watermarked ("HJ") laid paper is at the front and the back.

XV. *The Lesson of the Master*. The title-page is dated 1909. Collation: [unsigned, 1^2 (1_1+X_1) 2^6 3^1 4–26^8 27^2]; pp. [i–xx] [1–2], 3–[368] [369–370] plus 2. Contents: [i–ii] series half-title, verso blank; frontispiece with tissue guard tipped in (not in pagination); [iii–iv] title-page, verso copyright notice and arrangements notice; v–[xviii] "PREFACE"; [xix–xx] "CONTENTS", verso blank; [1–2] fly-title, verso blank; 3–[368] text; [369–370] blank, verso printer's imprint. Signature [1] is printed on watermarked ("HJ") laid paper, and the balance of the signatures are printed on unwatermarked laid paper. Signature [27] is printed on paper appreciably thinner than the papers used in the rest of the volume. A binder's fly-leaf of watermarked ("HJ") laid paper is at the front, but none at the back.

XVI. *The Author of Beltraffio*. The title-page is dated 1909. Collation: [unsigned, 1^2 (1_1+X_1) 2–28^8 29^4]; pp. [i–xiv][1–2], 3–[426][427–428][429–430] plus 2. Contents: [i–ii] series half-title, verso blank; frontispiece with tissue guard tipped in (not in the pagination); [iii–iv] title-page, verso copyright notice and arrangements notice; v–[xii] "PREFACE"; [xiii–xiv] "CONTENTS", verso blank; [1–2] fly-title, verso blank; 3–[426] text; [427–428] blank, verso printer's imprint; [429–430] blank leaf. Signatures [1–2] are printed on watermarked ("HJ") laid paper, and the balance of the signatures are printed on unwatermarked laid paper. A binder's fly-leaf of watermarked ("HJ") laid paper is at the front, but none at the back.

XVII. *The Altar of the Dead*. The title-page is dated 1909. Collation: [unsigned, 1^2 (1_1+X_1) 2–36^8 37^6]; pp. [i–xxxii] [1–2], 3–[542], [543–544] plus 2. Contents: [i–ii] series half-title, verso blank; frontispiece with tissue guard tipped in (not in the pagination); [iii–iv] title-page, verso copyright notice and arrangements notice; v–[xxix] "PREFACE"; [xxx] blank; [xxxi–xxxii] "CONTENTS", verso blank; [1–2] fly-title, verso blank; 3–[542] text; [543–544] blank, verso printer's imprint. Signatures [1–3] are printed on watermarked ("HJ") laid paper, and the balance of the signatures are printed on unwatermarked laid paper. A binder's fly-leaf of watermarked ("HJ") laid paper is at the front, but none at the back.

XVIII. *Daisy Miller*. The title-page is dated 1909. Collation: [unsigned, 1^2 (1_1+X_1) 2–34^8]; pp. [i–xxvi][1–2], 3–[506] plus 2. Contents: [i–ii] series half-title, verso blank; frontispiece with tissue guard tipped in (not in the pagination); [iii–iv] title-page, verso copyright notice and arrangements notice; v–[xxiv] "PREFACE"; [xxv–xxvi] "CONTENTS", verso blank; [1–2] fly-title, verso blank; 3–[506] text.

There is no printer's imprint. Signatures [1–2] and conjugate leaves [3$_4$] and [3$_5$] are printed on watermarked ("HJ") laid paper, and the balance of the leaves and signatures are printed on unwatermarked laid paper. A binder's fly-leaf of watermarked ("HJ") laid paper is at the front and the back.

XIX. *The Wings of the Dove*, Volume I. The title-page is dated 1909. Collation: [unsigned, 1² (1$_1$+X$_1$) 2–21⁸ 22²]; pp. [i–xxiv] [1–2], 3–[302] [303–304] plus 2. Contents: [i–ii] series half-title,verso blank; frontispiece with tissue guard tipped in (not in pagination); [iii–iv] title-page, verso copyright notice (no arrangements notice); v–[xxiii] "PREFACE"; [xxiv] blank; [1–2] divisional fly-title, verso blank; 3–[302] text; [303–304] blank leaf. There is no printer's imprint. Signature [1] is printed on watermarked ("HJ") laid paper, and the balance of the signatures are printed on unwatermarked laid paper. A binder's fly-leaf of watermarked ("HJ") laid paper is at the front, but none at the back.

XX. *The Wings of the Dove*, Volume II. The title-page is dated 1909. Collation: [unsigned, 1² (1$_1$+X$_1$) 2–26⁸ 27⁴]; pp. [i–iv] [1–2], 3–[405] [406] [407–408] plus 2. Contents: [i–ii] series half-title, verso blank; frontispiece with tissue guard tipped in (not in pagination); [iii–iv] title-page, verso copyright notice (no arrangements notice); [1–2] divisional fly-title, verso blank; 3–[405] text; [406] printer's imprint; [407–408] blank leaf. Signature [1] is printed on watermarked ("HJ") laid paper, and the balance of the signatures are printed on unwatermarked laid paper. A binder's fly-leaf of watermarked ("HJ") laid paper is at the front, but none at the back.

XXI. *The Ambassadors*, Volume I. The title-page is dated 1909. Collation: [unsigned, 1² (1$_1$+X$_1$) 2–20⁸ 21²]; pp. [i–xxiv] [1–2] 3–[286] [287–288] plus 2. Contents: [i–ii] series half-title, verso blank; frontispiece with tissue guard tipped in (not in pagination); [iii–iv] title-page, verso copyright notice and arrangements notice; v–[xxiii] "PREFACE"; [xxiv] blank; [1–2] divisional fly-title, verso blank; 3–[286] text; [287–288] blank leaf. There is no printer's imprint. Signature [1] is printed on watermarked ("HJ") laid paper, and the balance of the signatures are printed on unwatermarked laid paper. A binder's fly-leaf of watermarked ("HJ") laid paper is at the front, but none at the back.

XXII. *The Ambassadors*, Volume II. The title-page is dated 1909. Collation: [unsigned, 1² (1$_1$+X$_1$) 2–21⁸ 22⁴]; pp. [i–iv] [1–2], 3–[327] [328] plus 2.

Contents: [i–ii] series half-title, verso blank; frontispiece with tissue guard tipped in (not in pagination); [iii–iv] title-page, verso copyright notice and arrangements notice; [1–2] divisional fly-title, verso blank; 3–[327] text; [328] printer's imprint. Signature [1] is printed on watermarked ("HJ") laid paper, and the balance of the signatures are printed on unwatermarked laid paper. A binder's fly-leaf of watermarked ("HJ") laid paper is at the front and the back.

XXIII. *The Golden Bowl*, Volume I. The title-page is dated 1909. Collation: [unsigned, 1^2 (1_1+X_1) 2–27^8 28^4]; pp. [i–xxvi] [1–2], 3–[402] plus 2. Contents: [i–ii] series half-title, verso blank; frontispiece with tissue guard tipped in (not in pagination); [iii–iv] title-page, verso copyright notice (no arrangements notice); v–[xxv] "PREFACE"; [xxvi] blank; [1–2] divisional fly-title, verso blank; 3–[402] text. There is no printer's imprint. Signatures [1–3] are printed on watermarked ("HJ") laid paper, and the balance of the signatures are printed on unwatermarked laid paper. A binder's fly-leaf of watermarked ("HJ") laid paper is at the front and the back.

XXIV. *The Golden Bowl*, Volume II. The title-page is dated 1909. Collation: [unsigned, 1^2 (1_1+X_1) 2–24^8 25^2]; pp. [i–iv] [1–2], 3–[369] [370] [371–372] plus 2. Contents: [i–ii] series half-title, verso blank; frontispiece with tissue guard tipped in (not in pagination); [iii–iv] title-page, verso copyright notice (no arrangements notice); [1–2] divisional fly-title, verso blank; 3–[369] text; [370] printer's imprint; [371–372] blank leaf. Signatures [1–3] are printed on watermarked ("HJ") laid paper, and the balance of the signatures are printed on unwatermarked laid paper. A binder's fly-leaf of watermarked ("HJ") laid paper is at the front, but none at the back.

XXV. *The Ivory Tower*. The title-page is dated 1917. Collation: [unsigned, 1^8 (1_1+X_1) 2–23^8]; pp. [i–viii], 1–357 [358] [359–360] plus 2. Contents: [i–ii] series half-title, verso blank; frontispiece with tissue guard tipped in (not in pagination); [iii–iv] title-page, verso copyright notice (no arrangements notice); v–vi "PREFACE" [by Percy Lubbock]; [vii–viii] "CONTENTS", verso blank; 1–357 text; [358] blank; [359–360] blank leaf. There is no printer's imprint. The text is printed on unwatermarked laid paper throughout. There are no binder's fly-leaves.

XXVI. *The Sense of the Past*. The title-page is dated 1917. Collation: [unsigned, 1^8 (1_1+X_1) 2–23^8]; pp. [i–viii], 1–358 [359–360] plus 2.

THE NOVELS AND TALES OF HENRY JAMES

Contents: [i–ii] series half-title, verso blank; frontispiece with tissue guard tipped in (not in pagination); [iii–iv] title-page, verso copyright notice (no arrangements notice); [v–vi] "PREFACE" [by Percy Lubbock]; [vii–viii] "CONTENTS", verso blank; 1–358 text; [359–360] blank leaf. There is no printer's imprint. The text is printed on unwatermarked laid paper throughout. There are no binder's fly-leaves.

This set, formerly owned by James Gilvarry, was sold at Christie's on February 7, 1986, lot 106.

The John Hay Library at Brown University has a copy of the first impression (trade) of *The Novels and Tales* (New York Edition) in 24 volumes, 13 of which have dust-jackets on them (call number: Starred Books, PS2110 FO7, Volumes 1–24, copy 3). The dust-jackets are of cream wove paper printed in burgundy. The spine of the dust-jacket on Volume I reads: "THE NOVELS | AND TALES | OF | HENRY | JAMES | I | RODERICK | HUDSON | SCRIBNERS [all centered]". There is no lettering or decoration on the front or back covers, or on the front or back inner flaps.[46]

Both the American and English issues of *The Novels and Tales of Henry James* used an almost bewildering diversity of paper thickness in the various volumes. The problem that Scribner's had to address was how to make the volumes (the longest of which has 605 text pages and the shortest 284 pages) approximately equal in thickness so that the set would present a pleasing appearance. The issue was, among others, discussed in a letter of Scribner's to James of April 27, 1906 (quoted in Anesko, 151–152), in which Scribner's merely pointed out that he could make the thickness of the volumes approximately the same, without specifying the way this would be done. But measurement of the thickness of the paper in each volume of this edition shows that there is a close correlation between the length of the text and the thickness of the paper used, and that therefore the paper used resulted from a deliberate publishing decision, not the random choice of the printer. The measurements[47] are as follows:

---

46 I am indebted to Ann Morgan Dodge of the John Hay Library, for the above information and for providing me with a scan of the dust-jacket on *Roderick Hudson*.
47 These measurements were made with an electronic digital caliper with a specified accuracy of .02%. Measurements are of 200 text pages. Differences in

THE NOVELS AND TALES OF HENRY JAMES

Volume Number	Paper Thickness U.S. Trade	U.K. Issue	Number of Text Pages
1	.435	.435	527
2	.420	.435	540
9	.405	.440	543
10	.425	.465	498
11	.375	.400	575
13	.420	.460	548
14	.395	.405	605
17	.437	.435	540
18	.433	.448	504
3	.510	.530	428
4	.510	.530	438
6	.553	.575	429
12	.513	.550	411
16	.540	.540	424
23	.525	.525	424
5	.614	.636	361
7	.655	.675	372
8	.611	.640	439
15	.629	.650	366
19	.659	.672	300
20	.585	.615	403
21	.650	.685	284
22	.668	.688	235
24	.625	.639	367

Broadly speaking, the volumes fall into three major categories. Those with texts of between 498 and 605 pages used paper with a thickness of between .375 and .465; those with text between 411 and 438 pages used paper with a thickness of between .510 and .550; and finally those with texts of between 235 and 403 pages used paper with a thickness of

---

the text paper may be accounted for by the fact that different "batches" of paper of the same stated weight manufactured at different times may have differences in thickness. However, such differences may be slight. More significant errors in measurement may be due to the fact that the degree of the compression of the paper in the measurement process is most difficult to control. But this notwithstanding, it is believed that these measurements sustain the conclusion.

between .585 and .688. Volume VIII is a bit of an anomaly. These measurements indicates the lengths to which the printer and publisher went in the preparation of these volumes.

Printing History of the New York Edition: Scribner's Archive, Box 13–id-J.

Volume Number	Date Printed	Copies Printed	Copies Remaining 1913	1913[48] Imp.	1922[49] Imp.
I	Nov. 1907	1500	467	None	500
II	Nov. 1907	1500	484	None	500
III	Dec. 1907	1500	525	None	500
IV	Jan. 1908	1500	511	None	500
V	Dec. 1907	1500	509	None	500
VI	Dec. 1907	1500	509	None	500
VII	Feb. 1808	1500	510	None	500
VIII	Feb. 1908	1500	510	None	500
IX	Apr. 1908	1500	521	None	500
X	Apr. 1908	1500	510	None	500
XI	1909	1000	0	500	500
XII	1908	1000	11	500	500
XIII	1909	1000	40	500	500
XIV	1909	1000	0	500	500
XV	Feb. 1909	1000	23	500	500
XVI	Feb. 1909	1000	23	500	500
XVII	Mar. 1909	1000	47	500	500
XVIII	Mar. 1909	1000	16	500	500
XIX	Apr. 1909	1000	28	500	500
XX	Apr. 1909	1000	0	500	500
XXI	1909	1000	10	500	500
XXII	1909	1000	22	500	500
XXIII	July 1909	1000	22	500	500
XXIV[50]	July 1909	1000	16	500	500

48 The [no day or month] 1913 impression is the second impression of Volumes XI through XXIV.
49 The July 25, 1922 impression is the second impression of Volumes I to X, and the third impression of Volumes XI to XXIV.
50 The 1922 impression included Volumes XXV and XXVI. For the printing history of Volumes XXV and XXVI, see *The Ivory Tower* and *The Sense of the Past*, 77.3.0 and 78.4.0.

All copies were printed by H. O. Houghton & Co., Houghton, Mifflin's printing subsidiary. The type of paper is not specified on the cards, except in the case of the 1922 printing where there is the notation "laid – no deckle 33 1/2" x 44" [illegible]".

The record of the 1913 printing (second impression of Volumes XI–XXIV) is a continuation of the card devoted to each of the 24 Volumes. However, only a single card is devoted to the 1922 printing (which, it should be noted, includes both *The Ivory Tower* and *The Sense of the Past*). It is headed: "JAMES 26 Vols. New York Edition". The price is not specified. Under date [of printing] it reads: "1922 July 25[,] COPIES 500 PRINTER Houghton". Under the caption "INSERTS" it reads: "6/20/22 - 500 photogravures 26 V | Suffolk – 500 tissues HOH & Co." Under the caption "Houghton | Received from Binder" there is shown a "balance in the bindery" of 500 copies, with 89 copies delivered by the binder between September 7 1922, and April 1923, leaving a balance of 411 copies. There are three further notations under the heading "Binding Orders": "11/30/23 100S", "8/7/25 100S" and "1/24/28 100S", presumably binding orders for a further 300 sets.

The reason for the 1913 printing seems clear. By that date there were still on hand approximately 500 copies of each of the first 10 volumes, but almost no sheets left of the other 14. Since there appeared to be some continuing demand, Scribner's decided to print 500 copies of these last 14 volumes so that they could be sold as sets. By about 1918 or 1919, nearly all of the 1500 sets had been bound and presumably sold. By 1922, Scribner's must have felt that there was some continuing demand and accordingly printed 500 further sets of the 26 volumes to meet this demand.

There is only one reference in all of the cards to the limited edition. This is a pencil notation on the reverse of the card to *Roderick Hudson*, and reads: "6/1/16 Recd # 154, 155, 156 | Lt'd made up 1 complete | Delivery of Ltd Ed".

Some sheets of *The Selected Letters of Henry James*, selected and edited by Percy Lubbock (1920), were bound uniform with this edition and issued as volumes 27 and 28.[51] Examination of a copy of these two

---

[51] Scribner Archive, Box 13–1d-J. A card headed "Letters of Henry James" records that 100 copies of the 300 copies of the first edition, first impression, of *The Selected Letters* were bound for the New York Edition on March 27, 1920. The first impression was printed on February 27, 1920. A second impression of 2,000 copies, was printed on May 1, 1920.

volumes reveals that this is not entirely accurate. While 100 copies of the two volumes of *The Selected Letters* were published in the same smooth plum cloth, with a single-rule gilt border on the front cover and the centered circular device within which are the stylized initials "HJ", the page size of these two volumes is 8 $\sqrt[3]{4}$" x 5 $\sqrt[3]{4}$" and the volume size is 9" x 6", which is noticeably larger than the other 26 volumes. In addition, there is nothing on the spines of these two volumes to indicate that they are part of The *Novels and Tales*, as the spines merely read: "THE | LETTERS | OF | HENRY | JAMES | VOLUME I [II] | SCRIBNERS.

There are numerous references on the cards to sheets sold to Macmillan & Co. for the English issue, as follows:

Vol. I "6/25/09 105/106 [sic] Macmillan & Co @ 2/6 – fldg 1 ½ d. 1 set in cloth gratis 4/1/09 25 [sets of] sheets @ 2/6 fldg 1 ½ d" plus further orders dated 9/1/09, 2/5/10 and 10/31/10 each for 25 sheets;

Vol. II "6/25/09 Macmillan & Co. 105/100 @ 2/6 fld 1 ½ 1 cloth complimentary" plus orders dated 8/25/09, 10/21/09 and 8/3/10 each for 25 sets of sheets;

Vol. III "6/25/09 Macmillan & Co. 105/100 @ 2/6 + 1 ½ d 1 cloth gratis" plus orders dated 10/7/09 and 8/24/10 for 25 sets of sheets and 3/17/10 for 12 sets of sheets;

Vol. IV entry identical to Vol. III;

Vol. V "6/25/08 Macmillan & Co. 105/100 @ 2/6 + 1 ½ fldg 1 cloth gratis" plus orders dated 10/21/09 and 8/23/10 each for 25 sets of sheets;

Vol. VI "7/25/08 Macmillan & Co. 105/100 @ 2/6 + 1 ½ 1 cloth gratis" plus orders dated 10/21/09 and 8/26/10 each for 25 sets of sheets;

Vol. VII "7/25/09 Macmillan & Co. 105/100 @ 2/6 + 1 ½" plus order dated 10/21/09 for 25 sets of sheets;

Vol. VIII entry dated 9/27/08 otherwise identical to Vol. VII;

Vol. IX entry dated identical to Vol. VII;

Vol. X "7/25/08 Macmillan & Co. 105/100 @ 2/6 +1 ½ d 1 cloth grats [sic]" plus orders dated 10/21/09 and 10/31/10 each for 25 sets of sheets;

Vol. XI entry identical to Vol. X except orders dated 10/21/09 and 5/24/10 each for 25 sets of sheets;

Vol. XII "9/21/08 Macmillan & Co. 105/100 @ 2/6 + 1 ½ d" plus orders 10/21/09 and 8/26/10 each for 25 sets of sheets;

Vol. XIII "9/28/08 Macmillan & Co. 105/100 @ 2/6 + 1 ½" plus order 10/21/09 for 25 sets of sheets;

Vol. XIV entry identical to Vol. XIII;

Vol. XV "3/9/09 Macmillan & Co. 105/100 @ 2/6 + 1 ½ 1 cloth gratis" plus orders 10/21/09 for 25 and 3/10/11 for 12 sets of sheets with notation "no cancels";

Vol. XVI entry identical to Vol. XV except one order 10/21/09 for 25 sets of sheets;

Vol. XVII "4/5/09 – Macmillan & Co. 105/100 @ 2/6 + 1 ½ 1 cloth gratis" plus order 10/21/09 for 25 sets of sheets;

Vol. XVIII "4/5/09 Macmillan & Co. 105/100 @ 2/6 + 1 ½ d 1 cloth" plus order 10/21/09 for 25 sets of sheets;

Vol. XIX "5/3/09 Macmillan & Co. 105/100 @ 2/6 fld 1 ½ 1 cloth gratis" plus order 10/21/09 for 25 sets of sheets;

Vol. XX identical to Vol. XIX;

Vol. XXI "6/9/09 Macmillan & Co. 105/100 @ 2/6 + 1 ½ d 1 cloth gratis" plus orders 10/21/09 for 25 and 3/10/11 for 12 sets of sheets notation "no cancels";

Vol. XXII identical to Vol. XXI;

Vol. XXIII "Aug 3/09 Macmillan & Co. 105/100 @ 2/6 + 1 ½ 1 cloth grat" plus orders 10/21/09 for 25 and 3/10/11 for 12 sets of sheets notation "no cancels"; and

Vol. XXIV entry identical to Vol. XXIII except only one order dated 10/21/09 for 25 sets of sheets.

The fact that the total orders for sheets of some titles are greater than for others is, on the face of it, curious, and the record is clearly incomplete. However, it may also be explained by the likelihood that Macmillan not only sold this edition as sets, but also sold individual volumes; see the inserted ad in *Notes of a Son and Brother*, 72.3.0, where the volumes are advertised at 8s. 6d. each. This is also suggested by the fact that individual volumes of the English issue often turn up for sale, but that individual volumes of the American rarely do.

THE NOVELS AND TALES OF HENRY JAMES

64.2.0. *The Novels and Tales of Henry James*, first edition, limited impression, 26 volumes, New York 1907–1909 and 1917.

No copy in the collection.

James S. Jaffe Rare Books recorded in a catalogue published in March 2,000 a set of the large paper issue (limited impression) of The New York Edition which includes *The Ivory Tower* and *The Sense of the Past* (Volumes XXV and XXVI). It also records that this set has glassine dust-jackets.

64.3.0. *The Novels And Tales of Henry James*, first edition, English issue, (New York Edition), 24 volumes, London 1909 and 1913.

I. *Roderick Hudson*.

RODERICK | HUDSON [title in red] | BY | HENRY JAMES | [square device picturing the Brooklyn Bridge and ships in orange, white and brown] | MACMILLAN AND CO., LIMITED | ST. MARTIN'S STREET, LONDON | 1913 [all the foregoing within a black double-rule frame]

Size: 8 3/8″ x 5 1/2″.

Collation: [unsigned, 1^2 (1_1+X_1) 2^{10} 3^6 4^{10} 5^6 6^{10} 7^6 8^{10} 9^6 10^{10} 11^6 12^{10} 13^6 14^{10} 15^6 16^{10} 17^6 18^{10} 19^6 20^{10} 21^6 22^{10} 23^6 24^{10} 25^6 26^1, 27^6 28^{10} 29^6 30^{10} 31^6 32^{10} 33^6 34^{10} 35^6 36^2]; pp. [i–xxii], 1–[527] [528] [529–530] plus 2.

Contents: [i–ii] series half-title, verso blank; frontispiece with tissue guard tipped in, not reckoned in the pagination; [iii–iv] title-page, verso copyright notice and arrangements notice: "Copyright, 1875, by H. O. Houghton & Co., and | James R. Osgood & Co. | Copyright, 1882, by Henry James Jr. | Copyright, 1903, by Houghton Mifflin & Co. | Copyright, 1907, by Charles Scribner's Sons | Published under special arrangement with | Houghton Mifflin & Co."; v–[xx] "PREFACE"; [xxi–xxii] fly-title, verso blank; 1–[527] text; [528] centered, printer's imprint: "The Riverside Press [in Gothic type] | CAMBRIDGE [dot] MASSACHUSETTS | U [dot] S [dot] A"; [529–530] blank leaf.

Binding: sage-green buckram. The front cover has a stamped circular ornament of vines, leaves and flowers in gilt. The back cover is neither lettered nor decorated. The spine, which is lettered and decorated in gilt, reads: "THE NOVELS | [leaf device and dot] OF [dot and leaf device] | HENRY | JAMES | [dot] Vol. I [dot] | Roderick | Hudson | [long strapwork device of vines, leaves and flowers] | MACMILLAN [dot] &

[dot] Co." The "o" in "Co" is raised with a dot under it. The endpapers are of cream unwatermarked laid paper, and the text is printed on laid paper watermarked "HJ" throughout. A binder's fly-leaf of watermarked ("HJ") laid paper is at the front and the back. The top edge is gilt, and the other edges are untrimmed.

On the front pastedown of this and the other 23 volumes is the armorial bookplate of Francis Denis Lycett Green.

The other volumes, uniformly bound with Volume I, and having the titles on the title-page in red, the publisher's imprint in black and (with one exception noted below) cream endpapers of unwatermarked laid paper, are:

II. *The American*. The title-page is dated 1909. Collation: [unsigned, 1^2 (1_1+X_1) 2^2 $3-37^8$]; pp. [i–xxiv], 1–[540] [541–542] [543–544] plus 2. Contents: [i–ii] series half-title, verso blank; frontispiece with tissue guard tipped in (not in pagination); [iii–iv] title-page, verso copyright notice and arrangements notice; v–[xxiii] "PREFACE"; [xxiv] blank; 1–[540] text; [541–542] blank, verso printer's imprint; [543–544] blank leaf. The text is printed on watermarked ("HJ") laid paper throughout. A binder's fly-leaf of unwatermarked laid paper is at the front, but none at the back.

III. *The Portrait of a Lady*, Volume I. The title-page is dated 1909. Collation: [unsigned, 1^2 (1_1+X_1) $2-29^8$]; pp. [i–xxii], 1–[428] [429–430] plus 2. Contents: [i–ii] series half-title, verso blank; frontispiece with tissue guard tipped in (not in pagination); [iii–iv] title-page, verso copyright notice and arrangements notice; v–[xxi] "PREFACE"; [xxii] blank; 1–[428] text; [429–430] blank, verso printer's imprint. The text is printed on watermarked ("HJ") laid paper throughout. A binder's fly-leaf of watermarked ("HJ") laid paper is at the front, but none at the back.

IV. *The Portrait of a Lady*, Volume II. The title-page is dated 1909. Collation: [unsigned, 1^2 (1_1+X_1) $2-28^8$ 29^4]; pp. [i–iv], 1–[438] [439–440] plus 2. Contents: [i–ii] series half-title, verso blank; frontispiece with tissue guard tipped in (not in pagination); [iii–iv] title-page, verso copyright notice and arrangements notice; 1–[438] text; [439–440] blank, verso printer's imprint. The text is printed on watermarked ("HJ") laid paper throughout. A binder's fly-leaf of watermarked ("HJ") laid paper is at the front, but none at the back.

V. *The Princess Casamassima*, Volume I. The title-page is dated 1913. Collation: [unsigned, 1^2 (1_1+X_1) 2–25^8]; pp. [i–xxiv] [1–2], 3–[363] [364] plus 2. Contents: [i– ii] series half-title, verso blank; frontispiece with tissue guard tipped in (not in pagination); [iii–iv] title-page, verso copyright notice and arrangements notice; v- [xxiii] "PREFACE"; [xxiv] blank; [1–2] divisional fly-title, verso blank; 3–[363] text; [364] printer's imprint. The text is printed on watermarked ("HJ") laid paper throughout. A binder's fly-leaf of watermarked ("HJ") laid paper is at the front and the back.

VI. *The Princess Casamassima*, Volume II. The title-page is dated 1913. Collation: [unsigned, 1^2 (1_1+X_1) 2–28^8]; pp. [i–iv] [1–2], 3–[431] [432] plus 2. Contents: [i–ii] series half- title, verso blank; frontispiece with tissue guard tipped in (not in pagination); [iii–iv] title-page, verso copyright notice and arrangements notice; [1–2] divisional fly-title, verso blank; 3–[431] text; [432] printer's imprint. The text is printed on watermarked ("HJ") laid paper throughout. A binder's fly-leaf of watermarked ("HJ") laid paper is at the back, but none at the front.

VII. *The Tragic Muse*, Volume I. The title-page is dated 1913. Collation: [unsigned, 1^2 (1_1+X_1) 2–25^8 26^6]; pp. [i–xxii] [1–2], 3–[374] [375–376] [377–378] plus 2. Contents: [i–ii] series half-title, verso blank; frontispiece with tissue guard tipped in (not in pagination); [iii–iv] title-page, verso copyright notice and arrangements notice; v–[xxii] "PREFACE"; [1–2] divisional fly-title, verso blank; 3–[374] text; [375– 376] blank, verso printer's imprint; [377–378] blank leaf. The text is printed on watermarked ("HJ") laid paper throughout. A binder's fly-leaf of unwatermarked laid paper is at the front, but none at the back.

VIII. *The Tragic Muse*, Volume II. The title-page is dated 1913. Collation: [unsigned, 1^2 (1_1+X_1) 2–28^8 29^4 30^2]; pp. [i–iv] [1–2], 3–[441] [442] [443–444] plus 2. Contents: [i–ii] series half-title, verso blank; frontispiece with tissue guard tipped in (not in pagination); [iii–iv] title-page, verso copyright notice and arrangements notice; [1–2] divisional fly-title, verso blank; 3–[441] text; [442] printer's imprint; [443–444] blank leaf. The text is printed on watermarked ("HJ") laid paper throughout. A binder's fly-leaf of unwatermarked laid paper is at the front, but none at the back.

IX. *The Awkward Age*. The title-page is dated 1913. Collation: [unsigned, 1^2 (1_1+X_1) 2–36^8 37^4]; pp. [i–xxiv] [1–2], 3–[545] [546] [547–548] plus 2. Contents: [i–ii] series half-title, verso blank; frontispiece with tissue guard tipped in (not in pagination); [iii–iv] title-page, verso copyright notice and arrangements notice; v–[xxiv] "PREFACE"; [1–2] fly-title, verso blank; 3–[545] text; [546] printer's imprint; [547–548] blank leaf. The text is printed on watermarked ("HJ") laid paper throughout. A binder's fly-leaf of unwatermarked laid paper is at the front, but none at the back.

X. *The Spoils of Poynton*. The title-page is dated 1913. Collation: [unsigned, 1^2 (1_1+X_1) 2–33^8 34^6]; [i–xxvi] [1–2], 3–[500] [501–502] plus 2. Contents: [i–ii] series half-title, verso blank; frontispiece with tissue guard tipped in (not in pagination); [iii–iv] title-page, verso copyright notice and arrangements notice; v–[xxiv] "PREFACE"; [xxv–xxvi] "CONTENTS", verso blank; [1–2] fly-title, verso blank; 3–[500] text; [501–502] blank, verso printer's imprint. The text is printed on watermarked ("HJ") laid paper throughout. There are no binder's fly-leaves.

XI. *What Maisie Knew*. The title-page is dated 1913. Collation: [unsigned, 1^2 (1_1+X_1) 2–38^8 39^4]; pp. [i–xxiv] [1–2], 3–577 [578] [579–580] plus 2. Contents: [i–ii] series half-title, verso blank; frontispiece with tissue guard tipped in (not in pagination), [iii–iv] title-page, verso copyright notice and arrangements notice; v–[xxii] "PREFACE"; [xxiii–xxiv] "CONTENTS", verso blank; [1–2] fly-title, verso blank; 3–[577] text; [578] printer's imprint; [597–580] blank leaf. Signatures [1–3] are printed on watermarked ("HJ") laid paper, and the balance of the signatures are printed on unwatermarked laid paper. There are no binder's fly-leaves.

XII. *The Aspern Papers*. The title-page is dated 1913. Collation: [unsigned, 1^2 (1_1+X_1) 2–28^8 29^2]; pp. [i–xxvi] [1–2], 3–[413] [414] plus 2. Contents: [i–ii] series half-title, verso blank; frontispiece with tissue guard tipped in (not in pagination); [iii–iv] title-page, verso copyright notice and arrangements notice; v–[xxiv] "PREFACE"; [xxv–xxvi] "CONTENTS", verso blank; [1–2] fly-title, verso blank; 3–[413] text; [414] printer's imprint. Signatures [1–3] are printed on watermarked ("HJ") laid paper, and the balance of the signatures are printed on unwatermarked laid paper. A binder's fly-leaf of watermarked ("HJ") laid paper is at the front, but none at the back.

XIII. *The Reverberator*. The title-page is dated 1913. Collation: [unsigned, 1^2 (1_1+X_1) 2–36^8 37^6]; pp. [i–xxiv] [1–2], 3–[550] [551–552] plus 2. Contents: [i–ii] series half-title, verso blank; frontispiece with tissue guard tipped in (not in pagination); [iii–iv] title-page, verso copyright notice and arrangements notice; v–[xxi] "PREFACE"; [xxii] blank; [xxiii–xxiv] "CONTENTS", verso blank; [1–2] fly-title, verso blank; 3–[550] text; [551–552] blank, verso printer's imprint. Signatures [1–3] are printed on watermarked ("HJ") laid paper, and the balance of the signatures are printed on unwatermarked laid paper. The endpapers are of cream laid paper watermarked "[crown device] | Abbey Mills | Greenfield". There are no binder's fly-leaves.

The endpaper have been replaced, and the bookplate on the front pastedown has bled on to the series half-title rather than on to the front free endpaper prior to the time of the endpapers' replacement.

XIV. *Lady Barbarina*. The title-page is dated 1913. Collation: [unsigned, 1^2 (1_1+X_1) 2–40^8 41^2]; pp. [i–xxiv] [1–2], 3–[607] [608] plus 2. Contents: [i–ii] series half-title, verso blank; frontispiece with tissue guard tipped in (not in pagination); [iii–iv] title-page, verso copyright notice and arrangements notice; v–[xxii] "PREFACE"; [xxiii–xxiv] "CONTENTS", verso blank; [1–2] fly-title, verso blank; 3–[607] text; [608] printer's imprint. Signatures [1–3] are printed on watermarked ("HJ") laid paper, and the balance of the signatures are printed on unwatermarked laid paper. A binder's fly-leaf of watermarked ("HJ") laid paper is at the front and the back.

XV. *The Lesson of The Master*. The title-page is dated 1913. Collation: [unsigned, 1^2 (1_1+X_1) 2^6 3^{10} 4^6 5^{10} 6^6 7^{10} 8^6 9^{10} 10^6 11^{10} 12^6 13^{10} 14^6 15^{10} 16^6 17^{10} 18^6 19^{10} 20^6 21^{10} 22^6 23^{10} 24^6 25^{10} 26^1]; pp. [i–xx] [1–2], 3–[368] [369–370] plus 2. Contents: [i–ii] series half-title, verso blank; frontispiece with tissue guard tipped in (not in pagination); [iii–iv] title-page, verso copyright notice and arrangements notice; v–[xviii] "PREFACE"; [xix–xx] "CONTENTS", verso blank; [1–2] fly-title, verso blank; 3–[368] text; [369–370] blank, verso printer's imprint. Signature [1] is printed on watermarked ("HJ") laid paper, and the balance of the signatures are printed on unwatermarked laid paper There are no binder's fly-leaves.

XVI. *The Author of Beltraffio*. The title-page is dated 1909. Collation: [unsigned, 1^2 (1_1+x_1) 2–28^8 29^4]; pp. [i–xiv] [1–2], 3–[426] [427–428] [429–430] plus 2. Contents: [i–ii] series half-title, verso blank; frontispiece with tissue guard tipped in (not in pagination); [iii–iv] title-page, verso copyright notice and arrangements notice; v–[xxii]

"PREFACE"; [xxiii–xxiv] "CONTENTS", verso blank; [1–2] fly-title, verso blank; 3–[426] text; [427–428] blank, verso printer's imprint; [429–430] blank leaf. Signatures [1 - 2] are printed on watermarked ("HJ") laid paper, and the balance of the signatures are printed on unwatermarked laid paper. There are no binder's fly-leaves.

XVII. *The Altar of The Dead*. The title-page is dated 1913. Collation: [unsigned, 1^2 (1_1+X_1) $2-36^8$ 37^6]; pp. [i–xxxii] [1–2], 3–[542] [543–544] plus 2. Contents: [i–ii] series half-title, verso blank; frontispiece with tissue guard tipped in (not in pagination); [iii–iv] title-page, verso copyright notice and arrangements notice; v–[xxix] "PREFACE"; [xxx] blank; [xxxi–xxxii] "CONTENTS", verso blank; [1–2] fly-title, verso blank; 3–[542] text; [543–544] blank, verso printer's imprint. Signatures [1 - 3] are printed on watermarked ("HJ") laid paper, and the balance of the signatures are printed on unwatermarked laid paper. A binder's fly-leaf of watermarked ("HJ") laid paper is at the front, but none at the back.

XVIII. *Daisy Miller*. The title-page is dated 1913. Collation: [unsigned, 1^2 (1_1+X_1) $2-34^8$]; pp. [i–xxvi] [1–2], 3–[506] plus 2. Contents: [i–ii] series half-title, verso blank; frontispiece with tissue guard tipped in (not in pagination); [iii–iv] title-page, verso copyright notice and arrangements notice; v–[xxiv] "PREFACE"; [xxv-xxvi] "CONTENTS", verso blank; [1–2] fly-title, verso blank; 3–[506] text. There is no printer's imprint. Signatures [1 - 3] are printed on watermarked ("HJ") laid paper, and the balance of the signatures are printed on unwatermarked laid paper. A binder's fly-leaf of watermarked ("HJ") laid paper is at the front and the back.

XIX. *The Wings of The Dove*, Volume I. The title-page is dated 1913. Collation: [unsigned, 1^2 (1_1+X_1) $2-21^8$ 22^2]; pp. [i–xxiv] [1–2], 3–[302] [303–304] plus 2. Contents: [i–ii] series half-title, verso blank; frontispiece with tissue guard tipped in (not in pagination); [iii–iv] title-page, verso copyright notice (no arrangements notice); v–[xxiii] "PREFACE"; [xxiv] blank; [1–2] divisional fly-title, verso blank; 3–302 text; [303–304] blank leaf. There is no printer's imprint. Signature [1] is printed on watermarked ("HJ") laid paper, and the balance of the signatures are printed on unwatermarked laid paper. A binder's fly-leaf of watermarked ("HJ") laid paper is at the front, but none at the back.

XX. *The Wings of The Dove*, Volume II. The title-page is dated 1913. Collation: [unsigned, 1^2 (1_1+X_1) 2–26^8 27^4]; pp. [i–iv] [1–2], 3–[405] [406] [407–408] plus 2. Contents: [i–ii] series half-title, verso blank; frontispiece with tissue guard tipped in (not in pagination); [iii–iv] title-page, verso copyright notice (no arrangements notice); [1–2] divisional fly-title, verso blank; 3–[405] text; [406] printer's imprint; [407–408] blank leaf. Signature [1] is printed on watermarked ("HJ") laid paper, and the balance of the signatures are printed on unwatermarked laid paper. A binder's fly-leaf of watermarked ("HJ") laid paper is at the front, but none at the back.

XXI. *The Ambassadors*, Volume I. The title-page is dated 1913. Collation: [unsigned, 1^2 (1_1+X_1) 2–20^8 21^2]; pp. [i–xxiv] [1–2], 3–[286] [287–288] plus 2. Contents: [i–ii] series half-title, verso blank; frontispiece with tissue guard tipped in (not in pagination); [iii–iv] title-page, verso copyright notice and arrangements notice; v–[xxiii] "PREFACE"; [xxiv] blank; [1–2] divisional fly-title, verso blank; 3–[286] text; [287–288] blank leaf. There is no printer's imprint. Signature [1] is printed on watermarked ("HJ") laid paper, and the balance of the signatures are printed on unwatermarked laid paper. There are no binder's fly-leaves.

XXII. *The Ambassadors*, Volume II. The title-page is dated 1913. Collation: [unsigned, 1^2 (1_1+X_1) 2–21^8 22^4]; pp. [i–iv] [1–2], 3–[327] [328] plus 2. Contents: [i–ii] series half-title, verso blank; frontispiece with tissue guard tipped in (not in pagination); [iii–iv] title-page, verso copyright notice and arrangements notice; [1–2] divisional fly-title, verso blank; 3–[327] text; [328] printer's imprint. Signature [1] is printed on watermarked ("HJ") laid paper, and the balance of the signatures are printed on unwatermarked laid paper. A binder's fly-leaf of watermarked ("HJ") laid paper is at the back, but none at the front.

XXIII. *The Golden Bowl*, Volume I. The title-page is dated 1913. Collation: [unsigned, 1^2 (1_1+X_1) 2–27^8 28^4]; pp. [i–xxvi] [1–2], 3–[402] plus 2. Contents: [i–ii] series half-title, verso blank; frontispiece with tissue guard tipped in (not in pagination); [iii–iv] title-page, verso copyright notice (no arrangements notice); v–[xxv] "PREFACE"; [xxvi] blank; [1–2] divisional fly-title, verso blank; 3–[402] text. There is no printer's imprint. Signatures [1–3] are printed on watermarked ("HJ") laid paper, and the balance of the signatures are printed on unwatermarked laid paper. A binder's fly-leaf of watermarked ("HJ") laid paper is at the front and the back.

XXIV. *The Golden Bowl*, Volume II. The title-page is dated 1913. Collation: [unsigned, 1² (1₁+X₁) 2–24⁸ 25²]; pp. [i–iv] [1–2], 3–[369] [370] [371–372] plus 2. Contents: [i–ii] series half-title, verso blank; frontispiece with tissue guard tipped in (not in pagination); [iii–iv] title-page, verso copyright notice (no arrangements notice); [1–2] divisional fly-title, verso blank; 3–[369] text; [370] printer's imprint; [371–372] blank leaf. Signature [1] is printed on watermarked ("HJ") laid paper, and the balance of the signatures are printed on unwatermarked laid paper. There are no binder's fly-leaves.

The English issue of *The Novels and Tales of Henry James* is in 24 rather than the 26 volumes of the American edition, as neither *The Ivory Tower* nor *The Sense of the Past* were incoporated into it. There was also no limited impression published in England. Macmillan initially purchased 100 sets of sheets from Scribner's for the English issue and were given a further five sets of sheets "gratis". There were later order for further sets of sheets; see printing history following 64.1.0.

With regard to the 1913 dates on the title-pages of most of the above volumes, it is to be noted that the back covers of the dust-jackets on the first English edition, first impression, second state, of *A Small Boy and Others* (1913), 71.4.0, and the first English edition of *Notes of a Son and Brother* (1914), 72.4.0, have on them an ad for *The Novels of Henry James* in 24 volumes.

❧✠❦

65. *VIEWS AND REVIEWS*

65.1.0. *Views and Reviews*, first edition, trade impression, one volume, Boston 1908.

VIEWS | AND REVIEWS | BY | HENRY JAMES | NOW FIRST COLLECTED | INTRODUCTION BY | LE ROY PHILLIPS | COMPILER OF | "A BIBLIOGRAPHY OF THE WRITINGS | OF HENRY JAMES" | BOSTON | THE BALL PUBLISHING COMPANY | 1908

Size: 7 9/16″ x 5 3/16″.

Collation: [unsigned, 1–16⁸]; pp. [i–xiv], 1–241 [242].

Contents: [i–ii] half-title, verso blank; [iii–iv] title-page, verso copyright notice: "Copyright, 1908 [in italic] | By The Ball Publishing Co."; v–ix "INTRODUCTION [all in italic]"; [x] blank; [xi–xii] "CONTENTS", verso blank; [xiii–xiv] divisional fly-title, verso blank; 1–241 text; [242] blank.

Binding: olive-green vertical-rib-grain cloth. The front cover is decorated with a single-rule border in gilt. The back cover is neither lettered nor decorated. The spine, lettered and decorated in gilt, reads: "[rule] | VIEWS | AND | REVIEWS | [rule] | HENRY JAMES | THE BALL | PUBLISHING CO. | [rule]". The endpapers are of white wove paper, and the text is printed on wove paper. The top edge is gilt, the fore-edge is rough trimmed, and the bottom edge is untrimmed.

The trade impression was priced at $1.50 net, and the limited impression at $2.50 net. This title was not published in England.

65.2.0. *Views and Reviews*, first edition, limited impression, one volume, Boston 1908.

Size: 7 $^{11}/_{16}$″ x 5 $^{1}/_{8}$″.

The title-page, collation, and contents are identical to those of the first edition, trade impression, 65.1.0, except that on the verso of the title-leaf is the limitation notice: "This edition is limited to one hundred and sixty | copies, of which this is No. 105 [all in italic]".

Binding: cream paper wrappers over semi-flexible boards. The front cover is decorated with a single-rule border in gilt. The back cover is neither lettered nor decorated. The spine has a brown leather label, lettered and decorated in gilt, that reads: "[rule] | VIEWS | AND REVIEWS | [rule] | HENRY JAMES | [rule]". The endpapers are of white wove paper, and the text is printed on laid paper thinner that the paper used for the trade impression. All edges are untrimmed.

The publisher's ad in the trade impression describes the limited impression as: "160 Nunbered copies bound in Japan and boxed".

The difference in the text paper between this copy (laid paper) and 65.1.0 (wove paper) possibly indicates that they are of separate impressions.

JULIA BRIDE

66. *JULIA BRIDE*

66.1.0. *Julia Bride*, first separate edition, one volume, New York and London 1909.

JULIA BRIDE [in red] | BY | HENRY JAMES | ILLUSTRATED BY | W. T. SMEDLEY | [oval publisher's device] | NEW YORK AND LONDON | HARPER & BROTHERS PUBLISHERS [in red] | MCMIX [all of the foregoing within a black single-rule frame itself within a red double-rule border]

Size: 8″ x 5 1/8″.

Collation: [1]^8 (1$_1$+X$_1$) 2–6^8; pp. [2] [i–vi], 1–[84] [85–88] plus 2. The frontispiece with tissue guard, and three further full-page illustrations without tissue guards, all tipped in, and not reckoned in the pagination.

Contents: blank leaf; frontispiece with tissue guards tipped in not reckoned in the pagination; [i–ii] title-page, verso within a small single-rule frame copyright notice, reservation of rights and printing history: "Copyright, 1909, by Harper & Brothers. | [rule] | All rights reserved. [in italic] | Published September, 1909."; [iii–iv] "ILLUSTRATIONS [in italic]", verso blank; [v–vi] fly-title, verso blank; 1–[84] text; [85–88] blank leaves.

Binding: maroon diagonal-fine-ribbed cloth. The front cover has a decorative border in blind of entwined hearts and ribbon which is between two single-rule borders in blind, and a central panel lettered in gilt which reads: "JULIA | BRIDE | HENRY JAMES [author's name in sans-serif]". The back cover is neither lettered nor decorated. The spine, lettered in gilt, reads: "JULIA | BRIDE | [heart device] | JAMES [in sans serif] | HARPERS". The publisher's imprint on the spine is in a serif font with letters of uniform size 1/16″ high. The endpapers are of off-white wove paper, and the text is printed on wove paper. The frontispiece and three further illustrations tipped in are printed on smooth coated paper. The top edge is gilt, and the other edges are untrimmed.

Dust-jacket: white wove paper with a large pictorial panel on the front cover, printed in gray with a tinge of orange, replicating the frontispiece. This pictorial panel is framed by a narrow white frame, which is larger at the bottom and in the enlarged area printed in black is: "JULIA BRIDE by Henry James [in sans-serif]". This frame is in turn surrounded by a slightly wider orange border. The spine, with white with lettering in black running vertically down it, reads: "JULIA BRIDE. [space] By Henry James. [space] $1.25 [all in sans-serif]". The back cover of the dust-jacket is white with black lettering within a black single-rule border, which is headed: "By HENRY JAMES [in italic, underscored] | JULIA BRIDE", and is followed by a 15-line blurb for this title. Beneath the blurb is a rule, followed by: "Post 8vo, Cloth. Illuminated Wrapper. $1.25 [in italic]", a further rule and the publisher's imprint. The front inner flap, also white, has black lettering within a black single-ruled frame headed: "NOTICE | [double rule] | HOW | TO OPEN A BOOK | [single rule]", followed by 21 lines of text. The rear inner flap, which is also white, has black lettering within a black single-rule black frame, headed: "The | MOTHER | and the | FATHER | By | W. D. HOWELLS [all in sans-serif]", followed by 3 lines of text.

The ad on the back of this dust-jacket describes it as an "illuminated wrapper".

This is one of the two primary binding states (no priority) recorded in E&L A66. E&L records that on the second binding state the spine imprint is in sans-serif. Such a copy has not been seen. E&L also records three secondary binding states. BAL 10780 records one primary binding (this one), and five variants or remainder bindings. This title, as a separate edition, was not published in England.

The first appearance of *Julia Bride* in book form is in *The Novels and Tales of Henry James*, 64.1.0, Volume XVII, 489–[542] (1909).

66.2.0. *Julia Bride*, first separate edition, one volume, New York and London 1909.

Size: $7\,^3/_4''$ x $4\,^7/_8''$.

The title-page, collation, and contents are identical to those of the first separate edition (primary binding state), 66.1.0.

Binding: tan linen-grain cloth. The front cover, lettered and decorated in dark brown, reads: "JULIA | BRIDE | [daffodil device] | HENRY JAMES [author's name in sans-serif]". The back cover is neither lettered nor decorated. The spine, lettered and decorated in brown, reads: "JULIA | BRIDE | [heart device] | JAMES [in sans-serif] | [daffodil device] | HARPERS". The publisher's imprint at the foot of the spine is in a serif font with letters of uniform size $^3/_{32}''$ high. The endpapers are of off-white wove paper, and the text is printed on wove paper. All edges are trimmed, but the top edge is not gilt.

Dust-jacket: identical to the dust-jacket on 66.1.0, except that it has been cut down by the publisher or binder (or printed in this smaller format from the original plates) at the top and bottom, and folded further into the front and back covers to accommodate a smaller size book, thus reducing the width of the orange border on the front cover. In this case the dust-jacket is $1/4''$ shorter than the cover of the book, but it is the same size as the dust-jacket on the other copies catalogued below.

E&L A66 records three variant bindings. This copy is E&L's variant a.

Illustrated Plate 27.

66.3.0. *Julia Bride*, first separate edition, one volume, New York and London 1909.

Size: $7\,7/16''$ x $4\,7/8''$.

The title-page, collation, and contents are identical to those of the first separate edition (primary binding state), 66.1.0.

Binding: tan paper over boards, lettered and decorated in brown on the front cover and spine identically to the first edition (variant binding), 66.2.0, except that the daffodil device on the front cover is not present, and the publisher's imprint at the foot of the spine is in a serif font with letters of uniform size $1/16''$ high. The endpapers are of white wove paper, and the text is printed on wove paper. All edges are trimmed, but the top edge is not gilt.

This copy has a dust-jacket (cut down) identical to that on 66.1.0.

This copy is E&L variant b.

66.4.0. *Julia Bride*, first separate edition, one volume, New York and London 1909.

Size: $7\,7/16''$ x $4\,7/8''$.

The title-page, collation, and contents are identical to those of the first separate edition (primary binding state), 66.1.0.

Binding: pink quarter cloth, with buff paper over boards. The front cover, lettered in black, reads: "JULIA | BRIDE | HENRY JAMES [author's name in sans-serif]". The back cover is neither lettered nor decorated. The spine, lettered and decorated in black, reads: "JULIA | BRIDE | [heart device] | JAMES [in sans-serif] | Harpers". The publisher's imprint at the foot of the spine is in a serif font and has an "H" larger than the rest of the letters. The endpapers are of white wove paper, and the text is printed on wove paper. All edges are trimmed, but the top edge is not gilt.

This copy is E&L's variant c.

This copy has a dust-jacket (cut down), identical to that on the first separate edition, primary binding, 66.1.0.

66.5.0. *Julia Bride*, first separate edition, one volume, New York and London 1909.

Size: 7 $^5/_{16}$" x 4 $^7/_8$".

The title-page, collation, and contents are the same as those of the first separate impression (primary binding state), 66.1.0.

Binding: light aqua-blue smooth cloth. The front cover, lettered in black, reads: "JULIA | BRIDE | HENRY JAMES [author's name in sans-serif]". The back cover is neither lettered nor decorated. The spine, lettered and decorated in black, reads: "JULIA | BRIDE | [heart device] | JAMES | HARPERS". The publisher's imprint at the foot of the spine is in a sans-serif font with letters of uniform size $^1/_8$" high. The endpapers are of white wove paper, and the text is printed on wove paper. All edges are trimmed, but the top edge is not gilt.

Illustrated Plate 27.

This binding is not recorded in E&L or BAL.

66.6.0. *Julia Bride*, first separate edition, one volume, New York and London 1909.

Size: 7 $^5/_{16}$" x 4 $^7/_8$".

The title-page, collation, and contents are identical to those of the first separate edition (primary binding state), 66.1.0.

Binding: blue linen-grain cloth, lettered and decorated in black. The lettering on the front cover and the lettering and decoration on the spine are identical to those on the first edition (variant binding),

66.5.0, including the publisher's imprint at the foot of the spine is in a sans-serif font with letters of uniform size $1/8''$ high. The endpapers are of white wove paper, and the text is printed on wove paper. All edges are trimmed, but the top edge is not gilt.

On the front pastedown is the bookplate of Karl M. Armens.

Illustrated Plate 27

This binding is not recorded in E&L or BAL.

❧✢❧

67. ITALIAN HOURS

67.1.0. *Italian Hours*, first edition, one volume, London 1909.

ITALIAN HOURS [in red-brown] | BY | HENRY JAMES | AUTHOR OF "ENGLISH HOURS," "A LITTLE TOUR IN FRANCE," ETC. | ILLUSTRATED BY JOSEPH PENNELL | W [publisher's device of windmill] H | LONDON | WILLIAM HEINEMANN [in red-brown] | 1909

Size: $10\ 9/16''$ x $8\ 1/16''$

Collation: $[a]^4$ $([a]_1 + X_1)$ b^2 A–I K–U X–Z^8 2A^4; pp. [i–xii], [1]–364 [365–366] 367–376 plus 2. The frontispiece and a further 63 full-page illustrations tipped in, and not reckoned in the pagination.

Contents: [i–ii] half-title, verso ad headed: "OTHER WORKS ILLUSTRATED [in italic] | By Joseph Pennell", listing 4 titles, the first 2 by James; frontispiece with printed tissue guard tipped in not reckoned in the pagination; [iii–iv] title-page, verso copyright notice: "Copyright, London 1909, by William Heinemann | And Washington, U.S.A., by Houghton, Mifflin & Company"; v–[vi] "PREFACE", verso blank; vii–viii "CONTENTS", verso continuation of contents; ix–xi "LIST OF ILLUSTRATIONS; [xii] "ERRATA"; [1]–364 text; [365–366] divisional fly-title, verso blank; 367–376 "INDEX"; 376 at foot printer's imprint: "Printed by Ballantyne, Hanson & Co. | Edinburgh & London".

The 64 illustrations consist of the frontispiece and a further 31 color plates with printed tissue guards tipped onto inserted stubs, and 32 plates in brown and white monotone tipped in without tissue guards.

Binding: dull sage-green buckram. The front cover, lettered and decorated in gilt within a single-rule border in blind, reads: "ITALIAN

[dot] HOVRS | BY [dot] HENRY [dot] JAMES | ILLVSTRATED [colon] BY | JOSEPH [dot] PENNELL | [slightly oval device of an hourglass surrounded by angel wings]". The back cover is decorated in blind with the small square device of William Heinemann with a windmill flanked by "W" and "H". The spine, lettered and decorated in gilt, reads: "[single-rule] | ITALIAN | HOVRS | [three fleur-de-lys] | HENRY | JAMES | HEINEMANN [in serif type] | [single rule]". The endpapers are of cream laid paper, the text is printed on cream laid paper, and the illustrations are printed on wove paper. The top edge is gilt, and the other edges are untrimmed.

English Printing History. Heinemann Archive. First edition, one volume: *first* (and sole) *impression*: (number of copies not specified), published October 27, 1909, priced at 25s. E&L A67b records that the sole impression was of 1,000 copies, and that 300 sets of sheets were remaindered

67.2.0. *Italian Hours*, first edition, one volume, London 1909.

The title-page, size, collation, and contents are identical to those of the first edition, 67.1.0.

Binding: dull sage-green linen-grain cloth. The lettering and decoration on the front and back covers and spine are identical to those on 67.1.0, except that the publisher's imprint at the foot of the spine is in uniform sans-serif capitals, and the back cover has the same hourglass device as appears on the front cover, but in blind rather than gilt, in place of the William Heinemann device. The endpapers are of cream laid paper, the text is printed on cream laid paper, and the illustrations printed on wove paper. The top edge is trimmed and stained a light grey-blue, and the other edges are untrimmed.

This copy is one of the 300 that were remaindered.

67.3.0. *Italian Hours*, first American edition, first impression, one volume, Boston and New York 1909.

ITALIAN HOURS | BY HENRY JAMES | WITH ILLUSTRATIONS IN COLOR | BY JOSEPH PENNELL | [red vertical rectangular publisher's device] | BOSTON AND NEW YORK | HOUGHTON MIFFLIN COMPANY | MDCCCCIX

Size: 10 $^{9}/_{16}$" x 8".

ITALIAN HOURS

Collation: [unsigned, 1⁴ (1₂+X₁,₂) 2¹ 3–33⁸ 34⁴ 35¹]; pp. [2] [i–x] [1–2], 3–[505] [506] plus 2. Signature [1] has two additional non conjugate leaves, the frontispiece (not reckoned in the pagination) and the title-leaf (reckoned in the pagination), tipped in between the conjugate leaves [1₂] and [1₃]. A further 31 full-page color plates are tipped in, and not reckoned in the pagination.

Contents: blank leaf; [i–ii] half-title, verso blank; frontispiece with tissue guard tipped in not reckoned in the pagination; [iii–iv] title-page, verso copyright notice, reservation of rights and printing history: "COPYRIGHT, 1909, BY HENRY JAMES | ALL RIGHTS RESERVED | PUBLISHED NOVEMBER 1909"; [v–vi] "PREFACE", verso blank; vii–[viii] "CONTENTS", verso continuation of contents; ix–[x] "ILLUSTRATIONS", verso continuation of illustrations; [1–2] divisional fly-title, verso blank; 3–[505] text; [506] printer's imprint: "The Riverside Press [in Gothic type] | CAMBRIDGE [dot] MASSACHUSETTS | U [dot] S [dot] A".

Binding: terra-cotta smooth-linen-grain cloth. The front cover, which is lettered in the cloth color against a gilt ground within an elaborately decorated gilt mosaic background panel bordered with blue and green florets, ribbons, and garlands on which are imposed two gilt panels. The top panel reads: "ITALIAN | HOVRS | HENRY [small triangular device] JAMES", the lower panel reads: "ILLVSTRATED [small triangular device] BY | JOSEPH [small triangular device] PENNELL". The back cover is neither lettered nor decorated. The spine, lettered in gilt and decorated in gilt, green, and blue, reads: "ITALIAN | HOVRS | [mosaic panel with single rosette, ribbons, and suspended garland of leaves] | JAMES | ILLVSTRATED [small triangular device] BY | JOSEPH PENNELL | HOUGHTON | MIFFLIN CO." The endpapers are of off-white laid paper, the text is printed on laid paper, and the illustrations are printed on smooth coated paper. A binder's fly-leaf of laid paper is at the back, but none at the front. The top edge is gilt, and the other edges are rough trimmed.

On the front free endpaper is a small bookseller's label that reads: "W. B. CLARKE CO. | BOOKSELLERS AND STATIONERS | [rule] | 26 & 28 TREMONT ST. & | 30 COURT SQ., BOSTON."

Illustrated Plate 28.

This copy of the first impression lacks the slipcase box in which it was originally issued. The 32 brown and white monotone plates and the index, which are present in the first edition, 67.1.0, are not present in the first American edition.

American printing history. Houghton Mifflin Archive. First edition: Ms Am 2930(23), 215: "Holiday [Edition]" *first impression* November 9, 1909, 1510 copies, 1510 bound between November 9 and December 21, 1909; published November 1909; "Holiday [Edition]" *second impression* December 18, 1909, 504 copies, 485 bound between December 22, 1909, and August 6, 1910; notations: "4/7/09 rcvd. 2040 sets 32 col[ored] pl[ates] from Wm Heinemann", "12/18/09 ptd. 660 4pp. titles" and "12/23/09 ptd. 68 4pp. cancels". On January 5, 1910, June 4, 1910, and August 6, 1910, one copy (on each date) was bound in "full lev[ant]".

Both impressions were priced at $7.50.

67.4.0. *Italian Hours*, first American edition, second impression, one volume, Boston and New York 1909.

The title-page, size, collation, and contents are identical to those of the first American edition, first impression, 67.3.0, except that the verso of the title-page reads: "COPYRIGHT, 1909, BY HENRY JAMES | ALL RIGHTS RESERVED | PUBLISHED NOVEMBER 1909 | SECOND IMPRESSION".

Binding: terra-cotta smooth-linen-grain cloth, lettered and decorated identically to 67.3.0. The endpapers are of off-white laid paper, the text is printed on laid paper, and the illustrations are printed on coated wove paper. A binder's fly-leaf of laid paper is at the back, but none at the front. The top edge is gilt, and the other edges are rough trimmed.

68. *THE FINER GRAIN*

68.1.0. *The Finer Grain*, first edition, first impression, first binding state, one volume, New York 1910.

THE FINER GRAIN | BY | HENRY JAMES | NEW YORK | CHARLES SCRIBNER'S SONS | 1910

Size: $7 \frac{1}{2}''$ x $4 \frac{7}{8}''$.

THE FINER GRAIN

Collation: [unsigned, 1–20^8]; pp. [i–viii] [1–2], 3–312.

Contents: [i–ii] blank, verso ad headed: "BOOKS BY HENRY JAMES", listing 6 titles (including *The Novels and Tales*) with dollar prices; [iii–iv] half-title, verso blank; [v–vi] title-page, verso copyright notice, printing history and printer's device: "Copyright, 1910, by | CHARLES SCRIBNER'S SONS | [rule] | Published October, 1910 | [printer's device of the Scribner's Press]"; [vii–viii] "CONTENTS", verso blank; [1–2] divisional fly-title, verso blank; 3–312 text.

Binding: olive-brown sateen. The front cover, lettered in gilt within a single-rule gilt frame, reads: "THE FINER | GRAIN | By | HENRY JAMES". The back cover is neither lettered nor decorated. The spine, lettered and decorated in gilt, reads: "THE | FINER | GRAIN | [leaf ornament] | HENRY | JAMES | SCRIBNERS". The publisher's imprint on the spine is in uniform capitals 1/8" high. The endpapers are of white laid paper, and the text is printed on laid paper. The top edge is gilt, and the other edges are rough trimmed.

American printing history. Scribner's Archive. cards (2) Box 13: Id-J. First edition: *first impression* 3,000 copies printed September 20, 1910, all bound between September 30, 1910, and October 2, 1923; notation "9–30–10 CSS 3100 wraps"; published October 6, 1910; notations opposite binding orders (50 copies each) of April 14, 1919, and January 14, 1920, "omit gilt top-use cheap clo[th]. "NEW ED[ition]" 270 copies printed on May 24, 1924, all bound between July 18, 1924, and June 4, 1931; notations: "1931 June 4 Destroyed 71 [copies]" and "P.[lates] D.[estroyed] 6/13/38". It is unlikely that the "New Edition" was in fact a separate edition, but, as the small print run suggests, was a second impression of the first edition.

Both "editions" were printed and bound by Scribner's, but the type of paper used is not recorded. The first edition was initially priced at $1.25 net, but was later raised to $2.50 (date not recorded), but clearly for the "New Edition".

68.2.0. *The Finer Grain*, first edition, first impression, second binding state, one volume, New York 1910.

The title-page, size, collation, and contents are identical to the first edition, first impressin, first binding state, 68.1.0.

Binding: gray-green smooth cloth (not sateen). The front and back covers are neither lettered nor decorated. The spine, lettered and decorated in gilt, reads: "THE | FINER | GRAIN | [leaf ornament] | HENRY | JAMES | SCRIBNERS". The publisher's imprint on the spine is in uniform capitals $^3/_{16}$" high. The endpapers are of cream laid paper, and the text is printed on laid paper. The top edge is trimmed and stained light ochre, the fore-edge is untrimmed, and the bottom edge is rough trimmed.

On the rear pastedown is a small blue ticket lettered in dark blue reading: "BRENTANO'S | Booksellers & Stationers | Washington, D.C. [all within a single rule frame]".

This gray-green smooth cloth (not sateen) binding, is not recorded in E&L or BAL. It is undoubtedly one of the 100 copies of the first impression bound on April 14, 1919 and January 14, 1920 that omitted the gilt top and used cheaper cloth.

68.3.0. *The Finer Grain*, first English edition, first impression, English issue, one volume, London [n.d., 1910].

THE | FINER GRAIN | BY | HENRY JAMES | METHUEN & CO. LTD. | 36 ESSEX STREET W. C. | LONDON

Size: $7\,^7/_{16}$" x 5".

Collation: a^4 1–19^8 20^2; pp. [i–viii], 1–307 [308].

Contents: [i–ii] signature mark "*a*" at the foot, verso blank; [iii–iv] half-title, verso ad headed: "BY THE SAME AUTHOR", listing 3 titles; [v–vi] title-page, verso printing history: "First Published in 1910 [in italic]"; vii–[viii] "CONTENTS", verso blank; 1–307 text; [308] printer's imprint: "EDINBURGH | COLSTONS LIMITED | PRINTERS".

Binding: terra-cotta linen-grain cloth. The front cover, lettered in gilt within a single-rule border in blind, reads: "THE FINER GRAIN | HENRY JAMES". The back cover is neither lettered nor decorated. The spine, lettered and decorated in gilt, reads: "[double rule] | THE | FINER | GRAIN | HENRY | JAMES | [long strapwork device of intertwined vines with leaves] | METHUEN | [double rule]". The publisher's imprint at the foot of the spine is in uniform capitals $^5/_{32}$" high. The endpapers are of white wove paper, and the text is printed on wove paper. The top edge is trimmed and stained brown, the fore-edge is rough trimmed, and the bottom edge is untrimmed. A 32-page paginated publisher's catalogue, dated October 1910, printed on a lighter wove paper is bound in at the end, [32] of which is blank except for the printer's imprint.

E&L A68b notes first impressions with catalogues dated August, September, and October 1910.

English printing history. Methuen Archive Mss. LMC 2230, Stock Ledger, Vol. 4, p. 56. First edition: *first impression* September 14, 1910, 1,500 copies, with 9 over, all bound between September 26 and November 4, 1910, 1300 being bound for the English issue, and 209 for the colonial issue (all the colonial issue being bound in paper wrappers); notation: "Both Titles"; *second impression* October 8, 1910, 1,000 copies, with 10 over, 1006 being bound between October 31 and December 12, 1910, 731 for the English issue and 275 for the colonial issue (all the colonial issue being bound in cloth); notation: "Both Titles"; *third impression* December 7, 1910, 500 copies, none over, 465 bound between December 14, 1910, and October 15, 1912, all for the English issue; notation: "Both Titles". On that latter date 294 bound copies of the third impression, English issue, appear to have been remaindered to "Strake [?] & Son". Other notations: "Wrappers 1500 Sept. 20/10"; "Col[onial] Covers 500 Aug. 20/10" overwritten "Cancelled" and "500 Sept. 28/10" not overwritten; "from 1/[19]14 moulds and blocks destroyed", and "Type distributed Jan. 26/[19]11".

68.4.0. *The Finer Grain*, first English edition, first impression, English issue, one volume, London [n.d., 1910].

This copy is identical in every respect to the first English edition, first impression, English issue, 68.3.0, except that the 32-page publisher's catalogue bound in at the end is dated September 1910.

68.5.0. *The Finer Grain*, first English edition, second impression, English issue, one volume, London [n.d., 1910].

This copy is identical to the first English edition, first impression, English issue, 68.3.0, except that on the title-page "SECOND EDITION" appears between the author's name and the publisher's imprint, and the verso of the title-leaf reads: "Published … October 13th 1910 | Second Edition … October [space] 1910 [all in italic]".

Binding: terra-cotta linen-grain cloth, lettered in gilt, and decorated in gilt and in blind, identically to 68.3.0. The endpapers are of white wove paper, and the text is printed on wove paper. The top edge is trimmed and stained brown, and the other edges are untrimmed. A 32-page paginated publisher's catalogue, dated September 1910, (the last page of which is blank except for the printer's imprint) is bound in at the end. This catalogue is identical to that in 68.4.0. It is noted that this catalogue is earlier in date than that bound in at the end of one of the copies of the first impression, 68.3.0.

Another copy of the first English edition, second impression, English issue, has been examined, identical to this copy but with a 32-page paginated publisher's catalogue of ads dated October 1910, which catalogue is identical to that of the same date bound in 68.3.0.

68.6.0. *The Finer Grain*, first English edition, third impression, one volume, London [n.d., 1910].

The title-page, size, and collation are identical to those of the first English edition, first impression, English issue, 68.3.0, except that on the title-page "THIRD EDITION" appears between the author's name and the publisher's imprint, and the verso of the title-leaf reads: "First Published ... October 13, 1910 | Second Edition ... October [space] 1910 | Third Edition...December [space] 1910 [all in italic]".

Binding: tobacco-brown linen-grain cloth (distinctively less red than the cloth of the first impression). It is lettered in gilt, and decorated in gilt and blind, identically to 68.3.0, except that the publisher's imprint "METHUEN" at the foot of the spine is in uniform capitals $^1/_8"$ high as against uniform capitals $^5/_{32}"$ high on the first and second impressions. The endpapers are of white wove paper, and the text is printed on wove paper. The top edge is trimmed and stained brown, the fore-edge is rough trimmed, and the bottom edge is untrimmed. Bound in at the end are 8 pages of ads headed "METHUEN'S POPULAR NOVELS | Autumn 1912", printed on bookstock, followed by a 32-page paginated publisher's catalogue, dated July 1912, printed on thinner wove paper, [31] of which is blank except for the printer's imprint, and [32] of which is blank.

Although the verso of the title-page records that the third edition was printed in December 1910, the ads, printed on bookstock, are headed "METHUEN'S | POPULAR NOVELS | Autumn 1912". In addition, the

32-page publisher's catalogue bound in at the end is dated July 1912. Therefore the ads printed on bookstock were not printed at the time the third impression was printed and so are treated as inserted ads rather than as part of the third impression. This copy is a later binding up of third impression sheets.

68.7.0. *The Finer Grain*, first continental edition, one volume, Leipzig 1910.

THE FINER GRAIN | BY | HENRY JAMES | AUTHOR OF | "THE AMERICAN," "A LITTLE TOUR IN FRANCE," ETC. | COPYRIGHT EDITION [in italic] | LEIPZIG | BERNHARD TAUCHNITZ | 1910.

Size: 6 1/8″ x 4 5/16″.

Collation: $[1]^8$ $2-17^8$ 18^4; pp. [1–6], [7]–278 [279–280].

Contents: [1–2] series half-title, verso ad under the heading "TAUCHNITZ EDITION. | By the same Author," listing 14 titles the last of which is *A Little Tour in France*; [3–4] title-page, verso blank; [5–6] "CONTENTS.", verso blank; [7]–278 text; [279] printer's imprint: "[long rule] | PRINTING OFFICE OF THE PUBLISHER. | [long rule]"; [280] blank.

Binding: buff wove paper wrappers, cut flush, with lettering on the front cover in black within a black single-rule frame which is decorated with a flower like device at of the four corners with lettering above and below the frame. Within the frame the title and author's name are on one line. The spine is also lettered in black between a series of eight pairs of thick and thin black rules. The back cover, which is also lettered in black reads: "August 1911 | Tauchnitz Edition. | [rule] | Latest Volumes: | [followed by a list of 25 titles (two being in two volumes) volumes 2449 through 2275, the last of which is *A Rolling Stone* by B.M. Crocker] | [long rule] | The Tauchnitz Edition is sold by all Booksellers and Rail- | way Libraries on the Continent, price of each volume M 1, 60 | or francs 2,00 sewed, M 2, 20 or francs 2, 75 cloth (Original-Linen- | band), M 3,00 or francs 3, 75 in elegant soft binding (Original- | Geschenkband). A complete catalogue of the Tauchnitz Edition is attached to this work." The inside of the front and back covers are blank. A 32-page paginated publisher's catalogue dated July 1, 1911 is bound in at the end.

[535]

T&B 4224 records only one edition with one impression of this title. This is the first James title published by Tauchnitz since *A Little Tour in France* in 1885.

※✚※

69. *THE HENRY JAMES YEARBOOK*

69.1.0. *The Henry James Yearbook*, first edition, American issue, one volume, Boston [n.d., 1911].

THE | HENRY JAMES [in swash italic] | YEAR BOOK | [red rule] | SELECTED AND ARRANGED BY | EVELYN GARNAUT SMALLEY | WITH AN INTRODUCTION BY | HENRY JAMES AND WILLIAM DEAN HOWELLS | [red rule] | [publisher's device] | [red rule] | RICHARD G. BADGER | THE GORHAM PRESS | BOSTON [all the foregoing within a red single-rule border]

Size: $7\,^3/_8''$ x $4\,^{15}/_{16}''$.

Collation: [unsigned, 1^8 (1_1+X_1) $2-15^8$ 16^2]; [unpaginated, pp. 1–16, 17–245 246].

Contents: (unpaginated) [1–2] half-title, verso blank; [3–4] frontispiece photographic portrait of James tipped in, without a tissue guard; [5–6] title-page, verso copyright notice, acknowledgements and printer's imprint: "Copyright 1911 by Richard G. Badger | [rule] | All Rights Reserved | I acknowledge, with many thanks, the courtesy of | Messrs. Charles Scribner's Sons, | Messrs. Harper & Brothers, | The Houghton Mifflin Company, | The Macmillan Company and | Duffield & Company | in giving me their permission for the use of quotations | from the writings of Mr. Henry James published by them | and of which they have the copyright. | EVELYN GARNAUT SMALLEY | The Gorham Press, Boston, U.S.A."; [7–8] dedication, verso blank; [9–10] "PREFACE", verso blank; [11] first "INTRODUCTION", signed by James; [12–13] second "INTRODUCTION", verso introduction continued, signed by Howells; [14] blank; [15–16] divisional fly-title, verso blank; [17–245] text; [246] blank.

Binding: red leather over flexible boards. The front cover, lettered and decorated in gilt within a single-rule border in blind, reads: "[three leaf devices] THE [three leaf devices] | HENRY JAMES | [single leaf device] YEAR BOOK [single leaf device]", and on the lower right: "WITH AN INTRODUCTION BY | [facsimile signature of Henry James] | AND | [facsimile signature of W.D. Howells]". The back cover has centered the publisher's device in blind. The spine, lettered and decorated in gilt, reads: "THE | HENRY | JAMES | YEAR | BOOK | [single leaf device] | BADGER". The endpapers are of white laid paper, and the text is printed on India tint paper. The top edge is gilt, and the other edges are trimmed. A red ribbon marker is bound in.

This copy is in E&L A69a binding c, of which there was "no copy available for examination."

69.2.0. *The Henry James Yearbook*, first edition, English issue, one volume, London [n.d., 1912].

THE | HENRY JAMES [in swash italic] | YEAR BOOK | [red rule] | SELECTED AND ARRANGED BY | EVELYN GARNAUT SMALLEY | WITH AN INTRODUCTION BY | HENRY JAMES and WILLIAM DEAN HOWELLS | [red rule] | [publisher's device] | [red rule] | LONDON | J. M. DENT & SONS, Ltd. | COVENT GARDEN [all the foregoing within a red single-rule border]

Size: $7\,7/16''$ x $5''$.

Collation: [unsigned, $1^8(-1, \pm1_2 + X_1)$ 2–15^8 16^2]; [unpaginated, pp. 1–14, 15–243 244]. The excised leaf is the half-title, with a blank verso, in the first edition, American issue, 69.1.0. The title-leaf, [1_2], is a cancel.

Contents: (unpaginated) [1–2] recto blank, verso frontispiece photographic portrait of James tipped in, with a tissue guard; [3–4] title-page, verso blank; [5–6] dedication, verso blank; [7–8] "PREFACE", verso blank; [9] first "INTRODUCTION", signed by James; [10–11] second "INTRODUCTION", verso introduction continued, signed by Howells, [12] blank; [13–14] divisional fly-title, verso blank; [15–243] text; [244] blank.

Binding: burgundy fine-woven cloth. The front cover, lettered in gilt and decorated with a single-rule border in blind divided into three panels by two horizontal blind rules, reads: "[three leaf devices] THE [three leaf devices] | HENRY JAMES | [single leaf device] YEAR BOOK [single leaf device]", and at the foot centered: "WITH AN INTRODUCTION BY | [facsimile signature of Henry James] | AND | [facsimile signature of W. D. Howells." The back cover is neither lettered nor decorated. The spine, lettered in gilt within a single-rule border in blind, reads: "THE | HENRY | JAMES | YEAR | BOOK | [leaf device] | [blind rule] | [blind rule] | J. M. DENT | & SONS. LD [sic]". The endpapers are of white wove paper, and the text is printed on India tint paper. The top edge is gilt, and the other edges are trimmed. There is no ribbon marker bound in.

This issue is of imported American sheets.

❧+❧

70. THE OUTCRY

70.1.0. *The Outcry*, first edition, first impression, English issue, one volume, London [n.d., 1911].

THE OUTCRY | BY | HENRY JAMES | METHUEN & CO. LTD. | 36 ESSEX STREET W. C. | LONDON

Size: $7 \frac{1}{2}"$ x $4 \frac{7}{8}"$.

Collation: a^2 $1-19^8$ 20^4; pp. [i–iv] 1–[2], 3–311 [312].

Contents: [i–ii] half-title, with signature mark "*a*" at the foot, verso ad headed: "BY THE SAME AUTHOR", listing 6 titles; [iii–iv] title-page, verso printing history: "First Published in 1911 [in italic]"; 1–[2] divisional fly-title, verso blank; 3–311 text; [312] printer's imprint: "EDINBURGH | COLSTONS LIMITED | PRINTERS".

Binding: green coarse linen-grain cloth. The front cover, lettered in gilt within a single-rule border in blind, reads: "THE OUTCRY | HENRY JAMES". The back cover is neither lettered nor decorated. The spine, lettered and decorated in gilt, reads: "[double rules] | THE | OUTCRY | HENRY | JAMES | [long strapwork device of intertwined vines with leaves] | METHUEN | [double rules]". The endpapers are of white wove paper, and the text is printed on wove paper. The top edge is trimmed and stained light brown, the fore-edge is rough trimmed, and the bottom edge is untrimmed. A 32-page paginated publisher's catalogue, dated September 1911, printed on a lighter wove paper, is bound in at the end. Page [32] of the catalogue is blank except for the printer's imprint.

Dust-jacket: burgundy wove paper, lettered and decorated in black. The front cover has a double-rule border divided by two long horizontal rules into three panels. The top panel reads: "THE OUTCRY | BY | HENRY JAMES". The middle panel contains a blurb, which reads: "'The Outcry' deals with a question | sharply brought home of late to the | conscience of English Society – that of the | degree in which the fortunate owners of | precious and hitherto transmitted works | of art hold them in trust, as it were, for | the nation, and may themselves, as lax | guardians, be held to account by public | opinion. The situation represented in | Mr. Henry James's study of the larger | morality of the matter, if we may so call | it, and which is the case of a lax rather | than a jealous guardian, becomes conspic- | uous and acute. Hence springs the drama, | almost a national as well as a personal | crisis – a rapid, pre- | cipitated action, moving | through difficulties and dangers to a | happy issue." The bottom panel reads: METHUEN & CO. LTD. LONDON". The back cover has a single-rule border, similarly divided by two long rules into three panels. The top panel reads: "METHUEN'S POPULAR NOVELS | Crown 8vo. 6s. [in italic]". The middle panel lists 27 titles (one, this title, by James). The bottom panel reads: "METHUEN & CO. LTD. LONDON". The spine reads: "THE | OUTCRY | HENRY | JAMES | 6/- | METHUEN". The front inner flap has an ad for "UNDER WESTERN | EYES | by JOSEPH CONRAD" and "THE TAMING OF | JOHN BLUNT | by | ALFRED OLLIVANT", each title and author's name within a single-rule frame beneath which is a blurb. The back inner flap is headed "METHUEN'S SHILLING NOVELS [in sans serif]", beneath which are listed 9 titles (none by James).

E&L A70a quotes the blurb on the central panel of the front cover of the dust-jacket. However, the first four words of the second sentence of the blurb ("The situation represented in ..."), are not present in E&L's quotation. This could suggest that there are two states of this dust-jacket or, alternately, that E&L is in error.

Illustrated Plate 29.

BAL 10673 notes copies with catalogues dated March 1911, August 1911, and September 1911; see below.

English printing history. Methuen Archive. Mss. LMC 2230, Stock Ledger, Vol. 4, p. 198. First edition: *first impression* September 16, 1911, 2,000 copies, with 4 over, 2014 [sic] bound between between September 19 and October 17, 1911, 1814 of which were bound for the domestic issue, and 200 in cloth for the colonial issue; *second impression* September 29, 1911,

500 copies, with 10 over, 510 bound between October 17, 1911, and February 27, 1912, the entire impression being bound for the colonial market (250 being bound in cloth and 260 bound in paper wrappers); *third impression* October 18, 1911, 500 copies, with 3 over, 503 bound between October 27 and November 16, 1911; *fourth impression* November 4, 1911, 1,000 copies, with 5 over, 1005 bound between December 20, 1911, and March 17, 1916 (all but 30 being bound by May 11, 1912). The entire third and fourth impressions were bound for the domestic market. Notations: "Wrappers 2,000 Sept 16/11", "Col[onial] covers 500 Oct 5/11" and "Type distributed May 15/12". Next to each of the four impressions is the notation "Both Titles". The domestic copies were priced at 6s., and the colonial copies were priced at 2s. in cloth and 1s. 6d. in paper wrappers.

70.2.0. *The Outcry*, first edition, first impression, English issue, one volume, London [n.d., 1911].

This copy is identical to the first edition, first impression, English issue, 70.1.0, except that the 32-page publisher's catalogue at the end is dated August 1911.

70.3.0. *The Outcry*, first edition, first impression, English issue, one volume, London [n.d., 1911].

This copy is identical to the first edition, first impression, English issue, 70.1.0, except that the 32-page publisher's catalogue at the end is dated March 1911.

On the front pastedown is the bookplate of James Edmund Peter Leslie.

Loosely inserted in this copy is a two-page (one leaf) ad, on one side of which is a blurb for Marie Corelli's *The Life Everlasting*, which was to be "Ready About August 30", and on the other side a schedule of "Autumn 1911" publication of novels in Methuen's Popular Novels series, among which *The Outcry* is listed for September publication.

This copy with its publisher's catalogue of ads predating publication of this title by seven months is a good example of the practice of English binders to insert earlier dated publisher's catalogues when the supply of current catalogues ran out.

70.4.0. *The Outcry*, first edition, second impression (colonial), cloth binding state, one volume London [n.d., 1911].

THE OUTCRY | BY | HENRY JAMES | SECOND EDITION | METHUEN & CO. LTD. | 36 ESSEX STREET W.C. | LONDON | Colonial Library [in italic]

Size: 7 1/2" x 4 15/16".

Collation: a^2 1–19^8 20^4; pp. [i–iv] 1–[2], 3–311 [312].

Contents: [i–ii] half-title (with "Methuen's Colonial Library [in Gothic type, underscored]" at the top) with signature mark "*a*" at the foot, verso ad headed: "BY THE SAME AUTHOR", listing 6 titles; [iii–iv] title page, verso printing history: "First Published ... October 5th 1911 | Second Edition ... October 1911 [all in italic]; 1–[2] divisional fly-title, verso blank; 3–311 text; [312] printer's imprint: "EDINBURGH | COLSTONS LIMITED | PRINTERS".

Binding: purple linen-grain cloth. The front and back covers are neither lettered nor decorated. The spine, which is lettered and decorated in gilt, reads: "THE | OUTCRY | [dot] | HENRY | JAMES [all the foregoing within a frame with leaves and branches decoration above and below it] | METHUEN'S | COLONIAL LIBRARY [series title within an oblong frame]". The endpapers are of white wove paper with ads for Methuen's Colonial Library listing works of fiction on the pastedowns and the rectos and versos of the free endpapers, with the bottom half of the rear pastedown listing "General Literature". The text is printed on coarse wove paper. The top edge is trimmed and stained gray, the fore-edge is rough trimmed, and the bottom edge is untrimmed. Bound in at the end is a 32-page publisher's catalogue dated September 1911.

The entire second impression was devoted to the colonial market.

70.5.0. *The Outcry*, first edition, third impression, one volume, London [n.d., 1911].

The title-page, size, collation, and contents are identical to those of the first edition, first impression, English issue, 70.1.0, except that on the title-page "THIRD EDITION" appears between the author's name and the printer's imprint, and the title-leaf verso reads: "First Published ... October 5th 1911 | Second and Third Edition ... October [space] 1911 [all in italic]".

THE OUTCRY

Binding: green coarse linen-grain cloth, lettered and decorated identically to 70.1.0. The endpapers are of white wove paper, and the text is printed on wove paper. The top edge is trimmed and stained brown, the fore-edge is rough trimmed, and the bottom edge is untrimmed. Bound in at the end is a 32-page paginated publisher's catalogue dated March 1911.

70.6.0. *The Outcry*, first edition (American), one volume, New York 1911.

THE OUTCRY | BY | HENRY JAMES | NEW YORK | CHARLES SCRIBNER'S SONS | 1911

Size: 7 1/2" x 4 7/8".

Collation: [unsigned, 1–16^8 17^6]; pp. [i–vi] [1–2], 3–261 [262].

Contents: [i–ii] blank, verso ad headed: "BOOKS BY HENRY JAMES", listing 6 titles, and *The Novels and Tales* in 24 volumes, all with dollar prices; [iii–iv] half-title, verso blank; [v–vi] title-page, verso copyright notice and printing history: "Copyright, 1911, by | CHARLES SCRIBNER'S SONS | [rule] | Published September, 1911 | [device of the Scribner's Press]"; [1–2] divisional fly-title, verso blank; 3–261 text; [262] blank.

Binding: gray-brown sateen. The front cover, lettered in gilt within a gilt single-rule frame, reads: "THE OUTCRY | By | HENRY JAMES". The back cover is neither lettered nor decorated. The spine, lettered and decorated in gilt, reads: "THE | OUTCRY | [leaf device] | HENRY | JAMES | SCRIBNERS". The endpapers are of white wove paper, and the text is printed on wove paper. The top edge is gilt, and the other edges are untrimmed.

American printing history. Scribner's Archive. cards (2) Box 13: Id-J. First edition: *first impression* 3,000 copies printed on August 31, 1911, all bound between October 2, 1911, and November 13, 1923 (2452 bound in 1911); notations: "4/29/11 css 3100 wraps" and opposite a 1920 binding order "omit side stamps"; published October 5, 1911; *second impression* 550 copies printed December 27, 1923, 50 copies bound June 18, 1930. Notation: October 29, 1931 "job to Rock 515".

Both impressions were printed and bound by Scribner's. The paper used is not recorded.

The first edition was priced at $1.25 net, and later raised to $2.50.

THE OUTCRY

70.7.0. *The Outcry*, first continental edition, first impression, first binding state, one volume, 1912.

THE OUTCRY | BY | HENRY JAMES | AUTHOR OF "THE AMERICAN," "THE PORTRAIT OF A LADY," | "THE FINER GRAIN," ETC. | COPYRIGHT EDITION [in italic] | LEIPZIG | BERNHARD TAUCHNITZ | 1912.

Size: 6 7/16" x 4 5/8".

Collation: [1]^8 2–19^8; pp. [1–4], [5]–301 [302] [303–304].

Contents: [1–2] series half-title, verso ad listing 15 James titles, the last of which is *The Finer Grain*; [3–4] title-page, verso blank; [5]–301 text; [302] blank; [303–304] printer's imprint: "[rule] | PRINTING OFFICE OF THE PUBLISHER. | [rule]", verso blank.

Binding: buff wove paper wrappers, cut flush, with lettering on the front cover in black within a black single-rule frame which is decorated with floral devices at each of the four corners with lettering above and below the frame. Inside the front cover, under the heading "latest Volumes. – January 1912.", is a double-column list of Tauchnitz volumes 4282 to 4292, each volume being described in a separate blurb, which list continues on the inside of the back cover under the same heading for volumes 4293 to 4302, and continues on to the back cover for volumes 4303/4 to 4307 (which is the last title issued by Tauchnitz prior to this title, volume 4308). On the back cover following this listing is an ad for Dr. Leon Kellner's *Die Englische Literatur*, and following that the "Publishers' Notice" at the foot, which reads: "The Tauchnitz Edition is sold by all Booksellers and Rail- | way Libraries on the Continent, price of each volume M 1, 60 or | francs 2,00 sewed, M 2, 20 or francs 2, 75 cloth (Original-Leinen- | Band), M 3,00 or francs 3, 75 in elegant soft binding (Original- | Geschenkband). A List of such bound works selected from the | Tauchnitz Edition, and especially suitable for presents, etc., is now | obtainable everywhere in both English and German, entitled "Gift | Books," and "Geschenkliteratur." A complete Catalogue of the | Tauchnitz Edition is attached to this work. [all in italic]". A 32-page publisher's catalogue, dated December 1, 1911, is bound in at the end.

The fact that the series half-title verso lists 15 James titles, and the ads on the inside of the front and back covers, and on the back cover

THE OUTCRY

itself, list only works issued by Tauchnitz immediately prior to this title, and list none issued after the issuance of this title, indicates that this is a copy of the first impression, first binding state; see Appendix B. T&B 4308 records only one edition with one impression of this title.

70.8.0. *The Outcry*, first continental edition, first impression, second (?) binding state, one volume, Leipzig Bernhard Tauchnitz 1912.

The title-page, size, collation, and contents of this copy are identical to those of the first impression, first binding state, 70.7.0, including the 32-page publisher's catalogue, dated December 1, 1911, bound in at the end.

Binding: buff wove paper wrappers, cut flush, the front cover and spine of which are lettered and decorated identically to those of 70.7.0. However, both the inside of the front and back covers are blank. The rear cover has under the heading "June 1912. | Tauchnitz Edition. | [rule] | Latest Volumes:" a list of volumes 4308 (this title), and volumes 4309 to 4336, which were issued in 1912 by Tauchnitz after the issuance of this title. At the foot, following a rule, is the same notice as is at the foot of the back cover of 70.7.0, from which, however, the heading "Publishers' Notice" and the second sentence have been omitted.

On the front cover is a small green and white label reading: "LIBRERIA | DETKEN & ROCHOLL | DI B. JOHANNOWSKY | NAPOLI".

This wrapper date is not recorded in T&B.

A SMALL BOY AND OTHERS

71. *A SMALL BOY AND OTHERS*

71.1.0. *A Small Boy and Others*, first edition, first impression, first state, one volume, New York 1913.

A SMALL BOY | AND OTHERS | BY | HENRY JAMES | NEW YORK | CHARLES SCRIBNER'S SONS | 1913

Size: 8 $^{3}/_{16}$" x 5 $^{9}/_{16}$".

Collation: [unsigned, 1_8 (1_2+X_1) 2–26^8 27^6]; pp. [i–viii], 1–419 [420] plus 2. Frontispiece portrait with tissue guard, tipped in between [1_1] and [1_2] and not reckoned in the pagination.

Contents: [i–ii] blank, verso ad headed: "BOOKS BY HENRY JAMES", listing 7 Titles, and *The Novels and Tales* (The New York Edition) in 24 volumes, all with dollar prices; [iii–iv] half-title, verso blank; frontispiece portrait of James and his father with tissue guard tipped in and not reckoned in the pagination; [v–vi] title-page, verso copyright notice, printing history and printer's device: "Copyright, 1913, by | CHARLES SCRIBNER'S SONS | [rule] | Published March, 1913 | [printer's device of the Scribner's Press]"; [vii–viii] divisional fly-title, verso blank; 1–419 text; [420] blank.

Binding: greenish-brown sateen. The front cover, lettered in gilt within a single-rule gilt frame, reads: "A SMALL BOY | AND OTHERS | HENRY JAMES". The back cover is neither lettered nor decorated. The spine, lettered and decorated in gilt, reads: "A SMALL | BOY AND | OTHERS | [rule] | HENRY | JAMES | SCRIBNERS". The publisher's imprint at the foot of the spine is in uniform capitals $^{3}/_{16}$" high. The endpapers are of smooth white wove paper, and the text is printed on rough wove paper. The top edge is gilt, and the other edges are untrimmed.

Dust-jacket: off-white thin wove paper, lettered and decorated in black. The front cover, within a rectangular single-rule frame, reads: "A SMALL BOY | AND OTHERS | HENRY JAMES", and at the foot (outside the frame): "CHARLES SCRIBNER'S SONS". The spine lettering and decoration is identical to that on the spine of the book, with, however, the addition of the price, "$2.50 | NET [in sans-serif]" between the author's name and the publisher's imprint. The back cover, and the front and rear inner flaps, are neither lettered nor decorated.

On the rear pastedown are two small brown bookseller's ticket, both in the shape of a book, that read: "The White House | Books in various Languages | San Francisco", and "HARTMAN'S | BOOKS | INC. | Seattle".

This copy is of the first state with the ad on [ii] listing 7 James titles and *The Novels and Tales* in 24 Volumes, without the later inserted cancel of that leaf noting that *Notes of a Son and Brother* is "IN PREPARATION".

American printing history. Scribner's Archive. cards (2) Box 13: Id-J. First edition: *first impression* 2750 copies printed March 17, 1913, all bound between March 22, 1913, and December 14, 1914; notations: "3-5-13 Andrews & Son 2,020 prints $30.30", "3–22–13 css 2800 wraps", "2-17-13 Macmillan 1,000 frontis £5=24.30", "Andrews bill 1,010 – 15s", "4-29-13 Macmillan 500 Frontis £2.10" and "7/21/13 800 cancels and plate ptd for bal [illegible]"; published March 29, 1913; *second impression* 525 copies printed August 22, 1914, all but 122 bound between April 14, 1915, and March 23, 1929; notation: "1931 June 4 Destroyed 122". Notation opposite binding orders for 1919 and later: "omit gilt top & side stamps cheaper cloth".

Both impressions were printed and bound by Scribner's. The paper used is not recorded.

Priced at $2.50 net, raised for the second impression to $3.00.

71.2.0. *A Small Boy and Others*, first edition, second impression, second second state and second binding state, one volume, New York 1914.

The title-page and the title-leaf verso are identical to the first edition, first impression, first state, 71.1.0, except that the title-page is dated 1914 at the foot.

The size, collation, and contents are identical to 71.1.0, except that the ad on [ii] reads: "By HENRY JAMES | [rule] | A SMALL BOY AND OTHERS | NOTES OF A SON AND BROTHER | NOTES ON NOVELISTS | WITH SOME OTHER NOTES".

Binding: dull chocolate-brown fine-linen-grain cloth. The front and back covers are neither lettered nor decorated. The spine, lettered and decorated in gilt, reads: "A SMALL | BOY AND | OTHERS | [rule] | HENRY | JAMES | SCRIBNERS". The endpapers are of smooth white wove paper, and the text is printed on rough wove paper. The top edge is trimmed and stained ochre, and the other edges are untrimmed.

This copy is one of the copies of the second impression that was bound in cheaper cloth and with the gilt top and side stamping omitted.

A SMALL BOY AND OTHERS

71.3.0. *A Small Boy and Others*, first English edition, first impression, first state, one volume, London 1913.

A SMALL BOY | AND OTHERS | BY | HENRY JAMES | MACMILLAN & CO., LIMITED | ST. MARTIN'S STREET, LONDON | 1913

Size: 8 7/8" x 5 3/16".

Collation: $[A]^2 ([A]_1+X_1)$ B–I K–U X–Z 2A–2E^8 2F^4; pp. [i–iv], 1–436 [437–438] [339–340] plus 2. Frontispiece portrait with tissue guard tipped in between leaves $[A]_1$ and $[A]_2$, and not reckoned in the pagination.

Contents: [i–ii] half-title, verso publisher's device, frontispiece portrait of James with his father with tissue guard tipped in, and not reckoned in the pagination; [iii–iv] title-page, verso copyright notice: "COPYRIGHT"; 1–436 text; 436 at foot printer's imprint: "Printed by R. & R. Clark, Limited, Edinburgh. [all but publisher's name in italic]"; [437–438] ads headed on each page: "THE NOVELS OF | HENRY JAMES | In 24 Vols. [in italic]", followed by a list of the volumes which continues over on to [438], further followed by a rule and a list of 3 James titles: *French Poets and Novelists, Partial Portraits*, and *Nathanial Hawthorne*; [439–440] blank leaf.

Binding: blue smooth cloth. The front and back covers are not lettered, but are decorated in blind with two rules at the top, and two more widely spaced rules at the bottom. The spine, lettered and decorated in gilt, reads: "[two rules, the first thin, the second thicker] | A | SMALL | BOY | AND OTHERS | HENRY | JAMES | [thick rule] | MACMILLAN & Co. | [thinner rule]". The "o" in "Co" is raised above a dot. The endpapers are of white wove paper, and the text is printed on wove paper. All edges are untrimmed.

This copy is of the first state with a first signature of two leaves, without an "IN PREPARATION" notice tipped in 2F^4, with ads on 2F$_3$, [437–438], and with 2F$_4$, [439–440], blank.

English printing history: Macmillan Archive. MPL 55920, at 83 records that a print order for 1,000 copies of this title was placed on February 11, 1913, and on March 19, 1913 a print order was placed for "1,050 net envelopes", that is dust-jackets indicating that this book was designated a "net book" pursuant to the Net Book Agreement. No record was found of the June 1913 second impression; see 71.6.0 and 71.7.0. Both impressions were priced at 12s. net.

71.4.0. *A Small Boy and Others*, first English edition, first impression, second state, one volume, London 1913.

The title-page, size, collation, and contents are identical to those of the first English edition, first impression, first state, 71.3.0, except that an "IN PREPARATION" notice is tipped in 2F⁴ between 436 and [437] and is not reckoned in the pagination.

This is the second state, with the later inserted leaf after 436, on the recto of which is a notice that *Notes of a Son and Brother* is "IN PREPARATION", and the verso of which is blank. As in the first state, pages [437–438], leaf $2F_3$, are ads for "THE NOVELS OF | HENRY JAMES | In 24 Vols.", followed by a list of the volumes which continues over on to [438], further followed by a rule and a list of 3 James titles: *French Poets and Novelists, Partial Portraits,* and *Nathanial Hawthorne*; [439–440], leaf $2F_4$, are blank.

Binding: blue smooth cloth, lettered and decorated in gilt and in blind identically to 71.3.0. The endpapers are of white wove paper, and the text is printed on wove paper. All edges are untrimmed.

Dust-jacket: cream-yellow wove paper with an overall small interlocking design in orange of the publisher's device. The front cover, lettered and decorated in black, reads: "A SMALL BOY | AND OTHERS | HENRY JAMES, | [centered publisher's device]". The spine, which is lettered and decorated in black, reads: "A | SMALL | BOY | AND OTHERS | HENRY | JAMES | 12/- | NET | [publisher's device]". On the back cover, also lettered in black, is an ad for: "The Novels of Henry James | in 24 vols. With a new Preface and a | Frontispiece in each" (followed by a list of the volumes), followed after a short rule by 3 James titles: *French Poets and Novelists, Partial Portraits* and *Nathaniel Hawthorne*. At the foot is the publisher's imprint. No lettering (other than the overall design in orange, mentioned above) is present on the front or back inner flaps.

A circular stamp in blind is on the title-page with "presentation copy" embossed on it. On the front free endpaper is the inscription "Emorgan Humphreys. | Ehill. 1913."

The dust-jacket on this copy is uniform with that on the first English edition of *Notes of a Son and Brother* (1914), 72.4.0.

A SMALL BOY AND OTHERS

71.5.0. *A Small Boy and Others*, first English edition, first impression, second state, one volume, London 1913.

This copy is identical in all respects to the first English edition, first impression, second state, 71.4.0, except that the extra leaf inserted in 2F^4, between pages 436 and [437], has been inserted backwards, so that the recto is blank and the notice appears on the verso.

71.6.0. *A Small Boy and Others*, first English edition, second (?) impression, first state, one volume, London 1913.

The title-page and size are identical to those of the first English edition, first impression, first state, 71.3.0.

Collation: [A]^4 ([A]$_3$ +X$_1$) B–I K–U X–Z 2A–2E^8 2F^4; pp. [2] [i–vi], 1–436 [437–440] plus 2. Frontispiece portrait with tissue guard tipped in between [a]$_3$ and [A]$_4$, and not reckoned in the pagination.

Contents: blank leaf; [i–ii] blank, verso notice within a single-rule frame: "IN PREPARATION | BY THE SAME AUTHOR [first two lines in italic] | NOTES OF | A SON AND BROTHER"; [iii–iv] half-title, verso publisher's device and imprint; frontispiece portrait of James with his father with a tissue guard tipped in, not reckoned in the pagination; [v–vi] title-page, verso copyright notice: "COPYRIGHT"; 1–436 text; [437–440] ads: [437–438] as on those pages in both states of the first impression, 71.3.0–71.4.0, [439–440] both pages headed: "A SELECTION OF NEW BOOKS [in sans-serif]", the first title listed on [439] being *Gitanjali (Song Offerings)*, by Rabindranath Tagore.

The "IN PREPARATION" notice on [ii] of this state is the same as that which appears on the extra leaf inserted between 436 and [437] in the first English edition, first impression, second state, 71.4.0. The ads on [437–8] of this copy are the same as those that appear on those pages of 71.3.0 and 71.4.0; however, this copy has the additional ads on [439–440].

Binding: blue smooth cloth lettered and decorated in gilt and blind identically to 71.3.0, 71.4.0 and 71.5.0, except that the double rules across the front and back covers in blind and across the top and bottom of the spine in gilt are slightly thicker than those on first impression bindings. The endpapers are of white wove paper, and the text is printed on wove paper. All edges are untrimmed.

A SMALL BOY AND OTHERS

Dust-jacket: cream wove paper. The front cover, lettered and decorated in dark blue, reads: "A SMALL BOY | AND OTHERS | HENRY JAMES | [centered publisher's device]". The spine, lettered and decorated in dark blue, reads: "A | SMALL | BOY | AND OTHERS | HENRY | JAMES | 12/- | NET | [publisher's device as on the front cover]". On the back cover, also lettered in dark blue, is an ad for 4 James titles under the heading: "BY HENRY JAMES", followed by the heading: "THE NOVELS AND STORIES OF | HENRY JAMES | New and Complete Edition. In 35 Volumes. | Issued in two styles. Crown 8vo. 7s. 6d. net per volume. | Pocket Edition. F'cap 8vo. 7s. 6d. net per volume.", beneath which is a double-column list of the 35 volumes, at the foot of which is the publisher's imprint. The front and back inner flaps are blank.

This copy appears to be a sort of a hybrid in that its collation, contents (including the ads), and binding are identical to those of the first English edition, second impression, second state, 71.7.0, yet its title-page verso is identical to that of the first impression, first state, 71.3.0.

The dust-jacket, however, with the ad for *The Novels and Stories of Henry James* in 35 volumes, must have been printed in 1923 or later, as the volumes comprising that title were published in the period 1921–1923. However, the price on the spine, 12s., is the same price as a copy of *A Small Boy and Others* was priced in 1913.

71.7.0. *A Small Boy and Others*, first English edition, second impression, second state (?), one volume, London 1913.

This copy is identical to that believed to be of the first English edition, second impression, first state, 71.6.0, except that the verso of the title-page reads: "COPYRIGHT | First edition April 1913 | Reprinted June 1913 [printing history, except years, in italic]". This printing history is not present on the first state of the of the second impression, 71.6.0.

Binding: identical to that of 71.3.0, except that the double rules across the top and bottom of the front and back covers in blind, and across the top and bottom of the spine in gilt, are slightly thicker than those on the first impression bindings, 71.3.0–71.5.0. The endpapers are of white wove paper, and the text is printed on wove paper. The top and fore-edges are untrimmed, and the bottom edge is rough trimmed.

72. *NOTES OF A SON AND BROTHER*

72.1.0. *Notes of a Son and Brother*, first edition, binding state A, one volume, New York 1914.

NOTES OF A | SON AND BROTHER | BY | HENRY JAMES | ILLUSTRATED | NEW YORK | CHARLES SCRIBNER'S SONS | 1914

Size: $8\,1/8''$ x $5\,1/2''$.

Collation: [unsigned, 1^8 (1_2+X_1) $2-33^8$]; pp. [i–x], 1–515 [516] [517–518] plus 2. Frontispiece with tissue guard, tipped in between [1_2] and [1_3], and five further illustrations without tissue guards, also tipped in, and not reckoned in the pagination.

Contents: [i–ii] blank, verso ad headed: "By HENRY JAMES", listing 2 titles; [iii–iv] half-title, verso blank; frontispiece portrait of William James with tissue guard tipped in, and not reckoned in the pagination; [v–vi] title-page, verso copyright notice, printing history and printer's device: "Copyright, 1914, by | CHARLES SCRIBNER'S SONS | [rule] | Published March, 1914 | [printer's device of the Scribner's Press]"; [vii–viii] "ILLUSTRATIONS", verso blank; [ix–x] divisional fly-title, verso blank; 1–515 text; [516] blank; [517–518] blank leaf.

Binding: dull olive-brown smooth sateen. The front cover, lettered in gilt within a single-rule gilt frame, reads: "NOTES OF A SON | AND BROTHER | HENRY JAMES". The back cover is neither lettered nor decorated. The spine, lettered and decorated in gilt, reads: "NOTES OF | A SON AND | BROTHER | [rule] | HENRY | JAMES | SCRIBNERS". The publisher's imprint at the foot of the spine is in uniform capitals $3/16''$ high. The endpapers are of smooth cream wove paper, and the text is printed on wove paper. The top edge is gilt, and the other edges are untrimmed.

Dust-jacket: off-white thin wove paper, lettered and decorated in black. The front cover, within a rectangular single-rule frame, reads: "NOTES OF A SON | AND BROTHER | HENRY JAMES", and at the foot (outside the fame): "CHARLES SCRIBNER'S SONS". The spine lettering and decoration are identical to those on the spine of the book, with, however, the addition of the price "$2.50 | NET [in sans-serif]" between the author's name and the publisher's imprint. The back cover, and the front and rear inner flaps, are neither lettered nor decorated.

This binding and dust-jacket are uniform with those on the first edition of *A Small Boy and Others* (1913), 71.1.0.

American printing history. Scribner's Archive. card (1) Box 13: Id-J. First edition: *first* (and sole) *impression* 3,000 copies printed February 25, 1914, all but 250 bound between March 2, 1914, and May 24, 1927; notation: "1928 July Destroyed 250"; other notations: "2-10-14 css 4250 sets 5 cuts", "3-3-14 css 3100 wraps", "1/28/14 Macmillan & Co 1250 flat | illustrations (6) @ £12.00", "9/22/25 – 270 5 cuts Macmillan", and "10/26/25–275 photog Macmillan". Published March 7, 1914. The American edition was set from proofs of the English edition, which proofs were corrected by James; see Macmillan Archive, Vol. ccx, #54905, letter 20.

This edition was printed and bound by Scribner's. The paper used is not recorded.

Priced at $2.50 net.

72.2.0. *Notes of a Son and Brother*, first edition, binding state B, one volume, New York 1914.

The title-page, size, collation, and contents of this copy are identical to those of the first edition, first impression, binding state A, 72.1.0.

Binding: chocolate-brown linen-grain cloth (neither smooth nor sateen), with lettering and decoration in gilt on the front cover and spine identical to the lettering and decoration on 72.1.0. The endpapers are of cream wove paper, and the text is printed on wove paper of the same type as 72.1.0. The top edge is trimmed and stained light brown, and the other edges are untrimmed.

This variant binding is not noted in E&L or BAL.

72.3.0. *Notes of a Son and Brother*, first English edition, one volume, London 1914.

NOTES | OF | A SON & BROTHER | BY | HENRY JAMES | MACMILLAN AND CO., LIMITED | ST. MARTIN'S STREET, LONDON | 1914

Size: $8\,7/8''$ x $5\,5/8''$.

Collation: $[A]^4$ $([A]_2+X_1)$ B–I K–U X–Z 2A–2H^8; pp. [i–viii], 1–479 [480] plus 2. Frontispiece with tissue guard, tipped in between $[a]_2$ and $[a]_3$.

and five further illustrations also tipped in, all not reckoned in the pagination.

Contents: [i–ii] half-title, verso ad within a single-rule frame for *A Small Boy and Others*; [iii–iv] blank, verso publisher's device; frontispiece portrait of William James with tissue guard tipped in, not reckoned in the pagination; [v–vi] title-page, verso copyright notice: "COPYRIGHT"; vii–[viii] "ILLUSTRATIONS", verso blank; 1–479 text; 479 at foot printer's imprint: "Printed by R. & R. Clark, Limited, Edinburgh. [all except printer's name in italic]"; [480] blank.

Binding: blue smooth cloth. The front and back covers are not lettered, but are decorated in blind with two rules at the top and two more widely spaced rules at the bottom. The spine, lettered and decorated in gilt, reads: "[two rules, the first thin, the second thicker] | NOTES | OF | A SON | AND | BROTHER | HENRY | JAMES | [thick rule] | MACMILLAN & Co. | [thinner rule]". The "o" in "Co" is raised above a dot. The endpapers are of cream wove paper, and the text is printed on wove paper. All edges are untrimmed. Bound in at the end are two pages of unpaginated ads printed on bookstock headed on [1]: "By Henry James" followed by an ad for *A Small Boy and Others*, with extensive press commentary; and headed on [2]: "THE NOVELS OF HENRY JAMES | In 24 vols. 8vo. 8s.6d. net each.", listing the 24 volumes, followed by a rule, and a list of 3 James titles: *French Poets and Novelists*, *Partial Portraits*, and *Nathaniel Hawthorne*.

This binding is uniform with that of the first English edition, first impression, of *A Small Boy and Others* (1913), 71.3.0.

English printing history: Macmillan Archive. MPL 55920, at 165, records that a print order for 1250 copies of this title was placed on December 12, 1913, and that on March 6, 1914 a print order was placed for 1,300 envelopes (dust-jackets). It was published on March 13, 1914. No further impressions are recorded.

Priced at 12s. net.

72.4.0. *Notes of a Son and Brother*, first English edition, one volume, London 1914.

This copy is identical to the first English edition, 72.3.0, except that it has stamped in blind on the front cover a large circular device consisting of two concentric circles, the outer of which is 2 $^{7}/_{16}$" in diameter. Between the two concentric circles is stamped in blind: "[Maltese cross] PUBLIC [Maltese cross] LIBRARIES", and centered in the inner circle is: "CHELSEA". On the front pastedown is an engraved bookplate of "CHELSEA PUBLIC LIBRARIES", noting that this copy was "PRESENTED BY | The Henry James Memorial Fund, | 1919".

Dust-jacket: cream-yellow wove paper, with an overall design in orange of the publisher's device. The front cover, lettered and decorated in black, reads: "NOTES OF | A SON AND BROTHER | HENRY JAMES | [centered publisher's device]". The spine, lettered and decorated in black, reads: "NOTES | OF | A SON | AND | BROTHER | HENRY | JAMES | 12/- | NET | [publisher's device]". On the back cover, also lettered in black, is an ad for works: "By Henry James | A SMALL BOY | AND OTHERS | 8vo. 12s. net. | THE NOVELS OF HENRY JAMES | 24 vols. 8vo. 8s. 6d. net each | [followed by a list of the volumes]", further followed after a short rule by 3 James titles: *French Poets and Novelists*, *Partial Portraits* and *Nathaniel Hawthorne*. At the foot is the publisher's imprint.

The dust-jacket is pasted onto the rear free endpaper and is missing its front and rear inner flaps. It is uniform with the dust-jacket on the first English edition, first impression, second state, of *A Small Boy and Others*, 71.4.0.

Tanselle, 18, note 42, states: "in the earlier years of the [twentieth] century the Bodleian Library fastened jackets inside the books themselves."

❧✢❧

73. *NOTES ON NOVELISTS*

73.1.0. *Notes on Novelists*, first edition, one volume, London 1914.

NOTES ON NOVELISTS [in red] | WITH | SOME OTHER NOTES | BY | HENRY JAMES | [triangular publisher's device] | MCMXIV | J. M. DENT & SONS LTD. [in red] | ALDINE HOUSE, BEDFORD ST., W. C.

Size: 8 $^{3}/_{16}$" x 5 $^{15}/_{16}$".

Collation: [A]^8 B–I K–U X–Z^8; pp. [i–viii], [1]–360.

Contents: [i–ii] half-title, verso blank; [iii–iv] title-page, verso blank; v–vi "PREFACE", verso continuation of preface; vii–[viii] "CONTENTS", verso blank; [1]–360 text; 360 at foot printer's imprint: "THE TEMPLE PRESS, PRINTERS, LETCHWORTH".

Binding: green embossed calico-grain cloth. The front cover has a double-rule border in blind within which is centered a square publisher's device, also in blind. The back cover is neither lettered nor decorated. The spine, lettered and decorated in gilt, reads: "NOTES | ON | NOVELISTS | [round flower device] | HENRY | JAMES | J [dot] M [dot] DENT | & [dot] SONS [dot] Ld [sic]". The "d" in "Ld" is raised with no dot or line under it. The endpapers are of cream wove paper, and the text is printed on cream wove paper. The top edge is trimmed and stained brown, and the other edges are rough trimmed.

Dust-jacket: cream wove paper lettered and decorated in brown. The front cover, within a double-rule border (the outer rule being much thicker than the inner rule), reads: "NOTES ON | NOVELISTS | [small flower device] | HENRY JAMES"; followed by a 15-line blurb about this book. The spine reads: "[triple-rule] | NOTES | ON | NOVELISTS | [small flower device] | HENRY | JAMES | 7/6 | NET | [publisher's device] | J. M. DENT | & SONS, LTD. | [triple-rule]". The back cover has within a single-rule border an ad for "SOME RECENT BOOKS [underscored]", listing 4 titles (none by James), and, below a rule, "CHANNELS OF ENGLISH LITERATURE", listing 5 titles (none by James), and at the foot in a separate panel the publisher's imprint: "J. M. DENT & SONS LTD. BEDFORD STREET LONDON". The front and back inner flaps are blank.

E&L A73a notes that this edition was originally priced at 6s. when it was published in 1914, and that the price was raised to 7s. 6d. in early 1915 and to 9s.6d. in 1919 or 1920. This dust-jacket, with the 7/6 price on it, was therefore probably printed in 1915.

73.2.0. *Notes on Novelists*, first American edition, first impression, one volume, New York 1914.

NOTES ON NOVELISTS | WITH SOME OTHER NOTES | BY | HENRY JAMES | NEW YORK | CHARLES SCRIBNER'S SONS | 1914

Size: $8\,3/16''$ x $5\,9/16''$.

Collation: [unsigned, 1–29^8]; pp. [i–viii], 1–455 [456].

Contents: [i–ii] half-title, verso ad headed: "By HENRY JAMES", listing 3 titles; [iii–iv] title-page, verso copyright notice, printing history and printer's device: "Copyright, 1914, by | CHARLES SCRIBNER'S SONS | [rule] | Published October, 1914 | [printer's device of the Scribner's Press]"; v–vi "CONTENTS", verso continuation of contents; [vii–viii] divisional fly-title, verso blank; 1–455 text; [456] blank.

Binding: olive-drab sateen cloth. The front cover, lettered and decorated in gilt, reads: "NOTES ON NOVELISTS | WITH SOME OTHER NOTES | [two small gilt square dots] BY HENRY JAMES [two small gilt square dots]". The back cover is neither lettered nor decorated. The spine, lettered in gilt, reads: "NOTES ON | NOVELISTS | WITH SOME | OTHER NOTES | HENRY | JAMES | SCRIBNERS". The publisher's imprint at the foot of the spine is in uniform capitals ³⁄₁₆″ high. The endpapers are of smooth cream wove paper, and the text is printed on cream wove paper. The top edge is gilt, and the other edges are untrimmed.

Dust-jacket: tan wove paper, printed in black. The front cover reads: "NOTES ON NOVELISTS | WITH SOME OTHER NOTES | [two small square dots] BY HENRY JAMES [two small square dots] | CHARLES SCRIBNER'S SONS". The back cover is blank. The spine reads: "NOTES ON | NOVELISTS | WITH SOME | OTHER NOTES | HENRY | JAMES | $2.50 NET [in sans-serif] | SCRIBNERS". The front and rear inner flaps are blank. The lettering on the dust-jacket replicates (except the price on the spine) the lettering on the front cover and spine of the book.

American printing history. Scribner's Archive. card (1) Box 13: Id-J. First edition: *first impression* 1950 copies printed October 8, 1914, all bound between October 13, 1914, and December 2, 1915; published October 14, 1914; *second impression* 240 copies printed December 29, 1915, 277 [*sic*] bound between July 13, 1916, and March 6, 1918; notation: undated but opposite binding order of January 13, 1917, "22 over"; notation: "0 [copies] 11/14/22".

The two impression of this edition were printed and bound by Scribner's. The paper used is not recorded. Both impressions were priced at $2.50 net.

The American edition of this title was set from sheets of Dent's English edition; see letter of James to Pinker, dated September 11, 1914. Yale University Library, ZA James 1 v.3.

73.3.0. *Notes on Novelists*, first American edition, second impression, one volume, New York, 1916.

This copy is identical to the first American edition, first impression, 73.2.0, except that the title-page is dated 1916 at the foot.

❧✢❧

74. THE UNIFORM TALES OF HENRY JAMES

The 14 tales published by Martin Secker as the 14-volume *Uniform Edition of the Tales of Henry James* were published in England during the period 1915–1920.

The impetus to republish some of James's tales came from the publisher, Martin Secker, and the negotiations for their publication, were conducted through James's agent Pinker during the period September through November, 1914. In a letter to Pinker dated November 12, 1914, James stipulated that Secker adhere strictly to the text of his tales as he had revised them for his "definitive" New York Edition: "I shall *not* ask to see the proofs - I hate so reading over my old things! – if Mr Secker will please engage to see that the Edition de Luxe is utterly and absolutely conformed to, to the very most lurking comma, and still more to the most patent absence of one (emphasis in the original)."[52] Hence the declaration on the title-page verso of all but two (*The Lesson of the Master* and *Glasses*) of these volumes that "the text follows that of the Definitive Edition". This omission in *The Lesson of the Master* was clearly an oversight, which was corrected in the second impression. The other exception to this was the *Glasses*, which had its first book publication in *Embarrassments* in 1896 (although *Glasses* refers to *Embarrassments* being published in 1897, a reference no doubt to the one volume second edition). *Glasses* had not been included by James in The New York Edition. It was revised by James in 1915, shortly before his death, specifically for this edition.

James originally suggested to Pinker that some of the volumes should contain two stories, a strong lead story followed by a shorter one. He even suggested specific pairings, such as *The Alter of the Dead* and *The Pupil*, *The Beast in the Jungle* and *The Next Time*, and *The Death of the Lion* and *The Friend of the Friends*. But for reasons unknown, Pinker declined

---

52 Yale TS, Za James 1, v. 3, 53; quoted in Horne, 545.

to pass on this suggestion to Martin Secker, and James quickly dropped the idea; see letters of James to Pinker, September 11, 1914, and September 22, 1914, Yale TS, Za James v. 3.

Seven of the fourteen tales published in England in 1915–1916 were also published by Le Roy Phillips in America in 1917–18. BAL 10693 records that: "no trade notices found nor record of copyright deposit [in America]." But the lack of trade notices is not surprising given the small size of the American issue, and copyright was unnecessary as they already had that protection as part of *Embarrassments* and the New York Edition. These seven volumes constitute the American issue of the first edition, as they were printed and undoubtedly bound in England. They are not separate impressions, but are composed of sheets of the first impressions of the English edition. However, new half-title and title-leaves printed in England were substituted for [A]$_1$, $_2$ in each volume: the verso of the half-title sheet with the addition of an ad listing the 6 other titles in this issue, the title-page with the publisher's imprint "LE ROY PHILLIPS | BOSTON" at the foot, and the title-leaf verso as in the English edition, but with the addition of the rubric "Printed in Great Britain", except *The Turn of the Screw* which has "Printed in England".

Printing history. Martin Secker Archive. Martin Secker Publishing Ledgers, MS 1090, Ledger 1, 1910–1917, Ledger 2, 1917–1925, first uniform edition, in order of printings:

The Aspern Papers. Ledger 1, p. 161 and Ledger 2, p. 61: *first impression* 1500 copies printed December 1914, 1200 copies bound between March 1915 and May 1917; 200 copies exported to America in May 1917, and a further 200 copies exported in December 1917; *second impression* 750 copies printed in March 1919, 325 copies bound in May 1919 and a further 372 copies bound in February, July and November 1920. Total copies sold of both impressions by December 1923: 2,121. Mention of wrappers.

The Lesson of the Master. Ledger 1, p. 160, and Ledger 2, p. 63; *first impression* 1500 copies printed January 1915, 1,200 copies bound between March 1915 and May 1917; 200 copies exported to America in May 1917, and a further 200 copies exported in December 1917; *second impression* 750 copies printed in March 1919, 425 copies bound in May 1919, and a further 330 copies bound in July and September 1920. Total copies sold of both impressions by December 1923: 1,960. Mention of wrappers.

THE UNIFORM TALES OF HENRY JAMES

The Death of the Lion. Ledger 1, p. 174 and Ledger 2, p. 64; *first* (and sole) *impression* 1500 copies printed January 1915, 1,212 copies bound between March 1915 and August 1919, and a further 261 copies bound in February, July and September 1920; 30 copies exported to America in May 1922. Total copies sold by December 1923: 1272. Mention of wrappers.

Daisy Miller. Ledger 1, p. 173, and Ledger 2, p. 62; *first impression* 1500 copies printed January 1915, 1503 (sic) copies bound between March 1916 and July 1917; *second impression* 750 copies printed March 1919, 451 copies bound between May and December, 1919, and a further 282 copies bound between January and September 1920; 22 copies exported to America in May 1922. Total copies sold of both impressions by December 1922: 2,092. Mention of wrappers. A third impression, not recorded in the Ledgers, was published in 1924.

The Turn of the Screw. Ledger 1, p. 159, and Ledger 2, p. 60; *first impression* 1500 copies printed January 1915, 1,400 copies bound between March 1915 and August 1916; *second impression* 800 copies printed August 1917, 848 copies (*sic*) bound between June and September 1917; 400 copies exported to America in September 1917; *third impression* 500 copies printed February 1919, 489 copies bound in April and June 1919; *fourth impression* 1,000 copies printed January 1920, 1031 (*sic*) copies bound between February 1920 and August 1922. Total copies of all impressions sold by December 1922: 3,835. Mention of wrappers.

The Altar of the Dead. Ledger 1, p. 175, and Ledger 2, p. 69; *first impression* 1500 copies printed February 1915, 500 bound in August 1916; *second impression* 1,000 copies printed August 1916, 814 bound between June 1917 and June 1919, and a further 1196 copies bound between February and September 1920. Total copies sold by December 1923: 1,427. Mention of wrappers.

The Coxon Fund. Ledger 1, p. 176, and Ledger 2, p. 66; *first* (and sole) *impression* 1500 copies, 900 copies bound between February 1915 and March 1919, and a further 421 copies bound in July and September 1920; 30 copies exported to America in May 1922. Total copies sold by December 1923: 1236. Mention of wrappers.

The Reverberator. Ledger 1, p. 177; *first* (and sole) *impression* 1,500 copies printed March 1915, 1,450 copies bound between August 1915 and May 1917; 200 copies were exported to America in May 1917, and a further 200 exported in January 1918. Total copies sold by March 1919: 1,337. Mention of wrappers.

THE UNIFORM TALES OF HENRY JAMES

Glasses. Ledger 1, p. 207 and Ledger 2, p. 67; *first impression* 1,000 copies printed August 1916, 1,000 copies bound August 1916 and May 1917; 200 copies exported to America in May 1917, and a further 200 exported in December 1917; *second impression* 1,000 copies printed June 1918, 212 copies bound between July and September 1918, and a further 288 copies bound in July and September 1920. Total copies sold by December 1923: 1,384. No mention of wrappers.

The Figure in the Carpet. Ledger 1, p. 206 and Ledger 2, p. 70; *first impression* 1,000 copies printed August 1916, 1,000 copies bound between August and May 1917; 200 copies exported to America in May 1917, and a further 200 exported in December 1917; *second impression* 1,000 copies printed June 1919, 206 copies bound in July through December 1919, and a further 376 copies bound between July 1920 and July 1923. Total copies sold by December 1923: 1,466. Mention of wrappers.

The Beast in the Jungle. Ledger 1, p. 178, and Ledger 2, p. 65; *first* (and sole) *impression* 1500 copies printed July 1918, 1148 copies bound between August 1918 and August 1919. Total copies sold by December 1919: 975. Mention of wrappers.

In the Cage. Ledger 1, p. 205, and Ledger 2, p. 53; *first impression* 1,000 copies printed December 1919, 703 bound between January 1920 and August 1922. Total copies sold by December 1923: 645. Mention of wrappers. A second impression, not recorded in the Ledgers, was published in 1924.

No entries were found for *The Pupil* (1916) and *The Jolly Corner* (1919).

EC records that four volumes were published on April 15, 1915 (*The Aspern Papers*, *The Turn of the Screw*, *The Lesson of the Master*, and *Daisy Miller*), four volumes on November 15, 1915 (*The Beast in the Jungle*, *The Coxon Fund*, *The Death of the Lion*, and *The Reverberator*), four volumes on September 16, 1916 (*The Altar of the Dead*, *The Figure in the Carpet*, *Glasses*, and *The Pupil*), one volume in February 1919 (*The Jolly Corner*), and the final volume in 1920 (*In the Cage*). All were initially priced at 2s. 6d. net, except that the last two were priced at 3s. 6d. net.

All titles were published in dust-jackets. Both the absence of volume numbers and the reprinting history suggests that they were sold as single volumes rather than sets.

James received an advance of £1,000 against a royalty of 4d. per copy sold.

THE UNIFORM TALES OF HENRY JAMES

E&L A 74b records that because of a stock shortage of sheets of the first impression of *The Turn of the Screw*, Martin Seeker supplied Le Roy Phillips with sheets of the second impression (1917) for the American issue. However, this is not entirely correct, as the copy of the America issue catalogued in 74.2.0 is of the first (1915) impression. It is possible that sheets of both the first and second impressions were supplied to Le Roy Phillips.

74.1.0. *The Uniform Tales of Henry James*, first uniform edition, 14 volumes, London [n.d., 1915–1920].

The Lesson of the Master. First impression, 1915.

THE LESSON OF | THE MASTER | BY HENRY JAMES | [small leaf and branch ornament] | LONDON: MARTIN SECKER | NUMBER FIVE JOHN STREET ADELPHI

Size: 7 $3/4$" x 4 $5/16$".

Collation: $[A]^8$ B–G^8 $[H]^4$; pp. [1–4], 5–[118] [119–120].

Contents: [1–2] half-title, verso blank; [3–4] title-page, verso printing history: "This edition first printed in 1915" [no mention of the "Definitive Edition"]; 5–[118] text; [119–120] blank, verso printer's imprint: "THE BALLANTYNE PRESS | LONDON & EDINBURGH".

Binding: dark reddish-brown linen-grain cloth. The front cover is decorated with a double-rule border in blind divided by two vertical single rules in blind into three vertical panels. The center panel, which is lettered in gilt,[53] reads: "THE LESSON OF | THE MASTER | [leaf device] | HENRY | JAMES". The back cover is not lettered, but is similarly decorated in blind. The spine, which is lettered and decorated in gilt, reads: "[double rule] | THE | LESSON OF | THE MASTER | [leaf device] | HENRY | JAMES | MARTIN | SECKER | [double rule]". The publisher's imprint at the foot of the spine is in uniform capitals $1/8$" high. The endpapers are of cream wove paper, and the text is printed on laid paper. The top edge is gilt, the fore-edge is rough trimmed, and the bottom edge is untrimmed.

[53] Actually Dutch gold, "which actually is composed of brass ... an alloy of copper and zinc .... Unlike gold leaf, Dutch gold discolors, tarnishing more rapidly in polluted environments." Matt T. Roberts and Don Etherington, *Bookbinding and the Conservation of Books: A Dictionary of Descriptive Terminology* (Washington: Library of Congress, 1982), 84.

A second impression was published in 1919, identifiable by "SECOND IMPRESSION" on the title-page, and the title-leaf verso which reads: "This edition first published in 1915 | Reprinted 1919 | The text follows that of the | Definitive Edition | Date of original publication 1891".

The other titles uniformly bound (other than variations in cloth color) are:

> *The Turn of the Screw*. First impression, 1915. Collation: [A]⁸ B–I K–M N⁸; pp. [1–4], 5–[205] [206] [207–208]. Contents: [1–2] half-title, verso blank; [3–4] title-page, verso printing history: "This edition first published 1915 | The text follows that of the | Definitive Edition"; 5–[205] text; [206] blank; [207–208] printer's imprint: "THE BALLANTINE PRESS | LONDON & EDINBURG", verso blank. Bound in brown linen-grain cloth. The publisher's imprint on the spine is in uniform capitals ⅛" high. The endpapers are of cream wove paper, and the text is printed on laid paper. The top edge is gilt, and the other edges are rough trimmed.
>
> On the front pastedown is stamped "L. C. MARRAUD & CO., BOOKSELLER ETC., MADRAS."
>
> A fourth impression was printed in 1920. Collation: [A]⁸ B–I K–M⁸ N⁸ (–N₈); pp. [1–4], 5–[205] [206]. Contents: [1–2] half-title, verso ad listing 13 titles under the heading: "UNIFORM WITH THIS VOLUME [in italic]"; [3–4] title-page, verso printing history "This edition first published 1915 | Reprinted 1917, 1919 and 1920 | The text follows that of the | Definitive Edition | Date of original publication 1898"; 5–[205] text; [206] printer's imprint: "PRINTED IN ENGLAND BY | THE WESTMINSTER PRESS | 411a HARROW ROAD | LONDON". Bound in brown linen-grain cloth. The publisher's imprint on the spine is in uniform capitals 3/32" high. The endpapers are of cream laid paper, and the text is printed on laid paper. The top edge is gilt, and the other edges are rough trimmed.
>
> *The Aspern Papers*. First impression, 1915. Collation: [A]⁸ B–I K–L⁸; pp. [1–4], 5–[176]. Contents: [1–2] half-title, verso blank; [3–4] title-page, verso printing history: "This edition first published 1915 | The text follows that of the | Definitive Edition"; 5–[176] text; [176] at foot printer's imprint: "THE BALLANTYNE PRESS | LONDON & EDINBURGH". Bound in dark chocolate-brown linen-grain cloth. The publisher's imprint on the spine is in uniform capitals ⅛" high. The

endpapers are of cream wove paper, and the text is printed on laid paper. The top edge is gilt, and the other edges are rough trimmed.

A second impression was printed in 1919. Collation and contents are identical to those of the first impression, except that the title-page has on it "SECOND IMPRESSION", and the title-leaf verso reads: "This edition first published 1915 | Reprinted 1919 | The text follows that of the | Definitive Edition | Date of original publication 1888", and on [176] the printer's imprint reads: "PRINTED AT THE COMPLETE PRESS | WEST NORWOOD | LONDON". The publisher's imprint on the spine is in uniform capitals $3/32$" high. The endpapers are of cream wove paper, and the text is printed on laid paper. The top edge is gilt and the other edges are untrimmed.

This copy of the second impression has a dust-jacket of gray wove paper lettered and decorated in blue. The lettering and decoration on the front cover replicates the lettering and decoration in gilt and blind on the cover of the book. On the back cover within an oblong vertical double-rule frame is an ad for "UNIFORM EDITION | OF THE TALES OF | HENRY JAMES", listing 12 titles. The spine reads: "[double rule] | THE | ALTAR OF | THE DEAD | [leaf device] | HENRY | JAMES | PRICE | 3/6 | NET | MARTIN | SECKER". No lettering or decoration is present on the front and back inner flaps.

Daisy Miller. First impression, 1915. Collation: [A]^8 B–G^8 H^4; pp. [1–4], 5–[117] [118] [119–120]. Contents: [1–2] half-title, verso blank; [3–4] title-page, verso printing history: "This edition first published 1915 | The text follows that of the | Definitive Edition."; 5–[117] text; [118] printer's imprint: "THE BALLANTYNE PRESS | LONDON & EDINBURGH"; [119–120] blank leaf. Bound in dark chocolate-brown linen-grain cloth. The publisher's imprint on the spine is in uniform capitals $1/8$" high. The endpapers are of cream wove paper, and the text is printed on rough thick wove paper. The top edge is gilt, and the other edges are rough trimmed.

A second impression was published in 1919. Collation and contents are identical to the first impression, except that the title-page has on it "SECOND IMPRESSION", the title-leaf verso reads: "This edition first published 1915 | Reprinted 1919 | The text follows that of the | Definitive Edition | Date of original publication 1878", and on [118] the printer's imprint reads: "PRINTED AT THE COMPLETE PRESS | WEST NORWOOD | LONDON". The publisher's imprint on the spine is in uniform capitals 1/8" high. The endpapers are of cream wove paper, and the text is printed on laid paper. The top edge is gilt, and the other edges are untrimmed.

A third impression was published 1924, identifiable by "THIRD IMPRESSION" on the title-page, and the title-leaf verso which reads: "This edition first published in 1915 | Reprinted in 1919 and 1924 | The text follows that of the | Definitive Edition".

The Death of the Lion. First impression, 1915. Collation: [A]^8(–[A]$_1$) B–D^8 E^8 (–E$_8$); pp. [2], [1–4], 5–[73] [74]. Contents: blank leaf; [1–2] half-title, verso blank, [3–4] title-page, verso printing history: "This edition first published 1915 | The text follows that of the | Definitive Edition"; 5–[73] text, [74] printer's imprint: "THE BALLANTYNE PRESS | LONDON & EDINBURGH". Bound in brown linen-grain cloth. The publisher's imprint on the spine is in uniform capitals 1/8" high. The front and back pastedowns are of white wove paper, but there are no front or rear free endpapers, the blank leaf [A]$_1$, and the leaf E$_7$, with the printer's imprint on the verso, serving as the front and back free endpapers. The text is printed on thick rough wove paper. The top edge is gilt, and the other edges are rough trimmed.

There is a stamp of "County Londonderry Carnegie Library" on the title-page.

The Reverberator. First impression, 1915. Collation: [A]^8 B–I K–Q^8 R^2; pp. [1–4], 5–[259] [260]. Contents: [1–2] half-title, verso ad headed: "UNIFORM WITH THIS VOLUME [in italic]", listing 7 titles; [3–4] title-page, verso printing history: "This edition first published 1915 | The text follows that of the | Definitive Edition"; 5–[259] text; [260] printer's imprint: "THE BALLANTYNE PRESS | LONDON & EDIN-BURGH". Bound in reddish-brown linen-grain cloth. The publisher's imprint on the spine is in uniform capitals 1/8" high. The endpapers are of cream wove paper, and the text is printed on thin laid paper. The top edge is gilt, and the other edges are rough trimmed.

The Beast in the Jungle. First impression, 1915. Collation: [A]^8 B–E^8 F^4; pp. [1–4], 5–[87] [88]. Contents: [1–2] half-title, verso ad headed: "UNIFORM WITH THIS VOLUME [in italic]", listing 7 titles; [3–4] title-page, verso printing history: "This edition first published 1915 | The text follows that of the | Definitive Edition"; 5–[87] text;

[88] printer's imprint: "THE BALLANTYNE PRESS | LONDON & EDINBURGH". Bound in chocolate-brown linen-grain cloth. The publisher's imprint on the spine is in uniform capitals ⅛" high. The endpapers are of cream wove paper, and the text is printed on rough wove paper. The top edge is gilt, and the other edges are rough trimmed.

The Coxon Fund. First impression, 1915. Collation: [A]^8 B–G^8; pp. [1–4], 5–[111] [112]. Contents:[1–2] half-title, verso blank; [3–4] title-page, verso printing history: "This edition first published 1915 | The text follows that of the | Definitive Edition"; 5–[111] text; [111] at foot printer's imprint: "THE BALLANTYNE PRESS | LONDON & EDINBURGH"; [112] blank. Bound in reddish-brown linen-grain cloth. The publisher's imprint on the spine is in uniform capitals ⅛" high. The endpapers are of cream laid paper, and the text is printed on rough thick wove paper. The top edge is gilt, the fore-edge is rough trimmed, and the bottom edge is untrimmed.

The Altar of the Dead. First impression, 1916. Collation: [A]^8 B–D^8 E^4 F^2; pp. [1–4], 5–[73] [74] [75–76]. Contents: [1–2] half-title, verso blank; [3–4] title-page, verso printing history: "This edition first published 1915 | The text follows that of the | Definitive Edition"; 5–[73] text; [74] blank; [75–76] printer's imprint: "THE BALLANTYNE PRESS | LONDON & EDINBURGH", verso blank. Bound in light chocolate-brown linen-grain cloth. The publisher's imprint on the spine is in uniform capitals ⅛" high. The endpapers are of cream wove paper, and the text is printed on rough wove paper. The top edge is gilt, and the other edges are untrimmed.

EC records a publication date of September 1916 for this title. However, this copy has "This edition first published 1915" on the verso of the title-leaf; see BAL 10787 which states that the first impression was printed in 1915 but not published until 1916; also see the second impression below. A second impression was printed 1916, identifiable by the title-leaf verso which reads: "This edition first published 1916 | The text follows that of the | Definitive Edition".

This copy of the second impression has dust-jacket of gray wove paper, lettered and decorated in blue, which is uniform with the dust-jacket on the second impression of *The Aspern Papers* described above.

Glasses. First impression, 1916. Collation: [A]⁸ B–F⁸; pp. [1–4], 5–[93] [94] [95–96]. Contents: [1–2] half-title, verso ad headed: "UNIFORM WITH THIS VOLUME [in italic]", listing 11 titles; [3–4] title-page, verso printing history: "This edition first published 1916 | 'Glasses' is not included in the Definitive Edition: | it first appeared in the volume 'Embarrassments,' | published by Mr. William Heinemann in 1897 [*sic*, 1896]. The | text was revised by the author for this edition very | shortly before his death."; 5–[93] text; [94] blank; [95–96] printer's imprint: "PRINTED BY | KNIGHT'S WEST NORWOOD", verso blank. Bound in dark chocolate-brown linen-grain cloth. The publisher's imprint on the spine is in uniform capitals ³/₃₂" high. The endpapers are of cream wove paper, and the text is printed on rough wove paper. The top edge is gilt, and the other edges are rough trimmed.

A second impression was printed in 1919, with an ad on [2], headed: "UNIFORM WITH THIS VOLUME [in italic]", listing 13 titles, "SECOND IMPRESSION" on the title-page, and on the title-leaf verso the printing history: "This edition first published 1916 | Reprinted 1919 | 'Glasses' is not included in the Definitive | Edition: it [en quadrate present] first appeared in the volume | 'Embarrassments,' published by Mr. William | Heinemann in 1897 [*sic*, 1896]. The text was revised by | the Author for this edition very shortly before | his death." [95–96] blank, verso printer's imprint: "PRINTED IN ENGLAND BY | THE WESTMINSTER PRESS, 411A HARROW ROAD, | LONDON, W."

The Figure in the Carpet. First impression, 1916. Collation: [A]⁸ B–E⁸; pp. [1–4], 5–[78] [79–80]. Contents: [1–2] half-title, verso ad headed: "UNIFORM WITH THIS VOLUME [in italic]" listing 11 titles; [3–4] title-page, verso printing history: "This edition first published 1916 | The text follows that of the | Definitive Edition"; 5–[78] text; [79–80] printer's imprint: "PRINTED BY | KNIGHT'S WEST NORWOOD", verso blank. Bound in brown linen-grain cloth. The publisher's imprint on the spine is in uniform capitals ⅛" high. The endpapers are of cream wove paper, and the text is printed on rough wove paper. The top edge is gilt, and the other edges are rough trimmed.

A second impression was printed in 1919, with an ad on [2] headed: "UNIFORM WITH THIS VOLUME [in italic]", listing 13 titles, "SECOND IMPRESSION" on the title-page, and on the title-leaf verso the printing history: "This edition first published 1916 | Reprinted 1919 | The text follows that of the | Definitive Edition | Date [en quadrate present] of original publication 1896". [78] is blank. The printer's imprint on [79] reads: PRINTED IN ENGLAND BY | THE WESTMINSTER PRESS, 411A HARROW ROAD, | LONDON, W.".

This copy of the second impression has a dust-jacket of tan wove paper lettered and decorated in blue. The lettering and decoration on the front cover replicates the lettering and decoration in gilt and blind on the front cover of the book. The back cover has within an oblong double-rule frame an ad identical to that on the dust-jacket of the second impression of *The Aspern Papers*, above. The spine reads: "THE | FIGURE IN | THE CARPET | [leaf device] | HENRY | JAMES | PRICE | 3/6 | NET. | MARTIN | SECKER". No lettering or decoration is present on the front and back inner flaps.

The Pupil. First impression, 1916. Collation: [A]⁸ B–E⁸ F⁴; pp. [1–4], 5–[87] [88]. Contents: [1–2] half-title, verso ad headed: "UNIFORM WITH THIS VOLUME [in italic]", listing 11 titles; [3–4] title-page, verso printing history: "This edition first published 1916 | The text follows that of the | Definitive Edition"; 5–[87] text; [88] printer's imprint; "PRINTED AT | KNIGHT'S, WEST NORWOOD". Bound in chocolate-brown linen-grain cloth. The publisher's imprint on the spine is in uniform capitals ⅛" high. The endpapers are of cream wove paper, and the text is printed on wove paper. The top edge is gilt, the fore-edge is untrimmed, and the bottom edge is rough trimmed.

The Jolly Corner. First impression, 1918 [1919]. Collation: [A]⁸ B–D⁸ E⁴; pp. [1–4], 5–[72]. Contents: [1–2] half-title, verso ad headed: "UNIFORM WITH THIS VOLUME [in italic]", listing 13 titles; [3–4] title-page, verso printing history: "This edition first published 1918 | The text follows that of the | Definitive Edition"; 5–[72] text; [72] at foot printer's imprint: "PRINTED BY WILLIAM BRENDON & SON, LTD. | PLYMOUTH, ENGLAND". Bound in light chocolate-brown linen-grain cloth. The publisher's imprint on the spine is in uniform capitals 3/32" high. The endpapers are of cream wove paper, and the text is printed on laid paper. The top edge is gilt, the fore-edge is rough trimmed, and the bottom edge is untrimmed.

E&L A74a notes that the "issue" date of this impression is 1919.

However, this copy has the publication date 1918 on the verso of the title-leaf.

In the Cage. First impression, 1919 [1920]. Collation: [A]⁸ B–I K–L⁸; pp. [1–4], 5–[175] [176].The signature mark "L" is of damaged type, as is the last numeral "1" in the pagination of 131. Contents: [1–2] half-title, verso ad headed: "UNIFORM WITH THIS VOLUME [in italic]", listing 13 titles; [3–4] title-page, verso printing history: "This edition first published in 1919 | The text follows that of the | Definitive Edition | Date of original publication 1898"; 5–[175] text; [176] printer's imprint: "printed by | WILLIAM BRENDON AND SON, LTD. | PLYMOUTH ENGLAND". Bound in light reddish-brown linen-grain cloth. The publisher's imprint on the spine is in uniform capitals ³/₃₂" high. The endpapers are of cream wove paper, and the text is printed on rough wove paper. The top edge is gilt, the fore-edge is untrimmed, and the bottom edge is rough trimmed.

A second impression was printed in 1924, has "SECOND IMPRES-SION" on the title-page, and on the title-leaf verso the printing history: "This edition first published 1919 | Reprinted 1924 | The text follows that of the | Definitive Edition | Date of original publication 1898", and on [176] the printer's imprint: "Printed in Great Britain at | The Mayflower Press, Plymouth. [in italic] | William Brendon & Son, Ltd." Bound in reddish-brown linen-grain cloth.

74.2.0. *The Uniform Tales of Henry James*, first uniform edition, American issue, seven volumes, Boston [n.d., 1917–1918].

The Figure in the Carpet. First impression, 1916.

THE FIGURE IN | THE CARPET | BY HENRY JAMES | [leaf device] | LE ROY PHILLIPS | BOSTON

Size: 6 ⁵/₈" x 4 ³/₁₆".

Collation: π² [A]⁴ X² B–E⁸; pp. [1–4], 5–[78] [79–80].

Contents: [1–2] half-title, verso ad headed: "UNIFORM WITH THIS VOLUME [in italic]", listing the 6 other titles in this issue; [3–4] title-page, verso printing history: "This edition first published 1916 | The text follows that of the | Definitive Edition | Printed in Great Britain [in italic]"; 5–[78] text; [79] printer's imprint: "PRINTED BY | KNIGHT'S WEST NORWOOD"; [80] blank.

THE UNIFORM TALES OF HENRY JAMES

Binding: brown linen-grain cloth. The lettering and decoration in gilt and in blind on the front cover and spine, and the decoration in blind on the back cover are identical to those of the first uniform edition, 74.1.0, except that the publisher's imprint at the foot of the spine reads: "LE ROY | PHILLIPS | BOSTON". The endpapers are of cream wove paper, and the text is printed on wove paper. The top edge is trimmed and stained brown, and the other edges are rough trimmed.

Other titles uniformly bound (other than variations in cloth color) in the collection are:

The Turn of the Screw. First impression, 1915. Collation: [A]^8 ($\pm$[A]$_{1,2}$) B–I K–M N^8; pp. [1–4], 5–[205] [206] [207–208]. Contents: [1–2] half-title, verso ad headed: "UNIFORM WITH THIS VOLUME [in italic]", listing the 6 other titles in this issue; [3–4] title-page, verso printing history: "This edition first published 1915 | The text follows that of the | Definitive Edition | Printed in England [in italic]"; 5–[205] text; [206] blank; [207] printer's imprint: "PRINTED AT | KNIGHT'S, WEST NORWOOD", [208] blank. Bound in brown linen-grain cloth. The publisher's imprint on the spine is in uniform capitals ⅛" high. The endpapers are of cream wove paper, and the text is printed on wove paper. The top edge is trimmed and stained brown, and the other edges are rough trimmed.

The Reverberator. First impression, 1916. Collation: π^2 [A]^4 X^2 B–I K–Q^8 R^2; pp. [1–4], 5–[259] [260]. Contents: [1–2] half-title, verso ad headed: "UNIFORM WITH THIS VOLUME [in italic]", listing the 6 other titles in this issue; [3–4] title-page, verso printing history: "This edition first published 1916 | The text follows that of the | Definitive Edition | Printed in Great Britain [in italic]"; 5–[259] text; [259] at foot printer's imprint: "THE BALLANTYNE PRESS | LONDON & EDINBURGH"; [260] blank. The endpapers are of cream wove paper, the preliminaries, [1–4], are printed on wove paper, and the text is printed on laid paper. The top edge is trimmed and stained brown, and the other edges are rough trimmed.

The Aspern Papers. First impression, 1916. Collation: π^2 [A]^4 X^2 B–I K–L^8; pp. [1–4], 5–[176]. Contents: [1–2] half-title, verso ad headed: "UNIFORM WITH THIS VOLUME [in italic]", listing the 6 other titles in this issue; [3–4] title-page, verso printing history: "This edition first published 1916 | The text follows that of the | Definitive

Edition | Printed in Great Britain [in italic]"; 5–[176] text; [176] at foot printer's imprint: "THE BALLANTYNE PRESS | LONDON & EDINBURGH". Bound in brown linen-grain cloth. The endpapers are of white wove paper, the preliminaries, [1–4], are printed on wove paper, and the text is printed on laid paper. The top edge is trimmed and stained brown, and the other edges are rough trimmed.

The Lesson of the Master. First impression, 1916. Collation: π^2 [A]^4 X^2 B–G^8 H^4; pp. [1–4], 5–[118] [119–120]. Contents: [1–2] half-title, verso ad headed: "UNIFORM WITH THIS VOLUME" [in italic], listing the 6 other titles in this issue; [3–4] title-page, verso printing history: "This edition first published 1916 | The text follows that of the | Definitive Edition | Printed in Great Britain [in italic]"; 5–[118] text; [119] blank; [120] printer's imprint: "THE BALLANTYNE PRESS | LONDON & EDINBURGH". Bound in brown linen-grain cloth. The endpapers are of white wove paper, the preliminaries, [1–4], are printed on thin wove paper, and the text is printed on laid paper. The top edge is trimmed and stained brown, and the other edges are rough trimmed.

Glasses. First impression, 1916. Collation: π^2 [A]^4 X^2 B–F^8; pp. [1–4], 5–[93] [94–96]. Contents: [1–2] half-title, verso ad headed: "UNIFORM WITH THIS VOLUME" [in italic], listing the 6 other titles in this issue; [3–4], title-page, verso printing history: "This edition first published in 1916 | "Glasses" is not included in the Definitive Edition: | it first appeared in the volume "Embarrassements," | published by Mr. William Heinemann in 1897 [*sic*, 1896]. The | text was revised by the author for this edition very | shortly before his death. | Printed in Great Britain [in italic]"; 5–93 text; [94] blank; [95] printer's imprint: "PRINTED BY | KNIGHT'S WEST NORWOOD"; [96] blank. Bound in brown linen-grain cloth. The endpapers are of cream wove paper, and the text is printed on wove paper. The top edge is trimmed and stained brown, and the other edges are rough trimmed.

THE QUESTION OF THE MIND

75. THE QUESTION OF THE MIND

75.1.0. *The Question of the Mind*, first edition, self-wrapped pamphlet, London [n.d., 1915].

England [underscored] | at War: [underscored] | AN ESSAY | The Question of the Mind | by | Henry James | Issued by | THE CENTRAL COMMITTEE | For National Patriotic Organizations | C. P. BUILDING, 62 CHARING CROSS, LONDON, W. C. | [rule] | PRICE ONE PENNY.

Size: $8\,1/2''$ x $5\,1/2''$.

Collation [unsigned, 1^{10}]; [unpaginated pp. 1–20].

Contents: [1–2] title-page, verso copyright notice: "Copyright in | Great Britain and the U.S.A [*sic*, all in italic]"; 3–[20] text; [20] at foot printer's imprint: "[rule] | PRINTED BY THE PRESS PRINTERS, LTD., LONG ACRE, LONDON."

Binding: self wrapped. It is printed on cream laid paper, water-marked with a windmill and the date 1590. It is stapled, not sewn.

This copy has the circular ink stamp of the bibliographer Philip Gaskell on the title-page.

76. PICTURES AND OTHER PASSAGES FROM HENRY JAMES

76.1.0. *Pictures and Other Passages from Henry James*, first edition, English issue, one volume, London 1916.

PICTURES | And Other Passages from | HENRY JAMES | [square device of a bird perched on a leaf] | SELECTED BY | RUTH HEAD | LONDON | CHATTO & WINDUS | MCMXVI

Size: $7\,1/8''$ x $5''$.

Collation: $[A]^6$ $B–I^8$ K^4; pp. [i–xii], 1–[134] [135–136].

Contents: [i–ii] half-title, verso blank; [iii–iv] title-page, verso printer's imprint and reservation of rights: "PRINTED BY | WILLIAM CLOWES AND SONS, LIMITED, | LONDON AND BECCLES. | All rights reserved [in italic]"; v "PREFACE"; vi–ix continuation of preface;

[x] list of Heinemann editions quoted; [xi–xii] "CONTENTS", verso blank; 1–[134] text; [135] publisher's device; [136] printer's imprint as on [iv].

Binding: gray linen-grain quarter cloth, with black-on-white "spot" marbled paper over boards. The front and back covers are neither lettered nor decorated. The spine has a white paper label printed in black, which reads: "[thick followed by thin rule] | Pictures | & other | Passages | from | Henry | James | [thin followed by thick rule]". No publisher's imprint is present on the spine. The endpapers are of cream laid paper, and the text is printed on cream laid paper watermarked: "ANTIQUE DE LUXE". The top edge is trimmed and stained gray, and the other edges are untrimmed.

Printing history. Chatto & Windus Archive, Stock Book 8, p. 502 (CW B/2/19), and Profit and Loss Ledger 1910–1917, p. 32. First edition: *first (and sole) impression* 1,010 copies printed May 29, 1916. Also printed were 750 "dust covers" on June 1, 1916, 1,000 labels on July 26, 1916, and 320 title pages with the Frederick A. Stokes imprint on February 24, 1917. Three hundred and fifteen bound copies were exported to Frederick A. Stokes Company for the American issue, at a discounted price of 1s. 3d. per copy. Of the 695 copies of the English issue, 77 were distributed free to the press and others, 100 were sold to "Mussons (London)", with glassine dust-jackets, at a discounted price of 1s. 3d. per copy, and the balance were sold, presumably to distributors, at a discounted price of 2s. 4d. per copy. There are the notations that a half-tone was engraved, possibly for the dust-jacket, that the paper used for the covers was "spot marble" paper, and that on "Sept 15/30 1 zinco destroyed by Clowes".

EC records that the English issue was published on September 16, 1916, priced at 3s. 6. net. The American issue was published in October 1917.

76.2.0. *Pictures and Other Passages from Henry James,* first edition, American issue, one volume [n.d., 1917].

PICTURES | And Other Passages from | HENRY JAMES | [square device of a bird perched on a leaf] | SELECTED BY | RUTH HEAD | NEW YORK | FREDERICK A STOKES COMPANY | PUBLISHERS

Size: $7\,1/8''$ x $5''$.

Collation: [A⁶(±[A$_2$][A$_5$]+X$_1$)] B–I⁸ K⁴ (–K$_4$); pp. [i–xiv], 1–[134]. The title-leaf, [A$_2$], is a cancel, and there is additional leaf tipped in between [A]$_5$ and [A]$_6$, reckoned in the pagination. Leaf K$_4$, [135–136], excised in this American issue, has in the English issue the publisher's device on the recto, and the printer's imprint on the verso.

Contents: [i–ii] half-title, verso blank; [iii–iv] title-page, printer's imprint and reservation of rights as in the first edition, English issue, 76.1.0, except that after the word "PRINTED" there are the additional words "IN ENGLAND"; v "PREFACE"; vi–ix continuation of preface; [x] list of Heinemann editions quoted; [xi–xii] additional leaf tipped in headed: "Selections from the following books are used by permission | of and special arrangements with Messrs. Houghton Mifflin | Company", followed by citation of books of other American publishers from which quotations were taken, verso blank; [xiii–xiv] "CONTENTS", verso blank; 1–[134] text.

Binding: gray linen-grain quarter cloth, with black-on-white "spot" marbled paper over boards and a paper label on the spine, lettered and decorated identically to that on 76.1.0. The endpapers are of cream laid paper, and the text is printed on cream laid paper watermarked "ANTIQUE DE LUXE". The top edge is trimmed and stained gray, and the other edges are rough trimmed.

This issue was printed and bound in England.

⚜

77. THE IVORY TOWER

77.1.0. *The Ivory Tower*, first edition, first impression, one volume, London [n.d., 1917].

THE IVORY TOWER | BY | HENRY JAMES | LONDON: 48 PALL MALL | W. COLLINS SONS & CO. LTD. | GLASGOW MELBOURNE AUCKLAND

Size: 7 ⁵/₈" x 5 ⅛".

Collation: π⁴ (π$_1$ +X$_1$) A–I K–U X⁸ Y⁶; pp. [i–viii], 1–[348] plus 2.

Contents: [i–ii] half-title, verso blank; frontispiece photographic portrait of James with tissue guard tipped in not reckoned in the pagination; [iii–iv] title-page, verso copyright notice: "COPYRIGHT [in italic] | 1917"; v–vi "PREFACE [in italic]", verso continuation of preface; [vii–viii] "CONTENTS", verso blank; 1–[348] text; [348] at foot printer's imprint: "GLASGOW: PRINTED AT THE UNIVERSITY PRESS BY ROBERT MACLEHOSE AND CO. LTD."

Binding: dark blue smooth cloth. The front cover, lettered in gilt, reads: "THE IVORY TOWER | HENRY JAMES". The back cover is neither lettered nor decorated. The spine, lettered in gilt, reads: "THE | IVORY | TOWER | HENRY | JAMES | COLLINS". The endpapers are of cream wove paper, and the text is printed on cream wove paper. The top edge is trimmed, and the other edges are untrimmed.

This binding is uniform with those on the first edition, first impression, of *The Sense of the Past* (1917) and *The Middle Years* (1917), 78.1.0 and 79.1.0.

Dust-jacket: gray mottled wove paper. The front cover, lettered in brown, reads: "THE IVORY TOWER | HENRY JAMES | [within a brown thin single-rule frame is an applied black-and-white photographic portrait of James reproducing the frontispiece] | '[blurb] Printed with the novel is the unique sketch, written by | the author, outlining the story and indicating the method of | work of this great man of letters, whose death, in December, | 1915 [sic, February, 1916], was mourned by all lovers of literature.'" The spine, lettered in sage-green, reads: "THE | IVORY | TOWER | HENRY | JAMES | 6/- [in large bold type] | NET | COLLINS". The back cover, lettered in brown, reads: "Collins' Autumn Publications, 1917 | [long thin double rule] | [followed by 14 titles, including 3 by James] | [short rule] | LONDON 48 PALL MALL | W. COLLINS SONS & CO. LTD. | GLASGOW MELBOURNE AUCKLAND". The front and back inner flaps are blank.

Priced at 6s. The ad on the back cover of the dust-jacket states that *The Ivory Tower* and *The Sense of the Past* were also sold as a set "2 Vols. 12/- net".

It is highly unlikely that the difference between the color of the print on the spine of the dust-jacket and that on its front and back covers can be attributed to changes in the color of the ink over time.

77.2.0. *The Ivory Tower*, first edition, second impression, first binding state, one volume, London [n.d., 1917].

The title-page, size, collation, and contents (including the frontispiece photographic portrait of James tipped in after [ii]) are identical to those of the first edition, first impression, 77.1.0, except that the verso of the title-leaf reads: "COPYRIGHT [in italic] | First impression, September 1917 | Second impression, October 1917".

Binding: dark blue smooth cloth with lettering in gilt identical to that on 77.1.0. The endpapers are of cream wove paper, and the text is printed on cream wove paper. The top edge is trimmed, and the other edges are untrimmed.

On the front free endpaper is the inscription: "Violet- | Christmas. 1917. | From Father." On the rear pastedown is a small black ticket printed in gold that reads: "The Times Book Club | 380 Oxford St., London, W. 1."

77.2.1. *The Ivory Tower*, first edition, second impression, second binding state, one volume, London [n.d., 1917].

Size: 7 7/16" x 5".

The title-page, collation, and contents are identical to the first edition, first impression, 77.1.0, except that the frontispiece photographic portrait of James is not present, and the title-leaf verso reads: "COPYRIGHT [in italic] | First Impression, September 1917 | Second Impression, October 1917".

Binding: charcoal-gray linen-grain cloth lettered in red. The front cover reads: "THE IVORY TOWER | HENRY JAMES". The back cover is neither lettered nor decorated. The spine reads: "THE | IVORY | TOWER | HENRY | JAMES | COLLINS". The endpapers are of white wove paper, and the text is printed on wove paper. All edges are trimmed, and the top edge is stained brown.

This is the secondary binding state of the second impression. It is uniform with that on the first edition, second impression, second binding state, of *The Sense of the Past*, 78.3.0.

THE IVORY TOWER

77.3.0. *The Ivory Tower*, first American edition, first impression, one volume, New York 1917.

THE IVORY TOWER | BY | HENRY JAMES | NEW YORK | CHARLES SCRIBNER'S SONS | 1917

Size: $7\,3/8''$ x $4\,7/8''$.

Collation: [unsigned, $1–23^8$]; pp. $1\pi–2\pi$ [i–viii], 1–357 [358].

Contents: $1\pi–2\pi$ blank, verso ad headed: "BOOKS BY HENRY JAMES", listing 12 titles and *The Novels and Tales* (The New York Edition) in 26 volumes, all without dollar prices; [i–ii] half-title, verso blank; [iii–iv] title-page, verso copyright notice, printing history and printer's device: "Copyright, 1917, by | CHARLES SCRIBNER'S SONS | [rule] Published October, 1917 | [printer's device of the Scribner's Press]"; v–vi "PREFACE", verso continuation of preface; [vii–viii] "CONTENTS", verso blank; 1–357 text; [358] blank.

Binding: dull olive sateen. The front and back covers are neither lettered nor decorated. The spine, lettered and decorated in gilt, reads: "THE | IVORY | TOWER | [leaf device] | HENRY | JAMES | SCRIBNERS". The publisher's imprint at the foot of the spine is in uniform capitals $3/16''$ high. The endpapers are of cream wove paper, and the text is printed on cream wove paper. The top edge is gilt, the fore-edge is rough trimmed, and the bottom edge is trimmed.

Dust-jacket: cream smooth wove paper, lettered and decorated in black. The front cover reads: "THE IVORY TOWER | AN UNFINISHED NOVEL | By HENRY JAMES | CHARLES SCRIBNER'S SONS". The spine reads: "THE | IVORY | TOWER | [leaf device] | HENRY | JAMES | $1.50 | NET [this and the preceding line in sans-serif] | SCRIBNERS". The back cover is an ad headed: "By HENRY JAMES", followed by 12 titles (each of which is with a press opinion and the dollar price), with a double rule after the titles, and the publisher's imprint at the foot. The front and back inner flaps are blank.

American printing history. Scribner's Archive. cards (2) Box 13: Id-J. First edition: *first impression* 1,500 copies printed October 9, 1917, all bound between October 23, 1917, and June 6, 1924; published October 26, 1917; notations: "10/25/17 1,500 cover wraps". On December 18, 1917, three days after the second impression was printed, there were still 549 copies of the first impression in the bindery. Opposite the binding order of January 27, 1921, (when 248 copies remained in the bindery) is the notation "NEW ED[ition]"; *second impression* (on card headed James XXV Ivory Tower) 800 copies printed December 15, 1917, all but 150 bound between January [no day] 1918, and April 5, 1924; notations: "850 Frontis [$] 15.84 | 850 Tissues"; "Ltd Ed 140 [referring to copies bound uniformly with The New York Edition] | 1/31/18 [less]126 | [equals]14 [remaining] | Parker 191 | P.W 230 | 426. 4/5/24 – 4". Opposite the binding orders of May [no day] 1919 and October [no day] 1920, (each an order for 50 copies) are the notations: "3/5/19 50 N[ew]S[tyle]" and "5/4/20 50 N[ew] S[tyle]".

Priced at $1.50 net. Both impressions were printed and bound by Scribner's. The type of paper used is not recorded.

It would appear that the "New Edition" is not a new impression but merely a different binding, and that some of the second impression sheets were bound uniform with those of The New York edition and that others were bound in the so called "New Style" binding. The card for the second impression records two separate binding costs: 25.5 cents (per copy) and "Ltd 45 c[ents]". The references to frontispieces with a tissue guard indicates that the second impression copies have such a frontispiece, which was not included in the first impression copies. Copies of the second impression bound uniformly with the New York Edition have a frontispiece with a tissue guard. That frontispiece is entitled "On the Cliff Walk, Newport."

It is curious that a second impression of 800 copies was printed on December 15, 1917, when two days later 549 copies of the first impression were still in the bindery.

This was issued as a companion volume to the first American edition, first impression, of *The Sense of the Past* and hence it has a uniform binding. One hundred and forty-four sets of sheets of the second impression of this edition, in a larger page size and different binding, was also issued as Volume 26 of the American edition of *The Novels and Tales of Henry James*; see 64.1.0.

78. *THE SENSE OF THE PAST*

78.1.0. *The Sense of the Past*, first edition, first impression, one volume, London [n.d., 1917].

THE SENSE OF | THE PAST | BY | HENRY JAMES | LONDON: 48 PALL MALL | W. COLLINS SONS & CO. LTD. | GLASGOW MELBOURNE AUCKLAND

Size: $7\,^{11}/_{16}''$ x $5\,^{1}/_{8}''$.

Collation: π^4 (π_1 +X_1) A–I K–U X–Y^8; pp. [i–viii], 1–[351] [352] plus 2.

Contents: [i–ii] half-title, verso blank; frontispiece photographic portrait of James with tissue guard tipped in not reckoned in the pagination; [iii–iv] title-page, verso copyright notice: "Copyright [in italic] | 1917"; v–vi "PREFACE", verso continuation of preface; [vii–viii]. "CONTENTS", verso blank; 1–[351] text; [351] at foot printer's imprint: "GLASGOW: PRINTED AT THE UNIVERSITY PRESS BY ROBERT MACLEHOSE AND CO. LTD."; [352] blank.

Binding: dark blue smooth cloth. The front cover, lettered in gilt, reads: "THE | SENSE OF THE PAST | HENRY JAMES". The back cover is neither lettered nor decorated. The spine, lettered in gilt, reads: "THE | SENSE | OF THE | PAST | HENRY | JAMES | COLLINS". The endpapers are of cream wove paper, and the text is printed on cream wove paper. The top edge is trimmed and stained ochre, and the other edges are untrimmed.

This binding is uniform with those on the first edition, first impression, of *The Ivory Tower* and *The Middle Years*, 77.1.0 and 79.1.0

Dust-jacket: gray mottled wove paper. The front cover, lettered in brown, reads: "THE | SENSE OF THE PAST | HENRY JAMES | [within a thin brown single-rule frame is an applied black-and-white photographic portrait of James reproducing the frontispiece] | '[blurb] Printed with the novel is the unique sketch, written by | the author, outlining the story and indicating the method of | work of this great man of letters, whose death, in December, | 1915 [*sic*, February, 1916], was mourned by all lovers of literature.'" The spine, lettered in brown, reads: "THE | SENSE | OF THE | PAST | HENRY | JAMES | 6/- [in large bold type] | NET | COLLINS". The back cover, lettered in brown, reads: "Collins' Autumn Publications, 1917 | [long thin double rules] | [followed by 14 titles, including 3 by James] | [short rule] | London 48

THE SENSE OF THE PAST

Pall Mall | W. COLLINS SONS & CO. LTD. | GLASGOW MELBOURNE AUCKLAND". The front and back inner flaps are blank.

This dust-jacket is uniform with that on the first edition of *The Ivory Tower*, 77.1.0, except that the spine of this dust-jacket is lettered in brown rather than sage-green.

Priced at 6s. net, and as a set with *The Ivory Tower* at 12s. net.

78.2.0. *The Sense of the Past*, first edition, second impression, first binding state, one volume, London [n.d., 1917].

The title-page, size, collation, and contents (including the frontispiece photographic portrait of James tipped in after [ii]) are identical to the first edition, first impression, 78.1.0, except that the title-leaf verso reads: "COPYRIGHT [in italic] | First Impression, September 1917 | Second Impression, October 1917".

Binding: dark blue smooth cloth with lettering in gilt identical to that on 78.1.0. The endpapers are of cream wove paper, and the text is printed on wove paper. The top edge is trimmed and stained ochre, and the other edges are untrimmed.

This is the primary binding of the second impression.

78.3.0. *The Sense of the Past*, first edition, second impression, second binding state, one volume, London [n.d., 1917].

Size: $7\,3/8''$ x $4\,15/16''$.

The title-page, collation, and contents are identical to the first edition, first impression, 78.1.0, except that the frontispiece photographic portrait of James is not present, and the title-leaf verso reads: "COPYRIGHT [in italic] | First Impression, September 1917 | Second Impression, October 1917".

Binding: charcoal-gray linen-grain cloth lettered in red. The front cover reads: "THE | SENSE OF THE PAST | HENRY JAMES". The back cover is neither lettered nor decorated. The spine reads: "THE | SENSE | OF THE | PAST | HENRY | JAMES | COLLINS". The endpapers are of white wove paper, and the text is printed on wove paper. All edges are trimmed.

THE SENSE OF THE PAST

This is the secondary binding of the second impression which is uniform with the first edition, second impression, second binding state of *The Ivory Tower*, 77.2.1.

78.4.0. *The Sense of The Past*, first American edition, first impression, first binding state, one volume, New York 1917.

THE | SENSE OF THE PAST | BY | HENRY JAMES | NEW YORK | CHARLES SCRIBNER'S SONS | 1917

Size: 7 3/8″ x 4 7/8″.

Collation: [unsigned, 1–23^8]; pp. [i–x], 1–358.

Contents: [i–ii] blank, verso ad headed: "BOOKS BY HENRY JAMES", listing 12 titles and *The Novels and Tales* (The New York Edition) in 26 volumes, all without dollar prices; [iii–iv] half-title, verso blank; [v–vi] title-page, verso copyright notice, printing history and printer's device: "Copyright, 1917, by | CHARLES SCRIBNER'S SONS | [rule] | Published October, 1917 | [printer's device of the Scribner's Press]"; [vii–viii] "PREFACE", verso blank; [ix–x] "CONTENTS", verso blank; 1–358 text.

Binding: dull olive sateen. The front and back covers are neither lettered nor decorated. The spine, lettered and decorated in gilt, reads: "THE | SENSE OF | THE PAST | [leaf device] | HENRY | JAMES | SCRIBNERS". The publisher's imprint at the foot of the spine is in uniform capitals 3/16″ high. The endpapers are of cream wove paper, and the text is printed on cream wove paper. The top edge is gilt, the fore-edge is rough trimmed, and the bottom edge is trimmed.

Dust-jacket: cream smooth wove paper lettered and decorated in black. The front cover reads: "THE | SENSE OF THE PAST | AN UNFINISHED NOVEL | By HENRY JAMES | CHARLES SCRIBNER'S SONS". The spine reads: "THE | SENSE OF | THE PAST | [leaf device] | HENRY | JAMES | $1.50 | NET [this and the preceding line in sans-serif] | SCRIBNERS". The back cover is an ad for works "By HENRY JAMES", followed by 11 titles, each of which is with a press opinion and the dollar price, with a double rule after the titles, and the publisher's imprint at the foot.

This dust-jacket is uniform with the dust-jacket of the first American edition of *The Ivory Tower*, 77.3.0.

THE SENSE OF THE PAST

American printing history. Scribner's Archive. cards (2) Box 13: Id-J. First edition: *first impression* 1,500 copies printed October 15, 1917, all bound between October 23, 1917, and June 6, 1924; published October 26, 1917; notations: "10/25/17 1,500 cover wraps", and opposite the binding order of September 25, 1923, (when 153 copies remained unbound at the bindery) is the notation: "NEW ED[ition]"; *second impression* (on card headed "James XXVI Sense of the Past") 800 copies printed December 15, 1917, all but 150 bound between January [no day] 1918, and April 5, 1924; notations: "850 Frontis [$]15.84 | Tissues", "Ltd Ed 140 [referring to copies bound uniformly with The New York Edition] | 1/31/18 [less] 126 | [equals] 14 [remaining] | 4/5/24 [less] 4 | 10 [remaining]", and opposite binding order of April 5, 1924, "3/5/19 50 N.S. 5/6/20 50 N[ew].S[tyle]." Notation: "4/1/20 James Letters 2 Vols. From Binder 100 sets same style".

Priced at $1.50 net. Both impressions were printed and bound by Scribner's. The type of paper used is not recorded.

It would appear that the "New Edition" is not a new impression but merely a different binding, and that some of the second impression sheets were bound uniform with those of the New York edition and that others were bound in the so called "New Style" binding. The references to frontispieces with a tissue guard indicates that the second impression copies have such a frontispiece, which was not included in the first impression copies; see the printing history of *The Ivory Tower*, 77.3.0. Copies of the second impression bound uniformly with the New York Edition have a frontispiece with a tissue guard. That frontispiece is entitled: "31 Lowndes Square, Mr. Lowell's House while Minister in England."

This was issued as a companion volume to the first American edition, first impression, of *The Ivory Tower* and hence it has a uniform binding. One hundred and forty-four sets of sheets of the second impression of this edition, in a larger page size and different binding, was also issued as Volume XXVI of the American edition of *The Novels and Tales of Henry James*; see 64.1.0.

78.5.0. *The Sense of the Past*, first American edition, first (?) impression, second binding state, one volume, New York 1917.

The title-page, size, collation, and contents are identical to those of the first American edition, first impression, first binding state, 78.4.0.

Binding: brown smooth sateen cloth (slightly browner and less olive than the preceding copy), lettered and decorated identically to 78.4.0. The endpapers are of white wove paper, and the text is printed on wove paper. The top edge is trimmed and stained ochre, the fore-edge is untrimmed, and the bottom edge is trimmed.

This copy is in the secondary binding noted in E&L A78b, which records it as bound in linen-grain cloth, which is not the case with this copy.

⚜

79. THE MIDDLE YEARS

79.1.0. *The Middle Years*, first edition, first impression, one volume, London [n.d., 1917].

THE | MIDDLE YEARS | BY | HENRY JAMES | LONDON: 48 PALL MALL | W. COLLINS SONS & CO. LTD. | GLASGOW MELBOURNE AUCKLAND

Size: $7\,^{11}/_{16}''$ x $5\,^{3}/_{16}''$.

Collation: π^4 ($\pi_2 + X_1$)A–G^8 H^4; pp. [2] [i–vi], 1–[118] [119–120] plus 2.

Contents: blank leaf, [i–ii] half-title, verso copyright notice: "COPYRIGHT 1917 [in italic]"; frontispiece sketch of James with tissue guard tipped in not reckoned in the pagination; [iii–iv] title-page, verso blank; [v–vi] "EDITOR'S NOTE [in italic]", verso blank; 1–[118] text; [118] at foot printer's imprint: "GLASGOW: PRINTED AT THE UNIVERSITY PRESS BY ROBERT MACLEHOSE AND CO. LTD."; [119–120] blank leaf.

Binding: dark blue smooth cloth. The front cover, lettered in gilt, reads: "THE MIDDLE YEARS | HENRY JAMES". The back cover is neither lettered nor decorated. The spine, lettered in gilt, reads: "THE | MIDDLE | YEARS | HENRY | JAMES | COLLINS". The endpapers are of cream wove paper, and the text is printed on heavy stiff white wove paper. The top edge is trimmed, and the other edges are untrimmed. This binding is uniform with those on the first edition, first impression of *The Ivory Tower* and *The Sense of the Past*, 77.1.0 and 78.1.0.

Dust-jacket: gray mottled wove paper. The front cover, lettered in brown, reads: "THE MIDDLE YEARS | HENRY JAMES | [within a thin brown single-rule frame is an applied black-and-white sketch of Henry James reproducing the frontispiece] | '[blurb] A most interesting phase of the life of HENRY JAMES- | his first experience, as a man, of the London he loved so well.'" The spine, lettered in sage-green, reads: "THE | MIDDLE | YEARS | HENRY | JAMES | 5/- [in large bold type] | NET | COLLINS". The back cover, which is lettered in brown, reads: "COLLINS' AUTUMN PUBLICATIONS, 1917 | [a long thin double rule] | [followed by a list of 14 titles, including 3 by James] | [short rule] | London 48 Pall Mall | W. COLLINS SONS & CO. LTD. | GLASGOW MELBOURNE AUCKLAND". The front and back inner flaps are blank.

This dust-jacket is uniform with those of the first edition, first impression of *The Ivory Tower* and *The Sense of the Past*, 77.1.0 and 78.1.0, in all respects, including the ads.

The title-page has on it embossed in blind "REVIEW COPY".

Priced at 5s. net.

79.2.0. *The Middle Years*, first edition, second impression, one volume, London [n.d., 1917].

This copy is identical to the first edition, first impression, 79.1.0, except that the verso of the half-title-leaf reads: "COPYRIGHT [in italic] | First Impression, October 1917 | Second Impression, October 1917".

Noted in BAL 10699, but not in E&L.

79.3.0. *The Middle Years*, first American edition, one volume, New York 1917.

THE | MIDDLE YEARS | BY | HENRY JAMES | NEW YORK | CHARLES SCRIBNER'S SONS | 1917

Size: 8 3/16" x 5 1/2".

Collation: [unsigned, 1^8 (1$_2$ +X$_1$) 2–8^8]; pp. [i–viii], 1–119 [120] plus 2.

Contents: [i–ii] blank, verso ad headed: "By HENRY JAMES", listing 4 titles without dollar prices; [iii–iv] half-title, verso blank; photographic portrait of James with tissue guard tipped in not reckoned in the pagination; [v–vi] title-page, verso copyright notice, printing history and printer's device: "Copyright, 1917, by | CHARLES SCRIB-NER'S SONS | [rule] | Published November, 1917 | [printer's device of the Scribner's Press]"; [vii–viii] "EDITOR'S NOTE", verso blank; 1–119 text; [120] blank.

Binding: olive-brown sateen. The front cover, lettered in gilt within a single-rule gilt frame, reads: "THE MIDDLE | YEARS | HENRY JAMES". The back cover is neither lettered nor decorated. The spine, lettered and decorated in gilt, reads: "THE | MIDDLE | YEARS | [rule] | HENRY | JAMES | SCRIBNERS". The publisher's imprint at the foot of the spine is in uniform capitals $^{3}/_{16}$" high. The endpapers are of cream wove paper, and the text is printed on cream wove paper. The top edge is trimmed, and the other edges are untrimmed.

Dust-jacket: buff wove paper printed in black. The front cover reads: [within a small single-rule frame] "THE MIDDLE | YEARS | HENRY JAMES"; beneath the frame is a six-line blurb which reads: "These reminiscences cover Mr. James's memories of his | early London life, including recollections of Tennyson, | George Eliot, Lowell, when he held the English mis- | sion, and many others, besides delightful sketches of | the daily life and surroundings which then had for | James all the charm of novelty." At the foot of the front cover is the publisher's imprint. The spine reads: THE | MIDDLE | YEARS | [rule] | $1.25 | NET [this and the preceding line in sans-serif] | SCRIBNERS". The back cover is an ad for works: "By HENRY JAMES", listing 11 titles, each with press opinion and the dollar price, with a double-rule after the titles, and the publisher's imprint at the foot. The front and back inner flaps are blank.

This dust-jacket is uniform with those of the first American editions of *The Ivory Tower* (1917) and *The Sense of the Past* (1917), 77.3.0 and 78.4.0, in all respects, including the ads.

American printing history. Scribner's Archive. Card (1) Box 13: Id-J. First edition: *first* (and sole) *impression* 1,275 copies printed November 9, 1917, 1255 copies bound between November 21, 1917, and February 28, 1920; published November 23, 1917; notation: "11/17/17 1,300 cover wraps".

Priced at $1.25 net.

GABRIELLE DE BERGERAC

80. *GABRIELLE DE BERGERAC*

80.1.0. *Gabrielle de Bergerac*, first edition, first impression, one volume, New York 1918.

GABRIELLE De BERGERAC | BY HENRY JAMES | [vertical oval publisher's device reading "BL"] | NEW YORK | BONI AND LIVERIGHT | 1918

Size: 7 3/8″ x 4 5/8″.

Collation: [unsigned, 1–9⁸ 10⁶]; pp. [1–6], 7–153, [154] [155–156].

Contents: [1–2] half-title, verso blank; [3–4] title-page, verso copyright notice: "Copyright, 1918. | By BONI & LIVERIGHT, Inc."; [5–6] fly-title, verso blank; 7–153 text, [154] blank; [155–156] blank leaf.

Binding: white linen quarter cloth with green paper over boards. The front cover, lettered and decorated in black within a thick and thin black rule border with a fern leaf device inside each of the four corners, reads: "GABRIELLE DE | BERGERAC | BY | HENRY JAMES | [decorative rule] | BONI AND LIVERIGHT | NEW YORK". The back cover is neither lettered nor decorated. The spine, lettered and decorated in black, reads: "GABRIELLE | De BERGERAC | [rule] | JAMES [all the foregoing in sans-serif] | BONI AND LIVERIGHT". The endpapers are of smooth cream wove paper, and the text is printed on thick cream wove paper. There are no binder's fly-leaves. All edges are trimmed.

Dust-jacket: cream colored wove paper, the front and rear covers of which are green, and the spine is cream, all of which are lettered and decorated in black. The front cover of the dust-jacket exactly replicates the front cover of the book. The back cover has centered on it the oval Penguin logo in black, which is not on the back cover of the book. The spine reads: "GABRIELLE | DE | BERGERAC | $1.25 | net | BONI | & | LIVERIGHT". The front and back inner flaps are cream colored, and are lettered in black. On the front inner flap is an ad for: "THE PENGUIN SERIES", with a 10-line description of the series, followed by 4 new titles to be issued (including this one). On the back inner flap is an ad for: "The Modern Library", with a long run-on list of "Representative titles", starting with *The Red Lily* and ending with "Beardsley, etc."

Priced at $1.25. This title was not published in England.

Illustrated Plate 30.

80.2.0. *Gabrielle de Bergerac*, first edition, second impression, one volume, New York 1918.

The title-page, size, collation, and contents are identical to those of the first edition, first impression, 80.1.0, except that the title-page has between the author's name and the publisher's imprint the oval Penguin logo with lettering around the oval reading: "THE PENGUIN SERIES [in sans-serif]"; and the verso of the title-leaf reads: "Copyright, 1918. | By BONI & LIVERIGHT, Inc. | [rule] | First Printing...October, 1918 | Second Printing...December, 1918 [all after the rule in italic]".

Binding: identical to that of 80.1.0, except for the addition of the oval penguin logo (with lettering around the oval) on the spine between the author's name and the publisher's imprint. There is a binder's fly-leaf of wove paper at the back, but none at the front.

Dust-jacket: Identical to that on, 80.1.0, that is, without the rule and author's name on the spine.

80.3.0. *Gabrielle de Bergerac*, first edition, second impression, one volume, New York 1918.

The title-page, size, collation, contents and binding are identical to those of the first edition, second impression, 80.2.0.

Binding: identical to that on 80.2.0, except that there are no binder's fly-leaves.

Dust-jacket: identical to that on the first edition, first impression, 80.1.0, except that the spine reads: "GABRIELLE | DE | BERGERAC | [rule] | HENRY | JAMES | $ 1.25 | net | BONI | & | LIVERIGHT", that is a rule and the author's name have been added.

Illustrated Plate 30.

81. *WITHIN THE RIM*

81.1.0. *Within the Rim*, first edition, first impression, one volume, London [n.d., 1919].

WITHIN THE RIM | AND OTHER ESSAYS | 1914–15 | HENRY JAMES | [square publisher's device] | LONDON: 48 PALL MALL | W. COLLINS SONS & CO. LTD. | GLASGOW MELBOURNE AUCKLAND

Size: $7\,7/8''$ x $5\,3/16''$.

Collation: $[A]^8$ B–G^8 H^4; pp. [1–10], 11–[119] [120].

Contents: [1–2] half-title, verso blank; [3–4] title-page, verso copyright notice: "Copyright 1918"; [5–6] acknowledgements, verso blank; [7–8] "CONTENTS", verso blank; [9–10] divisional fly-title, verso blank; 11–[119] text; [119] at foot publisher's imprint: "GLASGOW: W. COLLINS SONS AND CO. LTD."; [120] blank.

Binding: smooth dark blue cloth. The front cover, lettered in gilt, reads: "WITHIN THE RIM | HENRY JAMES". The back cover is neither lettered nor decorated. The spine, lettered in gilt, reads: "WITHIN | THE | RIM | HENRY | JAMES | COLLINS". The endpapers are of cream wove paper, and the text is printed on stiff cream wove paper. The top edge is trimmed, and the other edges are untrimmed.

This binding is uniform with those on the first editions, first impressions of *The Ivory Tower*, *The Sense of the Past* and *The Middle Years*, 77.1.0, 78.1.0, and 79.1.0.

Dust-jacket: light gray wove paper, lettered and decorated in dark blue. The front cover has centered on it within a thin single-rule frame a 14-line blurb for this book, above which appears the title, and below which is the author's name. The spine reads: "WITHIN | THE | RIM | HENRY | JAMES | 6/- [in a very large and bold type] | NET | COLLINS". The rear cover is headed "COLLINS' PUBLICATIONS, 1918", followed by a double rule, below which is a double-column list of 25 titles (none by James), 12 in the first column, 13 in the second (the columns being separated by a long vertical single rule), with the publisher's imprint at the foot below a double rule. The dust-jacket is approximately $1/4''$ shorter in length than the cover of the book. The front and back inner flaps, which are only approximately $1\,1/2''$ wide, are blank. The dust-jacket has been on the book for some time as the upper portion of the covers and spine not covered by it are sunned.

TRAVELLING COMPANIONS

The title-page is blind stamped "review copy" within an oval.

A further impression was published by W. Collins and Co. Ltd., probably in the early 1920s as number 33 in their series Collins' Kings' Way Classics. It was priced at 3s. 6d. net. This title was not published in America.

81.2.0. *Within the Rim*, first edition, first impression, colonial issue, one volume, London [n.d., 1919].

The title-page, size, collation, and contents are identical to those of the first edition, first impression, 81.1.0.

Binding: smooth dark blue cloth, lettered in gilt on the front cover and spine identically to 81.1.0. The endpapers and the treatment of the edges are also identical to 81.1.0.

Dust-jacket: identical to the dust-jacket on 81.1.0, except that on the spine the price "6/-" has been covered by a paper label (1 $^1/_{16}$" (height) x $^7/_{16}$") on which, printed in dark blue, are two concentric ovals with the words "COLONIAL EDITION" printed in the space between them. As the label is wider than the spine of the dust-jacket, it extends slightly over the front and back covers.

Not noted in E&L.

❧✛❧

82. *TRAVELLING COMPANIONS*

82.1.0. *Travelling Companions*, first edition, first binding state, one volume, New York 1919.

TRAVELLING | COMPANIONS | BY | HENRY JAMES | [vertical oval publisher's device reading "BL"] | BONI AND LIVERIGHT | New York 1919

Size: 7 $^5/_{16}$" x 5".

Collation: [unsigned, 1–20^8]; pp. [i–x], 1–309 [310].

Contents: [i–ii] half-title, verso blank; [iii–iv] title-page, verso copyright notice and place of printing: "Copyright, 1919, | By Boni & Liveright, Inc. | Printed in the U.S.A. [in italic]"; [v–vi] "CONTENTS", verso blank; vii–ix "FOREWORD"; [x] blank; 1–309 text; [310] blank.

TRAVELLING COMPANIONS

Binding: Kelly-green linen-grain cloth. The front cover, lettered in gilt within a small gilt frame divided into two unequal panels by a horizontal gilt rule, reads: "Travelling | Companions | By Henry James". The back cover is neither lettered nor decorated. The spine, lettered and decorated in gilt, reads: "Travelling | Companions | [gilt rule] | by | Henry | James | BONI AND | LIVERIGHT". The publisher's imprint on the spine is in uniform capitals $3/4''$ wide. The endpapers are of smooth cream wove paper, and the text is printed on white wove paper. All edges are trimmed.

Dust-jacket: a pictorial dust-jacket of light tan wove paper. On the front cover, within a single-rule border, the title is in a freehand black printed script on two lines across the top, below which, on the left, is a freely rendered scene of a couple embarking at a train station, and on the right printed in red in a vertical column is a 22-line blurb about this book. Below this, across the bottom, is: "by [in black] | HENRY JAMES [in red]". On the lower left, in black, is the artist's name, "H. BRODZKY". The back cover, printed in black, reads: "[below a double rule] THE PENGUIN SERIES [in sans-serif] | [single rule] | [followed by a nine line description of the series] | Price $1.25 Each | To be Published April 20th | [followed by 2 titles] | Already Published | [followed by 4 titles]". At the bottom of the back cover is: "[single rule] | BONI & LIVERIGHT, Publishers, NEW YORK | [double rule]". The spine reads: "[in black] TRAVELLING | COMPANIONS | [single rule] | [in red] HENRY | JAMES | [in black and gray, a picture of a steam ship under sail] | [in red] 1.75 [sic] | net | [in a black script simulating handwriting] Boni & | Liveright". The front inner flap, printed in black, reads: "[double rule] | THE MODERN LIBRARY | OF THE WORLD'S BEST BOOKS | [double rule] | [nine line blurb] | [titles of volumes 1 to 36]". The back inner flap, also printed in black, continues the list with titles of volumes 37 to 68, followed by "To be Published April 20th", beneath which are titles of volumes 69 to 77.

Priced at $1.75. This title was not published in England.

Illustrated Plate 31.

BAL 10703 notes two states of the binding. The first with the publisher's imprint on the spine $3/4''$ wide, as on this copy (to which it assigns priority), and a second on which such imprint is $1''$ wide.

A LANDSCAPE PAINTER

83. *A LANDSCAPE PAINTER*

83.1.0. *A Landscape Painter*, first edition, first impression, trade issue, one volume, New York 1919 [1920].

A LANDSCAPE | PAINTER | By | HENRY JAMES | [triangular publisher's device] | New York | SCOTT AND SELTZER | 1919

Size: 7 1/4" x 4 15/16".

Collation: [unsigned, 1–17^8 18^4 19^8]; pp. [i–vi], 1–4 [5–6], 7–287 [288] [289–290].

Contents: [i–ii] half-title, verso blank; [iii–iv] title-page, verso copyright notice, place of printing and reservation of rights: "Copyright, 1919, | By Scott and Seltzer, Inc. | Printed in the United States of America | All rights reserved"; [v–vi] "CONTENTS", verso blank; 1–4 "PREFACE"; [5–6] divisional fly-title, verso blank; 7–287 text; [288] blank; [289–290] blank leaf.

Binding: dark green vertical-rib-grain cloth. The front cover is decorated in blind with a single-rule border and two long rules at right angles forming four panels. The back cover is neither lettered nor decorated. The spine, lettered and decorated in gilt, reads: "A | LANDSCAPE | PAINTER | [rule] | HENRY | JAMES | SCOTT | AND | SELTZER". The endpapers are of cream wove paper, and the text is printed on cream wove paper. All edges are trimmed, and the top edge appears to be stained ochre.

Dust-jacket: tan wove paper with all lettering and design elements printed in black. The front cover has a double-rule border divided by one horizontal double rule forming two panels. The upper panel reads: "A LANDSCAPE | PAINTER | By HENRY JAMES". The lower panel has a 12-line blurb about this book. The spine reads: "[double rule] | A | LANDSCAPE | PAINTER | [double rule] | HENRY JAMES | [double rule] | $1.75 | NET | [triangular publisher's device] | [double rule] | SCOTT | AND | SELTZER | [double rule]". The back cover, beneath a double rule, is entirely devoted to an ad for: "THE FORTUNE | A ROMANCE OF FRIENDSHIP | By DOUGLAS GOLDRING", with extensive press opinions. The publisher's imprint at the foot is between a set of double rules. The front inner flap has a blurb for *The Burning Secret* by Stephen Branch, with the publisher's imprint at the foot between a set of double rules, and the back inner flap has a blurb

A LANDSCAPE PAINTER

for *Sarah and Her Daughter* by Bertha Pearl, also with the publisher's imprint at the foot between a set of double rules.

This is a copy of the first impression dust-jacket with the first impression price of $1.75 net, which was raised to $2.00 for the second impression. The limited issue was priced at $5.00.

E&L A83a records the binding of this impression as dark green. BAL 10704 records the cloth color as green. The binding and dust-jacket are uniform with those on the first edition, trade issue, of *Master Eustace*, 85.1.0.

This impression was printed in December 1919 but was not published until January 2, 1920; see BAL 10704. This title was not published in England.

83.2.0. *A Landscape Painter*, first edition, first impression, limited issue, one volume, New York 1919 [1920].

Size: $7\,^{13}/_{16}$" x $5\,^{1}/_{4}$".

The title-page, collation, and contents are identical to those of the first edition, first impression, trade issue, 83.1.0. The limitation notice is on the paper label on the spine.

Binding: dark blue linen-grain cloth. The front and back covers are neither lettered nor decorated. The spine, which has a paper label lettered in black within a black double-rule border, reads: "A | LANDSCAPE | PAINTER | [rule] | HENRY | JAMES | [rule] | Special Issue of the | First Edition | Limited to 250 Copies | [rule] | SCOTT & SELTZER". The endpapers are of cream wove paper, and the text is printed on cream wove paper. All edges are untrimmed.

This copy is of untrimmed sheets of the first edition, first impression, trade issue, 83.1.0.

83.3.0. *A Landscape Painter*, first edition, second impression, one volume, New York 1919 [1920].

The title-page, size, collation, and contents of this copy are identical to those of the first edition, first impression, trade issue, 83.1.0 (including the 1919 date on the title-page), except that the verso of the title-leaf reads: "Copyright, 1919, | By Scott and Seltzer, Inc. | First printing, December, 1919. | Second printing, January, 1920. | Printed in the United States of America | All Rights Reserved".

Binding: dark green pebble-grain cloth, lettered and decorated identically to 83.1.0. The endpapers are of cream wove paper, and the text is printed on cream wove paper. All edges are trimmed, and the top edge appears to be stained ochre.

❦

84. *REFUGEES IN CHELSEA*

84.1.0. *Refugees in Chelsea*, first separate edition, one volume, Chelsea at the Ashendene Press [n.d., 1920].

REFUGEES IN CHELSEA | BY HENRY JAMES | Chelsea, at the Ashendene Press

Size: 11 3/8" x 8".

Collation: [unsigned, 1–4⁴]; pp. [8] [i–iv], 1–[12], [13–20].

Contents: eight blank pages (the first leaf serving as the front pastedown, and the second leaf serving as the front free endpaper); [i–ii] title-page, verso blank; [iii–iv] "FOREWORD", verso blank; 1–11 text (with a large rubricated "T" on 1); [12] colophon and limitation notice: "Printed by the kind permission of the Proprietors and Editor from 'The Times Literary Supplement' of March 23, 1916 by C. H. St J. Hornby at the Ashendene Press, Shelly House, Chelsea, in the month of April in the year 1920. | 50 copies on paper and 6 copies on vellum. For private circulation only"; [13–20] blank ([17–18] serving as the rear free endpaper and [19–20] serving as the rear pastedown).

Binding: quarter-bound light-brown linen shelfback, with blue-gray paper over boards. The front cover, lettered in black, reads: "REFUGEES IN CHELSEA | BY HENRY JAMES". The spine and back cover are neither lettered nor decorated. The text and other leaves are of hand made wove paper watermarked with a right facing arrow from the center of which is suspended a trumpet above a bar, and below which are the initials "C.H.StJ.H". All edges are untrimmed.

On [ii] is the bookplate of Clarence B. Hanson, Jr., and on [iii] the inscription "Graily Hewitt | from C.H.StJ. Hornby | Christmas, 1920".

Hornby was the printer of this book and Hewitt designed the rubricated "T" on 1.

The foreword was written by Logan Pearsall Smith. *Refugees in Chelsea* was first published in book form in *Within the Rim* (1919); see 81.1.0.

See C.H.St.J. Hornby, *A Descriptive Bibliography of Books Printed at the Ashendene Press 1895–1934* (Chelsea: Shelly House, 1935), 100, which records that this title was printed in Subiaco type, and that the six copies printed on velum were bound in morocco.

❧✚❧

85. MASTER EUSTACE

85.1.0. *Master Eustace*, first edition, trade issue, one volume, New York 1920.

MASTER EUSTACE | By | HENRY JAMES | [triangular publisher's device] | New York | THOMAS SELTZER | 1920

Size: 7 5/16" x 5".

Collation: [unsigned, 1–18^8]; pp. [i–vi] 1–4 [5–6], 7–280 [281–282].

Contents: [i–ii] half-title, verso blank; [iii–iv] title-page, verso copyright notice, place of printing and reservation of rights: "Copyright, 1920, by | THOMAS SELTZER, Inc. | Printed in the United States of America | All rights reserved"; [v–vi] "CONTENTS", verso blank; 1–4 "PREFACE"; [5–6] divisional fly-title, verso blank; 7–280 text; [281–282] blank leaf.

Binding: dark green vertical-rib-grain cloth. The front cover is decorated in blind with a single-rule border and two long rules at right angles forming four panels. The back cover is neither lettered nor decorated. The spine, lettered and decorated in gilt, reads: "MASTER | EUSTACE | [rule] | HENRY | JAMES | THOMAS | SELTZER". The endpapers are of cream wove paper, and the text is printed on cream wove paper watermarked with a circular device within which is a diamond shape containing the letter "D" and the words "MADE IN U.S.A.", and below that device the words "SUEDE FINISH". All edges are trimmed.

Dust-jacket: tan wove paper, lettered and decorated in olive-green. The front cover has a double ruled border divided by a horizontal double rule forming two panels. The upper panel reads: "MASTER | EUSTACE | By HENRY JAMES". The lower panel has a 12-line blurb for this work (the first six lines of which are set in a larger size type than the last six). The spine reads: "[double rule] | MASTER | EUSTACE | [double rule] | HENRY | JAMES | [double rule] | [triangular publisher's device] | [double rule] | THOMAS | SELTZER | [double rule]". The back cover, within a double ruled border, has two blurbs, the first for "MARIE-CLAIRE'S WORKSHOP | By MARGUERITE AUDOUX", and the second for "INVISIBLE TIDES | By BEATRICE KEAN SEYMOUR". At the foot between two sets of double rules is the publisher's imprint and address. The front inner flap has on the upper right the price, "$2.00", followed by a double rule, a blurb for "A LANDSCAPE PAINTER | By HENRY JAMES", a further double rule, and a second blurb for "SIDE ISSUES | By JEFFERY E. JEFFERY". At the bottom of this flap is a double rule. The back inner flap has beneath a double rule a blurb for "The Novel of the New Woman | [short rule] | WOMAN | By MAGDELEINE MARX", a double rule, followed by a second blurb for "THE DARK RIVER | By SARAH GERTRUDE MILLIN". At the bottom of this flap is a double rule.

This binding and dust-jacket are uniform with those of the first edition, trade issue, first impression, of *A Landscape Painter* (1920), 83.1.0.

Printing history. 1,500 copies of the trade issue were printed, and 300 of the limited issue. The trade issue was priced at $2.00, and the limited issue at $5.00. This title was not published in England.

85.2.0. *Master Eustace*, first edition, limited issue, one volume, New York 1920.

Size: 7 $^{11}/_{16}$" x 5 $^{1}/_{8}$".

The title-page, collation, and contents are identical to those of the first edition, trade issue, 85.1.0. There is no limitation notice.

Binding: dark blue smooth cloth, with no lettering or decoration on the front or back covers. The spine has a white paper applied label, reading: "MASTER | EUSTACE | [rule] HENRY | JAMES". There is no publisher's imprint at the foot of the spine. The endpapers are of cream wove paper, and the text is printed on cream wove paper watermarked as in 85.1.0. All edges are untrimmed.

This copy appears to be of untrimmed sheets of the first edition, trade issue, 85.1.0.

BAL 10707 notes a copy of this issue in The Library of Congress with the handwritten notation "300 copies".

❧✢❧

86. *THE NOVELS AND STORIES OF HENRY JAMES*

86.1.0. *Novels and Stories of Henry James*, first edition, "Crown Octavo" impression, 35 volumes, London 1921–1923.

[I] *Roderick Hudson.* One volume.

RODERICK HUDSON | BY | HENRY JAMES | MACMILLAN AND CO., LIMITED | ST. MARTIN'S STREET, LONDON | 1921

Size: 7 $^{9}/_{16}$" x 5".

Collation: $[a]^6$ b^8 B–I K–U X–Z 2A–2F^8 2G^{10}; pp. [i–xxviii], 1–[463] [464] [465–466] [467–468].

Contents: [i–ii] half-title, verso publisher's device, and office addresses; [iii–iv] title-page, verso copyright notice: "COPYRIGHT"; v–[vi] "NOTE", verso blank; vii–xxvii "PREFACE"; [xxviii] blank; 1–[463] text; [463] at foot printer's imprint: "Printed by R. & R. Clark, Limited, Edinburgh. [all except printer's name in italic]"; [464] blank; [465–466] ads headed on both pages: "THE NOVELS AND STORIES OF | HENRY JAMES [in sans-serif]", listing the 35 volumes; [467–468] blank leaf.

Binding: dark blue coarse linen-grain cloth. The front cover, lettered and decorated in gilt has the centered initials "HJ" intertwined with a flower and leaf device. The back cover is neither lettered nor decorated. The spine, lettered and decorated in gilt, reads: "[linear flower and intertwined leaf design] | RODERICK | HUDSON | HENRY | JAMES | MACMILLAN & Co. | [linear flower and intertwined leaf design]". The "o" in "Co" is raised above a dot. The endpapers are of white wove paper, and the text is printed on a slightly coarser wove paper. The top edge is untrimmed, and the fore-and bottom edges are rough trimmed.

The remaining 34 volumes are uniformly bound and decorated. The endpapers are of white wove paper, and the texts are printed on wove paper. Inserted ads, if present, are printed on bookstock. Titles that are in the collection are:

[III] *The Europeans.* One volume. Title-page dated 1921. Collation: [A]^2 B–I K–N^8 O^{10}; pp. [i–iv], 1–[209][210][211–212]. Leaf O$_{10}$ is two pages of ads, as in *Roderick Hudson.*

[IV] *Confidence.* One volume. Title-page dated 1921. Collation: [A]^2 B–I K–R^8 S^8 (–S$_8$); pp. [i–iv], 1–[270]. There are no ads at the end.

[V] *Washington Square.* One volume. Title-page dated 1921. Collation: [A]^2 B–I K–P^8 Q^6(–Q$_6$); pp. [i–iv], 1–[234]. There are no ads at the end.

[VI & VII] *The Portrait of a Lady.* Two volumes. Title-pages dated 1921. Collation: Volume I: [a]^4 b^8 B–I K–U X–Z 2A^8 2B^6; pp. [i–xxiv], [1–378][379–380]. Leaf 2B$_6$ is two pages of ads, as in *Roderick Hudson.* Volume II: [A]^2 B–I K–U X–Z 2A–2B^8; pp. [i–iv], [1–382][383–384]. Leaf 2B$_8$ is two pages of ads, as in *Roderick Hudson.*

[VIII & IX] *The Bostonians.* Two volumes. Title-pages dated 1921. Collation: Volume I: [A]^2 B–I K–S^8; pp. [i–iv][1–2], 3–[267][268][269–272]. Leaves S$_{7, 8}$ are four pages of ads, the first two as in *Roderick Hudson,* the third headed: "THE LETTERS OF HENRY JAMES", and the last headed: "BY HENRY JAMES", listing five titles. Volume II: [A]^2 B–I K–S^8 T^2; pp. [i–iv][1–2], 3–[276]. There are no ads at the end of Volume II.

[X & XI] *The Princess Casamassima.* Two volumes. Title-pages dated 1921. Collation: Volume I: [a]^8 b^8 B–I K–U^8 X^{10}; pp. [2] [i–xxx], 1–[2] 3–[321][322][323–324]. Leaf X$_{10}$ is two pages of ads, as in *Roderick Hudson.* Volume II: [A]^8 B–I K–U X–Z 2A–2B^8; pp. [i–iv], [1–2], 3–[382] [383–384]. Leaf 2B$_8$ is two pages of ads, as in *Roderick Hudson.*

[XIV] *The Awkward Age.* One volume. Title-page dated 1922. Collation: [a]^6 b^8 B–I K–U X–Z 2A–2G^8 2H^{10} (2H$_{10}$+X$_1$); pp. [i–xxviii], 1–[2] 3–[483][484] plus 2. There is an additional leaf inserted at the end with two pages of ads, as in *Roderick Hudson.*

[XV] *The Spoils of Poynton.* One volume. Title-page dated 1922. Collation: [a]^8 b^8 B–I K–U X–Z 2A–2E^8 2F^4; pp. [2] [i–xxx], 1–438 [439–440]. Leaf 2F$_4$ is two pages of ads, as in *Roderick Hudson.*

[XVI] *What Maisie Knew.* One volume. Title-page dated 1922. Collation: [a]^6 b^8 B–I K–U X–Z 2A–2I 2K^8; pp. [i–xxviii] 1–[2], 3–[511][512]. There are no ads at the end.

[XVII] *The Aspern Papers*. One volume. Title-page dated 1922. Collation: $[a]^8 b^8$ B–I K–U X–Z^8 2A^{10}; pp. [2], [i–xxx] 1–[2], 3–[370] [371–372]. Leaf 2A$_{10}$ is two pages of ads, as in *Roderick Hudson*.

[XVIII] *The Reverberator*. One volume. Title-page dated 1922. Collation: $[a]^6 b^8$ B–I K–U X–Z 2A–2I^8; pp. [2], [i–xxvi], 1–[2] 3–[494] [495–496]. Leaf 2I$_8$ is two pages of ads, as in *Roderick Hudson*.

[XIX] *Lady Barbarina*. One volume. Title-page dated 1922. Collation: $[a]^6 b^8$ B–I K–U X–Z 2A–2I 2K–2L^8 2M^6; pp. [i–xxviii] 1–[2], 3–[538] [539–540]. Leaf 2M$_6$ is two pages of ads, as in *Roderick Hudson*.

[XX] *The Lesson of the Master* One volume. Title-page dated 1922. Collation: $[a]^4 b^8$ B–I K–U X–Y^8; pp. [i–xxiv] 1–[2], 3–[331] [332–336]. Leaves Y$_{7,8}$ are four pages of ads, as in volume I of *The Bostonians*.

[XXI] *The Author of Beltraffio*. One volume. Title-page dated 1922. Collation: $[A]^8$ B–I K–U X–Z 2A^8 2B^6 (–2B$_6$); pp. [i–xvi] 1–[2], 3–[376] [377–378]. Leaf 2B$_5$ is two pages of ads, as in *Roderick Hudson*.

[XXII] *The Altar of the Dead*. One volume. Title-page dated 1922. Collation: $[a]^8 b^{10}$ B–I K–U X–Z 2A–2G^8 2H^8 (–H$_8$); pp. [i–xxxvi] 1–[2], 3–[478]. There are no ads at the end.

[XXIII] *Daisy Miller*. One volume. Title-page dated 1922. Collation: $[a]^6 b^8$ B–I K–U X–Z 2A–2E^8 2F^{10} (2F$_{10}$+X$_1$); pp. [i–xxviii] 1–[2] 3–[452] plus 2. There is an additional leaf inserted at the end with two pages of ads, as in *Roderick Hudson*.

[XXIV] *Watch and Ward*. One volume. Title-page dated 1923. Collation: $[A]^4$ B–I K–U X–Z 2A–2F^8 2G^6 (–2G$_6$); pp. [i–viii] 1–[2], 3–[457] [458]. There are no ads at the end.

[XXV] *The Diary of a Man of Fifty*. One volume. Title-page dated 1923. Collation: $[A]^4$ B–I K–U X–Z 2A–2I^8 (2I$_8$+X$_1$); pp. [i–viii] 1–[2], 3–[496] plus 2. There is an additional leaf inserted at the end with two pages of ads, as in *Roderick Hudson*.

[XXVI] *The Last of the Valerii*. One volume. Title-page dated 1923. Collation: $[A]^4$ B–I K–U X–Z 2A–2H^8 2I^4; pp. [i–viii] 1–[2], 3–[486] [487–488]. 485 is mispaginated 48. Leaf 2I$_4$ is two pages of ads, as in *Roderick Hudson*.

[XXVII] *Lord Beaupré*. One volume. Title-page dated 1923. Collation: $[A]^4$ B–I K–U X–Z 2A–2H^8; pp. [i–viii] 1–[2], 3–[475] [476] [477–478] [479–480]. Leaf 2H$_7$ is two pages of ads, as in *Roderick Hudson*.

[XXVIII] *Maud-Evelyn* One volume. Title-page dated 1923. Collation: [A]⁴ B–I K–U X–Z 2A–2G⁸ 2H⁶; pp. [i–viii] 1–[2], 3–[474] [475–476]. Leaf $2H_6$ is two pages of ads, as in *Roderick Hudson*.

[XXIX] *The Sacred Fount*. One volume. Title-page dated 1923. Collation: [A]² B–I K–Q⁸ R⁶ (–R_6); pp. [i–iv] [1–2], 3–[249] [250]. There are no ads at the end.

[XXX & XXXI] *The Wings of the Dove*. Two volumes. Title-pages dated 1923. Collation: Volume I: [a]⁶ b⁸ B–I K–R⁸ S⁶; pp. [2] [i–xxvi] 1–[2], 3–[266] [267–268]. Leaf S_6 is two pages of ads, as in *Roderick Hudson*. Volume II: [A]² B–I K–U X–Z⁸ 2A⁶; pp. [i–iv] 1–[2], 3–[359] [360] [361–362] [363–364]. Leaf $2A_5$ is two pages of ads, as in *Roderick Hudson*.

[XXXII & XXXIII] *The Ambassadors*. Two volumes. Title-page dated 1923. Collation: Volume I: [a]⁶ b⁸ B–I K–Q⁸ R⁸ (–$R_{7,8}$); pp. [i–xxviii] 1–[2], 3–[252]. Volume II: [A]² B–I K–T⁸ U⁴ (–U_4); pp. [i–iv] 1–[2] 3–[293] [294]. There are no ads at the end of either volume.

[XXXIV & XXXV] *The Golden Bowl*. Two volumes. Title-pages dated 1923. Collation: Volume I: [a]⁸ b⁸ B–I K–U X–Z⁸ 2A⁴ ($2A_4 + X_1$); pp. [2] [i–xxx] 1–[2], 3–[360] plus 2. There is an additional leaf inserted at the end with two pages of ads, as in *Roderick Hudson*. Volume II: [A]² B–I K–U X⁸ Y⁴; pp. [i–iv] 1–[2], 3–[325] [326] [327–328]. Leaf $2A_4$ is two pages of ads, as in *Roderick Hudson*.

Printing history: Macmillan Archive. The printing history of *The Novels and Stories of Henry James*, edited by Percy Lubbock, is recorded in MPL 255924 (Nov. 4, 1919–Nov. 21, 1921), 55925 (Nov. 22, 1921–Apr. 14, 1924), and on 16 "cards" in the Macmillan Archive at Basingstoke. As these sources record, the 35 volumes of this title were published in two styles: a Crown Octavo impression, and a Pocket impression.

The Crown Octavo impression was published between January 11, 1921 (*Roderick Hudson*), and November 30, 1923 (Volume II of *The Golden Bowl*). The print order and the number of copies delivered for each of these 35 volumes was 1,000 copies. In most cases there is recorded an order for dust-jackets (termed "envelopes" in MPL), usually some time after the print order. Also, in most cases dust-jacket print orders specify that it be printed with "7/6 net". Dust-jacket print orders for this impression were for 1050 copies for each volume, but in one case the order was for only 500 copies (*The Princess Casamassima*), and in three cases there is no record of dust-jackets ordered (undoubtedly an oversight). The Crown Octavo impression was printed from standing type.[54] The paper used for this impression was "Norvel Quad Crown Antique Wove B" (sheet size 40″ x 30″) of varying weights (55, 60, 70, 80 and 120), the heavier weight being used for the volumes with fewer pages to obtain size uniformity. No reprint orders for either texts or dust-jackets of this impression are recorded in these two Ledgers or the cards.

Titles in the "Pocket" impression was published on the same dates as the Crown Octavo impression, and were printed from the same standing type as the Crown Octavo impression. The print order for the first four volumes of the Pocket impression (*Roderick Hudson, The American, The Europeans* and *Confidence*) was for 2,000 copies of each, but commencing with the fifth volume (*Washington Square*), and for the 30 subsequent volumes, the print order was reduced to 1,000 copies for each volume. This decision to reduce the print order was made in March 1921, *after* the first volume was published on January 11, 1921. For the first four volumes, 2,100 copies of the dust-jacket were ordered for each volume, and 1,050 copies for the subsequent volumes, except in two case where 500 copies were ordered (*The Bostonians* and *The Princess Casamassima*), and four cases where there is no order recorded (again, surely an oversight). The print orders for the dust-jackets record in most cases that they were to be printed with "7/6 net". The paper used for the Pocket impression was 32, 36, 40, 50 or 52 weight Bible paper, sheet size 28 $1/4$″ x 36″, again for size uniformity. However, in one case (*The Lesson of the Master*) 85 Bible paper was used with a sheet size of 36″ x 52 $1/4$″. In the case of five of the volumes of the Pocket impression *(The Author of Beltraffio, Maud Evelyn, The Wings of the Dove*, Volume I, and *The Golden Bowl*, both Volumes) there is the notation "impose for 32 pp. 2/6 insert". No such inserts have been seen. Nine of the titles of the Pocket impression were reprinted in a third impression (the second of the Pocket Edition) on various dates between 1928 and 1937 (see below). These later impressions were printed from stereotype plates made from moulds of the standing type taken at the time the Pocket and Crown Octavo impressions were first printed.

54 Scribners, through Pinker, urged Macmillan to use the plates of the New York Edition for *The Novels and Stories of Henry James*, but Macmillan declined to use them. See Pinker correspondence with Macmillan & Co., Macmillan Archive, British Library, #54905.

The Crown Octavo and the Pocket, since both are printed from the same standing type, are of a single edition, but are believed to be separate impressions. This is suggested both by the different paper used and by the fact that separate print orders were given for each, although the dates of the print orders of the two in all but one case (*The Bostonians*) coincide.

Both the Crown Octavo and the Pocket impressions were initially priced at 7s. 6d. net per volume, although there is some evidence in the entries for the earliest published titles that a price of 7s. was initially contemplated, and in the agreement with Mrs. William James a price of 6s. was specified (see below). In the ledger entry for *What Maisie Knew*, Volume [XVI], there is recorded "100 3/6 env[elopes] ord[ered] 26/4/29". This suggests that in 1929 (or perhaps earlier) the price of the remaining unsold copies of the Pocket impression was reduced to 3s. 6d. net, and copies of the dust-jackets of some of the volumes were reprinted to reflect this price reduction, as well as a reduction to 5s. for the Crown Octave impression. Examples of such dust-jackets for *Roderick Hudson* and *The Golden Bowl* are described in 86.2.0.

There is no indication in the Macmillan records whether the Crown Octavo or the Pocket impressions were sold by subscription or as sets. The fact that except for the seven multi-volume titles, there were no volume numbers, the volumes were all priced individually, and were published over a period of almost two years, make it likely that they were sold as individual titles, and when the sets were completed, were sold as sets as well. The ad on the back cover of the dust-jacket of the pocket edition of *The Golden Bowl* records that the Crown Octavo edition was sold for £7 a set and the Pocket Edition for £5 a set, probably after 1923 when the sets were completed.

Print orders and dates of Publication of
The Novels and Stories of Henry James[55]

Volume	Date of Print Order	Date Sheets Received	Date of Publication	Date of Reprinting[56]
I	Mar. 17, 1920	Dec. 1920	Jan. 11, 1921	none
II	July 22, 1920	Dec. 1920	Feb. 1, 1921	none
III	July 22, 1920	Dec. 1920	Mar. 4, 1921	none
IV	Oct. 19, 1920	Dec. 1920	Apr. 12, 1921	none
V	Mar. 1, 1921	Apr. 1921	May 3, 1921	Mar. 1930
VI & VII	Mar. 18, 1921	Apr. 1921	June 3, 1921	Mar. 1928
VIII[57]	Apr. 14, 1921	June 1921	Aug. 5, 1921	none
IX	Apr. 18, 1921	June 1921	Aug. 5, 1921	none
X & XI	June 22, 1921	Sept. 1921	Oct. 4, 1921	none
XII & XIII	Sept. 21, 1921	Oct. 1921	Dec. 2, 1921	none
XIV	Nov. 8, 1921	Jan. 1922	Feb. 7, 1922	Feb. 1928
XV	Nov. 15, 1921	Jan. 1922	Mar. 10, 1922	none
XVI	Feb. 1, 1922	Apr. 1922	May 9, 1922	Mar. 1930
XVII	Mar. 15, 1922	Apr. 1922	May 9, 1922	June 1928
XVIII	May 3, 1922	May 1922	July 7, 1922	none
XIX	May 3, 1922	June 1922	July 7, 1922	none
XX	July 11, 1922	Aug. 1922	Sept. 12, 1922	none
XXI	July 25, 1922	Aug. 1922	Sept. 12, 1922	none

55 Unlike the Macmillan Editions Book, the two Ledgers cited above record print orders (dates and number of sheets) but do not record the date the sheets were received from the printer (in this case R. & R. Clark, which printed all 35 volumes), nor the dates of publication. This missing information is supplied by the cards.

56 It is not clear from the publisher's records whether this reprinting was in the Octavo Edition format or the Pocket Edition format. It is conjectured that it was reprinted in a size similar to the Pocket format but with a different binding, possibly light green.

57 Volumes VIII and IX are Volumes I and II of *The Bostonians*.

XXII	Oct. 4, 1922	Oct. 1922	Nov. 10, 1922	Sept. 1937
XXIII	Oct. 4, 1922	Oct. 1922	Nov. 10, 1922	June 1930
XXIV	Nov. 21, 1922	Dec. 1922	Jan. 9, 1923	none
XXV	Nov. 21, 1922	Dec. 1922	Jan. 9, 1923	none
XXVI	Jan. 24, 1923	Feb. 1923	Mar. 9, 1923	none
XXVII	Jan. 24, 1923	Feb. 1923	Mar. 9, 1923	none
XXVIII	Apr. 4, 1923	Apr. 1923	May 18, 1923	none
XXIX	Apr. 4, 1923	Apr. 1923	May 18, 1923	none
XXX[58]	May 2, 1923	July 1923	Aug. 14, 1923	Dec. 1936
XXXI	June 12, 1923	July 1923	Aug. 14, 1923	Dec. 1936
XXXII & XXXIII	July 24, 1923	Aug. 1923	Oct. 12, 1923	Sept. 1930
XXXIV[59]	Sept. 14, 1923	Nov. 1923	Nov. 30, 1923	Mar. 1934
XXXV	Oct. 25, 1923	Nov. 1923	Nov. 30, 1923	Mar. 1934

In an agreement dated September 3, 1919, between Macmillan and Mrs. William James, regarding the "cheap [later changed to "popular"] uniform edition of Henry James' books" it was provided that the published price of this edition was to be 6 shillings per volume, that Mrs. James was to receive a royalty of 10% of the published price of each volume sold, and that Macmillan was to have the exclusive licence to print and publish this edition in the United Kingdom and the British colonies and dependencies, with the exception of Canada. Pinker acted as the agent for Mrs. James in this connection; see Macmillan Archive, British Library, #54905, ff. 57, 58 and 60. However, when the first volume of the edition was published 16 months later, the price was fixed at 7s. 6d. net.

* * *

---

[58] Volumes XXX and XXXI are Volumes I and II of *The Wings of the Dove*.
[59] Volumes XXXIV and XXXV are Volumes I and II of *The Golden Bowl*.

86.2.0. *Novels and Stories of Henry James*, first "Pocket Edition", 35 volumes, London 1921–1923.

[I] *Roderick Hudson*. One volume.

RODERICK HUDSON | BY | HENRY JAMES | MACMILLAN AND CO., LIMITED | ST. MARTIN'S STREET, LONDON | 1921

Size: 6 7/8" x 4 1/4".

Collation: $[a]^6$ b^8 B–I K–U X–Z 2A–2F^8 2G^{10}; pp. [i–xxviii], 1–[463] [464] [465–466] [2].

Contents: [i–ii] half-title, verso publisher's device, and office addresses; [iii–iv] title-page, verso "COPYRIGHT"; v–[vi] "NOTE", verso blank; vii-xxvii "PREFACE"; [xxviii] blank; 1–[463] text; [463] at foot printer's imprint: "Printed by R. & R. Clark, Limited, Edinburgh. [all except printer's name in italic]"; [464] blank; [465–466] ads headed: "THE NOVELS AND STORIES OF | HENRY JAMES [in sans-serif]", listing the 35 volumes; [467–468] blank leaf.

Binding: dark blue linen-grain cloth. The front cover, lettered and decorated in gilt, reads within a floral frame: "NOVELS|AND|STORIES | OF | HENRY | JAMES". The back cover is neither lettered nor decorated. The spine, lettered and decorated in gilt, reads: "[double rule] | RODERICK | HUDSON | HENRY JAMES | [long floral strap-work decoration] | [double rule]". The endpapers are of white wove paper, and the text is printed on thin wove paper. All edges are trimmed, and the top edge is stained a light brown.

Dust-jacket: cream wove paper, lettered and decorated in dark blue. The front cover and spine of the dust-jacket replicates the front cover and spine of the book, except that the front cover of the dust-jacket has at the foot the price "3/6 NET". On the back cover is an ad headed: "THE NOVELS AND STORIES OF | HENRY JAMES | Crown 8vo 5s. net per volume. The set. £7 net. | Pocket Edition. F'cap 8vo. 3s. 6d. net per volume. | The set, £5 net.", followed by a list in two columns of the 35 volumes, and the publisher's imprint at the foot.[60]

The remaining 34 volumes are uniformly bound and decorated. They have endpapers of white wove paper, and the texts are printed on thin wove paper. Inserted ads, if present, are printed on bookstock. All

---

60 The prices on this dust-jacket indicate that it was probably printed in the late 1920s when the prices for these volumes were reduced.

edges are trimmed, and the top edges are stained light brown. Titles that are in the collection are:

[II] *The American.* One volume. Title-page dated 1921. Collation: [*a*]⁸ *b*⁸ B–I K–U X–Z 2A–2G⁸ 2H⁶; pp. [2] [i–xxx], 1–[474] [475–476]. Leaf 2H₆ is two pages of ads, as in *Roderick Hudson.*

[III] *The Europeans.* One volume. Title-page dated 1921. Collation: [A]² B–I K–N⁸ O¹⁰; pp. [i–iv], 1–[209] [210] [211–212]. Leaf O₁₀ is two pages of ads, as in *Roderick Hudson.*

[IV] *Confidence.* One volume. Title-page dated 1921. Collation: [A]² B–I K–S⁸; pp. [i–iv], 1–[270] [271–272]. Leaf S₈ is two pages of ads, as in *Roderick Hudson.*

[V] *Washington Square,* one volume. Title-page dated 1921. Collation: [A]⁴ B–I K–P⁸ Q⁶; pp. [i–iv], 1–[233] [235–236]. Leaf Q₆ is two pages of ads, as in *Roderick Hudson.*

[VI & VII] *The Portrait of a Lady.* Two volumes. Title-pages dated 1921. Collation: Volume I: [*a*]⁴ *b*⁸ B–I K–U X–Z 2A⁸ 2B⁶; pp. [i–xxiv], [1–378] [379–380]. Leaf 2B₆ is two pages of ads, as in *Roderick Hudson.* Volume II: [A]² B–I K–U X–Z 2A–2B⁸; pp. [i–iv], [1–382] [383–384]. Leaf 2B₈ is two pages of ads, as in *Roderick Hudson.*

Both title-pages are blindstamped "PRESENTATION COPY".

[VIII & IX] *The Bostonians.* Two volumes. Title-pages dated 1921. Collation: Volume I: [A]² B–I K–S⁸; pp. [i–iv] [1–2], 3–[267] [268] [269–272]. Leaves S₇,₈ are four pages of ads, the first two as in *Roderick Hudson,* the third headed: "THE LETTERS OF HENRY JAMES", and the last headed: "BY HENRY JAMES", listing 5 titles. Volume II: [A]² B–I K–S⁸ T² (T₂+X₁,₂); pp. [i–iv] [1–2], 3–[276] plus 4. Inserted at the end of Volume II are two conjugate leaves, the first with two pages of ads, as in *Roderick Hudson,* and the second a blank leaf.

[X & XI] *The Princess Casamassima.* Two volumes. Title-pages dated 1921. Collation: Volume I: [*a*]⁸ *b*⁸ B–I K–U⁸ X¹⁰ (–X₁₀); pp. [2] [i–xxx] [1–2], 3–[321] [322]. Volume II: [A]² B–I K–U X–Z 2A⁸ 2B⁸ (–2B⁸); pp. [i–iv] [1–2], 3–[382]. There are no ads at the end of either volume.

[XII & XIII] *The Tragic Muse.* Two volumes. Title-pages dated 1921. Collation: Volume I: [*a*]⁶ *b*⁸ B–I K–U X–Y⁸; pp. [2] [i–xxvi] [1–2], 3–[332] [333–334] [335–336]. Leaf Y₇ is two pages of ads, as in *Roderick Hudson,* and leaf Y₈ is blank. Volume II: [A]² B–I K–U X–Z 2A–2B⁸

($2B_8+X_1$); pp.[i–iv] [1–2], 3–[384] plus 2. There is an additional leaf inserted at the end with two pages of ads, as in *Roderick Hudson*.

[XIV] *The Awkward Age*. One volume. Title-page dated 1922. Collation: $[a]^6$ b^8 B–I K–U X–Z 2A–2G^8 2H^{10}; pp. [i–xxviii] 1–[2], 3–[483] [484]. There are no ads at the end.

[XVI] *What Maisie Knew*. One volume. Title-page dated 1922. Collation: $[a]^6$ b^8 B–I K–U X–Z 2A–2I 2K^8 (2$K_8+X_{1,2}$); pp. [i–xxviii] 1–[2], 3–[511][512] plus 4. There are two additional leaves inserted at the end with four pages of ads, as in Volume I of *The Bostonians*.

[XVIII] *The Reverberator*. One volume. Title-page dated 1922. Collation: $[a]^6$ b^8 B–I K–U X–Z 2A–2I^8; pp. [2] [i–xxvi] 1–[2], 3–[494] [495–496]. Leaf $2I_8$ is two pages of ads, as in *Roderick Hudson*.

[XIX] *Lady Barbarina*. One volume. Title-page dated 1922 (with a small upright vertical line between the "2's"). Collation: $[a]^6$ b^8 B–I K–U X–Z 2A–2I 2K–2L^8 2M^6; pp. [i–xxviii] 1–[2], 3–[538] [539–540]. Leaf $2M_6$ is two pages of ads, as in *Roderick Hudson*.

[XX] *The Lesson of the Master*. One volume. Title-page dated 1922. Collation: $[a]^4$ b^8 B–I K–U X^8 Y^8 ($-Y_8$); pp. [i–xxiv] 1–[2], 3–[331] [332] [333–334]. Leaf Y_7 is two pages of ads, as in *Roderick Hudson*.

[XXI] *The Author of Beltraffio*. One volume. Title-page dated 1922. Collation: $[A]^8$ B–I K–U X–Z 2A^8 2B^4 ($2B_4+X_1$); pp. [i–xvi] 1–[2] 3–[376] plus 2. There is an additional leaf inserted at the end with two pages of ads, as in *Roderick Hudson*.

[XXII] *The Altar of the Dead*. One volume. Title-page dated 1922. Collation: $[a]^8$ b^{10} B–I K–U X–Z 2A–2H^8; pp. [i–xxxvi] 1–[2], 3–[478] [479–480]. Leaf $2H_8$ is two pages of ads, as in *Roderick Hudson*.

[XXIII] *Daisy Miller*. One volume. Title-page dated 1922. Collation: $[a]^6$ b^8 B–I K–U X–Z 2A–2E^8, 2F^{10} ($2F_{10}+X_1$); pp. [i–xxviii] 1–[2], [3]–452 plus 2. There is an additional leaf inserted at the end with two pages of ads, as in *Roderick Hudson*.

[XXIV] *Watch and Ward*. One volume. The title-page dated 1923. collation: $[A]^4$ B–I K–U X–Z 2A–2F^8 2G^6; pp. [i–viii] 1–[2], 3–[457] [458] [459–460]. Leaf $2G_6$ is two pages of ads, as in *Roderick Hudson*.

This copy is blindstamped on the title-page "PRESENTATION COPY". Loosely inserted is a sheet of laid paper on the recto of which is printed: "Messrs. Macmillan & Co., Ltd., will | be glad to receive a copy of the issue | containing a notice of this work. | The price of the book is 7s. 6d. net."

[XXV] *The Diary of a Man of Fifty*. One volume. Title-page dated 1923. Collation: [A]⁴ B–I K–U X–Z 2A–2I⁸ (2I$_8$+X$_1$); pp. [i–viii] 1–[2], 3–[496], plus a 2. There are two pages of ads, as in *Roderick Hudson* inserted at the end.

[XXVI] *The Last of the Valerii*. One volume. Title-page dated 1923. Collation: [A]⁴ B–I K–U X–Z 2A–2H⁸ 2I⁴ (–2I$_4$); pp. [i–viii] 1–[2], 3–[486]. 485 is correctly paginated. There are no ads at the end.

[XXVII] *Lord Beaupré*. One volume. Title-page dated 1923. Collation: [A]⁴ B–I K–U X–Z 2A–2H⁸; pp. [i–viii] 1–[2], 3–[475] [476] [477–478] [479–480]. Leaf 2H$_7$ is two pages of ads, as in *Roderick Hudson*.

[XXVIII] *Maud-Evelyn*. One volume. Title-page dated 1923. Collation: [A]⁴ B–I K–U X–Z 2A–2G⁸ 2H⁶; pp. [i–viii] 1–[2], 3–[474] [475–476]. Leaf 2H$_6$ is two pages of ads, as in *Roderick Hudson*.

[XXIX] *The Sacred Fount*. One volume. Title-page dated 1923. Collation: [A]² B–I K–Q⁸ R⁶ (–R$_6$); pp. [i–iv] 1–[2], 3–[249] [250]. There are no ads at the end.

[XXX & XXXI] *The Wings of the Dove*. Two volumes. Title-pages dated 1923. Collation: Volume I: [*a*]⁶ *b*⁸ B–I K–R⁸ S⁶ (–S$_6$); pp. [2] [i–xxvi] 1–[2], 3–[266]. There are no ads at the end. Volume II: [A]² B–I K–U X–Z⁸ 2A⁶; pp. [i–iv] 1–[2], 3–[359] [360] [362–362] [363–364]. Leaf 2A$_5$ is two pages of ads, as in *Roderick Hudson*.

Both volumes have dust-jackets of cream wove paper, lettered and decorated in dark blue. The front covers and spines of the dust-jackets replicate the front covers and spines of the books, except that the front covers of the dust-jackets have at the foot the price "3/6 NET". On the back covers is an ad headed: "THE NOVELS AND STORIES OF | HENRY JAMES | Crown 8vo 5s. net per volume. The set. £7 net. | Pocket Edition. F'cap 8vo. 3s.6d. net per volume. | The set, £5 net.", followed by a list in two columns of the 35 volumes, and the publisher's imprint at the foot.

[XXXII & XXXIII] *The Ambassadors*. Two volumes. Title-pages dated 1923. Collation: Volume I: [*a*]⁸ *b*⁸ B–I K–Q⁸ R⁸ (–R$_{7,8}$); pp. [i–xxviii], 1–[2], 3–[252]. Volume II: [A]² B–I K–T⁸ U⁴ (–U$_4$); pp. [i–iv], 1–[2], 3–[293] [294]. There are no ads at the end of either volume.

[XXXIV & XXXV] *The Golden Bowl.* Two volumes. Title-pages dated 1923. Collation: Volume I: [*a*]⁸ *b*⁸ B–I K–U X–Z⁸ 2A⁴ (2A$_4$+X$_1$); pp. [2] [i–xxx] 1–[2], 3–[360], plus 2. There are two pages of ads as in *Roderick Hudson* inserted at the end. Volume II: [A]² B–I K–U X⁸ Y⁴; pp. [i–iv] 1–[2], 3–[325] [326] [327–328]. Leaf Y$_4$ is two pages of ads, as in *Roderick Hudson*. On the title-page of both volumes is blind-stamped "PRESENTATION COPY".

Sheets of some of the titles in this "Pocket Edition" have been examined bound in light aqua-green linen-grain cloth, with no lettering or decoration on the front or back covers, and lettered (but not decorated) in gilt on the spines. These copies have dust-jackets (printed in a slightly lighter blue) uniform with those described above, with the same "3/6 NET" price on the front cover of the dust-jacket. These are probably later (late 1920s) bindings-up of the later impressions of Pocket Edition sheets.

⚜

87. *NOTES AND REVIEWS*

87.1.0. *Notes and Reviews*, first edition, trade impression, one volume, Cambridge, 1921.

NOTES AND REVIEWS | By [in swash italic] | Henry James [in red gothic script] | With a Preface by Pierre de Chaignon la Rose | [rule] | A Series of Twenty-five Papers Hith- | erto Unpublished in Book Form | [rule] | [oval decorative device] | [rule] | DUNSTER HOUSE [in red] | Cambridge, Massachusetts [in swash italic] | MDCCCCXXI

Size: 8 $^{13}/_{16}$" x 5 $^{7}/_{8}$".

Collation: [unsigned, 1–14⁸ 15⁴ 16⁸]; pp. [i]–xx, 1–227 [228].

Contents: [i–ii] half-title, verso blank; [iii–iv] title-page, verso copyright notice and printer's imprint: "Copyright, 1921, by [in italic] | Dunster House Bookshop | THE UNIVERSITY PRESS, Cambridge, U.S.A."; v–xvi "Preface [in italic]"; xvii–xx "Contents [in italic]"; 1–227 text; [228] blank.

Binding: dark blue smooth quarter cloth with light blue paper over boards. The front cover, lettered in gilt, reads: "NOTES & REVIEWS |

BY HENRY JAMES". The back cover is neither lettered nor decorated. The spine, lettered and decorated in gilt, reads: "NOTES & | REVIEWS | [rule] | HENRY | JAMES | DUNSTER | HOUSE". The endpapers are of buff wove paper, and the text is printed on cream wove paper watermarked: "[eagle device] | Albion Text". There are no binder's fly-leaves. All edges are untrimmed.

Printing history. There were two impressions of this edition printed in 1921: the trade impression of 1,000 copies and the limited impression of 30 copies. The trade impression was priced at $5.00 and the limited impression at $10.00. This title was not published in England.

87.2.0. *Notes and Reviews*, first edition, limited impression, one volume, Cambridge 1921.

The title-page, size, collation, and contents are identical to those of 87.1.0, except that the verso of the title-leaf has the addition of a limitation notice that reads: "Of this Edition Thirty Copies have been | printed on Normandy Vellum, | of which this is | Number 24 [all in italic]".

Binding: mustard linen quarter cloth with beige paper over boards. The lettering and decoration are identical to that on 87.1.0. The endpapers are of cream wove paper, and the text is printed on wove Normandy Vellum. A binder's fly-leaf of bookstock is at both the front and the back. All edges are untrimmed.

Appendices

Appendix A
A Note on J. R. Osgood

A cataloguer of Henry James's American first editions is struck by the fact that a number of the first editions of James R. Osgood and Company sheets turn up in later binding states of other publishers (which are often erroneously catalogued as remainder bindings), that the James R. Osgood and Company imprint resurfaces in the 1880s after that firm was dissolved in 1878, and that the Osgood name resurfaces yet again in the 1890s as part of the English imprint James R. Osgood, McIlvaine & Co. In total, seventeen of James's first editions were published by firms in whose imprint the Osgood name appeared, and a better understanding of Osgood's checkered career as a publisher gives insight into this seeming confusion of publishing in America in the latter part of the Nineteenth Century.

James Ripley Osgood was a somewhat controversial figure in the American publishing world of the last four decades of the Nineteenth Century. Having joined the publisher Ticknor & Fields as a clerk in 1855, he rose quickly through the ranks under the mentorship of James T. Fields. Ticknor & Fields, under the conservative leadership of William Ticknor (who had trained at an investment firm and then a bank) and his decidedly junior partner Fields, was by the early 1860s the most prominent Boston publisher, with a list of authors, both English and American, that was the envy of its competitors. In April 1864, William Ticknor died, and a successor partnership was formed under the same name, Ticknor & Fields, the senior partner of which was James Fields and which included Osgood as a junior partner, even though he contributed no capital to the firm.

In October 1868, Fields, seemingly to free himself from the "Ticknor brotherhood", reorganized the firm under the name Fields, Osgood & Co., with Osgood as his working partner. The firm continued in the publishing business under that name until January 1871, when Fields, discouraged by the difficulties of publishing, retired at the age of 53 after 40 years of service with the firm. On January 1, 1871, Osgood acquired the assets of Fields, Osgood & Co. with two junior members

A NOTE ON J. R. OSGOOD

of that firm, John Spencer Clark and Benjamin Ticknor.

James R. Osgood and Company, as the new firm was named, was born at an unpropitious time. In November 1872, a fire destroyed the Boston warehouse where Osgood stored the steel plates used for printing illustrations. Two years after its formation the crash of September 1873 occurred. That crash was followed by several years of severe recession the effects of which were compounded by Osgood's practice of raising money by selling current titles at substantial discounts to jobbers, and by launching a new magazine, *The American Architect*. By the end of 1877, faced with the necessity of augmenting its dwindling capital, Osgood was in effect forced to bring in well capitalized partners, Henry O. Houghton (the owner of the prosperous Riverside Press) and George T. Mifflin, who could not resist the chance to acquire the copyrights and list of authors of J. R. Osgood and Company (and Ticknor & Fields' and Fields, Osgood & Co.). The new firm, styled Houghton, Osgood and Company, was established in January 1878.

As part of this transaction, Houghton, Osgood and Company acquired the unbound sheets of the first edition, first impression, of at least three of the four of Henry James's works which had first been published by James R. Osgood and Company, and issued them in bindings with the Houghton, Osgood imprint on the spines. These were *A Passionate Pilgrim*, *Transatlantic Sketches*, and *Roderick Hudson*. It also acquired the third impression sheets of *The American*, which was also issued in a Houghton, Osgood binding.

The relationship between the flamboyant and free spending Osgood, with his lack of attention to detail, and his conservative new partners, particularly H. O. Houghton, was troubled from the outset. Partly as a result of a disastrous fire in December 1879, which totally destroyed Houghton, Osgood's premises (but not the plates or printed sheets which were stored at the Riverside Press), and partly as a result of the continuing difficult economic environment, the new firm soon needed further capital. Whether Osgood refused to put up his share and consequently retired from the firm, or whether the silent financial partners of the firm made their continued support conditional on Osgood's departure, is not clear. What is clear is that on May 1, 1880, slightly more than two years after its formation, Houghton, Osgood and Company was voluntarily dissolved, Osgood was bought out, and the firm's assets were acquired by the newly

APPENDIX A

formed Houghton, Mifflin & Company (H. O. Houghton in partnership with G.H. Mifflin and Lawson Valentine). Among the assets that Houghton, Mifflin acquired were copyrights of books, the list of which ran to 48 pages and comprised the publications of Ticknor & Fields (two firms), Fields, Osgood & Company, James R. Osgood and Company (the first) and Houghton, Osgood & Company.

As a result, Houghton, Mifflin acquired the remaining unbound sheets of the first edition, first impression, of Henry James's *Transatlantic Sketches*, *Roderick Hudson* and *Confidence*, which had first been published by James R. Osgood and Company three years before, and issued them in bindings with the Houghton, Mifflin imprint on the spines. It also, no doubt, acquired the plates of two other of Henry James's works that had first been published by Houghton, Osgood and Company, *Watch and Ward* and *The Europeans*, and issued a reprint of these two title with new prelims in 1886 (and possibly earlier).

In that same year, 1880, Osgood, ever the optimist, set up a second James R. Osgood and Company in co-partnership with his brother, Edward, and John H. Ammon. Despite the fact that as part of the dissolution of Houghton, Osgood and Company, Osgood had agreed with Houghton, Mifflin that he would "respect the authors and enterprises belonging to the other" and "not seek by any influence ... to interfere with them", Osgood proceeded to poach Houghton, Mifflin authors by offering them advances and royalties well above standard, including Henry James. In the short run Osgood was successful, but in the not so long run his tactics proved ruinous. In May 1885, five years after its formation, the second James R. Osgood and Company failed, having nonetheless in the five years of its existence published six further James titles. Not having the means to reach a composition with the firm's creditors, most of the assets and the obligations of the firm were acquired by the newly formed Ticknor & Company (Benjamin and Thomas Ticknor and George Godfrey). But in the end Ticknor & Company was not a success, and in April 1889, its assets in turn were acquired by Houghton, Mifflin. As a result Houghton, Mifflin, which nine years earlier had bought out Osgood's interest in Houghton, Osgood and Company, acquired unbound sheets of a number of Henry James titles, including *A Little Tour in France*, which it issued with the original Osgood title-page but with the Houghton, Mifflin imprint at the foot of the spine. Anesko chronicles how Henry James was caught up in the James R. Osgood and Company's

A NOTE ON J. R. OSGOOD

bankruptcy, and as a consequence initially lost a significant portion of the $4000 that Osgood had agreed to pay him for *The Bostonians*.

Following the bankruptcy of the second James R. Osgood and Company in September 1885, Osgood took a position with Harper & Brothers in New York at the salary of $10,000 a year, an indication of the worth in which he was held by publishing circles. Less than a year later he moved to London where he served Harpers' as their London agent, and continued to follow his free spending ways. In the fall of 1890, while continuing to serve as Harpers' agent (and with Harpers' knowledge and consent), he, together with Clarence W. McIlvaine, a young apprentice in Harpers' New York office, founded the English publisher James R. Osgood, McIlvaine & Co. Osgood hoped to be able to use his excellent London connections to capitalize on the new American copyright law (which came into force in December 1891) which for the first time afforded American copyright protection to British works. Osgood, McIlvaine published four further James titles, but none of these had been issued when Osgood died (of chronic bronchitis) in May 1892. He was buried in Kensal Green Cemetery, Northwest London.[62]

---

62 The above information was derived, for the most part, from Carl J. Weber, *The Rise and Fall of James Ripley Osgood* (Waterville, Maine: Colby College Press, 1959), which is the only full-length biography of Osgood and presents a sympathetic account of his life and talents, and Ellen B. Ballou, *The Building of the House: Houghton, Mifflin's Formative Years* (Boston: Houghton, Mifflin Company, 1970), which presents a rather unsympathetic account, particularly of his dealings with Houghton, Mifflin after they bought him out. Warren S. Tryon and William Charvat, *The Cost Books of Ticknor and Fields* (New York: The Bibliographical Society of America, 1949), xiv–xxii, details the history of the firm to 1858 and the relationship between the two principal partners, Ticknor and Fields. Michael Anesko, *"Friction with the Market", Henry James and the Profession of Authorship* (New York: Oxford University Press, 1986), is a brilliant discussion, among other things, of James's earnings from his publications, as well, in Chapter V, of his financial travails with *The Bostonians* as a result of Osgood's bankruptcy.

Appendix B
A Note on Tauchnitz's James Editions

Tauchnitz International Editions in English 1841–1955 (Bibliographical Society of America New York, 1988) is the definitive bibliography of Tauchnitz editions in English. It records some 56,000 Tauchnitz copies by 783 authors, and among them 16 James titles first issued by Tauchnitz between 1878 and 1912.

As comprehensive as is this bibliography, Todd and Bowden are at pains to point out, as indeed certain items recorded in this Catalogue show, that their records may, in certain respects, be incomplete: "From recent experience....we fully expect that, as other copies appear, one in sixty will represent an impression not here defined, and one in twenty an unrecorded issue of an impression already identified. Within the general series no record based on merely 56,000 exemplars can entirely encompass the variations implicit in constantly reprinted runs exceeding forty million." Introduction, x.

As Todd and Bowden indicate, the problem of dating Tauchnitz editions is made more difficult by the fact of "Tauchnitz's almost invariable custom of retaining, through all subsequent impressions, the original imprint date."[63] Introduction, ix. Thus the title-page date is not necessarily an indication of the actual date of issue. During the period 1878 to 1912 it appears that there is only one variable between impressions, and that is the number and original issue dates of the titles of works by the same author listed on the verso of the half-title. One can be confident that a particular James title is of the first impression if none of the titles listed on the half-title verso had a date of first issue not later than the date on the title-page, and the date on the title-page is the original date of Tauchnitz's issuance of the work (the later is invariably assured as Tauchnitz did not change the

---

63 The only James edition or impression published by Tauchnitz recorded by T&B as not having a date on the title-page is the fourth impression of *Daisy Miller: A Study*, T&B 1819. It is also the only impression of a James title that has been found that was originally issue by Tauchnitz in both wrappers and in boards, although T&B does not record an issue of that title in boards. However, see 8.25.0. All other James titles, it is believed, were originally issued by Tauchnitz only in wrappers.

title-page date), subject to the proviso discussed below concerning the wrappers. The other "external leaves essential for precise identification", the title and the colophon, were all unchanged in the period during which James works were first issued by Tauchnitz (the colophon, "Printing Office of the Publisher", remained unchanged in the period 1859–1921, and the title-leaf imprint, "Leipzig | Bernard Tauchnitz | [date]", was unchanged in the period 1852–1930), and thus for the purpose of identifying first, and most subsequent, impressions of Tauchnitz first editions of James's works, can be ignored. This is also true of the wrapper styles (see below) and the price printed on the wrappers, which also remained essentially unchanged during the years 1878 to 1912.

Tauchnitz editions in this period were issued in dated wrappers (the back wrapper was dated by month and year at the head), with a dated publisher's catalogue invariably bound in at the end. Invariably the wrappers and catalogues did not survive the rebinding process that so many of the volumes underwent. However, wrapper and catalogue, when they survived, with dates later than the date on the title-page which cohere with the ad on the verso of the half-title, are catalogued by Todd and Bowden as a later binding-up of the first impression. Implicit in this is that Tauchnitz followed the practice of printing a large number of sheets of any given title and then binding and issuing them as needed with later dated wrappers and catalogues. Todd and Bowden record only one James title that went into a second edition (*i.e.* was reset), *The Europeans*, but they do not indicate a title-page date for that edition, which leads one to suspect that it was either undated (which would seem to be unlikely) or that it retained the original 1878 date.

However, to complicate matters further, it appears that Tauchnitz used two styles of wrappers simultaneously. As Todd and Bowden point out: "... copies with lists on back and inner wrappers may be adjudged as of the first issue but others with a heading of *identical date*, but also then reported as exhibiting a list on outer back wrapper only, are of later issue and usually cite books of a later date." 947 (emphasis in original). An example of this is the copy of the Tauchnitz edition of *Portraits of Places* recorded in this catalogue (21.13.0). The verso of its half-title lists twelve other James titles, none first issued after 1884. The title-page date is 1884, the wrapper, without a list on the inside back cover, is dated August 1884 at the back head, and the publisher's

APPENDIX B

Catalogue bound in at the end is also dated August 1884, which dates are the earliest recorded by Todd and Bowden at 2276a. However, based on the criteria set forth above regarding the two styles of wrappers, the absence of a list on the inside back wrapper would indicate that this is probably a second issue of the first impression. Of course, as with the verso of the half-title, first issue wrappers should not list titles published later than the first issue date of the title they cover.

From the above it can be seen that it is not difficult to identify first impressions from the verso of the half-title; and, provided the wrappers are intact, to date them. Subsequent issues of the first impression can only be dated by the wrapper and catalogue dates, the wrapper date, it would be thought, taking precedence over the catalogue date unless the catalogue date is later than the wrapper date.

Identifying subsequent impressions can also be made by reference to the half-title verso, but there is always a degree of uncertainty as to whether another impression intervened between the first impression and the impression one is attempting to identify, especially when separated by a number of years with no record of intervening impressions. The first impression of *The American*, for example, was issued in 1878, and since it was the first James title published by Tauchnitz, it has no titles "by the same author" listed on the verso of the half-title. The next impression of this title recorded by Todd & Bowden has thirteen titles listed on the verso of the half-title, which would indicate that it was printed between the publication of the first impressions of *Portrait of Places* in 1884, the thirteenth James title published by Tauchnitz, and *A Little Tour in France* in 1885, the fourteenth such title published. Thus one can date this impression of *The American* as between 1884 and 1885. But one can not be certain whether another impression intervened between 1878 and 1884. As Todd and Bowden recognize, one new copy in sixty may represent an impression not previously recorded.

Identifying subsequent issues of any given impression as well as dating them must, it would seem, be totally dependent on wrapper and catalogue dates, and given the significant number of issues of any given impression there can be little certainty as to how many such separate issues exist. As Todd and Bowden recognize one new copy in twenty may be an unrecorded issue.

Todd and Bowden record sixteen James titles issued by Tauchnitz prior to 1921. It has been thought worthwhile to list them below, with

A NOTE ON TAUCHNITZ'S JAMES EDITIONS

the date on the title-page, the number of Tauchnitz titles "by the same author" listed on the verso of the half-title of the first edition, first impression (of the first volume in the case of multiple volume editions, the other volumes having a blank verso), and the Todd and Bowden reference. These titles are:

Title	No. of volumes	Title-page date	No. of titles listed	T&B Ref.
The American	2	1878	–	1713 & 1714
The Europeans	1	1878	1	1792
Daisy Miller: A Study	1	1879	–	1819
Roderick Hudson	2	1879	3	1842 & 1843
The Madonna of the Future	1	1880	4	1881
Eugene Pickering	1	1880	5	1888
Confidence	1	1880	6	1901
Washington Square	2	1881	7	1977 & 1978
The Portrait of a Lady	3	1882	8	2042, 2043 & 2044
Foreign Parts	1	1883	9	2164
French Poets and Novelists	1	1883	10	2181
The Siege of London	1	1884	11	2234
Portraits of Places	1	1884	12	2276
A Little Tour in France	1	1885	13	2334
The Finer Grain	1	1910	14	4224
The Outcry	1	1912	15	4308

What is curious about the sequence of these Tauchnitz publications is that in the period 1878 to 1885 at least one (and sometimes two or three) new James titles were issued by Tauchnitz in each year; and yet in the twenty-five years between the publication of *A Little Tour in France* in 1885 and *The Finer Grain* in 1910 they published no new James titles; see T&B pages 451 and 455.

Appendix C
A Bundle of Letters: Points

Copy #	Size	Plaid Inside Wrappers	Author's Name: Style and Width
13.1.0.	6 3/4" x 5 3/8"	Yes	Wide serif narrow spaced: 1 15/16"
13.2.0.	6 3/4" x 5 3/8"	Yes	Wide serif narrow spaced: 1 15/16"
13.3.0.	6 5/8" x 5 3/8"	Yes	Wide serif narrow spaced: 1 15/16"
13.4.0.	6 5/8" x 5 3/8"	Yes	Wide serif narrow spaced: 1 15/16"
13.5.0.	6 1/2" x 5 5/16"	No	Wide serif narrow spaced: 1 15/16"
13.6.0.	6 3/4" x 5 7/16"	No	Small serif widely spaced: 2"
13.7.0.	6 3/4" x 5 7/16"	No	Small serif widely spaced: 2"

A BUNDLE OF LETTERS: POINTS

Comma After Jr.	Distance: "Letters" and "BY"	Distance: "Henry" and "Loring"	Sewn/ Stapled	Wrapper Color
Yes	$23/32''$	$1\,1/4''$	Stapled	Cream
Yes	$23/32''$	$1\,1/4''$	Stapled	Yellow
No	$31/32''$	$1\,1/32''$	Stapled	Blue
No	$31/32''$	$1\,1/32''$	Sewn	Cream
No	$28/32''$	$1\,1/32''$	Sewn	Cream
No	$27/32''$	$1\,1/4''$	Stapled	Pink
No	$27/32''$	$1\,1/4''$	Stapled	Blue

Appendix D
Second Edition, American Issue of *The Portrait of a Lady*: Points

	1st Imp. State A: 16.5.0	1st Imp. State A: 16.6.0	1st Imp. State A: 16.7.0
Title-Page	Singleton	Singleton	Singleton
Title-Page Type Dimensions	5.956″ (5 $^{31}/_{32}$″)	5.956″ (5 $^{31}/_{32}$″)	5.956″ (5 $^{31}/_{32}$″)
Title-Page Verso	Period after 1881	Period after 1881	Period after 1881
Cover Panel	Faint Mazelike Pattern	Faint Mazelike Pattern	Faint Mazelike Pattern
Last Signature: Collation	[23^8]	[23^8]	[23^8]
Endpapers	Brown	Brown	Brown
Ads	No	No	No
Ampersand in Imprint	Flat Top	Flat Top	Flat Top
Binding	Stapled	Stapled	Stapled
Cloth Color	Chocolate-Brown	Tan	Pea-Green
Title-Page Date	1882	1882	1882

SECOND EDITION OF *THE PORTRAIT OF A LADY*: POINTS

1st Imp. State B: 16.8.0	2nd Imp.: 16.9.0	2nd. or 3rd. Imp.: 16.10.0
Singleton	Conjugate	Conjugate
5.956″ (5 $^{31}/_{32}$″)	5.877″ (5 $^{7}/_{8}$″)	5.872″ (5 $^{7}/_{8}$″)
Period after 1881	Period after 1881	Period after 1881
Pronounced Mazelike Pattern	Faint Mazelike Pattern	No Mazelike Pattern
[23^8]	[22^{12} (-22 $_{11,12}$)]	[22^{12} (−22 $_{11,12}$)]
Olive gray-green	Brown	Brown
No	No	No
Rounded Top	Flat Top	Flat Top
Stapled	Stapled	Stapled
Chocolate-Brown	Pea-Green	Tan
1882	1882	1882

APPENDIX D

	2nd. or 3rd. Imp.: 16.11.0, 16.11.1, 16.11.2	4th. Imp.: 16.12.0, 16.12.1	5th Imp.: 16.13.0
Title-Page	Conjugate	Conjugate	Conjugate
Title-Page Type Dimensions	5.872″ ($5\,^{7}/_{8}″$)	5.901″ ($5\,^{29}/_{32}″$)	5.940″ ($5\,^{15}/_{16}″$)
Title-Page Verso	No Period After 1881	No Period After 1881	No Period After 1881
Cover Panel	Pronounced Mazelike Pattern	Pronounced Mazelike Pattern	Pronounced Mazelike Pattern
Last Signature: Collation	$[22^{12}(-22_{11,12})]$	$[22^{12}(-22_{12})]$	$[23^{6}(-23_{6})]$
Endpapers	Brown	Tan Floral	Tan Floral
Ads	No	No	Yes State A
Ampersand in Imprint	Flat Top	Flat Top	Flat Top
Binding	Stapled	Sewn	Sewn
Cloth Color	Tan, Chocolate-Brown, Pea-Green	Tan, Chocolate-Brown	Olive-green (Linen-grain)
Title-Page Date	1882	1882	1882

SECOND EDITION OF *THE PORTRAIT OF A LADY*: POINTS

5th or 6th Imp.: 16.14.0	5th or 6th Imp.: 16.15.0	7th Imp.: 16.16.0
Conjugate	Conjugate	Conjugate
5.940″ (5 $^{15}/_{16}$″)	5.963″ (5 $^{31}/_{32}$″)	5.934″ (5 $^{31}/_{32}$″)
No Period After 1881	No Period After 1881	No Period After 1881
Pronounced Mazelike Pattern	Pronounced Mazelike Pattern	Pronounced Mazelike Pattern
[23^6 (-23_6)]	[23^6 (-23_6)]	[23^6 (-23_6)]
Tan Floral	Tan Floral	Tan Floral
Yes, State A	Yes, State A	Yes, State B
Flat Top	Flat Top	Flat Top
Sewn	Sewn	Sewn
Chocolate-Brown	Pea-Green	Chocolate-Brown
1882	1882	1883

Appendix E
A Note on the Text of
The Portrait of a Lady

While the order in which the book texts of *The Portrait of a Lady* were published is clear, what that order conceals is the order in which those texts came into being. In a fascinating piece of bibliographical detective work, Simon Nowell-Smith revealed this in *The Texts of* The Portrait of a Lady *1881–1882: The Bibliographical Evidence, The Papers of The Bibliographical Society of America*, Volume 63:4, pages 304–310 (1969).

    The Portrait was first serialized in *Macmillan's Magazine* from October 1880 to November 1881. This serialization was set from James's manuscript which was sent to the printer in installments. The printer (R. Clay, Sons & Taylor) sent back to James two sets of proofs of each installment, which James corrected sending one set back to the English printer for inclusion in *Macmillan's Magazine*, and the second to the *Atlantic Monthly* in America for serialization (November 1880 to December 1881) in that magazine. Mr. Nowell-Smith notes that there are only "small variations in the two magazine texts", p. 306.

    James then revised the published serialization in *Macmillan's Magazine* for the book publication. These pages he sent to Clay, the English printer, which set the type for the one-volume edition of the book. Moulds were made of the type, and one set of stereotype plates was made from these moulds and sent to America. These plates were used to print the American one-volume edition between October 27 and November 2, 1881, which was published on November 16, 1881 under the Houghton, Mifflin imprint with an 1882 date on the title-page. While chronologically this was the second text published, it was the first book text to come into being.

    A second set of plates was cast from the same moulds, which was later used to print the first one-volume English edition which was published by Macmillan in June 1882. Mr. Nowell-Smith identifies four variants between the first impressions of the American and English one-volume editions (two errors corrected and two errors inadvertently created). This was the third text published but the second book text to come into being.

A NOTE ON THE TEXT OF *THE PORTRAIT OF A LADY*

In the period late August to 28 October 1881, after the moulds were made from the standing type, that type was "leaded out" by inserting leads in the metal (a sort of printer's hamburger extender) to bulk it up for the first English three-volume edition, and underwent a process of "correcting for press". It does not appear that James saw proofs of this three-volume edition, which was printed from this standing type (not plates), and published in the first week of November 1881, with a second impression from the same type (with one correction in the type which was also made in the plates cast for the first one-volume English edition) in January 1882. Needless to say, the "leading out" and correcting process introduced a number of errors in the text. Again, while this "three-decker" was chronologically the first published, it is actually the third book text, and arguably the most corrupt of the texts.

The text of *The Portrait of a Lady* was reset in its entirety by Macmillan in 1883 for the three-volume edition that is part of *The Novels and Tales of Henry James*, which Edel and Laurence call *The Collective Edition of 1883*. This edition, which used as its copytext the first English one-volume edition of 1882, corrected most of the errors in the 1882 one-volume edition. Arguably, it is the least corrupt of all the early texts in book form.

The Tauchnitz edition of 1881 was set from the text of the first impression of the three-volume edition of 1881, but apparently Tauchnitz, with his usual thoroughness, corrected some of the more obvious errors in it.

It is quite likely that most of Macmillan's multi-volume editions of James's works (11 in all) were similarly produced. That is the type was set for the second, usually one volume, edition, stereotype plates or (in a few cases) electrotypes were made for printing the second edition, and then the standing type was leaded out for the printing of the multi-volume first edition. In that process, not infrequently minor revisions were made to the standing type and slight redistributions of the type were made. See comment under 28.3.0. The one clear exception to this process that has been found are the English editions of *Roderick Hudson*, the first (i.e. multi-volume) edition of which was printed in pica, while the one-volume second edition was printed in long primer.

Appendix F
The Publishers of James's Non-Pirated Editions

An asterisk by the publisher's name indicates priority of publication in book form. A hash mark indicates that a pirated edition was also published. A double hash mark indicates that the title was not published for sale in the trade (i.e. that it was printed for copyright purposes or to provide acting copies).

Title	First published	English publisher	U.S. publisher
A Passionate Pilgrim	1875	n/a	James R. Osgood
Transatlantic Sketches	1875	n/a	James R. Osgood
Roderick Hudson	1875	Macmillan (1879)	James R. Osgood*
The American	1877#	Macmillan (1879)	James R. Osgood*
French Poets and Novelists	1878	Macmillan	n/a
Watch and Ward	1878	n/a	Houghton, Osgood
The Europeans	1878	Macmillan*	Houghton, Osgood
Daisy Miller: A Study	1878	Macmillan (1879)	Harper & Brothers*
An International Episode	1879	n/a	Harper & Brothers
The Madonna of the Future	1879	Macmillan	n/a
Confidence	1879	Chatto & Windus*	Houghton, Osgood (1880)
Hawthorne	1879	Macmillan*	Harper & Brothers (1880)
A Bundle of Letters	1880#	n/a	n/a
The Diary of A Man of Fifty	1880	n/a	Harper & Brothers
Washington Square	1880	Macmillan (1881)	Harper & Brothers*
The Portrait of a Lady	1881	Macmillan*	Houghton, Mifflin
The Point of View	1882##	n/a	n/a
Daisy Miller: A Comedy	1883	n/a	James R. Osgood
The Siege of London	1883	n/a	James R. Osgood
Collective Edition	1883	Macmillan	n/a
Portraits of Places	1883	Macmillan*	James R. Osgood (1884)
Notes on Drawings	1884	n/a	n/a
A Little Tour in France	1884	Heinemann (1900)	James R. Osgood*

[626]

THE PUBLISHERS OF JAMES'S NON-PIRATED EDITIONS

Title	First published	English publisher	U.S. publisher
Tales of Three Cities	1884	Macmillan	James R. Osgood*
The Art of Fiction	1885#	n/a	n/a
The Author of Beltraffio	1885	n/a	James R. Osgood
Stories Revived	1885	Macmillan	n/a
The Bostonians	1886	Macmillan*	Macmillan
The Princess Casamassima	1886	Macmillan*	Macmillan
Partial Portraits	1888	Macmillan*	Macmillan
The Reverberator	1888	Macmillan*	Macmillan
The Aspern Papers	1888	Macmillan*	Macmillan
A London Life	1889	Macmillan*	Macmillan
The Tragic Muse	1890	Macmillan	Houghton, Mifflin*
The American: A Comedy	1891##	n/a	n/a
The Lesson of the Master	1892	Macmillan	Macmillan*
The Real Thing	1893	Macmillan	Macmillan*
Picture and Text	1893	n/a	Harper & Brothers
The Private Life	1893	Osgood, McIlvaine*	Harper & Brothers
Essays in London and Elsewhere	1893	Osgood, McIlvaine*	Harper & Brothers
The Wheel of Time	1893	n/a	Harper & Brothers
Theatricals	1894	Osgood, McIlvaine*	Harper & Brothers
Guy Domville	1894##	n/a	n/a
Theatricals: 2nd Series	1894	Osgood, McIlvaine*	Harper & Brothers
Terminations	1895	Heinemann*	Harper & Brothers
Embarrassments	1896	Heinemann*	Macmillan
The Other House	1896	Heinemann*	Macmillan
The Spoils of Poynton	1897	Heinemann*	Houghton, Mifflin
What Maisie Knew	1897	Heinemann*	Herbert S. Stone
John Delavoy	1897##	n/a	n/a
In the Cage	1898	Duckworth & Co.*	Herbert S. Stone
The Two Magics	1898	Heinemann*	Macmillan
The Awkward Age	1899	Heinemann*	Harper & Brothers
The Soft Side	1900	Methuen & Co.*	Macmillan
The Sacred Fount	1901	Methuen & Co.	Scribner's*
The Wings of the Dove	1902	Constable	Scribner's*
The Better Sort	1903	Methuen & Co.*	Scribner's
The Ambassadors	1903	Methuen & Co.*	Harper & Brothers
William Wetmore Story	1903	Blackwood*	Houghton, Mifflin
The Golden Bowl	1904	Methuen & Co.	(1905)Scribner's*
The Question of Our Speech	1905	n/a	Houghton, Mifflin

APPENDIX F

Title	First published	English publisher	U.S. publisher
English Hours	1905	Heinemann*	Houghton, Mifflin
The American Scene	1907	Chapman & Hall*	Harper & Brothers
Novels and Tales	1907–9	Macmillan (1908–9)	Scribner's*
Views and Reviews	1908	n/a	Ball
Julia Bride	1909	n/a	Harper & Brothers
Italian Hours	1909	Heinemann*	Houghton, Mifflin
The Finer Grain	1910	Methuen & Co.	Scribner's*
The Henry James Yearbook	1911	J.M. Dent	Richard G. Badger*
The Outcry	1911	Methuen & Co.*	Scribner's
A Small Boy and Others	1913	Macmillan	Scribner's*
Notes of a Son and Brother	1914	Macmillan	Scribner's*
Notes on Novelists	1914	J.M. Dent*	Scribner's
Uniform Tales	1915–20	Martin Secker*	Le Roy Phillips (1917–1918)
The Question of the Mind	1915	n/a	n/a
Posthumous Works:			
Pictures and Other Passages	1916	Chatto & Windus*	F.A. Stokes Co. (1917)
The Ivory Tower	1917	W. Collins Sons*	Scribner's
The Sense of the Past	1917	W. Collins Sons*	Scribner's
The Middle Years	1917	W. Collins Sons*	Scribner's
Gabrielle de Bergerac	1918	n/a	Boni and Liveright
Within the Rim	1919	W. Collins Sons	n/a
Travelling Companions	1919	n/a	Boni and Liveright
A Landscape Painter	1920	n/a	Scott and Seltzer
Refugees in Chelsea	1920	Ashendene Press	n/a
Master Eustace	1920	n/a	Thomas Seltzer
Novels and Stories	1921–23	Macmillan	n/a
Notes and Reviews	1921	n/a	Dunster House

All of James's continental editions in English were published by Bernhard Tauchnitz, with the exception of *A London Life* which was published in 1891 and *The Lesson of the Master* which was published in 1892, in both cases by Heinemann and Balestier; see Appendix B for a listing of James titles issued by Tauchnitz. James three pirated editions were *The American* published by Ward, Lock & Co. in England in 1877, *A Bundle of Letters* published by Loring in America in 1879 or 1880, and *The Art of Fiction* published by Cupples, Upham & Co. in America in 1885.

Appendix G
Documents bearing on the Terms agreed between Scribners and Houghton, Mifflin relative to the New York Edition[62]

1. *Contract between Scribner's and Houghton, Mifflin, dated April 10, 1906*:

MEMORANDUM OF AGREEMENT, made this tenth day of April 1906, between CHARLES SCRIBNER'S SONS, Incorporated, of New York City, N.Y., and HOUGHTON, MIFFLIN & COMPANY, of Boston, Massachusetts, relative to a Subscription Edition of the Works of HENRY JAMES.

Said Houghton, Mifflin & Company agree that the novels and stories of Henry James which they now publish shall be included in said Edition, the new electrotype plates of said volumes to be made at the Riverside Press, and to remain in the keeping of H.O. Houghton & Company for not less than the term of three (3) years after the publication of said Edition, and the printing and binding of any editions during that period to be done at the Riverside Press; the volumes to be sold by Charles Scribner's Sons only by subscription and in complete sets, and each copy to bear the statement that it is published under special arrangement with Houghton, Mifflin & Company.

It is agreed that the price to be charged by Houghton, Mifflin & Company and paid by Charles Scribner's Sons for the electrotype plates and the printing and binding shall be mutually agreed upon and shall never exceed the current market rates of the Riverside Press. The plates shall of course be wholly the property of said Charles Scribner's Sons.

Said Charles Scribner's Sons further agree to pay to said Houghton, Mifflin & Company a royalty of FIVE (5) per cent. on the retail price of each volume, or part of a volume, sold by them which is made up of novels or stories published by Houghton, Mifflin & Company,

---

62 Reprinting of the documents, which are in the Houghton Library, Houghton, Mifflin & Co. records MS Am2346 (542), is by permission of the Houghton Library, Harvard University. The text of the Memorandum of Agreement, dated July 13, 1908, between Henry James and Macmillan and Co., Ltd. covering the terms of publication of the English issue of *The Novels and Tales of Henry James* may be found in Moore, 212–213.

APPENDIX G

in addition to such royalty as they shall pay directly to the Author; it being understood that the royalty on all copies, whether in the regular or large paper edition of such volumes, shall be based on the retail price of the cloth bound copies of the regular subscription edition; and that no royalty shall be paid on such few <u>short</u> stories as may be included in the same volumes with stories issued by other publishers.

Statements of sales and settlements for royalty to be made semi-annually.

This agreement is to be binding on the parties hereto and on their heirs and assigns.

In witness whereof the parties to this Agreement have hereunto set their hands and seals.

Witness to signature of <u>Charles Scribner's Sons</u>	/s/ Charles Scribner's Sons, Inc.
/s/ R.S. Watson	/s/ by Charles Scribner President
Witness to signature of <u>Houghton, Mifflin & Company</u>	
/s/ H. Garrison	/s/ Houghton, Mifflin & Co. [SEAL]

* * *

2. *Typed letter from Houghton, Mifflin to Scribner's, dated April 11, 1906:*

HOUGHTON, MIFFLIN AND COMPANY
Publishers
4 PARK STREET: BOSTON

April 11, 1906.

Messrs. Charles Scribner's Sons,
   New York City.

Dear Sirs:

We have your favour of yesterday enclosing duplicate agreements relative to the subscription edition of Henry James's works, and are returning one copy herewith duly signed by us. In re-reading the agreement it occurs to us that the third clause might perhaps have been made a little more explicit, as the royalty will of course attach to any and all editions printed from said plates, not only during the three years specified in the first clause, but subsequently, whether the printing shall be done at the Riverside Press or elsewhere. Of course there can be no other construction except by implication, and the matter is perfectly understood between us, but perhaps you will kindly attach this letter to your copy of the contract as a memorandum on this point.

      Yours very truly,
           Houghton, Mifflin & Co.
              /s/ HG

* * *

3. Typed letter from Scribner's to Houghton, Mifflin dated March 10, 1908:

CHARLES SCRIBNER'S SONS
   PUBLISHERS
 153–157 FIFTH AVENUE.
BETWEEN 21st AND 22nd STREETS.
           New-York March 10, 1908

Dear Sirs:
 Mr. Pinker is trying to secure an English publisher for the Henry James subscription edition and wishes us to supply sheets. As these books would be for English sale and therefore he ["he" struck out] Mr. Pinker [written in] would have to arrange with their English publishers, and the royalty also would be paid by the English publisher of the edition, we suppose you would make no claim for royalty on sheets so sold. But as technically they would be sold by us, we should like to be assured of your position before entering into any agreement.

      Yours faithfully
         /s/ Charles Scribner's Sons

To
 Messrs. Houghton, Mifflin & Company

* * *

APPENDIX G

4. *Handwritten internal Houghton, Mifflin memorandum dated March 13, 1908:*

3/13/08

E.G.R.

    Mr. Macmillan replied to this that of course we would ask no royalty on copies sold to England.

H.M. Co.
/s/ A. P

Appendix H
James Titles Listed For Sale in The Times Book Catalogue of 1905

Ambassadors, The, first English edition, first or second impression 1903 or 1904

American, The, Collective Edition of 1883, first or second impression, 1883 or 1886

Aspern Papers, The, second English edition, second impression, 1890

Awkward Age, The, first English edition, first impression, 1899

Better Sort, The, first English edition, first impression, 1903

Bostonians, The, second English edition, first impression, 1886

Daisy Miller: A Study, second English edition, first or second impression, 1879

Europeans, The, Collective Edition of 1883, first or second impression, 1883 or 1886

Golden Bowl, The, first English edition, first, second or third impression, 1905

In The Cage, first English edition, second impression, 1898

An International Episode, Collective Edition of 1883, first or second impression, 1883 or 1886

Lesson of the Master, The, first English edition, second impression, 1892

Madonna of the Future, The, Collective Edition of 1883, first or second impression, 1883 or 1886

Other House, The, second English edition, first impression, 1897

Passionate Pilgrim, The, edition not identified. See printing history, 1.1.0

Portrait of a Lady, The, Collective Edition of 1883, first or second impression, 1883 or 1886

Princess Casamassima, The, second English edition, second or third impression (yellowbacks), 1888

Private Life, The, first English edition, first impression, 1893

Real Thing, The, first English edition, first impression, 1893

Reverberator, The, second edition, second impression, English issue, 1888

Roderick Hudson, second English edition, revised, first impression, 1880

The Sacred Fount, first English edition, first impression, 1901

APPENDIX G

Siege of London, The, Collective Edition of 1883, first or second impression, 1883 or 1886
Soft Side, The, first English edition, first impression, 1900
Spoils of Poynton, The, first English edition, first impression, 1897
Terminations, first English edition, first or second impression, 1895
Tragic Muse, The, second English edition, third impression, 1891
Two Magics, The, first English edition, first or second impression, 1898
What Maisie Knew, first English edition, first, second or third impression, 1898 [1897]
Wings of the Dove, The, first English edition, first impression, 1902

Also sold by The Times Book Club, but not listed in the 1905 Catalogue was *Stories Revived*, second edition, first impression, 1885.

Index to James's Stories and Tales: First Magazine Publication and Subsequent Publication In Book Form, 1875–1923

Abasement of the Northmores, The: NPMP***; 54.1.0–54.6.0; 64.1.0–64.3.0; 86.1.0–86.2.0.

Adina: *Scribner's Monthly*, May-June 1874; 82.1.0.**

Altar of the Dead, The: NPMP; 45.1.0–45.7.0; 64.1.0–64.3.0; 74.1.0; 86.1.0–86.2.0.

Aspern Papers, The: *The Atlantic Monthly*, Mar.-May 1888; 32.1.0–32.5.0; 64.1.0– 64.3.0; 74.1.0–74.2.0; 86.1.0–86.2.0.

At Isella: *The Galaxy*, Aug. 1871; 82.1.0**.

Author of Beltraffio, The: *The English Illustrated Magazine*, June–July 1884 26.1.0–26.7.0; 27.1.0–27.5.0; 64.1.0–64.3.0; 86.1.0–86.2.0.

Beast in the Jungle, The: NPMP; 57.1.0–57.9.0; 64.1.0–64.3.0; 74.1.0; 86.1.0–86.2.0.

Beldonald Holbein, The: *Harper's Monthly*, Oct.1901; 57.1.0–57.9.0; 64.1.0–64.3.0; 86.1.0–86.2.0.

Bench of Desolation, The: *Putnam's Magazine*, Oct. 1909–Jan. 1910; 68.1.0–68.7.0; 86.1.0–86.2.0.

Benvolio: *The Galaxy*, Aug. 1875; 10.1.0–10.5.0, 10.8.0; 20.1.0–20.5.0; 85.1.0–85.2.0; 86.1.0–86.2.0.

Birthplace, The: NPMP; 57.1.0–57.9.0; 64.1.0–64.3.0; 86.1.0–86.2.0.

Broken Wings: *The Century Magazine*, Dec. 1900; 57.1.0–57.9.0; 64.1.0–64.3.0; 86.1.0–86.2.0.

Brooksmith: *Harper's Weekly* and *Black and White*, May 2, 1891; 36.1.0–36.6.0; 64.1.0–64.3.0; 86.1.0–86.2.0.

Bundle of Letters, A: *The Parisian*, 18 Dec. 1879; 13.1.0–13.7.0; 14.1.0–14.2.0; 15.3.0–15.6.0; 20.1.0–20.5.0; 64.1.0–64.3.0; 86.1.0–86.2.0; see also *Daisy Miller*, Harpers edition of 1883 (not in the collection).

Chaperone, The: *The Atlantic Monthly*, Nov.–Dec. 1891; 37.1.0–37.6.0; 64.1.0–64.3.0; 86.1.0–86.2.0.

Collaboration: *The English Illustrated Magazine*, Sept. 1892; 39.1.0–39.7.0; 41.1.0–41.2.0; 86.1.0–86.2.0.

Covering End: NPMP; 52.1.0–52.14.0; 86.1.0–86.2.0.

Coxon Fund, The: *The Yellow Book*, July 1894; 45.1.0–45.7.0; 64.1.0–64.3.0; 74.1.0; 86.1.0–86.2.0.

Cousin Maria: *Harper's Weekly*, 6, 13 and 20 Aug. 1887; retitled Mrs. Temperly for first book publication (q.v.).

Crappy Cornelia: *Harper's Magazine*, Oct. 1909; 68.1.0–68.7.0; 86.1.0–86.2.0.

Crawford's Consistency: *Scribner's Monthly*, August 1876; NSBP.

Daisy Miller: A Study: *The Cornhill Magazine*, June–July 1878 (two prior piracies: *Littell's Living Age*, 6 and 27 July 1878, and *Home Journal*, 31 July, 7 Aug. and 14 Aug. 1878); 8.1.0–8.25.0; 20.1.0–20.5.0; 64.1.0–64.3.0; 74.1.0; 86.1.0–86.2.0. See also Harpers edition of 1883 (not in the collection)

Day of Days, A: *The Galaxy*, 15 June 1866; 27.1.0–27.5.0; 83.1.0–83.3.0; 86.1.0–86.2.0.

Death of the Lion, The: *The Yellow Book*, Apr. 1894; 45.1.0–45.7.0; 64.1.0–64.3.0 74.1.0; 86.1.0–86.2.0.

De Grey: A Romance: *The Atlantic Monthly*, July 1868; 82.1.0**.

Diary of a Man of Fifty, The: *Harper's New Monthly Magazine* and *Macmillan's Magazine*, July 1879; 10.1.0–10.5.0, 10.8.0; 14.1.0–14.2.0; 20.1.0–20.5.0; 86.1.0–86.2.0; see also *Daisy Miller*, Harpers edition of 1883 (not in the collection).

Eugene Pickering: *The Atlantic Monthly*, Oct.–Nov. 1874; 1.1.0–1.11.0; 10.1.0–10.5.0, 10.8.0; 20.1.0–20.5.0; 86.1.0–86.2.0.

Europe: *Scribner's Magazine*, June 1899; 54.1.0–54.6.0; 64.1.0–64.3.0; 86.1.0–86.2.0.

Faces, The: *Harper's Bazar*, Dec. 1900; titled The Two Faces for first English magazine publication, *The Cornhill Magazine*, June 1901, and subsequent book publication (q.v.).

Figure in the Carpet, The: *Cosmopolitan*, Jan.–Feb. 1896; 46.1.0–46.7.0; 64.1.0–64.3.0; 74.1.0–74.2.0; 86.1.0–86.2.0.

Flickerbridge: *Scribner's Magazine*, Feb. 1902; 57.1.0–57.9.0; 64.1.0–64.3.0; 86.1.0–86.2.0.

Fordham Castle: *Harper's Magazine*, Dec. 1904; 64.1.0–64.3.0*; 86.1.0–86.2.0.

Four Meetings: *Scribner's Monthly*, Nov. 1877; 8.17.0–8.25.0; 20.1.0–20.5.0; 26.1.0–26.7.0; 64.1.0–64.3.0; 86.1.0–86.2.0.

Friends of the Friends, The: for first magazine and book publication see The Way It Came; subsequent book publication: 64.1.0–64.3.0; 86.1.0–86.2.0.

Gabrielle de Bergerac: *The Atlantic Monthly*, July–Sept. 1869; 80.1.0–80.3.0**.

Georgina's Reasons: *The New York Sun*, 20, 27 July, 3 Aug. 1884; 26.1.0–

26.7.0; 27.1.0–27.5.0; 86.1.0–86.2.0.
Given Case, The: *Collier's Weekly*, 31 Dec. 1898–7 Jan. 1899 and *Black & White*, Mar. 11 and 18, 1899; 54.1.0–54.6.0; 86.1.0–86.2.0.
Glasses: *The Atlantic Monthly*, Feb. 1896; 46.1.0–46.7.0; 74.1.0–74.2.0; 86.1.0–86.2.0.
Ghostly Rental, The: *Scribner's Monthly*, Sept. 1876; NSBP.
Great Condition, The: *The Anglo-Saxon Review*, June 1899; 54.1.0–54.6.0; 86.1.0–86.2.0.
Great Good Place, The: *Scribner's Magazine*, Jan. 1900; 54.1.0–54.6.0; 64.1.0–64.3.0; 86.1.0–86.2.0.
Greville Fane: *The Illustrated London News*, 17, 24 Sept. 1892; 37.1.0–37.6.0; 64.1.0–64.3.0; 86.1.0–86.2.0.
Guest's Confession: *The Atlantic Monthly*, Oct.–Nov. 1872; 82.1.0**.
Impressions of a Cousin, The: *The Century Magazine*, Nov.–Dec. 1883; 24.1.0– 24.11.0; 86.1.0–86.2.0.
International Episode, An: *The Cornhill Magazine*, Dec. 1878–Jan. 1879; 8.8.0–8.11.0, 8.15.0, 8.17.0–8.25.0; 9.1.0–9.7.0; 20.1.0–20.5.0; 64.1.0–64.3.0; 86.1.0–86.2.0.
In the Cage: NPMP; 51.1.0–51.6.0; 64.1.0–64.3.0; 74.1.0; 86.1.0–86.2.0.
Jersey Villas: *Cosmopolitan Magazine*, July–Aug. 1892; retitled Sir Dominique Ferraud for first book publication (q.v.).
John Delavoy: *Cosmopolis*, Jan.–Feb. 1898; **50**; 54.1.0–54.6.0; 86.1.0–86.2.0.
Jolly Corner, The: *English Review*, Dec. 1908; 64.1.0–64.3.0*; 74.1.0; 86.1.0–86.2.0.
Julia Bride: *Harper's Magazine*, Mar.–Apr. 1908; 64.1.0–64.3.0*; 66.1.0–66.6.0; 86.1.0–86.2.0.
Lady Barberina: *The Century Magazine*, May–July 1884; 24.1.0–24.11.0; 64.1.0–64.3.0; 86.1.0–86.2.0.
Landscape Painter, A: *The Atlantic Monthly*, Feb. 1866; 27.1.0–27.5.0; 83.1.0–83.3.0; 86.1.0–86.2.0.
Last of the Valerii, The: *The Atlantic Monthly*, Jan. 1874; 1.1.0–1.11.0; 27.1.0–27.5.0; 86.1.0–86.2.0.
Lesson of the Master, The: *The Universal Review*, July–Aug. 1888; 36.1.0–36.6.0; 64.1.0–64.3.0; 74.1.0–74.2.0; 86.1.0–86.2.0.
Liar, The: *The Century Magazine*, May–June 1888; 33.1.0–33.5.0; 64.1.0–64.3.0; 86.1.0–86.2.0.
Light Man, A: *The Galaxy*, July 1869; 27.1.0–27.5.0; 85.1.0–85.2.0; 86.1.0–86.2.0.
London Life, A: *Scribner's Magazine*, June 1888; 33.1.0–33.5.0; 86.1.0–86.2.0.

Longstaff's Marriage: *Scribner's Monthly*, Aug. 1878; 10.1.0–10.7.0; 20.1.0–20.5.0; 85.1.0–85.2.0; 86.1.0–86.2.0.

Lord Beaupré: *Macmillan's Magazine*, May–June 1892, under the title Lord Beauprey; 39.1.0.-39.7.0; 86.1.0–86.2.0.

Louisa Pallant: *Harper's New Monthly Magazine*, Feb. 1888; 32.1.0–32.5.0; 64.1.0–64.3.0; 86.1.0–86.2.0.

Madame de Mauves: *The Galaxy*, Feb.–Mar. 1874 under the title Mme. De Mauves; 1.1.0–1.11.0; 10.1.0–10.7.0; 20.1.0–20.5.0; 64.1.0–64.3.0; 86.1.0–86.2.0.

Madonna of the Future, The: *The Atlantic Monthly*, Mar. 1873; 1.1.0–1.11.0 10.1.0–10.7.0; 20.1.0–20.5.0; 64.1.0–64.3.0; 86.1.0–86.2.0.

Marriages, The: *The Atlantic Monthly*, Aug. 1891; 36.1.0–36.6.0; 64.1.0–64.3.0; 86.1.0–86.2.0.

Master Eustace: *The Galaxy*, Nov. 1871; 27.1.0–27.5.0; 85.1.0–85.2.0; 86.1.0–86.2.0.

Maud-Evelyn: *The Atlantic Monthly*, Apr. 1900; 54.1.0–54.6.0; 86.1.0–86.2.0.

Middle Years, The: *Scribner's Magazine*, May 1893; 45.1.0–45.7.0; 64.1.0–64.3.0; 86.1.0–86.2.0.

Miss Gunton of Poughkeepsie: *The Cornhill Magazine*, May 1900; 54.1.0–54.6.0; 64.1.0–64.3.0; 86.1.0–86.2.0.

Modern Warning, The: see Two Countries for first magazine publication; 32.1.0– 32.5.0; 86.1.0–86.2.0.

Mora Montravers: *The English Review*, Aug.–Sept. 1909; 68.1.0–68.7.0; 86.1.0–86.2.0.

Most Extraordinary Case, A: *The Atlantic Monthly*, Apr. 1868; 27.1.0–27.5.0; 83.1.0–83.3.0; 86.1.0–86.2.0.

Mrs. Medwin: *Punch*, 28 Aug. 4, 11, and 18 Sept. 1901; 57.1.0–57.9.0; 64.1.0–64.3.0; 86.1.0–86.2.0.

Mrs. Temperly: see Cousin Maria for first magazine publication; 33.1.0–33.5.0; 86.1.0–86.2.0.

My Friend Mr. Bingham: *The Atlantic Monthly*, Mar. 1868; NSBP***.

New England Winter, A: *The Century Magazine*, Aug.-Sept. 1884; 24.1.0–24.11.0; 86.1.0–86.2.0

Next Time, The: *The Yellow Book*, July 1895; 46.1.0–46.7.0; 64.1.0–64.3.0; 86.1.0–86.2.0.

Nona Vincent: *The English Illustrated Magazine*, Feb.–Mar. 1892; 37.1.0–37.6.0; 86.1.0–86.2.0.

Osborne's Revenge: *The Galaxy*, July 1868; NSBP.

Owen Wingrave: *The Graphic*, Christmas Number, 1892; 39.1.0; 41.1.0; 64.1.0–64.3.0; 86.1.0–86.2.0.

INDEX TO JAMES'S STORIES AND TALES

Pandora: *The New York Sun*, 1, 8 June 1884; 26.1.0–26.7.0; 27.1.0–27.5.0; 64.1.0–64.3.0; 86.1.0–86.2.0.

Papers, The: NPMP; 57.1.0–57.9.0; 86.1.0–86.2.0.

Passionate Pilgrim, A: *The Atlantic Monthly*, Mar.–Apr. 1871; 1.1.0–1.11.0; 19.13.0; 27.1.0–27.5.0; 64.1.0–64.3.0; 86.1.0–86.2.0.

Paste: *Frank Leslie's Popular Monthly*, Dec. 1899; 54.1.0–54.6.0; 64.1.0–64.3.0; 86.1.0–86.2.0.

Patagonia, The: *The English Illustrated Magazine*, Aug.–Sept. 1888; 33.1.0–33.5.0; 64.1.0–64.3.0; 86.1.0–86.2.0.

Path of Duty, The: *The English Illustrated Magazine*, Dec. 1884; 26.1.0–26.7.0; 27.1.0–27.5.0; 86.1.0–86.2.0.

Pension Beaurepas: *The Atlantic Monthly*, Apr. 1879; 15.3.0–15.6.0; 19.1.0–19.12.0; 20.1.0–20.5.0; 64.1.0–64.3.0; 86.1.0–86.2.0.

Point of View, The: *The Century Magazine*, Dec. 1882; 17; 19.1.0–19.12.0; 20.1.0–20.5.0; 64.1.0–64.3.0; 86.1.0–86.2.0.

Poor Richard: *The Atlantic Monthly*, June–Aug. 1867; 27.1.0–27.5.0; 83.1.0–83.3.0; 86.1.0–86.2.0.

Problem, A: *The Galaxy*, June 1868; NSBP.

Private Life, The: *The Atlantic Monthly*, Apr. 1892; 39.1.0–39.7.0; 64.1.0–64.3.0; 86.1.0–86.2.0.

Professor Fargo: *The Galaxy*, Aug. 1874; 82.1.0**.

Pupil, The: *Longman's Magazine*, Mar.–Apr. 1891; 36.1.0–36.6.0; 74.1.0–74.2.0; 86.1.0–86.2.0.

Real Right Thing, The: *Collier's Weekly*, 16 Dec. 1899; 54.1.0–54.6.0; 64.1.0–64.3.0; 86.1.0–86.2.0.

Real Thing, The: *Black and White*, 16 Apr. 1892; 37.1.0–37.6.0; 64.1.0–64.3.0; 86.1.0–86.2.0.

Reverberator, The: *Macmillan's Magazine*, Feb.–Apr. 1888; 31.1.0–31.5.0; 64.1.0–64.3.0; 74.1.0–74.2.0; 86.1.0–86.2.0.

Romance of Certain Old Clothes, The: *The Atlantic Monthly*, Feb. 1868; 1.1.0–1.11.0; 27.1.0–27.5.0; 86.1.0–86.2.0.

Rose-Agathe: see Theodolinde for first magazine publication; 27.1.0–27.5.0; 85.1.0–85.2.0 (under the title Theodolinde); 86.1.0–86.2.0.

Round of Visits, A: *The English Review*, Apr.–May 1910; 68.1.0–68.7.0; 86.1.0–86.2.0.

Siege of London, The: *The Cornhill Magazine*, Jan.–Feb. 1883; 19.1.0–19.13.0; 20.1.0–20.5.0; 64.1.0–64.3.0; 86.1.0–86.2.0.

Sir Dominick Ferrand: see Jersey Villas for first magazine publication; 37.1.0–37.6.0; 86.1.0–86.2.0.

Sir Edmund Orme: *Black and White*, 25 Nov. 1891 (Christmas number);

36.1.0–36.6.0; 64.1.0–64.3.0; 86.1.0–86.2.0.
Solution, The: *The New Review*, Dec. 1889, Jan.–Feb. 1890; 36.1.0–36.6.0; 86.1.0–86.2.0.
Special Type, The: *Collier's Weekly*, June 1900; 57.1.0–57.9.0; 86.1.0–86.2.0.
Story In It, The: *The Anglo-American Magazine*, Jan. 1902; 57.1.0–57.9.0; 64.1.0– 64.3.0; 86.1.0–86.2.0.
Story of a Masterpiece: *The Galaxy*, Jan.–Feb. 1868; NSBP.
Story of a Year: *The Atlantic Monthly*, Jan. 1865; NSBP.
Sweetheart of M. Briseux: *The Galaxy*, June 1873; 82.1.0**.
Tragedy of Errors, A: *Continental Monthly*, Feb. 1864; NSBP.
Theodolinde: *Lippincott's Magazine*, May 1878; retitled Rose-Agathe for first book publication (q.v.) but retitled Theodolinde in 85.1.0–85.2.0.
Third Person, The: NPMP; 54.1.0–54.6.0; 86.1.0–86.2.0.
Tone of Time, The: *Scribner's Magazine*, Nov. 1900; 57.1.0–57.9.0; 86.1.0–86.2.0.
Travelling Companions: *The Atlantic Monthly*, Nov.–Dec. 1870; 82.1.0**.
Tree of Knowledge, The: NPMP; 54.1.0–54.6.0; 64.1.0–64.3.0; 86.1.0–86.2.0.
Turn of the Screw, The: *Collier's Weekly*, 27 Jan.–16 Apr. 1898; 52.1.0–52.14.0; 64.1.0–64.3.0; 74.1.0–74.2.0; 86.1.0–86.2.0.
Two Countries: *Harper's New Monthly Magazine*, June 1888; retitled The Modern Warning for first book publication (q.v.).
Two Faces, The: see The Faces for first magazine publication; 57.1.0–57.9.0; 64.1.0– 64.3.0; 86.1.0–86.2.0.
Velvet Glove, The: *The English Review*, Mar. 1909; 68.1.0–68.7.0; 86.1.0–86.2.0.
Visits, The: *Black and White*, 28 May 1892; 39.1.0–39.7.0; 86.1.0–86.2.0.
Washington Square: *Cornhill Magazine*, June–Nov. 1880; 15.1.0–15.6.0; 20.1.0–20.5.0; 86.1.0–86.2.0.
Watch and Ward: *The Atlantic Monthly*, Aug.–Dec. 1871; 6.1.0–6.10.0; 86.1.0–86.2.0.
Way It Came, The: *The Chap Book* and *Chapman's Magazine of Fiction*, May 1896; 46.1.0–46.7.0; retitled The Friend of Friends for second and subsequent book publication (q.v.).
Wheel of Time, The: *Cosmopolitan Magazine*, Dec. 1892–Jan. 1893; 39.1.0–39.7.0; 41.1.0–41.4.0; 86.1.0–86.2.0.

INDEX TO JAMES'S STORIES AND TALES

* First book appearance is in *The Novels and Tales of Henry James*, (1907–1909) the New York Edition), 64.1.0–64.3.0.

** Not included in *The Novels and Stories of Henry James*, (1921–1923), 86.1.0–86.2.0. Seven of these missing stories were first published in book form in America by Boni & Liveright under the title *Travelling Companions* (1919), 82.1.0, and the eighth, *Gabrielle de Bergerac*, was first published in book form by Boni & Liveright in America under that title in 1918, 80.1.0. These titles were not published in England. As these stories comprise the entire contents of these two books, it is possible that Percy Lubbock, the editor of *The Novels and Stories of Henry James*, did not know of their existence.

*** NPMP indicates that there was no magazine publication prior to its appearance in book form. NSBP indicates that there was no subsequent book publication in the period to 1923.

Not included in the above index are 25 stories that were publish anonymously or under a nom de plume between 1852 and 1869 that have been identified by Floyd R. Horowitz as having been written by Henry James, as these stories were never previously published in book form. For these stories see Floyd R. Horowitz, *The Uncollected Henry James: Newly Discovered Stories* (New York: Carroll & Graf Publishers, 2004).

General Index

*Boldfaced numbers are references to section numbers.
Other numerical references are to entry numbers.*

Ambassadors, The, **58**
   American edition, 58.6.0-58.12.0
      dust-jackets, 58.6.0, 58.8.0
      printing history of, 58.6.0
   English edition, 58.1.0-58.5.0
      colonial impression, 58.4.0, 58.5.0
      printing history of, 58.1.0
      remainder bindings, 58.2.0
American, The, **4**
   American editions, 4.1.0-4.14.5
      dust-jackets, 4.13.0
      note on some binding states, 4.2.0
      presence of period on title-page, 4.1.0
      printing history of, 4.1.0
   Continental edition, 4.22.0
   English editions, 4.15.0-4.21.5
      bindings uniform with the second English edition of *The American*, 4.17.0
      identifying first impression, 4.15.0
      pirated editions of, 4.15.0-4.16.5
      printing history of, 4.15.0
American: A Comedy, The, **35**
American book prices, stability of, 52.13.0
American Scene, The, **63**
   American edition, 63.4.0-63.5.0
      dust-jacket, 63.5.0
      James outrage at mutilation of edition, 63.4.0
   English edition, 63.1.0-63.3.0
      colonial impression, 63.3.0
      dust-jacket, 63.2.0
Art of Fiction, The, **25**
   American edition, 25.1.0-25.5.0
      aquision of plates by De Wolfe, Fiske & Co., 25.2.0
Aspern Papers, The, **32**
   American edition, 32.5.0
   English editions 32.1.0-31.4.0
      binding error, 32.2.0
      Times Book Club states, 32.3.0-32.4.0
      printing history of, 32.1.0
The Atlantic Monthly Library of Travel, 23.15.0-23.16.0
Author of Beltraffio, The, **26**
   American edition, 26.1.0-26.7.0
   printing history of, 26.1.0
Awkward Age, The, **53**
   American edition, 53.6.0-53.7.0
      printing history of, 53.6.0
   English edition, 53.1.0-53.5.0
      colonial impression, 53.2.0
      colonial sheets bound for domestic market, 53.3.0-53.5.0
      printing history of, 53.1.0

Balestier, Charles Wolcott, 33.5.0
Better Sort, The, **57**
   American edition, 57.7.0-57.9.0
      printing history of, 57.7.0
   English edition, 57.1.0-57.6.0

INDEX

variant binding states, 57.4.0-57.5.0
    colonial impression, 57.6.0
    printing history of, 57.1.0
bindings uniform with
    second English edition of *The American*, 4.17.0
    first edition, second impression, of *A Little Tour in France*, 23.6.0
    second edition, first American impression, of *The Portrait of a Lady*, 1.7.0
    first edition of *The Spoils of Poynton*, 48.6.0, note 34
    first edition, later impression, of *Roderick Hudson*, 3.16.0
    See also, 1.1.0 and 8.15.0
Boni, Charles and Albert, 32.1.0
Booklovers Library, The, 48.8.0, 58.7.0; see also Tabbard Inn Library
Books published as periodicals, 24.7.0
Bostonians, The, 28
    American issue, 28.5.0-28.6.0
        priority of two binding states, 28.6.0
    English editions, 28.1.0-28.4.0
        printing history of, 28.1.0
        settings of first and second editions, 28.1.0
        variant or trial binding, 28.2.0
Brussel, I.R., 13.5.0
Bundle of Letters, A, 13
    American edition (unauthorized), 13.1.0-13.7.0
        dated copy, 13.5.0
        issue points, Appendix C
        printing history of, 13.1.0
Burn & Co., 10.1.0, 11.1.0, and 11.2.0

Chase Act of 1891, 36.1.0, 36.3.0, and following 59.6.0
Collective Edition of 1883, The, 20
    English edition, 20.1.0-20.5.0
    Overview of, 20
    printing history of, 20
    sold as boxed set, 20.1.0 and 20.4.5
    title of, 20, and note 27
Confidence, 11
    American edition, 11.3.0-11.7.5
        printing history of, 11.3.0
        sold as part of a set, 11.6.0
    English edition, 11.1.0-11.2.0
        A Note On, 11.1.0
        printing history of, 11.1.0
    Continental edition, 11.8.0
Continental editions
    published by Tauchnitz, Appendix B
    published by Heinemann & Balestier, 33.5.0, 36.6.0

Daisy Miller: A Comedy, 18
    American edition, 18.1.0-18.11.0
    printing history of, 18.1.0
Daisy Miller: A Study, 8
    American editions, 8.1.0-8.16.0
        dust-jacket, 8.3.0, 8.12.0, 8.13.5, and 8.15.0
        limited impression, 8.9.0
        printing history of, 8.1.0 and 9.6.0
        trade and limited impressions boxed, 8.8.0-8.9.0
        separate impressions of, 8.11.5-8.14.5 and 8.16.0
        dust-jacket, 8.12.0, 8.15.0
    Continental edition, 8.24.0-8.25.0
    English editions, 8.17.0-8.23.5
        differences between first and second impressions, 8.18.0
        dust-jacket, 8.23.5
        impressions with mixed sheets, 8.19.0, 8.22.0
        printing history of, 8.17.0
        Times Book Club states, 8.18.0, 8.19.0, 8.22.0
        yellowback, 8.23.0

INDEX

dating codes, see Harper & Brothers
Day, L. F., see yellowbacks
Diary of a Man of Fifty, The, **14**
    American edition, 14.1.0-14.2.0
        binding variants, 14.1.0
        printing history of, 14.1.0
dust-jackets, see individual titles
Dutch gold, 74.1.0

Eaton, Seymour, 56.5.0
Embarrassments, **46**
    American edition, 46.5.0-46.7.0
        printing history of, 46.5.0
    English edition, 46.1.0-46.4.0
        colonial impression, 46.3.0
        colonial sheets bound for domestic market, 46.4.0
        printing history of, 46.1.0
English Hours, **62**
    American edition, 62.7.0-62.11.0
        dust-jackets, 62.7.0, 62.8.0, 62.11.0
        limited format boxed, 62.7.0
        printing history of, 62.7.0
    English edition 62.1.0-62.6.0
        printing history of, 62.1.0
        remainder bindings, 62.2.0-62.6.0
English Library, The, 33.5.0, 36.6.0
English Men of Letters series, 12.1.0
Essays in London and Elsewhere, **40**
    American edition, 40.2.0
        printing history of, 40.2.0
    English edition, 40.1.0
Eugene Pickering, 10.8.0
Europeans, The, **7**
    American Edition, 7.6.0-7.15.0
        collations of first three impressions, 7.10.0
        printing history of, 7.6.0
    Continental edition, 7.16.0
    English editions, 7.1.0-7.5.5
        first and second impressions, distinguishing features, 7.2.0

        printing history of, 7.1.0
        Times Book Club state, 7.5.5
Eversley Series, 5.6.0, 30.2.0-30.5.0

Fields, Mary ("Kate"), 18.1.0
Fields, Osgood & Co., Appendix A
Finer Grain, The, **68**
    American edition, 68.1.0-68.2.0
        printing history of, 69.1.0
    Continental edition, 68.7.0
    English edition, 68.3.0-68.6.0
        printing history of, 68.3.0
Foreign Parts, 2.11.0-2.13.5
Fox, Duffield & Co., see Herbert S. Stone & Co.
French Poets and Novelists, **5**
    Continental editions, 5.7.0-5.8.0
    English editions, 5.1.0-5.6.5
        dust-jacket, 5.1.0
        plates for, purchased from Tauchnitz, 5.1.0
        printing history of, 5.1.0

Gabrielle de Bergerac, **80**
    American edition, 80.1.0-80.3.0
        dust-jackets, 80.1.0-80.3.0
Gaskell, Philip, 75.1.0
Golden Bowl, The, **60**
    American edition, 60.1.0-60.2.0
        mixed set, 60.2.0
        printing history of, 60.1.0
    English edition, 60.3.0-60.5.1
        printing history of, 60.3.0
Guy Domville, **43**

Harper & Brothers
    use of dating codes, 8.14.0
    moves offices, 8.15.0
Hawthorne, **12**
    American edition, 12.12.0-12.17.0
        first impression, typographical error in, 12.12.0
    English edition, 12.1.0-12.11.0
        index, first inclusion of, 12.10.0
        printing history of, 12.1.0

INDEX

Henry James Memorial Fund, 72.4.0
Heinemann & Balestier 33.5.0
   James titles published by, 33.5.0, 36.6.0
Higginson, F.L., 7.6.0
Henry James Yearbook, The, 69
   American edition, 69.1.0
   English edition, 69.2.0
Herbert S. Stone and Co.
   acquisition by Fox, Duffield & Co., 51.6.0
Holiday Edition, 7.14.0, 23.9.0, and 62.9.0
Houghton, Mifflin & Co.
   change of name, 4.12.0, 34.7.0
   formation and acquisition of other publishers, Appendix A
   use of backlist, 1.7.0
Houghton, Osgood & Co., Appendix A
Howells, W.D., 8.16.0, 23.20.0, 69.1.0, 69.2.0

International Episode, An, 9
   American editions, 9.1.0-9.7.0
     printing history of, 9.1.0
     third edition, separate impression of, 9.6.0-9.7.0
In The Cage, 51
   American edition, 51.5.0-51.6.0
     printing history of, 51.5.0
   English edition, 51.1.0-51.4.0
     binding states of first impression, 51.1.0-51.2.0
     Times Book Club states, 51.3.0, 51.4.0
Italian Hours, 67
   American edition, 67.3.0-67.4.0
     issued in slipcase box, 67.3.0
     printing history of, 67.3.0
   English edition, 67.1.0-67.2.0
     printing history of, 67.1.0
Ivory Tower, The, 77
   American edition, 77.3.0
     dust-jacket, 77.3.0
     inclusion in *The Novels and Tales of Henry James*, 64.1.0
     printing history of, 77.3.0
   English edition, 77.1.0-77.2.1
     dust-jacket, 77.1.0

James, Henry
   break with Macmillan, 34.8.0
   dropping use of "Jr.", 4.17.0, 12.9.0
   first published by Macmillan & Co., 5.1.0
   friendship with Balestier, 33.5.0
   possible plagiarism by, note 22
   publishers of his works, Appendix F
   speech at The Sesame Club, 61.7.0
   works of sold by The Times Book Club, Appendix H
James R. Osgood, McIlvaine & Co., Appendix A
John Delavoy, 50
J. R. Osgood & Co.
   history of, Appendix A
   monogram, 18.1.0
Julia Bride, 66
   American separate edition, 66.1.0-66.6.0
   dust-jackets, 66.1.0-66.4.0

Landscape Painter, A, 83
   American edition, 83.1.0-83.3.0
   dust-jacket, 83.1.0
   limited issue, 83.2.0
Leighton Son & Hodge, 40.1.0
Leighton, Archibald, see Leighton Son & Hodge
Lesson of the Master, The, 36
   American edition, 36.1.0-36.2.0
   Continental edition, 36.6.0
   English editions, 36.3.0-36.5.0
     colonial impression, 36.5.0
     distinction between American and English issues, 36.1.0

INDEX

Times Book Club state, 36.4.0
printing history of, 36.1.0
effects of copyright act on, 36.1.0
Library Edition, 12.10.0
Little Tour in France, A, 23
   American editions, 23.1.0-23.17.7
      "de-luxe" binding state, 23.11.5
      dust-jacket, 23.8.0, 23.17.0
      limited impression, 23.12.0
      misprint in, 23.1.0
      printing history of, 23.1.0
   Continental edition, 23.22.0-22.26.0
   English edition, 23.18.0-23.21.0
      dust-jacket, 23.19.0
      limited impression, 23.19.0
      printing history of, 23.18.0
London Life, A, 33
   American edition, 33.4.0
   Continental edition, 33.5.0
   English editions, 33.1.0-33.3.0
      binding error, 33.2.0
      printing history of, 33.1.0
Loomis, Richard S., Jr., note 25

Macmillan & Co.
   first James title published by, 5.1.0
   James titles published by, Appendix F
   relationship with James, break in, 34.8.0
Madonna of the Future, The, 10
   English editions, 10.1.0-10.5.0
      printing history of, 10.1.0
      Times Book Club state, 10.4.0
      yellowback, 10.5.0
   Continental edition, 10.6.0-10.7.0
      dust-jacket, 10.7.0
Master Eustace 85
   American edition, 85.1.0-85.2.0
      dust-jacket, 85.1.0
      limited issue, 85.2.0
      printing history of, 85.1.0
Middle Years, The, 79
   American edition, 79.3.0

      dust-jacket, 79.3.0
      printing history of, 79.3.0
   English edition, 79.1.0-79.2.0
      dust-jacket, 79.1.0

New York Edition, The. See *The Novels and Tales of Henry James*
Notes and Reviews 87
   American edition, 87.1.0-87.2.0
      limited impression, 87.2.0
Notes of a Son and Brother, 72
   American edition, 72.1.0-71.2.0
      dust-jacket, 72.1.0
      printing history of, 72.1.0
   English edition, 72.3.0-72.4.0
      dust-jacket, 72.4.0
      printing history of, 72.3.0
Notes on Drawings by George DuMaurier, 22
Notes on Novelists, 73
   American edition, 73.2.0-73.3.0
      dust-jacket, 73.2.0
      printing history of, 73.2.0
   English edition, 73.1.0
      dust-jacket, 73.1.0
Novels and Stories of Henry James, The, 86
   English edition, 86.1.0-86.2.0
      dust-jacket, 86.2.0
      printing history of, 86.1.0
Novels and Tales of Henry James, The, 64
   American edition, 64.1.0
      Its Background and Aftermath, 64
      ownership of plates, 3.16.0, Appendix G
      printing history of, 64.1.0
      Selected Letters, bound uniformly with, following 64.1.0
      terms of agreement between Scribner's and Houghton, Mifflin, Appendix G
      use of different thicknesses of text paper, following 64.1.0

INDEX

English edition, 64.3.0
    marketing in 1913-1914 of, following 64.3.0, 71.4.0, and 72.4.0

Osgood, James R.
    monogram, 18.1.0
    publishing career of, Appendix A
Other House, The, 47
    American edition, 47.10.0-47.12.0
        printing history of, 47.10.0
        spine lettering, 47.10.0
    English editions, 47.1.0-47.9.0
        colonial impression, 47.7.0
        colonial sheets bound for domestic market, 47.8.0-47.9.0
        printing history of, 47.1.0
Outcry, The, 70
    American edition, 70.6.0
        printing history of, 70.6.0
    Continental edition, 70.7.0-70.8.0
    English edition, 70.1.0-70.5.0
        colonial impression, 70.4.0
        dust-jacket, 70.1.0
        popularity of, 70.1.0
        printing history of, 70.1.0

Park Street Library, The, 62.11.0
Partial Portraits: 30
    English edition, 30.1.0-30.6.0
        distributed in America, 30.1.0
        printing history of, 30.1.0
Passionate Pilgrim, A, 1
    American editions, 1.1.0-1.11.0
        printing history of, 1.1.0
Pennell, Joseph, 7.14.0, 23.9.0, 23.10.0, 23.15.0, 62.7.0, 62.8.0, and 67.1.0
Periodical publication of books, 24.7.0
Pictures and Other Passages from Henry James, 76
    American issue, 76.2.0
    English edition, 76.1.0

    printing history of, 76.1.0
Picture and Text, 38
    American edition, 38.1.0-38.6.0
    "de-luxe" issue, 38.2.0
    printing history of, 38.1.0
    secondary bindings, 38.3.0-38.6.0
Pinker, James B., 4.21.5, 54.2.0, 63.4.0, 64, 73.2.0, 74, and 86.1.0
Point of View, The, 17
Portrait of a Lady, The, 16
    American editions, 16.5.0-16.21.0
        distinctive feature of the first impression, 16.5.0
        designated American impression, not issue, 16.5.0
        Points, Appendix D
        printing history of, 16.5.0
    English editions, 16.1.0-16.4.1
        note on the text of, Appendix E
        printing history of, 16.1.0
Portraits of Places, 21
    American edition, 21.5.0-21.12.0
        printing history of, 21.5.0
    Continental edition, 21.13.0-21.14.0
    English edition, 21.1.0-21.4.0
        printing history of, 21.1.0
Princess Casamassima, The, 29
    American edition, 29.7.0-29.8.0
        American sheets diverted to the English market, 29.3.0, 29.3.5
    English editions, 29.1.0-29.6.5
        yellowbacks, 29.3.5, 29.5.0-29.6.0
    printing history of, 29.1.0
Printing histories, *see* individual titles
Private Life, The, 39
    American edition, 39.2.0-39.7.0
        dust-jacket, 39.6.0
        secondary bindings, 39.3.0-39.7.0
    English edition, 39.1.0

INDEX

Question of Our Speech, The 61
   American edition, 61.1.0-61.13.0
      analysis of impressions and states of, following 61.13.0
      dust-jacket, 61.7.0
      impressions and states, distinguishing features, following 61.13.0
      limited format, 61.6.0
      printing history of, 61.1.0
Question of the Mind, The, 75
   English edition, 75.1.0
Quinn, John, 26.5.0

Real Thing, The 37
   American edition, 37.1.0-37.2.5
      cancel, 37.1.0
   English edition, 37.3.0-37.6.0
      colonial impressions, 37.5.0-37.6.0
      Times Book Club state, 37.4.0
   printing history of, 37.1.0
Refugees in Chelsea 84
   English edition, 84.1.0
Reverberator, The, 31
   American edition, 31.4.0-31.5.0
      variant sizes, 31.4.0-31.5.0
   English editions, 31.1.0-31.3.0
      binding states of second edition, 31.2.0-31.3.0
   printing history of, 31.1.0
Riverside Paper Series, 6.8.0
Riverside Pocket Series, 6.8.0
Roderick Hudson, 3
   American editions, 3.1.0-3.16.0
      note on the second edition, revised, American issue, following 3.1.0
      printing history of, 3.1.0
      suppression of first edition, 3.7.0
   Continental edition, 3.20.0-3.21.0
   English editions, 3.17.0-3.19.0
      note on binding uniform with the second edition, revised, English issue, following 4.17.0
      printing history of, 3.17.0
      yellowback, 3.19.0

Sacred Fount, The, 55
   American edition, 55.1.0-55.5.0
      binding states of first and second impressions, 55.1.0-55.4.0
      printing history of, 55.1.0
   English edition, 55.6.0-55.9.0
      colonial impression, 55.9.0
      printing history of, 55.6.0
Selected Letters of Henry James, The
   inclusion of in *The Novels and Tales of Henry James*, following 64.1.0
Sense of the Past, The, 78
   American edition, 78.4.0-78.5.0
      dust-jacket, 77.4.0
      inclusion in *The Novels and Tales of Henry James*, 64.1.0
      printing history of, 78.4.0
   English edition, 78.1.0-78.3.0
      dust-jacket, 78.1.0
Siege of London, The, 19
   American edition, 19.1.0-19.12.0
      dust-jacket, 19.12.0
      printing history of, 19.1.0
   Continental edition, 19.13.0
Silver lettering and decoration, 39.2.0
Small Boy and Others, A, 71
   American edition, 71.1.0-71.2.0
      dust-jacket, 71.1.0
      printing history of, 71.1.0
   English edition, 71.3.0-71.7.0
      dust-jackets, 71.4.0, 71.6.0
      hybrid impression, 71.6.0
      printing history of, 71.3.0
Soft Side, The, 54
   American edition, 54.4.0-54.6.0
   English edition, 54.1.0-54.3.0
      printing history of, 54.1.0

INDEX

Spoils of Poynton, The, 48
  American edition, 48.6.0–48.9.0
    printing history of, 48.6.0
    titles bound uniformly with, 48.6.0
  English edition, 48.1.0–48.5.0
    colonial impression, 48.3.0
    colonial sheets bound for domestic market, 48.5.0
    dust-jacket, 48.5.0
    mixed colonial and domestic sheets, 48.4.0
    printing history of, 48.1.0
staples, use of, 16.8.0
Stories Revived, 27
  English editions, 27.1.0–27.5.0
    printing history of, 27.1.0
    Times Book Club states, 27.4.0–27.5.0
    two volumes sold separately, 27.1.0

Tabard Inn Library, 48.8.0, 54.5.0, 56.2.0, and 58.7.0
Tales of Three Cities, 24
  American edition, 24.1.0–24.7.5
    bound as a paperback, 24.7.0
    printing history of, 24.1.0
  English edition, 24.8.0–24.11.0
    printing history of, 24.8.0
    Times Book Club state, 24.11.0
Tauchnitz, Bernhard
  competition from Heinemann & Balestier, 33.5.0
  editions of James's works, Appendix B
  publishing practices, Appendix B
  sale of plates of *French Poets and Novelists*, 5.1.0
Terminations, 45
  American edition, 45.6.0–45.7.0
    printing history of, 45.6.0
  English edition, 45.1.0–45.5.0
    colonial impression, 45.4.0
    colonial sheets bound for domestic market, 45.5.0
    printing history of, 45.1.0
Theatricals, 42
  American edition, 42.2.0
    dust-jacket, 42.2.0
  English edition, 42.1.0
Theatricals: Second Series, 44
  American edition, 44.2.0
    dust-jacket, 44.2.0
  English edition, 44.1.0
Times Book Club bindings, see individual titles and Appendix H
Thomas Nelson & Sons, James works published by, 4.21.5
Ticknor & Co. *See* Appendix A
Ticknor & Fields
  publishing history, Appendix A
  Ticknor Paper Series, 24.7.0
Transatlantic Sketches, 2
  American edition, 2.1.0–2.10.8
    printing history of, 2.1.0
  Continental edition, 2.11.0–2.13.0
  See also, *Foreign Parts*
Tragic Muse, The, 34
  American edition, 34.1.0–34.7.0
    printing history of, 34.1.0
  English editions, 34.8.0–34.12.0
    colonial impression, 34.9.0
    printing history of, 34.8.0
    Times Book Club states, 34.11.0–34.12.0
Two Magics, The, 52
  American edition, 52.6.0–52.14.0
    printing history of, 52.6.0
  English edition, 52.1.0–52.5.0
    colonial impression, 52.3.0
    colonial sheets bound for domestic market, 52.5.0
    mixed colonial and domestic sheets, 52.4.0
    printing history of, 52.1.0
Travelling Companions, 82
  American edition, 82.1.0
    dust-jacket, 82.1.0

INDEX

uniform bindings, see bindings uniform with

Uniform Tales of Henry James, The, **74**
    American issue, 74.2.0
    English edition, 74.1.0
        background, **74**
        dust-jackets, 74.1.0
    printing history of, **74**

Views and Reviews, **65**
    American edition, 65.1.0-65.2.0
        limited impression, 6.5.2.

Washington Square, **15**
    American edition, 15.1.0-15.2.0
        printing history of, 15.1.0
    Continental edition, 15.6.0
    English edition, 15.3.0-15.5.0
        printing history of, 15.3.0
Watch and Ward, **6**.
    American edition, 6.1.0-6.10.0
        printing history of, 6.1.0
        unrecorded impression, 6.8.0
Watt, A. P., 34.8.0
What Maisie Knew, **49**
    American edition, 49.6.0-49.10.0
        printing history of, 49.6.0
        watermarked paper used for, 49.6.0
    English edition, 49.1.0-49.5.0
        colonial impression, 49.4.0
        colonial sheets bound for domestic market, 49.5.0
        printing history of, 49.1.0
Wheel of Time, The, **41**
    American edition, 41.1.0-41.4.0
        printing history of, 41.1.0
William Wetmore Story and His Friends, **59**
    American edition, 59.5.0-59.6.0
    English edition, 59.1.0-59.4.0
        distinguishing features of first three impressions, following 59.6.0
        protruding en quadrate, 59.1.0
        trial binding, 59.1.0
Wings of the Dove, The, **56**
    American edition, 56.1.0-56.3.0
        printing history of, 5.6.1
    English edition, 56.4.0-56.5.0
Winterbottom Book Cloth Co., 40.1.0
Within the Rim, **81**
    English edition, 81.1.0
        colonial issue, 81.2.0
        dust-jackets, 81.1.0-81.2.0
Woolf, Leonard, 59.4.0
yellowbacks
    cover design of, 3.19.0
    titles published by Macmillan & Co., 3.19.0, 8.23.0, 10.5.0, 29.5.0, and 29.6.0